ADVANCED SOFTWARE ENGINEERING

THEORY AND PRACTICE

OTHER BOOKS BY THE SAME AUTHOR

- Solved Programming In C
- Solved Programming In C++
- Artificial Neural Networks
- Digital Image Processing
- Computer Oriented Numerical and Statistical
- Techniques
- Introduction to Microprocessors: 8085 and 8086
- Expert C Programming
- Expert C++ Programming
- C++ And Data Structures
- Data Structures
- Data Structures: An Algorithmic Approach Using C
- Data Structures: An Algorithmic Approach Using C++
- Electronics: Analog And Digital
- Soft Computing
- Fuzzy Systems
- Test Your C Programming Skills
- Mobile Computing
- Distributed Database Systems
- Fundamentals of Computers, Operating System and
- Information Technology
- Internet Applications
- Windows Based Computer Courses
- Computer Organization and Architecture

ADVANCED SOFTWARE ENGINEERING

THEORY AND PRACTICE

Dr. Ikvinderpal Singh

KHANNA BOOK PUBLISHING CO. (P) LTD.

Publisher of Engineering and Computer Books

4C/4344, Ansari Road, Darya Ganj, New Delhi-110002

Phone : 011-23244447-48 **Mobile:** +91-9910909320

E-mail : contact@khannabooks.com

Website : www.khannabooks.com

Dear Readers,

To prevent the piracy, this book is secured with HIGH SECURITY HOLOGRAM on the front title cover. In case you don't find the hologram on the front cover title, please write us to at contact@khannabooks.com or whatsapp us at +91-99109 09320 and avail special gift voucher for yourself.

Specimen of Hologram on front Cover title:

Moreover, there is a SPECIAL DISCOUNT COUPON for you with EVERY HOLOGRAM.

How to avail this SPECIAL DISCOUNT:

Step 1: Scratch the hologram
Step 2: Under the scratch area, your "coupon code" is available
Step 3: Logon to www.khannabooks.com
Step 4: Use your "coupon code" in the shopping cart and get your copy at a special discount
Step 5: Enjoy your reading!

Thanks,
Khanna Publishing House

Price: ₹ 785.00

ADVANCED SOFTWARE ENGINEERING

by **Dr. Ikvinderpal Singh**

ISBN: 978-93-82069-23-0

First Edition: 2014
Reprint: 2024

To view complete list of books, please scan the QR Code:

Published by:
Khanna Book Publishing Co. (P) Ltd.
CIN: U22110DL1998PTC095547

Visit us at: www.khannabooks.com
Write us at: contact@khannabooks.com

Printed in India.

Dedicated to My Parents

Preface

When a computer software succeeds—when it meets the needs of the people who use it, when it performs flawlessly over a long period of time, when it is easy to modify and even easier to use—it can and does change things for the better. But when software fails—when its users are dissatisfied, when it is error prone, when it is difficult to change and even harder to use—bad things can and do happen. We all want to build software that makes things better, avoiding the bad things that lurk in the shadow of failed efforts. To succeed, we need discipline when software is designed and built. We need an engineering approach.

Software engineering has evolved from an obscure idea practiced by a relatively small number of zealots to a legitimate engineering discipline. Today, it is recognized as a subject worthy of serious research, conscientious study, and tumultuous debate. Throughout the industry, software engineer has replaced *programmer* as the job title of preference. Software process models, software engineering methods, and software tools have been adopted successfully across a broad spectrum of industry applications.

Although managers and practitioners alike recognize the need for a more disciplined approach to software, they continue to debate the manner in which discipline is to be applied. Many individuals and companies still develop software haphazardly, even as they build systems to service the most advanced technologies of the day. Many professionals and students are unaware of modern methods. And as a result, the quality of the software that we produce suffers and bad things happen. In addition, debate and controversy about the true nature of the software engineering approach continue. The status of software engineering is a study in contrasts. Attitudes have changed, progress has been made, but much remains to be done before the discipline reaches full maturity. The Book of Advanced *Software Engineering: Theory and practice* is intended to serve as a guide to a maturing engineering discipline. it is intended for both students and practitioners, retaining its appeal as a guide to the industry professional and a comprehensive introduction to the student at the upper level undergraduate or first year graduate level. The format and style of the fifth edition have undergone significant change, making the presentation more reader-friendly and the content more easily accessible.

UNIT 1 Software Engineering: Chapter 1 presents an introduction to the software engineering milieu. It is intended to introduce the subject matter, and more important, to present concepts that will be necessary for later chapters. It gives Definition, Software characteristics, Software components, Software Applications.

UNIT 2 Software Development Process: Chapter 2 describe the Definition, Software Engineering Paradigms, waterfall method, prototyping, interactive Enhancement, The Spiral model, Requirements Engineering, requirements elicitation, Software Requirements Specification, requirements review, requirement management, Software Architecture and Design, Coding and Testing, Software maintenance and Customer Support.

UNIT 3 Planning and Estimation: Chapters 3 through 8 describe the Fundamentals of Software project planning , like Cost estimation, uncertainties in cost estimation, Single variable model, COCOMO model, On software size estimation, Project scheduling and milestones, Role of Metrics and measurement, Metrics for software productivity and quality, Measurement software, size-oriented metrics, function oriented metrics, Metrics for software quality, Integrating metrics within the software engineering process. It also includes Risk management, Software Quality, Software Quality Assurance Plan and software reliability. Conventional Software Management, Evolution of Software Economics, Improvement of Software Economics, Comparison of old and modern ways of Software Management.

UNIT 4 Software Reengineering: Chapters 9 through 11 discusses the Re-engineering, Restructuring and Reverse Engineering, Re-engineering existing systems, Data Re-engineering and migration, Software Reuse and Reengineering.

UNIT 5 Object-Oriented (OO) Measurements: Chapter 12 deals with metrics, Classification of OO metrics, Study of Design Metrics- method size, method internals, class size, class inheritance, Method inheritance, class intervals and class externals.

UNIT 6 Object-Oriented Analysis and Design: Chapters 13 and 14 describes the Structured System Analysis and Design, Object-Oriented analysis and Design, Object, Abstraction, Collaboration among Objects, Polymorphism, Classes, specifying State, Specifying Behavior, Class Relationships, Grouping, Hiding.

UNIT 7 Advanced Topics: Chapters 15 and 16 in the book integrates the Agents, Applications, Types and Classes, Multi-Agent systems, characteristics & Properties Agents.

The key advantage of this approach is that concepts and techniques are integrated into cohesive chapters. Hence many design and implementation details look 'obvious' when the reader encounters them. This fact helps to emphasize that the study of Advanced Software Engineering must be based on a sound understanding of concepts. This is the most important message a text can give to a student of Advanced Software Engineering who will face both a rich diversity and rapid changes in techniques of Advanced Software Engineering during his/her career.

We welcome comments from all readers to improve this book as a useful guide for the community of engineers and technologists who will become knowledgeable about the potential of Software Engineering for their use in solving the problems that challenge us each day.

DR. IKVINDERPAL SINGH

Contents

UNIT 2 : SOFTWARE DEVELOPMENT PROCESS

UNIT 3 : SOFTWARE PROJECT MANAGEMENT

UNIT 4 : SOFTWARE REENGINEERING

UNIT 5 : OBJECT ORIENTED MEASUREMENTS

UNIT 7 : SOFTWARE AGENTS

UNIT 1
SOFTWARE ENGINEERING

Introduction to Software Engineering

1

1.1 INTRODUCTION

Software is omnipresent in the lives of billions of human beings around the globe. Today, humans rely heavily on software systems. Software runs many aspects of our daily life. It helps us communicate, socialize, and perform day-to-day tasks at home and at office. Most importantly, software is a key player in the emerging knowledge-based service economy. However, there are many concerns about the quality and reliability, and hence the trustworthiness, of the software we produce and consume. Existing software is defected with thousands of defects. Some of the defects are known and have already been detected, while others have not manifested and are yet to be uncovered. The defects have caused many disasters, hence leading to huge financial losses, physical harm to humans, and resulting in life threatening situations. The main reasons for such a state of software are the lack of adequately trained software professionals and the lack of tools and techniques that can scale up the complexities of the needed software.

The nature and complexity of software have changed significantly in the last 30 years. In the 1970s, the applications ran on a single processor, produced alphanumeric output, and received their input from a linear source. Today's applications are far more complex, typically having graphical user interface and client-server architecture. They frequently run on two or more processors, under different operating systems, and on geographically distributed machines. Rarely, in history has field of endeavour evolved as rapidly as software development.

Therefore, there is an urgent need to adopt software engineering concepts, strategies, practices to avoid conflict, and to improve the software development process in order to deliver good quality maintainable software in time and within budget. In this chapter we give the readers an insight into what is meant by software, and software engineering, and what are the basic terminologies associated with the design of good quality software. Let us start with an introduction to software.

1.2 SOFTWARE

Software takes on a dual role. It is a product, as well as the vehicle for delivering the product. As a product, it delivers the computing potential embodied by computer hardware. Whether it resides within a mobile phone or operates inside a super-computer, software is information transformer, i.e. producing, managing, acquiring, modifying, displaying, or transmitting information that can be as simple as a single bit or as complex as a multimedia presentation derived from data acquired from dozens of independent sources. As the vehicle used to deliver the product, software acts as the basis for control of the computer, the communication of information, and the creation and control of other programs. Software delivers the most important product of our time, i.e. information.

Any software is described by its capabilities. The capabilities relate to the functions it executes, the features it provides, and the facilities it offers. Software written for sales-order processing would have different functions to process different types of sales orders from different market segments. The features, for example, would be to handle multi-currency computing, updating of product, sales, and tax status in MIS reports and books of accounts. The facilities could be printing of sales orders, e-mails to customers, reports, and advice to the store departments to dispatch the goods. The facilities and features could be optional and based on customer choices.

Software is developed keeping in mind certain hardware and operating system considerations, known as the platform. Hence, software is described along with its capabilities and the platform specifications that are required to run it.

1.2.1 Definition of Software

A computer has two aspects: (1) hardware and (2) software. The term hardware describes the physical aspects of computers and related devices. Detailed instructions in a form understandable to computer hardware need to be given for operating a computer and getting meaningful output from it. A set of instructions is called a computer program. The programs are often stored on computer storage devices so that they can be invoked when required. Software is a general term for the various programs and data stored on computer storage devices to operate the computer and related devices. Software controls the operation of computer hardware.

It has three principal functions:

- It helps in operating and managing the computer resources.
- It serves as an intermediary between the organization and its stored information.
- It helps in problem solving by using computer hardware.

Without the instructions provided by software, computer hardware is unable to perform any of the tasks associated with computers.

Software can be categorized into two types:

(1) Systems Software
(2) Applications Software

Systems software consists of generalized programs that manage computer resources such as the central processing unit (CPU), printers, terminals, communication links and peripheral equipment. In other words, systems software serves as the intermediary between the software used by end users and the computer itself. Applications software consists of programs designed for applying the computer to solve a specific problem. The programs for payroll processing or sales order entry are examples of applications software. Systems software provides the platform on which applications software runs. The relationship between user, applications software, systems software, and computer hardware is shown in Figure 1.1. The user sends instructions to the applications software, which "translates" the instructions for the systems software, which in turn forwards them to the hardware. Information flows in two directions: from the user working on the computer to the hardware and back again to the user.

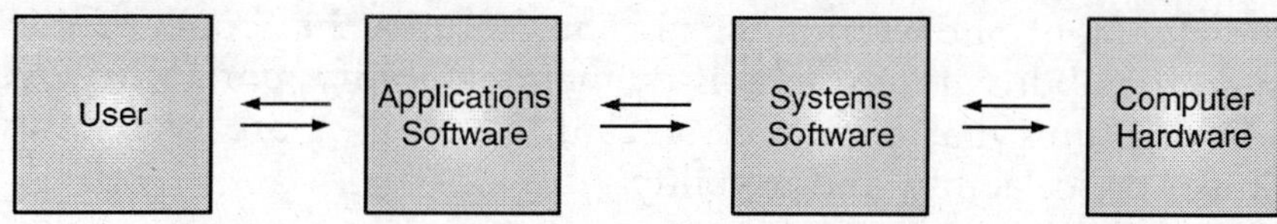

Figure 1.1: *Relationship between user, software and hardware*

Software is a set of instructions used to acquire inputs and to manipulate them to produce the desired output in terms of functions and performance as determined by the user of the software. It also includes a set of documents, such as the software manual, meant to help users understand the software system. Today's software is comprised of Source Code, Executables, Design Documents, Operations, and System Manuals and Installation and Implementation Manuals.

Software includes:

- Instructions (computer programs) that when executed provide desired functions and performance.
- Data structures that enable the programs to adequately manipulate information.
- Documents that describe the operation and use of the programs.

OR

"The term software refers to the set of computer programs, procedures, and associated documents (flowcharts, manuals, etc.) that describe the programs and how they are to be used. To be precise, software is a collection of programs whose objective is to enhance the capabilities of the hardware".

OR

Definition of software given by the IEEE:

Software is the collection of computer programs, procedure rules and associated documentation and data.

Computer software has become a driving force.

- It is the engine that drives business decision-making.
- It serves as the basis for modern scientific investigation and engineering problem-solving.
- It is embedded in all kinds of systems, such as transportation, medical, telecommunications, military, industrial processes, entertainment, office products, etc.

It is important as it affects nearly every aspect of our lives and has become pervasive in our commerce, our culture, and our everyday activities. Software's impact on our society and culture is significant. As software importance grows, the software community continually attempts to develop technologies that will make it easier, faster, and less expensive to build high-quality computer programs.

1.3 DESIRABLE SOFTWARE CAPABILITIES

The software capabilities determine the overall quality of the software product. Unfortunately, there is no quantitative assessment of such overall quality. However, the desirable capabilities should contribute positively to the overall software quality. When developing software, the desirable functionality of the product aimed for should always be kept in mind. Knowing the capabilities in advance helps promote more effective practices in software development and maintenance. The features that concern the developer or maintainer are flexibility, interoperability, maintainability, portability, reusability, and testability. The features that are more relevant to the users are availability, correctness, efficiency, integrity, scalability, and usability.

User-centered software capabilities are as follows:

- **Availability** is the degree to which the software system is available when its services are required. It can be quantified as the ratio of the actual availability of the software services to the expected availability during the same period.
- **Correctness** is the degree to which the software meets its requirements specifications. Correctness is affected positively by the completeness, consistency, and traceability of the software. Accuracy is a qualitative assessment of correctness.
- **Efficiency** is the degree to which the software system performs its functions using the least amount of computational and memory resources.
- **Integrity** is the degree to which the software system prevents unauthorised access to information or programs. Both integrity and availability contribute the security of the software system.
- **Reliability** is the ability of a software system to perform its functions under stated conditions and for a specified period of time. Reliability can be quantified using the mean time between failures. Reliability is affected positively by error recoverability and fault tolerance, modularity and simplicity, and other quality factors.
- **Scalability** is the ability of the software system to handle growing number of user requests up to a certain specified limit.
- **Usability** is the degree of ease with which the software system can be used. Usability is positively affected by learnability, readability, understandability, and other quality factors.

Developer-centered software capabilities are as follows:

- **Flexibility** is the measure of how easily the software system can be extended or expanded. Flexibility is positively affected by the simplicity, generality, and modularity of the software, and other quality factors.
- **Interoperability** is the ability of the software system to exchange information with other external systems.
- **Maintainability** is the measure of how easily the software system can be modified to fix errors, to improve its functions, or to adapt it to different environments. Maintainability is positively affected by adaptability, simplicity, modularity, traceability, and other quality factors.
- **Portability** is the ease with which the software system can be moved to a different software or hardware environment or platform. Portability is positively affected by generality and modularity and other quality factors.

- **Reusability** is the measure of how easily a software component can be reused in the same software system or utilized to build new systems. Reusability is positively affected by generality and modularity and other quality factors.
- **Testability** is the measure of how easily the test cases can be selected and executed to test the software. Testability is positively affected by modularity, simplicity and traceability, and other quality factors.

1.4 TYPES OF SOFTWARE

Computer software is often divided into two categories:

1. **System software.** The extensive use of systems software began with second-generation computers in early 1960s. Before this, the operation of a computer was controlled primarily by human operators. For example, the operator had to activate each peripheral device when that device was needed by the computer. This type of human intervention wasted large amounts of computer time and human resources. These functions were automated by software called operating systems.

   An operating system is a set of integrated programs that controls the execution of computer programs and manages the storage and processing resources of a computer system. These programs are stored in primary storage and partly in direct-access secondary storage. With operating systems, a queue of jobs that are awaiting execution is fed into a disk. The operating system starts each job as and when the system resources are available for its execution. Since human intervention is eliminated, computer idle time is significantly reduced.

   System software consists of three types of programs:

   (i) ***System Control Program.*** It controls the execution of programs, manages the storage and processing resources of the computer and performs other management and monitoring functions. The set of these programs constitutes the operating system.

   (ii) ***System Support Program.*** It provides services to other computer programs and to computer users for carrying out routine functions such as copying, deleting, merging or sorting files, directory checking etc. Most of these programs are also included in the operating system.

   (iii) ***System Development Program.*** It assists in the creation of application programs. Examples are language translators such as a BASIC interpreter and compilers such as FORTRAN, c/C++, Java, etc.

2. **Application software.** It applies the power of the computer to solve problems by performing specific tasks. It can support individuals, groups, and organizations. Companies can customize applications software, buy existing programs off-the-shelf or use a combination of customised and off-the-shelf application software. Electronic spreadsheet, word processing, graphics software and integrated software are general-purpose application software. Computer programs for payroll processing, inventory management and sales analysis are specific-purpose applications software. These are customised to meet the specific requirements of user organizations.

System software are low-level programs that interact with the computer at a very basic level and include the operating system and utilities for managing resources. In contrast, application software includes database programs, word processors, and spreadsheets. Application software sits above system software because it needs the help of system software to run. Figure 1.2 gives an overview of software classification and its types.

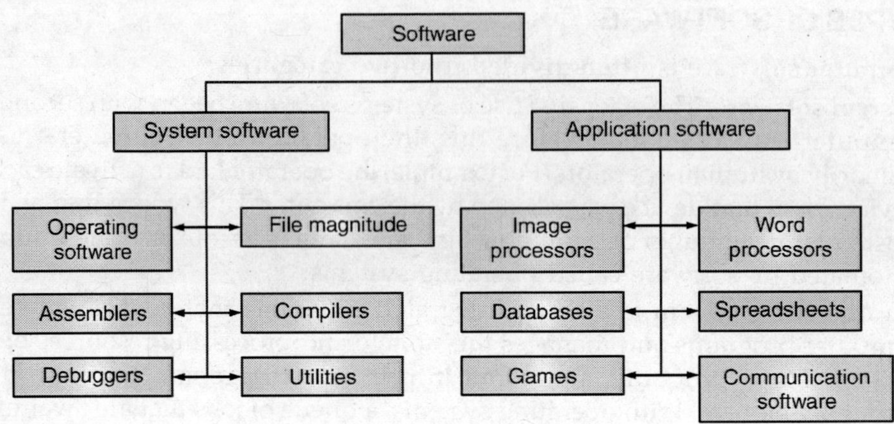

Figure 1.2: Types of Software

The following is an overview of the different classes of software:

1. **Operating Systems.** The operating system provides interface between the user and the hardware. It manages hardware, such as memory, CPU, input/ output devices, files, etc., for the user. Most commonly used operating systems include Microsoft Windows, DOS, Mac OS, OS/2, UNIX, etc.
2. **Utilities.** Utilities are programs that perform the specification tasks related to managing system resources. The operating system includes a number of utilities for managing disk printers and other devices.
3. **Compilers and Interpreters.** A complier is a program that translates source code into object code. The compiler derives its name from the way it works, looking at the entire piece of source code and collecting and reorganizing the instructions. Thus, a compiler differs from an interpreter, which analyses and executes each line of source code in succession, without looking at the entire program. The advantage of interpreters is that they can execute a program immediately. Compliers require some time before an executable program emerges. However, programs produced by compliers run much faster than the same programs executed by an interpreter.
4. **Word Processors.** A word processor is a program that enables you to perform word-processing functions. Word processors use a computer to create, edit, and print documents. Of all computer applications, word processors are the most common.

   To perform word processing, you need a computer, the word-processing software (word processor), and a printer. A word processor enables you to create a document, store it electronically on a disk, display it on a screen, modify it by entering commands and characters from the keyboard, and print it on a printer.

The great advantage of word processing over using a typewriter is that you can make changes without retyping the entire document. If you make a typing mistake, you simply back up the cursor and correct your mistake. If you want to delete a paragraph, you simply remove it, without leaving a trace. It is equally easy to insert a word, sentence, or paragraph in the middle of a document. Word processors also make it easy to move sections of text from one place to another within a document, or between documents. When you have made all the changes you want, you can send the file to a printer to get a hardcopy. Some of the commonly used word processors are Microsoft Word, WordStar, WordPerfect, etc.

5. **Spreadsheets.** A spreadsheet is a table of values arranged in rows and columns. Each value can have a predefined relationship to the other values. If you change one value, therefore, you may need to change other values as well.

   Spreadsheet applications (often referred to simply as spreadsheets) are computer programs that let you create and manipulate spreadsheets electronically. In a spreadsheet application, each value sits in a cell. You can define what type of data is in each cell and how different cells depend on one another. The relationships between cells are called formulas, and the names of the cells are called labels.

   Once you have defined the cells and the formulas for linking them together, you can enter your data. You can then modify selected values to see how all the other values change accordingly. This enables you to study various what-if scenarios.

   There are a number of spreadsheet applications on the market, Lotus 1-2-3 and Excel being among the most famous. These applications support graphic features that enable you to produce charts and graphs from the data.

   Some spreadsheets are multi-dimensional, meaning that you can link one spreadsheet to another. A three-dimensional spreadsheet, for example, is like a stack of spreadsheets all connected by formulae. A change made in one spreadsheet automatically affects other spreadsheets.

6. **Presentation Graphics.** Presentation graphics enable users to create highly stylized images for slide shows and reports. The software includes functions for creating various types of charts and graphs and for inserting text in a variety of fonts. Most systems enable you to import data from a spreadsheet application to create the charts and graphs. Presentation graphics are often called business graphics. Some of the popular presentation graphics software includes Microsoft PowerPoint, Lotus Freelance Graphics, Harvard Presentation Graphics, etc.

7. **Database Management System (DBMS).** A DBMS is a collection of programs that enable you to store, modify, and extract information from a database. There are many different types of DBMSs, ranging from small systems that run on personal computers to huge systems that run on mainframes. The following are some examples of database applications: computerized library systems, automated teller machines, flight and railway reservation systems, computerized inventory systems, etc.

   From a technical standpoint, a DBMS can differ widely. The terms relational, network, flat, and hierarchical all refer to the way a DBMS organizes information internally. The internal organization can affect how quickly and flexibly you can extract information.

Requests for information from a database are made in the form of a query, which is a stylized question. Different DBMSs support different query languages, although there is a semi-standardized query language called SQL (structured query language). Sophisticated languages for managing database systems are called fourth-generation languages, or 4GLs for short.

The information from a database can be presented in a variety of formats. Most DBMSs include a report-writer program that enables you to output data in the form of a report. Many DBMSs also include a graphics component that enables you to output information in the form of graphs and charts. Some examples of database management systems are IDMS, IMS, DB2, Oracle, Sybase, Informix, Ingress, MS-SQL Server, MS Access, etc.

8. **Image Processors.** Image processors or graphics programs enable you to create, edit, manipulate, add special effects, view, and print and save images, and include the following:
   (i) ***Paint Programs.*** A paint program is a graphics program that enables you to draw pictures on the display screen, which is represented as bitmaps (bit-mapped graphics). Most paint programs provide the tools in the form of icons. By selecting an icon, you can perform functions associated with the tool. In addition to these tools, paint programs also provide easy ways to draw common shapes, such as straight lines, rectangles, circles, and ovals.

   Sophisticated paint applications are often called image-editing programs. These applications support many of the features of draw programs, such as the ability to work with objects. Each object, however, is represented as a bitmap rather than as a vector image.

   (ii) ***Draw Programs.*** A draw program is another graphics program that enables you to draw pictures, then store the images in files, merge them into documents, and print them. Unlike paint programs, which represent images as bitmaps, draw programs use vector graphics, which makes it easy to scale images to different sizes. In addition, graphics produced with a draw program have no inherent resolution. Rather, they can be represented at any resolution, which makes them ideal for high-resolution output.

   (iii) ***Image Editors.*** An image editor is a graphics program that provides a variety of special features for altering bit-mapped images. The difference between image editors and paint programs is not always clear-cut, but in general, image editors are specialized for modifying bit-mapped images, such as scanned photographs, whereas paint programs are specialized for creating images. In addition to offering a host of filters and image transformation algorithms, image editors also enable you to create and superimpose layers.

1.5 LEGACY SOFTWARE

Hundreds of thousands of programs fall into one of the broad application domains discussed in the preceding subsection. Some of these are state-of-art software, just released to individuals, industry, and government. But other programs are older, in some cases much older.

These older programs, often referred to as legacy software, have been the focus of continuous attention and concern since 1960s. Dayani-Fard defined legacy software in the following way: "Legacy software systems were developed decades ago and have been continually modified to meet the changes in business requirements and computing platforms. The proliferation of such systems is causing headaches for large organizations who find them costly to maintain and risky to evolve."

Liu extends this description by noting that 'many legacy systems remain supportive to the core business functions and are indispensable to the business'. Hence, legacy software is characterized by longevity and business criticality.

If the legacy system meets the needs of the users and runs reliably, it is not broken and does not need to be fixed. However, when time passes, legacy systems often evolve for one or more of the following reasons:

- The software must be adapted to meet the needs of new computing environment or technology.
- The software must be enhanced to implement new business requirements.
- The software must be extended to make it interoperable with other more modern systems or databases.
- The software must be re-architectured to make it viable within a network environment.

When these modes of evolution occur, a legacy system must be re-engineered so that it remains viable to the future. The goal of modern software engineering is to devise methodologies that are founded on the notion of evolution, i.e. the notion that software systems continually change, new software systems are built from old ones, and all must interoperate and cooperate with each other.

1.6 SOFTWARE ENGINEERING

The term *software engineering* was first introduced in a 1968 North Atlantic Treaty Organization (NATO) conference held in Germany. During the late 1960s the computing field was starting to face a software 'crisis'. Computer hardware had made great leaps in computing power and storage capacity. This ushered in an era that saw the beginning of developing large and complex software that required a large number of programmers. The first wave involved system-level programs such as operating systems, file systems and access methods. With the recognition of huge potential of business automation, large and complex business applications software also started to emerge shortly afterward. Early experiences with writing programs proved to be insufficient for these large, complex projects. As a result, many software projects were delayed, and some were never completed. Others were completed but experience excessive budget overruns. The final software product often demonstrated unsatisfactory quality and performance. The users of these software systems were often subjected to incomprehensible manuals that were written by programmers who never met the users. These software releases needed continual support and maintenance that the original programmers were not trained to handle. The attendees of 1968 NATO conference recognized the need for a discipline much like the other engineering disciplines and thus formalised the concept of software engineering. In the past 40 years, great strides and improvements have been made in software industry and academia. But many more improvements are still needed for software engineering.

1.6.1 Definitions of Software Engineering

One of the earlier definitions of software engineering may be attributed to David Parnas, who stated that software engineering is a multiperson construction of multiversion software. This definition certainly brings out some of the aspects of software engineering that have been discussed until now.

Ian Sommerville states that 'software engineering is an engineering discipline whose focus is the cost-effective development of high quality software system'. He further explains that software is 'abstract and intangible' and defines software engineering as 'an engineering discipline that is concerned with all aspects of software production from the early stages of the system specification to maintaining the system after it has gone into use'. This definition certainly captures the software life cycle from inception to project sunset.

Shari Pfleeger uses the relationship between chemistry and chemical engineering as an analogy to discuss the relationship between computing and software engineering. She states that in computing we can focus on the "Computers and programming languages themselves or we can view them as tools to be used in designing and implementing a solution to a problem. Software engineering takes the latter view." According to her view, software engineering is the application of computing tools to solving problems.

The Software Engineering 2004 Curriculum Guidelines for Undergraduate Degree Programs in Software Engineering published by ACM and IEEE Computer Society recognizes the broad scope of the field and highlights three definitions from different sources:

- *From F. L. Bauer:* "The establishment and use of sound engineering principles (methods) in order to obtain economically software that is reliable and works on real machines."
- *From CMU:* "Software engineering is that form of engineering that applies the principles of computer science and mathematics to achieving cost-effective solution to software problems."
- *From IEEE:* "The application of a systematic, disciplined, quantifiable approach to development, operation, and maintenance of software."

The *Curriculum Guidelines* goes on further to state that "software engineering is about creating high-quality software in a systematic, controlled, and efficient manner. Consequently, there are important emphasis on analysis and evaluation, specification, design, and evolution of software. In addition, there are issues related to management and quality, to novelty and creativity, to standards, to individual skills, and to teamwork and professional practice that play a vital role in software engineering."

It is clear that capturing software engineering in a single sentence is very difficult due to its breadth and it short history. In the rest of this book we will cover many of these fundamental components of software engineering.

1.7 SOFTWARE ENGINEERING PRINCIPLES

Software-engineering principles deal with both the process of software engineering and the final product. The right process will help produce the right product, but the desired product will also affect the choice of which process to use. A traditional problem in software engineering has been the emphasis on either the process or the product to the exclusion of the other. Both are important.

The principles we develop are general enough to be applicable throughout the process of software construction and management. Principles, however, are not sufficient to drive software development. In fact, they are general and abstract statements describing desirable properties of software processes and products. But, to apply principles, the software engineer should be equipped with appropriate methods and specific techniques that help incorporate the desired properties into processes and products.

In principle, we should distinguish between methods and techniques. Methods are general guidelines that govern the execution of some activity; they are rigorous, systematic, and disciplined approaches. Techniques are more technical and mechanical than methods; often, they also have more restricted applicability. In general, however, the difference between the two is not sharp. We will therefore use the two terms interchangeably.

Sometimes, methods and techniques are packaged together to form a methodology. The purpose of a methodology is to promote a certain approach to solving a problem by preselecting the methods and techniques to be used. Tools, in turn, are developed to support the application of techniques, methods, and methodologies.

Figure 1.3 shows the relationship between principles, methods, methodologies, and tools. Each layer in the figure is based on the layer(s) below it and is more susceptible to change, due to the passage of time. This figure shows clearly that principles are the basis of all methods, techniques, methodologies, and tools.

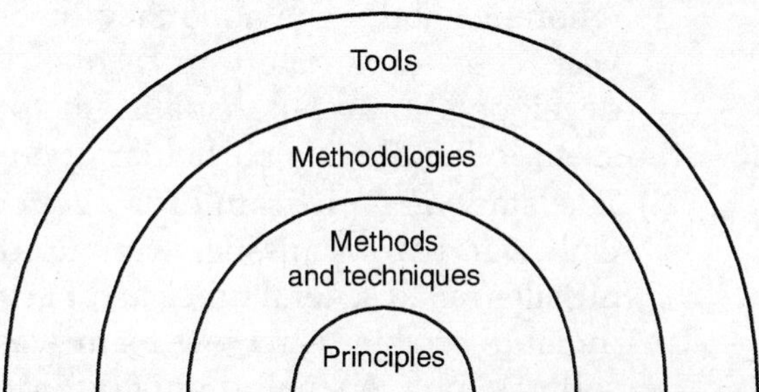

***Figure 1.3:** Relationship between Principles, Techniques, Methodologies, and Tools*

1.8 SOFTWARE CRISIS

Software engineering appears to be among the few options available to tackle the present software crisis. To explain the present software crisis in simple words, consider the following. The expenses that organizations all around the world are incurring on software purchases compared to those on hardware purchases have been showing a worrying trend over the years, as shown in Figure 1.4.

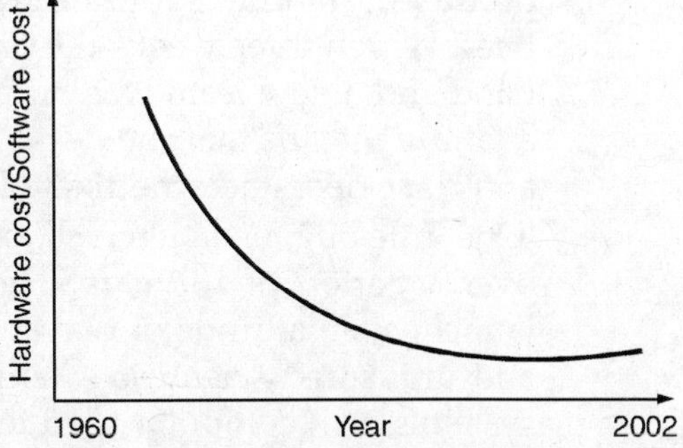

***Figure 1.4:** Change in the relative cost of Hardware and Software over Time*

Organizations are spending larger and larger portions of their money on software. Not only are the software products turning out to be more expensive than hardware, but they also present a host of other problems to the customers: software products ate difficult to alter, debug, and enhance; use resources non-optimally; often fail to meet the user requirements; are far from being reliable; frequently crash; and are often delivered late. Among these, the trend of increasing software costs is probably the most important symptom of the present software crisis. Remember that the cost we are talking about is not on account of increased features, but due to ineffective development of the product characterized by inefficient resource usage, and time and cost overruns.

The software crisis has been with us since 1970. Since then, the computer industry has progressed at a break-neck seed through the computer revolution, and recently, the network revolution triggered and/or accelerated by the explosive spread of the internet and most recently the web. Computer industry has been delivering exponential improvement in price-performance, but the problems with software have not been decreasing. Software still comes late, exceed budget and are full of residual faults. As per the latest IBM report, '31% of the projects get cancelled before they are completed, 53% over-run their cost estimates by an average of 189% and for every 100 projects, there are 94 restarts'. History has seen many software failures. Some of these are discussed here:

(i) The Y2K problem was the most crucial problem of the last century. It was somewhat ignorance about the adequacy or otherwise of using only the last two digits of the year. The 4-digit date format, like 1984, was shortened to 2-digit format, like 84. The developers could not visualise the problem of year 2000. Millions of rupees have been spent to handle this particular non-existent problem.

(ii) The 'star wars' program of USA produced 'Patriot missile' and was used first time in Gulf war. Patriot missiles were used as a defence for Iraqi Scud missiles. The Patriot missiles failed several times to hit Scud missiles, including one that killed 28 US soldiers in Saudi Arabia. A review team was constituted to find the reason and result was a software bug. A small timing error in the system's clock accumulated to the point that after 14 hours, the tracking system was no longer accurate. In the mentioned attack, the system had been operating for more than 100 hours causing the failure that lead to the death of soldiers.

(iii) In 1996, a US consumer group embarked on an 18-month, $1 million project to replace its customer database. The new system was delivered on time but did not work as promised, handling routine transactions smoothly but tripping over more complex ones. Within three weeks the database was shut down, transactions were processed by hand and a new team was brought in to rebuild the system. Possible reasons for such a failure may be that the design team was over optimistic in agreeing to requirements and developers became fixated on deadlines, allowing errors to be ignored.

(iv) 'One little bug, one big crash' of Ariane-5 space rocket, developed at a cost of $7000 M over a period of 10 years. The space rocket was destroyed after 39 seconds of its launch, at an altitude of two and a half miles along with its payload of four expensive and uninsured scientific satellites. The reason was very simple. When the guidance system's own computer tried to convert one piece of data, the sideways velocity of the rocket, from a 64-bit format to a 16-bit format, the number was too big, and an overflow error resulted after 36.7 seconds. When the guidance system shutdown. It passed control to an identical, redundant unit, which was there to provide backup in case of just such a failure. Unfortunately, the second unit had failed in the identical manner a few milliseconds before. In this case, the developers had decided that this particular velocity figure would never be large enough to cause the trouble; after all, it never had been before.

(v) The hole in the ozone layer over Antarctica remained undetected for a long period of time because the data analysis software used by NASA in its project to map the ozone layer had been designed to ignore values that deviated greatly from expected measurements. The project had been launched in 1978, but it wasn't until 1985 that the hole was discovered, and not by NASA. NASA didn't find the error until they reviewed their data, which indeed showed that there was a big hole in the ozone layer.

(vi) In 1980, NORAD reported that the US was under missile attack. The problem was caused by a faulty circuit, a possibility the reporting software hadn't taken into account. In 1983, a Soviet satellite reported incoming US missiles, but the officer in charge decided to follow his gut feeling that it was a false alarm and decided to do nothing. Luckily these false reports were never acted upon. If a counter strike had been launched in either case, a full-blown nuclear war would have been a fact and the world would have been a very different place today.

We may discuss many such failures which have played with human safety and caused the projects to fail in the past.

There are many factors that have contributed to the making of the present software crisis. Factors are larger problem sizes, lack of adequate training in software engineering, increasing skill shortage, and low productivity improvements. It is believed that the only satisfactory solution to the present software crisis can come possibly from a spread of software engineering practices among the engineers, coupled with further advancements to the software engineering discipline itself.

Hence, in order to handle such unfortunate events, a systematic and scientific discipline is required and this emerging discipline is software engineering.

1.9 SOFTWARE BEHAVIOUR, STRUCTURE, AND ARCHITECTURE

Like any other system, a software system can also be viewed as a static and dynamic entity that evolves over time after it has been subjected to both internal and external events from its executing environment.

The fixed set of instructions that makes a program provides the static structure of the software. This aspect of the software can be modelled at different levels of abstraction. Flowcharts can be used at the implementation level, structured charts or class diagrams can be used at the design level, and use case diagrams can be used at the requirements specifications level.

When subjected to internal events from timers and interrupts, or external inputs from other systems, devices, or users, the software behaves according to the behaviour specification by changing its internal state and by triggering the appropriate internal or external events. Software is mostly state-oriented. The reaction of the software to the various events depends on the state at which the software exists when the event occurs. All possible software reactions determine the behaviour of the software. Software behaviour can be modelled by diagrams, which can be state, sequence, and timing or activity diagrams. The diagrams and models can be used at different levels of abstraction. Thus software behaviour reflects the dynamic aspects of a software system.

Finally, the architectural aspect of software addresses some of the non-functional issues such as robustness, performance, resiliency, and security. Solutions affecting the software architecture include concurrency, distribution, synchronization, and multithreading. This aspect is gaining more attention because one of the main reasons for software failures if the misunderstanding or lack of handling of the non-functional requirements affecting the software architecture. Thus software architecture can be modelled by package and component diagrams. Figure 1.5 illustrates the three aspects of the software triad.

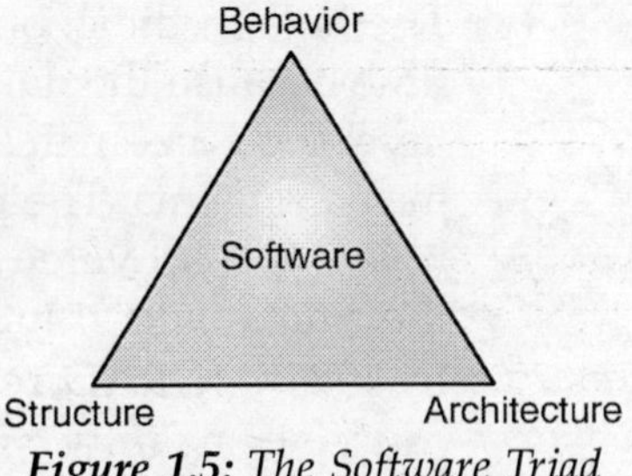

Figure 1.5: The Software Triad

To gain a better understanding of the software we develop, the behavioural, structural, and architectural issues of the software must be modelled and analysed. The three aspects of software should be part of any disciplined approach to software development.

1.10 SOFTWARE MYTHS

There are a number of myths associated with software development community. Some of them really affect the way, in which software development should take place. In this section, we list some of them, and discuss their applicability to standard software development.

1. **Software is easy to change.** It is true that the source code files are easy to edit, but that is quite different than saying that the entire software is easy to change. This is deceptive precisely because source code is easy to alter. But making changes without introducing errors is extremely difficult, particularly in organizations with poor process maturity. Every change requires the complete system to be re-verified. If we do not take proper care, this will be an extremely tedious and expensive process.
2. **Computers provide greater reliability than the devices they replace.** It is true that software does not fail in the traditional sense. There are no limits to how many times a given piece of code can be executed before it 'wears out'. In any event, the simple expression of this myth is that our general ledgers are still not perfectly accurate, even though they have been computerized. Back in the days of manual accounting systems, human error was a fact of life. Now, we have software error as well.
3. **Testing software or 'providing' software correct can remove all the errors.** Testing can only show the presence of errors. It cannot show the absence of errors. Our aim is to design effective test cases in order to find maximum possible errors. The more we test, the more we are confident about our design.
4. **Reusing software increases safety.** This myth is particularly troubling because of the false sense of security that code reuse can create. Code reuse is a very powerful tool that can yield dramatic improvement in development efficiency, but still requires analysis to determine its suitability and testing to determine if it works.
5. **Software can work right the first time.** If we go to an aeronautical engineer, and ask him to build fighter craft, he will quote us a price. If we demand that it is to be put in production without building a prototype, he will laugh and may refuse the job. Yet, software engineers are often asked to do precisely this sort of work, and they often accept the job.

6. **Software can be designed thoroughly enough to avoid most integration problems.** There is an old saying among software designers: "Too bad, there is no compiler for specifications". This point out the fundamental difficulty with detailed specifications. They always have inconsistencies, and there is no computer tool to perform consistency checks on these. Therefore, special care is required to understand the specifications, and if there is an ambiguity, that should be resolved before proceeding for design.
7. **Software with more features is better software.** This is, of course, almost the opposite of the truth. The best, most enduring programs are those which do one thing well.
8. **Addition of more software engineers will make up the delay.** This is not true in most cases. By the process of adding more software engineers during the project, we may further delay the project. This does not serve any purpose here, although this may be true for any civil engineering work.
9. **Aim is to develop working programs.** The aim has been shifted from developing working programs to good quality, maintainable programs. Maintaining software has become a very critical and crucial area for software engineering community.

This list is endless. These myths, poor quality of software, increasing cost and delay in the delivery of the software have been the driving forces behind the emergence of software engineering as a discipline. In addition, following are the contributing factors:

- Change in ratio of hardware to software costs
- Increasing importance of maintenance
- Advanced software techniques
- Increased demand for software
- Demand for larger and more complex software systems

1.11 SOFTWARE STAKEHOLDERS

Software products are complex to develop and maintain because of the many internal interactions within the software development group and the interactions with the external environment, including the various stakeholders. Software development stakeholders are those people who can affect or get affected by the software product that is to be developed. Various stakeholders are shown in Figure 1.6.

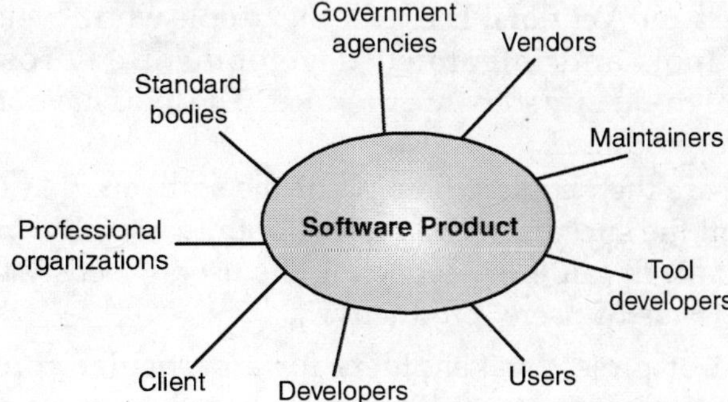

Figure 1.6: Stakeholders in a Software Product

The software stakeholders include:

- **Software Developers:** These are the people involved in the development of the software. A software developer might be involved in the various phases of the software development project, including requirements, specification, design, coding, and testing of the software.
- **Software Maintainers:** These are the people involved in the post-delivery and installation of the software, including maintenance, deployment, and configuration management.
- **Technical Writers:** These are the people involved in writing the various technical and user documentation that are needed to ensure the deployment of highly usable and maintainable software systems and applications.
- **Software Vendors:** These are the people responsible for marketing and selling the software application and use of various distribution channels.
- **Software Users:** These are the intended users of the software who can be classified according to the functionality offered to them and based on their roles or responsibilities. Possible types of software users include normal, administrative or privileged, executive management, and maintenance users.
- **Government Bodies:** These are the entities that might set and enforce rules and regulations to which the software must conform. Examples of such government bodies include environmental agencies, health agencies, and financial agencies.
- **Professional Organizations and Societies:** These are the entities involved in overseeing the state of the discipline and its body of knowledge in setting and maintaining the code of ethics for the profession. Moreover, professional organizations help in the life-long and continuous development of software professionals through administering professional certifications and organizing conferences, workshops, and other continuing education programs.
- **Standards Bodies:** These are the entities that are setting standards for software development, software environments, and software/hardware interfaces. In addition, standards bodies might be involved in setting application or context-specific standards in areas that include health, banking, and environment, and possibly, working in tandem with governmental agencies and professional organizations and societies.
- **Tool Developers and Vendors:** These are the people who develop and maintain software development tools and integrated development environments to facilitate the production of high-quality software products. The tools have an influence on the quality of the software produced.
- **Clients:** These are the people who pay for the software that is being developed. They are interested in the success of the project, both financially and technically. They have a substantial stake in faithfully reflecting the users' needs while ensuring a return on investment in terms of users' productivity.

The specific list of project stakeholders for a particular application depends on the complexity of the needed software and its application domain. For example, in a context in which a bank needs to outsource the development of a web-based application to provide value-added services to its customers, the stakeholders of this banking software might include those shown in Table 1.1.

Table 1.1: The Stakeholders in Banking Software

Stakeholder	Description
Client	Bank (paying for the software)
Developer	Software Company XYZ (selected to develop the software)
Users	Bank customers having online access
Technical writers	Employees of the bank or the software company
Government Bodies	Banking regulations related to privacy protection
Standard Bodies	Basel II for IT risk management
Professional Organizations	Banker's association
Software Maintainers	The bank, the software company, or a third party

1.12 ROLE OF MANAGEMENT IN SOFTWARE DEVELOPMENT

The management of software development is heavily dependent on four factors: People, Product, Process, and Project. Order of dependency of these factors is shown in Figure 1.7.

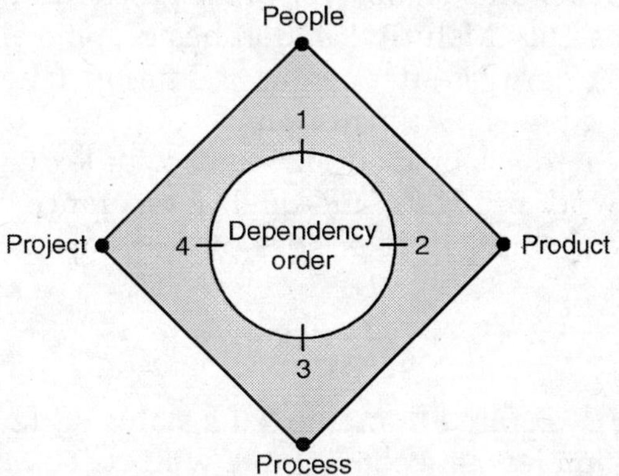

Figure 1.7: Factors of Management Dependency (from People to Project)

Software development is a people centric activity. Hence, success of the project is on the shoulders of the people who are involved in the development.

1.12.1 The People

Software development requires good managers. The managers should be able to understand the psychology of people and provide good leadership. A good manager cannot ensure the success of project, but can increase the probability of success. The areas to be given priority are: proper selection, training, compensation, and career development, work culture, etc.

Mangers face challenges. It requires mental toughness to endure inner pain. We need to plan for the best, be prepared for the worst, expect surprises, but continue to move forward anyway. Charles Maurice once rightly said 'I am more afraid of an army of one hundred sheep lead by a lion than an army of one hundred lions lead by a sheep'.

Hence, manager selection is most crucial and critical. After having a good manager, the project is in safe hands. It is the responsibility of a manager to manage, motivate, encourage, guide and control the people of his team.

1.12.2 The Product

What do we want to deliver to the customer? Obviously, a product, which is a solution to his problems. Hence, objectives and scope of work should be defined clearly to understand the requirements. Alternate solutions must be discussed. It may help the managers to select the 'best' approach within constraints imposed by delivery deadlines, budgetary restrictions, personnel availability, technical interfaces, etc. Without well-defined requirements, it may be impossible to define reasonable estimates of the cost, development time and schedule for the project.

1.12.3 The Process

The process is the way in which we produce software. It provides the framework from which a comprehensive plan for software development can be established. If the process is weak, the end product will undoubtedly suffer. There are many life cycle models and process improvement models. Depending on the type of the project, a suitable model is to be selected. Now-a-days CMM (capability Maturity Model) has become almost a standard for process framework. The process priority is after people and product; however, it plays a very crucial role for the success of the project. A small number of framework activities are applicable to all software projects, regardless of their size and complexity. A number of different task sets, tasks, milestones, work products, and quality assurance points, enable the framework activities to be adopted to the characteristics of the project and the requirements of the project team.

1.12.4 The Project

A proper planning is required to monitor the status of development and to control the complexity. Most of the projects are coming late with cost overruns of more than 100%. In order to manage a successful project, we must understand what we can go wrong and how to do it right. We should define concrete requirements (although very difficult) and freeze these requirements. Changes should not be incorporated to avoid software surprises. Software surprises are always risky and we should minimize them. We should have a planning mechanism to give warning before the occurrence of any surprise.

All four factors (People, Product, Process and Project) are important for the success of the project. Their relative importance helps us to organize development activities in more scientific and professional way.

1.13 PRINCIPLES OF SOFTWARE ENGINEERING

Many students of software engineering as well as practicing software engineers have asked if there are natural laws or principles in software engineering similar to those found in other disciplines such as laws of motion or laws of thermodynamics etc. We in software engineering do not have a set of laws, but we do have several sets of proposed principles of software engineering. These principles have evolved through numerous years of past experience and many are well accepted. Since software engineering is still young and developing, the existing principles will continue to be modified and new ones added. In this section, we will introduce some of them.

1.13.1 Davis's Early Principles of Software

Alan Davis (1994) is one of the earlier authorities to bring forward a set of principles that underlie software engineering. His article on the 15 principles of software engineering actually includes 30 principles. He later published a book entitled *201 Principles of Software Engineering*. Here we will introduce only the 15 'most important principles' as David saw them.

- **Make the quality Number 1:** It is short-sightedness to deliver a product that is of poor quality. Quality has many definitions and means different things to different constituents. For example, to the developer, it may mean 'elegant design', and to the customers, it may mean 'good response time'. IN any case, quality must be viewed as the first requirement.
- **High quality software is possible:** Large software systems can be built with good quality, although it may carry a high price.
- **Give products to customer early:** It is very difficult to completely understand and capture the users' needs during the requirements phase. Thus it is more effective to give the users a prototype of the product and let them play with it. Gather the feedback and then go into full-scale development of the product.
- **Determine the problem before writing the requirements:** Before the software engineers rush to offer the solution, ensure that the problem is well understood. Then explore the potential solution and various alternatives.
- **Evaluate design alternatives:** After the requirements are understood and agreed upon, explore a variety of design architecture and related algorithms. Ensure that the selected design and algorithms are best match to satisfy the goal of the requirement.
- **Use an appropriate process model:** Since there is no universal process model that applies to all projects, each project must select a process that fits the project based on parameters such as corporate culture, project circumstances, user expectations, requirements volatility, and resource experiences.
- **Use different language for different phases:** No one single language is optimal for all phases of software development. Therefore select the best methodology and language for different phases of software development. The difficulty in transition from one phase to another is not necessarily solved by using single language across all phases.
- **Minimize intellectual distance:** It is easier to create the solution if the distance between the real world problem and the computerized solution to that problem is minimized. That is, the software solution structure needs to be as close as possible to the real world problem structure.
- **Put technique before tools:** Before using the tool, the technique needs to be well understood. Otherwise, the tool just rushes us into performing the wrong thing faster.
- **Get it right before you make it faster:** It is essential to make the software execute correctly first and then work on improving it. Do not worry about optimization, both execution speed and code, during initial coding.

- **Inspect code:** Inspection as first proposed by IBM's Mike Fagan is a much better way to find errors than testing. Some early data in inspections showed a reduction of 50% to 90% of the time to test.
- **Good management is more important that good technology:** A good manager can produce extraordinary results even with limited resources. Even the best technology cannot compensate for terrible management because it cannot motivate people as well as managers can.
- **People are the key to success:** Software is a labour intensive profession, and people with experience, talent, and appropriate drive are the key. The right people can overcome may of the shortcomings in the process, methodology, and tools. There is no substitute for quality people.
- **Follow with care:** Be careful in adopting tools, processes, methodology, etc. Do not follow just because someone else is doing it or using it. Run some experiments before making a major commitment.
- **Take responsibility:** If you developed the system, then you should take responsibility to do it right. Blaming the failure or the problem on others or on the process is purely irresponsible.

All except two of David's 15 principles of software engineering address the management of and techniques of software development and support. The first two of David's principles address the software product quality attribute. It is interesting that quality is the only software product attribute mentioned in these principles. There is clearly a need to have more principles that address software product attributes. These product attributes might include the following:

- Maintainability
- Installability
- Usability
- Interoperability
- Modifiability

These attributes are still ill-defined. We must first clearly define them and then come to some consensus on which ones are important. As our field matures, the necessary software product attributes will gradually be developed.

1.13.2 Boyce's More Modern Principles

Building on David's list, Walker Royce (1998) in his book proposes a modern set. His top ten principles for modern software management are as follows:

- Base the process on an architecture-first approach.
- Establish an iterative process that addresses risks early in the process.
- Emphasize component based development to reduce the coding effort.
- Change management should be established to handle iterative process.
- Enhance the iterative development process environment, called round-trip engineering, where multiple changes may occur constantly across multiple artifacts with automated tools.

- Use model-based and machine-processable notation to capture design.
- Establish the process for objective quality control and project progress assessment that includes the assessment of all the intermediate artifacts.
- Use a demonstration-based approach where intermediate artifacts are transitioned to executable demonstration of the user scenario so that these artifacts can be accessed earlier.
- Plan to have incremental releases, each composed of a group of usage scenarios, with evolving levels of detail.
- Establish a configurable process since no one process is suitable for all software development.

These ten principles are heavily influenced by the assumption that the underlying development process should be iterative in nature. It is considered modern because it is becoming more evident that building a large, complex system in one iteration is extremely difficult. Simply understanding the requirements of a large system alone requires multiple iterations. A process that allows us to construct a software system iteratively and incrementally is crucial and is preferred as an alternative to the sequentially regimental phase approach such as the waterfall process model. We will discuss and expand on the different traditional and emerging software process models in Chapter 3.

1.13.3 Wasserman's Fundamental Software Engineering Concepts

Anthony Wasserman (1996) suggested that there are eight software engineering concepts that remained relatively constant even though the software industry has been changing. The following basic concepts thus form a 'foundation' to the software engineering discipline:

- Abstraction
- Analysis and design methods and notation
- User interface prototyping
- Modularity and architecture
- Reuse
- Life cycle and process
- Metrics
- Tools and integrated environment

The first concept, abstraction, is a technique that is often categorised as a design technique. It is in fact a broad method that software engineers employ to aid in generalization of a concept and postponing the concerns for the details. Proper analysis and design is the second concept and is a key to successfully developing software. Analysis provides us a clear set of requirements, and design transforms the requirements to solution structure. Many have attempted to omit or reduce these efforts, and such incomplete work has been the major cause of many software failures. In addition, the notation for analysis and design needs to be standardized to facilitate more universal communications.

Developing standard notation is crucial for software engineering to move toward a disciplined engineering profession. The third major concept, user interface prototyping contributes to a vital portion of understanding requirements and user preferences. It also contributes heavily to an iterative process approach to software development. Modularity in software architecture, the fourth concept, contributes heavily to the quality and maintainability of the software. In addition to modularity, Wasserman also focuses on design patterns and the need for standardizing architectures. Certainly, design patterns and standardization of architecture contributes heavily on the notion of reuse, which is listed as the fifth concept. Reuse is a long-standing practice in the software industry since the inception of macros in assembly language and standard math libraries. In operating systems and software tools, we find an abundance of libraries of general functions. Industry specific components that are easily identifiable and reusable need to be developed. Software process may not appear to be as significant to software engineering as concepts such as specification and analysis since there are software projects that have been successfully completed without much discipline or organized process. It is important to recognize, however, that most of the large, complex software projects have survived without some defined process. Thus the sixth major concept is life cycle and process. Employing metrics, the seventh concept, is an important engineering, as well as management, technique. It is impossible to measure any software attributes or software process without well-defined metrics and measurement techniques, let alone attempting to improve on these attributes and processes. Finally, tools and integrated environment, the eighth major concept, are necessary for the development and support of any large, complex software.

When each of Wasserman's ideas is viewed individually, the concepts do not appear extraordinarily exceptional. However, taken together, they certainly delineate many of the significant advances made in the software engineering field.

1.14 SOFTWARE ENGINEERING CODE OF ETHICS

Today, software is a valuable intellectual property, and software engineering is moving toward a more disciplined profession. Software plays a key role in all dimensions of our lives. As professionals, software engineers must conduct their practices at some level of professionalism to minimally ensure that their work results in no harm to society. An IEEE report has recommended eight principles for ethics and professional practices in software engineering.

1. Software engineers shall act consistently with the public interest.
2. Software engineers shall act in a manner that is in best interests of their client and employer, consistent with the public interest.
3. Software engineers shall ensure that their products and related modifications meet the highest professional standards possible.
4. Software engineers shall maintain integrity and interdependence in their professional judgement.
5. Software engineering managers and leaders shall subscribe to and promote an ethical approach to the management of software development and maintenance.
6. Software engineers shall advance the integrity and reputation of the profession consistent with the public interest.
7. Software engineers shall be fair to and supportive of their colleagues.
8. Software engineers shall participate in lifelong learning regarding the practice of their profession and shall promote an ethical approach to the practice of the profession.

Under each of these general principles, there are several sub-elements that further explain the principles. For example, the second principle of this code, which deals with client and employer, has nine more explanatory sub-principles regarding the duties of software engineers:

- Provide services in their areas of competence, being honest and forthright about any limitations of their experience and education.
- Not knowingly use software that is obtained or retained either illegally or unethically.
- Use the property of a client or employer only in ways properly authorized, and with the clients or employer's knowledge and consent.
- Ensure that any document upon which they rely has been approved, when required, by someone authorized to approve it.
- Keep private any confidential information gained in their professional work, where such confidentiality is consistent with the public interest and consistent with the law.
- Identify, document, collect evidence, and report to the client or employer promptly if, in their opinion, a project is likely to fail, to prove too expensive, to violate intellectual property law, or otherwise to be problematic.
- Identify, document, and report significant issues of social concern, of which they are aware, in software or related documents, to the employer or the client.
- Accept no outside work detrimental to the work they perform for their primary employer.
- Promise no interest adverse to their employer or client, unless a higher ethical concern is being compromised; in that case, inform the employer or another appropriate authority of the ethical concern.

Software engineering, to be judged as a professional engineering practice, must include the code and regulations that its members must uphold. Thus software engineering also includes directions for its members' knowledge acquisition and directions for its members' behavioural practices. This is particularly difficult as there are no government regulations and codes for software engineering as there are for civil or for chemical engineering. As mentioned earlier, there are laws for protecting intellectual properties, and software engineers can look to those for guidelines. The fact that there has been a task force effort on defining the code of conduct for software engineers already indicates that significant progress has been made in software engineering toward professionalism.

1.15 SOFTWARE QUALITY

In the most general sense, software quality can be defined as 'an effective software process applied in a manner that creates a useful product that provides measurable value for those who produce it and those who use it'. There is little question that the preceding definition could be modified or extended and debated endlessly. Here, the definition serves to emphasize three important points:

1. An *effective software process* establishes the infrastructure that supports any effort at building a high-quality software product. The management aspects of process create the checks and balances that help avoid project chaos which is a key contributor to poor quality. Software engineering practices allow the developer to analyse the problem

and design a solid solution, both critical to building high-quality software. Finally, umbrella activities such as change management and technical reviews have as much to do with quality as any other part of software engineering practice.

2. A *useful product* delivers the content, functions, and features that the end-user desires, but as important, it delivers these assets in a reliable, error-free way. A useful product always satisfies those requirements that have been explicitly stated by stakeholders. In addition, it satisfies a set of implicit requirements (e.g. ease of use) that are expected of high-quality software.
3. By *adding value for both the producer and user* of a software product, high-quality software provides benefits for the software organization and the end-user community. The software organization gains added value because high-quality software requires less maintenance effort, fewer bug fixes, and reduced customer support. This enables software engineers to spend more time creating new applications and less on rework. The user community gains added value because the application provides a useful capability in the way that expedites some business process. The end result is greater software product revenue, better profitability when an application supports a business process, and/or improved availability of information that is crucial for the business.

The modern view of quality associates a software product with several quality factors such as the following:

- **Portability:** A software product is said to be portable, if it can be easily made to work in different operating system environments, in different machines, with other software products, etc.
- **Usability:** A software product has good usability, if different categories of users (i.e. both expert and novice users) can easily invoke the functions of the product.
- **Reusability:** A software product has good reusability, if different modules of the product can easily be reused to develop new products
- **Correctness:** A software product is correct, if different requirements as specified in the SRS document have been correctly implemented.
- **Maintainability:** A software product is maintainable, if errors can be easily corrected as and when they show up, new functions can be easily added to the product, and the functionalities of the product can be easily modified, etc.

1.16 SOFTWARE QUALITY MANAGEMENT SYSTEM

A quality management system (often referred to as *quality system*) is the principle methodology used by organizations to ensure that the products they develop have the desired quality. A quality system consists of the following:

- **Managerial structure and individual responsibilities:** A quality system is actually the responsibility of the organization as a whole. However, many organizations have a separate quality department to perform several quality system activities. The quality system of an organization should have the support of the top management. Without support for the quality system at a high level in a company, few members of the staff will take the quality system seriously.

- **Quality system activities:** The quality system activities encompass the following:
  - Auditing of the projects
  - Review of quality system
  - Development of standards, procedures, and guidelines, etc.
  - Production of reports for top management summarizing the effectiveness of the quality system in the organization.

A good quality system must be well documented. Without a properly documented quality system, the application of quality controls and procedures become ad hoc, resulting in large variations in the quality of the product delivered. Also, an undocumented quality system sends clear messages to the staff about the attitude of the organization towards quality assurance. International standards such as ISO 9000 provide guidance on how to organize a quality system.

1.16.1 ISO 9000

As standards go, ISO 9000 is one of the most widely recognized in the world. ISO 9000 is a quality management standard that presents guidelines intended to increase business efficiency and customer satisfaction. The goal of ISO 9000 is to embed a quality management system within an organization, increasing productivity, reducing unnecessary costs, and ensuring quality of processes and products.

ISO 9001:2008 is applicable to businesses and organizations from every sector. The process oriented approach makes the standard applicable to service organizations as well. Its general guidelines allow for the flexibility needed for today's diverse business world.

We list here the ISO 9000 principles:

1. **A Customer Focus:** As stated before, the customer is the primary focus of a business. By understanding and responding to the needs of customers, an organization can correctly targeting key demographics and therefore increase revenue by delivering the products and services that the customer is looking for. With knowledge of customer needs, resources can be allocated appropriately and efficiently. Most importantly, a business's dedication will be recognized by the customer, creating customer loyalty. And customer loyalty is return business.
2. **Good Leadership:** A team of good leaders will establish unity and direction quickly in a business environment. Their goal is to motivate everyone working on the project, and successful leaders will minimize miscommunication within and between departments. Their role is intimately intertwined with the next ISO 9000 principle.
3. **Involvement of people:** The inclusion of everyone on a business team is critical to its success. Involvement of substance will lead to a personal investment in a project and in turn create motivated, committed workers. These people will tend towards innovation and creativity, and utilize their full abilities to complete a project. If people have a vested interest in performance, they will be eager to participate in the continual improvement that ISO 900 facilitates.
4. **Process approach to quality management:** The best results are achieved when activities and resources are managed together. This process approach to quality management can lower costs through the effective use of resources, personnel, and time. If a process

is controlled as a whole, management can focus on goals that are important to the big picture, and prioritize objectives to maximize effectiveness.

5. **Management system approach:** Combining management groups may seem like a dangerous clash of titans, but if done correctly can result in an efficient and effective management system. If leaders are dedicated to the goals of an organization, they will aid each other to achieve improved productivity. Some results include integration and alignment of key processes. Additionally, interested parties will recognize the consistency, effectiveness, and efficiency that come with a management system. Both suppliers and customers will gain confidence in a business's abilities.
6. **Continual Improvement:** The importance of this principle is paramount, and should a permanent objective of every organization. Through increased performance, a company can increase profits and gain an advantage over competitors. If a whole business is dedicated to continual improvement, improvement activities will be aligned, leading to faster and more efficient development. Ready for improvement and change, businesses will have the flexibility to react quickly to new opportunities.
7. **Factual approach to decision making:** Effective decisions are based on the analysis and interpretation of information and data. By making informed decisions, an organization will be more likely to make the right decision. As companies make this a habit, they will be able to demonstrate the effectiveness of past decisions. This will put confidence in current and future decisions.
8. **Supplier relationships:** It is important to establish a mutually beneficial supplier relationship; such a relationship creates value for both parties. A supplier that recognizes a mutually beneficial relationship will be quick to react when a business needs to respond to customer needs or market changes. Through close contact and interaction with a supplier, both organizations will be able to optimize resources and costs.

1.17 SOFTWARE PROCESSES CAPABILITY MATURITY MODEL

The Capability Maturity Model (CMM) was developed by W. Humphrey at the Software Engineering Institute at Carnegie Mellon University for the assessment of the development processes at software development companies. CMM was succeeded by the CMM Integration (CMMI) as a generalised model to assist in the assessment of the process maturity of different types of organizations and in various areas such as systems engineering, project management, and supply chain management. The CMM does not recommend any particular set of mature processes to be followed by an organization. However, the CMM can be used to assess the maturity of existing processes. The basis for the placement at a particular level is based on the availability of specific process areas defined for that level. As a result of the process maturity assessment, an organization is placed at one of five maturity levels: (1) initial, (2) repeatable, (3) defined, (4) managed, and (5) optimized, the best of which is obviously the optimized level. The different levels of SEI CMM have been designed so that it is easy for an organization to slowly build its quality system beginning from the scratch.

Level 1: Initial

At this level, the processes used are ad hoc, informal, and not documented. The knowledge and experiences are not archived and documented. Project success relies heavily on the efforts of some of the team members. However, due to lack of documented development methodologies and experiences, it might be impossible to repeat success in new projects of similar types and complexities. Completed projects in organizations at the initial level of maturity are characterized by low quality, numerous errors, and running time and over budget.

Level 2: Repeatable

At this level, the development methodology and all its phases are partially documented. The processes involved in the documented phases are repeatable, but the successful application of the processes is not guaranteed every time they are followed. The rigorous application of the documented phases varies from project to project. Project management techniques and tools are used to track project progress in terms of cost, schedule, and project deliverables. Software quality assurance is considered for the documented processes.

Level 3: Defined

At this level, the development processes are documented and well defined. Internal standards and documented methodology are used uniformly across the organization and in all development projects undertaken. The documented processes have also been updated over time using past experiences to improve performance. However, past experiences are assessed and documented qualitatively. Moreover, the documented processes are adapted to take into consideration the project complexity and context. Organizations at this level thoroughly consider all aspects of project management.

Level 4: Managed

At this level, developmental metrics are collected during the execution of the project to provide a quantitative basis for software quality management. The metrics allow the project manager to predict the future performance of the remaining phases of the project. The predictions allow the manager to closely track and control the project based on quantitative assessment. Consequently, this allows the manager to manage the risks more effectively and take the necessary and timely actions should any risk occur.

Level 5: Optimized

Using metrics collected during the execution of the project phases, and using the documented standards and processes, modifications to both standards and processes are implemented continuously during this level. The changes are also triggered by technology changes, the adoption of which can lead to improved performance. Performance indicators are developed and monitored. Changes to processes and standards show improvements in performance from project to project. Process and technology change management systems are in place to deal with changes in processes and in available technology. As the software development organization is maturing and gaining experience, the collected metrics are used to optimize the processes and the organization workflow leading to increased productivity while maintaining the product qualities.

An organization placed at a particular level is an indication that it meets all the requirements for that level and is showing clear indication that it is progressing toward the next higher level. The Software Engineering Institute (SEI) is maintaining a database of appraised organizations at levels 2 to 5. The characteristics of the five maturity levels are summarized in Table 1.2.

Table 1.2: Summary of the Characteristics of the Five Maturity Levels

Maturity Level	Characteristics
1. Initial	Ad hoc, informal, and non-documented processes
2. Repeatable	Processes and standards partially documented Software quality assurance considered Requirements management and project tracking in place
3. Defined	Development methodology and standards documented Risk management and qualitative assessment of project performance in place
4. Managed	Metrics on processes collected Quantitative assessment of process performance and software quality management in place
5. Optimized	Optimal processes and workflows in place Continuous process and standards improvements in place

The SEI has associated key process areas (KPAs) with each of the maturity levels except for Level 1. The KPAs describe those software engineering functions (e.g., software project planning, requirements management) that must be present to satisfy good practice at a particular level. Each KPA is described by identifying the following characteristics:

- *Goals*—the overall objectives that the KPA must achieve.
- *Commitments*—requirements (imposed on the organization) that must be met to achieve the goals or provide proof of intent to comply with the goals.
- *Abilities*—those things that must be in place (organizationally and technically) to enable the organization to meet the commitments.
- *Activities*—the specific tasks required to achieve the KPA function.
- *Methods for monitoring implementation*—the manner in which the activities are monitored as they are put into place.
- *Methods for verifying implementation*—the manner in which proper practice for the KPA can be verified.

Eighteen KPAs (each described using these characteristics) are defined across the maturity model and mapped into different levels of process maturity. The following KPAs should be achieved at each process maturity level:

Process maturity level 2

- Software configuration management
- Software quality assurance
- Software subcontract management
- Software project tracking and oversight
- Software project planning
- Requirements management

Process maturity level 3

- Peer reviews
- Intergroup coordination
- Software product engineering
- Integrated software management
- Training program
- Organization process definition
- Organization process focus

Process maturity level 4

- Software quality management
- Quantitative process management

Process maturity level 5

- Process change management
- Technology change management
- Defect prevention

Each of the KPAs is defined by a set of *key practices* that contribute to satisfying its goals. The key practices are policies, procedures, and activities that must occur before a key process area has been fully instituted. The SEI defines *key indicators* as 'those key practices or components of key practices that offer the greatest insight into whether the goals of a key process area have been achieved'. Assessment questions are designed to probe for the existence (or lack thereof) of a key indicator.

1.18 SIX SIGMA

General Electric (GE) first began Six Sigma in 1995 after Motorola and Allied Signal blazed the Six Sigma trial. Since then, thousands of companies around the world have discovered the far-reaching benefits of Six Sigma. The purpose of Six Sigma is to improve processes in order to do things better, faster, and at lower cost. It can be used to improve every facet of business, from production, to human resources, to order entry, to technical support. Six Sigma can be used for any activity that is concerned with cost, timeliness, and quality of results. Therefore, it is applicable to virtually every industry.

Six Sigma, at many organizations, simply means striving for near perfection. Six Sigma is a disciplined, data-driven approach to eliminate defects in any process, from manufacturing to transactional and from product to service.

The statistical representation of Six Sigma describes quantitatively how a process is performing. To achieve Six Sigma, a process must not produce more than 3-4 defects per million opportunities. A Six Sigma defect is defined as any system behaviour that is not as per customer specifications. The total number of Six Sigma opportunities is then the total number of chances for a defect. Process sigma can easily be calculated using a Six Sigma calculator.

The fundamental objective of Six Sigma methodology is the implementation of a measurement based strategy that focuses on process improvement and variation reduction through the application of Six Sigma improvement projects. This is accomplished through the use of two Six Sigma sub-methodologies: DMAIC and DMADV. The Six Sigma DMAIC process (define measure, analyse, improve, control) is an improvement system for existing processes falling below specification and thus looking for incremental improvement. The Six Sigma DMADV process (define, measure, analyse, design, verify) is an improvement system used to develop new processes or products at Six Sigma quality levels. It can also be employed if a current process requires more than just incremental improvement. Both Six Sigma processes are executed by Six Sigma Green Belts and Six Sigma Black Belts, and are overseen by Six Sigma Master Black Belts.

Many frameworks exist for implementing the Six Sigma methodology. Six Sigma Consultants all over the world have also developed proprietary methodologies for implementing Six Sigma quality, based on the similar change management philosophies and applications of tools.

1.19 GENERIC STAGES IN SOFTWARE DEVELOPMENT

As stated earlier, software engineering encompasses the use of a disciplined and systematic approach for the development and maintenance of computer software. The goals of software engineering are to deal with the software complexities, increase the reliability, and enhance the quality of the produced software.

One of the main features of a disciplined approach is to deal with complexity in a staged manner. In the initial stages, the software is tackled in different phases and at higher levels of abstraction. In the subsequent phases, the software is tackled at lower levels of abstraction by providing more details so that a proper implementation is obtained in the second stage. This process is also called top-down and stepwise refinement.

The three generic stages of software development and maintenance activities consist of the (1) **definition stage**, (2) **implementation stage**, and (3) **maintenance stage**. The definition stage is comprised of the requirements phase and the specification phase in which user requirements are collected and analysed to obtain a formal software specification. During the implementation stage, at a lower level of abstraction, the design phase refines the specifications to obtain a basis for a concrete implementation of the software. Coding of the design is performed and then tested for conformance to the specifications. The maintenance stage deals with the software change requests to correct software errors, adapt, or expand the software. The software changes could invoke a rework of the requirements, specifications, design, and implementation followed by a complete or regression testing to ensure the proper implementation of the needed software changes. The details of the generic stages are discussed in Chapter 2 in the context of Life Cycle Models. Figure 1.8 illustrates the three generic stages for software development and maintenance and their respective phases.

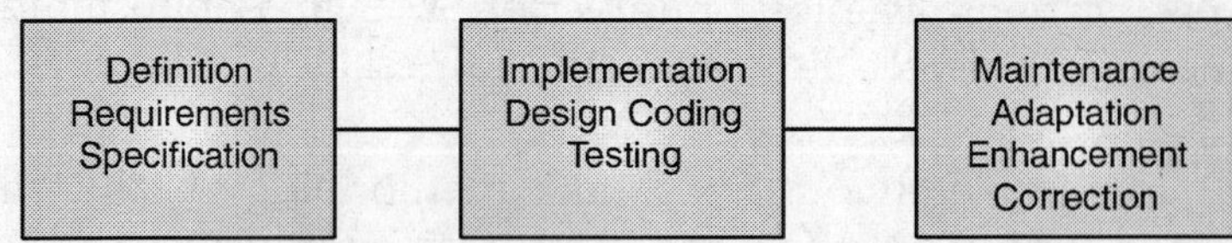

Figure 1.8: *The three Generic Stages for Software Development and Maintenance*

1.20 SOFTWARE DEVELOPMENT LIFE CYCLE

Alternatively referred to as software life cycle and software development phases, the software development process is a set of steps that a software program goes through when it is developed. In Figure 1.9, there is a waterfall type approach to software development and an example of the steps taken in the phases of software development.

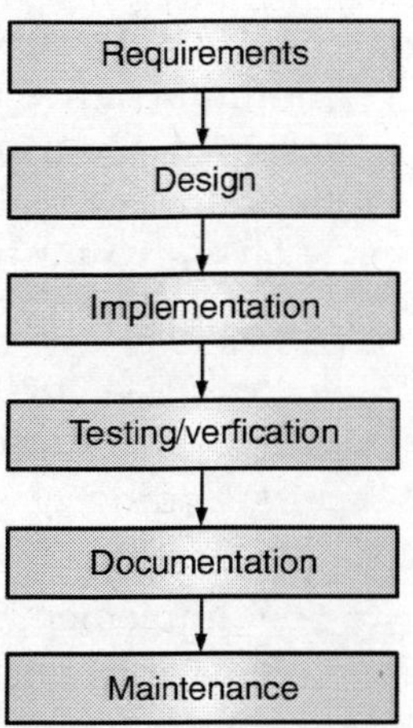

Figure 1.9: *Phases of Software Development*

First in the software development process, the requirements phase outlines the goals of what the program will be capable of doing. Next, the design phase covers how the program is going to be created, who will be doing what, etc. The implementation phase is where the programmers and other designers start work on the program. After the developers have a working copy, the testing and verification step can begin to help verify the program has no errors. During the testing phase, problems found are fixed, until the program meets the company's quality controls. After the program's development, the documentation phase on how to use the program can be completed. Finally, maintenance and updating the program must continue for several years after the initial release. A software development process makes everything easier and reduces the amount of problems encountered. Before going into details of each model in next chapter, let us have a look at the software development life cycle in general, and the phases it contains.

Definition: SDLC is an acronym for Software Development Life Cycle. It is also sometimes referred to as System Development Life Cycle. In simple words it the process or method applied to create or alter software projects. Each of these methodologies defines unique way to create a new software module or program.

The software-development life-cycle is used to facilitate the development of a large software product in a systematic, well-defined, and cost-effective way. It is the series of identifiable stages that a software product undergoes during its lifetime. A process model for software engineering is chosen based on the nature of the project and application, the methods and tools to be used, and the controls and deliverables that are required.

An information system goes through a series of phases from conception to implementation. This process is called the Software-Development Life-Cycle.

1.20.1 Entry and Exist Criteria

The software development life-cycle consists of several phases and these phases need to be identified along with defining the entry and exit criteria for every phase. A phase can begin only when the corresponding phase-entry criteria are satisfied. Similarly, a phase can be considered to be complete only when the corresponding exit criteria are satisfied.

If there is no clear indication of the entry and exit for every phase, it becomes very difficult to track the progress of the project.

1.21 SDLC PHASES

The software development life-cycle can be divided into 5-9 phases, i.e., it must have a minimum of five phases and a maximum of nine phases, depending upon the product being designed. On average it has seven or eight phases. In general, the process is divided into the following eight phases:

- Project initiation and planning/Recognition of need/Preliminary investigation
- Project identification and selection/Feasibility study
- Project analysis
- System design
- Coding
- Testing
- Implementation
- Maintenance

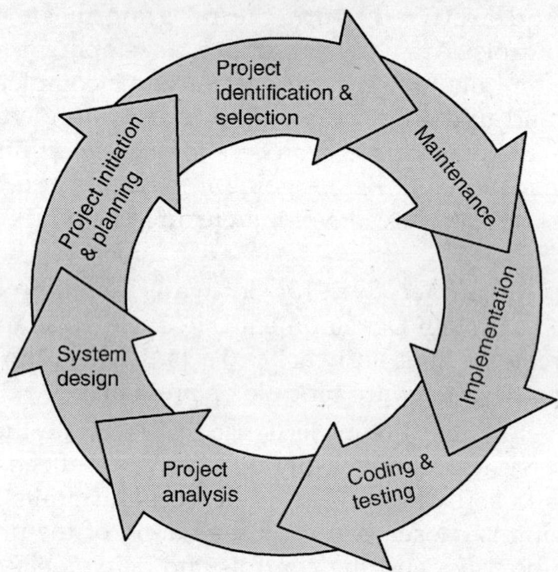

Figure 1.10: *Software Development Life Cycle*

Let us have a brief overview of each of these phases.

1.21.1 Recognition of Need

Recognition of need is nothing but the problem definition. It is the decision about problems in the existing system and the motivation for system change. The first stage of any project or system-development life-cycle is called the preliminary investigation. It is a brief investigation of the system under consideration. This investigation provides the organization's computer steering committee and any project team a set of terms or references for more detailed work. This is carried out by a senior manager and will result in a study proposal. At this stage the need for changes in the existing system are identified and shortcomings of the existing system are detected. These are stated clearly providing the basis for the initial or feasibility study.

1.21.2 Feasibility Study

A feasibility study is a preliminary study which investigates the information needs of prospective users and determines the resource requirements, costs, benefits, and feasibility of a proposed project.

The goal of feasibility studies is to evaluate alternative systems and to propose the most feasible and desirable systems for development. The feasibility of a proposed system can be evaluated in terms of four major categories, as illustrated in Table 1.3

Table 1.3: Key Features of Categories of Feasibility

Category	Features
Organizational Feasibility	How well the proposed system supports the strategic objectives of the organization.
Economic Feasibility	Cost savings Increased revenue Decreased investment Increased profits
Technical Feasibility	Hardware, software, and network capability, reliability and availability
Operational Feasibility	End-user acceptance Management support Customer, supplier, and government requirements

- **Organizational Feasibility:** Organizational feasibility is how well a proposed information system supports the objectives of the organization and is a strategic plan for an information system. For example, projects that do not directly contribute to meeting an organization's strategic objectives are typically not funded.
- **Economic Feasibility:** Economic feasibility is concerned with whether expected cost savings, increased revenue, increased profits, reductions in required investments, and other types of benefits will exceed the costs of developing and operating a proposed system. For example, if a project can't cover its development costs, it won't be approved, unless mandated by government regulations or other considerations.
- **Technical Feasibility:** Technical feasibility can be demonstrated if reliable hardware and software capable of meeting the needs of a proposed system can be acquired or developed by the business in the required time.
- **Operational Feasibility:** Operational feasibility is the willingness and ability of management, employees, customers, suppliers, and others to operate, use, and support a proposed system. For example, if the software for a new system is too difficult to use, employees may make too many errors and avoid using it. Thus, it would fail to show operational feasibility.

1.21.3 Project Analysis

Project analysis is a detailed study of the various operations performed by a system and their relationships within and outside the system. Detailed investigation is conducted with personnel closely involved with the area under investigation, according to the precise terms of reference arising out of the initial study reports. The tasks to be carried out are clearly defined such as:

- Examine and document the relevant aspects of the existing system, its shortcomings and problems.
- Analyse the findings and record the results.
- Define and document in an outline the proposed system.
- Test the proposed design against the known facts.
- Produce a detailed report to support the proposals.
- Estimate the resources required to design and implement the system.

The objectives at this stage are to provide solutions to stated problems, usually in the form of specifications to meet the users' requirements and to make recommendations for a new computer-based system. Analysis is an iterative and progressive process, examining information flows and evaluating various alternative design solutions until a preferred solution is available. This is documented as the system proposal.

1.21.4 System Design

It is the most creative as well as challenging phase of the system-development life-cycle. The term design describes the final system and process by which it is developed. Different stages of the design phase are shown in Figure 1.11.

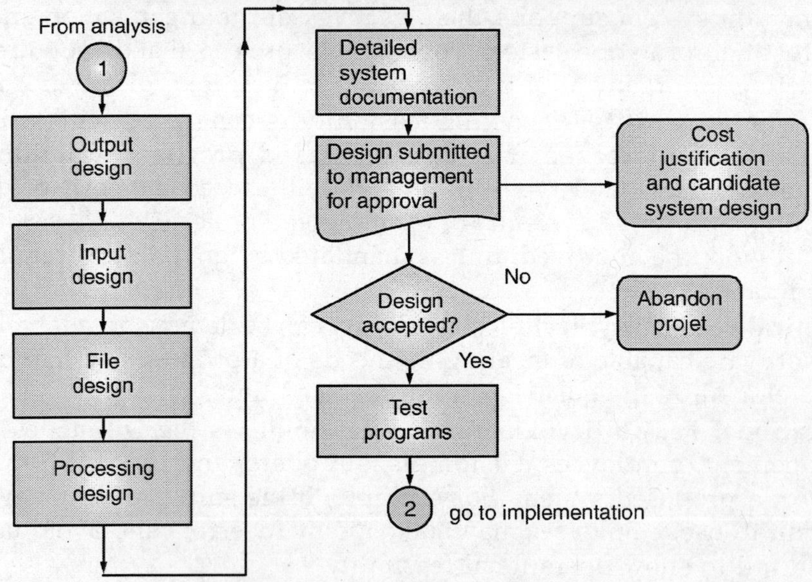

Figure 1.11: Cycle of Design Phase

Design activity includes the following tasks:

- Appraising the terms of reference
- Appraising the analysis of the existing system, particularly problem areas
- Defining precisely the required system output
- Determining data required to produce the output
- Deciding the medium and opening the files
- Devising processing methods and using software to handle files and to produce output
- Determining methods of data capture and data input
- Designing the output forms
- Defining detailed critical procedures
- Calculating timings of processing and data movements
- Documenting all aspects of design

1.21.5 Coding

The goal of the coding phase is to translate the design of the system into code in a given programming language, and hence to implement the design in the best possible manner. It affects both testing and maintenance phases. Well-written code can reduce the testing and maintenance effort. Hence, during coding the focus is on developing programs that are easy to read and understand and not simply on developing programs that are simple to write.

Coding can be subject to company-wide standards that may define the entire layout of programs, such as headers for comments in every unit, naming conventions for variables, classes and functions, the maximum number of lines in each component, and other aspects of standardization.

1.21.6 Testing

Testing is the major quality-control measure used during software development. Its basic function is to detect errors in the software. Thus, the goal of testing is to uncover requirement, design, and coding errors in the program.

Testing is an extremely critical and time-consuming activity. It requires proper planning of the overall testing process. During the testing of the unit, the specified test cases are executed and the actual results are compared with the expected output. The final output of the testing phase is the test report and the error report, or a set of such reports (one for each unit tested). Each test report contains the set of test cases and the result of executing the code with these test cases. The error report describes the errors encountered and the action taken to remove the errors. Testing cannot show the absence of defects; it can show only software errors present. During the testing phase emphasis should be on the following:

- Tests should be planned long before testing begins.
- All tests should be traceable to customer requirements.
- Tracing should begin "in the small" and progress toward testing "in the large."
- For most effective testing, independent, third parties should conduct testing.

1.21.7 Implementation

The implementation phase is mainly concerned with user training, site selection, and preparation and file conversion. Once the system has been designed, it is ready for implementation. Implementation is concerned with those tasks leading immediately to a fully operational system. It involves programmers, users, and operations management, but its planning and timing is a prime function of a systems analyst. It includes the final testing of the complete system to user satisfaction, and supervision of initial operation of the system. Implementation of the system also includes providing security to the system.

There are three types of implementation:

- Implementation of a computer system to replace a manual system.
- Implementation of a new computer system to replace an existing one.
- Implementation of a modified application (software) to replace an existing one using the same computer.

1.21.8 Maintenance

If there is any error to correct or change after the software has been implemented, then it is done in the maintenance phase. Maintenance of software is also a very necessary aspect related to software development. Many times maintenance may consume more time than the time consumed in the development. Also, the cost of maintenance varies from 50% to 80% of the total development cost. Maintenance is not as rewarding or exciting as developing the systems. It may have problems such as:

- Availability of only a few maintenance tools.
- User may not accept the cost of maintenance.
- Standards and guidelines of project may be poorly defined.
- A good test plan is lacking.
- Maintenance is viewed as a necessary evil often delegated to junior programmers.
- Most programmers view maintenance as low-level drudgery.

Maintenance may be classified as:

- **Corrective Maintenance:** Corrective maintenance means repairing processing or performance failures or making changes because of previously uncorrected problems.
- **Adaptive Maintenance:** Adaptive maintenance means changing the program function. This is done to adapt to the external environment change. For example, the current system was designed so that it calculates taxes on profits after deducting the dividend on equity shares. The government has issued orders now to include the dividend in the company profit for tax calculation. This function needs to be changed to adapt to the new system.
- **Perfective Maintenance:** Perfective maintenance means enhancing the performance or modifying the programs to respond to the user's additional or changing needs. For example, earlier data was sent from stores to headquarters on magnetic media but after the stores were electronically linked via leased lines, the software was enhanced to send data via leased lines. As maintenance is very costly and very essential, efforts have been done to reduce its costs. One way to reduce the costs is through maintenance

management and software modification audits. Software modification consists of program rewriting and system-level-upgrading.

- **Preventive Maintenance:** Preventive maintenance is the process by which we prevent our system from being obsolete. Preventive maintenance involves the concept of re-engineering and reverse engineering in which an old system with an old technology is re-engineered using new technology. This maintenance prevents the system from dying out.

SUMMARY

Software is the key element in the evolution of computer-based systems and products of one of the most important technologies on the world stage. Over the past 50 years, software has evolved from a specialized problem solving and information analysis tool to an industry in itself. Yet we still have trouble developing high quality software on time and within budget.

Software, i.e. programs, data and descriptive information, addresses a wide array of technology and application areas. Software engineering encompasses process, methods, and tools that enable complex computer-based systems to be built in a timely manner with quality. The software engineering practice is a problem solving activity that follows a set of core principles.

A wide array of software myths continue to lead managers and practitioners astray, even as our collective knowledge of software and technologies required to build it grows. As you learn more about software engineering, you will begin to understand why these myths should be debunked whenever they are encountered.

Concern for quality of the software-based systems has also grown as software becomes integrated into every aspect of our daily lives. But it is difficult to develop a comprehensive description of software quality. In this chapter users have learned that quality is an effective software process applied in a manner that creates a useful product that provides measurable value for those produce it and those who use it.

Every software organization is faced with the software quality dilemma. In essence, everyone wants to build high-quality systems, but the time and effort required to produce 'perfect' software are simply unavailable in the market-driven world. Software quality is achieved through the application of software engineering methods, solid management practices, and comprehensive quality control. SDLC is an acronym for Software Development Life Cycle. It is also sometimes referred to as System Development Life Cycle.

EXERCISES

1. Define software.
2. Describe the evolving role of software.
3. Discuss the characteristics of software.
4. Explain the different types of software?

5. Explain the various desirable software capabilities?
6. Explain the different types of system and application software's?
7. What do you mean by legacy software?
8. What is software engineering?
9. Explain the various principles of software engineering?
10. What is a software crisis? Explain the problems of a software crisis.
11. Explain the software behaviour, structure, and architecture?
12. What are software myths?
13. What are the different myths and realities about software?
14. Explain the various types of software stakeholders?
15. Explain the role of management in software development?
16. Explain the Davis's early principles of software engineering?
17. Explain the Boyce's more modern principles?
18. Explain the concepts of Wassermann's fundamental software engineering?
19. Explain the software engineering code of ethics?
20. What do you mean by software quality?
21. What do you mean by the software quality management system?
22. Explain the software processes capability maturity model?
23. Explain the concept of six sigma methodologies?
24. Explain the generic stages in software development?
25. Explain the various phases of SDLC?

❑

UNIT 2
SOFTWARE DEVELOPMENT PROCESS

Software Development Process

2

2.1 INTRODUCTION

A software development process makes everything easier and reduces the amount of problems encountered. An information system goes through a series of phases from conception to implementation. This process is called the Software-Development Life-Cycle.

The aim of requirements engineering is to convert the end-user requirements to a form that enables the development of some new methods to satisfy the needs of the user. In software engineering discipline, the new method involves the use of automated methods including the use of computers and associated technologies. This process is to be conducted very systematically and properly with utmost care. Thus, requirements must be written so they are meaningful not only to the customers but also to designers on the development team. Software Architecture is a branch of software engineering discipline. As it happens with every budding disciplines software architecture is defined in numerous ways. Each one of this definition highlights certain aspect of the software architecture. Our view of Software architecture is that of a discipline providing mechanisms to deal with ever increasing size and complexity of a software system. Software architecture manages the complexity of a software system by separating the computations performed by components from the interactions in which they involve with other components.

Software design can be started if the software project is found feasible and the software requirements specifications are formed. This is the most important stage in the software development process. Software design determines how a solution can be formulated to satisfy the user needs. Coding is the activity where a design is converted to runnable code. Depending on the details of the design specification, the coding activity may vary greatly. Many companies have coding standards that all the programmers must follow. The purpose of a coding standard is to make it easier for programmers to read each other's codes, and to make it easier to maintain the code. Software testing is an important process in the software development life cycle. It is also the most time consuming phase. Testing forms the last stage of any software development project before it can be released for implementation. It is mandatory for software to pass all the tests before implementation. Thus, testing process increases the reliability as well as quality of the software products. For testing software, different methods are available which are selected based on various criteria. The different tests measure different quality attributes of software. Testing process has become sophisticated and has grown into a specialised area requiring a deep knowledge and in-depth planning.

The testing strategy provides a road map that describes the steps to be conducted as part of testing, when these steps are planned and then undertaken, and how much effort, time, and resources will be required. On successful culmination of software testing, debugging is performed. Debugging is defined as a process of analysing and removing the error. It is considered necessary in most of the newly-developed software or hardware and in commercial products/personal application programs. For complex products, debugging is done at all the levels of the testing. Maintenance is the most expensive phase of software life cycle and therefore it is usually cost effective to invest in time and effort while developing the product and to emphasize on maintainability of the product to reduce the maintenance costs. A number of the product support and customer service models extend their support and service into a customer consulting practice. CASE stands for Computer-Aided Software Engineering. CASE is a tool that helps a software engineer maintain and develop software.

2.2 NEED FOR A LIFE CYCLE MODEL

Adherence to a life cycle model during software development has become universally accepted in all the modern software development organizations. We need to understand the basic need of the development team to adhere to a suitable life cycle model. The primary advantage of adhering to a life cycle model is that it encourages development of software in a systematic and disciplined manner. When a software product is developed by a single programmer, he has the freedom to decide the exact steps through which he will develop the program. But when a software product is developed by a team, it is necessary to have a precise understanding among the team members as to 'when to do what'. Otherwise, it may lead to chaos and project failure.

Hence various reasons for using a life-cycle model include:

- Helps to understand the entire process
- Enforces a structured approach to development
- Enables planning of resources in advance
- Enables subsequent controls of them
- Aids management to track progress of the system

If no life cycle model is followed, it becomes very difficult to chart the progress of the project. This usually leads to a problem that is identified as *99% complete syndrome.* This syndrome appears when there is no definite way to assess the progress of the project, and the optimistic team members may feel that the project is 99% complete even when the project is far from complete. Thus the chaos makes all the projections of the project manager about the completion time inaccurate.

2.3 STAGE DELIVERABLES

During each stage, additional information is gathered or developed, combined with the inputs, and used to produce the stage deliverables. It is important to note that the additional information is restricted in scope; "new ideas" that would take the project in directions not anticipated by the initial set of high-level requirements are not incorporated into the project. Rather, ideas for new capabilities or features that are out-of-scope are preserved for later consideration.

The six stages of the SDLC are designed to build on one another, taking the outputs from the previous stage, adding additional effort, and producing results that leverage the previous effort and are directly traceable to the previous stages. This top-down approach is intended to result in a quality product that satisfies the original intentions of the customer.

Too many software development efforts go awry when the development team and customer personnel get caught up in the possibilities of automation. Instead of focusing on high priority features, the team can become mired in a sea of "nice to have" features that are not essential to solve the problem, but in themselves are highly attractive. This is the root cause of a large percentage of failed and/or abandoned development efforts, and is the primary reason the development team utilizes the Waterfall SDLC (discussed in next section).

2.3.1 Planning Stage

The planning stage establishes a bird's eye view of the intended software product, and uses this to establish the basic project structure, evaluate feasibility and risks associated with the project, and describe appropriate management and technical approaches.

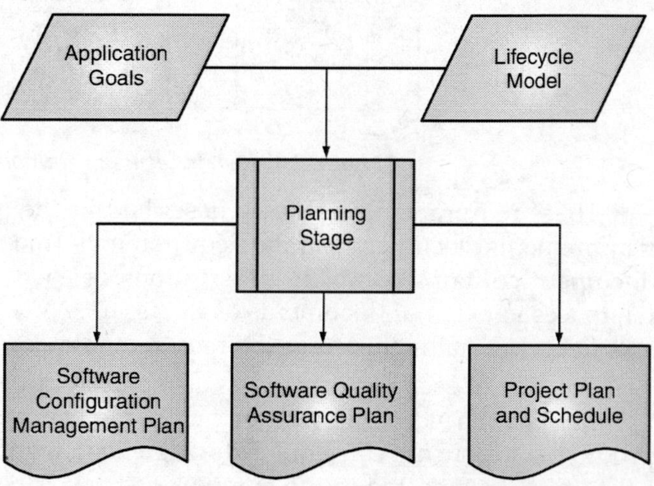

Figure 2.1: *Planning Stage Deliverables*

The most critical section of the project plan is a listing of high-level product requirements, also referred to as goals. All of the software product requirements to be developed during the requirements definition stage flow from one or more of these goals. The minimum information for each goal consists of a title and textual description, although additional information and references to external documents may be included.

The outputs of the project planning stage are the configuration management plan, the quality assurance plan, and the project plan and schedule, with a detailed listing of scheduled activities for the upcoming Requirements stage, and high level estimates of effort for the out stages.

2.3.2 Requirements Definition Stage

The requirements gathering process takes as its input the goals identified in the high-level requirements section of the project plan. Each goal will be refined into a set of one or more requirements. These requirements define the major functions of the intended application, define operational data areas and reference data areas, and define the initial data entities.

Major functions include critical processes to be managed, as well as mission critical inputs, outputs and reports. A user class hierarchy is developed and associated with these major functions, data areas, and data entities. Each of these definitions is termed a Requirement. Requirements are identified by unique requirement identifiers and, at minimum, contain a requirement title and textual description.

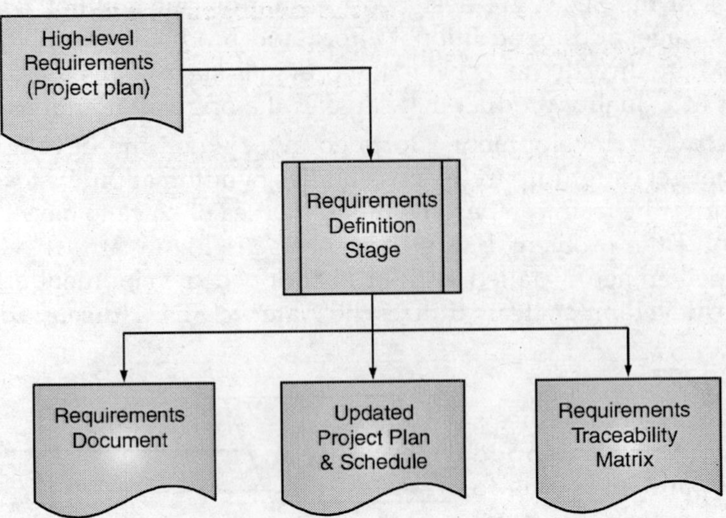

Figure 2.2: *Requirements Definition Stage Deliverables*

These requirements are fully described in the primary deliverables for this stage: the Requirements Document and the Requirements Traceability Matrix (RTM). The requirements document contains complete descriptions of each requirement, including diagrams and references to external documents as necessary. Note that detailed listings of database tables and fields are not included in the requirements document.

The title of each requirement is also placed into the first version of the RTM, along with the title of each goal from the project plan. The purpose of the RTM is to show that the product components developed during each stage of the software development lifecycle are formally connected to the components developed in prior stages.

In the requirements stage, the RTM consists of a list of high-level requirements, or goals, by title, with a listing of associated requirements for each goal, listed by requirement title. In this hierarchical listing, the RTM shows that each requirement developed during this stage is formally linked to a specific product goal. In this format, each requirement can be traced to a specific product goal, hence the term requirements traceability. The outputs of the requirements definition stage include the requirements document, the RTM, and an updated project plan.

2.3.3 Design Stage

The design stage takes as its initial input the requirements identified in the approved requirements document. For each requirement, a set of one or more design elements will be produced as a result of interviews, workshops, and/or prototype efforts.

Design elements describe the desired software features in detail, and generally include functional hierarchy diagrams, screen layout diagrams, tables of business rules, business process diagrams, pseudo code, and a complete entity-relationship diagram with a full data dictionary. These design elements are intended to describe the software in sufficient detail that skilled programmers may develop the software with minimal additional input.

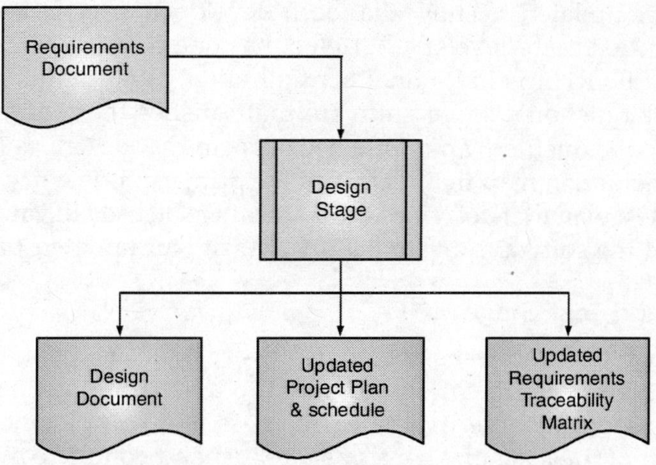

Figure 2.3: *Design Stage Deliverables*

When the design document is finalized and accepted, the RTM is updated to show that each design element is formally associated with a specific requirement. The outputs of the design stage are the design document, an updated RTM, and an updated project plan.

2.3.4 Development Stage

The development stage takes as its primary input the design elements described in the approved design document. For each design element, a set of one or more software artefacts will be produced. Software artefacts include but are not limited to menus, dialogs, data management forms, data reporting formats, and specialized procedures and functions. Appropriate test cases will be developed for each set of functionally related software artefacts, and an online help system will be developed to guide users in their interactions with the software.

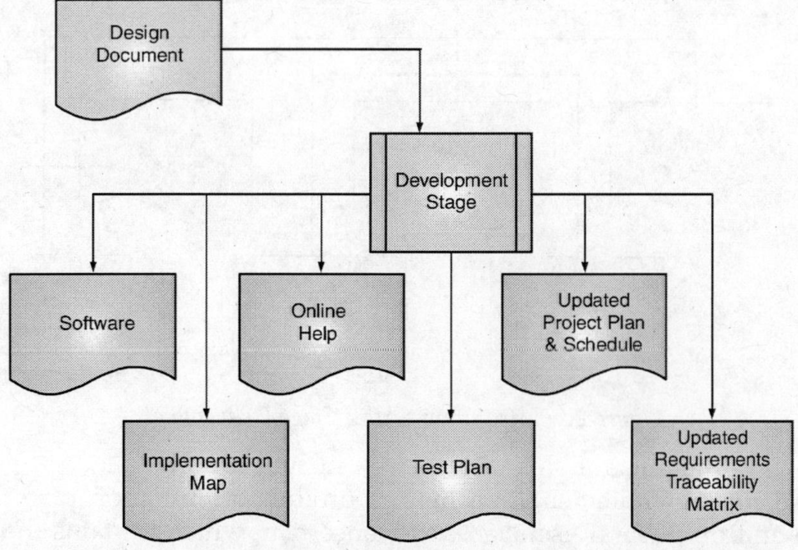

Figure 2.4: *Development Stage Deliverables*

The RTM will be updated to show that each developed artefact is linked to a specific design element, and that each developed artefact has one or more corresponding test case items. At this point, the RTM is in its final configuration. The outputs of the development stage include a fully functional set of software that satisfies the requirements and design elements previously documented, an online help system that describes the operation of the software, an implementation map that identifies the primary code entry points for all major system functions, a test plan that describes the test cases to be used to validate the correctness and completeness of the software, an updated RTM, and an updated project plan.

2.3.5 Integration and Test Stage

During the integration and test stage, the software artefacts, online help, and test data are migrated from the development environment to a separate test environment. At this point, all test cases are run to verify the correctness and completeness of the software. Successful execution of the test suite confirms a robust and complete migration capability.

During this stage, reference data is finalized for production use and production users are identified and linked to their appropriate roles. The final reference data (or links to reference data source files) and production user list are compiled into the Production Initiation Plan.

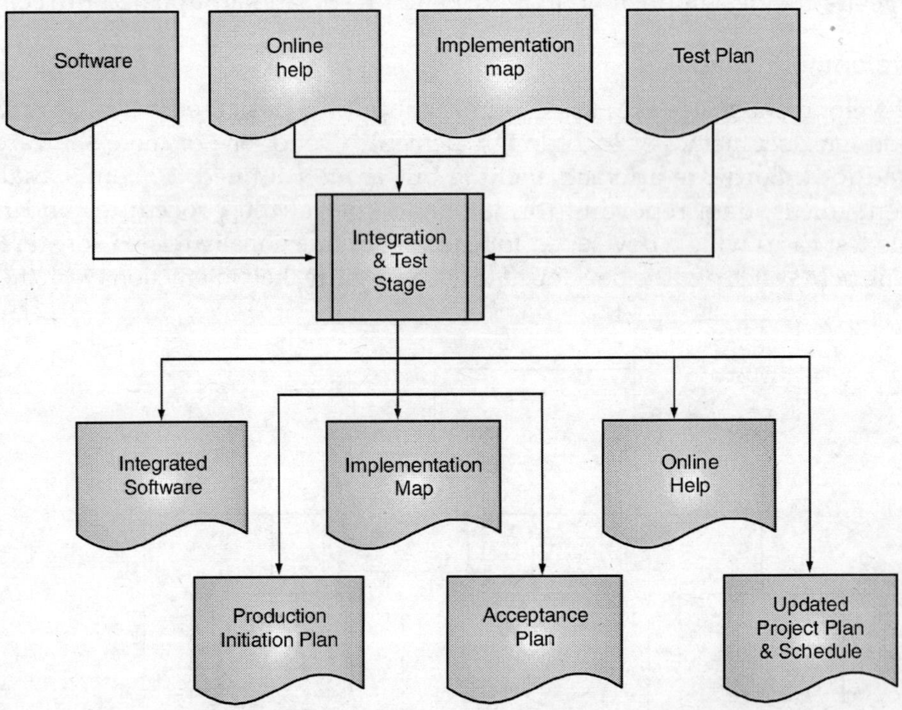

Figure 2.5: *Integration & Test Stage Deliverables*

The outputs of the integration and test stage include an integrated set of software, an online help system, an implementation map, a production initiation plan that describes reference data and production users, an acceptance plan which contains the final suite of test cases, and an updated project plan.

2.3.6 Installation and Acceptance Stage

During the installation and acceptance stage, the software artefacts, online help, and initial production data are loaded onto the production server. At this point, all test cases are run to verify the correctness and completeness of the software. Successful execution of the test suite is a prerequisite to acceptance of the software by the customer.

After customer personnel have verified that the initial production data load is correct and the test suite has been executed with satisfactory results, the customer formally accepts the delivery of the software.

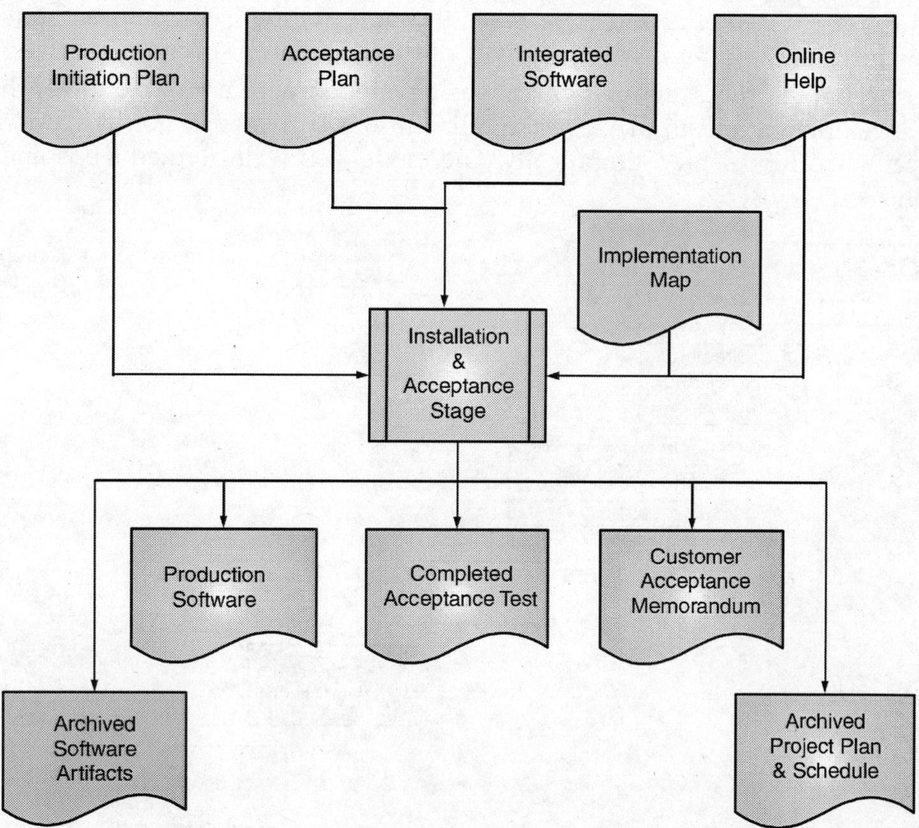

***Figure 2.6:** Installation & Acceptance Stage Deliverables*

The primary outputs of the installation and acceptance stage include a production application, a completed acceptance test suite, and a memorandum of customer acceptance of the software. Finally, the PDR enters the last of the actual labour data into the project schedule and locks the project as a permanent project record. At this point the PDR "locks" the project by archiving all software items, the implementation map, the source code, and the documentation for future reference.

2.4 PROCESS MODELS

Development process focuses on how the software is to be engineered. There are many different process models, each being well suited for some type of problems. Next we present the process models that are proposed over time, along with their advantages as well as disadvantages over the others.

2.4.1 Waterfall Model

The waterfall model is sometimes called the classical life cycle model as it suggests a systematic and sequential approach to software development that begins with customer specification of requirements and progresses through planning, modelling, construction, and deployment, ending in on-going support of the completed software.

This is a simple process model which was developed with a view to lower the cost of software development and to increase the reliability of software. It got its name from the appearance, when represented graphically. The model has well-defined steps and is quite popular and widely used.

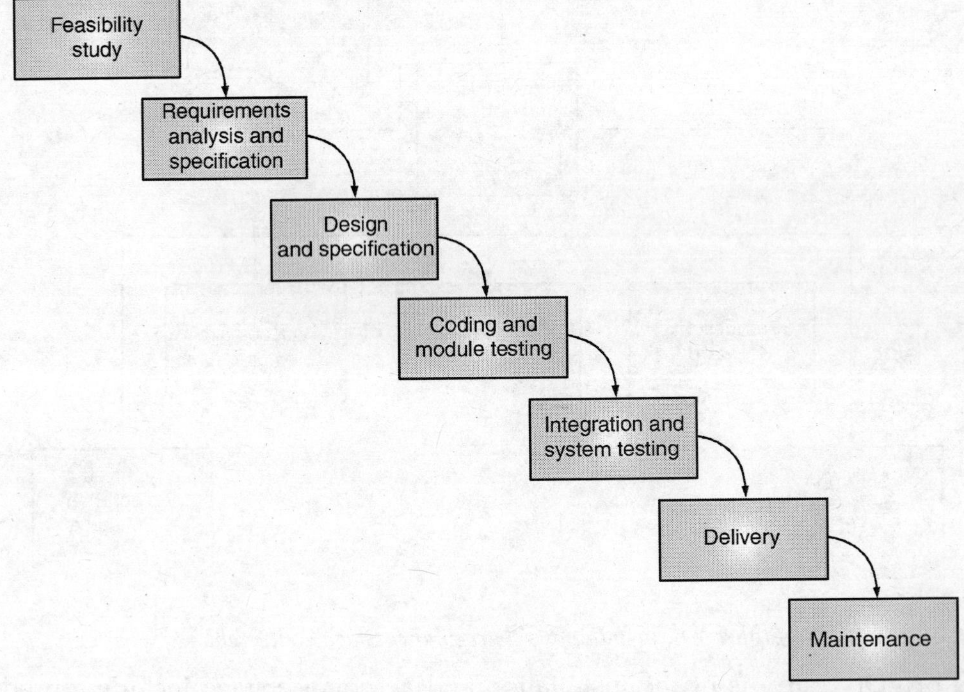

Figure 2.7: Waterfall Model

The waterfall model is illustrated in Figure 2.7. Because of the cascade from one phase to another, this model is known as the waterfall model or software lifecycle. As the figure shows, the process is structured as a cascade of phases, where the output of one phase constitutes the input to the next one. Each phase, in turn, is structured as a set of activities that might be executed by different people concurrently.

The phases shown in the figure are the following:

- Feasibility study
- Requirements analysis and specification
- Design and specification
- Coding and module testing
- Integration and system testing
- Delivery
- Maintenance

2.4.2 Iterative Waterfall Model

It is an enhancement to the original waterfall model. The classic waterfall model is an idealistic one since it assumes that no development error is ever committed by the engineers during any of the life cycle phases. However, practically the engineers do commit a large number of errors in almost every phase of life cycle. The source of the defects can be many, such as oversight, wrong assumptions, use of inappropriate technology, communication gap among project engineers etc. These defects usually get detected much later in the life cycle. But once a defect is detected, the engineers need to go back to the phase where the defect had occurred and redo some of the work done during that phase and the subsequent phases to correct the defect and its effect on the later phases. Therefore, in any practical software development work, it is not possible to strictly follow the classical waterfall model. Feedback paths are needed in the classical waterfall model from every phase to its preceding phases as shown in Figure 2.8 to allow for the correction of the errors committed during a phase that are detected in later phases.

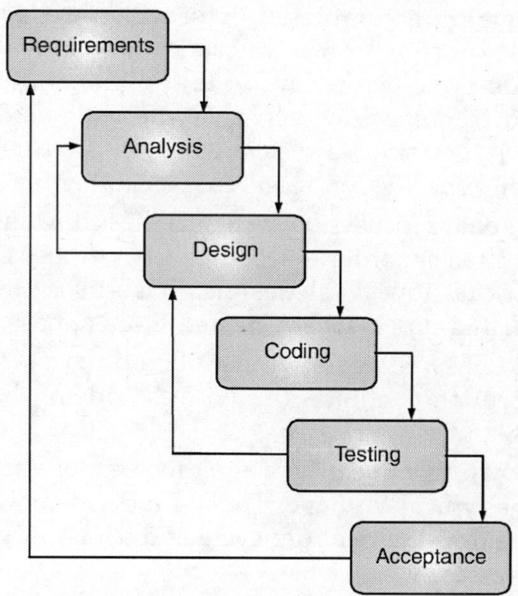

Figure 2.8: *Iterative Waterfall Model*

Though errors are inevitable in almost every phase of development, it is desirable to detect these errors in the same phase in which they occur. However, it may not always be possible to do so hence the errors must be detected as early as possible. For example, if a design error is detected in the design phase itself, then this problem can be taken care of much more easily than if the error is identified, say, after the testing phase. In the latter case, it would be necessary not only to rework the design, but also to appropriately redo the coding and system testing, hence incurring higher costs. The principle of detecting errors as close to their points of introduction is known as *phase containment of errors*, and is an important principle of software engineering.

An important technique used to achieve phase containment of errors is to conduct reviews after every milestone. In spite of the best effort put in to detect errors in the same phase in which they were committed, some errors do escape detection ad may get noticed only in the later phases. This necessitates rework of the already completed phases. Thus, the effort spent on a phase may require rework later due to errors in that phase which were detected in later phases.

In any practical development environment, several iterations through the waterfall stages are normally necessary to develop the final product. In spite of this, the final documents for the product should be written as if the product was developed using a pure classical waterfall model. Irrespective of life cycle model actually followed for the product development, if the final product is written to reflect a classical waterfall model of development, comprehension of the system documents becomes easy.

2.4.3 V-Shaped Model

Just like the waterfall model, the V-Shaped life cycle is a sequential path of execution of processes. Each phase must be completed before the next phase begins. Testing is emphasized in this model more than the waterfall model. The testing procedures are developed early in the life cycle before any coding is done, during each of the phases preceding implementation. Requirements begin the life cycle model just like the waterfall model. Before development is started, a system test plan is created. The test plan focuses on meeting the functionality specified in requirements gathering.

The high-level design phase focuses on system architecture and design. An integration test plan is created in this phase in order to test the pieces of the software systems ability to work together. However, the low-level design phase lies where the actual software components are designed, and unit tests are created in this phase as well.

The implementation phase is, again, where all coding takes place. Once coding is complete, the path of execution continues up the right side of the V where the test plans developed earlier are now put to use.

Instead of moving down in a linear way, the process steps are bent upwards after the coding phase, to form the typical V shape. The V-Model demonstrates the relationships between each phase of the development life cycle and its associated phase of testing. The V-model is depicted in Figure 2.9.

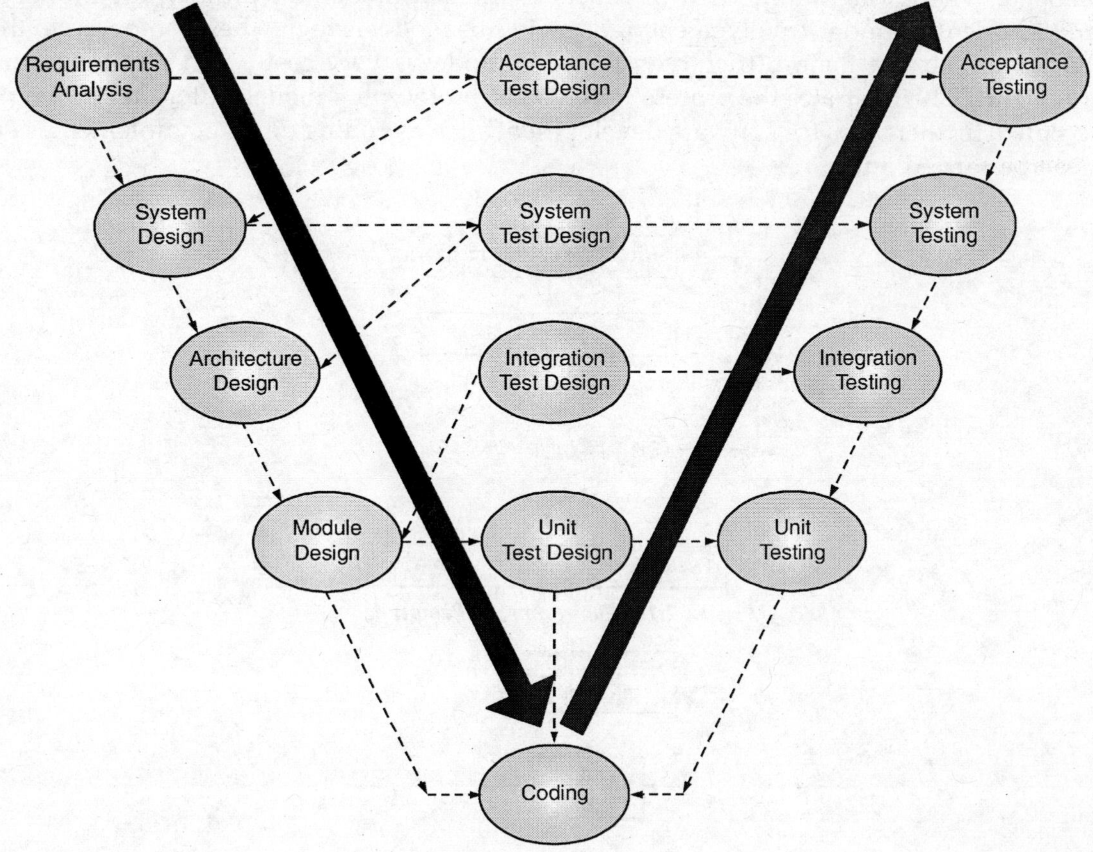

Figure 2.9: V-Model

2.4.4 Prototyping Model

The prototyping model suggests that before carrying out the development of the actual software, a working prototype of the system should be built. A prototype is a toy implementation of the system. A prototype usually exhibits limited functional capabilities, low reliability, and inefficient performance compared to the actual software as it is built using several shortcuts. These shortcuts might involve using inefficient, inaccurate, or dummy functions. The shortcut implementation of a function, for example, may produce the desired results by using a table look-up instead of performing the actual computations.

Developers and users work together for developing the prototype. Developed prototypes are the reviewed. The initial prototype may be having several shortcomings. Developers and users suggest modifications to the initial prototype. After these modifications are incorporated in the prototype, and another prototype is developed, it is again suggested some modifications if required. This process of modification, review and evaluation is continued until the model delivered exactly matches with the requirements needed. Based on this prototype, the system requirements are determined and the software system is developed. Where waterfall model was function-oriented model, the prototyping model is a process-oriented model. Involvement of users in this model is high when compared to the waterfall model. The main difficulty is that this model is very costly and requires more effort. Figure 2.10 illustrates the process followed in prototyping model. After the prototype is accepted, further steps for software development such as coding, testing, implementation etc. can be carried out.

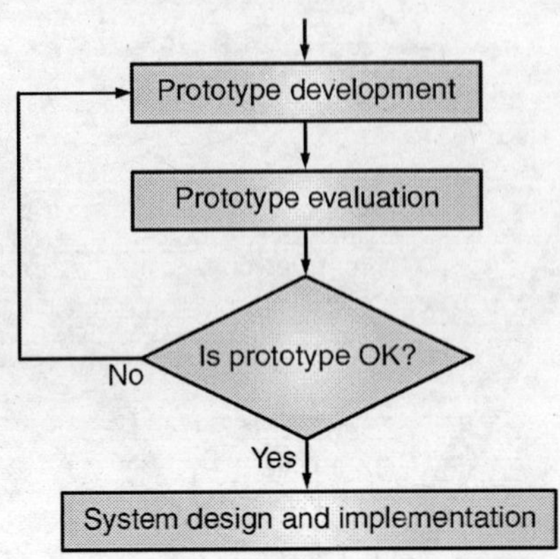

Figure 2.10: *Developing a Prototype*

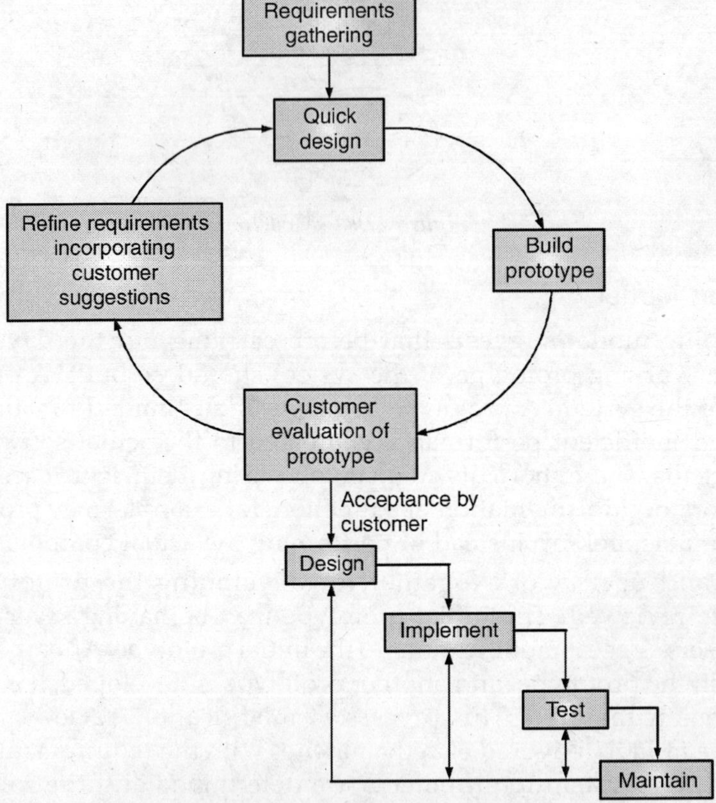

Figure 2.11: *Prototyping Model*

The prototyping model is shown in Figure 2.11. In this model, product development starts with an initial requirements gathering phase. A quick design is carried out and the prototype is built. The developed prototype is submitted to customer for his evaluation. Based on the customer feedback, the requirements are refined and the prototype is suitably modified. This cycle of obtaining customer feedback and modifying the prototype continues till the customer approves the prototype. The actual system is developed using the iterative waterfall approach. However, in the prototyping model of software development, the requirements analysis and specification phase becomes redundant as the working prototype approved by the customer becomes an animated requirements specification.

The code for the prototype is usually thrown away. However, the experience gathered from developing the prototype helps a great deal in developing the actual system. Therefore even though the construction of a working prototype may involve additional costs, for systems with unclear customer requirements and for systems with unresolved technical issues, the overall development cost might turn out to be lower in the prototype model than that of an equivalent system developed using iterative waterfall model. By constructing the prototype and submitting it for user evaluation, many customer requirements get properly defined and technical issues get resolved by experimenting with the prototype. This minimizes the change requests from the customer and the associated redesign costs..

Although prototyping model can be used as a standalone process model, it is more commonly used as a technique that can be implemented within the context of any one of the process models noted in this section. Regardless of the manner in which it is applied, the prototyping model assists the developers to better understand what is to be built when the requirements are fuzzy.

2.4.5 Spiral Model

The spiral model, originally proposed by Boehm, is an evolutionary software model that couples the iterative nature of prototyping with the controlled and systematic aspects of the linear segmental model.

The model got its name from its appearance when represented graphically. The graphical representation of the model appears in Figure 2.12. The exact number of spirals in a model is not fixed and it can vary depending upon many factors. The typical model can have only one spiral whereas another may have multiple spirals. Each loop represents a phase of software development. The model is flexible as number of loops representing phases can be suitably changed.

The goal of the spiral model of the software production process is to provide a framework for designing such processes, guided by the risk levels in the projects at hand. As opposed to the previously presented models, the spiral model may be viewed as a metamodel, because it can accommodate any process-development model. By using it as a reference, one may choose the most appropriate development model (e.g., evolutionary versus waterfall). The guiding principle behind such a choice is the level of risk; accordingly, the spiral model provides a view of the production process that supports risk management.

The spiral model is recommended where the requirements and solutions call for developing full-fledged, large, complex systems with many features and facilities from scratch. It is used when experimenting on technology, trying out new skills, and when the user is not able to offer requirements in clear terms. It is also useful when the requirements are not clear and when the solution intended has multi-users, multi-functions, multi-features, multi-location applications to be used on multiple platforms, where seamless integration, interfacing, data migration, and replication are the issues. The radial dimension of a cycle represents the cumulative costs, and the angular dimension represents the progress made in completing each cycle of the spiral.

Each phase in this model is split into four sectors (or quadrants) as shown in Figure 2.12.

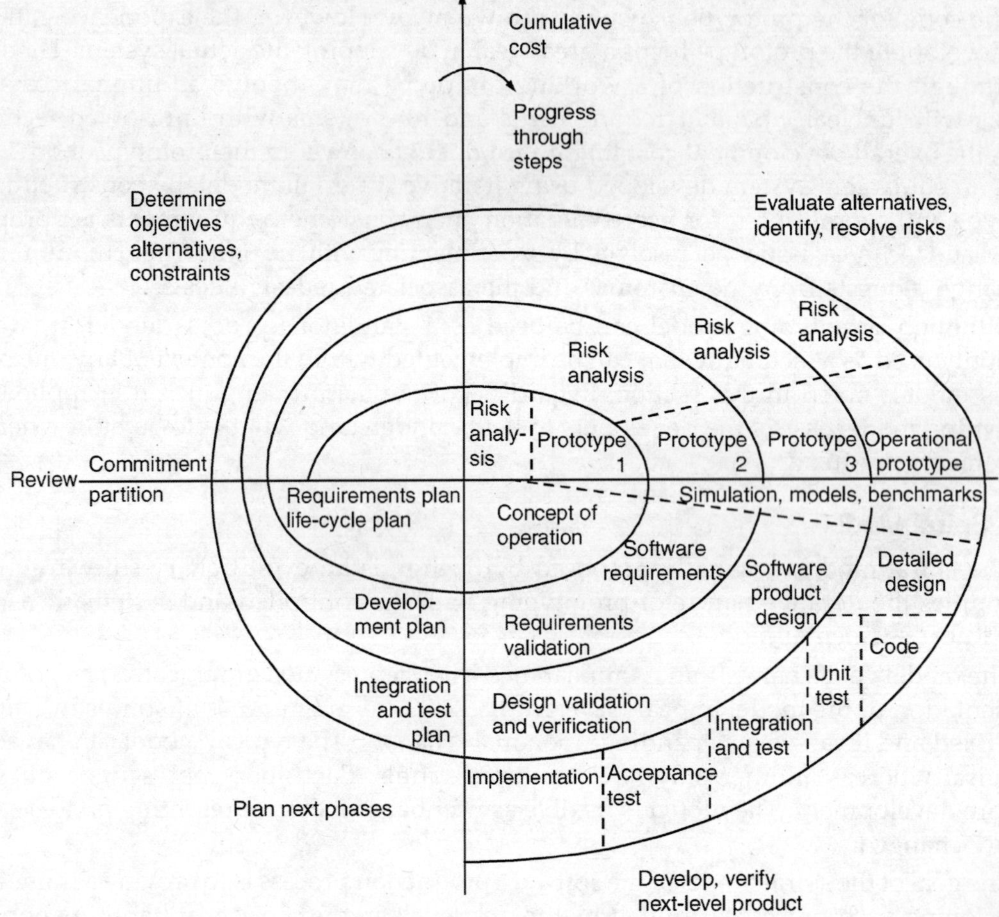

Figure 2.12: Spiral Model

The first quadrant identifies the objectives of the phase and the alternative solutions possible for the phase under consideration.

In the second quadrant we evaluate different alternatives based on the objectives and constraints. The evaluation is based on the risk perceptions for the project.

The third quadrant is the next step that emphasizes development of strategies that resolve the uncertainties and risks. This may involve activities, such as benchmarking, simulation, and prototyping.

In the last or fourth quadrant we determine the objective that should be fulfilled in the next cycle of our software development in order to build the complete system.

2.4.6 WinWin Spiral Model

The spiral model suggested a framework activity that addresses customer communication. The objective of this activity is to elicit project requirements from the customer. In an ideal context, the developer simply asks the customer what is required and the customer provides sufficient detail to proceed. Unfortunately, this rarely happens. In reality, the customer and the developer enter into a process of negotiation, where the customer may be asked to balance functionality, performance, and other product or system characteristics against cost and time to market.

The best negotiations strive for a "win-win" result. That is, the customer wins by getting the system or product that satisfies the majority of the customer's needs and the developer wins by working to realistic and achievable budgets and deadlines.

The Win-Win Spiral Model uses the theory W (win-win) approach to converge on a system's next-level objectives, constraints, and alternatives. This Theory W approach involves identifying the system's stakeholders and their win conditions, and using negotiation processes to determine a mutually satisfactory set of objectives, constraints, and alternatives for the stakeholders. In particular, the nine-step Theory W process translates into the following spiral model extensions:

- **Determine Objectives**
  Identify the system life-cycle stakeholders and their win conditions and establish initial system boundaries and external interfaces.
- **Determine Constraints**
  Determine the conditions under which the system would produce win-lose or lose-lose outcomes for some stakeholders.
- **Identify and Evaluate Alternatives**
  Solicit suggestions from stakeholders, evaluate them with respect to stakeholders' win conditions, synthesize and negotiate candidate win-win alternatives, analyse, assess, resolve win-lose or lose-lose risks, record commitments and areas to be left flexible in the project's design record and life cycle plans.
- **Cycle through the Spiral**
  Elaborate the win conditions evaluate and screen alternatives, resolve risks, accumulate appropriate commitments, and develop and execute downstream plans.

Boehm's WINWIN spiral model defines a set of negotiation activities at the beginning of each pass around the spiral. Rather than a single customer communication activity, the following activities are defined:

- Identification of the system or subsystem's key "stakeholders."
- Determinations of the stakeholders' "win conditions."
- Negotiations of the stakeholders' win conditions to reconcile them into a set of win-win conditions for all concerned (including the software project team).

Successful completion of these initial steps achieves a win-win result, which becomes the key criterion for proceeding to software and system definition. The WINWIN spiral model is illustrated in Figure 2.13.

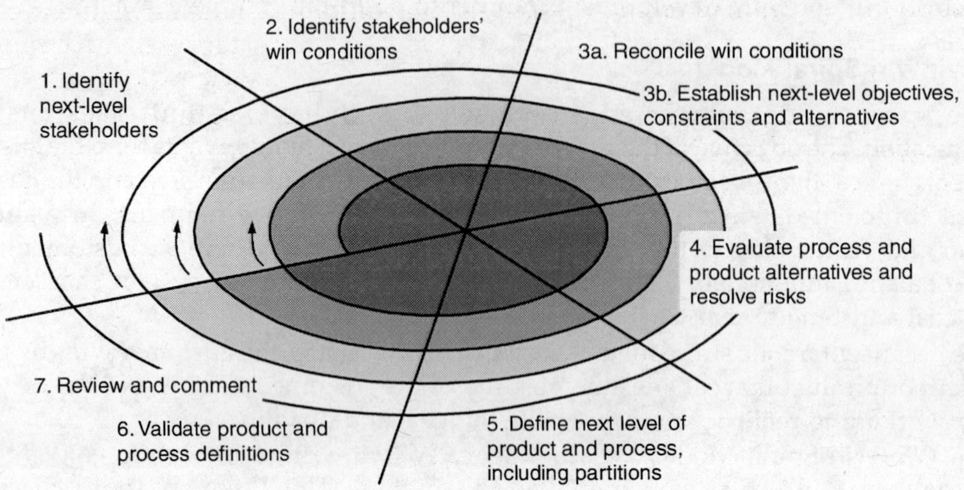

Figure 2.13: Win-Win Spiral Model

In addition to the emphasis placed on early negotiation, the WINWIN spiral model introduces three process milestones, called anchor points that help establish the completion of one cycle around the spiral and provide decision milestones before the software project proceeds.

In essence, the anchor points represent three different views of progress as the project traverses the spiral. The first anchor point, life cycle objectives (LCO), defines a set of objectives for each major software engineering activity. For example, as part of LCO, a set of objectives establishes the definition of top-level system/product requirements. The second anchor point, life cycle architecture (LCA), establishes objectives that must be met as the system and software architecture is defined. For example, as part of LCA, the software project team must demonstrate that it has evaluated the applicability of off-the-shelf and reusable software components and considered their impact on architectural decisions. Initial operational capability (IOC) is the third anchor point and represents a set of objectives associated with the preparation of the software for installation/distribution, site preparation prior to installation, and assistance required by all parties that will use or support the software.

2.4.7 Iterative Enhancement

The iterative-enhancement model combines elements of the linear sequential model (applied repetitively) with the iterative philosophy of prototyping. In this model, the software is broken down into several modules, which are incrementally developed and delivered. First, the development team develops the core module of the system and then it is later refined into increasing levels of capability of adding new functionalities in successive versions.

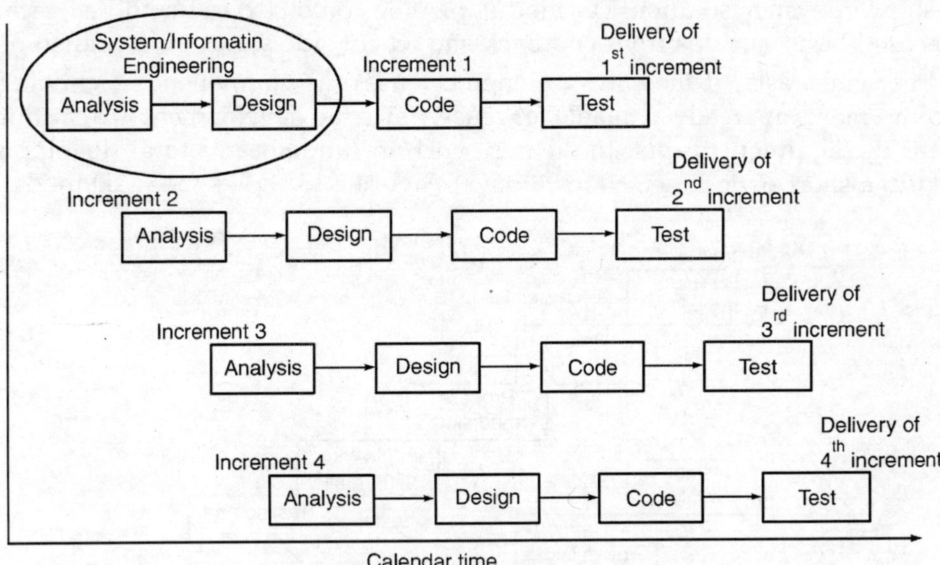

***Figure 2.14:** Iterative Enhancement Model*

Each linear sequence produces a deliverable increment of the software. For example, word-processing software developed using the iterative paradigm might deliver basis file management, editing, and document production functions in the first increment; more sophisticated editing and document production capabilities in the second increment; spelling and grammar checking in the third increment; and advanced page layout capability in the fourth increment. It should be noted that the process flow for any increment could incorporate the prototyping paradigm.

When an iterative-enhancement model is used, the first increment is often a core product. That is, basic requirements are addressed, but many supplementary features (some known, other unknown) remain undelivered. The core product is used by the customer (or undergoes detailed review). As a result of use and/or evaluation, a plan is developed for the next increment. The plan addresses the modification of the core product to better meet the needs of the customer and the delivery of additional features and functionality. This process is repeated following the delivery of each increment, until the complete product is produced.

2.4.8 RAD Model

The RAD (Rapid Application Development Model) model is an incremental software development process model that emphasizes an extremely short development cycle. It is a "high-speed" adaptation of the linear sequential model in which rapid development is achieved by using component-based construction. If requirements are well understood and project scope is constrained, the RAD process enables a development team to create a "fully functional system" within very short time periods.

The RAD model is proposed when requirements and solutions can be modularized as independent system or software components, each of which can be developed by different teams. After these smaller system components are developed, they are integrated to produce the large software system solution. The modularization could be on a functional, technology, or architectural basis, such as front-end-back-end, client side-server side, and so on.

RAD becomes faster if the software engineer uses the component's technology such that the components are really available for reuse. Since the development is distributed into component-development teams, the teams work in tandem and total development is completed in a short period (i.e., 60 to 90 days). Figure 2.15 shows the RAD model.

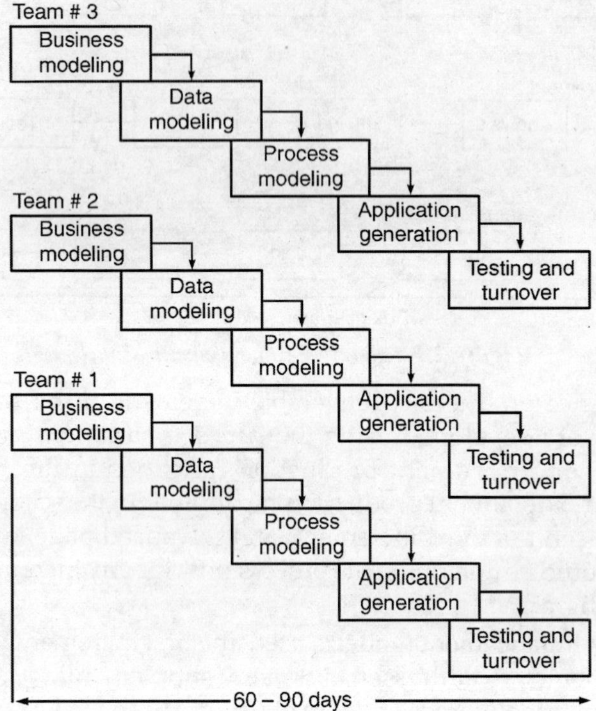

Figure 2.15: The RAD Model

Used primarily for information systems applications, the RAD approach encompasses the following phases:

1. **Business Modeling**

   It covers the following functions:
   - Where does information come from and go?
   - Who processes it?
   - What information drives the business process?
   - What information is generated?

2. **Data Modeling**

   The information flow defined as part of the business modeling phase is refined into a set of data objects that are needed to support the business. The characteristics of each object are identified and the relationships between these objects are defined.

3. **Process Modeling**
   In this model, information flows from object to object to implement a business function. To add, modify, delete, or retain a data object, there is a need for description which is done in this phase.
4. **Application Generation**
   RAD assumes the use of fourth-generation techniques. The RAD process works to reuse existing program components or create reusable components. To facilitate the construction of the software using the above cases, automated tools are used.
5. **Testing and Turnover**
   In this phase we have to test the programs, but we use some already existing programs which are already tested, so the time involved in testing is less. Only the new programs or components must be tested.

2.5 REQUIREMENTS ENGINEERING

Requirements form a set of statements that describe the user's needs and desires. In developing a software system, these requirements must be clearly and fully understood by the software developers. However, we often find requirements that encroach on the 'how' part and enter into the realm of solution design. Although we should try to limit the requirements to the 'what', it is not always that clear-cut.

The top reason for software project failures is incomplete requirements specification. At the same time, one of the important reasons for project success may be attributed to clear requirements statements. The significance of user requirements is now well appreciated. Managing requirements and user involvement is emerging as key task in software development process model.

A requirement is a feature of the system or a description of something the system is capable of doing in order to fulfil the system's purpose. Figure 2.16 illustrates the process of determining the requirements for a software-based system.

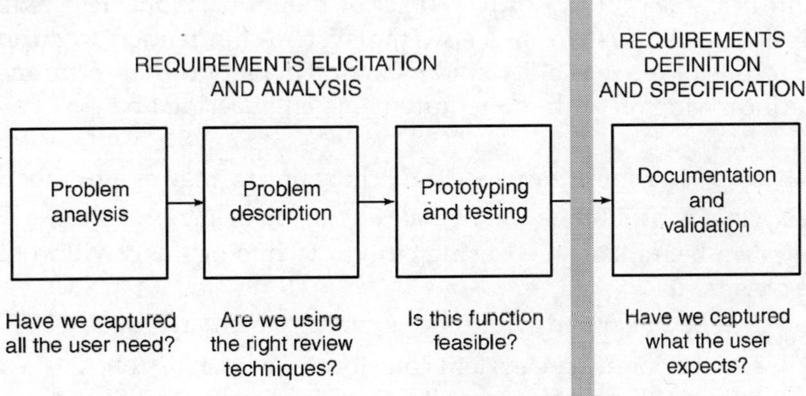

Figure 2.16: *The Process of Determining Requirements*

Requirements describe the "what" of a system, not the "how." Requirements engineering produces one large document, written in a natural language, and contains a description of what the system will do without describing how it will do it.

In the old days, requirements engineering used to be known as requirements analysis. Now, requirements engineering is becoming a discipline in its own right. **Requirements engineering** is a relatively recent term that denotes the set of activities that are associated with elicitation, specification, and management of requirements for a computer system. It is the systematic use of proven principles, techniques, and language tools for the cost-effective analysis, documentation, and on-going evaluation of the user's needs and the specifications of the external behaviour of a system to satisfy those user needs. It can be defined as a discipline, which addresses requirements of objects all along a system-development process.

The input to requirements engineering is the problem statement prepared by the customer. The output of the Requirements Engineering (RE) process is a system requirements specification called the Requirement Definition and Description (RDD). The system requirements specification forms the basis for designing software solutions.

Requirements engineer is a person who takes the concept of project and is responsible for creating the requirements documentation. He is also involved in various stages of software life-cycle to make sure that the documented requirements are met. In order to achieve the end result, a wide range of skill set is defined for a software engineer. He should possess the knowledge and experience in:

- Using CASE tools.
- Using general modeling techniques, including formal languages and conceptual modeling.
- Using particular modeling languages and ability to choose the best one among them for a given problem.
- Using management and traceability tools.
- Using tools and techniques in product planning and marketing.

2.6 FEASIBILITY STUDY

For all new systems, the requirements engineering process should start with a feasibility study. The input to the feasibility study is a set of preliminary business requirements, an outline description of the system and how the system is intended to support business processes. The results of the feasibility study should be a report that recommends whether or not it is worth carrying on with the requirements engineering and system development process.

A feasibility study is a short, focused study that aims to answer a number of questions:

- Does the system contribute to the overall objectives of the organisation?
- Can the system be implemented using current technology and within given cost and schedule constraints?
- Can the system be integrated with other systems which are already in place?

The issue of whether or not the system contributes to business objectives is critical. If a system does not support these objectives, it has no real value to the business. While this may seem obvious, many organisations develop systems which do not contribute to their objectives because they don't have a clear statement of these objectives, because they fail to define the business requirements for the system or because other political or organisation factors influence the system procurement.

Carrying out a feasibility study involves information assessment, information collection and report writing. The information assessment phase identifies the information that is required to answer the three questions set out above. Once the information has been identified, you should talk with information sources to discover the answers to these questions.

Some examples of possible questions that may be put are:

- How would the organisation cope if this system were not implemented?
- What are the problems with current processes and how would a new system help alleviate these problems?
- What direct contribution will the system make to the business objectives and requirements?
- Can information be transferred to and from other organisational systems?
- Does the system require technology that has not previously been used in the organisation?
- What must be supported by the system and what need not be supported?

In a feasibility study, you may consult information sources such as the managers of the departments where the system will be used, software engineers who are familiar with the type of system that is proposed, technology experts and end-users of the system. Normally, you should try to complete a feasibility study in two or three weeks.

Once you have the information, you write the feasibility study report. You should make a recommendation about whether or not the system development should continue. In the report, you may propose changes to the scope, budget and schedule of the system and suggest further high-level requirements for the system.

2.7 PROCESS OF REQUIREMENTS ENGINEERING

Once the preparation for requirements engineering is completed and the project is found to be feasible, the actual requirements development may commence. There are many different steps within requirements engineering. It is essential to ensure that the planned and agreed upon requirements engineering process is clear to all participants. Figure 2.17 illustrates the process steps of requirements engineering.

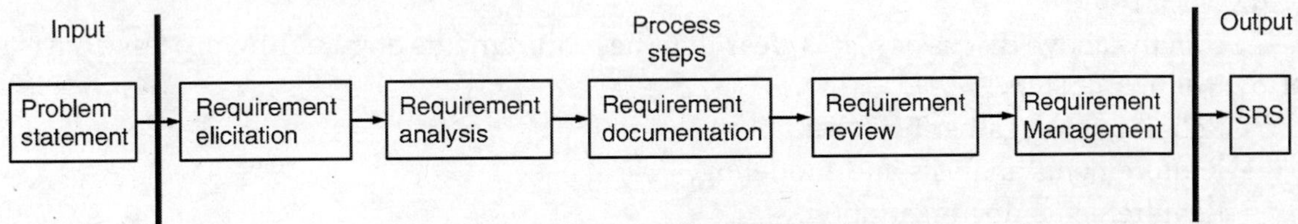

Figure 2.17: *Requirements Engineering Steps*

The process begins with requirements engineers performing the elicitation and gathering for requirements from the users and customers. The gathered information is then analysed. During the analysis step, the various requirements statements are checked for accuracy and conflict, categorized, and prioritized. The analysed material is then processed through three potential sub-activities which include requirement documentation, review and management.

Clearly, the analysed requirements must be properly defined and documented. The users must commit their time and people during the requirements elicitation and review steps.

As an output of the requirements engineering process, the finalized requirements specifications document is delivered. This document must be agreed upon and will serve as the 'contract' between the customer and the software development organization. Once the requirements specifications are agreed upon, they become the baseline. Thereafter, any modification or change request needs to be controlled and managed through a change control process to prevent the infamous project scope-creeping problem, where the project slowly grows in size without anyone's detection. Requirements scope-creep may happen any time during the software development life cycle and is one of the worst causes of schedule and cost overrun.

The mistake of not taking the time and effort to gather and understand the requirements can be costly, and it is not advisable for many good reasons. The following examples of negative consequences that occur if requirements engineering is not performed illustrate the positive reasons to perform requirements engineering:

- There are no documented requirements to base testing on.
- There are no agreed-upon requirements to control scope-creep.
- There are no documented requirements to base the customer training or customer support activities on.
- It is very difficult to manage project schedule and cost without clear and documented requirements.

It is thus clear that it is extremely unwise to base software development without any requirements engineering activities.

At the other end of the spectrum are the excessive costs of efforts devoted to reviews, the creation of voluminous documents, and other bureaucratic and wasteful activities. There is, however, time when the requirements engineer is asked to develop a requirements specification for the purpose of producing a document called a request for proposal (RFP) for inviting software development bids from many different software suppliers. In case of creating an RFP, requirements engineers are often found to err on the side of over-engineering. Most of the time, we need to be performing somewhere in between these two extreme ends of the spectrum.

From the above discussion, it is clear that the requirements engineering process consists of the following steps:

- Requirements gathering (elicitation).
- Requirements analysis and modeling.
- Requirements documentation.
- Requirements review.
- Requirements management.

2.7.1 Requirements Gathering/Elicitation

Requirements gathering/elicitation is the activity during which software requirements are discovered, articulated and revealed from the customers. Requirement elicitation is a communication process between the parties involved and affected in the problem situation. The tools in elicitation are meetings, interviews, video conferencing, e-mails, and existing documents study and facts findings. More than 90% to 95% elicitation should be complete in the initiation stage while the remaining 5% is completed during the development life-cycle. The requirements are gathered from various sources.

The sources are:

- Customer (Initiator)
- End Users
- Primary Users
- Secondary Users
- Stakeholders

2.7.2 Requirement Analysis And Modeling

After the requirements engineer has understood the exact customer requirements, he proceeds to identify and resolve the various requirements problems. The most important of these problems are the problems of anomalies, inconsistencies, and incompleteness.

2.7.3 Requirements Documentation

Requirements documentation is a very important activity, which is written after the requirements elicitation and analysis. This is the way to represent requirements in a consistent format. The requirements document is called the Software Requirements Specification (SRS).

The SRS is a specification for a particular software product, program, or set of programs that perform certain functions in a specific environment. It serves a number of purposes depending on who is writing it. First, the SRS could be written by the customer of a system. Second, the SRS could be written by a developer of the system. The two scenarios create entirely different situations and establish entirely different purposes for the document. In the first case, the SRS is used to define the needs and expectations of the users. In the second case, the SRS is written for a different purpose and serves as a contract document between customer and developer.

Thus, requirements must be written so they are meaningful not only to the customers but also to designers on the development team.

2.7.3.1 Software Requirements Specification Document

Software Requirements Specification (SRS) is a document specifying all user requirements in a neat and descriptive nature. The specification is aimed at various people in the development organization. SRS act as a medium of communication between the different departments in the development process. It acts as a set of standards for software development.

An SRS document is generated as the output of requirements engineering. Requirements engineering involves obtaining a clear and thorough understanding of the product to be developed. Thus, the SRS should be a consistent, correct, unambiguous, and complete document. The developer of the system can prepare an SRS after detailed communication with the customer.

An SRS clearly defines the following:

- *External interfaces of the system:* They identify the information that is to flow 'from and to' to the system.

- *Functional and non-functional requirements of the system:* They are the findings of the run-time requirements.

The functional requirements of the system as documented in the SRS document should clearly describe each function, which the system would support along with the corresponding input and output data set.

The non-functional requirements deal with the characteristics of the system that cannot be expressed as functions. Examples of non-functional requirements include aspects concerning maintainability, portability, and usability. The non-functional requirements include aspects concerning maintainability, portability, and usability. The non-functional requirements may also include reliability issues, accuracy of results, human-computer interface issues, and constraints on the system implementation.

2.7.3.2 Organisation of an SRS Document

There are many ways to structure a requirements document. There is no single method that is suitable for all projects. The IEEE and U.S. Department of Defence have proposed a candidate format for representing the SRS.

The general outline of the SRS document is given below:

1. Introduction
    - 1.1 Purpose
    - 1.2 Scope
    - 1.3 Definitions, Acronyms, and Abbreviations
    - 1.4 References
    - 1.5 Overview
2. The Overall Description
    - 2.1 Product Perspective
        - 2.1.1 System Interfaces
        - 2.1.2 Interfaces
        - 2.1.3 Hardware Interfaces
        - 2.1.4 Software Interfaces
        - 2.1.5 Communications Interfaces
        - 2.1.6 Memory Constraints
        - 2.1.7 Operations
        - 2.1.8 Site Adaptation Requirements
    - 2.2 Product Functions
    - 2.3 User Characteristics
    - 2.4 Constraints
    - 2.5 Operating Environment
    - 2.6 User Environment
    - 2.7 Assumptions and Dependencies
    - 2.8 Apportioning of Requirements

3. Specific Requirements
   3.1 External Interfaces
      (i) User Interface
      (ii) Hardware Interface
      (iii) Software Interface
      (iv) Communication Interface
   3.2 Functions
   3.3 Performance Requirements
   3.4 Logical Database Requirements
   3.5 Design Constraints
      3.5.1 Standards Compliance
   3.6 Software System Attribute
      3.6.1 Reliability
      3.6.2 Availability
      3.6.3 Security
      3.6.4 Maintainability
      3.6.5 Portability
   3.7 Organizing the Specific Requirements
      3.7.1 System Mode
      3.7.2 User Class
      3.7.3 Objects
      3.7.4 Feature
      3.7.5 Stimulus
      3.7.6 Response
      3.7.7 Functional Hierarchy
   3.8 Additional Comments
4. Supporting Information
   4.1 Table of Contents and Index
   4.2 Appendixes

The SRS document itself states in precise and explicit language those functions and capabilities a software system must provide, as well as states any required constraints by which the system must abide. The SRS also functions as a blueprint for completing a project with as little cost growth as possible. The SRS is often referred to as the 'parent document' as all subsequent project management documents, such as design specifications, statements of work, software architecture specifications, testing and validation plans, and documentation plans are related to it.

It is important to note that an SRS contains functional and non-functional requirements only. It does not offer any design suggestions, possible solutions to technology or business issues, or any other information other than what the development team understands the customer's system requirements to be.

2.7.4 Requirements Review

A requirements review is a manual process, which involves multiple readers from both client and contractor staff checking the requirements document for anomalies and omissions.

A requirements review can be informal or formal.

1. **Informal Review:** Informal reviews simply involve contractors discussing requirements with as many system stakeholders as possible. It is surprising how often communication between system developers and stakeholders ends after elicitation and there is no confirmation that the documented requirements are what the stakeholders really said they wanted.

   Many problems can be detected simply by talking about the system to stakeholders before making a commitment to a formal review.
2. **Formal Review:** In a formal requirements review, the development team should 'walk' the client through the system requirements, explaining the implications of each requirement. The review team should check each requirement for consistency and should check the requirements as a whole for completeness.

2.7.5 Requirements Management

Requirements define the capability that the software system solution must deliver and the intended results that must result on its application to business problems. In order to generate such requirements, a systematic approach is necessary, through a formal management process called Requirements Management.

Requirements management is defined as a systematic approach to eliciting, organizing, and documenting the requirements of the system, and a process that establishes and maintains agreement between the customer and project team on the changing requirements of the system.

The purpose of requirements management is to establish a common understanding between the customer and the software project of the customer's requirements that will be addressed by the software project. Requirements management involves establishing and maintaining an agreement with the customer on the requirements for the software project.

2.8 SOFTWARE ARCHITECTURE

Software Architecture is a branch of software engineering discipline. As it happens with every budding disciplines software architecture is defined in numerous ways. Each one of this definition highlights certain aspect of the software architecture.

One of the widely accepted definitions of the software architecture is due to Bass and Kazman. They define architecture of a software system as a structure of software depicted in terms of components, externally visible properties of components and the relationship among the components. This definition highlights the structural aspect of a software system.

Another, equally accepted definition of software architecture enumerates the design issues for specifying overall system structure that one must address at this level of abstraction. These issues are gross organization, global control structure, protocols for communication and synchronization, assignment of functionality to design elements, physical distribution of design elements, composition of design elements, scaling and performance, and selection among design alternatives.

Our view of Software architecture is that of a discipline providing mechanisms to deal with ever increasing size and complexity of a software system. Software architecture manages the complexity of a software system by separating the computations performed by components from the interactions in which they involve with other components. Hence, *architecture of a software system is depicted by specifying the constituent components and their interactions with each other*. Although, this definition misses other structural and design aspects of the software system it gives equal importance to computation and interaction.

To get better insight, software architecture is often compared with other architectural disciplines. In this respect, software architecture finds many similarities with building architecture. Like building architecture, software architecture is described by multiple views. Like building architecture, software architecture exhibits different architectural styles. Like building architecture, we find a close relationship between architectural style and engineering. Unlike building architecture, for software architecture boundaries between architecture, design, and implementation are not clearly defined.

So, to have a better understanding of what activities comes under software architecture, here, we are placing software architecture in the context of software engineering process. Normally, development cycle of a software project involves phases like requirement analysis, specifying architecture, specifying design, and implementing the software. Details of the activities that comes under each one of these phases are -

- *Requirement Analysis* is concerned with determination of the information, processing and characterizing of that information.
- *Architecture* is concerned with selection of architectural elements, their interactions and specifying the constraints on those elements and their interactions. Software Architecture provides a framework that satisfies the requirement and acts as a basis for the design.
- *Design* is concerned with the modularization, specifying detailed interfaces of the design elements, their algorithms and procedures, and the data types needed to support the architecture. Design must satisfy properties specified in the architecture and the requirement analysis.
- *Implementation* is concerned with the representations of the algorithms and data types. Implementation must satisfy the design, architecture, and requirements.

This rather vague term is defined by Bass, Clements, and Kazman in the following way:

"The software architecture of a program or computing system is the structure or structures of the system, which comprise software components, the externally visible properties of those components, and the relationships among them."

Thus it can be said that the architecture is not only the operational software. Rather, it is a representation that enables a software engineer to

- analyze the effectiveness of the design in meeting its mentioned requirements,
- consider various architectural alternatives at a stage when making design changes is still relatively easy, and
- reduce the potential risks associated with the construction of the software.

This definition emphasizes the role of "software components" in any architectural representation. In the context of architectural design, a software component can be something as simple as a program module, but it can also be extended to include databases and "middleware" that enable the configuration of a network of clients and servers. The properties of components are those characteristics that are necessary to an understanding of how the components interact with other components. At the architectural level, internal properties (e.g., details of an algorithm) are not specified. The relationships between components can be as simple as a procedure call from one module to another or as complex as a database access protocol. In this book the design of software architecture considers two levels of the design pyramid — data design and architectural design. As discussed earlier, data design enables us to represent the data component of the architecture, while architectural design focuses on the representation of the structure of software components, their properties, and interactions.

Shaw and Garlan describe software architecture as follows:

"Ever since the first program was divided into modules, software systems have had architectures, and programmers have been responsible for the interactions among the modules and the global properties of the assemblage." Historically, architectures have been implicit—accidents of implementation, or legacy systems of the past. Good software developers have often adopted one or several architectural patterns as strategies for system organization, but they use these patterns informally and have no means to make them explicit in the resulting system."

In recent times, effective software architecture and its categorical representation and design have become principal themes in software engineering.

2.8.1 Importance of Architectural Design

In a book dedicated to software architecture, Bass and his colleagues identify three key reasons that software architecture is important:

- Representations of software architecture are an enabler for communication between all parties (stakeholders) interested in the development of a computer-based system.
- The architecture highlights early design decisions that will have a profound impact on all software engineering work that follows and, as important, on the ultimate success of the system as an operational entity.
- Architecture "constitutes a relatively small, intellectually graspable model of how the system is structured and how its components work together".

The architectural design model and the architectural patterns contained within it are transferrable. That is, architecture styles and patterns can be applied to the design of other systems and represent a set of abstractions that enable software engineers to describe architecture in predictable ways.

2.9 DATA DESIGN

Like other software engineering activities, *data design* (sometimes referred to as *data architecture*) creates a model of data and/or information that is represented at a high level of abstraction (the customer/user's view of data). This data model is then refined into progressively more implementation-specific representations that can be processed by the computer-based system. In many software applications, the architecture of the data will have a profound influence on the architecture of the software that must process it.

The structure of data has always been an important part of software design. At the program component level, the design of data structures and the associated algorithms required to manipulate them is essential to the creation of high-quality applications. At the application level, the translation of a data model (derived as part of requirements engineering) into a database is pivotal to achieving the business objectives of a system. At the business level, the collection of information stored in disparate databases and reorganized into a "data warehouse" enables data mining or knowledge discovery that can have an impact on the success of the business itself. In every case, data design plays an important role.

2.10 ARCHITECTURAL STYLES

We now examine some of the broadly-used architectural styles. Our purpose is to illustrate the rich space of architectural choices, and indicate some of the trade-offs in choosing one style over another.

To make sense of the differences between styles, it helps to have a common framework from which to view them. The framework we will adopt is to treat an architecture of a specific system as a collection of computational components—or simply ***components***—together with a description of the interactions between these components—the ***connectors***. Graphically speaking, this leads to a view of an abstract architectural description as a graph in which the nodes represent the components and the arcs represent the connectors. As we will see, connectors can represent interactions as varied as procedure call, event broadcast, database queries, and pipes.

An architectural style, then, defines a family of such systems in terms of a pattern of structural organization. More specifically, an architectural style determines the vocabulary of components and connectors that can be used in instances of that style, together with a set of ***constraints*** on how they can be combined. These can include topological constraints on architectural descriptions (e.g., no cycles). Other constraints—say, having to do with execution semantics—might also be part of the style definition.

Given this framework, we can understand what a style is by answering the following questions:

- What is the structural pattern, i.e. the components, connectors, and constraints?
- What is the underlying computational model?
- What are the essential invariants of the style?
- What are some common examples of its use?
- What are the advantages and disadvantages of using that style?
- What are some of the common specializations?

In summary, each style describes a system category that encompasses the following attributes:

(1) a set of *components* (e.g., a database, computational modules) that perform a function required by a system;

(2) a set of *connectors* that enable "communication, coordination's and cooperation" among components;

(3) *constraints* that define how components can be integrated to form the system; and

(4) *semantic models* that enable a designer to understand the overall properties of a system by analyzing the known properties of its constituent parts.

An architectural style found in a software system is defined as a pattern of components and connectors that occur repeatedly. Usually an architectural style has similar type of components and connectors. They exhibit a particular way of interaction among the components. They are not a complete software system/subsystem. Architectural styles are intentionally ambiguous on the number of components and connectors present in it. An architectural style puts some constraints on components and connectors. Most of the ADL supports a mechanism to define architectural styles. The vast number of designed computer-based systems can be categorized into the underlying basic architectural styles. There are many more architectural styles which are available to a software designer.

2.11 ARCHITECTURAL DESCRIPTION LANGUAGES

Box-line diagrams are normally used to describe the structure of a software system. System modeling using box-line diagram is the simplest way to identify important elements of a software system and their relationship. However, the problem with the approach is that boxes and lines are overloaded with the meaning assigned to them. For example, a line in the diagram represents either a link between two software component, or an interdependence of a software component, or a procedure call. Earlier, Module Interconnection Languages (MIL) are used to describe the inter-relationship among the modules of software. Also, Interface Description Languages (IDL) are used for the same purpose in object and component oriented programming. MIL and IDL captures relationship between the source codes but fails to capture the dynamic relationship among the components of software. Hence, a different set of tools and techniques are required to define the structure of a software system. Architectural Description Languages (ADL) describes the structure of a software system at a level of abstraction that is closest to the intuition of a system designer.

2.12 SOFTWARE DESIGN AND SOFTWARE ENGINEERING

After the software requirements have been analyzed and specified, software design begins. It is the first of the three technical activities, viz. design, coding, and testing, that are necessary to build reliable software. Information transformation is the main aim of each of these activities, hence resulting in validated computer software. It can be said that software design is at the core of software engineering, and is applied regardless of the underlying software process model used.

There are four design models which are required to be built for a complete specification of design. This flow of information during software design is illustrated in Figure 2.18. Software requirements, established by the data, functional, and behavioral models, feed the design task. Using one of a number of design methods (discussed in later sections), the design task produces a data design, an architectural design, an interface design, and a component design.

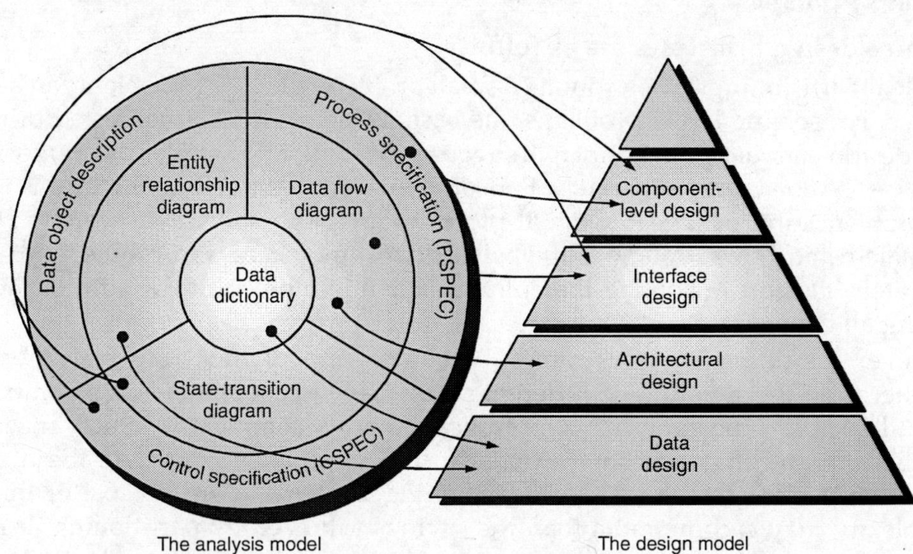

Figure 2.18: *Translating the analysis model into a software design*

- **Data Design:** The *data design* transforms the information domain model created during analysis into the data structures that will be required to implement the software. The data objects and relationships defined in the entity relationship diagram and the detailed data content depicted in the data dictionary provide the basis for the data design activity. Part of data design may occur in conjunction with the design of software architecture. More detailed data design occurs as each software component is designed.
- **Architectural Design:** The *architectural design* defines the relationships between major structural elements of the software, the "design patterns" that can be used to achieve the requirements that have been defined for the system, and the constraints that affect the way in which architectural design patterns can be applied. The architectural design representation— the framework of a computer-based system—can be derived from the system specification, the analysis model, and the interaction of subsystems defined within the analysis model.
- **Interface Design:** The *interface design* describes the software communications within itself, with systems that interoperate with it, and with humans who use it. An interface depicts a flow of information (e.g., data and/or control) along with its specific type of behavior. Therefore, data and control flow diagrams provide much of the information required for interface design.
- **Component Design:** The *component-level design* transforms structural elements of the software architecture into a procedural description of software components. Information obtained from the PSPEC, CSPEC, and STD serve as the basis for component design. During design, decisions are made that will ultimately affect the success of software construction and, as important, the ease with which software can be maintained.

2.12.1 Design Principles

The three design principles are as follows:

- **Problem Partitioning:** When solving a small problem, the entire problem can be tackled at once. For solving larger problems, the basic principle is the time-tested principle of "divide and conquer." This principle suggests dividing into smaller pieces, so that each piece can be conquered separately. For software design, therefore, the goal is to divide the problem into manageably small pieces that can be solved separately. The basic rationale behind this strategy is the belief that if the pieces of a problem are solvable separately, the cost of solving the entire problem is more than the sum of the cost of solving all the pieces.

  However, the different pieces cannot be entirely independent of each other as they together form the system. The different pieces have to cooperate and communicate to solve the larger problem. This communication adds complexity, which arises due to partitioning and may not have existed in the original problem. As the number of components increases, the cost of partitioning, together with the cost of this added complexity, may become more than the savings achieved by partitioning. It is at this point that no further partitioning needs to be done. The designer has to make the judgment about when to stop partitioning.

  Problem partitioning can be divided into two categories:

  (i) Horizontal Partitioning: Horizontal partitioning defines separate branches of modular hierarchy for each major program function. The simplest approach to horizontal partitioning defines three partitions: input, data transformation (often called processing), and output. Partitioning their architecture horizontally provides a number of distinct benefits:

  - Software that is easier to test.
  - Software that is easier to maintain.
  - Software that is easier to extend.
  - Propagation of fewer side effects.

  Conversely, horizontal partitioning often causes more data to be passed across module interfaces and can complicate the overall control of program flow.

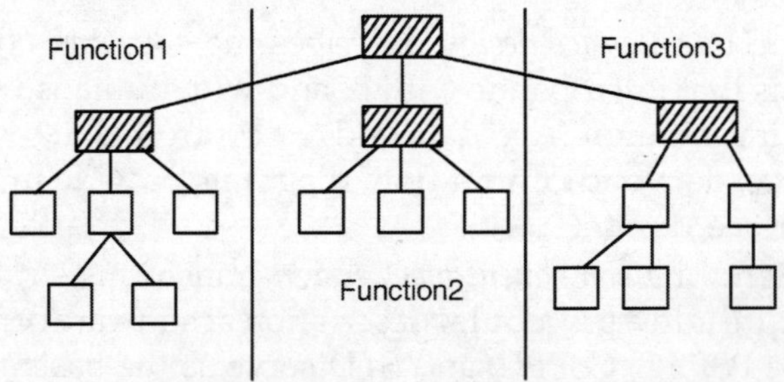

Figure 2.19: Horizontal Partitioning

  (ii) Vertical Partitioning: Vertical partitioning, often called factoring, suggests that control and work should be distributed from top-down in the program structure.

Top-level modules should perform control functions and do actual processing work. Modules that reside low in the structure should be the workers, performing all input, compilation, and output tasks.

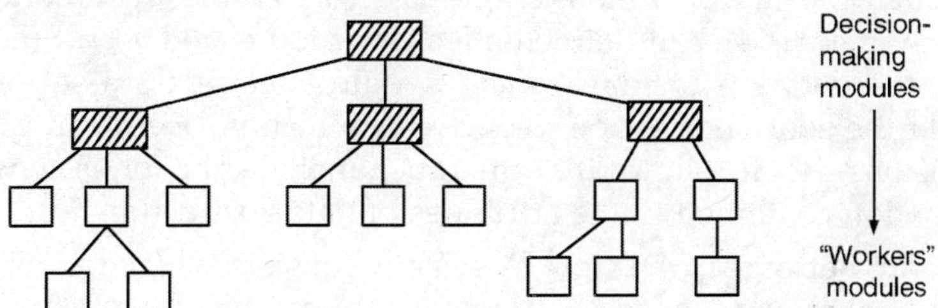

Figure 2.20: Vertical Partitioning

- **Abstraction:** An abstraction of a component describes the external behaviour of that component without bothering with the internal details that produce the behaviour. Abstraction is an indispensable part of the design process and it is essential for problem partitioning. Partitioning essentially is the exercise in determining the components of a system. However, these components are not isolated from each other, but interact with other components. In order to allow the designer to concentrate on one component at a time, abstraction of other components is used.
  Abstraction is used for existing components as well as components that are being designed. Abstraction of existing components plays an important role in the maintenance phase.
  During the design process, abstractions are used in a reverse manner not in the process of understanding a system. During design, the components do not exist, and in the design the designer specifies only the abstract specifications of the different components. The basic goal of system design is to specify the modules in a system and their abstractions. Once the different modules are specified, during the detailed design the designer can concentrate on one module at a time. The task in detailed design and implementation is essentially to implement the modules so that the abstract specifications of each module are satisfied.
  There are two common abstraction mechanisms for software systems:
  - ***Functional Abstraction:*** In functional abstraction, a module is specified by the function it performs. For example, a module to sort an input array can be represented by the specification of sorting. Functional abstraction is the basis of partitioning in function-oriented approaches. That is, when the problem is being partitioned, the overall transformation function for the system is partitioned into smaller functions that comprise the system function. An example of a functional abstraction would be the word *open* for a door. *Open* implies a long sequence of functional steps such as walk to the door, reach out and grasp knob, turn knob and pull door, step away from moving door, etc.
  - ***Data Abstraction:*** The second unit for abstraction is data abstraction. There are certain operations required from a data object, depending on the object and the environment in which it is used. Data abstraction supports this view. Data is not

treated simply as objects, but is treated as objects with some predefined operations on them. The operations defined on a data object are the only operations that can be performed on those objects. From outside an object, the internals of the object are hidden; only the operations on the object are visible. In the context of functional abstraction *open*, we can define data abstraction called *door*. Like any other data object, the data abstraction for *door* would encompass a set of attributes that describe the door, such as door type, swing direction, opening mechanism, weight, dimensions, etc. It follows that the functional abstraction *open* will make use of information contained in the attributes of data abstraction *door*.

- **Top-down and Bottom-up Design:** A system consists of components, which have components of their own; indeed a system is a hierarchy of components. The highest-level components correspond to the total system. To design such hierarchies there are two possible approaches: top-down and bottom-up. The top-down approach starts from the highest-level component of the hierarchy and proceeds through to lower levels. By contrast, a bottom-up approach starts with the lowest-level component of the hierarchy and proceeds through progressively higher levels to the top-level component.

  A top-down design approach starts by identifying the major components of the system, decomposing them into their lower-level components and iterating until the desired level of detail is achieved. Top-down design methods often result in some form of stepwise refinement. Starting from an abstract design, in each step the design is refined to a more concrete level, until we reach a level where no more refinement is needed and the design can be implemented directly. The top-down approach has been promulgated by many researchers and has been found to be extremely useful for design. Most design methodologies are based on the top-down approach.

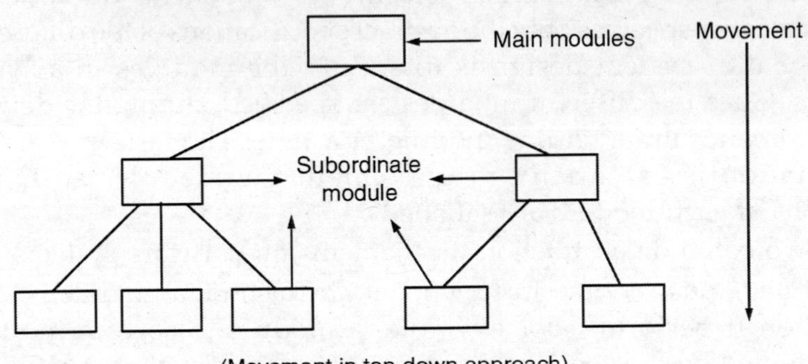

***Figure* 2.21:** *Top-Down Approach*

  A bottom-up design approach starts with designing the most basic or primitive components and proceeds to higher-level components that use these lower-level components. Bottom-up methods work with layers of abstraction. Starting from the very bottom, operations that provide a layer of abstraction are implemented. The operations of this layer are then used to implement more powerful operations and still a higher layer of abstraction, until the stage is reached where the operations supported by the layer are those desired by the system.

A top-down approach is suitable only if the specifications of the system are clearly known and the system development is from scratch. However, if a system is to be built from an existing system, a bottom-up approach is more suitable, as it starts from some existing components. So, for example, if an iterative enhancement type of process is being followed, in later iterations, the bottom-up approach could be more suitable (in the first iteration a top-down approach can be used).

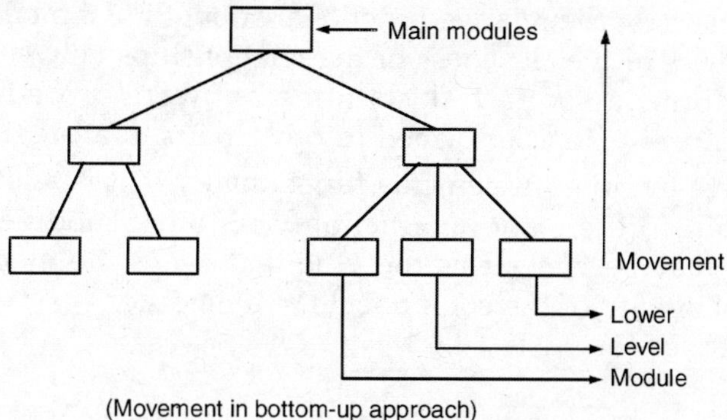

Figure 2.22: Bottom-Up Approach

2.12.2 Coupling

The coupling between two modules indicates the degree of interdependence between them. If two modules interchange a large amount of data, then they are highly interdependent. The degree of coupling between two modules depends on their interface complexity. The interface complexity is basically determined by the number of types of parameters that are interchanged while invoking the functions of the module.

- **Highly Coupled:** When the modules are highly dependent on each other then they are called highly coupled.
- **Loosely Coupled:** When the modules are dependent on each other but the interconnection among them is weak then they are called loosely coupled.

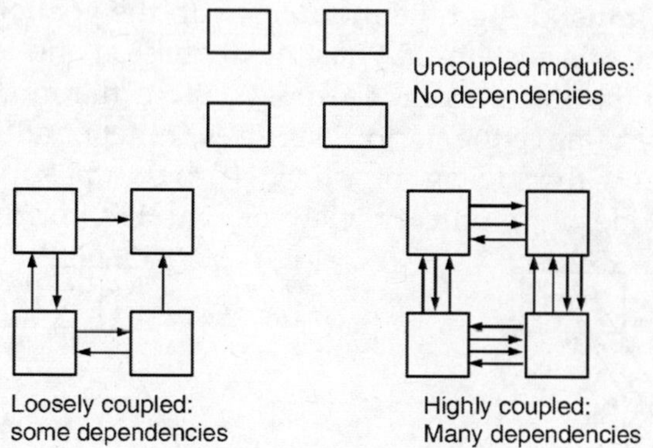

Figure 2.23: Coupling

- **Uncoupled:** When the different modules have no interconnection among them then they are called uncoupled modules.

2.12.3 Cohesion

One of the key notions related to the issue of keeping the design 'simple' so that it will have many of the desirable attributes is to ensure that each unit of the design, whether it is at the modular level or component level, is focused on a single purpose. Terms such as 'intramodular functional relatedness' or 'modular strength' have been used to address the notion of design cohesion.

Cohesion is a measure of the relative functional strength of a module. The cohesion of a component is a measure of the closeness of the relationships between its components. A cohesive module performs a single task within a software procedure, requiring little interaction with procedures being performed in other parts of a program.

A strongly cohesive module implements functionality that is related to one feature of the solution and requires little or no interaction with other modules. This is shown in Figure 2.24. Cohesion may be viewed as the glue that keeps the module together. It is a measure of the mutual officity of the components of a module.

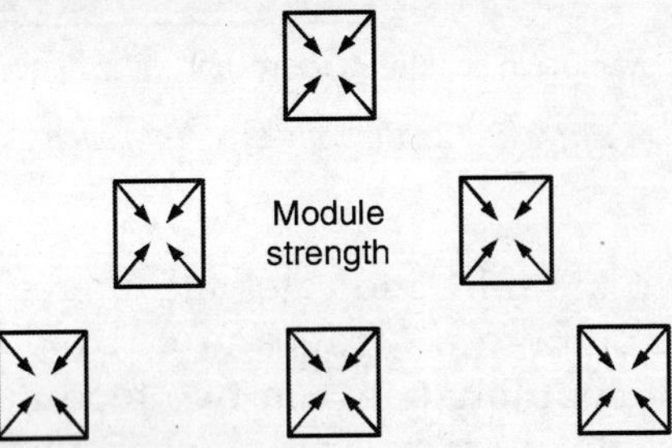

Figure 2.24: Cohesion-strength of Relation within Modules

Thus, we want to maximize the interaction within a module. Hence, an important design objective is to maximize the module cohesion and minimize the module coupling.

2.12.4 Relationship Between Coupling and Cohesion

A software engineer must design the modules with the goal of high cohesion and low coupling. A good example of a system that has high cohesion and low coupling is the 'plug and play' feature of a computer system. Various slots in the motherboard of the system simply facilitate to add or remove the various services/functionalities without affecting the entire system. This is because the add-on components provide the services in a highly cohesive manner. Figure 2.25 provides a graphical review of cohesion and coupling.

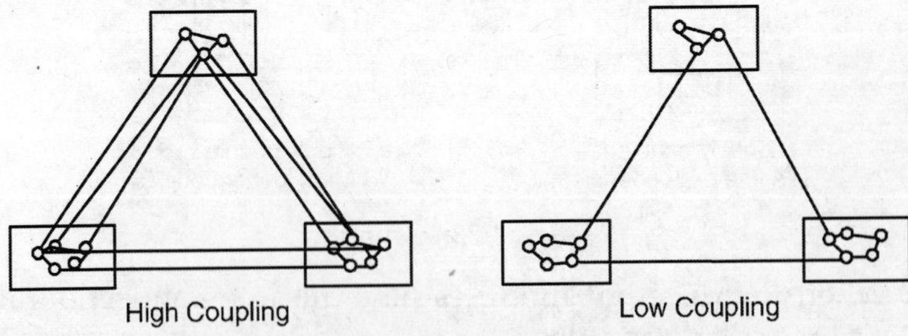

Figure 2.25: View of Cohesion and Coupling

Module design with high cohesion and low coupling characterizes a module as a black box when the entire structure of the system is described. Each module can be dealt with separately when the module functionality is described.

2.13 SOFTWARE DESIGN APPROACHES

There are fundamentally two different approaches to software design- function-oriented design and object-oriented design. However, these two design approaches are radically different. They are complementary rather than competing techniques. Each of these two techniques may be applicable at different stages of the design process. Salient features of these two approaches are discussed in the next sections.

2.13.1 Function-Oriented Design

The following are the salient features of a typical function-oriented design approach:

1. A system is viewed as something that performs a set of functions. Starting at this high-level view of the system, each function is successively refined into more detailed functions. For example, consider a function *create-new-library-member* which creates the record for a new member, assign a unique membership number to the new member, and prints a bill towards the membership charge. This function may consist of the following sub-functions:
    - *assign-membership-number*
    - *create-member-record*
    - *print-bill*

   Each of these sub-functions may be split into more detailed sub-functions and so on.
2. A system state is centralized and shared among different functions, e.g. data such as member-records is available for reference and updation to several functions such as:
    - *create-new-member*
    - *delete-member*
    - *update-member-record*

Several function-oriented design approaches have been developed.

These techniques, to start with, view a system as a black box that performs a set of high-level functions. During the design process, these high-level functions are successively decomposed into more detailed functions and finally the different identified functions are mapped into modules. The term top-down decomposition is often used to denote such successive decompositions of a set of high-level functions into more detailed functions.

The Structured Analysis/Structured Design (SA/SD) technique can be used to perform the high-level design of software. The details of the SA/SD technique are discussed below.

As the name implies, the SA/SD methodology consists of two distinct activities:

- Structured Analysis (SA)
- Structured Design (SD)

Structured analysis is the activity of deriving a structured model of the requirements of a system. Structured design, on the other hand, is the development of a blueprint of a computer system solution to a problem, having the same interrelationships and components as the original problem.

The aim of structured analysis activity is to transform a textual problem description into a graphic model. More precisely, structured analysis is used to carry out the top-down decomposition of the set of high-level functions depicted in problem description and to represent them graphically. During structured analysis, functional decomposition of the system is achieved, i.e. each function that the system performs is analysed and hierarchically decomposed into more detailed functions. On the other hand, during structured design, all functions identified during structured analysis are mapped to a module structure. This module structure is also called software architecture for the given problem and it can be directly implemented using a conventional programming language.

It is important to understand that the purpose of structured analysis is to capture the detailed structure of the system as perceived by the user, whereas the purpose of structured design is to define the solution that is suitable for implementation in some programming language. The results of structured analysis can therefore, be easily understood by the user since his terminology is used for naming different functions and data. The user can even review the results of the structured analysis to ensure that it captures all his requirements.

In the following section, we first discuss how to carry out structured analysis. Subsequently, we discuss how we can systematically transform the results of structured analysis into structured design.

2.13.1.1 Structured Analysis

During structured analysis, the major processing tasks (i.e. functions) of the system are analysed, and data flows among these processing tasks are represented graphically.

The analysis model must achieve these three primary objectives:

- Describe what the customer requires.
- Establish a basis for the creation of software design.
- Define a set of requirements that can be validated on the completion of software.

Structured analysis technique is based on the following essential underlying principles:

- Top-down decomposition approach
- Divide and conquer principle, where each function is decomposed independently
- Graphical representation of the analysis results

Special notations and graphical symbols are used to describe and partition the functionality of a system. The following tools are used for structured analysis:

- Data Flow Diagrams (DFD)
- Data Dictionary
- Context Diagrams
- Event Lists
- Entity-Relationship Diagram (ERD)
- State-Transition Diagram

2.13.1.2 Structured Design

The aim of structured design is to transform the results of structured analysis into a structure chart. A structure chart represents the software architecture, i.e. various modules making up the system, the module dependency, and the parameters that are passed among the different modules. Hence, the structure chart representation can be easily implemented using a programming language. Since the main focus in a structure chart is on module structure of software and the interaction among the different modules, the procedural aspects are not represented.

Software architecture is represented by a structure chart. The structure chart is the primary tool used in structured design. The structure chart is used to graphically depict the modular structure of software. It shows:

- how the program has been partitioned into smaller modules
- the hierarchy and organization of modules
- the communication interfaces between modules

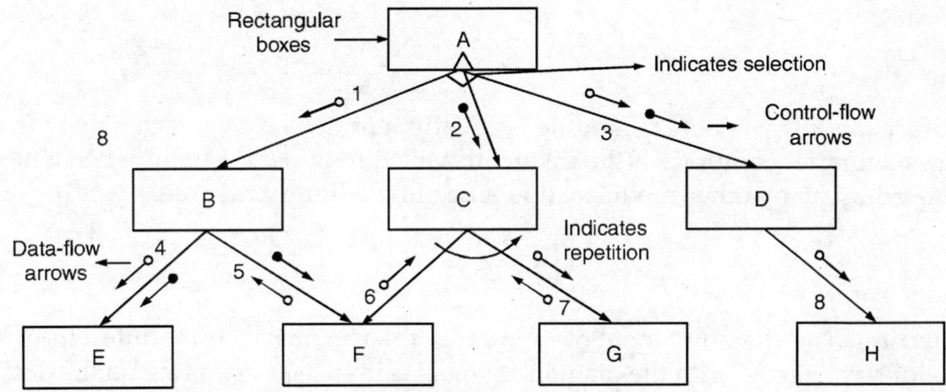

Figure 2.26: *(a) Hierarchical Format of a Structure Chart*

Here, black boxes are arranged in hierarchical format as shown in Figures 2.26 (*a*) and (*b*).

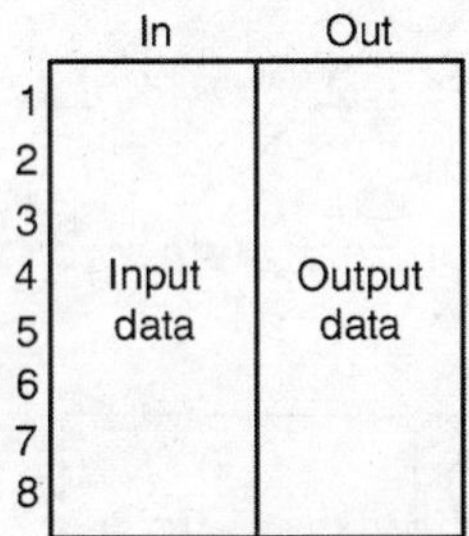

Figure 2.26: *(b) Format of a Structure Chart*

The basic building blocks used to design structure charts are as following:

- **Rectangle:** A rectangle represents a module. Usually, every rectangular box is annotated with the name of the module it represents.

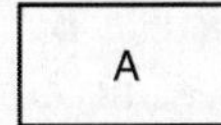

- **Module invocation arrow:** An arrow connecting two modules implies that during program execution, control is passed from one module to another in the direction of connecting arrow. However, just by looking at the structure chart, one cannot say whether a module calls another module just once or multiple times. Also, just by looking at the structure chart, one cannot tell the order in which the different modules are invoked.

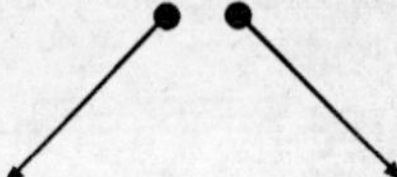

- **Data flow arrows:** These are small arrows appearing alongside the module invocation arrows. The data flow arrows are annotated with the corresponding data name. The data flow arrows represent the fact that the names data passes from one module to the other in the direction of the arrow.

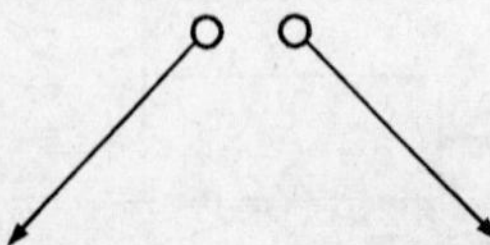

- **Library modules:** A library module is usually represented by a rectangle with double edges. Libraries comprise of the frequently called modules. Usually, when a module is invoked by many other modules, it is made into a library module.

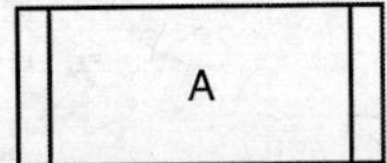

- **Selection:** The diamond symbol represents the fact that one module out of several modules connected with the diamond symbol is invoked depending on the outcome of the condition attached to the diamond symbol.

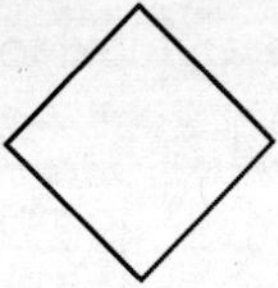

- **Repetition:** A loop around the control flowte arrows denotes that the respective modules are invoked repeatedly.

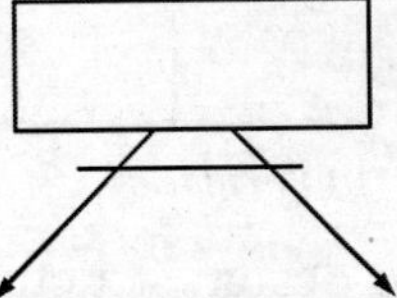

In any structure chart, there should be a single module at the top, called the *root*. There should be at most one control relationship between any two modules in the structure chart. This means that if module A invokes module B, module B cannot invoke module A. The main reason behind this restriction is that we can consider the different modules of a structure chart to be arranged in layers or levels. The principle of abstraction does not allow the lower-level modules to be aware of the existence of the higher-level modules. However, it is possible for the two higher-level modules to invoke the same lower-level module.

2.13.2 Object-Oriented Design

In the object-oriented design approach, the system is viewed as a collection of objects (i.e. entities). The system state is decentralized among the objects and each object manages its own state information. For example, in a Library Automation Software, each library member may be a separate object with its own data and functions to operate on these data. In fact, the functions defined for one object cannot refer or change data of other objects.

Objects have their own internal data which define their state. Similar objects constitute a class. In other words, each object is a member of some class. Classes may inherit features from a super class. Conceptually, objects communicate by message passing.

Object-oriented (OO) approaches for software development have become extremely popular in recent years. Much of the new development is now being done using OO techniques and languages. There are many advantages that OO systems offer. An OO model closely represents the problem domain, which makes it easier to produce and understand designs. As requirements change, the objects in a system are less immune to these changes, thereby permitting changes more easily. Inheritance and close association of objects in design to problem domain entities encourage more re-use, i.e., new applications can use existing modules more effectively, thereby reducing development cost and cycle time. Object-oriented approaches are believed to be more natural and provide richer structures for thinking and abstraction. Common design patterns have also been uncovered that allow reusability at a higher level.

The object-oriented design approach is fundamentally different from the function-oriented design approaches primarily due to the different abstraction that is used. It requires a different way of thinking and partitioning. It can be said that thinking in object-oriented terms is most important for producing truly object-oriented designs.

Object-oriented design is part of object-oriented development where an object-oriented strategy is used throughout the development process:

- ***Object-oriented analysis*** is concerned with developing an object-oriented model of the application domain. The objects in that model reflect the entities and operations associated with the problem to be solved.
- ***Object-oriented design*** is concerned with developing an object-oriented model of a software system to implement the identified requirements. The objects in an object-oriented design are related to the solution to the problem. There may be close relationships between some problem objects and some solution objects, but the designer inevitably has to add new objects and to transform problem objects to implement the solution.
- ***Object-oriented programming*** is concerned with realising a software design using an object-oriented programming language, such as Java. An object-oriented programming language provides constructs to define object classes and a run-time system to create objects from these classes.

The transition between these stages of development should, ideally, be seamless, with compatible notations used at each stage. Moving to the next stage involves refining the previous stage by adding detail to existing object classes and devising new classes to provide additional functionality. As information is concealed within objects, detailed design decisions about the representation of data can be delayed until the system is implemented. In some cases, decisions on the distribution of objects and whether objects can be sequential or concurrent may also be delayed.

This means that software designers can devise designs that can be adapted to different execution environments. This is exemplified by the Model Driven Architecture (MDA) approach, which proposes that systems should be explicitly designed in two levels, an implementation-independent level and an implementation-dependent level. An abstract model of the system is designed at the implementation-independent level, and this is mapped to a more detailed platform-dependent model that can be used as a basis for code generation.

Object-oriented systems are easier to change than systems developed using other approaches because the objects are independent. They may be understood and modified as standalone entities. Changing the implementation of an object or adding services should not affect other system objects. Because objects are associated with things, there is often a clear mapping between real-world entities (such as hardware components) and their controlling objects in the system. This improves the understandability and hence the maintainability of the design.

Objects are, potentially, reusable components because they are independent encapsulations of state and operations. Designs can be developed using objects that have been created in previous designs. This reduces design, programming and validation costs. It may also lead to the use of standard objects (hence improving design understandability) and reduce the risks involved in software development.

2.13.3 Function-Oriented Versus the Object-Oriented Approach

The following are some of the important differences between the function-oriented and object-oriented design approach.

Functional-oriented Approach	**Object-oriented Approach**
In the functional-oriented design approach, the basic abstractions, which are given to the user, are real-world functions, such as sort, merge, track, display, etc.	In the object-oriented design approach, the basic abstractions are not the real-world functions, but are the data abstraction where the real-world entities are represented, such as picture, machine, radar system, customer, student, employee, etc.
In function-oriented design, functions are grouped together by which a higher-level function is obtained. An example of this technique is SA/SD.	In this design, the functions are grouped together on the basis of the data they operate on, such as in class person, function displays are made member functions to operate on its data members such as the person name, age, etc.
In this approach, the state information is often represented in a centralized shared memory.	In this approach, the state information is not represented in a centralized shared memory but is implemented/ distributed among the objects of the system.

2.14 DETAILED DESIGN

In the previous two sections we discussed two different approaches for system design: function-oriented and object-oriented. In system design we concentrate on the modules in a system and how they interact with each other. Once the modules are identified and specified during the high-level design, the internal logic that will implement the given specifications can be designed, and is the focus of this section.

The detailed design activity is often not performed formally and archived as it is almost impossible to keep the detailed design document consistent with the code. Due to this, developing the detailed design is useful for the more complex and important modules, and is often done informally by the programmer as part of the personal process of developing code.

2.14.1 Program Design Language

Program design language (PDL), also called *structured English* or *pseudocode*, is "a pidgin language in that it uses the vocabulary of one language (i.e., English) and the overall syntax of another (i.e., a structured programming language)". In this section, PDL is used as a generic reference for a design language. At first glance PDL looks like a modern programming language. The difference between PDL and a real programming language lies in the use of narrative text (e.g., English) embedded directly within PDL statements. Given the use of narrative text embedded directly into a syntactical structure, PDL cannot be compiled (at least not yet). However, PDL tools currently exist to translate PDL into a programming language "skeleton" and/or a graphical representation (e.g., a flowchart) of design. These tools also produce nesting maps, a design operation index, cross-reference tables, and a variety of other information.

2.14.2 Logic Algorithm Design

The basic goal in detailed design is to specify the logic for the different modules that have been specified during system design. Specifying the logic will require developing an algorithm that will implement the given specifications. Here we consider some principles for designing algorithms or logic that will implement the given specifications.

The term algorithm is quite general and is applicable to a wide variety of areas. For software we can consider an **algorithm** to be an unambiguous procedure for solving a problem. A **procedure** is a finite sequence of well-defined steps or operations, each of which requires a finite amount of memory and time to complete. In this definition we assume that termination is an essential property of procedures.

2.15 USER-INTERFACE (UI) DESIGN

Up until now, we have focused on software units and the interactions among them. In this section, we will concentrate on user-interface (UI) design, i.e. the interactions between a human user and software. Instead of worrying about reducing software defects, we must now worry about reducing human errors. Although some designers may believe that having a graphical user interface solves many of user anxiety problems with computing systems, it is still important to understand what is it that makes the interface easier to understand, navigate, and use. What is user-friendliness, and what characterizes a good user-interface design? The important characteristic here is that the interface has more to do with people rather than software systems.

The user interface portion of a software product is responsible for all interactions with the user. In early days of computing, no software product had any user interface. The computer those days were batch systems and no interactions with the users were supported. Today the things are very different, and almost every software product has a user interface, and is highly interactive. Hence no wonder that many users judge a software product based on its user interface. Aesthetics apart, an interface that is difficult to use leads to higher levels of user errors and ultimately leads to user dissatisfaction. Users become particularly irritated when a system behaves in unexpected ways, i.e. issued commands do not carry out actions according to the intuitive expectations of the user. Normally, when a user starts using a system, he builds a mental model of the system and expects the system behaviour to conform to it. For example, if a user action causes one type of system activity and response under some context, then the user would expect similar system activity and response to occur for similar user actions in identical contexts. Therefore, sufficient care and attention should be paid to the design of the user interface of any software product.

Systematic development of the user interface is also important from another consideration. Development of a good user interface usually takes significant portion of the total system development effort. For many interactive applications, as much as 50% of the total development effort is spent on developing the user interface part. Unless the user interface is designed and developed in a systematic manner, the total effort required to develop he interface will increase tremendously. Therefore, it is necessary to carefully study various systematic techniques available for the development of user interface.

2.16 CODING

Coding is the activity where a design is converted to runnable code. Depending on the details of the design specification, the coding activity may vary greatly. Many companies have coding standards that all the programmers must follow. The purpose of a coding standard is to make it easier for programmers to read each other's codes, and to make it easier to maintain the code.

When a programmer writes initial code for a program, he has certain ideas on the overall structure of the program. These ideas determine how modifications should be done. Unfortunately, since the program is only one example of these ideas, it is usually not sufficient to simply read the program in order to understand these underlying ideas. Therefore, the program must be accompanied by some kind of documentation, whether in the form of comments or in the form of separate documents. In both cases, the purpose of the documentation is not to repeat what is already known from the program itself, nut to serve as a complement to the program. In short, documentation contains what the program does not contain.

So far, the skills we have learned have helped us to understand the customers and users problem and to devise a high-level solution for it. Now, the focus needs to be shifted on implementing the solution as software, i.e. programs must be written that correctly implement the design. This task can be daunting for several reasons. First, the designers may not have addressed all of the idiosyncrasies of the platform and programming environment, i.e. structures and relationships that are easy to describe with charts and tables are not always straightforward to write as code. Second, the code must be written in such a way that is understandable not only to us when we revisit it for testing, but also to others as the system evolves over time. Third, we must take advantage of the characteristic of the design's organization, the data's structure, and the programming language's constructs while still creating code that is easily reusable.

Clearly, there are many ways to implement a design and many languages and tools are also available, we cannot hope to cover all of them in this book. The programming guidelines are generally applicable to any implementation. Hence, the chapter does not teach the developers how to program; rather it explains some of the software engineering practices that should be kept in mind while writing the code.

The input to coding phase is design document. During the coding phase, different modules identified in the design document are coded according to the respective module specifications. Recall that at the end of the design phase, the developers have the module structure of the system and the module specifications where the data structures and algorithms for each module are specified. Therefore, the objective of the coding phase is to transform the design of a system, as given by its module specification, into a high-level language code and to unit test this code.

Good software development organizations require their programmers to follow some well-defined and standard style of coding called coding standards. Most software development organizations formulate their own coding standards that suit them the most, and require their engineers to follow these standards rigorously due to the following reasons:

- A coding standard gives a uniform appearance to the codes written by various engineers.
- It provides sound understanding of the code.
- It encourages good programming practices.

A coding standard lists several rules to be followed during coding, such as the way variables should be named, the way the code should be laid out, error return conventions, and so forth. Besides the coding standards, several coding guidelines are also suggested by software companies. Coding guidelines provide general suggestions regarding the coding style to be followed and leave the actual implementation of these guidelines to the discretion of the individual engineers.

After a module has been coded, usually code reviews are carried out to ensure that coding standards are followed and to detect as many errors possible before testing. It is important to detect as many errors as possible during code reviews and during unit testing, because an error detected at these stages would require much less effort for debugging compared to that needed for fixing errors, if the same error was detected during integration or system testing.

2.16.1 Code Reviews

Code review is the process by which code is authorized to enter the development tree. We use code review to keep defects from entering the development tree, and to assure that we're constructing a product that matches the requirements.

The goal of the code review process is to save time, by catching defects before they affect others and before they get lost in the sea. Defects are functional problems (bugs), maintenance problems such as fragile or incomprehensible code, and traceability problems such as unnecessary features or features that don't match the requirements.

The goals of this document are to describe the process that we actually use to make changes to the development tree, and to make this process consistent. It's a starting point, not a destination: like a piece of software, we will debug it and optimize it as we gain experience as a team. It does derive from code review processes we've used successfully in the past, so it's known to work in principle.

Code reviews have multiple objectives.

(a) Evaluate conformance to specifications and standards

(b) Find anomalies

(c) Verify quality

(d) Forum for learning

2.16.2 Code Walkthrough

Code walkthrough is an informal code analysis technique. In this technique, after the code has been coded, it is successfully compiled and all syntax errors are eliminated. Some members of the development team are given the code a few days before the walkthrough meeting to read and understand the code. Each member selects some test cases and simulates execution of the code by hand. The main objectives of the walkthrough are to discover the algorithmic and logical errors in the code. The members note down their findings to discuss these in a walkthrough meeting where the coder of the module is also present.

Regular code walkthrough is a very useful tool in development as people tend to overlook mistakes that they have implemented themselves. Code walkthrough also helps to spread expert knowledge throughout a development team. The suggestions and ideas which evolve during review sessions often take the process big steps forward. It thus has a positive effect on software quality, readability, and ease of understanding.

Even though a code walkthrough is an informal analysis technique, several guidelines have evolved over the years for making this naive technique more effective and useful. Of course, these guidelines are based on personal experience, common sense, and several objective factors. Therefore, these guidelines should be considered as examples rather than as rules to that can be applied dogmatically. Some of these guidelines are the following:

- The team performing the code walkthrough should not be either too big or too small. Ideally it should comprise of three to seven members.
- Discussion should focus on discovery of errors and not on how to fix the discovered errors. Meeting coordinators must not let the meeting degenerate into a problem solving session. Problems must be identified and assigned as action items to discuss in a follow-up meeting, after a solution has been devised.
- In order to foster cooperation and to avoid the feeling among the engineers that they are being evaluated in the code walkthrough meeting, managers should not attend the walkthrough meetings.
- The duration of a code walkthrough should be of reasonable duration. A balance should be made between the length of the walkthrough and the attention span of the team.

2.16.3 Code Inspection

Code inspection is one of the most powerful tools for eliminating bugs. Formal code inspections are probably the most important tool one can use to get the code fast with fewer bugs. The goal of code inspection is to identify and remove bugs before testing the code. The best code inspection comes about from properly organized teams. Experience indicates that when management is involved usually only the most superficial bugs are caught, since no one wishes to show the author to be the cause of major program defects.

- **Moderator**
  The moderator must be very competent technically, as he has to lead the inspection process. He paces the meetings, coaches other team members, deals with scheduling a meeting place and disseminating materials before the meeting, and follows up on the rework, if any.
- **Reader**
  The reader takes the team through the code by paraphrasing its operation. The author is never allowed to take this role, since he may read what he meant instead of what was actually implemented.
- **Recorder**
  The recorder notes each error on a standard form. This frees the other team members to focus on thinking deeply about the code.
- **Author**
  The author's role is to understand the errors found and to illuminate unclear areas. As code inspections are never confrontational, the author should never be in a position of defending the code.

2.17 SOFTWARE DOCUMENTATION

We have already seen that when we develop a software product, we not only develop the executable files and the source code, but also develop various kinds of documents such as users' manual, software requirements specifications (SRS) document, design document, test document, installation manual, etc. as a part of any software development process. All these documents are an important part of any software development process. Good documents are very useful and serve the following purposes:

- Good documents enhance understandability and maintainability of a software product. They reduce the effort and time required for maintenance.
- Good documents help the users to effectively exploit the system.
- Good documents help in effectively overcoming the manpower turnover problem, where even when an engineer leaves the organization, the newcomer can build up the required knowledge quickly.
- Good documents help the manager in effectively tracking the progress of the project. The project manager knows that measurable progress is achieved if a piece of work is done and the required documents are produced and reviewed.

The main document that results from coding activity is the code itself. Contrary to what some people think, the main purpose of the code as a document is to be read by other programmers. The fact that the code also serves as input to a translator that generates machine readable code, is secondary. Therefore, it is important to structure the code so that it is readable to humans. Comments are an important part of the code. The code itself is usually supplemented by other documentation. The purpose of this documentation is to explain choices that were made during the coding phase. That way, the program can be altered in a clean and consistent way during the maintenance phase.

Based on this discussion, software documentation can be categorized as two basic types: one **external**, addressing information about the program. The other is **internal**, which has to be closed to the program, program statement and program block to explain it, then and there.

2.18 SOFTWARETESTING

Software testing is a process used to identify the correctness, completeness, and quality of developed computer software. It includes a set of activities conducted with the intent of finding errors in software so that it could be corrected before the product is released to the end users. In simple words, software testing is an activity to check whether the actual results match the expected results and to ensure that the software system is defect free.

Software testing is an important process in the software development life cycle. It is also the most time consuming phase. Testing forms the last stage of any software development project before it can be released for implementation. It is mandatory for software to pass all the tests before implementation. Thus, testing process increases the reliability as well as quality of the software products.

Software is developed for specific purposes. It can be used and can be marketed only if it is working properly. Actually testing is a process that is not to be done at the end of software development process, but both coding and testing have to go simultaneously. Testing of software modules and their integration with the main module needs to be done continuously. Every upgrade version, module addition or enhancement or a new implementation also needs to be tested, thus making the testing process very time consuming and complex. Lack of testing results in the development of unstable systems. Several cases can be narrated where businesses suffered huge financial and credibility losses due to the deployment of under-tested systems.

With the change in technology and the nature of conducting businesses, every small module of software has become very important. An error in any of the modules can make the entire application a failure, thereby causing much loss to the organizations. Thus testing process has become more important and significant.

Software testing thus provides confidence to the developers in the product or applications. Testing also increases the quality of the product. Testing detects weaknesses in the application and helps to strengthen the identified weaknesses. Testing ensures the usability as well as the operability of the system. It also determines the extent up to which the requirements have been met.

For testing software, different methods are available which are selected based on various criteria. The different tests measure different quality attributes of software. Testing process has become sophisticated and has grown into a specialised area requiring a deep knowledge and in-depth planning. Several companies spend more than 50% of their budget for testing purposes only. Hence shows the importance given to the software testing processes.

2.18.1 Basic Definitions

Here we give a list of terms that are to be used throughout the section with a brief introduction to each of them.

2.18.1.1 Error

People make errors. Mistake can be used as a synonym to error. The mistakes made while coding are commonly called bugs. Errors have a property of propagation. For example, a requirements error is magnified during design and further amplified during coding.

Errors can be classified into two categories:

- **Syntax Error**
  A syntax error is a program statement that violates one or more rules of the language in which it is written.
- **Logic Error**
  A logic error deals with incorrect data fields, out-of-range terms, and invalid combinations.

2.18.1.2 Fault

A fault is a result of an error. Defect can be used as a synonym to fault. It can be said that a fault is a representation of an error, where the representation is the mode of expression, such as narrative text, dataflow diagrams, hierarchy charts, source code, and so on. There can be two types of faults in software:

- **Faults of Omission**
  A fault of omission occurs when something is missing that should be present in the representation, or when we fail to enter correct information.
- **Faults of Commission**
  A fault of commission occurs when we enter something into a representation that is incorrect.

  Of these two types, faults of omission are more difficult to detect and resolve.

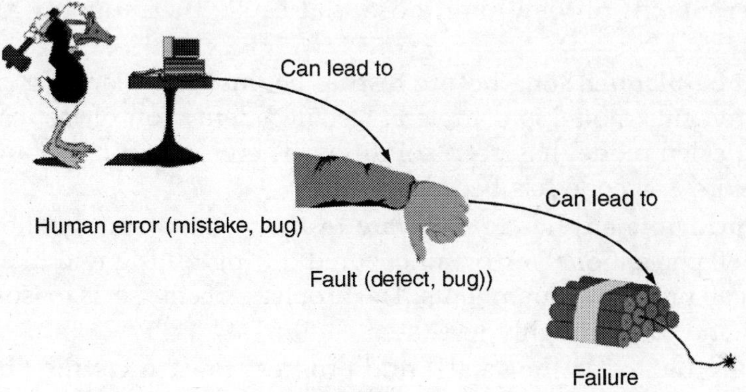

Figure 2.27: Error, Fault and Failure.

2.18.1.3 Failure

A failure occurs when a fault executes. Two refinements arise here; one is that failures only occur in an executable representation, which is usually taken as the source code, or more precisely loaded object code; the second refinement is that this definition relates failure only to faults of commission.

Thus a failure is the inability of the software to perform a required function to its specification. In other words, when software goes ahead in processing without showing error or fault even though certain input and process specification are violated, then it is called a software failure.

A software failure occurs when the behaviour of software is different from the required behaviour. It is produced only when there is a fault in the system. Hence it can be said that faults have the potential to cause failures and their presence is a necessary but not a sufficient condition for failure to occur.

2.18.1.4 Incident

When a failure occurs, it may or may not be readily apparent to the user. An incident is the synonym associated with the failure the alerts the users to the occurrence of a failure.

2.18.1.5 Test

Testing is concerned with errors, faults, failures and incidents. A test is an act of exercising software with test cases. A test has two distinct goals, i.e. to find failures and to demonstrate correct execution.

2.19 TESTING PRINCIPLES

Before applying methods to design effective test cases, a software engineer must understand the basic principles that guide software testing. Davis suggests a set1 of testing principles that have been adapted for use in this book:

- **All tests should be traceable to customer requirements:** As we have seen, the objective of software testing is to uncover errors. It follows that the most severe defects (from the customer's point of view) are those that cause the program to fail to meet its requirements.
- **Tests should be planned long before testing begins:** Test planning can begin as soon as the requirements model is complete. Detailed definition of test cases can begin as soon as the design model has been solidified. Therefore, all tests can be planned and designed before any code has been generated.
- **The Pareto principle applies to software testing:** Stated simply, the Pareto principle implies that 80 percent of all errors uncovered during testing will likely be traceable to 20 percent of all program components. The problem, of course, is to isolate these suspect components and to thoroughly test them.
- **Testing should begin "in the small" and progress toward testing "in the large."** The first tests planned and executed generally focus on individual components. As testing progresses, focus shifts in an attempt to find errors in integrated clusters of components and ultimately in the entire system.

- **Exhaustive testing is not possible:** The number of path permutations for even a moderately sized program is exceptionally large. For this reason, it is impossible to execute every combination of paths during testing. It is possible, however, to adequately cover program logic and to ensure that all conditions in the component-level design have been exercised.
- **To be most effective, testing should be conducted by an independent third party:** By *most effective,* we mean testing that has the highest probability of finding errors (the primary objective of testing).

2.20 TESTING LIFE CYCLE

Figure 2.28 depicts a life cycle model for testing. In the development phases, three opportunities arise for errors to be made, resulting in faults that propagate through the remainder of the development process. Hence, the first three phases are *'Putting Bugs IN'*, the Testing phase is *'Finding Bugs'*, and the last three phases are *'Getting Bugs OUT'*. The Fault Resolution step is another opportunity for errors and new faults to creep in.

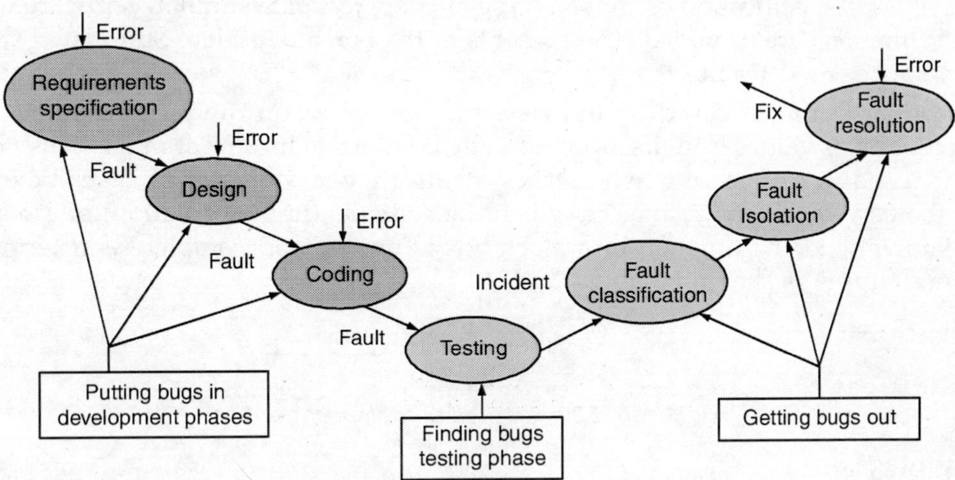

Figure 2.28: A Testing Life Cycle.

2.21 TEST CASES

The goal of testing is to find errors, and a good test case is the one that has a high probability of finding an error. At the same time, testing must be carried out to achieve the goal of finding most errors within a minimum amount of time.

Ideally we would like to develop a set of test cases such that successful execution of all of them implies that there are no errors in the program. But as each test case causes money, because effort is needed to generate the test case, machine time is needed to execute the program for that test case, and even more effort is needed to evaluate the results. Therefore, we would like to minimize the number of test cases that are needed to detect errors. There are two fundamental goals of a testing activity:

- *Maximize the number of errors detected, and*
- *Minimize the number of test cases.*

A **successful test case** is the one that uncovers an as-yet-undiscovered error.

2.22 TAXONOMY OF SOFTWARE TESTING

Two fundamental approaches are used to identify test cases, known as black box (functional) and white box (structural) testing. Another approach known as grey box testing is a combination of both the above mentioned approaches. Each of these approaches has several distinct test case identification methods, more commonly called testing methods. We present a brief introduction to each of them before going into the details of each of them.

2.22.1 Black Box Testing

Black box testing approach focuses on inputs, outputs, and principle function of a software module. It is also known as functional testing. The starting point of black box testing is either a specification or code. In case of code, test data simulate software to check if desired functions are provided. The contents of the box are hidden. Stimulated software must produce desired results.

Functional testing is based on the view that any program can be considered to be a function that maps values from its input domain to values in its output range. This notion is commonly used in engineering, when the systems are considered to be black boxes. This leads to the term black box testing, in which the contents (implementation) of a black box are not known, and the function of a black box is understood completely in terms of its inputs and outputs as shown in Figure 2.29.

Figure 2.29: An engineer's black box

Advantages:

- Well suited and efficient for large code segments.
- Code Access not required.
- Clearly separates user's perspective from the developer's perspective through visibly defined roles.
- Large numbers of moderately skilled testers can test the application with no knowledge of implementation, programming language or operating systems

Disadvantages:

- Limited Coverage, since only a selected number of test scenarios are actually performed.
- Inefficient testing, due to the fact that the tester only has limited knowledge about an application.
- Blind Coverage, since the tester cannot target specific code segments or error prone areas.
- The test cases are difficult to design.

2.22.2 White Box Testing

White box testing approach looks into the structure of code for a software module. It is also known as structural testing. This form of testing focuses on the detailed design of the software rather than on functions (black boxes). In structural testing, statements, paths, and branches are checked for correct execution.

Structural testing is the other fundamental approach to test case identification. To contrast it with functional testing, it is sometimes called white box (or even clear box) testing. The clear box metaphor is probably more appropriate; because the essential difference is that the implementation of the box is known and used to identify test cases. The ability to 'see inside' the black box allows the tester to identify test cases based on how the function is actually implemented.

Advantages:

- As the tester has knowledge of the source code, it becomes very easy to find out which type of data can help in testing the application effectively.
- It helps in optimizing the code.
- Extra lines of code can be removed which can bring in hidden defects.
- Due to the tester's knowledge about the code, maximum coverage is attained during test scenario writing.

Disadvantages:

- Due to the fact that a skilled tester is needed to perform white box testing, the costs are increased.
- Sometimes it is impossible to look into every nook and corner to find out hidden errors that may create problems as many paths will go untested.
- It is difficult to maintain white box testing as the use of specialized tools like code analyzers and debugging tools are required.

2.22.3 Grey Box Setting

Grey Box testing is a technique to test the application with limited knowledge of the internal workings of an application. In software testing, the term the more you know the better carries a lot of weight when testing an application.

Mastering the domain of a system always gives the tester an edge over someone with limited domain knowledge. Unlike black box testing, where the tester only tests the application's user interface, in grey box testing, the tester has access to design documents and the database. Having this knowledge, the tester is able to better prepare test data and test scenarios when making the test plan.

Advantages:

- Offers combined benefits of black box and white box testing wherever possible.
- Grey box testers don't rely on the source code; instead they rely on interface definition and functional specifications.
- Based on the limited information available, a grey box tester can design excellent test scenarios especially around communication protocols and data type handling.
- The test is done from the point of view of the user and not the designer.

Disadvantages:

- Since the access to source code is not available, the ability to go over the code and test coverage is limited.
- The tests can be redundant if the software designer has already run a test case.
- Testing every possible input stream is unrealistic because it would take an unreasonable amount of time; therefore, many program paths will go untested.

2.22.4 Black Box vs Grey Box vs White Box

Black Box Testing	Grey Box Testing	White Box Testing
The Internal Workings of an application are not required to be known	Somewhat knowledge of the internal workings are known	Tester has full knowledge of the Internal workings of the application
Also known as closed box testing, data driven testing and functional testing	Another term for grey box testing is translucent testing as the tester has limited knowledge of the insides of the application	Also known as clear box testing, structural testing or code based testing
Performed by end users and also by testers and developers	Performed by end users and also by testers and developers	Normally done by testers and developers
Testing is based on external expectations-Internal behavior of the application is unknown	Testing is done on the basis of high level database diagrams and data flow diagrams	Internal workings are fully known and the tester can design test data accordingly
This is the least time consuming and exhaustive	Partly time consuming and exhaustive	The most exhaustive and time consuming type of testing
Not suited to algorithm testing This can only be done by trial and error method	Not suited to algorithm testing Data domains and Internal boundaries can be tested, if known	Suited for algorithm testing Data domains and Internal boundaries can be better tested

2.23 LEVELS OF SOFTWARE TESTING

There are many strategies that can be used to test software. At one extreme, one could wait until the system is fully constructed and then construct tests on the overall system to find errors. This approach would result in buggy software that disappoints all concerned. At the other extreme, one could conduct tests on a daily basis or whenever a new part of the system is constructed. This approach may seem unappealing, although it is very effective technique.

A testing strategy chosen by the developers lies between these two extremes. It takes an incremental view of testing, beginning with the testing if individual program units, moving to tests conducted on the integration of individual units, and concluding with the tests that exercise the fully constructed system. Each of these classes of tests is described by various levels described ahead.

Levels of testing echo with the levels of abstraction found in the Waterfall Model of the software development life cycle. Although the Waterfall Model has its disadvantages, it is useful for testing as a means of identifying distinct levels of testing and for clarifying the objectives that pertain to each level.

Software testing is carried out at different levels throughout the entire software development life cycle. Testing starts with individual software units (modules). Each unit should be checked functionally and structurally. Testing is also necessary during the integration of software units to ensure that each combination of units is satisfactory. System and acceptance testing follow unit and integration testing. Hence four levels of testing are identified, which are given in table below:

Testing	Definition	Purpose	Traceability
Unit	Verify the implementation of design of software element (e.g. function, module)	Ensure program logic is complete and correct. Ensure that component works as designed.	Trace each test to detailed design.
Integration	Hardware and software elements are combined and tested until the entire system has been integrated.	Ensures that design objectives are satisfied.	Trace each test to a high level design.
System	Test integration of entire hardware and software.	Ensure that software as a complete entity compiles with its operational requirements.	Trace test to system requirements.
Acceptance	Determine if test results satisfy acceptance criteria of project stakeholders.	Ensures that objectives of stakeholders are satisfied.	Trace each test to stakeholder requirements.

The span of each level of testing (testing traceability) throughout the system development life cycle is illustrated in the figure 2.30.

The different levels of testing attempt to detect different types of faults. The first level of testing is called **unit testing**, where various modules are tested against the specifications produced during design for the modules. Unit Testing is done at the lowest level. It tests the basic unit of software, which is the smallest testable piece of software, and is often called "unit", "module", or "component" interchangeably. It is essentially performed for the verification of the code produced during the coding phase, and hence the goal is to test the internal logic of the modules.

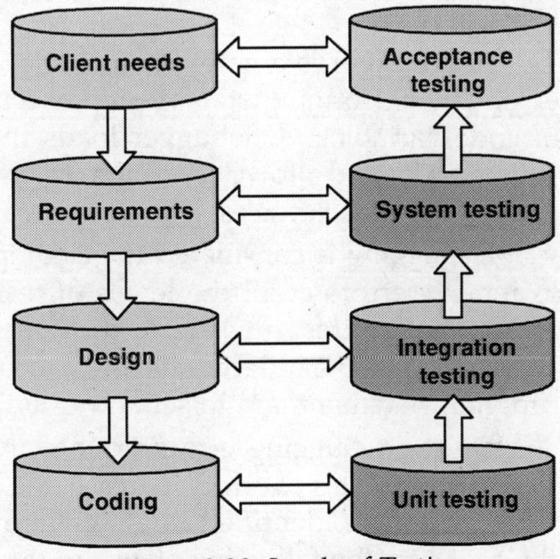

Figure 2.30: Levels of Testing

This testing is particularly performed by the programmer of the module. A module can be considered for integration with other modules only after it is unit tested satisfactorily. Due to such close association of coding and unit testing, the coding phase if frequently named as 'coding and unit testing' phase. As the focus of this level of testing is on testing the code, structural testing is best suited approach for this level.

The next level of testing is called **integration testing**, where many unit tested modules are combined into subsystems, which are then tested. Integration Testing is performed when two or more tested units are combined into a larger structure. The test is often done on both the interfaces between the components and the larger structure being constructed, if its quality property cannot be assessed from its components. Hence, the emphasis is on the interfaces between modules, thereby focusing the concern on the design phase.

The next two levels are **system testing** and **acceptance testing**, where the entire software system is tested. The reference document that is used for this testing is the requirement specification document. System Testing tends to affirm the end-to-end quality of the entire system. System test is often based on the functional/requirement specification of the system. Non-functional quality attributes, such as reliability, security, and maintainability, are also checked. Acceptance Testing is done when the completed system is handed over from the developers to the customers or users. The purpose of acceptance testing is rather to give confidence that the system is working than to find errors. The main goal of these levels of testing is to see if the software meets all the specified requirements. As these levels focus on the external behaviour of system, without any emphasis on the internal logic, functional testing is the right choice.

2.24 DEBUGGING

On successful culmination of software testing, debugging is performed. Debugging is defined as a process of analysing and removing the error. It is considered necessary in most of the newly-developed software or hardware and in commercial products/personal application programs. For complex products, debugging is done at all the levels of the testing.

A **debugger** is a software tool that is used to detect the source of program or script errors, by performing step-by-step execution of application code and viewing the content of code variables. A debugger loads in a program (compiled executable, or interpreted source code) and allows the user to trace through the execution. Debuggers typically can do disassembly, stack traces, expression watches, and more.

Debugging is considered to be complex and time-consuming process since it attempts to remove errors at all the levels of testing. To perform debugging, debugger is used to reproduce failures, investigate the state of programs and find the corresponding defect. Debuggers enable programmers to execute programs step by step, to halt a program at any program statement and to set and examine program variables.

During debugging, errors are encountered that range from less damaging to catastrophic. The various levels of errors increase, the amount of effort to find their causes also increases. Once errors are identified in a software system, the next step is to debug. For debugging the problem, the following steps are used.

1. **Defect confirmation/identification:** A problem is identified in a system and a defect report is created. A software engineer maintains and analysis this error report and finds solution to the following questions.
   - What is the expected/desired behaviour of the system?
   - What is the actual behaviour Brute force?
   - Does a defect exist in the system?
2. **Defect analysis:** If the defect is genuine, the next step is to understand the root cause of the problem. Generally, engineers debug by starting a debugging tool and they try to understand the root cause of the problem by the following a step-by-step execution of the program.
3. **Defect resolution:** Once the root cause of a problem is identified, the error can be resolved by making an appropriate change to the system by fixing the problem.

After the debugging process ends, the software is retested to ensure that no errors are left undetected. Moreover, it checks that no new errors are left undetected. Moreover, it checks that no new errors are introduced in the software as a result of change made to it during the debugging process.

In this section, we summarize the important approaches that are available to identify the error locations. Each of these approaches has its own advantages and disadvantages and therefore each will be useful only in appropriate circumstances.

]2.24.1 DEBUGGING GUIDELINES

Some guidelines that are followed while performing debugging are as follows:

- Debugging is the process of solving problems. Hence, individuals involved in debugging should understand all the causes of an error before starting with debugging.
- No experimentation should be done while performing debugging. The experimental changes instead of removing often increase the problem by adding new errors in it.
- When there is an error in one segment of a program, there is a high possibility of the presence of another error in that program. So, when an error is found in one segment of program, the rest of the program should be properly examined for the presence of errors.
- It is necessary to confirm that new code added in a program to fix errors is correct and is not introducing any new error in it. Thus, to verify the correctness of a new code and to ensure that no new errors are introduced, regression testing should be performed.

2.25 SOFTWARE MAINTENANCE

Software maintenance is the general process of changing a system after it has been delivered. The term is usually applied to custom software in which separate development groups are involved before and after delivery. The changes made to the software may be simple changes to correct coding errors, more extensive changes to correct design errors, or significant enhancements to correct specification errors or accommodate new requirements. Changes are implemented by modifying existing system components and, where necessary, by adding new components to the system.

Maintenance begins almost immediately after the software is released to end users. Within days, bug reports filter back to the software engineering organization. Within weeks, one class of users indicates that the software must be changed so that it can accommodate the special needs of their environment. Within months, another corporate group who wanted nothing to do with the software when it was released now recognizes that it may provide them with unexpected benefit. They might need a few enhancements to make it work in their world.

The challenge of software maintenance begins here, when the organization is faced with a growing queue of bug fixes, adaptation requests, and outright enhancements that must be planned, scheduled and ultimately accomplished. Before long, the queue has grown long and the work it implies threatens to overwhelm the available resources. As the time passes, the organization may find itself spending more money and time maintaining existing programs than it is engineering new applications. In some situations, it is not unusual for a software organization to expend as much as 60-70% of all available resources on software maintenance.

Another reason for software maintenance problem is the mobility of software people. It is likely that the software team which carried out the original work is no longer available. Even worse situation may arise when the newer generations of people have modified the system and moved on. An today, there may be no one left who has the direct knowledge of the legacy system.

2.25.1 Types of Software Maintenance

The requirement of software maintenance arises on account of three main reasons:

- **Corrective Maintenance**
  Corrective maintenance of a software product becomes necessary to rectify the errors observed while the system is in use. Coding errors are usually relatively cheap to correct; design errors are more expensive as they may involve rewriting several program components. Requirements errors are the most expensive to repair because of the extensive system redesign which may be necessary.
- **Adaptive Maintenance**
  A software product might need maintenance when the customers need the product to run on new platforms, on new operating systems, or when they need the product to be interfaced with the new hardware or software. The application system must be modified to adapt it to cope with these environmental changes.
- **Perfective Maintenance**
  A software product needs maintenance to support the new features that users want it to support, to change different functionalities of the system according to customer demands, or to enhance the performance of the system. The scale of the changes required to the software is often much greater than for the other types of maintenance.
- **Preventative Maintenance**
  When computer programmers engage in preventative software maintenance they try to prevent problems with software programs before they occur. Programmers seek to prevent corrective maintenance as much as possible, while also anticipating adaptive

maintenance needs before users experience problems. Computer programmers test software, as automotive companies test the vehicles they make, to make sure the software can handle high data loads and other stressful operations without problems. Computer programmers also test the software with other programs users likely will use on their computers, making sure compatibility issues do not arise.

2.25.2 Factors Affecting Maintenance Costs

Following are the factors affecting maintenance costs:

- **Module Independence:** This is the ability to modify one part of the system.
- **Programming Language:** For the higher the level of the language, the maintenance is cheaper.
- **Programming Style:** The way in which a program is written makes difference in the cost.
- **Program Validation and Testing:** the more time and effort spent on design validation and program testing, the fewer errors and the less the need for corrective maintenance.
- **Quality of Program Documentation:** The better the documentation, the easier it is to maintain.
- **Configuration Management Techniques:** Keeping track of all the system documents and ensuring they are consistent is a major cost of maintenance.
- **Application Domain:** If the application domain is not well understood then the chances of errors are more. This causes high cost on maintenance.
- **Staff Stability:** Maintenance costs are reduced if developers have to maintain their own systems.
- **Age of the System:** Older systems are difficult to maintain
- **Dependence of the System on the External Environment:** If the system is highly dependent upon external environment then lot of maintenance is needed.
- **Hardware Stability:** If the hardware platform will not change over the life of the system then the maintenance will not be needed.

2.26 CUSTOMER SUPPORT

As we know that large software products go through a very lengthy and expensive development process, however the post-release product support and maintenance cycles are several times longer than the development cycle. The software product life span after the initial release lasts several years. The success is dependent on the real users' experience with the software. Despite developers' hopes to have 'user friendly' and 'high quality' software, many large software products are complex and contain defects at product release time. Furthermore, due to a variety of reasons such as resource and schedule constraints, the first release of a product may not include everything in the requirements list. Thus it is extremely important that there is a good understanding of and extensive preparation made for post-release customer support. The customer support and services include two main types of activities:

- Product defect support
- Product non-defect support and services

In addition, most of the customer support and service for large software products charges a fee. Many software organizations charge as much as 10% to 20% of the original product price for one year of post-release product support and customer service. Some charge a fee on a 'per-call' basis where each telephone call to the customer support service requires the caller to pay for the service/support effort. These paying customers and users clearly expect a professional level of services and product maintenance updates. A number of the product support and customer service models extend their support and service into a customer consulting practice. The consulting service will include customer product education and mentoring as well as performing product extensions and customizations. In general, once a software product is modified and customized, that portion is not covered by the general product support contract and must be supported by the consulting service contract.

2.27 COMPUTER AIDED SOFTWARE ENGINEERING (CASE)

CASE stands for Computer-Aided Software Engineering. CASE is a tool that helps a software engineer maintain and develop software. The workshop for software engineering is called an Integrated Project Support Environment (IPSE) and the tool-set that fills the workshop is called CASE. CASE is an automated support tool for software engineers in any software engineering process.

Software engineering mainly includes the following processes:

- Translation of user needs into software requirements
- Transaction of software requirements into design specifications
- Implementation of design into code
- Testing of the code
- Documentation

CASE technology provides software-process support by automating some process activities and by providing information about the software being developed. Examples of activities, which can be automated using CASE, include:

- The development of graphical system models as part of the requirements specification or the software design.
- Understanding a design using a data dictionary which holds information about the entities and relations in a design.
- The generation of user interfaces from a graphical interface description, which is created interactively by the user.
- Program debugging through the provision of information about an executing program.
- The automated translation of programs from an old version of a programming language, such as COBOL, to a more recent version.

A good workshop for any craftsperson—a mechanic, a carpenter, or a software engineer—has three primary characteristics: (1) a collection of useful tools that will help in every step of building a product, (2) an organized layout that enables tools to be found quickly and used efficiently, and (3) a skilled artisan who understands how to use the tools in an effective manner. Software engineers now recognize that they need more and varied tools along with an organized and efficient workshop in which to place the tools.

The workshop for software engineering has been called an *integrated project support environment* and the tools that fill the workshop are collectively called *computer-aided software engineering*.

CASE provides the software engineer with the ability to automate manual activities and to improve engineering insight. Like computer-aided engineering and design tools that are used by engineers in other disciplines, CASE tools help to ensure that quality is designed in before the product is built.

We first need to define what a CASE environment is. A CASE tool is generic term used to denote any form of automated support for software engineering. In a more restricted sense, a CASE tool can mean any tool used to automate some activity associated with software engineering. Many CASE tools are now available, where some of these assist in phase-related tasks such as specification, structured analysis, design, coding, testing, etc. and others are related to non-phase activities such as project management etc. The primary objectives of deploying a CASE tool are:

- An increase in productivity
- Production of better quality software at a lower price

2.27.1 Case Environment

Although individual CASE tools are useful, the true power of a tool set can be realised only when these set of tools are integrated into a common framework of environment. If the different CASE tools are not integrated, then the data generated by one tool would have to input to other tools. This may also involve format conversions as the tools developed by different vendors are likely to use differing formats. This results in an additional effort of exporting data from one tool and importing data to another. Also, many tools do not allow exporting data and maintain the data in proprietary formats.

CASE tools are characterised by the stage or stages of software development life cycle on which they focus. Since different tools covering different stages share common information, it is required that they integrate through some central repository to have a consistent view of information associated with the software. This central repository is usually a data dictionary containing the definitions of all composite and elementary items. Through the central repository, all the CASE tools in a CASE environment share common information among themselves. Thus a CASE environment facilitates the automation of the step-by-step methodologies for software development. In contrast to a CASE environment, a programming environment is an integrated collection of tools to support only the coding phase of software development. The tools commonly integrated in a programming environment are a text editor, a compiler, and a debugger. The different tools are integrated to the extent that once the compiler detects an error, the editor automatically goes to the statements in error and the error statements are highlighted. Examples of popular programming environments are Turbo C environment, Visual Basic, Visual C++, etc. A schematic representation of a CASE environment is shown in Figure 2.31.

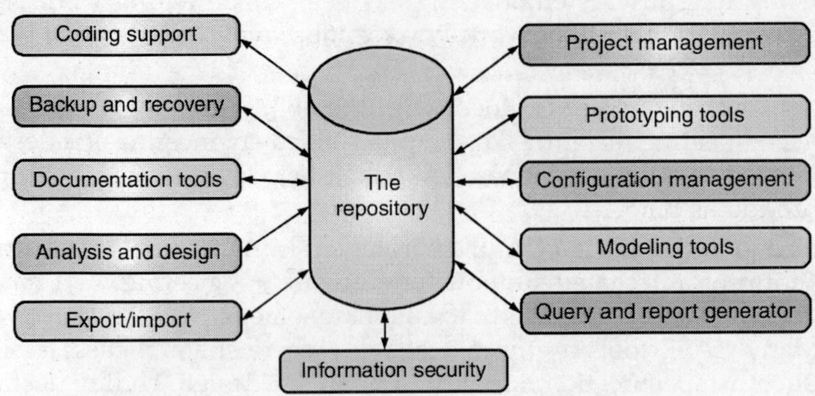

Figure 2.31: A CASE Environment

The standard programming environments such as Turbo C, Visual C++, and more come equipped with a program editor, complier, debugger, linker, etc. All these tools are integrated. If you click on an error reported by compiler, not only does it take you into the editor, but also takes the cursor to the specific line or statement causing the error.

SUMMARY

A software development process makes everything easier and reduces the amount of problems encountered. An information system goes through a series of phases from conception to implementation. This process is called the Software-Development Life-Cycle.

The waterfall model is conceptually the simplest model of software development, where the requirement, design, coding, and testing phases are performed in linear progression. It has been very widely used, and is suitable for well-understood problems. In the prototyping model, a prototype is built before building the final system, which is used to further develop the requirements leading to more stable requirements. This is useful for projects where requirements are not clear. In the iterative enhancement model, software is developed in iterations, each iteration resulting in a working software system. This model does not require all requirements to be known at the start, allows feedback from earlier iterations for next ones, and reduces risk as it delivers value as the project proceeds.

The aim of requirements engineering is to convert the end-user requirements to a form that enables the development of some new methods to satisfy the needs of the user. In software engineering discipline, the new method involves the use of automated methods including the use of computers and associated technologies. This process is to be conducted very systematically and properly with utmost care. Thus, requirements must be written so they are meaningful not only to the customers but also to designers on the development team.

Software Architecture is a branch of software engineering discipline. As it happens with every budding disciplines software architecture is defined in numerous ways. Each one of this definition highlights certain aspect of the software architecture. Our view of Software architecture is that of a discipline providing mechanisms to deal with ever increasing size and complexity of a software system. Software architecture manages the complexity of a software system by separating the computations performed by components from the interactions in which they involve with other components. Software design can be started if the software project is found feasible and the software requirements specifications are formed. This is the most important stage in the software development process. Software design determines how a solution can be formulated to satisfy the user needs.

Coding is the activity where a design is converted to runnable code. Depending on the details of the design specification, the coding activity may vary greatly. Many companies have coding standards that all the programmers must follow. The purpose of a coding standard is to make it easier for programmers to read each other's codes, and to make it easier to maintain the code.

Software testing is an important process in the software development life cycle. It is also the most time consuming phase. Testing forms the last stage of any software development project before it can be released for implementation. It is mandatory for software to pass all the tests before implementation. Thus, testing process increases the reliability as well as quality of the software products. For testing software, different methods are available which are selected based on various criteria. The different tests measure different quality attributes of software. Testing process has become sophisticated and has grown into a specialised area requiring a deep knowledge and in-depth planning. A testing strategy for software testing integrates software test case design methods into a well-planned series of steps that result in the successful construction of software. The strategy provides a road map that describes the steps to be conducted as part of testing, when these steps are planned and then undertaken, and how much effort, time, and resources will be required. On successful culmination of software testing, debugging is performed. Debugging is defined as a process of analysing and removing the error. It is considered necessary in most of the newly-developed software or hardware and in commercial products/personal application programs. For complex products, debugging is done at all the levels of the testing. Maintenance is the most expensive phase of software life cycle and therefore it is usually cost effective to invest in time and effort while developing the product and to emphasize on maintainability of the product to reduce the maintenance costs. A number of the product support and customer service models extend their support and service into a customer consulting practice.

CASE stands for Computer-Aided Software Engineering. CASE is a tool that helps a software engineer maintain and develop software.

EXERCISES

1. Discuss the SDLC in brief.
2. Give the basic phases in the software-development life-cycle.
3. What are the different steps in the software-development life-cycle?
4. What are the important activities that are carried out during the feasibility study phase?
5. Why we need for a life cycle model?

6. Draw the schematic diagram of the waterfall model of software development. Also discuss its phases in brief.
7. Explain the waterfall model in detail with the help of a diagram.
8. Draw the schematic diagram of the V-Shaped life cycle of software development. Also discuss its phases in brief.
9. What is a prototype? Draw the schematic diagram of the prototyping model of software development. Also discuss its phases in brief.
10. Explain the spiral model in detail with the help of a diagram.
11. Explain the Win-Win spiral model in detail with the help of a diagram.
12. Explain the Iterative Enhancement Model in detail with the help of a diagram.
13. Explain the RAD Model in detail with the help of a diagram.
14. What do you mean by requirement engineering?
15. What do the term requirements mean? Explain various types of requirements?
16. What are the preparations for Requirements Engineering?
17. What do you mean by feasibility study?
18. What are the crucial process steps of requirement engineering? Discuss with the help of a diagram.
19. Explain the process of requirements documentation or Software Requirements Specification?
20. Explain the structure of an SRS document?
21. Define software architecture?
22. Explain the role of data design in software architectural design?
23. Explain the different architectural designs?
24. Define Architectural Description language?
25. Explain the relationship between software design and software engineering?
26. Explain the various design principles of software design?
27. What is abstraction? Explain the different types of abstraction?
28. Define coupling?
29. Define cohesion?
30. Explain the relationship between coupling and cohesion?
31. Explain the various software design approaches?
32. Comparison between function and object oriented approach?
33. Explain the concept of detailed design?
34. What is coding?
35. What are code reviews?
36. Define code walkthrough?
37. Define code inspection?
38. Explain the concept of software documentation?
39. What do you understand by the terms error, fault, and failure?
40. Define the various principles of testing.
41. What is a test case?

42. Define testing life cycle?
43. Explain the different approaches of testing?
44. Explain the black-box testing?
45. Explain the white-box testing?
46. Explain the grey-box testing?
47. Comparison between black-box, white-box and grey-box testing?
48. Explain the levels of software testing?
49. Define the term "debugging."
50. What are the guidelines for debugging?
51. Define software maintenance?
52. What are the factors that affecting maintenance costs?
53. Define customer support?
54. Explain Computer-Aided Software Engineering (CASE) and the various types of CASE tools.
55. Give the architecture of a CASE environment.

❑

UNIT 3
SOFTWARE PROJECT MANAGEMENT

Software Project Management and Metrics

3

3.1 INTRODUCTION

The challenges of constructing a software product have no easy solution. To put together a large software product takes time as well as resources. And, like any other large construction project, careful planning at the beginning of the project is thus the single most important factor that distinguishes success from failure. This initial planning, however, by no means is enough, and must continue throughout the software development and maintenance process. Notwithstanding the need for continual planning, these activities reach a peak after the specifications have been drawn up but before design activities commence. At this point in the process, meaningful duration and cost estimates are computed and a detailed plan for completing the project produced.

In this chapter, we cover both these types of planning, the planning that proceeds throughout the project and the intense planning that must be carried out once the specifications are complete.

3.2 PROJECT

A project can be defined in many ways:

"A project is a temporary endeavour undertaken to create a unique product, service, or result". Operations, on the other hand, is work done in organizations to sustain the business. Projects are different from operations in that they end when their objectives have been reached or the project has been terminated.

A project is *temporary*. A project's duration might be just one week or it might go on for years, but every project has an end date. You might not know that end date when the project begins, but it's there somewhere in the future. Projects are not the same as on-going operations, although the two have a great deal in common.

A project is an *endeavour*. Resources, such as people and equipment, need to do work. The endeavour is undertaken by a team or an organization, and therefore projects have a sense of being intentional, planned events. Successful projects do not happen spontaneously; some amount of preparation and planning happens first.

Finally, every project creates a *unique product* or *service*. This is the deliverable for the project and the reason, why that project was undertaken.

3.2.1 Project Attributes

Projects come in all shapes and sizes. The following attributes help us to define a project further:

- ***A project has a unique purpose.*** Every project should have a well-defined objective. For example, many people hire firms to design and build a new house, but each house, like each person, is unique.
- ***A project is temporary.*** A project has a definite beginning and a definite end. For a home construction project, owners usually have a date in mind when they'd like to move into their new homes.
- ***A project is developed using progressive elaboration or in an iterative fashion.*** Projects are often defined broadly when they begin, and as time passes, the specific details of the project become clearer. For example, there are many decisions that must be made in planning and building a new house. It works best to draft preliminary plans for owners to approve before more detailed plans are developed.
- ***A project requires resources, often from various areas.*** Resources include people, hardware, software, or other assets. Many different types of people, skill sets, and resources are needed to build a home.
- ***A project should have a primary customer or sponsor.*** Most projects have many interested parties or stakeholders, but someone must take the primary role of sponsorship. The project sponsor usually provides the direction and funding for the project.
- ***A project involves uncertainty.*** Because every project is unique, it is sometimes difficult to define the project's objectives clearly, estimate exactly how long it will take to complete, or determine how much it will cost. External factors also cause uncertainty, such as a supplier going out of business or a project team member needing unplanned time off. This uncertainty is one of the main reasons project management is so challenging.

3.2.2 Features of Projects

Following are the various features of projects:

- Projects are often carried out by a team of people who have been assembled for that specific purpose. The activities of this team may be coordinated by a project manager.
- Project teams may consist of people from different backgrounds and different parts of the organisation. In some cases project teams may consist of people from different organisations.
- Project teams may be inter-disciplinary groups and are likely to lie outside the normal organisation hierarchies.
- The project team will be responsible for delivery of the project end product to some sponsor within or outside the organisation. The full benefit of any project will not become available until the project as been completed.

3.2.3 Project Classification

In recent years more and more activities have been tackled on a project basis. Project teams and a project management approach have become common in most organisations. The basic approaches to project management remain the same regardless of the type of project being considered. You may find it useful to consider projects in relation to a number of major classifications:

(a) Engineering and construction

The projects are concerned with producing a clear physical output, such as roads, bridges or buildings. The requirements of a project team are well defined in terms of skills and background, as are the main procedures that have to be undergone. Most of the problems which may confront the project team are likely to have occurred before and therefore their solution may be based upon past experiences.

(b) Introduction of new systems

These projects would include computerisation projects and the introduction of new systems and procedures including financial systems. The nature and constitution of a project team may vary with the subject of the project, as different skills may be required and different end-users may be involved. Major projects involving a systems analysis approach may incorporate clearly defined procedures within an organisation.

(c) Responding to deadlines and change

An example of responding to a deadline is the preparation of an annual report by a specified date. An increasing number of projects are concerned with designing organisational or environmental changes, involving developing new products and services.

3.3 PROJECT CONSTRAINTS

Like any human undertaking, projects need to be performed and delivered under certain constraints. Traditionally, these constraints have been listed as scope, time, and cost. These are also referred to as the Project Management Triangle, where each side represents a constraint. One side of the triangle cannot be changed without impacting the others. A further refinement of the constraints separates product 'quality' or 'performance' from scope, and turns quality into a fourth constraint.

The time constraint refers to the amount of time available to complete a project. The cost constraint refers to the budgeted amount available for the project. The scope constraint refers to what must be done to produce the project's end result. These three constraints are often competing constraints: increased scope typically means increased time and increased cost, a tight time constraint could mean increased costs and reduced scope, and a tight budget could mean increased time and reduced scope.

The discipline of project management is about providing the tools and techniques that enable the project team (not just the project manager) to organize their work to meet these constraints.

Another approach to project management is to consider the three constraints as finance, time and human resources. If you need to finish a job in a shorter time, you can allocate more people at the problem, which in turn will raise the cost of the project, unless by doing this task quicker we will reduce costs elsewhere in the project by an equal amount.

3.3.1 Time

For analytical purposes, the time required to produce a product or service is estimated using several techniques. One method is to identify tasks needed to produce the deliverables documented in a work breakdown structure or WBS. The work effort for each task is estimated and those estimates are rolled up into the final deliverable estimate.

The tasks are also prioritized, dependencies between tasks are identified, and this information is documented in a project schedule. The dependencies between the tasks can affect the length of the overall project (dependency constraint), as can the availability of resources (resource constraint). Time is not considered a cost nor a resource, since the project manager cannot control the rate at which it is expended. This makes it different from all other resources and cost categories.

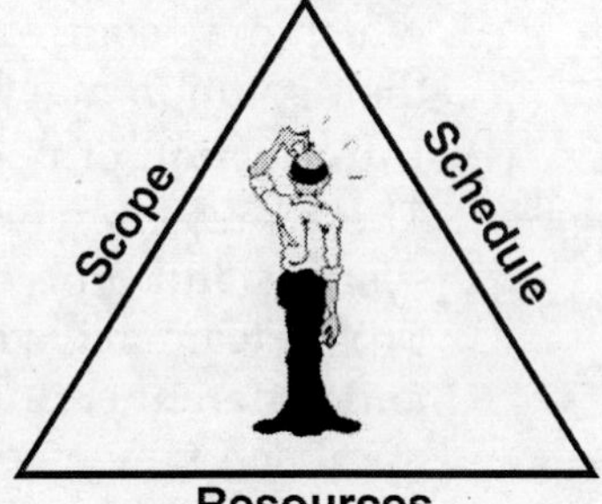

***Figure 3.1:** The Project Management Triangle*

3.3.2 Cost

Cost to develop a project depends on several variables including: labour rates, material rates, risk management, plant (buildings, machines, etc.), equipment, and profit. When hiring an independent consultant for a project, cost will typically be determined by the consultant's or firm's per diem rate multiplied by an estimated quantity for completion.

3.3.3 Scope

Scope is requirement specified for the end result. The overall definition of what the project is supposed to accomplish, and a specific description of what the end result should be or accomplish can be said to be the scope of the project. A major component of scope is the quality of the final product. The amount of time put into individual tasks determines the overall quality of the project. Some tasks may require a given amount of time to complete adequately, but given more time could be completed exceptionally. Over the course of a large project, quality can have a significant impact on time and cost or vice versa.

Together, these three constraints viz. Scope, Schedule & Resources have given rise to the phrase *"On Time, On Spec, On Budget"*. In this case, the term "scope" is substituted with "spec(ification)"

3.4 PROJECT MANAGERS

When the plan starts to involve different things happening at different times, some of which are dependent on each other, plus resources required at different times and in different quantities and perhaps working in different rates, the paper plan could start to cover a vast area and be unreadable.

Nevertheless, the idea that the complex plans could be analysed by a computer to allow someone to control a project is the basis of much of the development in technology that now allows projects of any size and complexity, not only to be planned, but also modeled to answer 'what if?' questions.

The original programs and computers tended to produce answers long after an event had taken place. Now, there are many project planning and scheduling programs that can provide real time information, as well as linking to risk analysis, time recording, and costing, estimating and other aspects of project control.

But computer programs are not project management: they are tools for project managers to use. Project management is all that mix of components of control, leadership, teamwork, resource management, etc. that goes into a successful project.

Project managers can be found in all industries. Their numbers have grown rapidly as industry and commerce has realised that much of what it does is project work. And as project-based organizations have started to emerge, project management is becoming established as both a professional career path and a way of controlling business.

So opportunities in project management now exist not only in being a project manager, but also as part of the support team in a project or program office or as a team leader for part of a project. There are also qualifications that can be attained through the professional associations.

3.4.1 Software Project Manager

Software project managers take the overall responsibility of steering a project to success. The job responsibilities of a project manager range from invisible activities such as building up team morale to highly visible customer presentations. Most managers take responsibility for project proposal writing, project cost estimation, scheduling, project staffing, software process tailoring, project monitoring and control, software configuration management, risk management, interfacing with clients, managerial report writing and presentations, and so forth. These activities are numerous, varied and difficult to enumerate, but we can broadly classify them into project planning, and project monitoring and control activities. The project planning activity is undertaken before the development starts. The project monitoring and control activities are undertaken once the development has begun, the aim being to ensure that the development proceeds as per plan. The changes to the pan whenever required are made to continuously cope with the solution.

A theoretical knowledge of different project management techniques is certainly necessary to become a successful project manager. However, effective software project management frequently calls for good qualitative judgement and decision making capabilities. In addition to having a good grasp of the latest software project management techniques such as cost estimation, risk management, configuration management, project managers need good communication skills and the ability to get work done. However, some skills such as tracking and controlling the process of the project, customer interaction, managerial presentations, and team building are largely acquired through experience. Nonetheless, the importance of sound knowledge of the prevalent project management techniques cannot be over-emphasized.

3.5 PROJECT MANAGEMENT

Project management is the art of maximizing the probability that a project delivers its goals on Time, to Budget, and at the required Quality. The art of planning for the future has always been a human trait. In essence a project can be captured on paper with a few simple elements: a start date, and end date, the tasks that have to be carried out and when they should be finished, and some idea of the resources (people, machines, etc.) that will be needed during the course of the project.

Project management is the application of knowledge, skills, tools, and techniques to project activities to meet project requirements. Project management is accomplished through the use of the processes such as: initiating, planning, executing, controlling, and closing. It is important to note that many of the processes within project management are iterative in nature. This is in part due to the existence of and the necessity for progressive elaboration in a project throughout the project life cycle, i.e. the more you know about your project, the better you are able to manage it.

Project management is also defined as a strategic competency that has successfully been applied in such high profile projects as the construction of silk root, organizing and managing the Olympics Games, and the construction of Delhi-Amritsar highway, just to name a few. If project management can play a major role in these success stories, just imagine what it might be able to do for your own organization.

The term project management is sometimes used to describe an organizational approach to the management of ongoing operations. This approach, more properly called management by projects, treats many aspects of ongoing operations as projects to apply project management techniques to them

Almost any human activity that involves carrying out a non-repetitive task can be a project. So we all are project managers. We all practice project management (PM). But there is a big difference between carrying out a very simple project involving one or two people and one involving a complex mix of people, organizations and tasks.

3.5.1 Software Project Management

Software project management encompasses a set of activities that are performed during the phases of a typical software development cycle. The software project manager continuously ensures that the software product is developed according to the client's business requirements, within the allocated time, and within budget. Many software projects fail because of poor management. The manager could have overlooked one or more of the crucial elements of project management. These elements include risk engineering and management, human resource management, effort and cost estimation, project monitoring, tracking and control, time and financial management, and the proper use of project management tools. The manager must develop a management plan to follow closely during the execution of the project. This plan must be monitored and necessary modifications made by the manager to ensure the timely delivery of a quality software product.

The main goal of software project management is to enable a group of software engineers to work efficiently towards successful completion of the project. For small software development projects, one of the software engineers assumes the responsibility of software project management in addition to his normal responsibilities. However, the large products usually have full-time project managers.

3.6 SOFTWARE PROJECT MANAGEMENT PROCESS

Software project management involves the application of good management practices to the development and support of software. By necessity, it is a multidisciplinary subject. In terms of Figure 3.2, software project management is concerned with ensuring that, for a software project, the most appropriate process and methodologies are chosen, the desired internal product structure is attained, and the external product properties are achieved. In addition, the project management constraints of schedule and resources must be met.

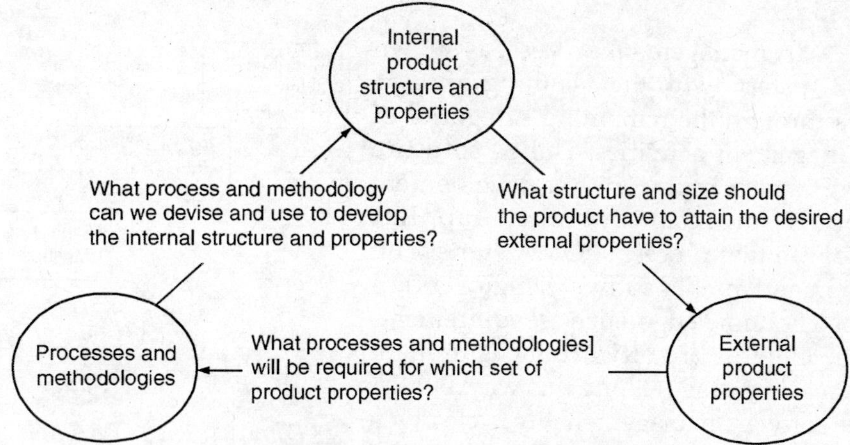

Figure 3.2: *Software Engineering*

In terms of Figure 3.3, software project management may be viewed as applying sufficient resources to ensure that the software artefacts evolve in a manner such that:

- They meet all the product functional and other requirements.
- They are developed within the cost constraints.
- They are developed within the allotted schedule.

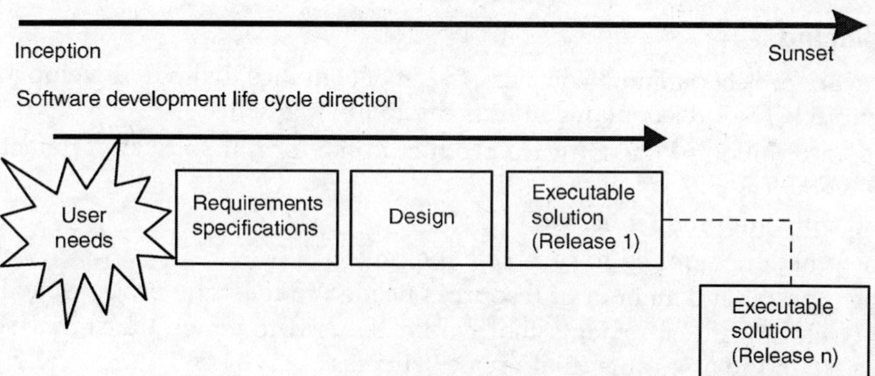

Figure 3.3: *The Software Product Life Cycle*

Satisfying the product requirements, budgetary, and schedule constraints is the essence of product management. Because software projects heavily depend on the availability of human resources, software project management also requires people management.

3.7 POMA: THE PHASES OF SOFTWARE PROJECT MANAGEMENT

Software project management, much like other project management, has four major phases, called POMA:

- Planning
- Organizing
- Monitoring
- Adjusting

The POMA management process, as shown in Figure 3.4, starts with the planning of tasks and moves through the remaining categories of project management activities. Unlike software engineering, which begins with a development and support process and then applies management to that process, POMA starts with management and applies software engineering's domain specific knowledge, such as requirements solicitation method or software measurement method, at various stages along this way. POMA models the software management life cycle much as waterfall software process models the software development life cycle.

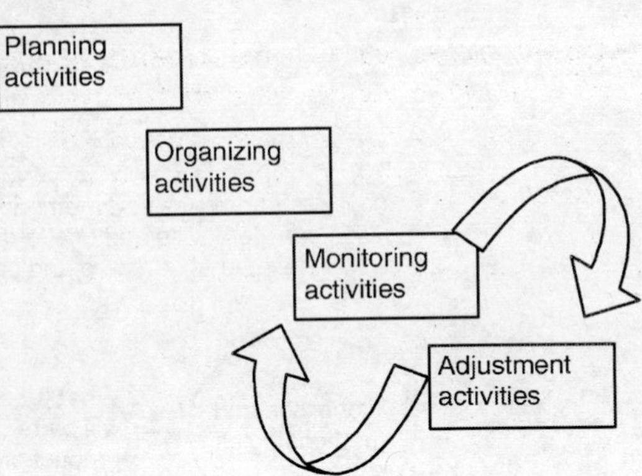

Figure 3.4: The POMA Management Process

Note that the activities in the four process categories of POMA are not necessarily sequential. Some activities within each category may overlap, and the categories themselves may overlap. For example, the monitoring and adjustment categories are likely to iterate. In this iteration between monitoring and adjustment, the project manager may adjust the original plan, the original organization, or both.

3.7.1 Planning

Software project planning consists of a set of activities that will develop a plan of attack for the project. The project plan contains the following items:

- The description of the software product in the form if software artefact contents and deliverables.
- The software product attributes.
- The schedule required to complete the project.
- The types of and amount of resources needed to meet the project schedule.
- The relevant measurements that would be used to gauge the status of the software project and to assess the final project 'success'.
- The risks associated with the project.

Project planning includes a time-consuming and very important set of tasks that is, unfortunately, often rushed. It is much wiser to spend the appropriate time needed to develop a good plan initially than to have to make multiple and costly adjustments later. Even with a well-conceived plan, it is unusual not to encounter some conditions that require unexpected changes during the project. However, having a well-thought-out plan facilitates making project adjustments even at a much later phase.

3.7.2 Organizing

Software project organization seeks to construct a software development, support, and service organization based on the project plan. To build and implement the software project organization, several activities are undertaken: acquiring the various skilled individuals needed for the project, defining a process and a set of methodologies that will be utilized for the software project, obtaining a set of tools that will support the process and the methodologies, and creating a well-defined set of metrics that will be used to track and gauge the project.

A significant portion of the task of organizing activities is ensuring that all personnel brought on board are properly equipped to perform their designated tasks. This equipping of personnel includes obtaining needed tools and preparing facilities for initiation of the project, and it also includes educating the personnel in using those tools, the methodology selected, and the metrics chosen.

In addition, as part of the organizing activities, project managers need to ensure that adequate financial funding has been set aside and will be made available in a timely manner. Thus, the software project management team must either include financial management and personnel management members or have well-defined interfaces with these other organizations. Just like any organizational interface, the software project organization relies on human relationships that need to be established, nurtured, and maintained. The 'people management' aspect of organizing is critically important. Managers should always be cognizant of the fact that the morale of the organization affects its productivity.

3.7.3 Monitoring

Software project monitoring focuses on the following activities:

- Consistently and regularly collecting measurements.
- Analysing the data.
- Representing and presenting the data for a defined set of reports.
- Making projections and making recommendations based on the analysis of the data.

Software project management, like any other project management situation, involves a heavy dosage of 'people' management. Therefore, the project monitoring component must include the soft art of both physically and virtually 'walking around the hallway' and tapping into day-to-day issues, concerns, and morale.

3.7.4 Adjusting

Adjustments and changes are a very important set of activities for software project managers. It is a rare situation in which we can develop a perfect plan and put together a perfect organization. Most of the time, we will need to make mid-course adjustments, sometimes several times. The monitoring of projects ensures that the correct adjustments can be made at a relatively early stage in the development process. In a situation that is often encountered, the design of a software artefact is found to have a high number of errors that are attributable to unclear requirements. In this situation, the software project managers might need to commission a rework on the requirements and ask for adjustments in the project schedule, resources, or content. For a software project manager to make adjustment, he/she must first recognize the need for making a change, and the risks of not doing so. Then a potential set of adjustments must be available, along with some prioritization scheme.

Unfortunately, many adjustments might be needed, for example, because of the loss of a skilled team member or the discovery of an unfeasible design. Adjustments and changes are often made under pressure and in uncomfortable conditions. Nevertheless, project managers must have the courage to stand up and take action. Sometimes even changes to the original plan or organizational structure are required. Later, the software project managers must continue to monitor the project after appropriate adjustments are made. If the information from the monitoring activities dictates that further adjustments and modifications are needed, then the software project management must make these additional changes. This potentially extensive, iterative process continues until the project is completed.

3.7.5 POMA At All Management Levels

All managers at different levels are involved in the four major activity categories of POMA. The difference is merely the degree to which they are involved.

Higher-level managers, including executives, tend to be more intimately involved in establishing the general plans and overall organization of the project. As a consequence, they tend to focus more on the planning and the organizing portions of POMA.

Middle managers are involved in building more specific project plans and specific organizations. They also participate in monitoring project status and help in making adjustments. These managers are the management 'work horses' in that they are involved equally heavily in all four categories of project management.

Lower level managers and project leaders perform daily project monitoring and device instant adjustments, if they become necessary. Although these first-line managers and project leaders play important roles in higher-level planning and organizing, most of the time they focus more intently on planning and organizing just their portion of the project responsibilities. The lower-level managers therefore tend to concentrate on the monitoring and adjustment categories of POMA.

3.8 PRINCIPLES OF SOFTWARE PROJECT MANAGEMENT

This section introduces 14 principles of software project management that are based upon the experience of seasoned software managers. To make these principles useful, each is related to the primary functions software managers perform. These principles are based on fundamental premise that good engineering and classical project management methods, tools, and techniques can be applied in a cost-effective manner to cope with the challenges associated with delivering high-quality software products on schedule and within budget.

The principles of software management revolve around five primary functions software managers perform to get their job done effectively: planning, organizing, staffing, directing, and controlling. Software managers must develop skills, knowledge, and abilities in each of these functions to successfully deliver an acceptable product in schedule and within budget. They start by planning their projects thoroughly and creating the road map that they will use to create baselines and expectations. Then they create organizations, staff them with the right mix of talent and capability, develop teams and teamwork, and motivate and direct their human resources toward achieving project related goals. They have to integrate the work of many participants to pull the pieces of this puzzle together in such a manner that they can achieve aggressive budgets and schedules. They put into place controls and use them to track status and determine whether or not their teams are making suitable progress. They manage risk and deal with the day-to-day issues that can, if left unchecked, impede progress. They replan, refocus, and reenergize their teams as they take detours to overcome the obstacles that get in the way of achieving their goals. Software project managers are focused on delivering acceptable products on schedule and within budget. They intentionally avoid doing things that would distract them from accomplishing this goal.

3.8.1 Planning

Planning is defined as deciding what has to be done, when and how to do it, and who should do it. It encompasses many related disciplines, such as estimating, budgeting, and scheduling. Software managers get involved in many types of planning exercises. For example, they plan projects, capital acquisitions, and/or training/skill development. Plans form the basis against which schedule and budgetary performance are assessed and project control is implemented. Plans create the foundations that project managers use to gain visibility into and control over progress. Based upon the experience of seasoned managers and the software project management body of knowledge, the following three principles establish the basis for project planning:

- **Principle 1- Planning Takes Precedence:** Planning logically takes precedence over all other management functions. While often difficult and time consuming to perform, plans form the basis of all future work. Mangers are encouraged to devote the time needed to figure out what needs to be done, when to do it, who should do it, and how to address the contingencies. Budgets are financial plans, whereas schedules create a viable project time line.
- **Principle 2- Effective Plans Tap the Infrastructure:** Plans are most effective when they are consistent with policies and take full advantage of the organization's existing management infrastructure. This is especially true for those organizations that have initiated a software process improvement program aimed at institutionalizing a 'preferred process' and 'best practices' across groups.
- **Principle 3- Plans Should be Living Documents:** Plans should be maintained as living documents or they will quickly become outdated and lose their value as control tools. Plans need to be periodically updated to add detail and reflect the current situation.

Because of their short timetable, most project plans tend to be tactical (near-term) instead of strategic (long-term). When capital and research budgets are impacted, this is a mistake because implementation of project plans may become dependent on others for their realization. The most basic elements of a project plan are its budgets (financial plans) and schedules (delivery timetables). The parts of these documents with the highest leverage are the risk management and contingency plans. It is not uncommon for a manager to spend as much as fifty percent of his/her time early in the project on planning. The better the plans, the more visibility and control you have over task progress. In addition, the higher in management you move, the more strategic your plans become. For example, product line or line-of-business managers generate product plans whose horizons may be 10 to 20 years long. Independent of the level of planning, each plan you develop represents a guide to some future course of action.

To establish a budget, you will have to prepare a resource estimate (time, staff, budget, etc.) based upon your understanding of what is that must be done and the resources you have available to handle the job. The ability to estimate resources accurately is a skill every software manager must possess. Poor resource estimates can lead to problems that no amount of dedication, perseverance and hard work can correct. The more accurate the estimate, the higher your chances of success will be.

3.8.2 Organizing

Managers create organizations to achieve their goals and get the work they are responsible for done as efficiently as possible. Such organizations provide a structure that lets managers get work done by assigning responsibilities, delegating authority, and holding people accountable for results. Most managers work within an existing organizational structure. Their function is to build teams, staff them, provide them with leadership, direct them, integrate their results, and manage communications up, down, and across the organization. Based upon extensive software engineering project management experience, these tasks lead to the following two organizational principles:

- **Principle 4- Assign your Software Manager Early:** Recruit your software manager early in the project and empower this professional to perform all of the tasks for which he/she will be held responsible. Ensure that this person occupies a high enough position in the hierarchy to successfully compete for needed resources (staff, budget, etc.), talent, and maintain management support.
- **Principle 5- Give Authority Commensurate with Responsibility:** The software manager's responsibility should commensurate with his/her authority. Because software managers are not always masters of their own destiny, they should not be held accountable for results when others' actions impede their performance. Such problems often occur when dealing with requirements. Software managers are not in charge of requirements, but rely on them to form the foundation of their architecture and design.

Many of the organizational factors that impact the performance of software managers fall outside their sphere of control. For example, marketing is often responsible for developing requirements (and their frequent change) and for customer liaison. Influence is the key for gaining control over this untenable situation. The software manager must be able to communicate effectively with others within, across, and up and down the existing organizational framework. Working groups and use of integrated product teams are mechanisms that can be used specifically for this purpose.

Communications must flow up and down and across the organization to keep people influenced. Staff members must keep abreast of current events or they will lose focus and their performance will be negatively impacted. Newsletters, colloquiums, brown-bag lunches, weekly team meetings and monthly 'all hands' meetings, are proven mechanisms for improving communications. They should be exploited, along with software peer reviews and inspections.

3.8.3 Staffing

Staffing refers to recruiting, growing, and keeping the people you need to get the job done properly. Organizations are only as good as the people who populate them. Software managers must be able to recognize talent, breed competence, and weed out deadwood. They must be able to attract the right people to fill key slots within their organizations. Based upon a great deal of software engineering experience, the following two principles establish the basis for staffing:

- **Principle 6- Care about Your People:** Software managers must be able to show their people that they truly care about them, their careers, and their goals. Because actions speak louder than words, managers must demonstrate their devotion by fighting for promotions, salary increases, and better working conditions for their people. They must also be able to coach poor achievers and be able to improve their job-related performance.
- **Principle 7- Provide Dual-Career Ladders:** Promotion should be possible up either a technical or managerial career ladder. Technical people who do not want to move into management slots should be given the opportunity to follow other career paths. Chief software engineer positions that are equivalent to middle- and upper-level management slots should be made visible part of the organizational chart.

In many organizations, dual-career paths act as powerful incentives for technical people who may or may not want to move into management. Knowing what is required to progress along dual lines provides software people with the growth and opportunity they desire. It acts as a motivator and stimulates high levels of achievement. It also makes career counselling easier, especially when people are not satisfied.

As in many other scientific disciplines, good technical performers are often promoted prematurely to management positions. This is frequently a mistake because the skills required for management differ from those required for engineering. Good software managers have to be developed. Training must be provided for those who have demonstrated management potential. Mentoring and other forms of coaching need to be available to help develop individual skills and abilities. In addition, new supervisors should be taught the fundamentals of management.

3.8.4 Directing

Managers get things done through the actions of others. They communicate their goals and lead and motivate their subordinates to achieve these goals typically under deadline pressures. Direction tends to be difficult because software people are highly creative and individualistic. Leadership and direction are needed to eliminate mistrust and provide focus for work activities. Based upon lessons learned managing software projects, the following three direction principles create a foundation for our discussions on direction:

- **Principle 8- Provide your People with an Opportunity to Excel:** Interesting work and the opportunity to excel will motivate your people to do best that they can. Software managers need to understand how to channel their behaviour so that it is directed toward achieving work-related goals.
- **Principle 9- Lead by Satisfying Goals:** People will follow those individuals who lead by example and represent a means to satisfy their own personal goals. Success will

come to those managers who can make satisfying personal and work-related goals possible on the job.

- **Principle 10- Keep Key People Focused:** Avoid giving your best people too much to do. Too many diversions cause a loss of efficiency that talent alone cannot correct. Learn to say 'no' to distractions. To succeed, keep your people focused on the task at hand.

We would like to populate our organizations with talented, self-motivated professionals. Under such a system, tasks would be completed with little or no management interference. Unfortunately, such situations do not exist in most firms. Managers, like coaches, must build synergistic teams and motivate their players to perform at their fullest capability. Managers must be able to communicate, lead, and motivate the players so that they can survive the trials of combat. In addition, they must be able to focus the team, as necessary, to meet deadlines.

3.8.5 Controlling

Planning and control tend to be closely related activities. Managers control by tracking progress against plans and acting on observed deviations. They track actual against targets and forecast trends. Controls should be diagnostic, therapeutic, accurate, timely, understandable, and most important, economical. They should call attention to significant deviations from the norm and suggest ways of fixing the problems. They should be forward-looking and emphasize what you need to do in the future to make corrections relative to your plans.

To be in control, managers must experience risks and use metrics to manage. Based upon extensive project management experience, thus leads to the following control principles:

- **Principle 11- Focus on the Significant Deviations:** Controls should be implemented to alert managers promptly to significant deviations from plans. the philosophy of 'if it isn't broke, don't fix it' should be remembered. In other words, don't interfere if things are going well and the prognosis looks good for the future.
- **Principle 12- You Cannot Control What You Cannot Measure:** Effective control requires that we measure performance against standards. Normally, these standards are budgets and schedules established as targets within your project plan. However, other standards may exist, especially when metrics and other indicators are used to track status and measure progress. Independent of the system you use, you cannot determine where you are going if you do not know where you are or have been.
- **Principle 13- Make Risk Abatement Your Goal:** Risk management and abatement must be an integral part of any control system or else it will cease to work. Identifying obstacles and figuring out ways to avoid them in advance is an essential part of the control progress.

Controls close the loop in the feedback system. They provide managers with the visibility and insight needed to make better and timely decisions. Software managers rely on configuration management, metrics and measurements, quality assurance, software inspections, risk management, and verification and validation techniques to provide them with visibility into the project's status and control over its progress.

3.8.6 Instituting Technology Change

The software industry is in constant state of change. Managers need to be aware of advances that are being made in order to harness them for their benefit. Although using new technology may lie risky, software managers must be able to figure out when and how to put it work for their organization's benefit. Otherwise, the ability to get the job done may be hindered. Experience with such new technology gives rise to the following final principle of software project management:

- **Principle 14- Match Technology Risk with Expected Benefits:** Technology should be used only when the risk associated with its use is applicable. For projects on a tight schedule, the introduction of something new may be unacceptable. Yet, the same technology may be defensive on another project where adequate resources are available to insert it operationally.

We firmly believe that technology transfer is the primary means we have to alleviate most of the software problems the industry if experiencing. We need to figure out how to tap the benefits of new technologies, without paying too high a price. We need to work smarter and harder, or we may not be able to handle the workload in the future.

3.9 SOFTWARE METRICS

Poor size estimation is one of the main reasons major software-intensive acquisition programs ultimately fail. Size is the critical factor in determining cost, schedule, and effort. The failure to accurately predict (usually too small) results in budget overruns and late deliveries which undermine confidence and erode support for your program. Size estimation is a complicated activity, the results of which must be constantly updated with actual counts throughout the life cycle. Size measures include source lines-of-code, function points, and feature points. Complexity is a function of size, which greatly impacts design errors and latent defects, ultimately resulting in quality problems, cost overruns, and schedule slips. Complexity must be continuously measured, tracked, and controlled. Another factor leading to size estimate inaccuracies is requirements creep which also must be baselined and diligently controlled.

"Software metrics are quantifiable measures that could be used to measure different characteristics of a software system or the software-development process."

Metrics and measurements are necessary aspects of managing a software development project. For effective monitoring, management needs to get information about the project: how far it has progressed, how much development has taken place, how far behind schedule it is, and the quality of the development so far. Based on this information, decisions can be made about the project. Without proper metrics to quantify the required information, subjective opinion would have to be used, which is often unreliable and goes against the fundamental goals of engineering. Hence, we can say that metrics-based management is also a key component in the software-engineering strategy to achieve its objectives.

3.9.1 Definition

Software metrics can be defined as *"The continuous application of measurement-based techniques to the software-development process and its products to supply meaningful and timely management information, together with the use of those techniques to improve that process and its products."*

Metrics ensure that the final product is of high quality and the productivity of the project stays high. In this sequence metrics for intermediate products of requirements and design is to predict or get some idea about the metrics of the final product. Several metrics have been designed for coding; namely, size, complexity, style, and reliability.

3.9.2 Categories of Metrics

There are three categories of software metrics, which are as follows:

1. ***Product Metrics.*** Product metrics describe the characteristics of the product, such as size, complexity, design features, performance, efficiency, reliability, portability, etc.
2. ***Process Metrics.*** Process metrics describe the effectiveness and quality of the processes that produce the software product. Examples are:
   - Effort required in the process
   - Time to produce the product
   - Effectiveness of defect removal during development
   - Number of defects found during testing
   - Maturity of the process
3. ***Project Metrics.*** Project metrics describe the project characteristics and execution. Examples are:
   - Number of software developers
   - Staffing pattern over the life-cycle of the software
   - Cost and schedule
   - Productivity

3.9.3 Attributes of Effective Software Metrics

Hundreds of metrics have been proposed for computer software, but not all provide practical support to the software engineer. Some demand measurement that is too complex, others are so esoteric that few real-world professionals have any hope of understanding them, and others violate the basic intuitive notions of what high-quality software really is.

Ejiogu defines a set of attributes that should be encompassed by effective software metrics. The derived metric and the measures that lead to it should be:

- *Simple and computable:* It should be relatively easy to learn how to derive the metric, and its computation should not demand inordinate effort or time.
- *Empirically and intuitively persuasive:* The metrics should satisfy the engineer's intuitive notions about the product attribute under consideration.
- *Consistent and objective:* The metric should always yield results that are unambiguous.
- *Consistent in the use of units and dimensions:* The mathematical computation of the metric should use measures that do not lead to bizarre combinations of units.
- *Programming-language independent:* Metrics should be based on the analysis model, the design model, or the structure of the program itself.
- *An effective mechanism for high-quality feedback:* That is, the metric should lead to a higher-quality end product.

3.10 SOURCE LINES OF CODE (SLOC) METRIC

Source lines of code (SLOC or simply LOC) is a software metric used to measure the size of a computer program by counting the number of lines in the text of the program's source code. SLOC is typically used to predict the amount of effort that will be required to develop a program, as well as to estimate programming productivity or maintainability once the software is produced.

It is the simplest among tall metrics available to estimate project size. Most SLOC estimates count all executable instructions and data declarations but exclude comments, blanks, and continuation lines. SLOC can be used to estimate size through analogy, i.e. by comparing the new software's functionality to similar functionality found in other historic applications. Obviously, having more detailed information available about the functionality of the new software provides the basis for a better comparison. In theory, this should yield a more credible estimate. The relative simplicity of the SLOC size measure facilitates automated and consistent (repeatable) counting of actual completed software size. It also enables recording size data needed to prepare accurate estimates for future efforts. The most significant advantage of SLOC estimates is that they directly relate to the software to be built. The software can then be measured after completion and compared with your initial estimates. If you are using SLOC with a predictive model (e.g., Barry Boehm's COnstructive COst MOdel (COCOMO)), your estimates will need to be continually updated as new information is available. Only through this constant re-evaluation can the predictive model provide estimates that approximate actual costs.

A large body of literature and historical data exists that uses SLOC, or thousands of source lines-of-code (KSLOC), as the size measure. Source lines-of-code are easy to count and most existing software estimating models use SLOCs as the key input. However, it is virtually impossible to estimate SLOC from initial requirements statements. Their use in estimation requires a level of detail that is hard to achieve (i.e., the planner must often estimate the SLOC to be produced before sufficient detail is available to accurately do so.)

Because SLOCs are language-specific, the definition of how SLOCs are counted has been troublesome to standardize. This makes comparisons of size estimates between applications written in different programming languages difficult even though conversion factors are available. From SLOC estimates a set of simple, size-oriented productivity and quality metrics can be developed for any given on-going program. These metrics can be further refined using productivity and quality equations such as those found in the basic COCOMO model.

Determining SLOC count at the end of a project is a very simple job. However, accurate estimation of SLOC count at the beginning of a project is very difficult. In order to estimate the SLOC count at the beginning of beginning of a project, project managers usually divide the problem into modules, and each module into submodules, and so on, until the sizes of the different leaf-level modules can be approximately predicted. To be able to do this, past experience in developing similar projects proves helpful. By using the estimation of lowest level modules, project managers arrive at the total size estimation.

There are two major types of SLOC measures: **physical SLOC** and **logical SLOC**. The most common definition of physical SLOC is a count of "non-blank, non-comment lines" in the text of the program's source code. Logical SLOC measures attempt to measure the number of "statements", but their specific definitions are tied to specific computer languages (one simple logical SLOC measure for C-like languages is the number of statement-terminating semicolons). It is much easier to create tools that measure physical SLOC, and physical SLOC definitions are easier to explain. However, physical SLOC measures are sensitive to logically irrelevant formatting and style conventions, while logical SLOC is less sensitive to formatting and style conventions. Unfortunately, SLOC measures are often stated without giving their definition, and logical SLOC can often be significantly different from physical SLOC.

There are several cost, schedule, and effort estimation models which use SLOC as an input parameter, including the widely-used Constructive Cost Model (COCOMO) series of models invented by Dr. Barry Boehm. While these models have shown good predictive power, they are only as good as the estimates (particularly the SLOC estimates) fed to them.

3.10.1 Advantages

Following are the advantages of SLOC:

- **Scope for Automation of Counting:** Since Line of Code is a physical entity; manual counting effort can be easily eliminated by automating the counting process. Small utilities may be developed for counting the SLOC in a program. However, a code counting utility developed for a specific language cannot be used for other languages due to the syntactical and structural differences among languages.
- **An Intuitive Metric:** Line of Code serves as an intuitive metric for measuring the size of software due to the fact that it can be seen and the effect of it can be visualized. Function Point is more of an objective metric which cannot be imagined as being a physical entity, it exists only in the logical space. This way, SLOC comes in handy to express the size of software among programmers with low levels of experience.

3.10.2 Disadvantages

Following are the disadvantages of SLOC:

- **Lack of Accountability:** Lines of code measure suffers from some fundamental problems. First and foremost, it is completely inaccurate and unfortunate to have to measure the productivity of a development project with the outcome of one of the phases (coding phase) which usually accounts for only 30% to 35% of the overall effort.
- **Lack of Cohesion with Functionality:** Though experiments have repeatedly confirmed that effort is highly correlated with SLOC, functionality is less well correlated with SLOC. That is, skilled developers may be able to develop the same functionality with far less code, so one program with less SLOC may exhibit more functionality than another similar program. In particular, SLOC is a poor productivity measure of individuals, since a developer can develop only a few lines and still be more productive than a developer creating more lines of code.
- **Adverse Impact on Estimation:** As a consequence of the lack of accountability, estimates done based on lines of code can adversely go wrong, in all possibility.

- **Developer's Experience:** Implementation of a specific logic differs based on the level of experience of the developer. Hence, number of lines of code differs from person to person. An experienced developer may implement certain functionality in fewer lines of code than another developer of relatively less experience does, though they use the same language.
- **Difference in Languages:** Consider two applications that provide the same functionality (screens, reports, databases). One of the applications is written in C++ and the other application written a language like COBOL. The number of function points would be exactly the same, but aspects of the application would be different. The lines of code needed to develop the application would certainly be not the same. As a consequence, the amount of effort required to develop the application would be different (hours per function point). Unlike Lines of Code, the number of Function Points (discussed next) will remain constant.
- **Advent of GUI Tools:** With the advent of GUI-based languages/tools such as Visual Basic, much of development work is done by drag-and-drops and a few mouse clicks, where the programmer virtually writes no piece of code, most of the time. It is not possible to account for the code that is automatically generated in this case. This difference invites huge variations in productivity and other metrics with respect to different languages, making the Lines of Code more and more irrelevant in the context of GUI-based languages/tools, which are prominent in the present software development arena.
- **Far from OO Development:** Line of Code makes no meaning in the case of Object-Oriented development where everything is treated in terms of Objects and classes. Since object is a true representation of data and functionality and so is a Function Point, FPA remains more relevant for Object-Oriented software development.
- **Problems with Multiple Languages:** In today's software scenario, never a single language is used for development. Very often, number of languages are employed depending upon the complexity and requirements. Tracking and reporting of productivity and defect rates poses a serious problem in this case since defects cannot be attributed to a particular language subsequent to integration of the system. Function Point stands out to be the best measure of size in this case.
- **Lack of Counting Standards:** There is no standard definition of what a line of code is. Do comments count? Are data declarations included? What happens if a statement extends over several lines? These are the questions that often arise. Though organizations like SEI and IEEE have published some guidelines in an attempt to standardize counting, it is difficult to put these into practice especially in the face of newer and newer languages being introduced every year.

3.11 FUNCTION POINT METRIC

Function point metric was proposed by Albrecht in 1983. It overcomes many of the shortcomings of the SLOC metric. Since its inception, function point metric has been slowly gaining popularity. One of the important advantages of using function point metric is that it can be used to easily estimate the size of a software product directly from the problem specification. This is in contrast to the SLOC metric, where the size can be accurately determined only after the product has been completely developed.

Function Point Analysis is an objective and structured technique to measure software size by quantifying its functionality provided to the user, based on the requirements and logical design. This technique breaks the system into smaller components so they can be better understood and analysed. Function Point count can be applied to Development projects, Enhancement projects, and existing applications as well. There are 5 major components of Function Point Analysis which capture the functionality of the application. These are: External Inputs (EIs), External Outputs (EOs), External Inquiries (EQs), Internal Logical Files (ILFs) and External Interface Files (EIFs). First three are treated as Transactional Function Types and last two are called Data Function Types. Function Point Analysis consists of performing the following steps:

- Determine the type of Function Point count
- Determine the application boundary
- Identify and rate transactional function types to calculate their contribution to the
- Unadjusted Function Point count (UFP)
- Identify and rate the data function types to calculate their contribution to the UFP
- Determine the Value Adjustment Factor (VAF) by using General System Characteristics (GSCs)
- Finally, calculate the adjusted Function Point count

Each of the components of Function Point Analysis is explained in brief in the following sub-sections.

1. **External Input (EI)**

   External Input is an elementary process in which data crosses the boundary from outside to inside. This data may come from a data input screen or another application. The data may be used to maintain one or more internal logical files. The data can be either control information or business information.

2. **External Output (EO)**

   External Output is an elementary process in which derived data passes across the boundary from inside to outside. Additionally, an EO may update an internal logical file. The data creates reports or output files sent to other applications. These reports and files are created from information contained in one or more internal logical files and external interface files. Derived Data is data that is processed beyond direct retrieval and editing of information from internal logical files or external interface files.

3. **External Inquiry (EQ)**

   External Inquiry is an elementary process with both input and output components that results in data retrieval from one or more internal logical files and external interface files. The input process does not update or maintain any FTRs (Internal Logical Files or External Interface Files) and the output side does not contain derived data.

4. **Internal Logical File (ILF)**

   Internal Logical File is a user identifiable group of logically related data that resides entirely within the application boundary and is maintained through External Inputs. Even though it is not a rule, at least one external output and/or external inquiry should include the ILF as an FTR.

5. **External Interface File (EIF)**
External Interface File is a user identifiable group of logically related data that is used for reference purposes only. The data resides entirely outside the application boundary and is maintained by external inputs of another application. That is, the external interface file is an internal logical file for another application. At least one transaction, external input, external output or external inquiry should include the EIF as a File Type Referenced.
6. **Rating the Transactional and Data Function Types**
Each of the identified components is assigned a rating (as Low, Average, and High). Transactional Function Types are given the rating depending upon the number of Data Element Types (DET), File Types Referenced (FTR) associated with them. Data Function Types are assigned ratings based on the number of Data Element Types (DET), and Record Element Types (RET) associated. A DET is a unique user recognizable, non-recursive (non-repetitive) field. A DET is information that is dynamic and not static. A dynamic field is read from a file or created from DETs contained in an FTR. A RET is user recognizable sub group of data elements within an ILF or an EIF. An FTR is a file type referenced by a transaction. An FTR must also be an internal logical file or external interface file.
The total number of EIs, EOs, EQs, ILFs, and EIFs, after applying the weights corresponding to the ratings (Low, Average, and High) will give the Unadjusted Function Point count (UFP).
7. **General System Characteristics (GSCs)**
The value adjustment factor (VAF) is calculated based on 14 General System Characteristics that rate the general functionality of the application being counted. The GSCs are: Data communications, Distributed data processing, Performance, Heavily used configuration, Transaction rate, On-line data entry, End-user efficiency, On-line update, Complex processing, Reusability, Installation ease, Operational ease, Multiple sites, and Facilitate change. The degree of influence of each characteristic has to be determined as a rating on a scale of 0 to 5 as defined below.
   - *0: Not present, or no influence*
   - *1: Incidental influence*
   - *2: Moderate influence*
   - *3: Average influence*
   - *4: Significant influence*
   - *5: Strong influence throughout*

   Once all the GSCs have been rated, Total Degrees of Influence (TDI) is obtained by summing up all the ratings. Now, Value Adjustment Factor is calculated using the formula:

$$VAF = 0.65 + TDI/100$$

8. **Final FP Count**
After determining the Unadjusted Function Point count (UFP) out of transactional and data function types, and calculating the Value Adjustment Factor (VAF) by rating the general system characteristics, the final Function Point count can be calculated using the formula:

FP = Unadjusted Function Point count (UFP) * Value Adjustment Factor (VAF)

3.11.1 Advantages

Function Point Analysis provides the best objective method for sizing software projects, and for managing the size during development. Following are some of the many advantages that FPA offers.

- **Helps Comparison:** Since Function Points measures systems from a functional perspective, hence they are independent of technology. Regardless of language, development method, or hardware/platform used, the number of FP for a system will remain constant. The only variable is the amount of effort needed to deliver a given set of FP; therefore, Function Point Analysis can be used to determine whether a tool, an environment, a language is more productive compared with others within an organization or among organizations. This is a critical point and one of the greatest values of Function Point Analysis.
- **Helps Monitor Scope Creep:** Function Point Analysis can provide a mechanism to track and monitor scope creep. FP counts at the end of requirements, analysis, design, code, testing and deployment can be compared. The FP count at the end of requirements and/or designs can be compared to FP actually delivered. If the project has grown, there has been scope creep. The amount of growth is an indication of how well requirements were gathered by and/or communicated to the project team. If the amount of growth of projects declines over time it is a natural assumption that communication with the user has improved.
- **Ease of Contract Negotiations:** From a customer view point, Function Points can be used to help specify to a vendor, the key deliverables, to ensure appropriate levels of functionality will be delivered, and to develop objective measures of cost-effectiveness and quality. They are most effectively used with fixed price contracts as a means of specifying exactly what will be delivered. From a vendor perspective, successful management of fixed price contracts depends absolutely on accurate representations of effort. Estimation of this effort (across the entire life cycle) can occur only when a normalized metric such as the one provided by Function Points is applied.

  Here, the meaning of the word 'normalized metric' is that Function Point truly accounts for the entire gamut of software development spreading across all the phases from Requirements through Testing, whereas SLOC pertains to and is an outcome of only one of the phases.
- **Handling Volatility:** The advantage that Function Points bring to early estimation is the fact that they are derived directly from the requirements and hence show the current status of requirements completeness. As new features are added, the function point total will go up accordingly. If the organization decides to remove features or defer them to a subsequent release, the function point metric can also handle this situation very well, and reflect true state.
- **Use of Historic Data:** Once project size has been determined in Function Points, estimates for Duration, Effort, and other costs can be computed by using historic

data. Since FP is independent of languages or tools, data from similar past projects can be used to produce consistent results, unlike Lines of Code data which is much tightly tied to languages requiring many other parameters to be taken into account.

- **Availability of Empirical Formulae:** Unlike lines of code, FP can be used more effectively to develop many predictive formulae such as defect potential, maintenance effort which can help pinpoint opportunities for improvement. Caper Jones estimates that Function Points raised to the 1.2 power (FP1.2) estimates the number of test cases. That is, test cases grow at a faster rate than Function Points. This is logically valid because as an application grows, the number of interrelationships within the application becomes more complex, requiring more test cases. Many empirical formulae have been suggested by Caper Jones which are in wide use among FP practitioners.
- **Enables Better Communication:** FP can help improve communications with senior management since it talks in terms of functionality rather than any implementation details, technical aspects, or physical code. Furthermore, Function Points are easily understood by the non-technical user. This helps communicate sizing information to a user (or customer) as well.
- **Offers Better Benchmarking:** Since FP is independent of language, development methodology, programming practices, and technology domain, projects using FP become better candidates for benchmarking across organizations and geographies.

3.11.2 Disadvantages

Function Points offer vast number of benefits by capturing the size of the software from its functionality standpoint. FPA does have some disadvantages. However, organizations can easily overcome these problems by practicing FPA consistently over a period of time.

- **Requires Manual Work:** Due to its very nature, Function Points have to be counted manually. The counting process cannot be automated.
- **Necessitates Significant Level of Detail:** A great level of detail is required to estimate the software size in terms of Function Points. Information on inputs, outputs, screens, database tables, and even records and fields will be required to perform FPA accurately. Typically this is not the case with any development project where the requirements are not clear to this level of detail, in the beginning.
- **Requires Experience:** Function Point Analysis requires good deal of experience if it were to be done precisely. FPA inherently requires sufficient knowledge of the counting rules, which are comparatively difficult to understand.

3.12 FEATURE POINT METRIC

A major shortcoming of the function point measure is that it does not take into account the algorithmic complexity of software, i.e. the function point metric implicitly assumes that the effort required to design and develop any two functionalities of the system is same. But, as we know that it is normally not true. The effort required to design and develop various facilities of a system varies a lot.

Feature point metric incorporates algorithm complexity as an extra parameter, which ensures that the compound size using the feature point metric reflects the fact that the more is the complexity of the module, the greater is the effort required to develop it and therefore its size should be larger as compared to the simpler functions.

Proponents of function point and feature point metrics claim that these metrics are language-independent and can be easily computed from the SRS document during project planning, whereas the opponents claim that these metrics are subjective and require a sleight of hand. An example of the subjective nature of the function point metric can be that the way one would group logically related data items can be very subjective. Therefore, there is sufficient scope for different project managers to arrive at different function point measures for the same problem.

3.13 COST ESTIMATION

Most information for initial cost estimation comes from the feasibility study and requirement analysis. When we estimate costs very early, there is less information upon which to base estimates and, therefore, this information is less detailed and the estimates may be less accurate. Software cost estimation is important for making good management decisions. It is also connected to determining how much effort and time a software project requires. Cost estimation has several uses:

- It establishes a firm, reliable budget for an in-house project.
- It facilitates competitive contract bids.
- It determines what is most cost effective for the organization.

Software cost estimation provides the vital link between the general concepts and techniques of economic analysis and the particular world of software engineering. There is no good way to perform a software cost-benefit analysis, break-even analysis, or make-or-buy analysis without some reasonably accurate method of estimating software costs, and their sensitivity to various product, project, and environmental factors. These methods provide an essential part of the foundation for good software management. Without a reasonably accurate cost-estimation capability, software projects often experience the following problems:

1. Software project personnel have no firm basis for telling a manager, customer, or salesperson that their proposed budget and schedule are unrealistic. This leads to optimistic over promising on software development, low-balling on competitive software contract bids and the inevitable overruns and performance compromises as a consequence.
2. Software analysts have no firm basis for making realistic hardware-software trade-off analysis during the system design phase. This often leads to a design in which the hardware cost is decreased, at the expense of an even larger increase in the software cost.
3. Project managers have no firm basis for determining how much time and effort each software phase and activity should take. This leaves managers with no way to tell whether or not the software is proceeding according to plan. That basically means that the software portion of the project is out of control from its beginning.

The cost of medium and large software projects is determined by the cost of developing the software, plus the cost of equipment and supplies. The latter is generally a constant for most projects.

The cost of developing the software is simply the estimated effort, multiplied by presumably fixed labour costs. For this reason, we will concentrate on estimating the development effort, and leave the task of converting the effort to money to each company.

There are two basic models for estimating software development effort (or cost): holistic and activity-based. The single biggest cost driver in either model is the estimated project size.

Holistic models are useful for organizations that are new to software development, or that do not have baseline data available from previous projects to determine labour rates for the various development activities.

Estimates produced with activity-based models are more likely to be accurate, as they are based on the software development rates common to each organization. Unfortunately, you require related data from previous projects to apply these techniques.

3.13.1 Holistic Models for Cost Estimating

Holistic models relate size, effort, and (sometimes) schedule by applying equations to determine the overall cost, and then applying a percent of the overall cost to each development activity. They do not consider the actual labour rates and costs of each activity.

Popular holistic models include the following:

- SDM (Software Development Model - Putnam - 1978)
- SLIM (Software Lifecycle Management - Putnam – 1979)
- COCOMO (Constructive Cost Model - Boehm - 1981)
- COPMO (Cooperative Programming Model - Conte, Dunsmuir, Shen - 1986)

Of these models, COCOMO is most widely used, and will suffice if there is insufficient data to carry out activity-based cost estimation.

3.13.2 Activity-based Models for Cost Estimating

The activity-based model uses data from the metrics database to determine the labour rates for the various development activities. For this reason, you can only apply it once the metrics program is established and there is a baseline from which to work.

3.14 COCOMO

The COCOMO cost estimation model is used by thousands of software project managers, and is based on a study of hundreds of software projects. Unlike other cost estimation models, COCOMO is an open model, so all of the details are published, including:

- The underlying cost estimation equations
- Every assumption made in the model (e.g. "the project will enjoy good management")

- Every definition (e.g. the precise definition of the Product Design phase of a project)
- The costs included in an estimate are explicitly stated (e.g. project managers are included, secretaries aren't)

The original COCOMO stands for Constructive Cost Model. The word "constructive" implies that the complexity of the model can be understood because of the openness of the model, which permits exactly to know *WHY* the model gives the estimates it does. The model was first published by Dr. Barry Boehm in 1981, and reflected the software development practices of these days. Since this time many efforts were done in the improvement of the software development techniques. Some of the changes were moving away from mainframe overnight batch processing to real time applications, strenuousness in effort in building software for reusing, new kind of system development in including off-the-shelf software components (COTS) and spending as much effort on designing and managing the software development process as was once spent creating the software product.

These changes urged to revise the existing model. By the joint efforts of USC-CSE (University of California, Center for Software Engineering) and the COCOMO II Project Affiliate Organizations the COCOMO II model was presented, which should remedy all deficiencies. This new, improved COCOMO (COCOMO II) is now ready to assist professional software cost estimators.

3.14.1 COCOMO I

COCOMO I or COCOMO '81 provides a well-defined, open engineering basis for reasoning about the cost and schedule implications of a software solution. Boehm postulated that any software development project can be classified into one of the following three categories based on the development complexity: *organic, semidetached,* and *embedded*. In order to classify a product into the identified categories, Boehm requires us to consider not only the characteristics of the product but also those of the development team and development environment. Roughly, these three product classes correspond to application, utility, and system programs, respectively. Normally, data processing programs are considered to be application programs. Compilers, linkers, etc, are utility programs. Operating systems and real-time system programs are system programs. System programs interact directly with the hardware and typically involve meeting timing constraints and concurrent processing.

It is also stated that utility programs are roughly three times as difficult to write as application programs and system programs are roughly three times as difficult as utility programs. Thus, the ratios of the relative levels of product development complexity of the three categories of products are 1:3:9 for application, utility, and system programs.

The three levels in the COCOMO hierarchy are given as below:

- **Basic COCOMO**: computes software development effort and cost as a function of program size expressed in estimated lines of source code. There are three modes within Basic COCOMO:
  - *Organic Mode:* Development projects typically are uncomplicated and involve small experienced teams. The planned software is not considered innovative and requires a relatively small amount of SLOC (typically under 50,000).

- *Semidetached Mode:* Development projects typically are more complicated than in Organic Mode and involve teams of people with mixed levels of experience. The software requires no more than 300,000 SLOC. The project has characteristics of both projects for Organic Mode and projects for Embedded Mode.
- *Embedded Mode:* Development projects must fit into a rigid set of requirements because the software is to be embedded in a strongly joined complex of hardware, software, regulations and operating procedures.

- **Intermediate COCOMO:** an extension of the Basic model that computes software development effort by adding a set of "cost drivers," that will determine the effort and duration of the project, such as assessments of personnel and hardware.
- **Detailed COCOMO:** an extension of the Intermediate model that adds effort multipliers for each phase of the project to determine the cost drivers' impact on each step.

3.14.1.1 Basic Cocomo Model

The basic COCOMO model gives an approximate estimate of the project parameters. The basic COCOMO estimation model is given by the following expressions:

$$\text{Effort} = a_1 \times (\text{KLOC})^{a_2} \quad \text{PM}$$

$$\text{Tdev} = b_1 \times (\text{Effort})^{b_2} \quad \text{Months}$$

where KLOC is the estimated size of the software product expressed in Kilo Lines of Code and a_1, a_2, b_1, b_2 are constants of the software product.

Tdev is the estimated time to develop the software, expressed in months. Effort is the total effort required to develop the software product, expressed in person-months (PM).

The person-month curve is shown in Figure 3.5.

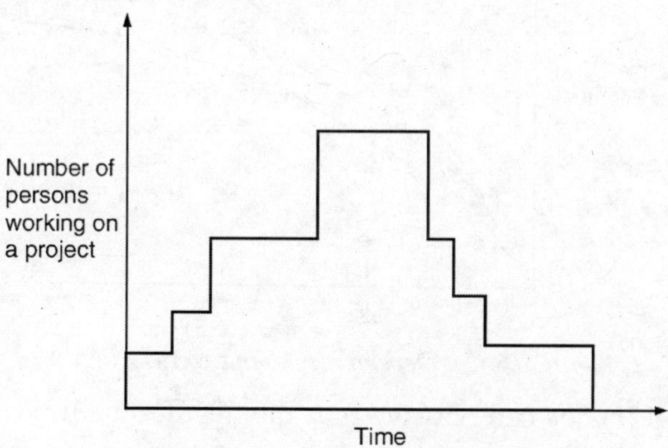

***Figure 3.5:** Person Month Curve*

Estimation of Development Effort

Organic:	Effort = 2.4 $(\text{KLOC})^{1.05}$ PM
Semi-detached:	Effort = 3.0 $(\text{KLOC})^{1.12}$ PM
Embedded:	Effort = 3.6 $(\text{KLOC})^{1.20}$ PM

Figure 3.6 (*a*) shows a plot of the estimated effort versus the size for various product sizes.

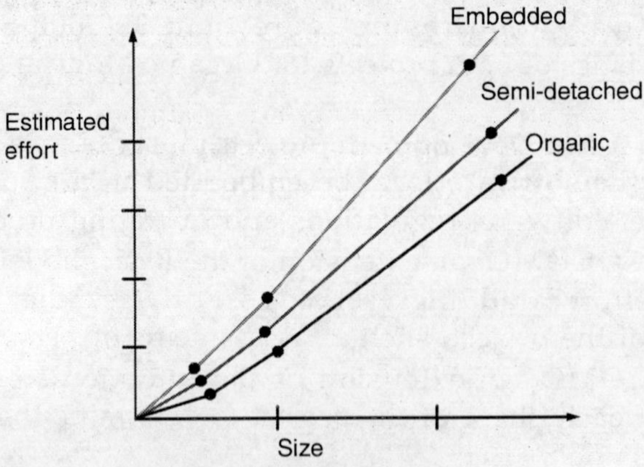

Figure 3.6 (a): *Effort Versus Size*

From Figure 3.6 (*a*), we can observe that the effort is almost linearly proportional to the size of the software product.

Estimation of Development Time

Organic: $T_{dev} = 2.5\ (\text{Effort})^{0.38}$ Months

Semi-detached: $T_{dev} = 2.5\ (\text{Effort})^{0.35}$ Months

Embedded: $T_{dev} = 2.5(\text{Effort})^{0.32}$ Months

Figure 3.6 (*b*) shows a plot of development time versus product size.

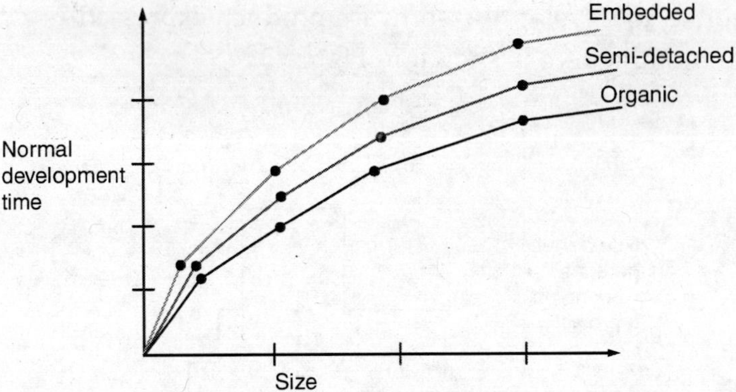

Figure 3.6 (b): *Development Time Versus Product Size*

From Figure 3.6 (*b*), we can observe that the development time is a sub-linear function of the size of the product.

3.14.1.2 Intermediate COCOMO Model

The intermediate COCOMO model recognizes this fact and refines the initial estimate obtained through the basic COCOMO expression by using a set of 15 cost drivers (multipliers) based on various attributes of software development.

Table 3.1: COCOMO Intermediate Cost Drivers

Driver Type	Code	Cost Driver
Product attributes	RELY	Required software reliability
	DATA	Database size
	CPLX	Product complexity
Computer attributes	TIME	Execution time constraints
	STOR	Main storage constraints
	VIRT	Virtual machine volatility–degree to which the operating system changes
	TURN	Computer turnaround time
Personnel attributes	ACAP	Analyst capability
	AEXP	Application experience
	PCAP	Programmer capability
	VEXP	Virtual machine (i.e., operation system) experience
	LEXP	Programming-language experience
Projects attributes	MODP	Use of modern programming practices
	TOOL	Use of software tools
	SCED	Required development schedule

3.14.1.3 Complete COCOMO Model

The shortcomings of both basic and intermediate COCOMO models are that they:

- Consider a software product a single homogenous entity. However, most large systems are made up of several smaller subsystems. Some subsystems may be considered organic, some embedded, etc. For some, the reliability requirements may be high, and so on.
- Consider the cost of each subsystem separately.
- Consider the costs of the subsystems but add them separately to obtain total cost.
- Reduce the margin of error in the final estimate.

A large amount of work has been done by Boehm to capture all significant aspects of software development. It offers a means for processing all the project characteristics to construct a software estimate. The complete model introduces two more capabilities:

1. **Phase-Sensitive Effort Multipliers.** Some phases (design, programming, and integration/test) are more affected than others by factors defined by the cost drivers. The complete model provides a set of phase-sensitive effort multipliers for each cost driver. This helps in determining the manpower allocation for each phase of the project.
2. **Three-Level Product Hierarchy.** Three product levels are defined. These are module, subsystem, and system levels. The ratings of the cost drivers are done at appropriate levels; that is, the level at which it is most susceptible to variation.

Advantages of COCOMO I

Following are the advantages of COCOMO I:

- COCOMO is transparent, one can see how it works unlike other models such as SLIM
- Drivers are particularly helpful to the estimator to understand the impact of different factors that affect project costs

Drawbacks of COCOMO I

Following are the drawbacks of COCOMO I:

- It is hard to accurately estimate KDSI early on in the project, when most effort estimates are required KLOC, actually, is not a size measure it is a length measure
- Extremely vulnerable to mis-classification of the development mode
- Success depends largely on tuning the model to the needs of the organization, using historical data which is not always available

3.14.2 COCOMO II

COCOMO II was developed from earlier COCOMO cost estimation model, which was largely based on original code development. The COCOMO II model takes into account more modern approaches to software development, such as rapid development using dynamic languages, development by component composition, and use of database programming. COCOMO II supports the spiral model of development, described in Chapter 3, and embeds sub models that produce increasingly detailed estimates.

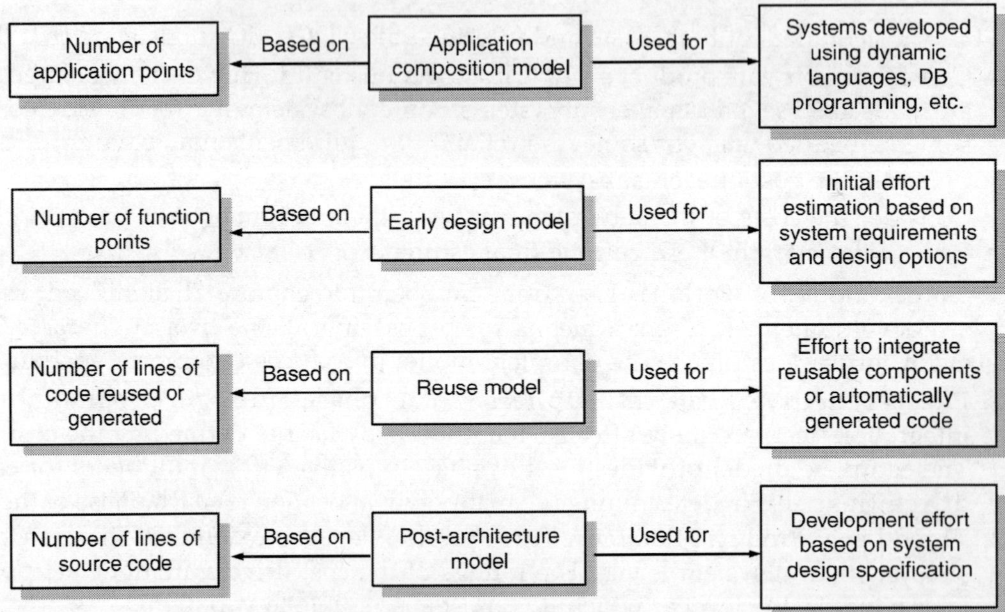

Figure 3.7: COCOMO II estimation models

The sub models (Figure 3.7) that are part of the COCOMO II model are:

- **An application-composition model:** This model models the effort required to develop systems that are created from reusable components, scripting, or database programming. Software size estimates are based on application points, and a simple size/productivity formula is used to estimate the effort required. The number of application points in a program is a weighted estimate of the number of separate screens that are displayed, the number of reports that are produced, the number of modules in imperative programming languages (such as Java), and the number of lines of scripting language or database programming code.
- **An early design model:** This model is used during early stages of the system design after the requirements have been established. The estimate is based on the standard estimation formula, with a simplified set of seven multipliers. Estimates are based on function points, which are then converted to number of lines of source code. Function points are a language-independent way of quantifying program functionality. Total number of function points in a program is computed by measuring or estimating the number of external inputs and outputs, user interactions, external interfaces, and files or database tables used by the system.
- **A reuse model:** This model is used to compute the effort required to integrate reusable components and/or automatically generated program code. It is normally used in conjunction with the post-architecture model.
- **A post-architecture model:** Once the system architecture has been designed, a more accurate estimate of the software size can be made. Again, this model uses the standard formula for cost estimation discussed above. However, it includes a more extensive set of 17 multipliers reflecting personnel capability, product, and project characteristics.

Of course, in large systems, different parts of the system may be developed using different technologies and you may not have to estimate all parts of the system to the same level of accuracy. In such cases, you can use the appropriate submodel for each part of the system and combine the results to create a composite estimate.

3.15 STAFFING

Once the effort required to develop software has been determined, it is necessary to determine the staffing requirement for the project. Putnam first studied the problem of what should be a proper staffing pattern for software projects. He extended the work of Norden who had earlier investigated the staffing pattern of research and development (R&D) type of projects. In order to appreciate the staffing pattern of software projects, Norden's and Putnam's results must be understood.

3.15.1 Norden's Work

Norden studied the staffing patterns of several R & D projects. He found that the staffing pattern can be approximated by the Rayleigh distribution curve (as shown in Figure 3.8). Norden represented the Rayleigh curve by the following equation:

$$E = K/t_d^2 * t * e^{-t^2/2t^2} d$$

Where E is the effort required at time t. E is an indication of the number of engineers (or the staffing level) at any particular time during the duration of the project, K is the area under the curve, and td is the time at which the curve attains its maximum value. It must be remembered that the results of Norden are applicable to general R & D projects and were not meant to model the staffing pattern of software development projects.

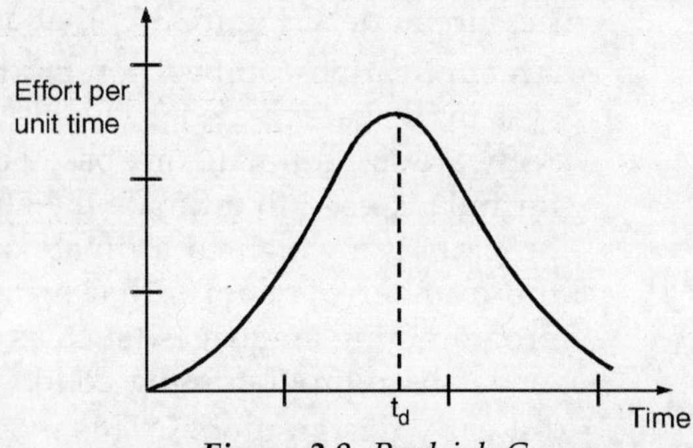

Figure 3.8: Rayleigh Curve

3.15.2 Putnam's Work

Putnam studied the problem of staffing of software projects and found that the software development has characteristics very similar to other R & D projects studied by Norden and that the Rayleigh-Norden curve can be used to relate the number of delivered lines of code to the effort and the time required to develop the project. By analysing a large number of army projects, Putnam derived the following expression:

$$L = C_k K^{1/3} t_d^{4/3}$$

The various terms of this expression are as follows:

- K is the total effort expended (in PM) in the product development and L is the product size in KLOC.
- t_d corresponds to the time of system and integration testing. Therefore, td can be approximately considered as the time required to develop the software.
- C_k is the state of technology constant and reflects constraints that impede the progress of the programmer. Typical values of C_k = 2 for poor development environment (no methodology, poor documentation, and review, etc.), C_k = 8 for good software development environment (software engineering principles are adhered to), C_k = 11 for an excellent environment (in addition to following software engineering principles, automated tools and techniques are used). The exact value of C_k for a specific project can be computed from the historical data of the organization developing it.

Putnam suggested that optimal staff build-up on a project should follow the Rayleigh curve. Only a small number of engineers are needed at the beginning of a project to carry out planning and specification tasks. As the project progresses and more detailed work is required, the number of engineers reaches a peak. After implementation and unit testing, the number of project staff falls.

However, the staff build-up should not be carried out in large instalments. The team size should either be increased or decreased slowly whenever required to match the Rayleigh-Norden curve. Experience shows that a very rapid build-up of project staff any time during the project development correlates with schedule slippage.

It should be clear that a constant level of manpower throughout the project duration would lead to wastage of effort and increase the time and effort required to develop the product. If a constant number of engineers are used over all the phases of a project, some phases would be overstaffed and the other phases would be understaffed causing inefficient use of manpower, leading to schedule slippage and increase in cost.

3.15.2.1 Effect of Schedule Change On Cost

By analysing a large number of army projects, Putnam derived the following expression:

$$L = C_k K^{1/3} t_d^{4/3}$$

Where, K is the total effort expended (in PM) in the product development and L is the product size in KLOC, t_d corresponds to the time of system and integration testing and C_k is the state of technology constant and reflects constraints that impede the progress of the programmer

Now by using the above expression it is obtained that,

$$K = L^3/C_k^3 t_d^4$$

or,

$$K = C/t_d^4$$

For the same product size, $C = L^3 / C_k^3$ is a constant,

or, $$K = K_1/K_2 = t_{d2}^4/t_{d1}^4$$

or, $$K \propto 1/t_d^4$$

or, $$\text{cost} \propto 1/t_d$$

(as project development effort is equally proportional to project development cost)

From the above expression, it can be easily observed that when the schedule of a project is compressed, the required development effort as well as project development cost increases in proportion to the fourth power of the degree of compression. It means that a relatively small compression in delivery schedule can result in substantial penalty of human effort as well as development cost. For example, if the estimated development time is 1 year, then in order to develop the product in 6 months, the total effort required to develop the product (and hence the project cost) increases 16 times.

3.16 SCHEDULING

Following the definitions of project activities, the activities are associated with time to create a project schedule. The project schedule provides a graphical representation of predicted tasks, milestones, dependencies, resource requirements, task duration, and deadlines. The project manager's schedule interrelates all tasks on a common time scale. The project schedule should be detailed enough to show each Work Breakdown Structure (WBS) task to be performed, the name of the person responsible for completing the task, the start and end date of each task, and the expected duration of the task.

Like development of each of the project plan components, developing a schedule is an iterative process. Milestones may suggest additional tasks, tasks may require additional resources, and task completion may be measured by additional milestones. For large, complex projects, detailed sub-schedules may be required to show an adequate level of detail for each task.

During the life of the project, actual progress if frequently compared with the original schedule. This allows for evaluation of development activities. The accuracy of the planning process can be assessed. Basic efforts associated with developing a project schedule include the following:

3.16.1 Define the Type of Schedule

The type of schedule associated with a project relates to the complexity of the implementation. For large, complex projects with a multitude of interrelated tasks, a PERT chart (or activity network) may be used. PERT charts depict interdependencies and associations and allow planning to include these relationships. A key feature of the PERT method is the ability to determine and to show the critical path of the project (see below for a discussion on critical path). A sample PERT chart is shown in Figure 3.9.

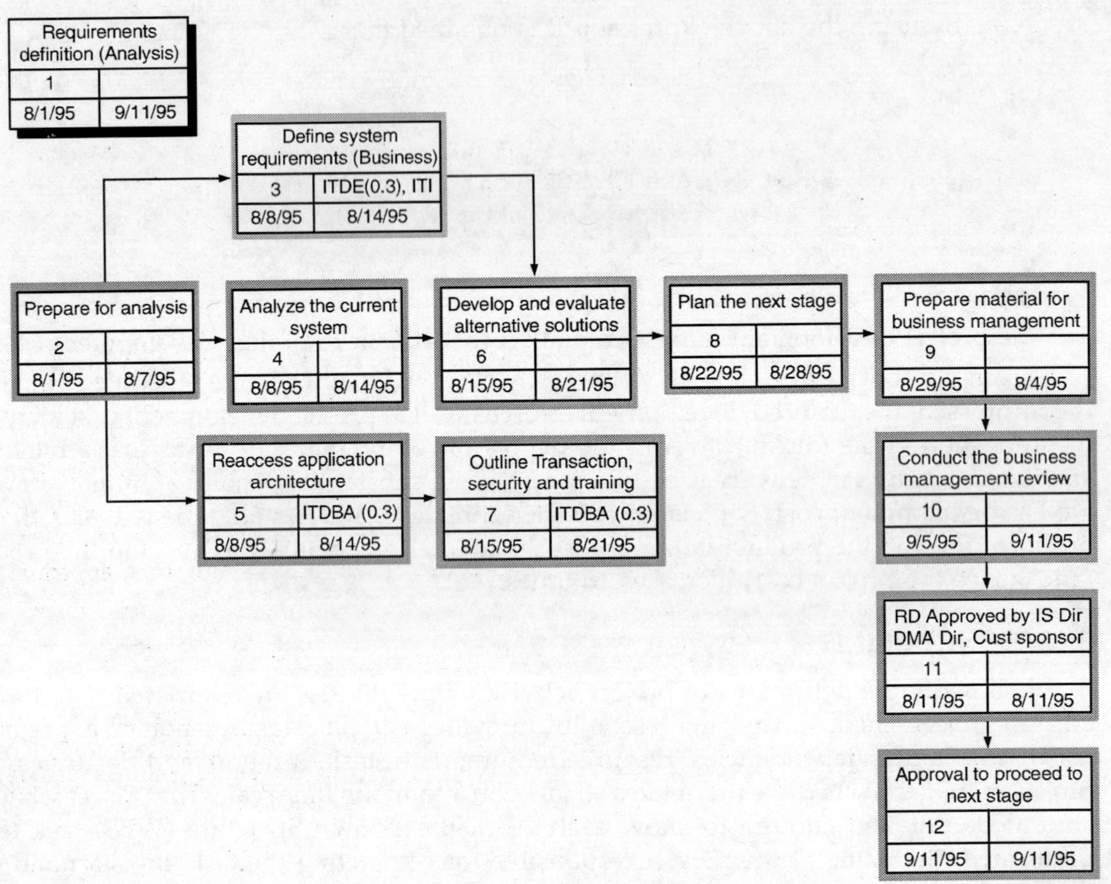

Figure 3.9: A Sample PERT Chart

For small projects, a GANTT chart (or bar graph) is adequate. These schedules are two-dimensional representations that show the tasks and the timeframe for completion. Since task interrelationships are not easily shown on a GANTT chart, it is considered a weak planning tool for complex information technology projects. However, the GANTT chart is common in reporting status and in defining the schedule for small, simple projects with few interrelationships. A sample GANTT chart is shown in Figure 3.10.

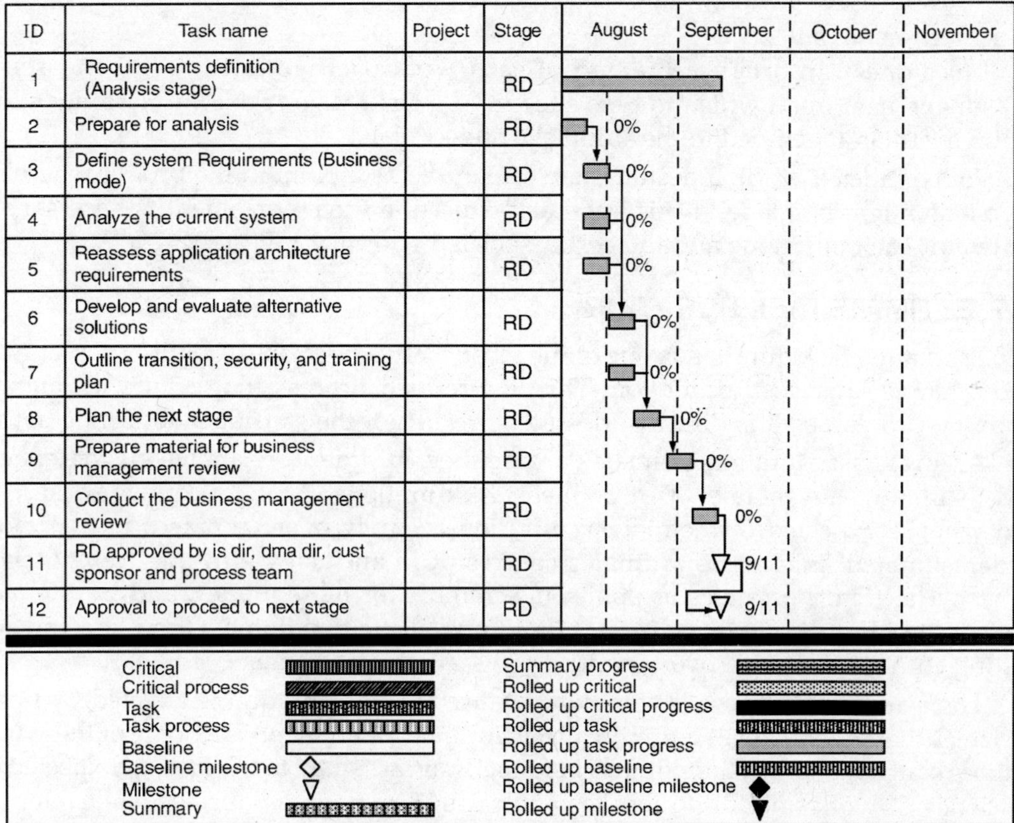

Figure 3.10: *A Sample GANTT Chart*

3.16.2 Define Precise and Measurable Milestones

The completion of key actions is important in all projects. These completions are denoted by milestones. These events have no duration. For example, deliverables often are represented as milestones, while the effort to product the deliverables is referred to as a task.

While milestones are unique to each project, some example project milestones are shown below:

- Requirements Approval
- Phase Review Approval
- Prototype Approval
- Design Reviews Complete
- Code Reviews Complete
- Unit Test Complete
- Integration Test Complete
- Acceptance Test Complete
- System Acceptance by User

- Customer Shipment
- Document Delivery

Milestones can occur at the end of each work package in the WBS and serve as a measurable item upon which to base success of a task. Major project milestones should be summarized and included in the summary project plan.

For contracted work, milestones are often used as a point in the project where interim payments might be made. If this approach is used, mutual agreement is necessary on the content of each milestone and the cost associated with that milestone.

3.17 ESTIMATE TASK DURATION

Estimating task duration is one of the most challenging aspects of project planning. It is also a key to later cost estimation. This is a refined process that occurs throughout the planning process, as it is directly affected by results of the staffing and costing activities.

Accurate ask duration estimates are defined in order to stabilize customer relations and maintain team morale. With defined task durations, the team knows what to expect and what is expected of them. Task duration is rarely overestimated, but is frequently underestimated. Inaccurate estimates can result in an increase in the 'frenzy level' of a project. The frenzy escalates as sponsors scramble for more money, and/or the technical staffs scrambles to complete a project in an unrealistic timeframe. Often, the end result is cutting corners, excessive overtime, and a dissatisfied customer.

The estimation process is complex because activity duration is affected by numerous variables that must be dealt with concurrently in the planning phase. Some of these variables include staff availability, the skill level of the person assigned to the task, unexpected events, efficiency of work time, and mistakes and misunderstandings during the development of the project.

When estimating the duration of the task, reality is a major factor. The knowledgeable factor takes into account absenteeism, meetings, discussions and interaction among the staff. No one is 100% productive every hour of the workday. If a scheduled task assumes 100% productivity, the schedule rapidly falls apart. A successful schedule builds these types of factors into the duration estimate.

There are several techniques that support task duration estimation. The most common technique is based on the historical experience of a similar scope work performed by the estimator. Collected and archived historical project data are used successfully by many organizations to achieve quality performance on project deliveries.

Historical records greatly support both the duration and the cost estimations that are so important in this phase. Data based on staff skills are far more valuable than generalized 'industry' estimates. If historical data does not exist, seek the advice of experts and others who have completed similar tasks.

When historical data or experts are not available, use a technique of getting estimates from multiple sources, comparing results and estimating the duration based on multiple inputs. The nature of this method is predicated on finding good sources for providing the estimates.

3.18 DEFINE PRIORITIES

Clearly defining the task priorities helps to resolve any scheduling and/or resource conflicts. Understanding the priorities and relationships of the tasks assists in resolving difficult scheduling conflicts.

3.19 DEFINE CRITICAL PATH

The critical path is the longest path through a project. It determines the earliest possible completion of the work. The critical path is carefully managed because if critical path tasks slip, the entire project is delayed. In order to manage the project, the project manager determines the critical path and remains aware of its importance throughout the implementation of the plan.

The successful scheduler considers availability of both labour and non-labour resources. Equipment availability in a long lead item often drives the critical path of a schedule. If installation equipment is required, for example, and the equipment cannot be delivered for six months, the installation phase is help up for that period of time.

3.20 DOCUMENT ASSUMPTIONS

Documentation of the assumptions made in developing the project schedule is critical to the later success of the project. Without clear documentation of these assumptions, later changes to the schedule ate very difficult and risky.

If, for example, a schedule was shortened because it was assumed that a highly skilled person would be performing the work, that assumption should be documented. Then, if a less skilled person is actually assigned to perform the task, the project manager can recognize the risk and make necessary changes and decisions. Without documentation of the assumption, the schedule could be later placed in serious risk without the project manager realizing it.

3.21 IDENTIFY RISKS

Risks are inherently involved with scheduling limited resources. Good scheduling makes allowances for risks in one or more of the following ways:

- Where significant schedule risks are identified, add an additional WBS task for risk management/risk reduction, where financial reserves can be set aside to deal with potentially delayed schedules.
- Add additional time to those tasks where risks are inherent. There is no rule of thumb for this multiplier; it depends on the degree of risk and overall importance of the schedule to the project.
- Add a percentage time multiplier to the schedule for particular individuals, particularly if new technology is being used or if the person providing the estimate is extremely optimistic. Technical staffs often underestimate the time required to do any particular task.

3.22 REVIEW RESULTS

The development of a schedule requires input from more than one person. No one possesses all the knowledge or understanding of all the factors that affect the schedules in every aspect of the project Schedule review also prompts but-in to the schedule. But-in on the schedule by the people who will actually perform the work is critical to success. Participation in scheduling gives staff a stake in the outcome of the project. On the other hand, imposed schedules offer the opportunity for sabotage.

Once an initial cut at the schedule is ready, a team should perform a review. The work descriptions and the schedule should be reviewed by the people named to do the work (and who did not participate in the initial estimates). Interview the people and determine if the work descriptions are complete and accurate.

Determine if there is a common understanding of what has to be done. Get their independent estimates as to how long it will take to do their job. Where there are significant differences between the current schedule and the new estimates, determine the reasons and either redefine the work packages or review and iterate the schedule estimates.

SUMMARY

The challenges of constructing a software product have no easy solution. To put together a large software product takes time as well as resources. And, like any other large construction project, careful planning at the beginning of the project is thus the single most important factor that distinguishes success from failure. Software project managers take the overall responsibility of steering a project to success. The job responsibilities of a project manager range from invisible activities such as building up team morale to highly visible customer presentations. Most managers take responsibility for project proposal writing, project cost estimation, scheduling, project staffing, software process tailoring, project monitoring and control, software configuration management, risk management, interfacing with clients, managerial report writing and presentations, and so forth. These activities are numerous, varied and difficult to enumerate, but we can broadly classify them into project planning, and project monitoring and control activities. The project planning activity is undertaken before the development starts. The project monitoring and control activities are undertaken once the development has begun, the aim being to ensure that the development proceeds as per plan. The changes to the pan whenever required are made to continuously cope with the solution. A theoretical knowledge of different project management techniques is certainly necessary to become a successful project manager. However, effective software project management frequently calls for good qualitative judgement and decision making capabilities.

EXERCISES

1. What do you mean by project?
2. What are the attributes of project?
3. What are the various project constraints?

4. What do you mean by project management?
5. What are the responsibilities of software project managers?
6. Explain the various phases of software project management?
7. what are the various principles of software project management?
8. What are software metrics?
9. Explain the various categories of metrics?
10. What are the attributes of effective software metrics?
11. Explain the source lines of code (SLOC) metric in detail?
12. What are the advantages of disadvantages of SLOC?
13. Explain the function point metric in detail?
14. What are the components of Function Point Analysis?
15. What are the advantages of disadvantages of function point metric?
16. Explain the concept of feature point metric?
17. What do you mean by cost estimation?
18. Explain the models of cost estimation?
19. Explain the COCOMO cost estimation model?
20. Explain the COCOMO I cost estimation model?
21. Explain the advantages and disadvantages of COCOMO I.
22. Explain the COCOMO II cost estimation model?
23. Explain the advantages and disadvantages of COCOMO II.
24. What is staffing? Explain the staffing pattern of software projects?
25. Explain the concept of project scheduling?
26. What do you mean by estimating task duration?
27. Define priorities?
28. Define critical path?
29. What are document assumptions?
30. Explain the concept of identify risks and review results?

❑

Risk Analysis and Management

4

4.1 INTRODUCTION

Risk analysis and management are a series of steps that help a software team to understand and manage uncertainty. Many problems can plague a software project. A risk is a potential problem, i.e. it might happen or it might not. But, regardless of the outcome, it's a really good idea to identify it, assess its probability of occurrence, estimate its impact, and establish a contingency plan should the problem actually occur.

4.2 RISK

A risk is the possibility that an undesirable event (called the risk event) could happen. Risks involve both uncertainty (events that are guaranteed to happen are not risks) and loss (events that don't negatively affect the project are not risks). Proactive risk management is the process of trying to minimize the possible bad effects of risk events happening.

There is disagreement about what risks should be managed. Some experts suggest that only risks that are unique to the current project should be considered in risk analysis and management. Their view is that the management of risks common to most projects should be incorporated into the software process.

4.3 RISK MANAGEMENT

Risk management is the area that tries to ensure that the impact of risks on cost, quality, and schedule is minimal. It is a scientific process based on the application of game theory, decision theory, probability theory, and utility theory. The Software Engineering Institute (SEI) classifies the risk hierarchy as shown in Figure 4.1.

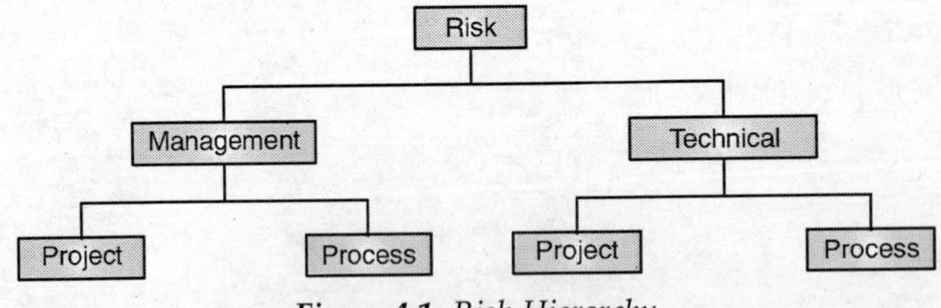

Figure 4.1: Risk Hierarchy

Risk scenarios may emerge out of management challenges and technical challenges in achieving specific goals and objectives.

Risk management must be performed regularly throughout the achievement life-cycle. Risks are dynamic, as they change over time. Risk management should not be regarded as an activity integral to the main process of achieving specific goals and objectives. Risk and its management should not be treated as an activity outside the main process of achievement. Risk is managed best when risk management is implemented as a mainstream function in the software-development and goal-achievement processes.

Risk management plays an important role in ensuring that the software product is error-free. Firstly, risk management takes care that the risk is avoided, and if it is not avoidable, then the risk is detected, controlled, and finally recovered.

4.4 TYPES OF RISKS

There are three types of risks, which are discussed as follows:

1. ***Product Risks.*** *Project risks* threaten the project plan. That is, if project risks become real, it is likely that project schedule will slip and that costs will increase. Project risks identify potential budgetary, schedule, personnel (staffing and organization), resource, customer, and requirements problems and their impact on a software project.
2. ***Business Risks.*** Business risks are risks that affect the organization developing or procuring the software. For example, technology changes and product competition. The top five business risks are:
   - Building an excellent product or system that no one really wants (market risks).
   - Building a product that no longer fits into the overall business strategy for the company (strategic risk).
   - Building a product that the sales force doesn't understand how to sell.
   - Losing the support of senior management due to a change in focus or a change in people (management risk).
   - Losing budgetary or personnel commitment (budget risks).
3. ***Project Risks.*** *Business risks* threaten the viability of the software to be built. Business risks often jeopardize the project or the product. Candidates for the top five business risks are (1) building an excellent product or system that no one really wants (market risk), (2) building a product that no longer fits into the overall business strategy for the company (strategic risk), (3) building a product that the sales force doesn't understand how to sell, (4) losing the support of senior management due to a change in focus or a change in people (management risk), and (5) losing budgetary or personnel commitment (budget risks). It is extremely important to note that simple categorization won't always work. Some risks are simply unpredictable in advance.

4.5 CATEGORIES OF RISK MANAGEMENT

Risk management is particularly important for software projects because of the inherent uncertainties that most projects face. These stem from loosely defined requirements, requirements changes due to changes in customer needs, difficulties in estimating the time and resources required for software development, and differences in individual skills. The project manager needs to anticipate risks; understand the impact of these risks on the project, the product, and the business; and take steps to avoid these risks. He may also need to draw up contingency plans so that, if the risks do occur, one can take immediate recovery action.

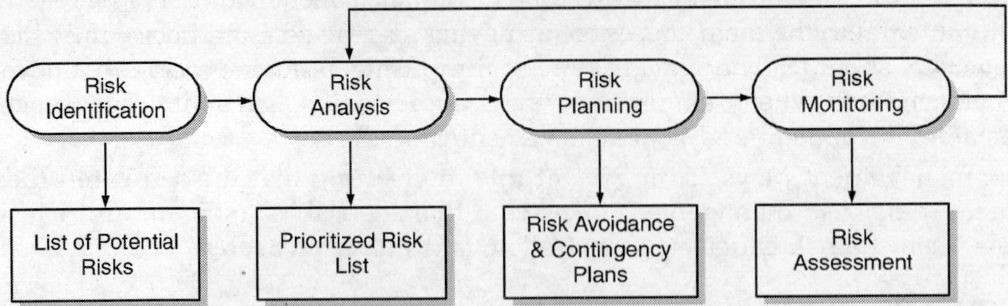

***Figure 4.2:** The Risk Management Process*

An outline of the process of risk management is illustrated in Figure 4.2. It involves several stages:

- *Risk identification:* The possible project, product, and business risks are identified during this stage.
- *Risk analysis:* The likelihood and consequences of these risks is assessed during this stage.
- *Risk planning:* Plans are made to address the risk, either by avoiding it or minimizing its effects on the project.
- *Risk monitoring:* The risk and plans for risk mitigation are regularly assessed and revised when something is learnt about the risk.

The project manager should document the outcomes of the risk management process in a risk management plan. This should include a discussion of the risks faced by the project, an analysis of these risks, and information on how he proposes to manage the risk if it seems likely to be a problem.

The risk management process is an iterative process that continues throughout the project. Once an initial risk management plan has been drawn, the situation needs to be monitored to detect emerging risks. As more information about the risks becomes available, the risks have to be analysed and one has to decide if the risk priority has changed. The plans for risk avoidance and contingency management may then have to be changed.

4.5.1 Risk Identification

Risk identification is the first stage of the risk management process. It is concerned with identifying the risks that could pose a major threat to the software engineering process, the software being developed, or the development organization. Risk identification may be a team process where a team get together to brainstorm possible risks. Alternatively, the project manager may simply use his or her experience to identify the most probable or critical risks.

As a starting point for risk identification, a checklist of different types of risk may be used. There are at least six types of risk that may be included in a risk checklist:

- *Technology risks:* These are the risks that derive from the software or hardware technologies that are used to develop the system.
- *People risks:* These are the risks that are associated with the people in the development team.
- *Organizational risks:* These are the risks that derive from the organizational environment where the software is being developed.
- *Tools risks:* These are the risks that derive from the software tools and other support software used to develop the system.
- *Requirements risks:* These are the risks that derive from changes to the customer requirements and the process of managing the requirements change.
- *Estimation risks:* These are the risks that derive from the management estimates of the resources required to build the system.

Risk type	Possible risks
Technology	The database used in the system cannot process as many transactions per second as expected. (1) Reusable software components contain defects that mean they cannot be reused as planned. (2)
People	It is impossible to recruit staff with the skills required. (3) Key staff are ill and unavailable at critical times. (4) Required training for staff is not available. (5)
Organizational	The organization is restructured so that different management are responsible for the project. (6) Organizational financial problems force reductions in the project budget. (7)
Tools	The code generated by software code generation tools is inefficient. (8) Software tools cannot work together in an integrated way. (9)
Requirements	Changes to requirements that require major design rework are proposed. (10) Customers fail to understand the impact of requirements changes. (11)
Estimation	The time required to develop the software is underestimated. (12) The rate of defect repair is underestimated. (13) The size of the software is underestimated. (14)

Figure 4.3: *Examples of different types of risks*

Figure 4.3 gives some examples of possible risks in each of these categories. When the risk identification process is finished, the project manager should have a long list of risks that could occur and which could affect the product, the process, and the business. He then needs to prune this list to a manageable size. If there are too many risks, it is practically impossible to keep track of all of them.

4.5.2 Risk Analysis

During the risk analysis process, the project manager has to consider each identified risk and make a judgment about the probability and seriousness of that risk. There is no easy way to do this. He has to rely on his own judgment and experience of previous projects and the problems that arose in them. It is not possible to make precise, numeric assessment of the probability and seriousness of each risk. Rather, he should assign the risk to one of a number of bands:

1. The probability of the risk might be assessed as very low (< 10%), low (10–25%), moderate (25–50%), high (50–75%), or very high (> 75%).
2. The effects of the risk might be assessed as catastrophic (threaten the survival of the project), serious (would cause major delays), tolerable (delays are within allowed contingency), or insignificant.

Risk	Probability	Effects
Organizational financial problems force reductions in the project budget (7).	Low	Catastrophic
It is impossible to recruit staff with the skills required for the project (3).	High	Catastrophic
Key staff are ill at critical times in the project (4).	Moderate	Serious
Faults in reusable software components have to be repaired before these components are reused (2).	Moderate	Serious
Changes to requirements that require major design rework are proposed (10).	Moderate	Serious
The organization is restructured so that different management are responsible for the project (6).	High	Serious
The database used in the system cannot process as many transaction per second as expected (1).	Moderate	Serious
The time required to develop the software is underestimated (12).	High	Serious
Software tools cannot be integrated (9).	High	Tolerable
Customers fail to understand the impact of requirements changes (11).	Moderate	Tolerable
Required training for staff is not available (5).	Moderate	Tolerable
The rate of defect repair is underestimated (13).	Moderate	Tolerable
The size of the software is underestimated (14).	High	Tolerable
Code generated by code generation tools is inefficient (8).	Moderate	Insignificant

Figure 4.4: *Risk Types and Examples*

The results of this analysis process should then be tabled using a table ordered according to the seriousness of the risk. Figure 4.4 illustrates this for the risks that have been identified in Figure 4.3. Obviously, the assessment of probability and seriousness is arbitrary here. To make this assessment, the detailed information is needed about the project, the process, the development team, and the organization.

Of course, both the probability and the assessment of the effects of a risk may change as more information about the risk becomes available and as risk management plans are implemented. Therefore, this table should be updated during each iteration of the risk process.

Once the risks have been analysed and ranked, it should be assessed that which of these risks are most significant. This judgment must depend on a combination of the probability of the risk arising and the effects of that risk. In general, catastrophic risks should always be considered, as should all serious risks that have more than a moderate probability of occurrence.

Boehm recommends identifying and monitoring the top 10 risks, but this figure should be thought of as rather arbitrary. The right number of risks to monitor must depend on the project. It might be 5 or it might be 15. However, the number of risks chosen for monitoring should be manageable. A very large number of risks would simply require too much information to be collected. From the risks identified in Figure 4.4, it is appropriate to consider the 8 risks that have catastrophic or serious consequences (Figure 4.5).

Risk	Strategy
Organizational financial problems	Prepare a briefing document for senior management showing how the project is making a very important contribution to the goals of the business and presenting reasons why cuts to the project budget would not be cost-effective.
Recruitment problems	Alert customer to potential difficulties and the possibility of delays; investigate buying-in components.
Staff illness	Reorganize team so that there is more overlap of work and people therefore understand each other's jobs.
Defective components	Replace potentially defective components with bought-in components of known reliability.
Requirements changes	Derive traceability information to assess requirements change impact; maximize information hiding in the design.
Organizational restructuring	Prepare a briefing document for senior management showing how the project is making a very important contribution to the goals of the business.
Database performance	Investigate the possibility of buying a higher-performance database.
Underestimated development time	Investigate buying-in components; investigate use of a program generator.

Figure 4.5: *Strategies to help manage risks*

4.5.3 Risk Planning

The risk planning process considers each of the key risks that have been identified, and develops strategies to manage these risks. For each of the risks, the project manager has to think of actions that he might take to minimize the disruption to the project if the problem identified in the risk occurs. He also should think about information that he might need to collect while monitoring the project so that problems can be anticipated.

Again, there is no simple process that can be followed for contingency planning. It relies on the judgment and experience of the project manager.

Figure 4.5 shows possible risk management strategies that have been identified for the key risks (i.e., those that are serious or intolerable) shown in Figure 4.4.

These strategies fall into three categories:

1. *Avoidance strategies:* Following these strategies means that the probability that the risk will arise will be reduced. An example of a risk avoidance strategy is the strategy for dealing with defective components shown in Figure 4.5.
2. *Minimization strategies:* Following these strategies means that the impact of the risk will be reduced. An example of a risk minimization strategy is the strategy for staff illness shown in Figure 4.5.
3. *Contingency plans:* Following these strategies means that you are prepared for the worst and have a strategy in place to deal with it. An example of a contingency strategy is the strategy for organizational financial problems that has been shown in Figure 4.5.

A clear analogy can be seen here with the strategies used in critical systems to ensure reliability, security, and safety, where one must avoid, tolerate, or recover from failures. Obviously, it is best to use a strategy that avoids the risk. If this is not possible, a strategy that reduces the chances that the risk will have serious effects needs to be used. Finally, the strategies must be in place to cope with the risk if it arises. These should reduce the overall impact of a risk on the project or product.

4.5.4 Risk Monitoring

Risk monitoring is the process of checking that the assumptions about the product, process, and business risks have not changed. The project manager should regularly assess each of the identified risks to decide whether or not that risk is becoming more or less probable. He should also think about whether or not the effects of the risk have changed. To do this, he has to look at other factors, such as the number of requirements change requests, which gives clues about the risk probability and its effects. These factors are obviously dependent on the types of risk. Figure 4.6 gives some examples of factors that may be helpful in assessing these risk types. The risks must be monitored regularly at all stages in a project. At every management review, each of the key risks should be considered and discussed separately. It should be decided if the risk is more or less likely to arise and if the seriousness and consequences of the risk have changed.

Risk	Potential indicators
Technology	Late delivery of hardware or support software; many reported technology problems.
People	Poor staff morale; poor relationships amongst team members; high staff turnover.
Organizational	Organizational gossip; lack of action by senior management.
Tools	Reluctance by team members to use tools; complaints about CASE tools; demands for higher-powered workstations.
Requirements	Many requirements change requests; customer complaints.
Estimation	Failure to meet agreed schedule; failure to dear reported defects.

Figure 4.6: *Risk Indicators*

4.6 SOURCES OF RISKS

There are two major sources of risk, which are as follows:

1. ***Generic Risks.*** Generic risks are the risks common to all software projects. For example, requirement misunderstanding, allowing insufficient time for testing, losing key personnel, etc.
2. ***Project-Specific Risks.*** A vendor may be promising to deliver particular software by a particular date, but is unable to do it.

4.7 SAFETY RISKS AND HAZARDS

Risk is not limited to the software project itself. Risks can occur after the software has been successfully developed and delivered to the customer. These risks are typically associated with the consequences of software failure in the field.

In the early days of computing, there was reluctance to use computers (and software) to control safety critical processes such as nuclear reactors, aircraft flight control, weapons systems, and large-scale industrial processes. Although the probability of failure of a well-engineered system was small, an undetected fault in a computer-based control or monitoring system could result in enormous economic damage or, worse, significant human injury or loss of life. But the cost and functional benefits of computer-based control and monitoring far outweigh the risk. Today, computer hardware and software are used regularly to control safety critical systems.

When software is used as part of a control system, complexity can increase by an order of magnitude or more. Subtle design faults induced by human error—something that can be uncovered and eliminated in hardware-based conventional control—become much more difficult to uncover when software is used.

Software safety and *hazard analysis* are software quality assurance activities that focus on the identification and assessment of potential hazards that may affect software negatively and cause an entire system to fail. If hazards can be identified early in the software engineering process, software design features can be specified that will either eliminate or control potential hazards.

SUMMARY

Risk analysis and management are a series of steps that help a software team to understand and manage uncertainty. Many problems can plague a software project. A risk is a potential problem, i.e. it might happen or it might not. But, regardless of the outcome, it's a really good idea to identify it, assess its probability of occurrence, estimate its impact, and establish a contingency plan should the problem actually occur. Risk management is the area that tries to ensure that the impact of risks on cost, quality, and schedule is minimal. It is a scientific process based on the application of game theory, decision theory, probability theory, and utility theory. Risk management must be performed regularly throughout the achievement life-cycle. Risks are dynamic, as they change over time. Risk management should not be regarded as an activity integral to the main process of achieving specific goals and objectives. Risk and its management should not be treated as an activity outside the main process of achievement. Risk management plays an important role in ensuring that the software product is error-free. Firstly, risk management takes care that the risk is avoided, and if it is not avoidable, then the risk is detected, controlled, and finally recovered.

EXERCISES

1. What is risk?
2. Explain the concept of risk management?
3. What are the three types of risks?
4. Explain the different categories of risk management?
5. What do you mean by risk identification?
6. Explain the risk analysis process?
7. What do you mean by risk planning?
8. Explain the concept of risk monitoring?
9. What are two major sources of risk?
10. Explain the concept of safety risks and hazards?

❑

Software Configuration Management

5

5.1 INTRODUCTION

Software engineers usually find coding to be the most satisfying aspect of their job. This is easy to understand because programming is a challenging, creative activity requiring extensive technical skills. It can mean getting to "play" with state-of-the-art tools, and it provides almost instant gratification in the form of immediate feedback. Programming is the development task that most readily comes to mind when the profession of software engineering is mentioned.

That said, seasoned engineers and project managers realize that programmers are part of a larger team. All of the integral tasks, such as quality assurance and verification and validation, are behind-the-scenes activities necessary to turn standalone software into a useful and usable commodity. Software configuration management (SCM) falls into this category—it can't achieve star status, like the latest "killer app," but it is essential to project success. The smart software project manager highly values the individuals and tools that provide this service.

This section will answer the following questions about software configuration management.

Change is inevitable when computer software is built. And change increases the level of confusion among software engineers who are working on a project. Confusion arises when changes are not analyzed before they are made, recorded before they are implemented, reported to those with a need to know, or controlled in a manner that will improve quality and reduce error. Babich discusses this when he states:

The art of coordinating software development to minimize confusion is called *configuration management*. Configuration management is the art of identifying, organizing, and controlling modifications to the software being built by a programming team. The goal is to maximize productivity by minimizing mistakes.

Software configuration management (SCM) is an umbrella activity that is applied throughout the software process. Because change can occur at any time, SCM activities are developed to (1) identify change, (2) control change, (3) ensure that change is being properly implemented, and (4) report changes to others who may have an interest.

It is important to make a clear distinction between software support and software configuration management. Support is a set of software engineering activities that occur after software has been delivered to the customer and put into operation. Software configuration management is a set of tracking and control activities that begin when a software engineering project begins and terminate only when the software is taken out of operation.

A primary goal of software engineering is to improve the ease with which changes can be accommodated and reduce the amount of effort expended when changes must be made. In this chapter, we discuss the specific activities that enable us to manage change.

5.2 SOFTWARE CONFIGURATION MANAGEMENT

Software configuration management (SCM) is the organization of the components of a software system so that they fit together in a working order, never out of synch with each other. Those who have studied the best way to manage the configuration of software parts have more elegant responses.

Roger Pressman says that SCM is a "set of activities designed to control change by identifying the work products that are likely to change, establishing relationships among them, defining mechanisms for managing different versions of these work products, controlling the changes imposed, and auditing and reporting on the changes made."

We think that Pressman's description is a better description because we often view SCM as meaning software change management.

Wayne Babich describes SCM as "the art of identifying, organizing, and controlling modifications to the software being built by a programming team. It maximizes productivity by minimizing mistakes."

The Software Engineering Institute says that it is necessary to establish and maintain the integrity of the products of the software project throughout the software life cycle. Activities necessary to accomplish this include identifying configuration items/units, systematically controlling changes, and maintaining the integrity and the traceability of the configuration throughout the software life cycle. Military standards view configuration as the functional and/or physical characteristics of hardware/software as set forth in technical documentation and archives in a product. In identifying the items that need to be configured, we must remember that all project artifacts are candidates—documents, graphical models, prototypes, code, and any internal or external deliverable that can undergo change. In SW PM terminology, a configuration item might be a proposal/estimate or bid, project plan, risk management plan, quality assurance plan, CM plan itself, test plan, system requirements specification, system design document, review metric, code, test result, tool (editors, compilers, CASE), and so on. There are basic objects and aggregate objects to be configured. The number of relationships among them reflects the complexity of the configuration task.

The output of the software process is information that may be divided into three broad categories: (1) computer programs (both source level and executable forms); (2) documents that describe the computer programs (targeted at both technical practitioners and users), and (3) data (contained within the program or external to it). The items that comprise all information produced as part of the software process are collectively called a *software configuration.*

As the software process progresses, the number of *software configuration items* (SCIs) grows rapidly. A *System Specification* spawns a *Software Project Plan* and *Software Requirements*

Specification (as well as hardware related documents). These in turn spawn other documents to create a hierarchy of information. If each SCI simply spawned other SCIs, little confusion would result. Unfortunately, another variable enters the process—*change*. Change may occur at any time, for any reason. In fact, the First Law of System Engineering [BER80] states: "No matter where you are in the system life cycle, the system will change, and the desire to change it will persist throughout the life cycle."

What is the origin of these changes? The answer to this question is as varied as the changes themselves. However, there are four fundamental sources of change:

- New business or market conditions dictate changes in product requirements or business rules.
- New customer needs demand modification of data produced by information systems, functionality delivered by products, or services delivered by a computer-based system.
- Reorganization or business growth/downsizing causes changes in project priorities or software engineering team structure.
- Budgetary or scheduling constraints cause a redefinition of the system or product.

Software configuration management is a set of activities that have been developed to manage change throughout the life cycle of computer software. SCM can be viewed as a software quality assurance activity that is applied throughout the software process. In the sections that follow, we examine major SCM tasks and important concepts that help us to manage change.

Virtually everyone on a software project is affected by SCM. From the framers of the project plan to the final tester, we rely on it to tell us how to find the object with the latest changes. During development, when iterations are informal and frequent, little needs to be known about a change except what it is, who did it, and where it is. In deployment and baselining, changes must be prioritized, and the impact of a change upon all customers must be considered. A change control board (CCB) is the governing body for modifications after implementation.

5.3 SCM PRINCIPLES

SCM can be viewed as a pyramid, as shown in Figure 5.1. Let's explore each of the six layers, starting at the bottom and working to the top. Then we'll look at two other faces of the pyramid—the training plan and the transition plan.

5.3.1 Understanding of SCM

An understanding of SCM is critical to the organization attempting to institute any system of product control. Understanding through training is a key initial goal, as shown in the pyramid. Executives and management must understand both the benefits and the cost of SCM to provide the needed support in its implementation. Software

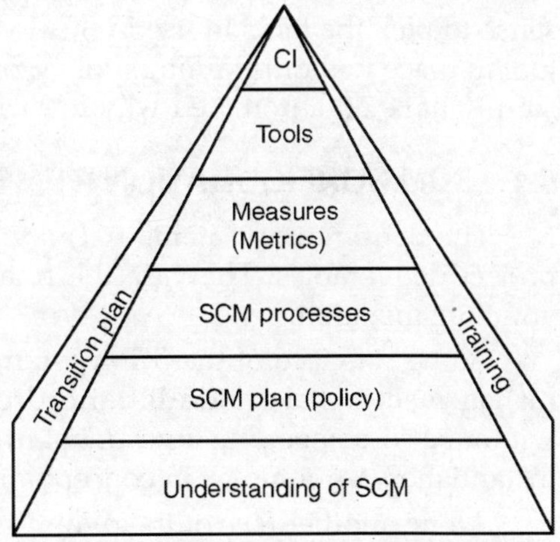

Figure 5.1: *Software Configuration Management Pyramid*

developers must understand the basics of SCM because they are required to use the tool in building their software products. Without a total understanding, a partial implementation of SCM with workarounds and back doors will result in disaster for an SCM system.

5.3.2 SCM Plans and Policies

Development of an SCM policy for an organization and the subsequent plans for each product developed is crucial to successful SCM implementation. Putting SCM into an organization is a project like any other, requiring resources of time and money. There will be specific deliverables and a timeline against which to perform. The policy for the organization lays out in a clear, concise fashion the expectations that the organizational leadership has for its system. It must lay out the anticipated benefits and the method to measure the performance to those benefits.

5.3.3 SCM Processes

The specific processes of SCM are documented for all users to recognize. Not all SCM processes need to be used within an organization or on a product. Yet, it is important to have available, in "plain sight," those processes that are used specifically in your organization. This also maps those processes to how they are implemented.

5.3.4 Metrics

The measures used to show conformance to policy and product plans are important details. These measures show where the organization is along the path to reaping the benefits of SCM.

5.3.5 Tools for SCM

The tools used to implement SCM are the next-to-last item on the pyramid. For too many managers, this is often the first instead of the fifth stem in SCM—many organizations and projects simply buy a tool, plop it in place, and expect magic. Actually, it makes little sense to pick the tools to use in SCM without having done all the previous work. Putting a tool in place without training, policy, or metrics is an exercise in automating chaos. You will simply have an automated way to turn out the wrong product faster.

5.4 SCM CONFIGURATION ITEMS

The configuration items (CI) are those "things" that represent internal and external project deliverables. They are the final result of all the work done to implement SCM in your organization.

Along one face of the SCM pyramid is the training plan and its execution. A common management mistake is to arbitrarily drop an SCM requirement on a development organization without a corresponding investment in training. The process of SCM and the tools used in its instantiation are complex in concept and execution, making training a true requirement.

Along another face of the pyramid, we indicate the transition plan to get to an effective SCM implementation. The introduction of configuration management is a project in and of itself, requiring a project plan within the context of the organization. Just like planning for development, plans for improving product quality and reducing development time must be followed to reap the benefits.

SCM is the identification scheme for the software components of a system. It controls changes to the configuration and maintains integrity and traceability of the configuration.

Software in this context refers to all deliverables: documentation, test scripts, test data files, code, and so on. Change control is the management of change as one part of the SCM process.

Version control is the management of the product versions generated as part of the SCM process. Release control is the transformation of configuration items into a deliverable product. A configuration item (CI) is a standalone part of the product development that is combined with other CIs into a release. Examples of software CIs include design documents, manuals and tutorials, measurement data, program trouble reports, requirements, source code, and test cases.

5.4.1 SCM Is An Sei Cmm Level 2 Key Process Area

(SEI) Capability Maturity Model (CMM) levels of maturity. At Level 2 of CMM, an organization moves beyond just getting the job done and into an environment where a software project management process is in place, the organization sets expectations via policies, and projects have disciplined phases and milestones. This level is described as the repeatable level, built upon key process areas of requirements management, software project planning, software project tracking and oversight, software subcontract management, software quality assurance, and software configuration management. The goals for SCM at maturity Level 2 are:

- Software configuration management activities are planned.
- Selected software work products are identified, controlled, and available.
- Changes to identified software work products are controlled.
- Affected groups and individuals are informed of the status and content of software baselines.

Questions that assessors might ask include:

- Is a mechanism used for controlling changes to the software requirements?
- Is a mechanism used for controlling changes to the software design?
- Is a mechanism used for controlling changes to the code?
- Is a mechanism used for configuration management of the software tools used in the development process?

5.5 THE FOUR BASIC REQUIREMENTS FOR AN SCM SYSTEM

Identification, control, audit, and status accounting are the four basic requirements for a software configuration management system. These requirements must be satisfied regardless of the amount of automation within the SCM process. All four may be satisfied by an SCM tool, a tool set, or a combination of automated and manual procedures.

- **Identification:** Each software part is labeled so that it can be identified. Furthermore, there will be different versions of the software parts as they evolve over time, so a version or revision number will be associated with the part. The key is to be able to identify any and all artifacts that compose a released configuration item. Think of this as a bill of materials for all the components in your automobile. When the manufacturer realizes that there has been a problem with parking brakes purchased from a subcontractor, it needs to know all the automobile models using that version of the parking brake. It is the same with software. If we are building a multimedia system that has audio MPEG3 drivers for Windows 98, Windows 2000, Windows CE, Linux, and FreeBSD operating systems, how do we find out which releases are impacted when we find an error in the Linux product? You must go back to your SCM system to identify all the common components in all operating system releases that are impacted.

- **Control:** In the context of configuration management, "control" means that proposed changes to a CI are reviewed and, if approved, incorporated into the software configuration. The goal is to make informed decisions and to acknowledge the repercussions associated with a change to the system. These changes may impact budgets, schedules, and associated changes to other components. If a problem is reported in a released product, software engineers must act quickly to evaluate repercussions—a "fix" for one client's version of the product may be dangerous to another. The control inherent in an SCM system shows each version in which the flawed component appears.
- **Auditing:** Auditing an SCM system means that approved requested changes have indeed been implemented. The audits allow managers to determine whether software evolution is proceeding both logically and in conformance with requirements for the software. The SCM system should document changes, versions, and release information for all components of each configuration item. When such documentation is in place, auditing becomes a straightforward analysis task.
- **Status accounting:** Reports and documentation produced by the status accounting function are the auditable entries. All approved parts of a software configuration must be accounted for, and the software parts list must reflect the transition from part CI_n to CI_{n+1}. This accounting provides the historic information to determine both what happened and when on the software project. Status accounting enables the auditing requirement of the SCM. As a project manager, the status accounting holds a wealth of information on the amount of effort required throughout the life cycle of the product in its development and maintenance. This is critical to the software project manager in making estimates for new systems based on historic information. The SCM can be used as one of the key components of the project managers' metrics system.

5.6 PLANNING AND ORGANIZING FOR SCM

Software configuration management is an important element of software quality assurance. Its primary responsibility is the control of change. However, SCM is also responsible for the identification of individual SCIs and various versions of the software, the auditing of the software configuration to ensure that it has been properly developed, and the reporting of all changes applied to the configuration.

Any discussion of SCM introduces a set of complex questions:

- How does an organization identify and manage the many existing versions of a program (and its documentation) in a manner that will enable change to be accommodated efficiently?

- How an organization control changes does before and after software is released to a customer?
- Who has responsibility for approving and ranking changes?
- How can we ensure that changes have been made properly?
- What mechanism is used to appraise others of changes that are made?

When planning for SCM in your product development organization, you must first understand the classes of potential problems that can exist. Once the classes are understood, the inherent problems that are causing configuration management issues may be easily identified.

5.6.1 Potential SCM Problem Classes

Following are the potential SCM problem classes:

1. **Multiple developer syndrome:** When you have a project that requires more than one developer, there is the problem with multiple people working on one product base. This could be a test plan, requirements specification, or code. Effort is wasted when two or more people work on the same file and then save it. Without SCM control, the last person to save the file has those changes saved. All the other changes are lost. The simplistic method of locking a file while one person reads it prevents others from simultaneously working on the file.
2. **Multiple releases**: Enhancements to the base product should result in additional releases of the product containing the latest changes. Once the second release is available, some users are on an earlier release. Having an SCM makes managing those releases possible. When bugs are reported, changes must be made across all impacted releases. As new features become available in the product, they must be made available to all current users, no matter what the release date.
3. **Product family**: As products are built that offer the same capabilities across a heterogeneous set of hardware platforms, both the common and the platform-specific software bases must be managed. If a product operates on four versions of Windows, three versions of UNIX, Red Hat Linux, and FreeBSD the user manual may be significantly the same. But there is a different installation process for all nine platforms. Without SCM, nine individual manuals must be written and maintained. With SCM, one documentation configuration item with nine versions will suffice, with the differences being only the installation procedure.
4. **Requirements change**: The first law of systems engineering is that no matter where we are in the system life cycle, the system/software will change, and the desire to change it will persist throughout the life cycle. Dealing with this change represents a major management challenge. Having an SCM in place will ease the management of these changes to the requirements of the products that will occur. An SCM allows the easy identification of feature sets that group the requirements satisfied by a release or version of the product. These feature sets are tracked through development to delivery.
5. **Schedule change**: As requirements change, so must the schedule. Mapping the feature sets for release to the schedule allows project managers to more accurately estimate the effort required for generating that next release. Having the SCM in place allows

the project manager to look at historic effort levels in getting out releases. This is an enormous aid in estimating the "what if" scenarios that result from taking on new product users or providing customized solutions to other clients.

6. **Software changes**: No product developer has the luxury to write code once and forget about it. Along with requirements and schedules, the software being developed changes in response to those other changes. Software is not static. That is its inherent power. It can be changed, so it will be changed. SCM systems track those changes so that, if the wrong change is made, a previous working version is available. This capability alone has saved enormous amounts of time as developers have tried out specific solutions that did not work in the product environment and were able to rapidly back up to a working version.
7. **Staff changes**: In the best of organizations, people get promoted, take other jobs, and leave. When that happens in the midst of a development project, not just the technology knowledge goes out the door. The long-learned knowledge of how things are done is also gone. So when a replacement person is brought on board, they may know the technology, but without a documented SCM process, they will have no real idea how to do product development. SCM provides the framework and knowledge base of what has gone on before in the project. A new staff member has one place to go to understand the "how" of the organization's development process and the "what" of the project to date.
8. **System/user documentation change**: No product developer has the luxury to produce in a technology or tool vacuum. All product developers use hardware microcode, operating systems, tools, and documentation that are not under their control. When a major operating system change occurs (e.g., the next "best" release of Windows), an SCM will allow tracing all the CIs, components, and subcomponents that are impacted by that change. The change is isolated, and the amount of effort required to respond to the change can be estimated. This provides a responsible schedule for an upgrade based on situations beyond the organization's control.

5.7 SCM STAFFING

On any given project, a few engineers or developers specialize in and become your SCM experts. While they are the gurus, everyone on your project will be a user of the product that they select, develop, and maintain. It is better to have a few highly experienced people than a large number of inexperienced people. These experienced few must be able to see congruence between software products and perceive what is missing from a software product.

We can group the characteristics and abilities needed by the four SCM functions: identification, control, auditing, and status accounting.

- **Identification**
  - Ability to see partitions
  - Ability to see relationships
  - Some technical ability
  - System engineering orientation
  - Programming

- **Control**
  - Ability to evaluate benefits versus cost
  - System viewpoint (balance of technical/managerial, user/buyer/seller)
  - An appreciation of what is involved in engineering a software change
- **Auditing**
  - Extreme attention to detail
  - Ability to see congruence
  - Ability to perceive what is missing
  - Extensive experience with technical aspects of system engineering or software engineering
- **Status Accounting**
  - Ability to take notes and record data
  - Ability to organize data
  - Some technical familiarity
  - System engineering orientation
  - Programming

Once the staffing of the SCM function is complete and the overall organization's SCM policy is established, the configuration control board (CCB) is identified. The CCB is the heart of the control function. It infuses sustained visibility into the process of change throughout the system life cycle and traceability into the process of change. The membership in the CCB is not limited to the developers or product line management. All stakeholders in the product must be represented. This includes the end-user usually represented by marketing, subcontractors used in the product development, product development funders, and the product developers. The CCB is the final decision maker as to what bug fixes, enhancements, and feature sets get included in the next product release.

The CCB has periodic meetings, with the results documented. These meetings can be done in a rapid fashion, and doing them online or via email is an adequate way to gain consensus and come to a decision. Important to status accounting is the documentation of CCB meeting minutes. The basic purpose of the minutes is to provide the CCB decision makers with the information needed to make intelligent, informed decisions. The amount of detail varies with the meeting frequency and technical content.

5.8 SCM TOOLS

The minimum features for SCM tools are closely related to the task of handling the different product deliverables produced within the project software engineering process. Tool requirements and selection criteria are based on a series of features that provide a consistent look and feel with state-of-the-art software development environments. An SCM tool must have multiuser support, an intuitive graphical user interface, conformity to the organization's development environment, scalability, flexibility in integrating other software development tools, ease of setup, modifiable models, process management, extensive support for the development phase, and management of non-development objects.

Basic selection criteria include the following:

- **Multiuser support:** Tools are to be used concurrently by several users. They have to store all acquired information in a central, shared repository, and the SCM tool has to allow controlled parallel work on the different project documents.
- **Intuitive GUI:** Because the tools will be used throughout the project and not only by developers, an intuitive, easy-to-use graphical user interface is considered very important.
- **Conformity to the organization's development environment:** The organization must define up front the hardware and software development platforms used. For example, the project may work on a heterogeneous network of Unix-based workstations (mainly Sun Sparc stations) and PCs. The workstations may be used for some part of the development and as a file server and communication server. The PCs may be using MS Windows 2000 NT. PCs and workstations may be interconnected using the NFS protocol (especially Sun PC-NFSpro on the PCs). The tool has to be able to store its shared repositories on a workstation and has to allow PC clients as well as workstation clients supporting the operating systems and protocols.
- **Scalability:** The tool should work equally well for smaller projects as for larger ones.
- **Flexibility in integrating other software development tools:** The tool must allow the integration of all the other development tools to provide a highly homogeneous environment. Especially the tools for design, implementation, and testing will have to co-operate on the common SCM repository.
- **Ease of setup:** The SCM tool should allow an easy installation and setup, and should be able to run nearly "out of the box." It should contain predefined, immediately usable models describing the types of items, the life cycle, and the roles of the different users. The importance of existing projects and their directory structures should be made as easy as possible.
- **Modifiable models:** Though a working set of models should be predefined, each of these should be modifiable and extensible. This is especially important because project managers and developers want to adapt these models to the software development process as defined for the company. Role models must be adapted to the roles assigned to the different employees on the project. Object-type models must be extensible to reflect different types of objects used in the environment and especially with respect to non-development objects.
- **Process management:** Process management comprises efficient support of object life cycles and object promotion, together with a flexible and extensible approach to life cycle models. Based on a concept of object types, it should be possible to attach different life cycles to different types of objects.
- **Extensive support for the development phase:** During development when checkout and update of objects is frequent, the tool should aid a developer in determining the set of objects that need an update or renewed check-in. Although this requirement seems to be trivial at first, the latest version of the tool you plan to use must be evaluated with emphasis on the environment prior to the first build. These do a good job in change management once the first release has been produced.

- **Management of non-development objects:** SCM tools must manage all artifacts of the project, not just code. These will mainly be documents and their versions and releases. The tool must be able to support that.
- **Permission management:** Everyone should not have access to make changes to different pieces of the software. In many situations, check-in and checkout only will not prevent integration from being broken by multiple people modifying code for their own designs and interfaces.

Many configuration management tools in the market promise to fulfill more or less all of the requirements. The keys to any tool selection are to know your project's tool requirements, to understand how tools relate to the project's success factors, and to do a current market search for tools. The following is an example of using that tool selection method for an SCM tool. This is simply an example, and it must be updated with individual key project success factors, tool requirements, and the tools available in the market based on the project's schedule requirements.

5.8.1 Benefits of SCM Process and Tools

SCM benefits an organization in four areas: control, management, cost savings, and quality (Figure 5.2). These four benefits are mapped to an organization's overall goals and objectives when the decisions are made to bring a SCM tool in-house. The features of a SCM tool further support these benefits.

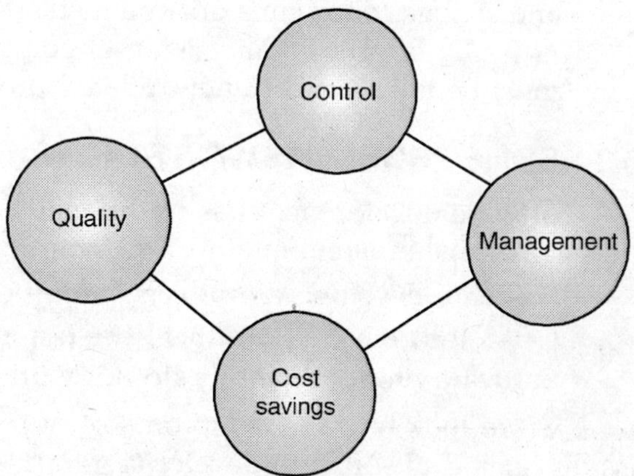

***Figure 5.2:** SCM Benefits the Organization in Four Major Ways*

1. **Control:** Control in SCM provides the ability to review, approve, and incorporate changes into a configuration item. There must be one controlling SCM tool so that there is only one set of training, license management, installation, and user procedures. All project personnel use the tool. Inherent in the tool is a standardized, measurable process for change. Integrity maintenance of CIs is enforced throughout the product life cycle. The tool permits only controlled change to the baseline CIs, and all changes are tracked.
2. **Management:** Management in SCM is concerned with the automation of identifying and guiding configuration items through their life cycle to final assembly as part of product and delivery. Identification of CIs through a unique naming convention allows version, release, update, and full change tracking. Baselining of CIs with the ability to produce product deltas from the baseline satisfies requirement and schedule changes along with product family support. Rapid reviews and audits of CIs are accomplished through the analysis of historic information collected. Project status reporting is accomplished in a clear and consistent format based on SCM collected information on all CIs under configuration management.

3. **Cost Savings:** Cost savings are realized across the entire product development life cycle with SCM. Maintaining product integrity through defined, tracked, and audited CIs provides a managed bill of materials for the product released to customers. Cost savings scale with SCM use and application across applications. This scaling is dependent on the depth of control needed for each application product release tree. Deep combinations for product families can be analyzed for risk exposure and cost savings directly impacted by the amount of configuration management applied. Side effects are reduced through controlled change by understanding the impact on all versions and releases. Accurate and repeatable release control is produced in a repeatable fashion over entire product families for all customers and users.
4. **Quality:** Software development is a people-intensive activity, and quality must be considered at every person-to-tool interface. Ensuring a high-quality work environment must address the process of building software products in an automated fashion. This must include tracking CIs to the tools that produced them and the clients that ultimately receive the product. Measuring the end product to ensure high quality is done through tracking the changes made to a product throughout its life cycle. Repeatable management and change control in a documented and measured fashion allows accurate estimation of future efforts. Quality is an ongoing process. The lessons learned in one product must be transferred to new, related products and entire product families.

5.9 SOME PROBLEMS WITH SOFTWARE

Software development has traditionally suffered from producing end products with a definite lack of inherent quality. The symptoms of this quality lack are listed here:

- Software development projects are often delivered late and over budget.
- Often the delivered product does not meet customer requirements and is never used.
- Software products simply do not work right.

As we look into the symptoms of our software development malaise, five principal issues related to software development arise.

- **Lack of Visibility:** Software is conceptual in nature. Unlike a bridge, a building, or another physical structure, it is not easy to look at software and assess how close it is to completion. Without strong project management, "software is 90% complete 90% of the time." Through the adoption of SCM policy and the definition of the configuration management model of the software under development, all CIs, components, and subcomponents are immediately visible for versions, releases, and product families.
- **Lack of Control:** Because software is inherently intangible, it is also more difficult to control. Without an accurate assessment of progress, schedules slip and budgets are overrun. It is hard to assess what has been accomplished and what remains to be done. SCM provides the mechanism for controlling the project through measuring the amount of effort compared to the project management plan and estimating the future effort based on past work.
- **Lack of Traceability:** A lack of linkage between project events contributes to project failures. The main benefit of SCM is providing the traceability among versions, releases, and product families. The value of this traceability is enormous when a problem arises

in one release or product family that impacts other client releases and products. Making one change and promoting that through the entire product software base is an incredible cost savings in time, money, and client good will. A lack of linkage between project events contributes to project failures where solving one problem either exacerbates a problem in another area or fails to fix the same problem elsewhere. A traceability thread allows management to examine the chain of events that caused a project to encounter difficulty as an integral process within the auditing capability of SCM. A project becomes a year late one day at a time unless the effort reported on the schedule maps to the actual work being done and traced within the software configuration management system.

- **Lack of Monitoring:** Without traceability and visibility, monitoring of software development projects becomes extremely difficult. Management cannot make informed decisions, and thus schedules slip further and costs continue to exceed budget. There is no way to monitor a project when the project manager has no tools to look into the actual product development within the project. SCM provides the tools that open up the process to external monitoring. With SCM in place and a policy of traceability and visibility accepted, monitoring of software development projects becomes a simple part of the overall project management task. Management makes informed decisions avoiding schedule slips and budget excesses through the monitoring available with SCM tools and the integral workings of the CCB.
- **Uncontrolled Change:** Software is very malleable; it is idea-stuff, and customers constantly have new ideas for it. People would rarely ask a bridge constructor to make the kinds of changes mid project that software customers tend to request. The impact of such changes can be just as great. All SCM tools, along with the CCB, support a mechanism for appropriate change control.

SUMMARY

Software configuration management is an umbrella activity that is applied throughout the software process. SCM identifies controls, audits, and reports modifications that invariably occur while software is being developed and after it has been released to a customer. All information produced as part of software engineering becomes part of a software configuration. The configuration is organized in a manner that enables orderly control of change.

The software configuration is composed of a set of interrelated objects, also called software configuration items that are produced as a result of some software engineering activity. In addition to documents, programs, and data, the development environment that is used to create software can also be placed under configuration control.

Once a configuration object has been developed and reviewed, it becomes a baseline. Changes to a baselined object result in the creation of a new version of that object. The evolution of a program can be tracked by examining the revision history of all configuration objects. Basic and composite objects form an object pool from which variants and versions are created. Version control is the set of procedures and tools for managing the use of these objects. Change control is a procedural activity that ensures quality and consistency as changes are made to a configuration object. The change control process begins with a change request, leads to a decision to make or reject the request for change, and culminates with a controlled update of the SCI that is to be changed. The configuration audit is an SQA activity that helps to ensure that quality is maintained as changes are made. Status reporting provides information about each change to those with a need to know.

EXERCISES

1. What do you mean by Software configuration management (SCM)?
2. Explain the various principles of SCM?
3. Explain, in detail, the SEI-CMM model?
4. What are the four basic requirements for an SCM system?
5. Explain the planning and organizing for SCM?
6. Explain the potential SCM problem classes?
7. What is SCM staffing?
8. Explain the various tools for SCM?
9. What are the benefits of SCM process and tools?
10. What are the problems with software development?

❑

Software Quality

6

6.1 INTRODUCTION

The software engineering approach described in this book works toward a single goal: to produce high-quality software. Yet many readers will be challenged by the question: "What is software quality?"

Philip Crosby, in his landmark book on quality, provides an ironic answer to this question:

The problem of quality management is not what people don't know about it. The problem is what they think they do know.

Some software developers continue to believe that software quality is something you begin to worry about after code has been generated. Nothing could be further from the truth! *Software quality assurance* (SQA) is an umbrella activity that is applied throughout the software process.

SQA encompasses:

(1) a quality management approach,
(2) effective software engineering technology (methods and tools),
(3) formal technical reviews that are applied throughout the software process,
(4) a multi-tiered testing strategy,
(5) control of software documentation and the changes made to it,
(6) a procedure to ensure compliance with software development standards (when applicable), and
(7) measurement and reporting mechanisms.

In this chapter, we focus on the management issues and the process-specific activities that enable a software organization to ensure that it does "the right things at the right time in the right way."

We examine the qualities that are pertinent to software products and software production processes. These qualities will become our goals in the practice of software engineering. The basic goal of software engineering is to produce quality software. Software quality is a broad and important field of software engineering addressed by several standardization bodies, such as ISO, IEEE, ANSI, etc.

6.2 QUALITY CONCEPTS

It has been said that no two snowflakes are alike. Certainly when we watch snow falling it is hard to imagine that snowflakes differ at all, let alone that each flake possesses a unique structure. In order to observe differences between snowflakes, we must examine the specimens closely, perhaps using a magnifying glass. In fact, the closer we look the more differences we are able to observe.

This phenomenon, *variation between samples*, applies to all products of human as well as natural creation. For example, if two "identical" circuit boards are examined closely enough, we may observe that the copper pathways on the boards differ slightly in geometry, placement, and thickness. In addition, the location and diameter of the holes drilled in the boards varies as well.

All engineered and manufactured parts exhibit variation. The variation between samples may not be obvious without the aid of precise equipment to measure the geometry, electrical characteristics, or other attributes of the parts. However, with sufficiently sensitive instruments, we will likely come to the conclusion that no two samples of any item are exactly alike.

Variation control is the heart of quality control. A manufacturer wants to minimize the variation among the products that are produced, even when doing something relatively simple like duplicating diskettes. Surely, this cannot be a problem—duplicating diskettes is a trivial manufacturing operation, and we can guarantee that exact duplicates of the software are always created.

Or can we? We need to ensure the tracks are placed on the diskettes within a specified tolerance so that the overwhelming majority of disk drives can read the diskettes. In addition, we need to ensure the magnetic flux for distinguishing a zero from a one is sufficient for read/write heads to detect. The disk duplication machines can, and do, wear and go out of tolerance. So even a "simple" process such as disk duplication may encounter problems due to variation between samples.

But how does this apply to software work? How might a software development organization need to control variation? From one project to another, we want to minimize the difference between the predicted resources needed to complete a project and the actual resources used, including staff, equipment, and calendar time. In general, we would like to make sure our testing program covers a known percentage of the software, from one release to another. Not only do we want to minimize the number of defects that are released to the field, we'd like to ensure that the variance in the number of bugs is also minimized from one release to another. (Our customers will likely be upset if the third release of a product has ten times as many defects as the previous release.) We would like to minimize the differences in speed and accuracy of our hotline support responses to customer problems. The list goes on and on.

6.3 QUALITY

The *American Heritage Dictionary* defines *quality* as "a characteristic or attribute of something." As an attribute of an item, quality refers to measurable characteristics— things we are able to compare to known standards such as length, color, electrical properties, and malleability. However, software, largely an intellectual entity, is more challenging to characterize than physical objects.

Nevertheless, measures of a program's characteristics do exist. These properties include cyclomatic complexity, cohesion, number of function points, lines of code, and many others. When we examine an item based on its measurable characteristics, two kinds of quality may be encountered: quality of design and quality of conformance.

Quality of design refers to the characteristics that designers specify for an item. The grade of materials, tolerances, and performance specifications all contribute to the quality of design. As higher-grade materials are used, tighter tolerances and greater levels of performance are specified, the design quality of a product increases, if the product is manufactured according to specifications.

Quality of conformance is the degree to which the design specifications are followed during manufacturing. Again, the greater the degree of conformance, the higher is the level of quality of conformance.

In software development, quality of design encompasses requirements, specifications, and the design of the system. Quality of conformance is an issue focused primarily on implementation. If the implementation follows the design and the resulting system meets its requirements and performance goals, conformance quality is high.

But are quality of design and quality of conformance the only issues that software engineers must consider? Robert Glass argues that a more "intuitive" relationship is in order:

User satisfaction = compliant product + good quality + delivery within budget and schedule

At the bottom line, Glass contends that quality is important, but if the user isn't satisfied, nothing else really matters. DeMarco reinforces this view when he states: "A product's quality is a function of how much it changes the world for the better." This view of quality contends that if a software product provides substantial benefit to its end-users, they may be willing to tolerate occasional reliability or performance problems.

6.4 SOFTWARE QUALITY

Software quality is the:

Conformance to explicitly stated functional and performance requirements, explicitly documented development standards, and implicit characteristics that are expected of all professionally developed software.

The above definition emphasizes three important points:

1. Software requirements are the foundation from which quality is measured. Lack of conformance to requirements is lack of quality.
2. Specified standards define a set of development criteria that guide the manner in which software is engineered. If the criteria are not followed, lack of quality will almost surely result.
3. There is a set of implicit requirements that often goes unmentioned. If software conforms to its explicit requirements but fails to meet implicit requirements, software quality is suspect.

Our introduction to software components and to errors and their causes, and our knowledge that errors harm the quality of the software, have prepared us to define our target – software quality.

Software quality – IEEE definition

Software quality is:

1. The degree to which a system, component, or process meets specified requirements.
2. The degree to which a system, component, or process meets customer or user needs or expectations.

These are two alternative definitions of software quality, held by the founders of modern quality assurance, Philip B. Crosby and Joseph M. Juran. Each definition reflects a different conception of software quality:

- "Quality means conformance to requirements".
- "(1) Quality consists of those product features which meet the needs of customers and thereby provide product satisfaction. (2) Quality consists of freedom from deficiencies".

Crosby's definition of software quality refers to the degree to which the written software me team. This means that errors included in the software specification are not considered and do not reduce the software quality, a characteristic that can be considered the approach's deficiency.

Juran's definition is aimed at achieving customer satisfaction, and views the fulfillment of customers' real needs as the true goal of software quality. Adopting the second definition demands that a developer must invest significant professional efforts in examining and correcting the customer's requirements specifications. The main deficiency of this definition is the fact that it frees the customer of any professional responsibility for the accuracy and completeness of the software specifications. Also, following this conception, the customer is allowed to express his real needs, which may differ from the project specifications on one or more issues, at a very late stage of the project, even at the final stage. As a result, difficulties are expected to arise during the development process of the project, especially when attempting to prove how well the program fulfills the user's needs.

Software quality – Pressman's definition

Software quality is defined as:

Conformance to explicitly stated functional and performance requirements, explicitly documented development standards, and implicit characteristics that are expected of all professionally developed software.

Pressman's definition suggests three requirements for quality assurance that are to be met by the developer:

- Specific functional requirements, which refer mainly to the outputs of the software system.
- The software quality standards mentioned in the contract.
- Good Software Engineering Practices (GSEP), reflecting state-of-the-art professional practices, to be met by the developer even though not explicitly mentioned in the contract.

In effect, Pressman's definition provides operative directions for testing the degree to which the requirements are met.

6.5 CLASSIFICATION OF SOFTWARE QUALITIES

There are many desirable software qualities. Some of these apply both to the product and to the process used to produce the product. The user wants the software products to be reliable, efficient, and easy to use. The producer of the software wants it to be verifiable, maintainable, portable, and extensible. The manager of the software project wants the process of software development to be productive and easy to control.

In this section, we consider two different classifications of software-related qualities: internal versus external and product versus process.

6.5.1 External Versus Internal Qualities

We can divide software qualities into external and internal qualities. The external qualities are visible to the users of the system: the internal qualities are those that concern the developers of the system. In general, users of software only care about the external qualities, but it is the internal qualities, which deal largely with the structure of the software, that help developers achieve the external qualities. For example, the internal quality of verifiability is necessary for achieving the external quality of reliability. In many cases, however, the qualities are related closely and the distinction between internal and external is not sharp.

6.5.2 Product and Process Qualities

We use a process to produce the software product. We can also attribute some qualities to the process, although process qualities often are closely related to product qualities. For example, if the process requires careful planning of system test data before any design and development of the system starts, products reliability will increase. Some qualities, such as efficiency, apply both to the product and to the process.

It is interesting to examine the word product here. It usually refers to what is delivered to the customer. Even though this is an acceptable definition from the customer's perspective, it is not adequate for the developer who requires a general definition of a software product that encompasses not only the object code and the user manual that are delivered to the customer but also the requirements, design, source code, test data, etc. In fact, it is possible to deliver different subsets of the same product to different customers.

6.6 SOFTWARE QUALITY ATTRIBUTES

Software quality is comprised of six main attributes (called characteristics) as shown in Figure 6.1. These six attributes have detailed characteristics which are considered the basic ones and which can and should be measured using suitable metrics.

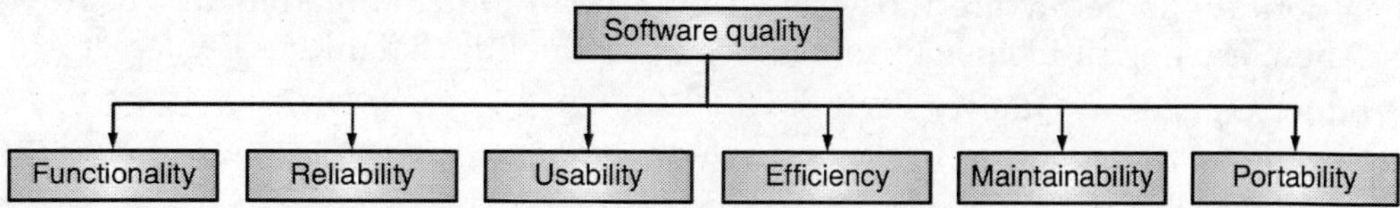

Figure 6.1: *Software Quality Attributes*

At the top level, for software products, these attributes can be defined as follows:

1. **Functionality:** The capability to provide functions which meet stated and implied needs when the software is used.
2. **Reliability:** The capability to maintain a specified level of performance.
3. **Usability:** The capability to be understood, learned, and used.
4. **Efficiency:** The capability to provide appropriate performance relative to the amount of resources used.
5. **Maintainability:** The capability to be modified for purposes of making corrections, improvements, or adaptation.
6. **Portability:** The capability to be adapted for different specified environments without applying actions or means other than those provided for this purpose in the product.

6.7 McCALL'S QUALITY FACTORS

McCall, Richards, and Walters propose a useful categorization of factors that affect software quality. These software quality factors, shown in Figure 6.2, focus on three important aspects of a software product: its operational characteristics, its ability to undergo change, and its adaptability to new environments.

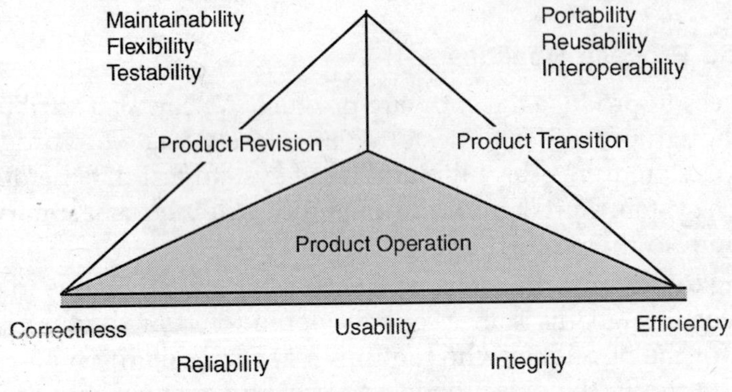

Figure 6.2: McCall's Software Quality Factors

One attempt to identify specific product qualities that are appropriate to software has been that of James A. McCall. He grouped software qualities into three sets of quality factors:

- Product operation qualities;
- Product revision qualities; and
- Product transition qualities.

The definitions below are those given by McCall, but the reader may come across others. These are not all inclusive: sometimes other qualities might be of interest.

Product Operation Quality Factors

- *Correctness:* The extent to which a program satisfies its specifications and fulfills the user's objectives.
- *Reliability:* The extent to which a program can be expected to perform its intended function with required precision.

- *Efficiency:* The amount of computer resources required by the software.
- *Integrity:* The extent to which access to software or data by unauthorized persons can be controlled.
- *Usability:* The effort required for learning, operating, preparing input, and interpreting output.

Product Revision Quality Factors

- *Maintainability:* The effort required to locate and fix an error in an operational program.
- *Testability:* The effort required to test a program to ensure it performs its intended function.
- *Flexibility:* The efforts required to modify an operational program.

Product Transition Quality Factors

- *Portability:* The effort required for transferring a program from one hardware configuration and software system environment to another.
- *Reusability:* The extent to which a program can be used in other applications.
- *Interoperability:* The efforts required to couple one system to another.

6.8 SOFTWARE QUALITY CRITERIA

The software quality criteria of various quality factors are depicted in Table 6.1.

Table 6.1: Software Quality Criteria

Quality	Factor Quality Criteria
Correctness	Traceability, consistency, completeness
Reliability	Error tolerance, consistency, accuracy, simplicity
Efficiency	Execution efficiency, storage efficiency
Integrity	Access control, access audit
Usability	Operability, training, communicativeness, input/output volume, input/output area
Maintainability	Consistency, simplicity, conciseness, modularity, self-descriptiveness
Testability	Simplicity, modularity, instrumentation, self-descriptiveness
Flexibility	Modularity, generality, expandability, self-descriptiveness
Portability	Modularity, self-descriptiveness, machine independence, software system independence
Reusability	Generality, modularity, software system independence, machine independence, self-descriptiveness
Interperability	Modularity, communications commonality, data commonality

6.9 REPRESENTATIVE QUALITIES

In this section, we present the most important qualities of software products and processes.

1. ***Correctness.*** A program is functionally correct if it behaves according to the specification of the functions it should provide (called functional requirements specifications). It is common simply to use the term "correct" rather than "functionally correct"; similarly, in this context, the term "specifications" implies "functional requirements specification." We will follow this convention when the context is clear.

   The definition of correctness assumes that a specification of the system is available and that it is possible to determine unambiguously whether or not a program meets the specifications. With most current software systems, no such specification exists. If a specification does exist, it is usually written in an informal style using natural language.

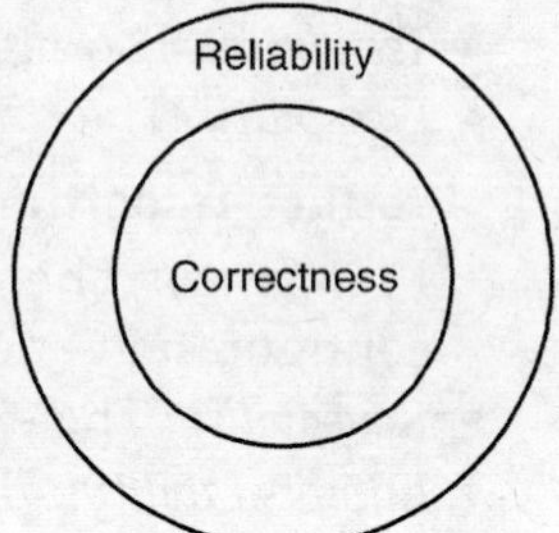

Figure 6.3: Relationship between Correctness and Reliability in the Ideal Case

2. ***Reliability.*** Informally, software is reliable if the user can depend on it. The specialized literature on software reliability defines reliability in terms of statistical behavior—the probability that the software will operate as expected over a specified time interval.

   Figure 6.3 illustrates the relationship between reliability and correctness. This figure shows that the set of all reliable programs includes the set of correct programs, but not vice versa.

3. ***Robustness.*** A program is robust if it behaves "reasonably," even in circumstances that were not anticipated in the requirements specification— for example, when it encounters incorrect input data or some hardware malfunction (say, disk crash). Obviously, robustness is a difficult-to-define quality; after all, if we could state precisely what we should do to make an application robust, we would be able to specify its "reasonable" behavior completely. The robustness would become equivalent to correctness (or reliability in the sense of Figure 6.3).

4. ***Performance.*** Performance is important because it affects the usability of the system. If a software system is too slow, it reduces the productivity of the users, possibly to the point of not meeting their needs. If a software system uses too much disk space, it may be too expensive to run. If a software system uses too much memory, it may affect the other applications that are run on the same system, or it may run slowly while the operating system tries to balance the memory usage of the different applications. Performance is also important because it affects the scalability of a software system.

5. ***Verifiability.*** A software system is verifiable if its properties can be verified easily. For example, it is important to be able to verify the correctness or the performance of a software system. Verifiability is usually an internal quality, although it sometimes becomes an external quality also. For example, in many security-critical applications, the customer requires the verifiability of certain properties. The highest level of the security standard for a trusted computer system requires the verifiability of the operating system kernel.

6. ***Repairability.*** A software system is repairable if it allows the correction of its defects with a limited amount of work. In many engineering products, repairability is a major

design goal. For example, automobile engines are built with the parts that are most likely to fail as the most accessible. In computer hardware engineering, there is a subspecialty called Repairability, Availability, and Serviceability (RAS).

7. ***Evolvability.*** Like other engineering products, software products are modified over time to provide new functions or to change existing functions. Indeed, the fact that software is so malleable makes modifications extremely easy to apply to an implementation.
8. ***Understandability.*** Some software systems are easier to understand than others. Of course, some tasks are inherently more complex than others. Given tasks of inherently similar difficulty, we can follow certain guidelines to produce more understandable designs and to write more understandable programs. For example, abstraction and modularity enhance a system's understandability.
9. ***Interoperability.*** "Interoperability" refers to the ability of a system to coexist and cooperate with other systems. With interoperability, a vendor can produce different products and allow the user to combine them if necessary. This makes it easier for the vendor to produce the products, and it gives the user more freedom in exactly what functions to pay for and to combine. Interoperability can be achieved through standardization of interfaces.
10. ***Productivity.*** Productivity is a quality of the software-production process; it measures the efficiency of the process and, as we said before, is the performance quality applied to the process. An efficient process results in faster delivery of the product. Productivity offers many trade-offs in the choice of a process. For example, a process that requires specialization of individual team members may lead to productivity in producing a certain product, but not in producing a variety of products. Software reuse is a technique that leads to the overall productivity of an organization that is involved in developing many products, but developing reusable modules is harder than developing modules for one's own use, thus reducing the productivity of the group that is developing reusable modules as part of their product development.
11. ***Timeliness.*** Timeliness is a process-related quality that refers to the ability to deliver a product on time. Timeliness requires careful scheduling, accurate estimation of work, and clearly specified and verifiable milestones.
12. ***Visibility.*** A software-development process is visible if all of its steps and its current status are documented clearly. Another term used to characterize this property is transparency. The idea is that the steps and the status of the project are available and easily accessible for external examination.

6.10 IMPORTANCE OF SOFTWARE QUALITY

We would expect quality to be a concern of all producers of goods and services. However, the special characteristics of software, and in particular, its intangibility and complexity, make special demands.

1. ***Increasing Criticality of Software.*** The final customer or user is naturally anxious about the general quality of software, especially its reliability. This is increasingly the case as organizations become more dependent on their computer systems and software is used more and more in areas which are safety critical; for example, to control aircraft.

2. ***The Intangibility of Software.*** This makes it difficult to know whether a particular task in a project has been completed satisfactorily. The results of these tasks can be made tangible by demanding that the developers produce 'deliverables' that can be examined for quality.
3. ***Accumulating Errors during Software Development.*** As computer system development is made up of a number of steps where the output from one step is the input to the next, the errors in the earlier deliverables will be added to those in the later steps leading to an accumulating detrimental effect, and generally, the later in a project that an error is found the more expensive it will be to fix. In addition, because the number of errors in the system is unknown the debugging phases of a project are particularly difficult to control.

For these reasons quality management is an essential part of effective overall project management.

6.11 QUALITY CONTROL

Variation control may be equated to quality control. But how do we achieve quality control? *Quality control* involves the series of inspections, reviews, and tests used throughout the software process to ensure each work product meets the requirements placed upon it. Quality control includes a feedback loop to the process that created the work product. The combination of measurement and feedback allows us to tune the process when the work products created fail to meet their specifications. This approach views quality control as part of the manufacturing process.

Quality control activities may be fully automated, entirely manual, or a combination of automated tools and human interaction. A key concept of quality control is that all work products have defined, measurable specifications to which we may compare the output of each process. The feedback loop is essential to minimize the defects produced.

6.12 QUALITY ASSURANCE

Quality assurance consists of the auditing and reporting functions of management. The goal of quality assurance is to provide management with the data necessary to be informed about product quality, thereby gaining insight and confidence that product quality is meeting its goals. Of course, if the data provided through quality assurance identify problems, it is management's responsibility to address the problems and apply the necessary resources to resolve quality issues.

6.12.1 Cost of Quality

The *cost of quality* includes all costs incurred in the pursuit of quality or in performing quality-related activities. Cost of quality studies are conducted to provide a baseline for the current cost of quality, identify opportunities for reducing the cost of quality, and provide a normalized basis of comparison. The basis of normalization is almost always dollars. Once we have normalized quality costs on a dollar basis, we have the necessary data to evaluate where the opportunities lie to improve our processes. Furthermore, we can evaluate the effect of changes in dollar-based terms.

Quality costs may be divided into costs associated with prevention, appraisal, and failure. *Prevention costs* include

- quality planning
- formal technical reviews
- test equipment
- training

Appraisal costs include activities to gain insight into product condition the "first time through" each process. Examples of appraisal costs include

- in-process and interprocess inspection
- equipment calibration and maintenance
- testing

Failure costs are those that would disappear if no defects appeared before shipping a product to customers. Failure costs may be subdivided into internal failure costs and external failure costs. *Internal failure costs* are incurred when we detect a defect in our product prior to shipment. Internal failure costs include

- rework
- repair
- failure mode analysis

External failure costs are associated with defects found after the product has been shipped to the customer. Examples of external failure costs are

- complaint resolution
- product return and replacement
- help line support
- warranty work

As expected, the relative costs to find and repair a defect increase dramatically as we go from prevention to detection to internal failure to external failure costs. Anecdotal data reported by Kaplan, Clark, and Tang reinforces earlier cost statistics and is based on work at IBM's Rochester development facility:

A total of 7053 hours was spent inspecting 200,000 lines of code with the result that 3112 potential defects were prevented. Assuming a programmer cost of $40.00 per hour, the total cost of preventing 3112 defects was $282,120, or roughly $91.00 per defect.

Compare these numbers to the cost of defect removal once the product has been shipped to the customer. Suppose that there had been no inspections, but that programmers had been extra careful and only one defect per 1000 lines of code [significantly better than industry average] escaped into the shipped product. That would mean that 200 defects would still have to be fixed in the field. At an estimated cost of $25,000 per field fix, the cost would be $5 million, or approximately 18 times more expensive than the total cost of the defect prevention effort.

It is true that IBM produces software that is used by hundreds of thousands of customers and that their costs for field fixes may be higher than those for software organizations that build custom systems. This in no way negates the results just noted. Even if the average software organization has field fix costs that are 25 percent of IBM's (most have no idea what their costs are!), the cost savings associated with quality control and assurance activities are compelling.

6.12.2 The Quality Movement

Today, senior managers at companies throughout the industrialized world recognize that high product quality translates to cost savings and an improved bottom line. However, this was not always the case. The quality movement began in the 1940s with the seminal work of W. Edwards Deming and had its first true test in Japan. Using Deming's ideas as a cornerstone, the Japanese developed a systematic approach to the elimination of the root causes of product defects. Throughout the 1970s and 1980s, their work migrated to the western world and was given names such as "total quality management" (TQM). Although terminology differs across different companies and authors, a basic four step progression is normally encountered and forms the foundation of any good TQM program.

The first step, called *kaizen,* refers to a system of continuous process improvement. The goal of *kaizen* is to develop a process (in this case, the software process) that is visible, repeatable, and measurable.

The second step, invoked only after *kaizen* has been achieved, is called *atarimae hinshitsu.* This step examines intangibles that affect the process and works to optimize their impact on the process. For example, the software process may be affected by high staff turnover, which itself is caused by constant reorganization within a company. Maybe a stable organizational structure could do much to improve the quality of software. *Atarimae hinshitsu* would lead management to suggest changes in the way reorganization occurs.

While the first two steps focus on the process, the next step, called *kansei* (translated as "the five senses"), concentrates on the user of the product (in this case, software). In essence, by examining the way the user applies the product *kansei* leads to improvement in the product itself and, potentially, to the process that created it.

Finally, a step called *miryokuteki hinshitsu* broadens management concern beyond the immediate product. This is a business-oriented step that looks for opportunity in related areas identified by observing the use of the product in the marketplace. In the software world, *miryokuteki hinshitsu* might be viewed as an attempt to uncover new and profitable products or applications that are an outgrowth from an existing computer-based system.

For most companies *kaizen* should be of immediate concern. Until a mature software process has been achieved, there is little point in moving to the next steps.

6.13 SOFTWARE QUALITY ASSURANCE

Even the most jaded software developers will agree that high-quality software is an important goal. But how do we define quality? A wag once said, "Every program does something right, it just may not be the thing that we want it to do."

Many definitions of software quality have been proposed in the literature. For our purposes, *software quality* is defined as

Conformance to explicitly stated functional and performance requirements, explicitly documented development standards, and implicit characteristics that are expected of all professionally developed software.

There is little question that this definition could be modified or extended. In fact, a definitive definition of software quality could be debated endlessly. For the purposes of this chapter, the definition serves to emphasize three important points:

1. Software requirements are the foundation from which quality is measured. Lack of conformance to requirements is lack of quality.
2. Specified standards define a set of development criteria that guide the manner in which software is engineered. If the criteria are not followed, lack of quality will almost surely result.
3. A set of implicit requirements often goes unmentioned (e.g., the desire for ease of use and good maintainability). If software conforms to its explicit requirements but fails to meet implicit requirements, software quality is suspect.

In this section we discuss:

- The alternative SQA definitions
- Software quality assurance compared with software quality control
- The objectives of SQA.ets the specifications prepared by the customer and his professional

6.13.1 Background Issues

Quality assurance is an essential activity for any business that produces products to be used by others. Prior to the twentieth century, quality assurance was the sole responsibility of the craftsperson who built a product. The first formal quality assurance and control function was introduced at Bell Labs in 1916 and spread rapidly throughout the manufacturing world. During the 1940s, more formal approaches to quality control were suggested. These relied on measurement and continuous process improvement as key elements of quality management.

Today, every company has mechanisms to ensure quality in its products. In fact, explicit statements of a company's concern for quality have become a marketing ploy during the past few decades.

The history of quality assurance in software development parallels the history of quality in hardware manufacturing. During the early days of computing (1950s and 1960s), quality was the sole responsibility of the programmer. Standards for quality assurance for software were introduced in military contract software development during the 1970s and have spread rapidly into software development in the commercial world. Extending the definition presented earlier, software quality assurance is a "planned and systematic pattern of actions" that are required to ensure high quality in software. The scope of quality assurance responsibility might best be characterized by paraphrasing a once-popular automobile commercial: "Quality Is Job #1." The implication for software is that many different constituencies have software quality assurance responsibility—software engineers, project managers, customers, salespeople, and the individuals who serve within an SQA group.

The SQA group serves as the customer's in-house representative. That is, the people who perform SQA must look at the software from the customer's point of view. Does the software adequately meet the quality factors? Has software development been conducted according to pre-established standards? Have technical disciplines properly performed their roles as part of the SQA activity? The SQA group attempts to answer these and other questions to ensure that software quality is maintained.

6.13.2 Software Quality Assurance Definitions

One of the most commonly used definitions of software quality assurance (SQA) is offered by the IEEE Glossary, cited below.

Software quality assurance – The IEEE definition

Software quality assurance is:

1. A planned and systematic pattern of all actions necessary to provide adequate confidence that an item or product conforms to established technical requirements.
2. A set of activities designed to evaluate the process by which the products are developed or manufactured. Contrast with quality control.

This definition may be characterized in the following:

- Plan and implement systematically. SQA is based on planning and the application of a variety of actions that are integrated into all the stages of the software development process. This is done in order to substantiate the client's confidence that the software product will meet all the technical requirements.
- Refer to the software development process.
- Refer to the specifications of the technical requirements.

Despite its emphasis on planning and systematic implementation, the IEEE definition restrains the scope of SQA in several directions, excluding maintenance and timetable and budget issues. This author adopts a broader conception of SQA that, of course, affects its definition. A broader definition, though placing additional burdens on the SQA function, is expected to yield better results and greater customer satisfaction.

The main deviations from the IEEE definition are:

- SQA should not be limited to the development process. Instead, it should be extended to cover the long years of service subsequent to product delivery. Adding issues directly related to the software product introduces quality issues that integrate software maintenance functions into the overall conception of SQA.
- SQA actions should not be limited to the technical aspects of the functional requirements, but should include also activities that deal with scheduling and the budget. The reasoning behind this expansion in scope is the close relationship between timetable or budget failure and the meeting of functional technical requirements. Very often, when projects are under severe time constraints, professionally "dangerous" changes that can seriously harm the prospects of meeting the functional requirements are made in the project schedule.

Similar undesirable results can be expected with projects that are under budgetary constraints and unable to cope with the inadequate resources allocated to the project and its maintenance.

SQA – expanded definition

Software quality assurance is:

A systematic, planned set of actions necessary to provide adequate confidence that the software development process or the maintenance process of a software system product conforms to established functional technical requirements as well as with the managerial requirements of keeping the schedule and operating within the budgetary confines.

The aim of the Software Quality Assurance (SQA) process is to develop a high quality software product. Software Quality Assurance is a set of activities designed to evaluate the process by which software is developed and/or maintained. Quality assurance is a planned and systematic pattern of all actions necessary to provide adequate confidence that the item or product conforms to established technical requirements.

The purpose of a software quality assurance group is to provide assurance that the procedures, tools, and techniques used during product development and modification are adequate to provide the desired level of confidence in the work products.

The process of the SQA includes the following:

1. Defines the requirements for software controlled system fault/failure detection, isolation, and recovery;
2. Reviews the software-development processes and products for software error prevention and/or controlled change to reduced functionality states; and
3. Defines the process for measuring and analyzing defects as well as reliability and maintainability factors.

The various objectives of SQA are as follows:

- Quality management approach.
- Measurement and reporting mechanisms.
- Effective software-engineering technology.
- A procedure to assure compliance with software-development standards where applicable.
- A multi-testing strategy is drawn.
- Formal technical reviews that are applied throughout the software process.

The major goals of SQA are as follows:

- SQA activities are planned.
- Non-compliance issues that cannot be resolved within the software project are addressed by senior management.
- Adherence of software products and activities to the applicable standards, procedures, and requirements is verified objectively.
- Affected groups and individuals are informed of SQA activities and results.

6.14 SQA ACTIVITIES

Software quality assurance is composed of a variety of tasks associated with two different constituencies—the software engineers who do technical work and an SQA group that has responsibility for quality assurance planning, oversight, record keeping, analysis, and reporting.

Software engineers address quality (and perform quality assurance and quality control activities) by applying solid technical methods and measures, conducting formal technical reviews, and performing well-planned software testing. Only reviews are discussed in this chapter.

The charter of the SQA group is to assist the software team in achieving a high quality end product. The Software Engineering Institute recommends a set of SQA activities that address quality assurance planning, oversight, record keeping, analysis, and reporting. These activities are performed (or facilitated) by an independent SQA group that:

- **Prepares an SQA plan for a project.** The plan is developed during project planning and is reviewed by all interested parties. Quality assurance activities performed by the software engineering team and the SQA group are governed by the plan. The plan identifies
  - evaluations to be performed
  - audits and reviews to be performed
  - standards that are applicable to the project
  - procedures for error reporting and tracking
  - documents to be produced by the SQA group
  - amount of feedback provided to the software project team
- **Participates in the development of the project's software process description.** The software team selects a process for the work to be performed. The SQA group reviews the process description for compliance with organizational policy, internal software standards, externally imposed standards (e.g., ISO-9001), and other parts of the software project plan.
- **Reviews software engineering activities to verify compliance with the defined software process.** The SQA group identifies, documents, and tracks deviations from the process and verifies that corrections have been made.
- **Audits designated software work products to verify compliance with those defined as part of the software process.** The SQA group reviews selected work products; identifies, documents, and tracks deviations; verifies that corrections have been made; and periodically reports the results of its work to the project manager.
- **Ensures that deviations in software work and work products are documented and handled according to a documented procedure.** Deviations may be encountered in the project plan, process description, applicable standards, or technical work products.
- **Records any noncompliance and reports to senior management.** Noncompliance items are tracked until they are resolved.

In addition to these activities, the SQA group coordinates the control and management of change and helps to collect and analyze software metrics.

6.14.1 The Objectives of SQA Activities

The objectives of SQA activities refer to the functional, managerial and economic aspects of software development and software maintenance.

Software development (process-oriented):

4. Assuring an acceptable level of confidence that the software will conform to functional technical requirements.
5. Assuring an acceptable level of confidence that the software will conform to managerial scheduling and budgetary requirements.

6. Initiating and managing of activities for the improvement and greater efficiency of software development and SQA activities. This means improving the prospects that the functional and managerial requirements will be achieved while reducing the costs of carrying out the software development and SQA activities.

Software maintenance (product-oriented):

1. Assuring with an acceptable level of confidence that the software maintenance activities will conform to the functional technical requirements.
2. Assuring with an acceptable level of confidence that the software maintenance activities will conform to managerial scheduling and budgetary requirements.
3. Initiating and managing activities to improve and increase the efficiency of software maintenance and SQA activities. This involves improving the prospects of achieving functional and managerial requirements while reducing costs.

6.15 THE SQA PLAN

An SQA plan defines the quality processes and procedures that should be used. This involves selecting and instantiating standards for products and processes and defining the required quality attributes of the system.

The SQA plan provides a roadmap for instituting software quality assurance. Developed by the SQA group (or the software team if a SQA group does not exist), the plan serves as a template for SQA activities that are instituted for each software project.

The quality plan should select those organizational standards that are appropriate to a particular product and development process. New standards may have to be defined if the project uses new methods and tools. An outline structure for a quality plan includes:

1. *Product introduction:* A description of the product, its intended markets, and the quality expectations for the product.
2. *Product plans:* The critical release dates and responsibilities for the product along with plans for distribution and product servicing.
3. *Process descriptions:* The development and service processes that should be used for product development and management.
4. *Quality goals:* The quality goals and plans for the product including an identification and justification of critical product quality attributes.
5. *Risks and risk management:* The key risks that might affect product quality and the actions to address these risks.

Preparation of a Software Quality Assurance Plan for each software project is a primary responsibility of the software quality assurance group.

Topics in a Software Quality Assurance Plan include:

- Purpose-scope of plan;
- List of references to other documents;
- Management, including organization, tasks, and responsibilities;
- Documentation to be produced;
- Standards, practices, and conventions;
- Reviews and audits;

- Testing;
- Problem reporting and corrective action;
- Tools, techniques, and methodologies;
- Code, media, and supplier control;
- Records collection, maintenance, and retention;
- Training;
- Risk management—the methods of risk management that are to be used.

A standard for SQA plans has been recommended by the IEEE. Initial sections describe the purpose and scope of the document and indicate those software process activities that are covered by quality assurance. All documents noted in the *SQA Plan* are listed and all applicable standards are noted. The management section of the plan describes SQA's place in the organizational structure, SQA tasks and activities and their placement throughout the software process, and the organizational roles and responsibilities relative to product quality.

The documentation section describes (by reference) each of the work products produced as part of the software process. These include

- project documents (e.g., project plan)
- models (e.g., ERDs, class hierarchies)
- technical documents (e.g., specifications, test plans)
- user documents (e.g., help files)

In addition, this section defines the minimum set of work products that are acceptable to achieve high quality. The standards, practices, and conventions section lists all applicable standards and practices that are applied during the software process (e.g., document standards, coding standards, and review guidelines). In addition, all project, process, and (in some instances) product metrics that are to be collected as part of software engineering work are listed.

The reviews and audits section of the plan identifies the reviews and audits to be conducted by the software engineering team, the SQA group, and the customer. It provides an overview of the approach for each review and audit. The test section references the *Software Test Plan and Procedure*. It also defines test record-keeping requirements. Problem reporting and corrective action defines procedures for reporting, tracking, and resolving errors and defects, and identifies the organizational responsibilities for these activities.

The remainder of the *SQA Plan* identifies the tools and methods that support SQA activities and tasks; references software configuration management procedures for controlling change; defines a contract management approach; establishes methods for assembling, safeguarding, and maintaining all records; identifies training required to meet the needs of the plan; and defines methods for identifying, assessing, monitoring, and controlling risk.

6.16 SOFTWARE QUALITY ASSURANCE AND SOFTWARE QUALITY CONTROL

Two phrases are constantly repeated within the context of software quality: "Quality control" and "quality assurance". Are they synonymous? How are they related? According to the IEEE software quality assurance definition, "quality control" is to be contrasted with "quality assurance".

These two terms represent separate and distinct concepts:

- **Quality control** is defined as "a set of activities designed to evaluate the quality of a developed or manufactured product"; in other words, activities whose main objective is the withholding of any product that does not qualify. Accordingly, quality control inspection and other activities take place as the development or manufacturing of the product is completed yet before the product is shipped to the client.
- The main objective of **quality assurance** is to minimize the cost of guaranteeing quality by a variety of activities performed throughout the development and manufacturing processes/stages. These activities prevent the causes of errors, and detect and correct them early in the development process. As a result, quality assurance activities substantially reduce the rate of products that do not qualify for shipment and, at the same time, reduce the costs of guaranteeing quality in most cases.

In sum:

(1) Quality control and quality assurance activities serve different objectives.

(2) Quality control activities are only a part of the total range of quality assurance activities.

6.17 SOFTWARE QUALITY ASSURANCE AND SOFTWARE ENGINEERING

According to the IEEE (1991), **software engineering** is defined as follows:

(1) The application of a systematic, disciplined, quantifiable approach to the development, operation and maintenance of software; that is, the application of engineering to software.

(2) The study of approaches as in (1).

The characteristics of software engineering, especially the systematic, disciplined and quantitative approach at its core, make the software engineering environment a good infrastructure for achieving SQA objectives. The methodologies and tools that are applied by software engineering determine, to a considerable extent, the level of quality to be expected from the software process and the maintenance services. Therefore, it is desirable that when making decisions about software methodologies and tools, SQA considerations be added to the efficiency and economy considerations associated with software engineering.

It is commonly accepted that cooperation between software engineers and the SQA team is the appropriate way to achieve efficient and economic development and maintenance activities that, at the same time, assure the quality of the product of these activities.

6.18 SOFTWARE REVIEWS

Software reviews are a "filter" for the software engineering process. That is, reviews are applied at various points during software development and serve to uncover errors and defects that can then be removed. Software reviews "purify" the software engineering activities that we have called *analysis, design*, and *coding.*

Freedman and Weinberg discuss the need for reviews this way:

Technical work needs reviewing for the same reason that pencils need erasers: *To err is human.* The second reason we need technical reviews is that although people are good at catching some of their own errors, large classes of errors escape the originator more easily than they escape anyone else. The review process is, therefore, the answer to the prayer of Robert Burns:

O wad some power the giftie give us to see ourselves as other see us

A review—any review—is a way of using the diversity of a group of people to:

1. Point out needed improvements in the product of a single person or team;
2. Confirm those parts of a product in which improvement is either not desired or not needed;
3. Achieve technical work of more uniform, or at least more predictable, quality than can be achieved without reviews, in order to make technical work more manageable.

Many different types of reviews can be conducted as part of software engineering. Each has its place. An informal meeting around the coffee machine is a form of review, if technical problems are discussed. A formal presentation of software design to an audience of customers, management, and technical staff is also a form of review. In this section, however, we focus on the *formal technical review,* sometimes called a *walkthrough* or an *inspection.* A formal technical review is the most effective filter from a quality assurance standpoint. Conducted by software engineers (and others) for software engineers, the FTR is an effective means for improving software quality.

6.19 FORMAL TECHNICAL REVIEWS

A formal technical review is a software quality assurance activity performed by software engineers (and others). The objectives of the FTR are (1) to uncover errors in function, logic, or implementation for any representation of the software; (2) to verify that the software under review meets its requirements; (3) to ensure that the software has been represented according to predefined standards; (4) to achieve software that is developed in a uniform manner; and (5) to make projects more manageable. In addition, the FTR serves as a training ground, enabling junior engineers to observe different approaches to software analysis, design, and implementation. The FTR also serves to promote backup and continuity because a number of people become familiar with parts of the software that they may not have otherwise seen.

The FTR is actually a class of reviews that includes walkthroughs, inspections, round-robin reviews and other small group technical assessments of software. Each FTR is conducted as a meeting and will be successful only if it is properly planned, controlled, and attended. In the sections that follow, guidelines for a walkthrough are presented as a representative formal technical review.

6.20 THE REVIEW MEETING

Regardless of the FTR format that is chosen, every review meeting should abide by the following constraints:

- Between three and five people (typically) should be involved in the review.
- Advance preparation should occur but should require no more than two hours of work for each person.
- The duration of the review meeting should be less than two hours.

Given these constraints, it should be obvious that an FTR focuses on a specific (and small) part of the overall software. For example, rather than attempting to review an entire design, walkthroughs are conducted for each component or small group of components. By narrowing focus, the FTR has a higher likelihood of uncovering errors. The focus of the FTR is on a work product (e.g., a portion of a requirements specification, a detailed component design, a source code listing for a component). The individual who has developed the work product—the *producer*—informs the project leader that the work product is complete and that a review is required. The project leader contacts a *review leader,* who evaluates the product for readiness, generates copies of product materials, and distributes them to two or three reviewers for advance preparation. Each reviewer is expected to spend between one and two hours reviewing the product, making notes, and otherwise becoming familiar with the work. Concurrently, the review leader also reviews the product and establishes an agenda for the review meeting, which is typically scheduled for the next day.

The review meeting is attended by the review leader, all reviewers, and the producer. One of the reviewers takes on the role of the *recorder;* that is, the individual who records (in writing) all important issues raised during the review. The FTR begins with an introduction of the agenda and a brief introduction by the producer. The producer then proceeds to "walk through" the work product, explaining the material, while reviewers raise issues based on their advance preparation. When valid problems or errors are discovered, the recorder notes each.

At the end of the review, all attendees of the FTR must decide whether to (1) accept the product without further modification, (2) reject the product due to severe errors (once corrected, another review must be performed), or (3) accept the product provisionally (minor errors have been encountered and must be corrected, but no additional review will be required). The decision made, all FTR attendees complete a sign-off, indicating their participation in the review and their concurrence with the review team's findings.

6.21 REVIEW REPORTING AND RECORD KEEPING

During the FTR, a reviewer (the recorder) actively records all issues that have been raised. These are summarized at the end of the review meeting and a review issues list is produced. In addition, a formal technical review summary report is completed.

A *review summary report* answers three questions:

1. What was reviewed?
2. Who reviewed it?
3. What were the findings and conclusions?

The review summary report is a single page form (with possible attachments). It becomes part of the project historical record and may be distributed to the project leader and other interested parties.

The *review issues list* serves two purposes:

(1) to identify problem areas within the product and

(2) to serve as an action item checklist that guides the producer as corrections are made.

An issues list is normally attached to the summary report.

It is important to establish a follow-up procedure to ensure that items on the issues list have been properly corrected. Unless this is done, it is possible that issues raised can "fall between the cracks." One approach is to assign the responsibility for follow-up to the review leader.

6.22 REVIEW GUIDELINES

Guidelines for the conduct of formal technical reviews must be established in advance, distributed to all reviewers, agreed upon, and then followed. A review that is uncontrolled can often be worse that no review at all. The following represents a minimum set of guidelines for formal technical reviews:

1. *Review the product, not the producer.* An FTR involves people and egos. Conducted properly, the FTR should leave all participants with a warm feeling of accomplishment. Conducted improperly, the FTR can take on the aura of an inquisition. Errors should be pointed out gently; the tone of the meeting should be loose and constructive; the intent should not be to embarrass or belittle. The review leader should conduct the review meeting to ensure that the proper tone and attitude are maintained and should immediately halt a review that has gotten out of control.
2. *Set an agenda and maintain it.* One of the key maladies of meetings of all types is *drift*. An FTR must be kept on track and on schedule. The review leader is chartered with the responsibility for maintaining the meeting schedule and should not be afraid to nudge people when drift sets in.
3. *Limit debate and rebuttal.* When an issue is raised by a reviewer, there may not be universal agreement on its impact. Rather than spending time debating the question, the issue should be recorded for further discussion off-line.
4. *Enunciate problem areas, but don't attempt to solve every problem noted.* A review is not a problem-solving session. The solution of a problem can often be accomplished by the producer alone or with the help of only one other individual. Problem solving should be postponed until after the review meeting.
5. *Take written notes.* It is sometimes a good idea for the recorder to make notes on a wall board, so that wording and priorities can be assessed by other reviewers as information is recorded.
6. *Limit the number of participants and insist upon advance preparation.* Two heads are better than one, but 14 are not necessarily better than 4. Keep the number of people involved to the necessary minimum. However, all review team members must prepare in advance. Written comments should be solicited by the review leader (providing an indication that the reviewer has reviewed the material).
7. *Develop a checklist for each product that is likely to be reviewed.* A checklist helps the review leader to structure the FTR meeting and helps each reviewer to focus on important issues. Checklists should be developed for analysis, design, code, and even test documents.
8. *Allocate resources and schedule time for FTRs.* For reviews to be effective, they should be scheduled as a task during the software engineering process. In addition, time should be scheduled for the inevitable modifications that will occur as the result of an FTR.
9. *Conduct meaningful training for all reviewers.* To be effective all review participants should receive some formal training. The training should stress both process-related issues and the human psychological side of reviews. Freedman and Weinberg estimate a one-month learning curve for every 20 people who are to participate effectively in reviews.

10. *Review your early reviews.* Debriefing can be beneficial in uncovering problems with the review process itself. The very first product to be reviewed should be the review guidelines themselves.

Because many variables (e.g., number of participants, type of work products, timing and length, specific review approach) have an impact on a successful review, a software organization should experiment to determine what approach works best in a local context. Porter and his colleagues provide excellent guidance for this type of experimentation.

SUMMARY

Software quality assurance is an umbrella activity that is applied at each step in the software process. SQA encompasses procedures for the effective application of methods and tools, formal technical reviews, testing strategies and techniques, procedures for change control, procedures for assuring compliance to standards, and measurement and reporting mechanisms.

SQA is complicated by the complex nature of software quality—an attribute of computer programs that is defined as "conformance to explicitly and implicitly specified requirements." But when considered more generally, software quality encompasses many different product and process factors and related metrics.

Software reviews are one of the most important SQA activities. Reviews serve as filters throughout all software engineering activities, removing errors while they are relatively inexpensive to find and correct. The formal technical review is a stylized meeting that has been shown to be extremely effective in uncovering errors.

To properly conduct software quality assurance, data about the software engineering process should be collected, evaluated, and disseminated. Statistical SQA helps to improve the quality of the product and the software process itself. Software reliability models extend measurements, enabling collected defect data to be extrapolated into projected failure rates and reliability predictions.

The objectives of SQA activities for software development and maintenance are:

(1) Assuring, with acceptable levels of confidence, conformance to functional technical requirements.

(2) Assuring, with acceptable levels of confidence, conformance to managerial requirements of scheduling and budgets.

(3) Initiating and managing activities for the improvement and greater efficiency of software development and SQA activities.

Quality control is a set of activities carried out with the main objective of withholding products from shipment if they do not qualify. In contrast, quality assurance is meant to minimize the costs of quality by introducing a variety of activities throughout the development and maintenance process in order to prevent the causes of errors, detect them, and correct them in the early stages of development. As a result, quality assurance substantially reduces the rates of non-qualifying products.

Software engineering is the application of a systematic, disciplined, quantifiable approach to the development, operation and maintenance of software. The characteristics of software engineering, especially its systematic, disciplined and quantitative approach, make software engineering a good environment for achieving SQA objectives. It is commonly accepted that cooperation between software engineers and the SQA team is the way to achieve efficient and economic development and maintenance activities that, at the same time, assure the quality of the products of these activities.

We recall the words of Dunn and Ullman: "Software quality assurance is the mapping of the managerial precepts and design disciplines of quality assurance onto the applicable managerial and technological space of software engineering." The ability to ensure quality is the measure of a mature engineering discipline. When the mapping is successfully accomplished, mature software engineering is the result.

EXERCISES

1. What do you mean by quality?
2. What is software quality?
3. Explain the classification of software qualities?
4. What are the various attributes of software quality?
5. State some of the software quality factors that are proposed by McCall.
6. Explain the criteria for software quality?
7. Define representative qualities.
8. State the importance of software quality.
9. What is quality control?
10. What is quality assurance?
11. What is software quality assurance (SQA)?
12. What are the various background issues of quality assurance?
13. What are the goals of software quality assurance?
14. What are the objectives of software quality assurance?
15. Explain the various activities of SQA?
16. Define an SQA plan.
17. Explain the relationship between software quality assurance and software quality control?
18. Explain the relationship between software quality assurance and software engineering?
19. What are software reviews?
20. What are formal technical reviews?
21. What is review meeting?
22. Explain the review reporting and record keeping?
23. What are the guidelines for reviews?

❑

Software Reliability

7

7.1 INTRODUCTION

There is no doubt that the reliability of a computer program is an important element of its overall quality. If a program repeatedly and frequently fails to perform, it matters little whether other software quality factors are acceptable.

Software reliability, unlike many other quality factors, can be measured directed and estimated using historical and developmental data. Software reliability is defined in statistical terms as "the probability of failure-free operation of a computer program in a specified environment for a specified time". To illustrate, program X is estimated to have a reliability of 0.96 over eight elapsed processing hours. In other words, if program X were to be executed 100 times and require eight hours of elapsed processing time (execution time), it is likely to operate correctly (without failure) 96 times out of 100.

Whenever software reliability is discussed, a pivotal question arises: What is meant by the term failure? In the context of any discussion of software quality and reliability, failure is nonconformance to software requirements. Yet, even within this definition, there are gradations. Failures can be only annoying or catastrophic. One failure can be corrected within seconds while another requires weeks or even months to correct. Complicating the issue even further, the correction of one failure may in fact result in the introduction of other errors that ultimately result in other failures.

7.2 SOFTWARE TRAGEDIES

With the advent of the computer age, computers, as well as the software running on them, are playing a vital role in our daily lives. We may not have noticed, but appliances such as washing machines, telephones, TVs, and watches, are having their analog and mechanical parts replaced by CPUs and software. The computer industry is booming exponentially. With a continuously lowering cost and improved control, processors and software controlled systems offer compact design, flexible handling, rich features and competitive cost. Like machinery-replaced craftsmanship in the industrial revolution, computers and intelligent parts are quickly pushing their mechanical counterparts out of the market.

People used to believe that "software never breaks". Intuitively, unlike mechanical parts such as bolts, levers, or electronic parts such as transistors, capacitor, software will stay "as is" unless there are problems in hardware that changes the storage content or data path. Software does not age, rust, wearout, deform or crack. There is no environmental constraint for software to operate as long as the hardware processor it runs on can operate.

Furthermore, software has no shape, color, material, and mass. It cannot be seen or touched, but it has a physical existence and is crucial to system functionality. Without being proven to be wrong, optimistic people would think that once after the software can run correctly, it will be correct forever. A series of tragedies and chaos caused by software proves this to be wrong. These events will always have their place in history.

Tragedies in Therac 25, a computer-controlled radiation-therapy machine in the year 1986, caused by the software not being able to detect a race condition, alerts us that it is dangerous to abandon our old but well understood mechanical safety control and surrender our lives completely to software controlled safety mechanism.

Software can make decisions, but can just as unreliable as human beings. The British destroyer Sheffield was sunk because the radar system identified an incoming missile as "friendly". The defense system has matured to the point that it will not mistake the rising moon for incoming missiles, but gasfield fire, descending space junk, etc. were also examples that can be misidentified as incoming missiles by the defense system. Software can also have small unnoticeable errors or drifts that can culminate into a disaster. On February 25, 1991, during the Golf War, the chopping error that missed 0.000000095 second in precision in every 10th of a second, accumulating for 100 hours, made the Patriot missile fail to intercept a scud missile. 28 lives were lost.

Fixing problems may not necessarily make the software more reliable. On the contrary, new serious problems may arise. In 1991, after changing three lines of code in a signaling program which contains millions lines of code, the local telephone systems in California and along the Eastern seaboard came to a stop.

Once perfectly working software may also break if the running environment changes. After the success of Ariane 4 rocket, the maiden flight of Ariane 5 ended up in flames while design defects in the control software were unveiled by faster horizontal drifting speed of the new rocket.

There are much more scary stories to tell. This makes us wondering whether software is reliable at all, whether we should use software in safety-critical embedded applications. You can hardly ruin your clothes if the embedded software in your washing machine issues erroneous commands; and 50% of the chances you will be happy if the ATM machine miscalculates your money; but in airplanes, heart pace-makers, radiation therapy machines, a software error can easily claim people's lives. With processors and software permeating safety critical embedded world, the reliability of software is simply a matter of life and death.

7.3 SOFTWARE RELIABILITY

Software reliability is defined as the probability of failure-free operation of a computer program in a specified environment for a specified time. Reliability of a software product essentially denotes its trustworthiness or dependability. Reliability of a software product can also be defined as the probability of the product working "correctly" over a given period of time.

The expected curve for software is given in Figure 7.1.

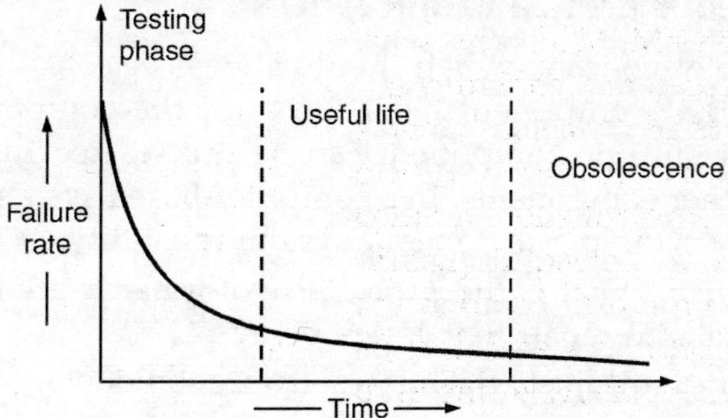

***Figure 7.1:** Software Reliability Curve (Failure Rate versus Time)*

Software may be retired only if it becomes obsolete. Some of the contributing factors are given below:

- Change in environment
- Change in infrastructure/technology
- Major change in requirements
- Increase in complexity
- Extremely difficult to maintain
- Deterioration in structure of the code
- Slow execution speed
- Poor graphical user interfaces

According to ANSI, Software Reliability is defined as: the probability of failure-free software operation for a specified period of time in a specified environment. Although Software Reliability is defined as a probabilistic function, and comes with the notion of time, we must note that, different from traditional Hardware Reliability, Software Reliability is not a direct function of time. Electronic and mechanical parts may become "old" and wear out with time and usage, but software will not wear-out during its life cycle. Software will not change over time unless intentionally changed or upgraded.

Software Reliability is an important attribute of software quality, together with functionality, usability, performance, serviceability, capability, installability, maintainability, and documentation. Software Reliability is hard to achieve, because the complexity of software tends to be high. While any system with a high degree of complexity, including software, will be hard to reach a certain level of reliability, system developers tend to push complexity into the software layer, with the rapid growth of system size and ease of doing so by upgrading the software. For example, large next-generation aircraft will have over one million source lines of software on-board; next-generation air traffic control systems will contain between one and two million lines; the upcoming international Space Station will have over two million lines on-board and over ten million lines of ground support software; several major life-critical defense systems will have over five million source lines of software. While the complexity of software is inversely related to software reliability, it is directly related to other important factors in software quality, especially functionality, capability, etc. Emphasizing these features will tend to add more complexity to software.

7.4 SOFTWARE RELIABILITY SPECIFICATIONS

Reliability is a complex concept, which should always be considered at the system level rather than the individual component level. Because the components in a system are interdependent, a failure in one component can be propagated through the system and affect the operation of other components. In a computer-based system, you have to consider three dimensions when specifying the overall system reliability:

1. ***Hardware Reliability.*** What is the probability of a hardware component failing and how long does it take to repair that component?
2. ***Software Reliability.*** How likely is it that a software component will produce an incorrect output? Software failures are different from hardware failures in that software does not wear out. It can continue operating correctly after an incorrect result has been produced.
3. ***Operator Reliability.*** How likely is it that the operator of a system will make an error? The reliability of a system depends upon a number of factors rather than the sum of all the probabilities (failure probabilities of each factor).

$$PS = PA + PR + \dots\dots\dots\dots\dots + PN,$$

where

PS = Probability of system failure
PA = Probability of component A failure
PB = Probability of component B failure
PN = Probability of component N failure

As the number of factors increase, the overall probability of system failure increases.

Reliability Terminologies

- *System failure:* An event that occurs at some point in time when the system does not deliver a service as expected by its users.
- *System error:* Erroneous system behavior where the behavior of the system does not conform to its specifications.
- *System fault:* An incorrect system state, i.e., a system state that is unexpected by the designers of the system.
- *Human errors or mistakes:* Human behavior that results in the introduction of faults into a system.

7.5 SOFTWARE FAILURE MECHANISMS

The software failure may be classified as:

- *Transient failure:* These failures only occur with certain inputs.
- *Permanent failure:* this failure occurs on all inputs.
- *Recoverable failure:* System can recover without operator help.
- *Unrecoverable failure:* System can recover with operator help only.
- *Non-corruption failure:* Failure does not corrupt system state or data.
- *Corrupting failure:* It corrupts system state or data.

Software failures may be due to errors, ambiguities, oversights or misinterpretation of the specification that the software is supposed to satisfy, carelessness or incompetence in writing code, inadequate testing, incorrect or unexpected usage of the software or other unforeseen problems. While it is tempting to draw an analogy between Software Reliability and Hardware

Reliability, software and hardware have basic differences that make them different in failure mechanisms. Hardware faults are mostly physical faults, while software faults are design faults, which are harder to visualize, classify, detect, and correct. Design faults are closely related to fuzzy human factors and the design process, which we don't have a solid understanding. In hardware, design faults may also exist, but physical faults usually dominate.

In software, we can hardly find a strict corresponding counterpart for "manufacturing" as hardware manufacturing process, if the simple action of uploading software modules into place does not count. Therefore, the quality of software will not change once it is uploaded into the storage and start running. Trying to achieve higher reliability by simply duplicating the same software modules will not work, because voting cannot mask off design faults.

A partial list of the distinct characteristics of software compared to hardware is listed below:

- **Failure cause:** Software defects are mainly design defects.
- **Wear-out:** Software does not have energy related wear-out phase. Errors can occur without warning.
- **Repairable system concept:** Periodic restarts can help fix software problems.
- **Time dependency and life cycle:** Software reliability is not a function of operational time.
- **Environmental factors:** Do not affect Software reliability, except it might affect program inputs.
- **Reliability prediction:** Software reliability cannot be predicted from any physical basis, since it depends completely on human factors in design.
- **Redundancy:** Cannot improve Software reliability if identical software components are used.
- **Interfaces:** Software interfaces are purely conceptual other than visual.
- **Failure rate motivators:** Usually not predictable from analyses of separate statements.
- **Built with standard components:** Well-understood and extensively tested standard parts will help improve maintainability and reliability.

But in software industry, we have not observed this trend. Code reuse has been around for some time, but to a very limited extent. Strictly speaking there are no standard parts for software, except some standardized logic structures.

7.6 THE BATHTUB CURVE FOR SOFTWARE RELIABILITY

Over time, hardware exhibits the failure characteristics shown in following Figure 7.2, known as the bathtub curve. Period A, B and C stand for burn-in phase, useful life phase and end-of-life phase respectively.

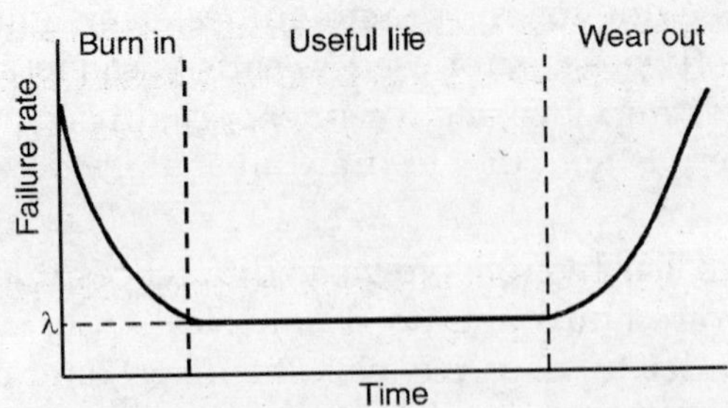

Figure 7.2: Bathtub curve for hardware reliability

Software reliability, however, does not show the same characteristics similar as hardware. A possible curve is shown in following Figure 7.3 if we projected software reliability on the same axes. There are two major differences between hardware and software curves. One difference is that in the last phase, software does not have an increasing failure rate as hardware does. In this phase, software is approaching obsolescence; there are no motivations for any upgrades or changes to the software. Therefore, the failure rate will not change. The second difference is that in the useful-life phase, software will experience a drastic increase in failure rate each time an upgrade is made. The failure rate levels off gradually, partly because of the defects found and fixed after the upgrades.

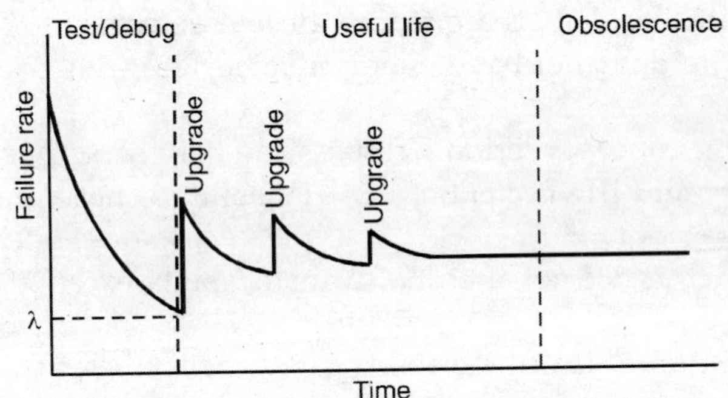

Figure 7.3: Revised bathtub curve for software reliability

The upgrades in above Figure imply feature upgrades, not upgrades for reliability. For feature upgrades, the complexity of software is likely to be increased, since the functionality of software is enhanced. Even bug fixes may be a reason for more software failures, if the bug fix induces other defects into software. For reliability upgrades, it is possible to incur a drop in software failure rate, if the goal of the upgrade is enhancing software reliability, such as a redesign or reimplementation of some modules using better engineering approaches, such as clean-room method.

Figure 7.4 shows the testing results of fifteen POSIX compliant operating systems. From the graph we see that for QNX and HP-UX, robustness failure rate increases after the upgrade. But for SunOS, IRIX and Digital UNIX, robustness failure rate drops when the version numbers go up. Since software robustness is one aspect of software reliability, this result indicates that the upgrade of those systems shown in following Figure 7.4 should have incorporated reliability upgrades.

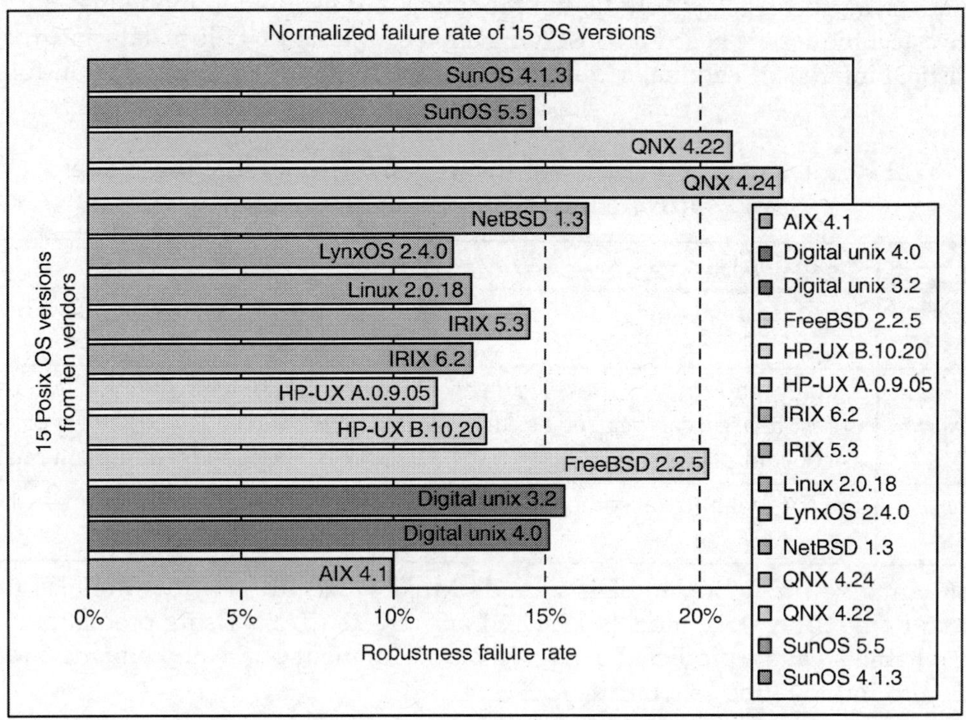

Figure 7.4: *Test Results of POSIX compliant operating system*

7.7 AVAILABLE TOOLS, TECHNIQUES, AND METRICS

Since Software Reliability is one of the most important aspects of software quality, Reliability Engineering approaches are practiced in software field as well. Software Reliability Engineering (SRE) is the quantitative study of the operational behavior of software-based systems with respect to user requirements concerning reliability.

7.7.1 Software Reliability Models

A proliferation of software reliability models have emerged as people try to understand the characteristics of how and why software fails, and try to quantify software reliability. Over 200 models have been developed since the early 1970s, but how to quantify software reliability still remains largely unsolved. As many models as there are and many more emerging, none of the models can capture a satisfying amount of the complexity of software; constraints and assumptions have to be made for the quantifying process.

Therefore, there is no single model that can be used in all situations. No model is complete or even representative. One model may work well for a set of certain software, but may be completely off track for other kinds of problems.

Most software models contain the following parts: assumptions, factors, and a mathematical function that relates the reliability with the factors. The mathematical function is usually higher order exponential or logarithmic. Software modeling techniques can be divided into two subcategories: prediction modeling and estimation modeling. Both kinds of modeling techniques are based on observing and accumulating failure data and analyzing with statistical inference. The major differences of the two models are shown in following Table 7.1.

Table 7.1: Difference between software reliability prediction models and software reliability estimation models

Issues	Prediction Models	Estimation Models
Data Reference	Uses historical data	Uses data from the current software development effort
When Used in Development Cycle	Usually made prior to development or test phases; can be used as early as concept phase	Usually made later in life cycle (after some data have been collected); not typically used in concept of development phases
Time Frame	Predict reliability at some future time	Estimate reliability at either present or some future time

Representative prediction models include Musa's Execution Time Model, Putnam's Model, and Rome Laboratory models TR-92-51 and TR-92-15, etc. Using prediction models, software reliability can be predicted early in the development phase and enhancements can be initiated to improve the reliability.

Representative estimation models include exponential distribution models, Weibull distribution model, Thompson and Chelson's model, etc. Exponential models and Weibull distribution model are usually named as classical fault count/fault rate estimation models, while Thompson and Chelson's model belong to Bayesian fault rate estimation models.

The field has matured to the point that software models can be applied in practical situations and give meaningful results and, second, that there is no one model that is best in all situations. Because of the complexity of software, any model has to have extra assumptions. Only limited factors can be put into consideration. Most software reliability models ignore the software development process and focus on the results — the observed faults and/or failures. By doing so, complexity is reduced and abstraction is achieved, however, the models tend to specialize to be applied to only a portion of the situations and a certain class of the problems. We have to carefully choose the right model that suits our specific case. Furthermore, the modeling results cannot be blindly believed and applied.

7.7.2 Software Reliability Metrics

Measurement is commonplace in other engineering field, but not in software engineering. Though frustrating, the quest of quantifying software reliability has never ceased. Until now, we still have no good way of measuring software reliability.

Measuring software reliability remains a difficult problem because we don't have a good understanding of the nature of software. There is no clear definition to what aspects are related to software reliability. We cannot find a suitable way to measure software reliability, and most of the aspects related to software reliability. Even the most obvious product metrics such as software size have not uniform definition.

It is tempting to measure something related to reliability to reflect the characteristics, if we cannot measure reliability directly. The current practices of software reliability measurement can be divided into four categories:

7.7.2.1 Product Metrics

Software size is thought to be reflective of complexity, development effort and reliability. Lines of Code (LOC), or LOC in thousands (KLOC), is an intuitive initial approach to measuring software size. But there is not a standard way of counting. Typically, source code is used (SLOC, KSLOC) and comments and other non-executable statements are not counted. This method cannot faithfully compare software not written in the same language. The advent of new technologies of code reuse, and code generation technique also cast doubt on this simple method.

Function point metric is a method of measuring the functionality of a proposed software development based upon a count of inputs, outputs, master files, inquires, and interfaces. The method can be used to estimate the size of a software system as soon as these functions can be identified. It is a measure of the functional complexity of the program. It measures the functionality delivered to the user and is independent of the programming language. It is used primarily for business systems; it is not proven in scientific or real-time applications.

Complexity is directly related to software reliability, so representing complexity is important. Complexity-oriented metrics is a method of determining the complexity of a program's control structure; by simplify the code into a graphical representation. Representative metric is McCabe's Complexity Metric.

Test coverage metrics are a way of estimating fault and reliability by performing tests on software products, based on the assumption that software reliability is a function of the portion of software that has been successfully verified or tested.

7.7.2.2 Project Management Metrics

Researchers have realized that good management can result in better products. Research has demonstrated that a relationship exists between the development process and the ability to complete projects on time and within the desired quality objectives. Costs increase when developers use inadequate processes. Higher reliability can be achieved by using better development process, risk management process, configuration management process, etc.

7.7.2.3 Process Metrics

Based on the assumption that the quality of the product is a direct function of the process, process metrics can be used to estimate, monitor and improve the reliability and quality of software. ISO-9000 certification, or "quality management standards", is the generic reference for a family of standards developed by the International Standards Organization (ISO).

7.7.2.4 Fault and Failure Metrics

The goal of collecting fault and failure metrics is to be able to determine when the software is approaching failure-free execution. Minimally, both the number of faults found during testing (i.e., before delivery) and the failures (or other problems) reported by users after delivery are collected, summarized and analyzed to achieve this goal. Test strategy is highly relative to the effectiveness of fault metrics, because if the testing scenario does not cover the full functionality of the software, the software may pass all tests and yet be prone to failure once delivered. Usually, failure metrics are based upon customer information regarding failures found after release of the software.

The failure data collected is therefore used to calculate failure density, Mean Time Between Failures (MTBF) or other parameters to measure or predict software reliability.

- **Mean Time to Failure (MTTF):** MTTF is a basic measure of reliability for non-repairable systems. It is the mean time expected until the first failure of a piece of equipment. MTTF is a statistical value and is meant to be the mean over a long period of time and large number of units. For constant failure rate systems, MTTF is the inverse of the failure rate. If failure rate is in failures/million hours, MTTF = 1,000,000 / Failure Rate for components with exponential distributions.

  Technically MTBF should be used only in reference to repairable items, while MTTF should be used for non-repairable items. However, MTBF is commonly used for both repairable and non-repairable items.
- **Mean Time between Failures (MTBF):** MTBF is a basic measure of reliability for repairable items. It can be described as the number of hours that pass before a component, assembly, or system fails. It is a commonly-used variable in reliability and maintainability analyses.

  MTBF can be calculated as the inverse of the failure rate for constant failure rate systems. For example: If a component has a failure rate of 2 failures per million hours, the MTBF would be the inverse of that failure rate.

  MTBF = (1,000,000 hours) / (2 failures) = 500,000 hours

  Actually MTBF is the summation of MTTF and MTRF (Mean Time To Repair).

  MTBF = MTTF+MTTR
- **Availability:** It is a measure of the time during which the system is available. It may be stated as:

  Availability = MTBF / (MTBF + MMTR)
- **Probability of Failure on Demand (POFOD):** It is defined as the probability that the system will fail when a service is requested.
- **Rate of occurrence of failure (ROCOF):** It may be defined as the number of failures in unit time interval.

7.7.3 Software Reliability Improvement Techniques

Good engineering methods can largely improve software reliability. Before the deployment of software products, testing, verification and validation are necessary steps. Software testing is heavily used to trigger, locate and remove software defects. Software testing is still in its infant stage; testing is crafted to suit specific needs in various software development projects in an ad-hoc manner. Various analysis tools such as trend analysis, fault-tree analysis, Orthogonal Defect classification and formal methods, etc. can also be used to minimize the possibility of defect occurrence after release and therefore improve software reliability.

After deployment of the software product, field data can be gathered and analyzed to study the behavior of software defects. Fault tolerance or fault/failure forecasting techniques will be helpful techniques and guide rules to minimize fault occurrence or impact of the fault on the system.

7.8 SOFTWARE FAULT TOLERANCE

Software fault tolerance is the ability for software to detect and recover from a fault that is happening or has already happened in either the software or hardware in the system in which the software is running in order to provide service in accordance with the specification. Software fault tolerance is a necessary component in order to construct the next generation of highly available and reliable computing systems from embedded systems to data warehouse systems.

In order to adequately understand software fault tolerance it is important to understand the nature of the problem that software fault tolerance is supposed to solve. Software faults are all design faults. Software manufacturing, the reproduction of software, is considered to be perfect. The source of the problem being solely design faults is very different than almost any other system in which fault tolerance is a desired property. This inherent issue, that software faults are the result of human error in interpreting a specification or correctly implementing an algorithm, creates issues, which must be dealt with in the fundamental approach to software fault tolerance.

Current software fault tolerance methods are based on traditional hardware fault tolerance. The deficiency with this approach is that traditional hardware fault tolerance was designed to conquer manufacturing faults primarily, and environmental and other faults secondarily. Design diversity was not a concept applied to the solutions to hardware fault tolerance, and to this end, N-Way redundant systems solved many single errors by replicating the same hardware. Software fault tolerance tries to leverage the experience of hardware fault tolerance to solve a different problem, but by doing so creates a need for design diversity in order to properly create a redundant system.

Design diversity is a solution to software fault tolerance only so far as it is possible to create diverse and equivalent specifications so that programmers can create software, which has different enough designs that they don't share similar failure modes. Design diversity and independent failure modes have been shown to be a particularly difficult problem though. The issue still remains that for a complex problem, the need for humans to solve that problem error free is not easily solvable.

Fault tolerance is defined as how to provide, by redundancy, service complying with the specification in spite of faults having occurred or occurring. Laprie argues that fault tolerance is accomplished using redundancy. This argument is good for errors which are not caused by design faults, however, replicating a design fault in multiple places will not aide in complying with a specification. It is also important to note the emphasis placed on the specification as the final arbiter of what is an error and what is not. Design diversity increases pressure on the specification creators to make multiple variants of the same specification, which are equivalent in order to aid the programmer in creating variations in algorithms for the necessary redundancy. The definition itself may no longer be appropriate for the type of problems that current fault tolerance is trying to solve, both hardware and software.

Randell argues that the difference between fault tolerance versus exception handling is that exception handling deviates from the specification and fault tolerance attempts to provide services compliant with the specification after detecting a fault. This is an important difference to realize between trying to construct robust software versus trying to construct reliable software. Reliable software will accomplish its task under adverse conditions while robust software will be able to indicate a failure correctly, (hopefully without the entire system failing.)

7.8.1 Software Bugs

Software faults are most often caused by design faults. Design faults occur when a programmer either misunderstands a specification or simply makes a mistake. Software faults are common for the simple reason that the complexity in modern systems is often pushed into the software part of the system. It is estimated that 60-90% of current computer errors are from software faults. Software faults may also occur from hardware; these faults are usually transitory in nature, and can be masked using a combination of current software and hardware fault tolerance techniques.

7.9 SOFTWARE FAULTTOLERANCETECHNIQUES

Software fault tolerance techniques are designed to allow a system to tolerate software faults that remain in the system after its development. Software fault tolerance techniques are employed during the procurement, or development, of the software. When a fault occurs, these techniques provide mechanisms to the software system to prevent system failure from occurring.

Software fault tolerance techniques provide protection against errors in translating the requirements and algorithms into a programming language, but do not provide explicit protection against errors in specifying the requirements. Software fault tolerance techniques have been used in the aerospace, nuclear power, healthcare, telecommunications and ground transportation industries, among others.

7.9.1 Recovery Blocks

The recovery block method is a simple method developed by Randell from what was observed as somewhat current practice at the time. The recovery block operates with an adjudicator, which confirms the results of various implementations of the same algorithm. In a system with recovery blocks, the system view is broken down into fault recoverable blocks. The entire system is constructed of these fault tolerant blocks. Each block contains at least a primary, secondary, and exceptional case code along with an adjudicator. The adjudicator is the component, which determines the correctness of the various blocks to try. The adjudicator should be kept somewhat simple in order to maintain execution speed and aide in correctness. Upon first entering a unit, the adjudicator first executes the primary alternate. (There may be N alternates in a unit which the adjudicator may try.) If the adjudicator determines that the primary block failed, it then tries to roll back the state of the system and tries the secondary alternate. If the adjudicator does not accept the results of any of the alternates, it then invokes the exception handler, which then indicates the fact that the software could not perform the requested operation.

Recovery block operation still has the same dependency, which most software fault tolerance systems have: design diversity. The recovery block method increases the pressure on the specification to be specific enough to create different multiple alternatives that are functionally the same. This issue is further discussed in the context of the N-version method.

The recovery block system is also complicated by the fact that it requires the ability to roll back the state of the system from trying an alternate. This may be accomplished in a variety of ways, including hardware support for these operations. This try and rollback ability has the effect of making the software to appear extremely transactional, in which only after a transaction is accepted is it committed to the system. There are advantages to a system built with a transactional nature, the largest of which is the difficult nature of getting such a system into an incorrect or unstable state. This property, in combination with check pointing and recovery may aide in constructing a distributed hardware fault tolerant system.

7.9.2 N-Version Software

The N-version software concept attempts to parallel the traditional hardware fault tolerance concept of N-way redundant hardware. In an N-version software system, each module is made with up to N different implementations. Each variant accomplishes the same task, but hopefully in a different way. Each version then submits its answer to voter or decider, which determines the correct answer, and returns that as the result of the module. This system can hopefully overcome the design faults present in most software by relying upon the design diversity concept. An important distinction in N-version software is the fact that the system could include multiple types of hardware using multiple versions of software. The goal is to increase the diversity in order to avoid common mode failures. Using N-version software, it is encouraged that each different version be implemented in as diverse a manner as possible, including different tool sets, different programming languages, and possibly different environments. The various development groups must have as little interaction related to the programming between them as possible. N-version software can only be successful and successfully tolerate faults if the required design diversity is met.

The dependence on appropriate specifications in N-version software, (and recovery blocks,) cannot be stressed enough. The delicate balance required by the N-version software method requires that a specification be specific enough so that the various versions are completely inter-operable, so that a software decider may choose equally between them, but cannot be so limiting that the software programmers do not have enough freedom to create diverse designs. The flexibility in the specification to encourage design diversity, yet maintain the compatibility between versions is a difficult task, however, most current software fault tolerance methods rely on this delicate balance in the specification.

7.9.3 N-Version Software and Recover Block - Comparison

The differences between the recovery block method and the N-version method are not too numerous, but they are important. In traditional recovery blocks, each alternative would be executed serially until an acceptable solution is found as determined by the adjudicator. The recovery block method has been extended to include concurrent execution of the various alternatives. The N-version method has always been designed to be implemented using N-way hardware concurrently. In a serial retry system, the cost in time of trying multiple alternatives may be too expensive, especially for a real-time system. Conversely, concurrent systems require the expense of N-way hardware and a communications network to connect them. Another important difference in the two methods is the difference between an adjudicator and the decider. The recovery block method requires that each module build a specific adjudicator; in the N-version method, a single decider may be used. The recovery block method, assuming that the programmer can create a sufficiently simple adjudicator, will create a system, which is difficult to enter into an incorrect state. The engineering tradeoffs, especially monetary costs, involved with developing either type of system have their advantages and disadvantages, and it is important for the engineer to explore the space to decide on what the best solution for his project is.

7.10 RELIABILITY MODELS

A reliability growth model is a mathematical model of software reliability, which predicts how software reliability should improve over time as faults are discovered and repaired. These models help the manager in deciding how much efforts should be devoted in testing. The goal of project manager is to test and debug the system until the required level of reliability is reached.

There are various models, which have been derived from reliability experiments in a number of application domains. These models are usually based on formal testing data. The quality of their results depends upon the input data, the better the outcome. The more data points available the better the model will perform. When using calendar time for large projects, you need to verify homogeneity of testing effort.

Software reliability growth models fall into two major categories:

- **Time between failure models (MTBF):** In this class of models the process under study is the time between failures. The most common approach is to assume that the time between, say, the (i - 1)st and the ith failures, follows a distribution whose parameters depend on the number of faults remaining in the program during this interval. Estimates of the parameters are obtained from the observed values of times between failures and estimates of software reliability, mean time to next failure, etc., are then obtained from the fitted model. Another approach is to treat the failure times as realizations of a stochastic process and use an appropriate time-series model to describe the underlying failure process.
- **Fault count models (faults or time normalized rates):** The interest of this class of models is in the number of faults or failures in specified time intervals rather than in times between failures. The failure counts are assumed to follow stochastic process with a time dependent discrete or continuous failure rate. Parameters of the failure rate can be estimated from the observed values of failure counts or from failure times. Estimates of software reliability mean time to next failure, etc., can again be obtained from the relevant equations.

7.10.1 Times Between Failures Models

This is one of the earliest classes of models proposed for software reliability assessment. When interest is in modeling times between failures, it is expected that the successive failure times will get longer as faults are removed from the software system. For a given set of observed values, this may not be exactly so due to the fact that failure times are random variables and observed values are subject to statistical fluctuations.

A number of models have been proposed to describe such failures. Let a random variable T_i denote the time between the (i-1)st and the ith failures, Basically, the models assume that T_i follows a known distribution whose parameters depend on the number of faults remaining in the system after the (i-1)st failure. The assumed distribution is supposed to reflect the improvement in software quality as faults are detected and removed from the system. The key models in this class are described below.

7.10.1.1 Jelinski-Moranda (JM) De-Eutrophication Model

Jelinski-Moranda model developed by Jelinski and Moranda in 1972 was one of the first software reliability growth models. This is one of the earliest and probably the most commonly used model for assessing software reliability. It assumes that there are N software faults at the start of testing, each is independent of others and is equally likely to cause a failure during testing. A detected fault is removed with certainty in a negligible time and no new faults are introduced during the debugging process. The software failure rate, or the hazard function, at any time is assumed to be proportional to the current fault content of the program. In other words, the hazard function during t_i, the rime between (i – 1)st and ith failures, is given by:

$$Z(t_i) = \Phi[N - (i - 1)]$$

where Φ is a proportionality constant. Note that this hazard function is constant between failures but decreases in steps of size Φ following the removal of each fault.

A variation of the above model was proposed by Moranda to describe testing situations where faults are not removed until the occurrence of a fatal one at which time the accumulated group of faults is removed. In such a situation, the hazard function after a restart can be assumed to be a fraction of the rate which attained when the system crashed. For this model, the hazard function during the ith testing interval is given by:

$$Z(t_i) = Dk^{i-1}$$

where D is the fault detection rate during the first interval and k is a constant ($0 < k < 1$).

7.10.1.2 Schick and Wolverton (SW) Model)

This model is based on the same assumptions as the JM model except that the hazard function is assumed to be proportional to the current fault content of the program as well as to the time elapsed since the last failure is given by:

$$Z(t_i) = \Phi\{(N - (i - 1))\}\ t_i$$

where various quantities are as defined above. Note that in some texts t_i has been taken to be the cumulative time from the beginning of testing. That interpretation of t_i seems to be inconsistent.

We note that the above hazard rate is linear with time within each future interval, returns to zero at the occurrence of a failure and increases linearly again but at a reduced slope, the decrease in the slope being proportional to Φ. A modification of the above model is also proposed whereby the hazard function is assumed to be parabolic in test time and is given by:

$$Z(t_i) = \Phi\,[N - (i - 1)]\,(- a t_i^2 + b t_i + c)$$

where a, b, c are constants and the other quantities are as defined above. This function consists of two components. The first is basically the hazard function of the JM model and the superimposition of the second term indicates that the likelihood of a failure occurring increases rapidly as the test time accumulates within a testing interval. At failure times ($t_i = 0$), the hazard function is proportional to that of the JM model.

7.10.1.3 Goel-Okumoto (GO) Imperfect Debugging Model

The above models assume that the faults are removed with certainty when detected. However, in practice that is not always true. To overcome this limitation, Goel and Okumoto proposed an imperfect debugging model which is basically an extension of the JM model. In this model, the number of faults in the system at time t, X(t), is treated as a Markov process whose transition probabilities are governed by the probability of imperfect debugging. Times between the transitions of X(t) are taken to be exponentially distributed with rates dependent on the current fault content of the system. The hazard function during the interval between the (i – 1)st and the ith failures is given by:

$$Z(t_i) = [N - p\,(i - 1)]\,\lambda$$

where N is the initial fault content of the system, p is the probability of imperfect debugging, and λ is the failure rate per fault.

7.10.1.4 Littlewood-Verall Bayesian Model

Littlewood and Verall took a different approach to the development of a model for times between failures. They argues that software reliability should not be specified in terms of the number of errors in the program. Specifically, in their model, the times between failures are assumed to follow an exponential distribution but the parameter of this distribution is treated as a random variable with a gamma distribution, viz.

$$f(t_i \mid \lambda_i) = \lambda_i\, e^{-\psi i t i}$$

and

$$f(\lambda_i \mid \alpha, \psi(i)) = [\{\psi(i)\}^{\alpha}\, \lambda_i^{\alpha - 1}\, e^{-\psi(i)\lambda i}] / \tau_{\alpha}$$

In the above, ψ(i) describes the quality of the programmer and the difficulty of the programming task. It is claimed that the failure phenomenon in different environments can be explained by this model by taking different forms of the parameter ψ(i).

7.10.2 Fault Count Models

This class of models is concerned with modeling the number of failures seen or faults detected in the given testing intervals. As faults are removed from the system, it is expected that the observed number of failures per unit time will decrease. If this is so, then the cumulative number of failures versus time curve will eventually level off. Note that time here can be calendar time, CPU time, number of test cases run or some other relevant metric. In this setup, the time intervals may be fixed a priori and the observed number of failures in each interval is treated as a random variable.

Several models have been suggested to describe such failure phenomenon. The basic idea behind most of these models is that of a Poisson distribution whose parameter takes different forms for different models. It should be noted that Poisson distribution has been found to be an excellent model in many fields of application where interest is in number of occurrences.

One of the earliest models in this category was proposed by Shooman. Taking a somewhat similar approach, Musa later proposed another failure count model based on execution time. Schneidewind took a different approach and studied the fault counts over a series of time intervals. Goel and Okumoto introduced a time dependent failure rate of the underlying Poisson process and developed the necessary analytical details of the models. These and some other in this class are described below.

7.10.2.1 Goel-Okumoto Non-Homogeneous Poisson Process Model

In this model Goel and Okumoto assumed that a software system is subject to failures at random times caused by faults present in the system. Letting N(t) be the cumulative number of failures observed by time t, they proposed that N(t) can be modeled as a nonhomogeneous Poisson process, i.e. as a Poisson process with a time dependent failure rate. Based on their study of actual failure data from many systems, they proposed the following form of the model:

$$P\{N(t) = y\} = [(m(t))^y / y!\,] * e^{-m(t)}, \; y = 0, 1, 2, \ldots$$

where

$$m(t) = a(1 - e^{-bt})$$

and

$$\lambda(t) \equiv m'(t) = abe^{-bt}$$

Here m(t) is the expected number of failures observed by time t and $\lambda(t)$ is the failure rate.

Using somewhat different approach than described above, Schneidewind had earlier studied the number of faults detected during a time interval and failure counts over a series of time intervals. He assumed that the failure process is a nonhomogeneous Poisson process with an exponentially decaying intensity function given by

$$d(i) = \alpha e^{-\beta i}, \; \alpha, \beta > 0, I = 1, 2, \ldots$$

where α and β are the parameters of the model.

7.10.2.2 Goel Generalized Non-Homogeneous Poisson Process Model

Most of the times between failures and failure count models assume that a software system exhibits a decreasing failure rate pattern during testing. In other words, they assume that software quality continues to improve as testing progresses. In practice, it has been observed that in many testing situations, the failure rate first increases and then decreases. In order to model this increasing/decreasing failure rate progress, Goel proposed the following generalization of the Goel-Okumoto NHPP model.

$$P\{N(t) = y\} = [(m(t))^y / y!\ ] * e^{-m(t)},\ y = 0, 1, 2, \ldots$$

and

$$m(t) = a\,(1 - e^{-bt^c})$$

where a is expected number of faults to be eventually detected, and b and c are constants that reflect the quality of testing. The failure rate for the model is given by

$$\lambda(t) \equiv m'(t) = abc\ e^{-bt^c}\ t^{c-1}$$

7.10.2.3 Musa Execution Time Model

In this model Musa makes assumptions that are similar to those of the JM model except that the process modeled is the number of failures in specified execution time intervals. The hazard function for this model is given by

$$z(\tau) = \Phi\, f(N - n_c)$$

where τ is the execution time utilized in executing the program up to the present, f is the linear execution frequency (average instruction execution rate divided by the number of instructions in the program), Φ is a proportionality constant, which is a fault exposure ratio that relates fault exposure frequency to the linear execution frequency, and n_c is the number of faults corrected during $(0, \tau)$.

One of the main features of this model is that it explicitly emphasizes the dependence of the hazard function on execution time. Musa also provides a systematic approach for converting the model so that it can be applicable for calendar time as well.

7.10.2.4 Shooman Exponential Model

This model is essentially similar to the JM model. For this model the hazard function is of the following form

$$z(t) = k\,[(N/I) - n_c(\tau)]$$

where t is the operating time of the system measured from its initial activation, I is the total number of instructions in the program, τ is the debugging time since the start of system integration, $n_c(\tau)$ is the total number of faults since corrected during τ, normalized with respect to I, and k is a proportionality constant.

7.10.2.5 Generalized Poisson Model

This is a variation of the NHPP model of Goel and Okumoto and assumes a mean value function of the following form:

$$m(t_i) = \Phi\,(N - M_{i-1})\,t_i^{\alpha}$$

where M_{i-1} is the total number of faults removed up to the end of the $(i - 1)^{st}$ debugging interval, Φ is a constant of proportionality, and ψ is a constant used to rescale time t_i.

7.10.2.6 IBM Binomial and Poisson Models

In these models Brooks and Motley consider the fault detection process during software testing to be discrete process, following a binomial or a Poisson distribution. The software system is assumed to be developed and tested incrementally. They claim that both models can be applied at the module or the system level.

7.10.2.7 Musa-Okumoto Logarithmic Poisson Execution Time Model

In this model the observed number of failures by some time τ is assumed to be a NHPP, similar to the Goel-Okumoto model, but with a mean value function which is a function of τ, viz.

$$\mu(\tau) = (1/\theta) * \ln(\lambda_0 \, \theta_\tau + 1)$$

where λ_0 and θ represent the initial failure intensity and the rate of reduction in the normalized failure intensity per failure, respectively. This model is also closely related to Moranda's geometric de-eutrophication model and can be viewed as a continuous version of this model.

7.11 SOFTWARE SAFETY

Before software was used in safety critical systems, they were often controlled by conventional (nonprogrammable) mechanical and electronic devices. System safety techniques are designed to cope with random failures in these [nonprogrammable] systems. Human design errors are not considered since it is assumed that all faults caused by human errors can be avoided completely or removed prior to delivery and operation.

When software is used as part of the control system, complexity can increase by an order of magnitude or more. Subtle design faults induced by human error—something that can be uncovered and eliminated in hardware-based conventional control— become much more difficult to uncover when software is used.

Software safety is a software quality assurance activity that focuses on the identification and assessment of potential hazards that may affect software negatively and cause an entire system to fail. If hazards can be identified early in the software engineering process, software design features can be specified that will either eliminate or control potential hazards.

A modeling and analysis process is conducted as part of software safety. Initially, hazards are identified and categorized by criticality and risk. For example, some of the hazards associated with a computer-based cruise control for an automobile might be

- causes uncontrolled acceleration that cannot be stopped
- does not respond to depression of brake pedal (by turning off)
- does not engage when switch is activated
- slowly loses or gains speed

Once these system-level hazards are identified, analysis techniques are used to assign severity and probability of occurrence. To be effective, software must be analyzed in the context of the entire system. For example, a subtle user input error (people are system components) may be magnified by a software fault to produce control data that improperly positions a mechanical device. If a set of external environmental conditions are met (and only if they are met), the improper position of the mechanical device will cause a disastrous failure. Analysis techniques such as *fault tree analysis*, *real-time logic*, or *petri net models* can be used to predict the chain of events that can cause hazards and the probability that each of the events will occur to create the chain.

Once hazards are identified and analyzed, safety-related requirements can be specified for the software. That is, the specification can contain a list of undesirable events and the desired system responses to these events. The role of software in managing undesirable events is then indicated.

Although software reliability and software safety are closely related to one another, it is important to understand the subtle difference between them. Software reliability uses statistical analysis to determine the likelihood that a software failure will occur. However, the occurrence of a failure does not necessarily result in a hazard or mishap. Software safety examines the ways in which failures result in conditions that can lead to a mishap. That is, failures are not considered in a vacuum, but are evaluated in the context of an entire computer-based system.

SUMMARY

Software reliability is a key part in software quality. Software Reliability is defined as: the probability of failure-free software operation for a specified period of time in a specified environment. The study of software reliability can be categorized into three parts: modeling, measurement and improvement. Reliability of the software depends on the faults in the software. To assess the reliability of software, reliability models are required. To use the model, data is collected about the software. Most reliability models are based on the data obtained during the system and acceptance testing.

Software reliability modeling has matured to the point that meaningful results can be obtained by applying suitable models to the problem. There are many models exist, but no single model can capture a necessary amount of the software characteristics. Assumptions and abstractions must be made to simplify the problem. There is no single model that is universal to all the situations.

Software reliability measurement is *naive*. Measurement is far from commonplace in software, as in other engineering field. "How good is the software, quantitatively?" As simple as the question is, there is still no good answer. Software reliability cannot be directly measured, so other related factors are measured to estimate software reliability and compare it among products. Development process, faults and failures found are all factors related to software reliability.

Software reliability improvement is *hard*. The difficulty of the problem stems from insufficient understanding of software reliability and in general, the characteristics of software. Until now there is no good way to conquer the complexity problem of software. Complete testing of a moderately complex software module is infeasible. Defect-free software product cannot be assured. Realistic constraints of time and budget severely limit the effort put into software reliability improvement.

As more and more software is creeping into embedded systems, we must make sure they don't embed disasters. If not considered carefully, software reliability can be the reliability bottleneck of the whole system. Ensuring software reliability is no easy task. As hard as the problem is, promising progresses are still being made toward more reliable software. More standard components and better process are introduced in software engineering field.

EXERCISES

1. Explain the concept of software tragedies?
2. What is software reliability?
3. What are the specifications of software reliability?
4. Explain the various software failure mechanisms?
5. Explain the bathtub curve for software reliability?
6. What are the available tools, techniques, and metrics for software reliability?
7. Explain the various software reliability metrics?
8. Define software fault tolerance?
9. Define software bugs?
10. Explain the various software fault tolerance techniques?
11. Explain the different reliability models?
12. What do you understand by software safety?

❑

Software Economics

8

8.1 INTRODUCTION

Software economics is the study of how scarce project resources are allocated for software projects. Software economics helps software managers allocate those resources in the most efficient manner. The process of counting function points, gathering data, analyzing data is commonly referred to as Software Metrics, but in reality is a branch of economics which should be called Software Economics.

8.2 EVOLUTION OF SOFTWARE ECONOMICS

Software engineering is dominated by intellectual activities that are focused on solving problems of immense complexity with numerous unknowns in competing perspectives. The early software approaches of the 1960s and 1970s can best be described as craftsmanship, with each project using a custom process and custom tools. In the 1980s and 1990s, the software industry matured and transitioned to more of an engineering discipline. However, most software projects in this era were still primarily research-intensive, dominated by human creativity and diseconomies of scale.

Most cost models can be abstracted into a function of five basic parameters, which are as follows:

- **Size:** The size of the end product (in human-generated components), which is typically quantified in terms of the number of source instructions or the number of function points required to develop the required functionality.
- **Process:** The process used to produce the end product, in particular the ability of the process to avoid non-value-adding activities (rework, bureaucratic delays, communications overhead)
- **Personnel:** The capabilities of software engineering personnel, and particularly their experience with the computer science issues and the applications domain issues of the project.
- **Environment:** The environment, which is made up of the tools and techniques available to support efficient software development and to automate the process.
- **Quality:** The required quality of the product, including its features, performance, reliability, and adaptability.

The relationships among these parameters and the estimated cost can be written as follows:

$$\text{Effort} = (\text{Personnel})(\text{Environment})(\text{Quality})(\text{Size}^{\text{Process}})$$

Several parametric models have been developed to estimate software costs. All of them can be generally abstracted into this form. One important aspect of software economics is that the relationship between effort and size exhibits a diseconomy of scale. The diseconomy of scale of software development is a result of the process exponent being greater than 1.0. Contrary to most manufacturing processes, the more software you build, the more expensive it is per unit item.

For example, for a given application, a 10,000-line software solution will cost less per line than a 100,000-line software solution. Assume that a 100,000-line system requires 900 staff-months for development, or about 111 lines per staff-month, or 1.37 hours per line. If this same system were only 10,000 lines, and all other parameters were held constant, this project would be estimated at cost 62 staff-months, or about 175 lines per staff-month, or 0.87 hour per line. The per-line cost for smaller application is much less than for the larger application. The reason is primarily the complexity of managing interpersonal communications as the number of team members scales up. The diseconomy of scale is characteristic of any research project in which the product is a one-of-a-kind instance of intellectual property.

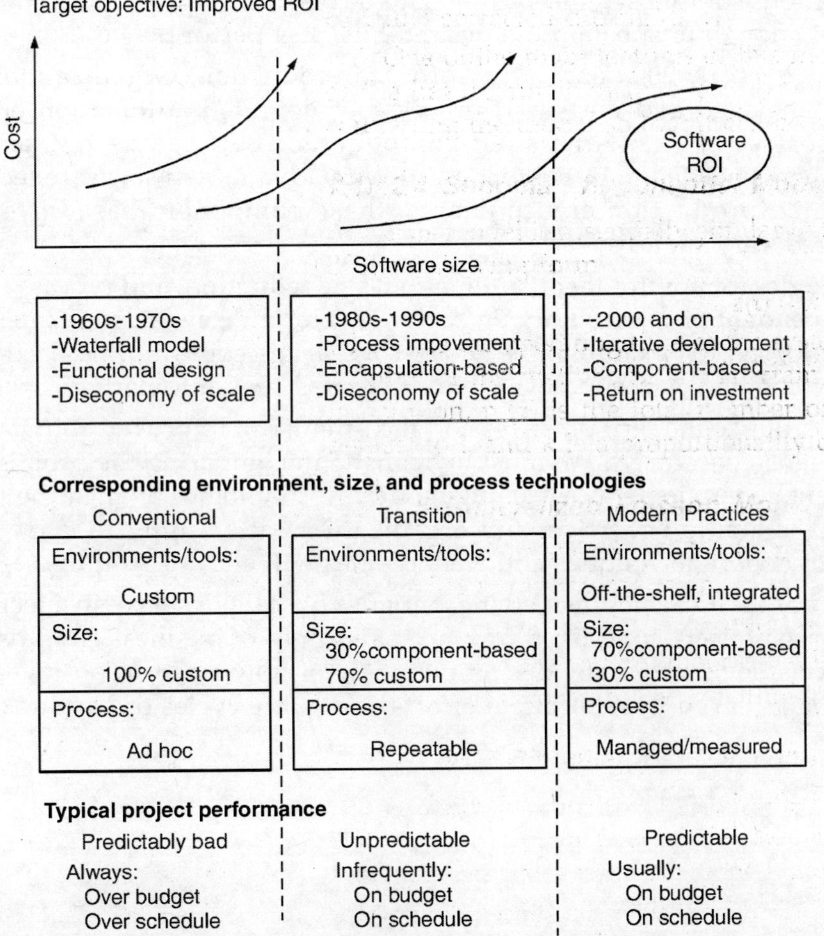

***Figure 8.1:** Three Generations of Software Economics leading to the Target Objective*

Figure 8.1 shows three generations of basic technology advancements in tools, components and processes. The required level of quality and personnel are assumed to be constant. The ordinate of the graph refers to software unit costs realized by an organization. The abscissa represents the life cycle of the software business engaged in by the organization. The three generations of software development are defined as follows:

1. *Conventional:* 1960s and 1970s, craftsmanship. Organizations used custom tools, custom processes, and virtually all custom components built in primitive languages. Project performance was highly predictable in that cost, schedule and quality objectives were almost always underachieved.
2. *Transition:* 1980s and 1990s, software engineering. Organizations used more-repeatable processes and off-the-shelf tools, and mostly (>70%) custom components built in higher level languages. Some of the components (<30%) were available as commercial products, including the operating system, database management system, networking, and graphical user interface. During the 1980s, some organizations began achieving economies of scale, but with the growth in applications complexity, the existing languages, techniques, and technologies were just not enough to substain the desired business performance.
3. *Modern Practices:* 2000 and later, software production. Organizations started the use of managed and measured processes, integrated automation environments, and mostly (70%) off-the-shelf components. Perhaps as few as 30% of the components needed to be custom built. With advances in software technology and integrated production environments, these component-based systems can be produced very rapidly.

Technologies for environment automation, size reduction, and process improvement are not independent of one another. In each new era, the key is complementary growth in all technologies. For example, the process advances could not be used successfully without new component technologies and increased tool automation.

The transition to modern practices and the promise of improved software economics are by no means guaranteed. We must be realistic in comparing the promises of a well-executed, next generation process using modern technologies against the ugly realities of history. It is a sure bet that many organizations attempting to carry out modern projects with modern techniques and technologies will end up with the same old delay.

Organizations are achieving better economies of scale in successive technology eras, with very large projects, long-lived products, and lines of business comprising multiple similar projects. Figure 8.2 provides an overview of how a return on investment (ROI) profile can be achieved in subsequent efforts across life cycles of various domains.

Achieving ROI across a line of business

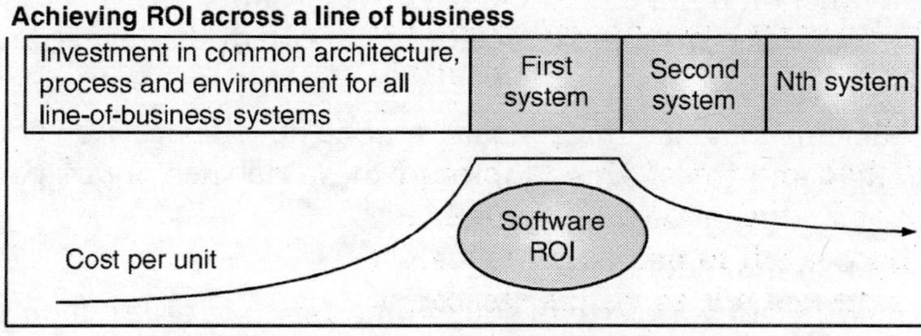

Achieving ROI across project with multiple iterations

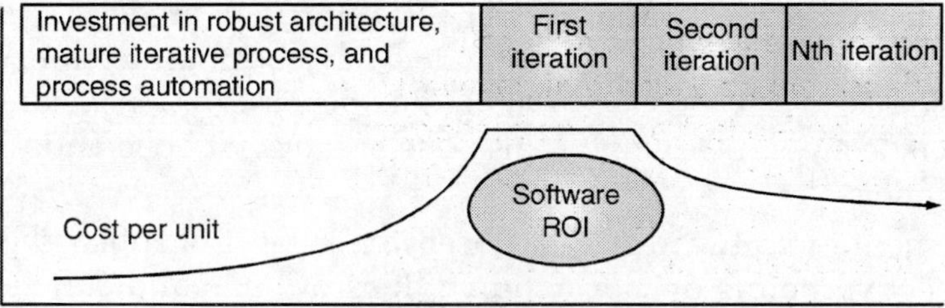

Achieving ROI across a life cycle of product releases

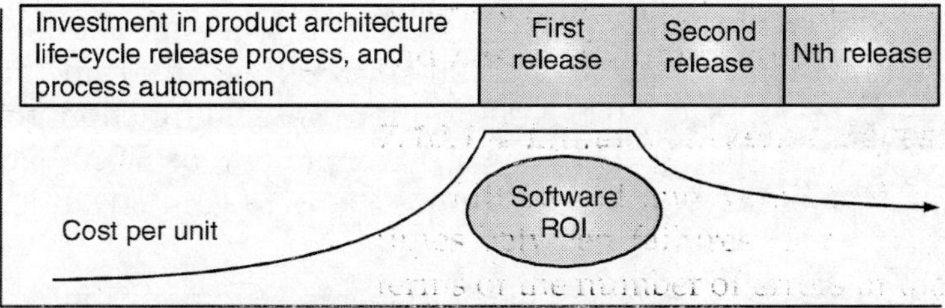

Figure 8.2: Return on Investment in Different Domains

8.3 PRAGMATIC SOFTWARE COST ESTIMATION

One critical problem in software cost estimation is a lack of well-documented case studies of projects that used an iterative development approach. Although cost model vendors claim that their tools are suitable for estimating iterative development projects, few are based on empirical project databases with modern iterative development success stories. Furthermore, because the software industry has inconsistently defined metrics or atomic units of measure, the data from actual projects are highly suspect in terms of consistency and comparability. It is hard enough to collect a homogeneous set of project data within one organization. It is extremely difficult to homogenize data across different organizations with different processes, languages, domains, and so on. For example, the fundamental unit of size can be counted differently across the industry. It is surprising that modern language standards do not make it simple definition of a source line reportable by the compiler. The exact definition of a function point or a SLOC is not very important, just as the exact length of a foot or a meter is equally arbitrary. It is simply important that everyone uses the same definition.

There have been many long-standing debates among developers and vendors of software cost estimation models and tools. Three topics of these debates are of particular interest here:

1. Which cost estimation model to use?
2. Whether to measure software size in source lines of code or function points?
3. What constitutes a good estimate?

About 50 vendors of software cost estimation tools, data, and services compete within the software industry. There are several popular cost estimation models as well as numerous organization-specific models. All the recent models have been centered on COCOMO and its successors, Ada COCOMO and COCOMO II, it is the basis of many software economics arguments and perspectives. COCOMO is also one of the most open and well-documented cost estimation models.

The measurement of software size has been the subject of much rhetoric. There are basically two objective points of view: source lines of code and function points. Both perspectives have proven to be more valuable than a third, which the subjective or ad hoc point of view practiced by many immature organizations that use no systematic measurement of size.

Many software experts have argued that SLOC is a lousy measure of size. However, when a code segment is described as a 1,000-source-line program, most people feel comfortable with its general 'mass'. If the description were 20 function points, 6 classes, 5 use cases, 4 object points, 6 files, 2 subsystems, 1 component, or 6,000 bytes, most people, including software experts, would ask further questions to gain an understanding of the subject code.

Today, language advances and the use of components, automatic source code generation, and object orientation have made SLOC a much more ambiguous measure.

The use of function points has a large following. The International Function Point User's Group, formed in 1984, is the dominant software measurement association in the industry. The primary advantage of using function points is that this method is independent of technology and is therefore a much better primitive unit for comparisons among projects and organizations. The main disadvantage is that the primitive definitions are abstract and measurements are not easily derived directly from the evolving artefacts.

Although both measures of size have their drawbacks, an organization can make either one work. The use of some measure is better than none at all. Anyone doing a cross-product or cross-organization comparisons should be using function points as the measure of size. Function points are also probably a more accurate estimator in the early phases of a project life cycle. In the later phases, however, SLOC becomes a more useful and precise measurement basis of various metrics perspectives.

The general accuracy of conventional cost models (such as COCOMO) has been described as 'within 20% of actuals, 70% of the time'. This level of unpredictability in the conventional software development process should be truly frightening to every investor, especially in light of the fact that few projects miss their estimate by doing better than expected. This is an interesting phenomenon to be considered when scheduling labour-intensive efforts. Unless specific incentives are provided for beating the overall schedule, projects rarely do better than planned. Teams and individuals perform subplanning to meet their objectives. If the time objective is lenient, they either expend energy elsewhere or they continue to add quality beyond what is necessary. They almost never propose to accelerate the schedule. If they did, their suggestion would most likely meet their resistance from other stakeholders who are expecting to synchronize. So plans to be ambitious as can possibly be achieved.

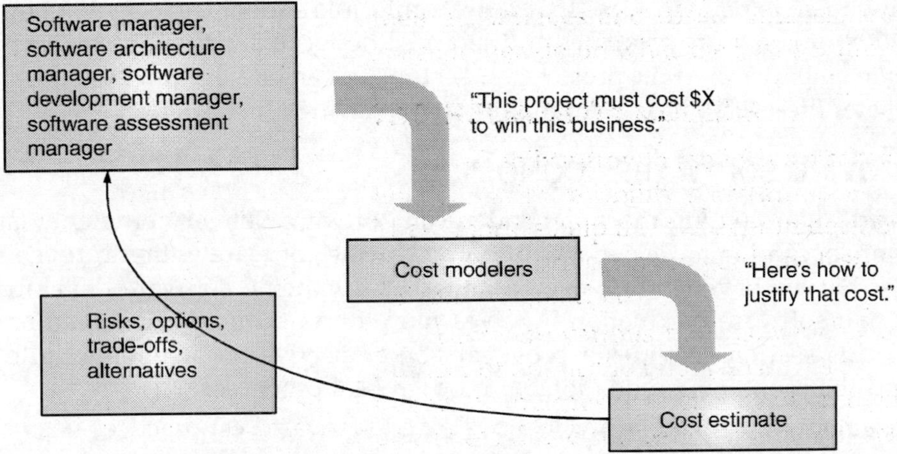

Figure 8.3: *The Predominant Cost Estimation Process*

Most real-world use of cost models is bottom-up rather than top-down. Figure 8.3 illustrates the predominant practice: The software manager defines the target cost of the software, and then manipulates the parameters and sizing until the target cost can be justified. The rationale for the target cost may be to win a proposal, to solicit customer funding, to attain internal corporate funding, or to achieve some other goal.

The process described in Figure 8.3 is not all bad. In fact, it is absolutely necessary to analyse the cost risks and understand the sensitivities and trade-offs objectively. It forces the software manager to examine the risks associated with achieving the target costs and to discuss this information with other stakeholders. The result is usually various perturbations in the plans, designs, process, or scope being proposed. This process provides a good vehicle for a basis of estimate and overall cost analysis.

A practical lesson learned from the field is that independent cost estimates are usually inaccurate. The only way to produce a credible estimate is for a competent team, the software project manager and the software architecture, development, and test managers, to iterate through several estimates and sensitivity analyses. This team must then take ownership of that cost estimate for the project to succeed.

Thus, in summary, a good estimate has the following attributes:

- It is conceived and supported by the project manager, architecture team, development team, and test team accountable for performing the work.

- It is accepted by all stakeholders as ambitious but realizable.
- It is based on a well-defined software cost model with credible basis.
- It is based on a database of relevant project experience that includes similar processes, similar technologies, similar environments, similar quality requirements, and similar people.
- It is defined in enough detail so that its key areas are understood and the probability of success is objectively assessed.

Extrapolating from a good estimate, an ideal estimate would be derived from a mature cost model with an experience base that reflects multiple similar projects done by the same team with the same mature processes and tools. Although this situation rarely exists when a project team embarks on a new project, good estimates can be achieved in a straightforward manner in later life-cycle phases of a mature project using a mature process.

8.4 IMPROVING SOFTWARE ECONOMICS

The world is becoming more dependent on software delivery efficiency and world economies are becoming more dependent on producing software with improved economic outcomes. What we have learned over decades of advancing software development best practice is that software production involves more of an economics than an engineering discipline. This section provides a provocative perspective on achieving agile software delivery and the economic foundations of modern best practices.

Improvement in software lifecycle models and software best practices has been a long slog that accelerated in the 1980s as the engineering roots of software management methods continued to fail in delivering acceptable software project performance.

Most organizations that depend on software are struggling to transform their lifecycle model from a development focus to a delivery focus. This subtle distinction in wording represents a dramatic change in the principles that are driving the management philosophy and the governance models. Namely, a "software development" orientation focuses on the various activities required in the development process, while a "software delivery" orientation focuses on the results of that process. Organizations that have successfully made this transition — perhaps thirty to forty percent by our estimate — have recognized that engineering discipline is trumped by economics discipline in most software- intensive endeavours.

Table 8.1: Differentiating conventional engineering governance from economically driven governance

Software Development: Engineering Driven	Software Delivery: Economics Driven
Distinct development phases	Continuously evolving systems
Distinct handoff from development team to maintenance team	Common process, platform, and team for development and maintenance
Distinct and sequential activities from requirements to design to code to test to operations	Sequence of usable capabilities with ever-increasing value

Phase and role specific processes and tools	Collaborative platform of integrated tools and process enactment
Collocated teams	Geographically distributed, web-based collaboration
Early precision in complete plans and requirements	Evolving precision as uncertainties are resolved
Governance through measurement of artefact production and activity completion	Governance through measurement of incremental outcomes, and progress/quality trends
Engineering discipline: precisely define requirements/plans completely, then track progress against static plans and scope	Economic discipline: reduce uncertainties, manage variance, measure trends, adapt and

Table 8.1 provides a few differentiating indicators of successfully making the transformation from conventional engineering governance to more economically driven governance.

It is not that much easy to improve the software economics but also difficult to measure and validate. There are many aspects are there in order to improve the software economics they are, Size, Process, Personnel, Environment and quality. These parameters (aspects) are not independent they are dependent. For example, tools enable size reduction and process improvements, size-reduction approaches lead to process changes, and process improvements drive tool requirements.

1. Reducing the *size* or complexity of what needs to be developed.
2. Improving the development *process*.
3. Using more-skilled *personnel* and better teams.
4. Using better *environments*.
5. Trading off or backing off on *quality* thresholds.

These parameters are given in priority order for most software domains. Table 8.2 lists some of the technology developments, process improvement efforts, and management approaches targeted at improving the economics of software development and integration.

Table 8.2: Important Trends in Improving Software Economics

Cost Model Parameters	**Trends**
Size Abstraction and component-based development technologies	Higher order languages (C++, Ada 95, Java, Visual Basic, etc.) Object-oriented (analysis, design, programming) Reuse Commercial components
Process Methods and techniques	Iterative development Process maturity models Architecture-first development Acquisition reform

Personnel People factors	Training and personnel skill development Teamwork Win-win cultures
Environment Automation technologies and tools	Integrated tools (visual modeling, compiler, editor, debugger, change management, etc.) Open systems Hardware platform performance Automation of coding, documents, testing, analysis
Quality Performance, reliability, accuracy	Hardware platform performance Demonstration-based assessment Statistical quality control

Most software experts would also stress the significant dependencies among these trends. For example, tools enable size reduction and process improvements, size reduction approaches lead to process changes, and process improvements drive toll requirements. Consider the domain of user interface software. Two decades ago, teams developing a user interface would spend extensive time analysing operations, human factors, screen layouts, and screen dynamics. All this would be done on paper because it was extremely expensive to commit designs, even informal prototypes, to execute code. Therefore, the process emphasized a fairly heavyweight set of early paper artefacts and user concurrence so that these 'requirements' could be frozen and the high construction costs could be minimized.

Graphical User Interface (GUI) technology is a good example of tools enabling a new and different process. As GUI technology matured, the conventional user interface process became obsolete. GUI builder tools permitted engineering teams to construct an executable user interface faster and at less cost. The paper descriptions were now unnecessary; in fact, they were an obstacle to the efficiency of the process. Operations analysis and human factors analysis were still important, but these activities could now be done in a realistic target environment using existing primitives and building blocks. Engineering and feedback cycles that used to take months could now be done in days or weeks. The old process was geared toward ensuring that the user interface was completely analysed and designed, because the project could afford only one construction cycle. The new process was geared toward taking the user interface through a few realistic versions, incorporating user feedback all along the way, and achieving a stable understanding of the requirements and the design issues in balance with one another.

It could be argues that the process advances drove the development of the tools, or that the technology advances drove the process change. Reality is probably a mixture of both. The point is that the five basic parameters of the cost estimation equation are not mutually exclusive, nor are they independent of each other. They are interrelated.

Another important factor that has influenced software technology improvements across the board is the ever-increasing advances in hardware performance. The availability of more cycles, more memory, and more bandwidth has eliminated many sources of software implementation complexity. Simpler, brute-force solutions are now possible, and hardware improvements are probably the enabling advance behind most software technology improvements of substance.

8.4.1 Reducing Software Product Size

- By choosing the type of the language
- By using Object-Oriented methods and visual modeling
- By reusing the existing components and building reusable components &
- By using commercial components, we can reduce the product size of a software

Here UPFs (Universal Function Points) are useful estimators for language-independent in the early life cycle phases. The basic units of function points are:

- External user inputs
- External outputs
- Internal logical data groups
- External data Interfaces
- External inquiries

8.4.1.1 Object Oriented Methods and Visual Modeling

There has been a widespread movement in the 1990s toward Object-Oriented technology. Some studies concluded that Object-Oriented programming languages appear to benefit both software productivity and software quality. One of such Object-Oriented method is UML (Unified Modeling Language). Booch described the following three reasons for the success of the projects that are using Object-Oriented concepts:

1. An OO-model of the problem and its solution encourages a common vocabulary between the end user of a system and its developers, thus creating a shared understanding of the problem being solved.
2. The use of continuous integration creates opportunities to recognize risk early and make incremental corrections without weaken the entire development effort.
3. An OO-architecture provides a clear separation among different elements of a system, crating firewalls that prevent a change in one part of the system from the entire architecture.

He also suggested five characteristics of a successful OO-Project,

1. A cruel focus on the development of a system that provides a well understood collection of essential minimal characteristics.
2. The existence of a culture that is centered on results, encourages communication, and yet is not afraid to fail.
3. The effective use of OO modeling.
4. The existence of a strong architectural vision.
5. The application of a well-managed iterative and incremental development life cycle.

8.4.1.2 Reuse

Organizations that translate reusable components into commercial products have the following characteristics:

- They have an economic motivation for continued support.
- They take ownership of improving product quality, adding new features and transitioning to new technologies.
- They have a sufficiently broad customer base to be profitable.

8.4.1.3 Commercial Components

A common approach being pursued today in many domains is to maximize integration of commercial components and off-the-shelf products. While the use of commercial components is certainly desirable as a means of reducing custom development, it has not proven to be straightforward in practice. Table 8.3 identifies some of the advantages and disadvantages of using commercial components. Because the trade-offs frequently have global effect on quality, cost, and supportability, the selection of commercial components over development of custom components has significant impact on a project's overall architecture. The paramount message here is that these decisions must be made early in the life cycle as part of the architectural design.

Table 8.3: Advantages and Disadvantages of Commercial Components versus Custom Software

Approach	Advantages	Disadvantages
Commercial Components	Predictable license costs Broadly used, mature technology Available now Dedicated support organization Hardware/software independence Rich in functionality	Frequent upgrades Up-front license fees Recurring maintenance fees Dependency in vendor Run-time efficiency sacrifices Functionality constraints Integration not always trivial No control over upgrades and maintenance Unnecessary features that consume extra resources Often inadequate reliability and stability Multiple-vendor incompatibilities
Custom Development	Complete change freedom Smaller, often simpler implementations Often better performance Control of development and enhancement	Expensive, unpredictable development Unpredictable availability date Undefined maintenance model Often immature and fragile Single-platform dependency Drain on expert requires

8.4.2 Improving Software Processes

There are three distinct process perspectives:

1. **Meta process:** It is an Organization's policies, procedures, and practices for pursuing a software intensive line of business. The focus of this process is of organizational economics, long-term strategies, and software ROI.
2. **Macro process:** A project's policies, and practices for producing a complete software product within certain cost, schedule, and quality constraints. The focus of the macroprocess is on creating an sufficient instance of the metaprocess for a specific set of constraints.

3. **Micro process:** A projects team's policies, procedures, and practices for achieving an artefact of a software process. The focus of the microprocess is on achieving an intermediate product baseline with sufficient functionality as economically and rapidly as practical.

The objective of process improvement is to maximize the allocation of resources to productive activities and minimize the impact of overhead activities on resources such as personnel, computers, and schedule.

Schedule improvement has at least three dimensions:

1. We could take an N-step process and improve the efficiency of each step.
2. We could take an N-step process and eliminate some steps so that it is now only an M-step process.
3. We could take an N-step process and use more concurrency in the activities being performed or the resources being applied.

Table 8.4: Three Levels of Process and their Attributes

Attributes	MetaProcess	MacroProcess	MicroProcess
Subject	Line-of-business	Project	Iteration
Objectives	Line-of-business Profitably Competitiveness	Project profitability Risk management Project budget, schedule, quality	Resource management Risk resolution Milestone budget, schedule, quality
Audience	Acquisition authority, customers Organizational management	Software project managers Software engineers	Subproject managers Software engineers
Metrics	Project predictability Revenue, market share	On budget, on schedule Major milestone success Project scrap and rework	On budget, on schedule Major milestone progress Release/iteration scrap and rework
Concerns	Bureaucracy vs. standardization	Quality vs. financial performance	Content vs. schedule
Time scales	6 to 12 months	1 to many years	1 to 6 months

8.4.3 Improving Team Effectiveness

COCOMO model suggests that the combined effects of personnel skill and experience can have an impact on productivity as much as a factor of four over the unskilled personnel. Balance and coverage are two of the most important features of excellent teams. Whenever a team is in out of balance then it is vulnerable. It is the responsibility of the project manager to keep track of his teams. Since teamwork is much more important than the sum of the individuals.

Boehm proposes the following staffing principles:

1. **The principle of top talent:** Use better and fewer people.
2. **The principle of job matching:** Fit the tasks to the skills and motivation of the people available.
3. **The principle of career progression:** An organization does best in the long run by helping its people to self-actualize.
4. **The principle of team balance:** Select people who will complement and synchronize with one another.
5. **The principle of phase-out:** Keeping a misfit on the team doesn't benefit anyone.

In general, staffing is achieved by these common methods:

- If people are already available with required skill set, just take them
- If people are already available but do not have the required skills, re-train them
- If people are not available, recruit trained people
- If you are not able to recruit skilled people, recruit and train people

Staffing of key personnel is very important, i.e. Project Manager and Software Architect.

Important Project Manager Skills are listed as follows:

- **Hiring skills.** Few decisions are as important as hiring decisions. Placing the right person in the right job seems obvious but is surprisingly hard to achieve.
- **Customer-interface skill.** Avoiding adversarial relationships among stake-holders is a prerequisite for success.
- **Decision-making skill.** The jillion books written about management have failed to provide a clear definition of this attribute. We all know a good leader when we run into one, and decision-making skill seems obvious despite its intangible definition.
- **Team-building skill.** Teamwork requires that a manager establish trust, motivate progress, exploit eccentric prima donnas, transition average people into top performers, eliminate misfits, and consolidate diverse opinions into a team direction.
- **Selling skill.** Successful project managers must sell all stakeholders (including themselves) on decisions and priorities, sell candidates on job positions, sell changes to the status quo in the face of resistance, and sell achievements against objectives. In practice, selling requires continuous negotiation, compromise, and empathy.

Important Software Architect Skills are listed as follows:

- **Technical Skills**: the most important skills for an architect. These must include skills in both, the problem domain and the solution domain
- **People Management Skills**: must ensure that all people understand and implement the architecture in exactly the way he has conceptualized it. This calls for a lot of people management skills and patience.
- **Role Model**: must be a role model for the software engineers – they would emulate all good things that the architect does

8.4.4 Improving Automation Through Software Environments

The following are the some of the configuration management environments which provide the foundation for executing and implementing the process:

Planning tools, Quality assurance and analysis tools, Test tools, and User interfaces provide crucial automation support for evolving the software engineering artefacts.

- ***Round-trip engineering:*** is a term used to describe the key capability of environments that support iterative development.
- ***Forward engineering:*** is the automation of one engineering artefact from another, more abstract representation. Ex: compilers and linkers
- ***Reverse engineering:*** is the generation or modification of a more abstract representation from an existing artefact, for example creating visual design model from a source code.

8.4.5 Achieving Required Quality

Key elements that improve overall software quality include the following:

- Focusing on powerful requirements and critical use case early in the life cycle
- Focusing on requirements completeness and traceability late in the life cycle
- Focusing throughout the life cycle on a balance between requirements evolution, design evolution, and plan evolution
- Using metrics and indicators to measure the progress and quality of an architecture as it evolves from high-level prototype into a fully biddable product
- Providing integrated life-cycle environments that support early and continuous configuration control, change management, rigorous design methods, document automation, and regression test automation
- Using visual modeling and higher level languages that support architectural control, abstraction, reliable programming, reuse, and self-documentation
- Early and continuous close look into performance issues through demonstration-based evaluations

In order to evaluate the performance the following sequence of events are necessary,

1. Project inception
2. Initial design review
3. Mid-life-cycle design review
4. Integration and test

Table 8.5: General Quality Improvements with a Modern Process

Quality Driver	Conventional Process	Modern Iterative Processes
Requirements misunderstanding	Discovered late	Resolved early
Development risk	Unknown until late	Understood and resolved early
Commercial components	Mostly unavailable	Still a quality driver, but trade-offs must be resolved early in life cycle
Change management	Late in the life cycle, chaotic and malignant	Early in the life cycle, straight-forward and benign
Design errors	Discovered late	Resolved early

Automation	Mostly error-prone manual procedures	Mostly automated, error-free evolution of artefacts
Resource adequacy	Unpredictable	Predictable
Schedules	Overconstrained	Tunable to quality, performance feedback, quantitative understanding
Target performance	Paper-based analysis or separate simulation	Executing prototypes, early performance feedback, quantitative understanding
Software process rigor	Document-based	Managed, measured, and toll-supported

Improved insight into run-time performance issues is even more important as projects incorporate mixtures of commercial components and custom-developed components. Conventional development processes stressed early sizing and timing estimates of computer program resource utilization.

However, the typical chronology of events in performance assessment was as follows:

- **Project Inception:** The proposed design was asserted to be low risk with adequate performance margin.
- **Initial design review:** Optimistic assessments of adequate design margin were based mostly on paper analysis or rough simulation of the critical threads. In most cases, the actual application algorithms and database sizes were fairly well understood. However, the infrastructure, including the operating system overhead, the database management overhead, and the inter-process and network communications overhead, and all the secondary threads were typically misunderstood.
- **Mid-life-cycle design review:** The assessments started whittling away at the margin, as early benchmarks and initial tests began exposing the optimism inherent in earlier estimates.
- **Integration and Test:** Serious performance problems were uncovered, necessary fundamental changes in the architecture. The underlying infrastructure was usually the scapegoat, but the real culprit was immature use of the infrastructure, immature architectural solutions, or poorly understood early design trade-offs.

8.5 COMPARISON OF OLD AND NEW WAYS OF SOFTWARE MANAGEMENT

Over the past two decades software development is a re-engineering process. Now it is replaced by advanced software engineering technologies. This transition was motivated by the insatiable demand for more software features produced more rapidly under more competitive pressure to reduce cost. In the commercial software industry, the combination of competitive pressures, profitability, diversity of customers, and rapidly changing technology caused many organizations to initiate new management approaches.

Conventional software engineering has numerous well-established principles. Many are still valid, while the others are obsolete. A modern software management process will incorporate many conventional principles but will also transition to some substantially new approaches.

8.5.1 The Principles of Conventional Software Engineering

Based on many years of software development experience, the software industry proposed so many principles (nearly 201 by – Davis's). Of which Davis's top 30 principles are:

1. **Make quality #1:** Quality must be quantified and mechanisms put into place to motivate its achievement.
2. **High-quality software is possible:** In order to improve the quality of the product we need to involve the customer, select the prototyping, simplifying design, conducting inspections, and hiring the best people.
3. **Give products to customers early:** No matter how hard you try to learn user's needs during the requirements phase, the most effective way to determine real needs is to give users a product and let them play with it.
4. **Determine the problem before writing the requirements:** Whenever a problem is raised most engineers provide a solution. Before we try to solve a problem, be sure to explore all the alternatives and don't be blinded by the understandable solution.
5. **Evaluate design alternatives:** After the requirements are agreed upon, we must examine a variety of architectures and algorithms and choose the one which is not used earlier.
6. **Use an appropriate process model:** For every project, there are so many prototypes (process models). So select the best one that is exactly suitable to our project.
7. **Use different languages for different phases:** Our industry's main aim is to provide simple solutions to complex problems. In order to accomplish this goal choose different languages for different modules/phases if required.
8. **Minimize intellectual distance:** We have to design the structure of software is as close as possible to the real-world structure.
9. **Put techniques before tools:** An undisciplined software engineer with a tool becomes a dangerous, undisciplined software engineer.
10. **Get it right before you make it faster:** It is very easy to make a working program run faster than it is to make a fast program work. Don't worry about optimization during initial coding.
11. **Inspect the code:** Examine the detailed design and code is a much better way to find the errors than testing.
12. **Good management** is more important than good technology.
13. **People are the key to success:** Highly skilled people with appropriate experience, talent, and training are the key. The right people with insufficient tools, languages, and process will succeed.
14. **Follow with care:** Everybody is doing something but does not make it right for you. It may be right, but you must carefully assess its applicability to your environment.
15. **Take responsibility:** When a bridge collapses we ask "what did the engineer do wrong?" Similarly if the software fails, we ask the same. So the fact is in every engineering discipline, the best methods can be used to produce poor results and the most out of date methods to produce stylish design.
16. **Understand the customer's priorities**. It is possible the customer would tolerate 90% of the functionality delivered late if they could have 10% of it on time.

17. **The more they see, the more they need**. The more functionality (or performance) you provide a user, the more functionality (or performance) the user wants.
18. **Plan to throw one away** .One of the most important critical success factors is whether or not a product is entirely new. Such brand-new applications, architectures, interfaces, or algorithms rarely work the first time.
19. **Design for change**. The architectures, components, and specification techniques you use must accommodate change.
20. **Design without documentation is not design**. I have often heard software engineers say, "I have finished the design. All that is left is the documentation."
21. **Use tools, but be realistic**. Software tools make their users more efficient.
22. **Avoid tricks**. Many programmers love to create programs with tricks constructs that perform a function correctly, but in an obscure way. Show the world how smart you are by avoiding tricky code.
23. **Encapsulate**. Information-hiding is a simple, proven concept that results in software that is easier to test and much easier to maintain.
24. **Use coupling and cohesion**. Coupling and cohesion are the best ways to measure software's inherent maintainability and adaptability.
25. **Use the McCabe complexity measure**. Although there are many metrics available to report the inherent complexity of software, none is as intuitive and easy to use as Tom McCabe's.
26. **Don't test your own software**. Software developers should never be the primary testers of their own software.
27. **Analyse causes for errors**. It is far more cost-effective to reduce the effect of an error by preventing it than it is to find and fix it. One way to do this is to analyse the causes of errors as they are detected.
28. **Realize that software's entropy increases**. Any software system that undergoes continuous change will grow in complexity and become more and more disorganized.
29. **People and time are not interchangeable**. Measuring a project solely by person-months makes little sense.
30. **Expert excellence**. Your employees will do much better if you have high expectations for them.

8.5.2 The Principles of Modern Software Management

Here we present the ten principles of modern software management. The principles are in priority order.

1. **Base the process on an architecture-first approach:** *(Central design element)* This requires that a demonstrable balance be achieved among the driving requirements, the architecturally significant design decisions, and the life cycle plans before the resources are committed for full-scale development.
2. **Establish an iterative life-cycle process:** *(The risk management element)* With today's sophisticated systems, it is not possible to define the entire problem, design the entire solution, build the software, then test the end product in sequence. Instead, and iterative process that refines the problem understanding, an effective solution, and an effective

plan over several iterations encourages balanced treatment of all stakeholder objectives. Major risks must be addressed early to increase predictability and avoid expensive downstream scrap and rework.

3. **Transition design methods to emphasize component-based development:** *(The technology element)* Moving from LOC mentally to component-based mentally is necessary to reduce the amount of human-generated source code and custom development. A component is a cohesive set of pre-existing lines of code, either in source or executable format, with a defined interface and behaviour.
4. **Establish a change management environment:** *(The control element)* The dynamics of iterative development, include concurrent workflows by different teams working on shared artefacts, necessitates objectively controlled baseline.
5. **Enhance change freedom through tools that support round-trip engineering:** *(The automation element)* Round-trip engineering is the environment support necessary to automate and synchronize engineering information in different formats. Change freedom is necessary in an iterative process.

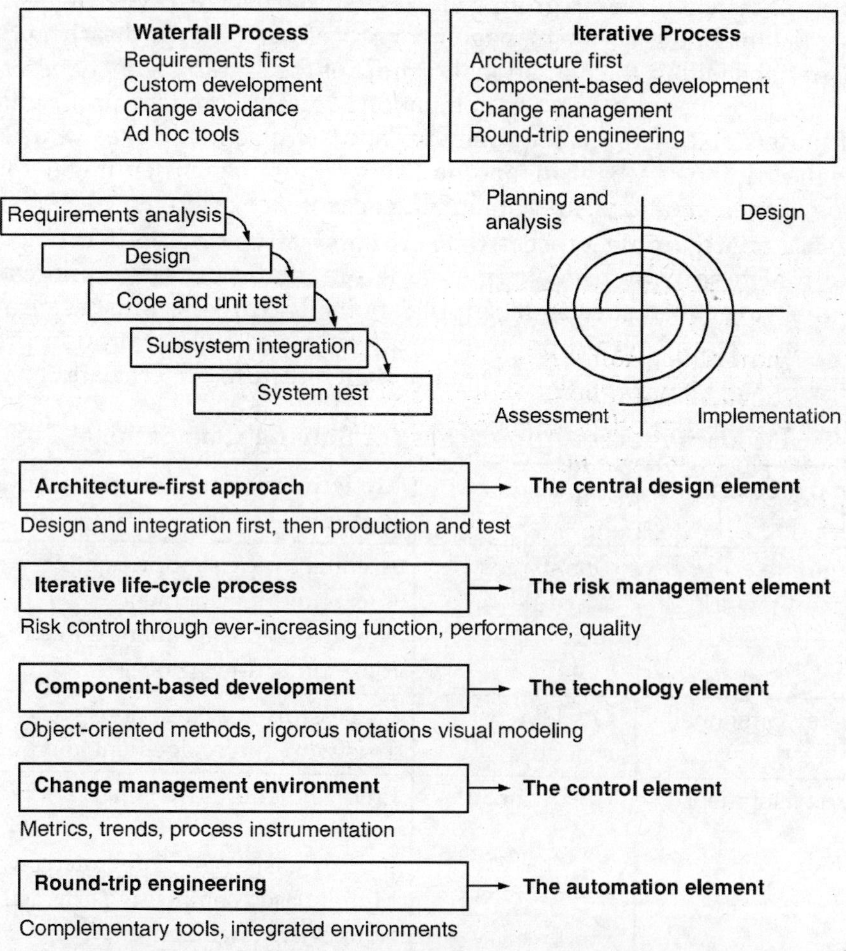

Figure 8.4: *The Top Five Principles of a Modern Process*

6. **Capture design artefacts in rigorous, model-based notation:** A model-based approach supports the evolution of semantically rich graphical and textual design notations. Visual modeling with rigorous notations and formal machine- process able language provides more objective measures than the traditional approach of human review and inspection of ad hoc design representations in paper doc.
7. **Instrument the process for objective quality control and progress assessment:** Life-cycle assessment of the progress and quality of all intermediate product must be integrated into the process. The best assessment mechanisms are well-defined measures derived directly from the evolving engineering artefacts and integrated into all activities and teams.
8. **Use a demonstration-based approach to assess intermediate artefacts:** Transitioning from whether the artefact is an early prototype, a baseline architecture, or a beta capability into an executable demonstration of relevant provides more tangible understanding of the design trade-offs, early integration and earlier elimination of architectural defects.
9. **Plan intermediate releases in groups of usage scenarios with evolving levels of detail:** It is essential that the software management process drive toward early and continuous demonstrations within the operational context of the system, namely its use cases. The evolution of project increments and generations must be commensurate with the current level of understanding of the requirements and architecture. Cohesive usage scenarios are then the primary mechanism for organizing requirements, defining iteration content, assessing implementations, and organizing acceptance testing.
10. **Establish a configurable process that economically scalable:** No single process is suitable for all software developments. A pragmatic process framework must be configurable to a broad spectrum of applications. The process must ensure that there is economy of sale and return on investment by exploiting a common process spirit, extensive process automation, and common architecture patterns and components.

Table 8.6: Modern Process Approaches for Solving Conventional Problems

Conventional Process: Top 10 Risks	Impact	Modern Process: Inherent Risk Resolution Features
Late breakage and excessive scrap/rework	Quality, cost, schedule	Architecture first approach Interactive development Automated change management Risk-confronting process
Attrition of key personnel	Quality, cost, schedule	Successful, early iterations Trustworthy management and planning
Inadequate development resources	Cost, schedule	Environments as first-class artefacts of the process Industrial-strength, integrated environments Model-based engineering artefacts Round-trip engineering

Adversarial stakeholders	Cost, schedule	Demonstration-based review Use-case-oriented requirements/testing
Necessary technology insertion	Cost, schedule	Architecture-first approach Component-based development
Requirements creep	Cost, schedule	Iterative development Use case modeling Demonstration-based review
Analysis paralysis	Schedule	Demonstration-based review Use-case-oriented requirements/testing
Inadequate performance	Quality	Demonstration-based performance assessment Early architecture performance feedback
Overemphasis on artefacts	Schedule	Demonstration-based assessment Objective quality control
Inadequate fashion	Quality	Interactive development Early prototypes, incremental releases

SUMMARY

Software economics is the study of how scarce project resources are allocated for software projects.Softwareeconomicshelpssoftwaremanagersallocatethoseresourcesinthemost efficient manner. The process of counting function points, gathering data, analyzing data is commonly referred to as Software Metrics, but in reality is a branch of economics which should be called Software Economics. Software engineering is dominated by intellectual activities that are focused on solving problems of immense complexity with numerous unknowns in competing perspectives. The world is becoming more dependent on software delivery efficiency and world economies are becoming more dependent on producing software with improved economic outcomes. Improvement in software lifecycle models and software best practices has been a long slog that accelerated in the 1980s as the engineering roots of software management methods continued to fail in delivering acceptable software project performance. Over the past two decades software development is a re-engineering process. Now it is replaced by advanced software engineering technologies. Conventional software engineering has numerous well-established principles. Many are still valid, while the others are obsolete. A modern software management process will incorporate many conventional principles but will also transition to some substantially new approaches.

EXERCISES

1. What do you mean by software economics?
2. Explain the evolution of software economics?
3. What do you understand pragmatic software cost estimation?
4. How can you improve software economics?
5. Explain the various parameters of cost model?
6. How can you reduce software product size?
7. What are the advantages and disadvantages of Commercial Components versus Custom Software?
8. Explain the procedure of improving software processes?
9. Explain the general quality improvements with a modern process?
10. Comparison of old and new ways of software management?

❑

UNIT 4
SOFTWARE REENGINEERING

Software Reengineering

9

9.1 INTRODUCTION

The re-engineering re-use things already in the old software to avoid waste of material and spiritual reduce maintenance costs take to bring about the economic value, the most effective. The growth in costs and the importance of software companies, agencies, small and medium enterprises and large organizations were forced to attempt re-engineering software. Basically, the software re-engineering is to take and pass the existing software. It is the software maintenance costs, repair expensive or system architecture and performance have failed to do. We take it with technology software and hardware available. However, the difficulty here lies in understanding the current system. Usually the requirements, design and document source code (code) is not available or has expired long ago so it's not clear. What is at, functions to move? Usually the system will include features not needed; it will need to be removed in the new software system.

Large number of systems built from scratch is decreasing, while the number of legacy systems in usability was very high. While the functionality of the system remains unchanged as the application environment, system level hardware and software are different. To enhance the existing functionality may be needed. Although the re-engineering efforts to improve, it does not incorporate until reengineering is completed. This allows comparison of the functionality of existing systems and new systems.

The problem is that systems are in use today, the basic system, to be a lack of well-designed structure and organization of code changes the whole software system is difficult and expensive. Corporations do not want to destroy the system because it was built for many subsidiaries of the Group which, if destroyed will result in the application process may have made will be lost. Often the developers of the legacy systems are not always acceptable or correct the information that was lost this is the only remaining source of the code of existing software. The initial cost for developing logic and the components of the system software should not be wasted. Therefore, re-use through reengineering is desired.

The challenge in software re-engineering is to take existing systems and imbued with good features and attributes of the software developer, created a new system where the goal is to maintain the required functions in the application of new technologies. Although the specific objectives of a reengineering task are determined by the objectives of each company, but overall achievement has four main objectives of the re-engineering software:

- Prepare for enhanced functionality.
- Improve maintenance.
- Access to the new platform.
- Improved reliability.

Although re-engineering should not be taken to enhance the functionality of existing systems, it is frequently used to prepare for advanced functionality. The legacy system, through amendment and supplement the annual improvement in error or by more difficult or expensive. The source (code) no longer clears, and reference materials may not exist and if there is often outdated. Re-engineering determines the characteristics of existing systems can be compared with the specifications of the desired system. Reconstruct the target can be improved to facilitate the improvements. For example, if you want to improve the system based on object-oriented design, the objective of the system can be developed using object-oriented technology to prepare for the enhanced functionality to the system base. As the system developed and advanced, maintenance costs increased due to changes more difficult and time consuming. The goal of re-engineering is to redesign the system with the appropriate function module and clear interface. Document internal and outside addition will be in circulation thus improving maintainability.

Computer industry is developing at very high speeds. New hardware and system software include new features become obsolete quickly. Since the system changed so that skilled workers move to work with newer technology, leaving some employees to maintain the old system. In a short time, the manufacturer no longer supports addition. Software products and hardware become quite expensive to maintain. Even as the compatibility of legacy systems with newer ones. That's why software companies have to move to newer platform hardware, operating systems, and programming languages.

The main goal is to achieve higher reliability. Although reliability cannot always be very high, more likely, over time and may have changed on the reliability, the system time much has changed, and it raises many problems such as maintenance and continues to change. For maintenance and further changes to the software reliability will decrease until no longer acceptable.

9.2 REENGINEERING

Reengineering involves the process of taking existing legacy software that will have become expensive to maintain or whose system architecture or implementation are now obsolete, and redoing it with current software and/or hardware technology or, technically, it is the examination, analysis, and alteration of an existing software system to reconstitute it in a new and better form, and the subsequent implementation of the new form, thereof. The difficult part lies in understanding the existing system. In most cases, the requirements, design and code documentation will no longer be available, or will be out of date, so it is really not clear what functions are to be moved. Generally the system would contain functions that will no longer be needed, and they would thus not be moved to the new system.

Re-engineering is a process that involves the examination, analysis and alteration of an existing software system to reconstitute it in a new form, and the subsequent implementation of the new form.

The reengineering process encompasses a combination of other processes such as:

- reverse engineering,
- redocumentation,
- restructuring,
- translation,
- forward engineering

The goal is to understand the existing software and then to re-implement it to improve the system's functionality, performance or implementation. The objective is to maintain the existing functionality and prepare for functionality to be added later.

9.3 TAXONOMY OF SOFTWARE REENGINEERING

In this section, the following key terms provide a clear scope and taxonomy of the domain of software reengineering:

1. **Forward engineering** is the traditional process of moving from high level abstractions and logical, implementation-independent designs to the physical implementation of a system.
2. **Reverse engineering** is the process of analyzing a subject system to
   (1) identify the system's components and their interrelationships and
   (2) create representations of the system in another form or higher level of abstraction.
3. **Redocumentation** is the creation or revision of a semantically equivalent representation within the same relative abstraction level. The resulting forms of representation are usually considered alternate views (for example, data flow, data structures, and control flow) intended for a human audience. Redocumentation is the simplest and oldest form of reverse engineering and can be considered to be an unintrusive, weak form of restructuring.
4. **Design recovery or reverse design** is a subset of reverse engineering in which domain knowledge, external information, and deduction or fuzzy reasoning are added to the observations of the subject system to identify meaningful higher-level abstractions beyond those obtained directly by examining the system itself. Design recovery recreates design abstractions from a combination of code, existing design documentation (if available), personal experience, and general knowledge about problem and application domains.
5. **Program understanding or program comprehension** is a term related to reverse engineering. Program understanding implies always that understanding begins with the source code while reverse engineering can start at a binary and executable form of the system or at high-level descriptions of the design. The science of program understanding includes the cognitive science of human mental processes in program understanding. Program understanding can be achieved in an ad hoc manner, and no external representation has to arise. While reverse engineering is the systematic approach to developing an external representation of the subject system, program understanding is comparable with design recovery because both of them start at source code level.
6. **Restructuring** is the transformation from one representation form to another at the same relative abstraction level, while preserving the subject system's external behavior (i.e., functionality and semantics).

7. **Reengineering** is the examination and alteration of a subject system to reconstitute it in a new form and the subsequent implementation of the new form. The process of reengineering computing systems involves three main steps: reverse engineering, functional restructuring, and forward engineering.
8. **Reverse specification** is a kind of reverse engineering where a specification is abstracted from the source code or design description. Specification in this context means an abstract description of what the software does. In forward engineering, the specification tells us what the software has to do. However, this information is not included in the source code. Only in rare cases, it can be recovered from comments in the source code and from the people involved in the original forward engineering process.
9. **Recode** involves changing the implementation characteristic of the source code. Language translation and control flow restructuring are source-code-level changes. Other possible changes include conforming to coding standards, improving source code readability, and renaming program items.
10. **Redesign** involves changing the design characteristics. Possible changes include restructuring design architecture, altering a system's data model as incorporated in data structures or in a database, and improving an algorithm.
11. **Respecify** involves changing the requirement characteristics. This type of change can refer to changing only the form of existing requirements (i.e., taking informal requirements expressed in English and generating a formal specification expressed in a formal language, such as Z). This type of change can also refer to changing system requirements, such as the addition of new requirements, or the deletion or alteration of existing requirements.

Figure 9.1 presents a general model of reverse engineering, and Figure 9.2 presents a general model of reengineering, in terms of the above definitions.

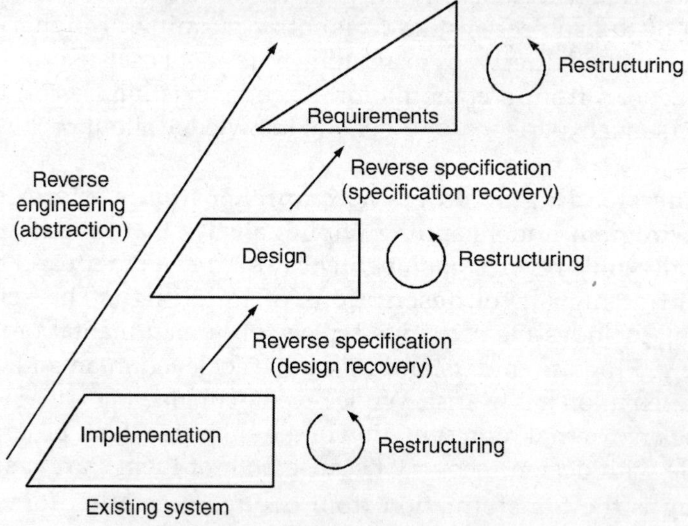

Figure 9.1: General model for reverse engineering.

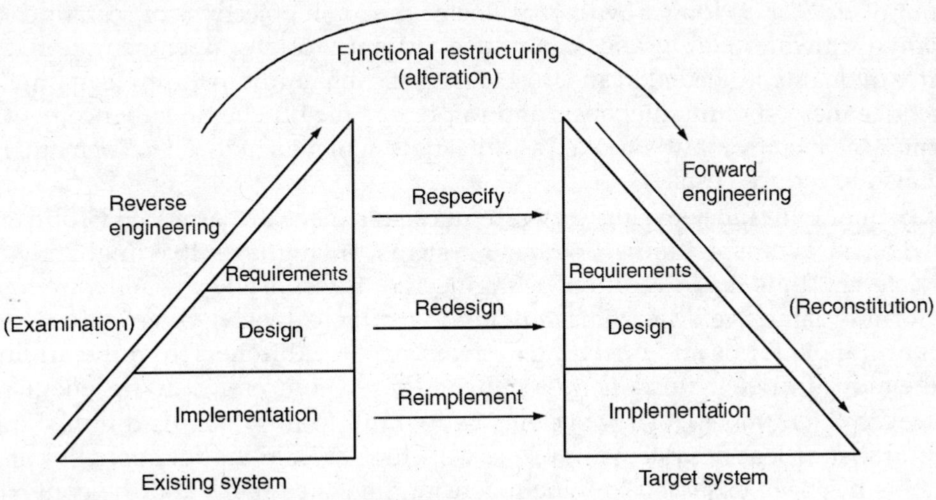

Figure 9.2: *General model for software reengineering.*

9.4 REENGINEERING BENEFITS

Following are the various benefits of reengineering:

1. *Lower costs:* Evidence from a number of US projects suggests that reengineering an existing system costs significantly less than new system development. Ulrich, for example reports on a reengineering project that cost $12 million, compared to estimated redevelopment costs of $50 million.
2. *Lower risks:* Reengineering is based on incremental improvement of systems, rather than radical system replacement. The risk of losing critical business knowledge, which may be embedded in a legacy system, or of producing a system that does not meet its users' real needs, is drastically reduced.
3. *Better use of existing staff:* Existing staff expertise can be maintained and extended accommodate new skills during reengineering. The incremental nature of reengineering means that existing staff skills can evolve as the system evolves. The approach carries less risk and expense which is associated with hiring new staff.
4. *Revelation of business rules:* As a system is reengineered, business rules that are embedded in the system are rediscovered. This is particularly true where the rules govern exceptional situations.
5. *Incremental development*: Reengineering can be carried out in stages, as budget and resources are available. The operational organisation always has a working system, and end users are able to gradually adapt to the reengineered as it is delivered in increments.

9.5 REENGINEERING OBJECTIVES

There are two general reengineering objectives:

- **Quality Improvement:** The existing software will be of low quality, due to many modifications during the course of time. The user and system documentation will often be out-of-date or no longer available. One of the main objectives of reengineering is to improve software quality and to produce current working documentation. A higher degree of quality is needed in an effort to increase reliability, to improve maintainability, to reduce the cost of maintenance, and to prepare for functional enhancement. Object-oriented technology may be applied as a means to achieve a higher level of maintainability and also to reduce costs.

- **Mitigation:** Old and working software may still meet the user needs but it may be based on hardware platforms, operating systems, or languages that might have become obsolete and thus may need to be reengineered, transporting the software to a newer platform or language. Migration may involve quite extensive redesigning of the new supporting platforms and operating systems are very different from the original, such as the move from a mainframe to a network-based computing environment.

However, the number of large systems being built from scratch is diminishing, while the number of legacy systems in use is very high. While the functionality of existing systems has been observed to remain constant, on the other hand the context of new systems, such as the application environment, system level hardware and software, has proved to be different. Enhancements to the functionality of the existing system may also be needed, but although the reengineering effort may be configured for enhancements, they should be incorporated until after the reengineering is complete. This facilitates the comparison of functionality between the existing system and the new system.

The root of the problem is that the systems currently in use, 'legacy' systems, have become lacking in good design structure and code organization, making changes to the software difficult and costly. Corporations do not want to throw away these systems because there are many built in subtle business application processes that have evolved over time that would be lost. In most cases the original developers of the legacy systems are not available to verify or explain this information. The only available source is the current software source code. The original expense if developing the logic and components of the software systems should not be wasted, so reuse through reengineering is desired.

The challenge in software engineering is to take existing systems and instil good software development methods and properties, generating a new target system that maintains the required functionality while applying new technologies. Although specific objectives of a reengineering task are determined by the goals of the corporations, there are four reengineering objectives.

- **Preparation for functional enhancement:** The reengineered target system can be built to easily facilitate the enhancements. For example, if the desired system enhancements build to on object-oriented design, the target system can be developed using object oriented technology in preparation to increase on the functionality of the legacy system.
- **Improve maintainability:** As systems grow and evolve, maintainability becomes a bottleneck and very time consuming. An objective of reengineering is to re-design the system with more appropriately functional modules and explicit interfaces. Documentation, internal and external, will also be current, hence improving maintainability.

- **Migration:** The computer industry continues to grow at a fast rate. New hardware and software systems include new features, quickly outdating current systems. For these reasons, companies with working software that meets their needs might need to migrate to a new hardware platform, operating system or language.
- **Improve reliability:** Although it is possible that reliability was never very high in the first place, more likely, over time and with multiple changes, there have been problems, one change causing multiple additional problems. As maintenance and changes continue, the reliability of the software steadily decreases to the point of being unacceptable.

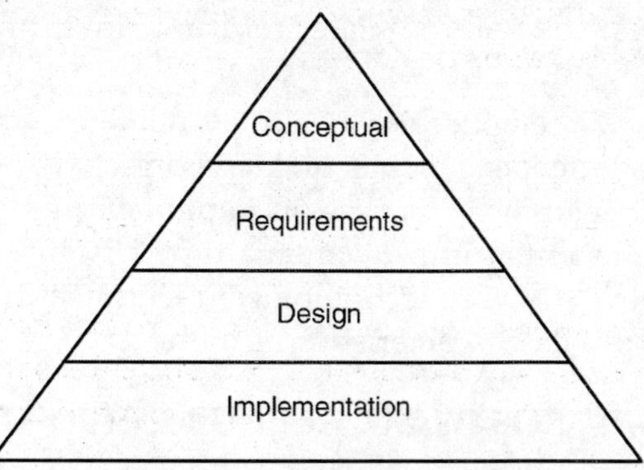

Figure 9.3: *Levels of Abstraction*

Although reengineering should not be done to enhance the functionality of an existing system, it is often used in preparation for enhancement. Legacy systems, through years of modifications due to errors or enhancements, become difficult and expensive to change. The code no longer has a clear, logical structure and documentation may not exist, and if it exists, it is often outdated. Reengineering specifies the characteristics of the existing systems that can be compared to the specifications of the characteristics of the desired system. The reengineered target system can be built to easily facilitate the enhancements. For example, if the desired system enhancements built on object-oriented design, the target system can be developed using object-oriented technology in preparation for increasing the functionality of the legacy system. As systems grow and evolve, maintainability costs increase because changes become difficult and time consuming. An objective of reengineering is to redesign the system with more appropriately functional modules and explicit interfaces. Documentation, internal and external, will also be current, hence improving maintainability.

9.6 BENEFITS OF REENGINEERING A LEGACY SYSTEM

Although many application development tool vendors emphasize new development in the form of tools to drive multi-tier application development or web-enablement, the notion of how to leverage past IT investments has largely been overlooked. Since business rules define the active policy of an organization, an ability to identify, understand and leverage these rules is a key prerequisite to evolving an organization's IT infrastructure.

Until recently, software engineering concentrated almost exclusively on the definition and improvement of the software development process. And this produced a lot of important results, ranging from structured analysis, to object oriented analysis, domain and component analysis, CASE environments, etc., which are very useful in developing new systems and forward engineering existing systems well maintained and documented. But legacy systems, created prior these methodologies and tools, usually are very poor in documentation and suffer of years of personnel change and ad-hoc maintenance interventions. This is where reengineering steps in.

"**Reengineering** *is the systematic transformation of an existing system into a new form to realize quality improvements in operation, system capability, functionality, performance, or evolvability at a lower cost, schedule, or risk to the customer.*"

This definition emphasis's the focus that reengineering puts on improving existing systems with a greater return of investment (ROI) than could be obtained through a new development.

Reengineering is closely related to traditional maintenance, as defined by ANSI-IEEE: maintenance entails making corrective, perfective, and adaptive changes to software, while development focuses on implementing new capabilities, adding functionalities, or making substantial improvements typically by using new computer resources and incorporating new software technologies; reengineering spans the gap between these two activities and exhibits characteristics of both.

9.7 SOFTWARE REENGINEERING CYCLE

To understand better the process of software reengineering, we first examine the reengineering cycle chart (Figure 9.4) introduced by Bachman, which features both forward and reverse engineering. Reverse engineering begins at the bottom left of Figure 9.4 with the definition of existing applications and raises the applications to successively higher levels of abstraction. At the top of Figure 9.4, the design objects created by the reverse engineering steps are enhanced and validated to become the revised design objects that may be used in the forward engineering process. At the bottom of Figure 9.4, a new application system becomes an existing application system at the moment that it goes into production.

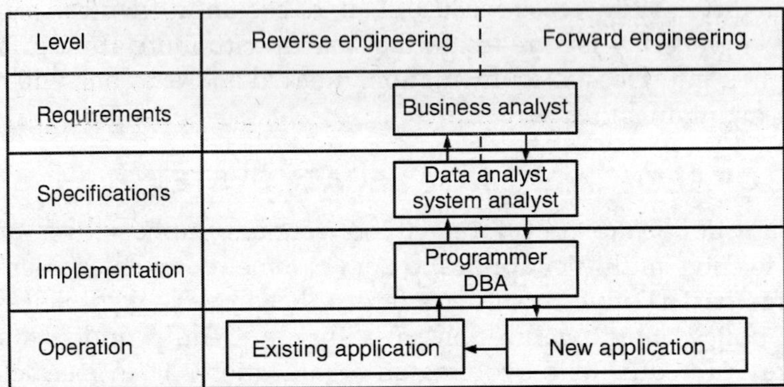

Figure 9.4: Bachman's reengineering cycle.

To generalize this model, many software systems typically undergo the following stages:

Specification → Design → Implementation → Design → Specification

This represents a process whereby before implementing a program, a specification was written first. Then, a design was derived from the given specification, and the program was implemented and operated for a period of time. When the program needed to be changed, a design or specification (which may be different from the original one) was obtained through reverse engineering (the design or specification can be used for such purposes as maintenance and reengineering). A specification states what a program does; a design states both what a program does and how it does it, and the program itself implements how to do the job. Therefore the above process can be represented as follows:

what? → what & how? → how? → what & how? → what?

A specification, a design, and an implementation of a program usually entail different levels of abstraction. To move from one stage (e.g., the specification stage) to another stage (e.g., the design stage) involves a process of crossing levels of abstraction. Usually a specification is more abstract than its implementation; therefore, the above process can again be represented as follows:

abstract → less abstract → concrete → more abstract → abstract

This suggests that the abstraction level of software is an important feature when both forward and reverse engineering are carried out and therefore that abstraction is significant for both reverse and forward engineering.

9.8 GENERAL MODEL OF SOFTWARE REENGINEERING

Re-engineering starts with the source code of the basic system exist, and ends with the source code of the system will target. This process can be as simple as using the translation tool to translate source code from one language into another language (FORTRAN to C) or from one operating system to other operating systems (UNIX to DOS). On the other hand, the task of re-engineering can be very complex, using existing source code to recreate the design, determine the requirements in existing systems and then compare them to current requirements now, remove things no longer apply, the system design using object-oriented design and the last code into a new system. Figure 9.5 the general pattern of re-engineering software for engineering and process for all levels of re-engineering based on the level of software development level abstractions mentioned above.

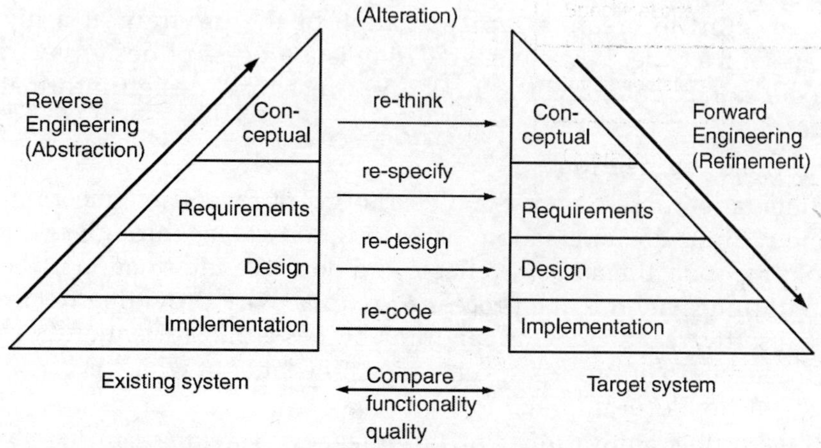

Figure 9.5: *General Pattern of Re-engineering Software*

The model in Figure 9.5 applies three principles of reengineering: abstraction, the amendment and refinement. This abstraction level is a gradual increase in the level of abstraction of the system. The present system was created by replacing a row of information is the information that is more abstract. Abstractions make the description emphasize the characteristics of the system. The upward movement is called reverse engineering and related accessories to the process, tools and techniques. The amendment is to create one or more to convert a representation of the system without changing the level of abstraction in which additional, delete and modify information. The refinement (Refinement) is the gradual reduction in the level of abstraction of the system caused by the continuous replacement information in existing systems with more detailed information. It is technically forward (Forward engineering) as software developers with the code (code) but with some new screening process.

To change a feature of the system, the work is done at the level of abstraction at which information about characteristics that are clearly presented. To translate the code (code) as a language aiming to reverse engineering are necessary changes made at the level of implementation.

9.8.1 Reverse Engineering

The term *reverse engineering* has its origins in the hardware world. A company disassembles a competitive hardware product in an effort to understand its competitor's design and manufacturing "secrets." These secrets could be easily understood if the competitor's design and manufacturing specifications were obtained. But these documents are proprietary and unavailable to the company doing the reverse engineering. In essence, successful reverse engineering derives one or more design and manufacturing specifications for a product by examining actual specimens of the product.

Reverse engineering for software is quite similar. In most cases, however, the program to be reverse engineered is not a competitor's. Rather, it is the company's own work (often done many years earlier). The "secrets" to be understood are obscure because no specification was ever developed. Therefore, reverse engineering for software is the process of analysing a program in an effort to create a representation of the program at a higher level of abstraction than source code. Reverse engineering is a process of design recovery. Reverse engineering tools extract data, architectural, and procedural design information from an existing program.

Types of reverse engineering:

1. **Re-documentation:** It is one of the oldest forms of reverse engineering. One way of producing accurate documentation for existing software is through re-documentation. In lack of proper document only reliable and objective information is the source code itself. Re-documentation is the process of retro activity providing documentation for an existing software system. One can think of it as a transformation from source code to pseudocode and /or process specification. The latter of which is considered to be at higher abstraction level than the former.
2. **Structural Re-documentation:** For large legacy system, an understanding of the structural aspect of system architects is more important than any single algorithmic

component. Program understanding is especially problematic for software engineer and technical managers. The doc that exists usually describes the isolated parts of the system; it does not describe the overall architecture. Moreover the documentation

9.8.2 Forward Engineering

A program with control flow that is the graphic equivalent of a bowl of spaghetti, with "modules" that are 2,000 statements long, with few meaningful comment lines in 290,000 source statements and no other documentation must be modified to accommodate changing user requirements.

We have the following options:

1. We can struggle through modification after modification, fighting the implicit design and source code to implement the necessary changes.
2. We can attempt to understand the broader inner workings of the program in an effort to make modifications more effectively.
3. We can redesign, recode, and test those portions of the software that require modification, applying a software engineering approach to all revised segments.
4. We can completely redesign, recode, and test the program, using CASE (reengineering) tools to assist us in understanding the current design.

There is no single "correct" option. Circumstances may dictate the first option even if the others are more desirable.

Rather than waiting until a maintenance request is received, the development or support organization uses the results of inventory analysis to select a program that (1) will remain in use for a preselected number of years, (2) is currently being used successfully, and (3) is likely to undergo major modification or enhancement in the near future. Then, option 2, 3, or 4 is applied.

This preventative maintenance approach was pioneered by Miller under the title *structured retrofit*. This concept is defined as "the application of today's methodologies to yesterday's systems to support tomorrow's requirements." At first glance, the suggestion that we redevelop a large program when a working version already exists may seem quite extravagant.

Before passing judgment, consider the following points:

1. The cost to maintain one line of source code may be 20 to 40 times the cost of initial development of that line.
2. Redesign of the software architecture (program and/or data structure), using modern design concepts, can greatly facilitate future maintenance.
3. Because a prototype of the software already exists, development productivity should be much higher than average.
4. The user now has experience with the software. Therefore, new requirements and the direction of change can be ascertained with greater ease.
5. CASE tools for reengineering will automate some parts of the job.
6. A complete software configuration (documents, programs, and data) will exist upon completion of preventive maintenance.

When a software development organization sells software as a product, preventive maintenance is seen in "new releases" of a program. A large in-house software developer (e.g., a business systems software development group for a large consumer products company) may have 500–2000 production programs within its domain of responsibility. These programs can be ranked by importance and then reviewed as candidates for preventive maintenance.

The forward engineering process applies software engineering principles, concepts, and methods to re-create an existing application. In most cases, forward engineering does not simply create a modern equivalent of an older program. Rather, new user and technology requirements are integrated into the reengineering effort. The redeveloped program extends the capabilities of the older application.

9.8.3 Reverse, Forward and Reengineering (A Brief Overview)

We give a comparison of the three terms viz. Reverse Engineering, Forward Engineering, and Reengineering, in Figure 9.6.

Reverse Engineering	Forward Engineering	Reengineering
It performs transformation from a lower abstraction to higher one.	The traditional process of moving from high level abstractions and logical, implementation-independent designs to the physical implementations of a system.	Reengineering is to examine the finished product and build it again, but better.
Usually done when documents are not appropriate or missing.	Modification of the system is done. For example, use of different programming language introduction of new DBMS transfer of software to new hardware platform	Usually done for improvements in the system.
Reverse engineering is finding out how a product works from the finished product.	In forward engineering, one designs a machine to do something.	After finding out how the product works, it is done or implemented with new technology or methodology.
Reverse engineering is trying to recreate the source code from the complied code. This is trying to figure out how a piece of software works given only the final system.	Forward engineering is normal engineering. It builds devices that can do certain useful things for us: bridges, furnaces, cars, planes. We build the devices by applying the principles of physics and previous engineering.	Reengineering on the other hand is creating a new piece of software with similar functionality as an existing one. But you may be 'improving' the way it was built.
Reverse engineering is taking apart a finished product for the purposes of learning how it works.	It usually consists of modifying software that has been already written-this is because software is normally continually changed over a period of years until it becomes obsolete.	Reengineering is simply a new re-implementation of a product with better engineering.

Reverse engineering is to take a bridge apart to see how it was built. Any activity that requires program understanding at any level may fall within the scope of reverse engineering.	It sometimes consists of developing completely new software.	Reengineering is to throw a bridge away and rebuild it from scratch. Reengineering may be useful for the modification of the legacy code or software.

Figure 9.6: *Comparison of Reverse Engineering, Forward Engineering and Reengineering*

9.9 RE-ENGINEERING APPROACHES

There are three different approaches to software re-engineering. The approaches differ in the amount and rate of replacement of the existing system with the target system. Each approach has its own benefits and risks.

9.9.1 Big Bang Approach

The "Big Bang" approach, also known as the "Lump Sum" approach, replaces the entire system at one time, as shown in Figure 9.7. This approach is often used by projects that need to solve an immediate problem, such as migration to different system architecture.

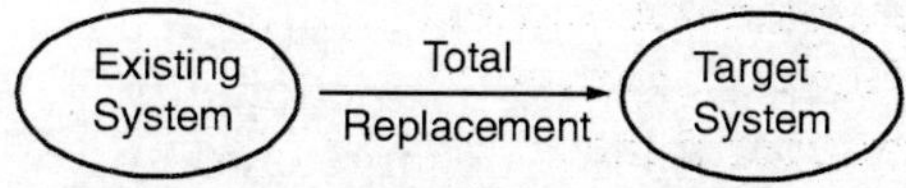

Figure 9.7: *Big Bang Approach*

The advantage to this approach is that the system is brought into a new environment all at once. No interfaces between old and new components must be developed; no mingled environments must be operated and maintained. . The disadvantage with this approach is the result tends to be monolithic projects that may not always be suitable. For large systems, this approach may consume too many resources or require large amounts of time before the target system is produced. The risk with this approach is high; the system must be functionally intact and work in parallel with the old system to assure functionality. This parallel operation may be difficult and expensive to do. A major difficulty is change control; between the time the new system is started and finished, many changes are likely to be made to the old system, which have to be reflected in the new system. It is a lot of work to stay current and not to lose a capability that has been put in the old system. That is, what is being reengineered is likely to change.

9.9.2 Incremental Approach

The "Incremental" approach to re-engineering is also known as "Phase-out". In this approach, shown in Figure 9.8, system sections are re-engineered and added incrementally as new versions of the system are needed to satisfy new goals. The project is broken into re-engineering sections based on the existing system's sections.

The advantages to this approach are that the components of the system are produced faster and it is easier to trace errors since the new components are clearly identified. Since interim versions are released, the customer can see progress and quickly identify lost functionality. A benefit is that change to the old system can be easier dealt with, since changes to components that are not being re-engineered have no impact on the current component. A disadvantage to the Incremental approach is that the system takes longer to complete with multiple interim version that require careful configuration control. Another disadvantage is that the entire structure of the system cannot be altered; only the structure within the specific component sections being reengineered.

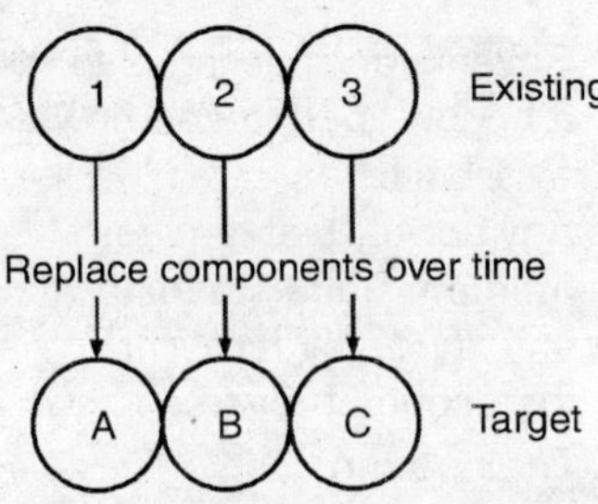

Figure 9.8: Incremental/Phase-out Re-engineering Approach

This requires careful identification of components in the existing system and extensive planning of the structure of the target system. This approach has a lower risk than the Big Bang because as each component starts re-engineering, the risks for that portion of the code can be identified and monitored.

9.9.3 Evolutionary Approach

In the "Evolutionary" approach, as in the Incremental approach, sections of the original system are replaced with newly re-engineered system sections. In this approach however, the sections are chosen based on their functionality, not on the structure of the existing system. The target system is built using functionally cohesive sections as needed. The Evolutionary approach allows developers to focus re-engineering efforts on identifying functional objects regardless of where the tasks reside in the current system. As shown in Figure 9.9, components of the current system are broken by functions and re-engineered into new components.

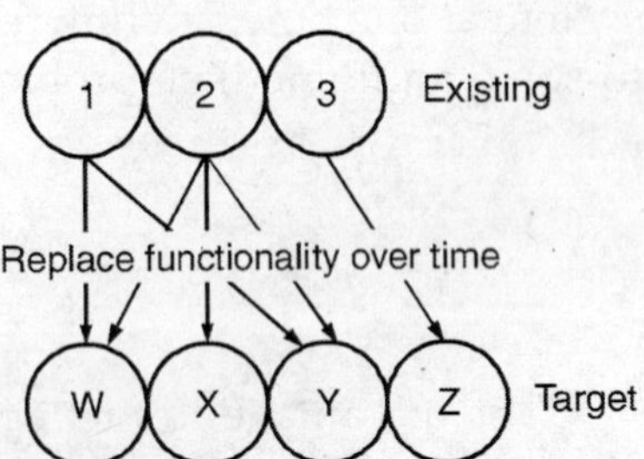

Figure 9.9: Evolutionary Re-engineering Approach

The advantages of Evolutionary re-engineering are the resulting modular design and the reduced scope for a single component. This approach works well when converting to object-oriented technology. One disadvantage is that similar functions must be identified throughout the existing system then refined as a single functional unit. There may also be interface problems and response time degradation since functional sections of the original system are being reengineered instead of architectural sections.

9.10 RE-ENGINEERING PHASES AND TASKS

There is a core process that every organization should follow when re-engineering. Re-engineering

Poses its own technical challenges and without a comprehensive development process will waste time and money. Automation and tools can only support this process, not preempt it. The re-engineering process can be broken into five phases and associated tasks, starting with the initial phase of determining the feasibility and cost effectiveness of reengineering, and concluding with the transition to the new target system.

These five reengineering development phases are: (1) Re-engineering team formation; (2) Project feasibility analysis; (3) Analysis and planning; (4) Re-engineering implementation; and (5) Transition and testing.

9.10.1 Re-engineering Team Formation

This team will manage the re-engineering effort from start to conclusion and will need comprehensive training in how to manage the technological change, the basics of re-engineering, and the use of target development and maintenance processes. Their tasks will be diverse, starting with establishing goals, strategies and an action plan within the current environment and based on the identified business needs including cost justifications. Although team members must have the "standard" software development skills, they will need additional, specific skills. They will be responsible for identifying, testing and purchasing new tools, then making sure personnel are properly trained on the tools and the tools are being effectively used. The team will need to provide internal marketing of the re-engineering work, consulting with personnel to verify the process is correctly being applied. These tasks will require team members to have good interpersonal skills to resolve rejection of new concepts and perceptions of software ownership. Since the field of re-engineering continues to evolve, the team members will also need to continue research in this technology.

9.10.2 Project Feasibility Analysis

The initial task of the re-engineering team is to evaluate the organizational needs and goals that the existing system meets. It is important that the re-engineering strategy fit with the organization's cultural norms. Software products currently in use must be analyzed in terms of problem specification including objectives, motivation, constraints and business rules. The value of the applications must be investigated to determine what is the expected return on investment from the re-engineering effort: the degree the software quality is expected to increase, the maintenance process efficiency improve, and the business value enhanced. Once the expectations are established, they must be expressed in a measurable way - reduction in cost of sustaining engineering, reduction in operations, improvement in performance, etc. Then the costs of reengineering must be compared to the expected cost savings and the increase in value of the system.

9.10.3 Analysis and Planning

This re-engineering phase has three steps: analyze the legacy system, specify the characteristics of the target system, and create a standard testbed or validation suite to validate the correct transfer of functionality. The analysis step begins by locating all available code and documentation, including user manuals, design documents and requirement specifications. Once all of the information on the legacy system is collected, it is analyzed to identify its unique aspects. The current condition of the existing system, its maintainability and operability, must be specified in order to show a return on investment with the target system. A set of software metrics should be selected to assist in identifying the quality problems with the current system and the prioritization of applications that are candidates for re-engineering according to their technical quality and business value. The metrics should include measurements of the costs of changes to the software, if an increase in maintainability is one of the goals of the reengineering process. At the conclusion of the re-engineering effort the same metrics should be used to identify the quality of the new system and the return on investment. The collection of metrics on the new system should continue throughout development to identify if what is happening is normal or expected and in order to react quickly to abnormal signs. Once the legacy system and its quality characteristics have been specified, the step of stating the desired characteristics and specification of the target system begins. The characteristics of the existing system that must be changed are specified, such as its operating system, hardware platform, design structure, and language.

Finally, a standard testbed and validation suite must be created. These will be used to prove the new system is functionally equivalent to the legacy system and to demonstrate functionality has remained unchanged after re-engineering. The testbed for the target system may be implemented incrementally if necessary, but traceability to the functions of the legacy system is important.

9.10.4 Re-engineering Implementation

Now that the re-engineering objectives have been specified, the approach has been defined, and the legacy system analyzed, the reverse and forward engineering are started. Using the Levels of Abstraction, the actual functions of the legacy system are unraveled by reverse engineering. Various tools are available for this task. These tools must be examined for usability in the context of the objectives of the reengineering process. They must integrate easily into the process with minimum massaging.

After the desired level of abstraction is reached, forward engineering can begin. Forward engineering corresponds exactly to the normal software development process, starting from the abstraction level reached in the reverse engineering process. That is, if the software is to be redesigned to fit new overall system architecture, the reverse engineering process should extract the software requirements, and the forward engineering process would start with the development of a new design. In forward engineering, any change or increase in functionality must be avoided since this complicates the validation process. Throughout this phase, quality assurance and configuration management disciplines and techniques must be applied. Measurement techniques use should continue to assess the improvement to the software and to identify potential areas of risk.

9.10.5 Testing and Transition

As the functionality of the new system grows, testing must be done to detect errors introduced during re-engineering. The testing techniques and methods are the same as those used during a "from scratch" system development. Assuming the requirements for the new system are the same as those for the legacy system the test suite and test bed developed in the planning phase can be used. The same test cases can be applied to both the legacy system and the target system, comparing the results to validate the functionality of the target system. Software documentation on the legacy must be updated, rewritten or replaced during this phase so that they apply to the new system, and contain the information needed to operate and maintain it.

9.11 BUSINESS PROCESS REENGINEERING

Business process reengineering (BPR) extends far beyond the scope of information technologies and software engineering. Among the many definitions (most somewhat abstract) that have been suggested for BPR is one published in Fortune magazine: "the search for, and the implementation of, radical change in business process to achieve breakthrough results." But how is the search conducted, and how is the implementation achieved? More important, how can we ensure that the "radical change" suggested will in fact lead to "breakthrough results" instead of organizational chaos?

9.11.1 Business Processes

A *business process* is "a set of logically related tasks performed to achieve a defined business outcome". Within the business process, people, equipment, material resources, and business procedures are combined to produce a specified result. Examples of business processes include designing a new product, purchasing services and supplies, hiring a new employee, and paying suppliers. Each demands a set of tasks and each draws on diverse resources within the business.

Every business process has a defined customer—a person or group that receives the outcome (e.g., an idea, a report, a design, a product). In addition, business processes cross organizational boundaries. They require that different organizational groups participate in the "logically related tasks" that define the process.

A business is actually a hierarchy of subsystems. The overall business is segmented in the following manner:

The business
- business systems
  - business process
    - business subprocesses

Each business system (also called *business function*) is composed of one or more business processes, and each business process is defined by a set of subprocesses. BPR can be applied at any level of the hierarchy, but as the scope of BPR broadens (i.e., as we move upward in the hierarchy), the risks associated with BPR grow dramatically. For this reason, most BPR efforts focus on individual processes or subprocesses.

9.11.2 Principles of Business Process Reengineering

In many ways, BPR is identical in focus and scope to business process engineering. In an ideal setting, BPR should occur in a top-down manner, beginning with the identification of major business objectives and goals and culminating with a much more detailed specification of the tasks that define a specific business process.

Hammer suggests a number of principles that guide BPR activities when they begin at the top (business) level:

- **Organize around outcomes, not tasks.** Many companies have compartmentalized business activities so that no single person (or organization) has responsibility (or control) of a business outcome. It such cases, it is difficult to determine the status of work and even more difficult to debug process problems if they do occur. BPR should design processes that avoid this problem.

- **Have those who use the output of the process perform the process.** The intent of this recommendation is to allow those who need business output to control all of the variables that allow them to get the output in a timely manner. The fewer separate constituencies involved in a process, the smoother is the road to a rapid outcome.
- **Incorporate information processing work into the real work that produces the raw information.** As IT becomes more distributed, it is possible to locate most information processing within the organization that produces the raw data. This localizes control, reduces communication time, and puts computing power in the hands of those that have a vested interest in the information that is produced.
- **Treat geographically dispersed resources as though they were centralized.** Computer-based communications have become so sophisticated that geographically diverse groups can be placed in the same "virtual office." For example, instead of running three engineering shifts at a single location, a global company can run one shift in Europe, a second shift in North America, and a third shift in Asia. In each case, engineers will work during daylight hours and communicate via high-bandwidth networks.
- **Link parallel activities instead of integrating their results.** When different constituencies perform work in parallel, it is essential to design a process that demands continuing communication and coordination. Otherwise, integration problems are sure to result.
- **Put the decision point where the work is performed, and build control into the process.** Using software design jargon, this principle suggests a flatter organizational architecture with reduced factoring.
- **Capture data once, at its source.** Data should be stored on-line so that once collected it need never be re-entered.

Each of these principles represents a "big picture" view of BPR. Guided by these principles, business planners and process designers must begin process redesign.

9.12 REENGINEERING ECONOMICS

The decision to reengineer is usually fiscal, rather than technical. Systems become increasingly expensive to maintain as they age and 'bit rot' sets in – the increasing occurrence of errors induced through miscomprehension of increasingly contorted code. However, the criteria from which arises the decision to redevelop or reengineer a system are diverse and extremely fuzzy. Sneed lays out a simple framework for judging the derived benefit.

Management is typically first concerned with the cost of reengineering relative to the cost of redevelopment and the cost of maintenance. The choice between redevelopment and reengineering is principally one involving the difference in value attached to the old and new system, balanced by the risks associated with the anticipated costs of (in)action:

Reengineering Benefit =

[Old_Value – (Reeng_Cost * Reeng_Risk)] – [New_Value – (Dev_Cost * Dev_Risk)]

The life-expectancy of the existing system relative to the time required to reengineer it and the time required to redevelop it should appear as weights in the risk terms. Note that it is quite possible to derive negative benefit if the cost or risk of reengineering the system is sufficiently high compared to the costs of just starting over from scratch.

The choice between continued maintenance and reengineering is structured similarly:

Reengineering Benefit = [Old_Maint_Cost – Reeng_Maint_Cost]
+ [Old_Value – (Reeng_Cost * Reeng_Risk)]
– [New_Value – (Dev_Cost * Dev_Risk)]

factoring in an additional term addressing the expected difference in maintaining the old versus reengineered system. The *added* value of reengineering a new system must be balanced against the *current* value of the present system. This is effectively the risk of reengineering relative to the risk of a new development and the risk of doing nothing.

9.13 COST/BENEFIT ANALYSIS MODEL

In a perfect world, every unmaintainable program would be retired immediately; to be replaced by high-quality, reengineered applications developed using modern software engineering practices. But we live in a world of limited resources. Reengineering drains resources that can be used for other business purposes. Therefore, before an organization attempts to reengineer an existing application, it should perform a cost/benefit analysis.

A cost/benefit analysis model for reengineering has been proposed by Sneed. Nine parameters are defined:

- P_1 = current annual maintenance cost for an application.
- P_2 = current annual operation cost for an application.
- P_3 = current annual business value of an application.
- P_4 = predicted annual maintenance cost after reengineering.
- P_5 = predicted annual operations cost after reengineering.
- P_6 = predicted annual business value after reengineering.
- P_7 = estimated reengineering costs.
- P_8 = estimated reengineering calendar time.
- P_9 = reengineering risk factor ($P9$ = 1.0 is nominal).
- L = expected life of the system.

The cost associated with continuing maintenance of a candidate application (i.e., reengineering is not performed) can be defined as

$$C_{\text{maint}} = [P_3 - (P_1 + P_2)] \times L$$

The costs associated with reengineering are defined using the following relationship:

$$C_{\text{reeng}} = [P_6 - (P_4 + P_5) \times (L - P_8) - (P_7 \times P_9)]$$

Using the costs presented in equations above, the overall benefit of reengineering can be computed as

$$\text{cost benefit} = C_{\text{reeng}} - C_{\text{maint}}$$

The cost/benefit analysis presented in the equations can be performed for all high-priority applications identified during inventory analysis. Those applications that show the highest cost/benefit can be targeted for reengineering, while work on others can be postponed until resources are available.

9.14 REENGINEERING RISKS

In order to factor risk into an economic decision model such as the one above, it is first necessary to understand just where risks lie, and the form that they might take. Arnold elaborates the following framework for categorizing risk in the reengineering of software:

Process risks

Extremely high manual reengineering costs

Cost benefits not realized in required time frame

Cannot economically justify the reengineering effort

Reengineering effort drifts

Lack of management commitment to ongoing reengineering solution

Personnel risks

Programmers inhibiting the start of reengineering

Programmers performing less effectively to make an unpopular reengineering project look less effective

Application risks

Reengineering with no local application experts available

Existing business knowledge embedded in source code is lost

Reengineered system does not perform adequately

Technology risks

Recovered information is not useful or used

Reverse engineering to representations that cannot be shared

Reengineering technology inadequate to accomplish reengineering goals

Tool risks

Dependence on tools that do not perform as advertised

Not using installed tools

Strategy risks

Premature commitment to a reengineering solution for an entire system

Failure to have a long-term vision with interim goals

Lack of global view: code, data, process reengineering

No plan for using reengineering tools

This list compresses into three core concerns: the organizational will to follow a reengineering project through to completion, the skill and commitment of the technical staff involved, and the existence of the information necessary to accomplish the task.

9.15 RESTRUCTURING

Software restructuring modifies source code and/or data in an effort to make it amenable to future changes. In general, restructuring does not modify the overall program architecture. It tends to focus on the design details of individual modules and on local data structures defined within modules. If the restructuring effort extends beyond module boundaries and encompasses the software architecture, restructuring becomes forward engineering.

Arnold defines a number of benefits that can be achieved when software is restructured:

- Programs have higher quality—better documentation, less complexity, and conformance to modern software engineering practices and standards.
- Frustration among software engineers who must work on the program is reduced, thereby improving productivity and making learning easier.
- Effort required to perform maintenance activities is reduced.
- Software is easier to test and debug.

Restructuring occurs when the basic architecture of an application is solid, even though technical internals need work. It is initiated when major parts of the software are serviceable and only a subset of all modules and data need extensive modification.

9.15.1 Code Restructuring

The most common type of reengineering (actually, the use of the term *reengineering* is questionable in this case) is code restructuring. Some legacy systems have a relatively solid program architecture, but individual modules were coded in a way that makes them difficult to understand, test, and maintain. In such cases, the code within the suspect modules can be restructured.

To accomplish this activity, the source code is analysed using a restructuring tool. Violations of structured programming constructs are noted and code is then restructured (this can be done automatically). The resultant restructured code is reviewed and tested to ensure that no anomalies have been introduced. Internal code documentation is updated.

Code restructuring is performed to yield a design that produces the same function but with higher quality than the original program. In general, code restructuring techniques model program logic using Boolean algebra and then apply a series of transformation rules that yield restructured logic. The objective is to take "spaghetti-bowl" code and derive a procedural design that conforms to the structured programming philosophy.

Other restructuring techniques have also been proposed for use with reengineering tools. A *resource exchange diagram* maps each program module and the resources (data types, procedures and variables) that are exchanged between it and other modules. By creating representations of resource flow, the program architecture can be restructured to achieve minimum coupling among modules.

9.15.2 Data Restructuring

A program with weak data architecture will be difficult to adapt and enhance. In fact, for many applications, data architecture has more to do with the long-term viability of a program that the source code itself.

Unlike code restructuring, which occurs at a relatively low level of abstraction, data structuring is a full-scale reengineering activity. In most cases, data restructuring begins with a reverse engineering activity. Current data architecture is dissected and necessary data models are defined. Data objects and attributes are identified, and existing data structures are reviewed for quality.

When data structure is weak (e.g., flat files are currently implemented, when a relational approach would greatly simplify processing), the data are reengineered. Because data architecture has a strong influence on program architecture and the algorithms that populate it, changes to the data will invariably result in either architectural or code-level changes.

Before data restructuring can begin, a reverse engineering activity called *analysis of source code* must be conducted. All programming language statements that contain data definitions, file descriptions, I/O, and interface descriptions are evaluated. The intent is to extract data items and objects, to get information on data flow, and to understand the existing data structures that have been implemented. This activity is sometimes called *data analysis*.

Once data analysis has been completed, *data redesign* commences. In its simplest form, a *data record standardization* step clarifies data definitions to achieve consistency among data item names or physical record formats within an existing data structure or file format. Another form of redesign, called *data name rationalization,* ensures that all data naming conventions conform to local standards and that aliases are eliminated as data flow through the system.

When restructuring moves beyond standardization and rationalization, physical modifications to existing data structures are made to make the data design more effective. This may mean a translation from one file format to another, or in some cases, translation from one type of database to another.

9.16 REVERSE ENGINEERING

Reverse engineering conjures an image of the "magic slot." We feed an unstructured, undocumented source listing into the slot and out the other end comes full documentation for the computer program. Unfortunately, the magic slot doesn't exist. Reverse engineering can extract design information from source code, but the abstraction level, the completeness of the documentation, the degree to which tools and a human analyst work together, and the directionality of the process are highly variable.

The *abstraction level* of a reverse engineering process and the tools used to effect it refers to the sophistication of the design information that can be extracted from source code. Ideally, the abstraction level should be as high as possible. That is, the reverse engineering process should be capable of deriving procedural design representations (a low-level abstraction), program and data structure information (a somewhat higher level of abstraction), data and control flow models (a relatively high level of abstraction), and entity relationship models (a high level of abstraction). As the abstraction level increases, the software engineer is provided with information that will allow easier understanding of the program.

The *completeness* of a reverse engineering process refers to the level of detail that is provided at an abstraction level. In most cases, the completeness decreases as the abstraction level increases. For example, given a source code listing, it is relatively easy to develop a complete procedural design representation. Simple data flow representations may also be derived, but it is far more difficult to develop a complete set of data flow diagrams or entity-relationship models.

Completeness improves in direct proportion to the amount of analysis performed by the person doing reverse engineering. *Interactivity* refers to the degree to which the human is "integrated" with automated tools to create an effective reverse engineering process. In most cases, as the abstraction level increases, interactivity must increase or completeness will suffer.

If the *directionality* of the reverse engineering process is one way, all information extracted from the source code is provided to the software engineer who can then use it during any maintenance activity. If directionality is two way, the information is fed to a reengineering tool that attempts to restructure or regenerate the old program.

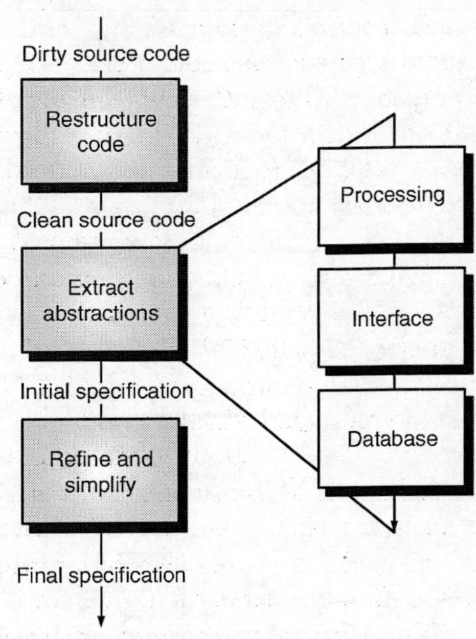

Figure 9.10:
The reverse engineering process

The reverse engineering process is represented in Figure 9.10. Before reverse engineering activities can commence, unstructured ("dirty") source code is *restructured* so that it contains only the structured programming constructs. This makes the source code easier to read and provides the basis for all the subsequent reverse engineering activities.

The core of reverse engineering is an activity called *extract abstractions*. The engineer must evaluate the old program and from the (often undocumented) source code, extract a meaningful specification of the processing that is performed, the user interface that is applied, and the program data structures or database that is used.

9.17 REVERSE ENGINEERING PROCEDURE

Reverse engineering is the process of analyzing a subject system to identify the system's components and their interrelationships and create representations of the system in another form or at a higher level of abstraction. In reverse engineering, the requirements and the essential design, structure and content of the legacy system must be recaptured. In addition to capturing technical relationships and interactions, information and rules about the business application and process that have proved useful in running the business must also be retrieved. This involves extracting design artifacts and building or synthesizing abstractions that are less implementation dependent. The key objectives in reverse engineering are to generate alternative views, recover lost information, detect side effects, synthesize higher abstractions, and facilitate reuse. The effectiveness of this process will affect the success of the reengineering project. Reverse engineering does not involve changes to the system or creating a new system, it is the process of examination without changing its overall functionality.

The reverse engineering process, shown in Figure 9.11, begins by extracting the requirements and detailed design information from the source code and existing documents. A requirements document is created and a high level design abstraction is extracted and expressed using dataflow and control-flow diagrams. The recovered design is reviewed for consistency and correctness.

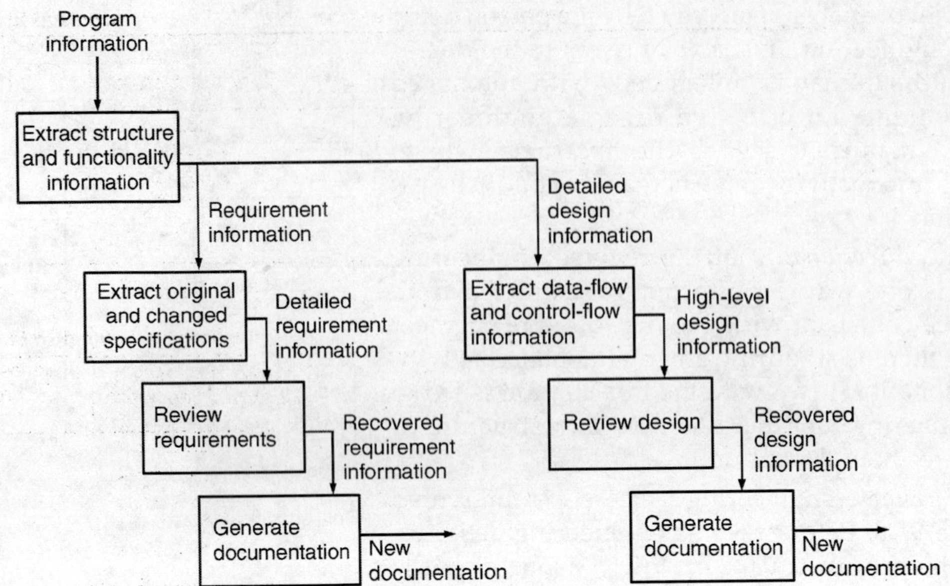

Figure 9.11: Reverse Engineering Procedure

Slicing, or code isolation, is a method for pulling out from a program those parts that are concerned with a specified behavior of interest. It is a means of locating the minimum amount of data and code that is required to derive a desired data item at a particular point in the program. Conceptually, slicing is easy - accrue all data definitions and control flow which contribute to the desired data element values at the slice points and discard anything that does not contribute to those values. The objective of slicing is to compute the minimal subset of code required for a function. However, in reality slicing is very difficult.

There are three approaches to slicing: conditional-based, forward, and backward. Conditional-based slicing utilizes the concept that business functions are structured along conditional tests. This slicing method is potentially useful to identify areas of the program reachable under globally specified conditions since the user specifies logical express and operationally slicing range (where to start and end slicing). All reachable program statements along control flow paths for which given expression is true are included in the slice segment. Forward slicing uses functions that normally process input values. The objective in this method is to find all areas of code that depend on the values of input variables. Ripple effect analysis is applied; given a variable and slicing range, statements in that range that can be potentially affected by the variable are defined. The statements can be affected in terms of data flow, control dependency, or recursive process; variables on the left and right of the statement are included. In backward slicing, the process starts with the results of the existing program. Areas of code that contribute to values of output variables are a part of the slice. Given a variable and range, this method of slicing returns statements that can potentially affect the value of variable; variable only on right side of the equation are used. Tools are available to facilitate slicing, but the process is still difficult and time consuming.

9.18 REVERSE ENGINEERING TO UNDERSTAND PROCESSING

The first real reverse engineering activity begins with an attempt to understand and then extract procedural abstractions represented by the source code. To understand procedural abstractions, the code is analysed at varying levels of abstraction: system, program, component, pattern, and statement.

The overall functionality of the entire application system must be understood before more detailed reverse engineering work occurs. This establishes a context for further analysis and provides insight into interoperability issues among applications within the system. Each of the programs that make up the application system represents a functional abstraction at a high level of detail. A block diagram, representing the interaction between these functional abstractions, is created. Each component performs some sub-function and represents a defined procedural abstraction. A processing narrative for each component is created. In some situations, system, program and component specifications already exist. When this is the case, the specifications are reviewed for conformance to existing code.

Things become more complex when the code inside a component is considered. The engineer looks for sections of code that represent generic procedural patterns. In almost every component, a section of code prepares data for processing (within the module), a different section of code does the processing, and another section of code prepares the results of processing for export from the component. Within each of these sections, we can encounter smaller patterns; for example, data validation and bounds checking often occur within the section of code that prepares data for processing.

For large systems, reverse engineering is generally accomplished using a semi-automated approach. CASE tools are used to "parse" the semantics of existing code. The output of this process is then passed to restructuring and forward engineering tools to complete the reengineering process.

9.19 REVERSE ENGINEERING TO UNDERSTAND DATA

Reverse engineering of data occurs at different levels of abstraction. At the program level, internal program data structures must often be reverse engineered as part of an overall reengineering effort. At the system level, global data structures (e.g., files, databases) are often reengineered to accommodate new database management paradigms (e.g., the move from flat file to relational or object-oriented database systems). Reverse engineering of the current global data structures sets the stage for the introduction of a new system-wide database.

9.19.1 Internal Data Structures

Reverse engineering techniques for internal program data focus on the definition of classes of objects. This is accomplished by examining the program code with the intent of grouping related program variables. In many cases, the data organization within the code identifies abstract data types. For example, record structures, files, lists, and other data structures often provide an initial indicator of classes.

Breuer and Lano suggest the following approach for reverse engineering of classes:

1. Identify flags and local data structures within the program that record important information about global data structures (e.g., a file or database).
2. Define the relationship between flags and local data structures and the global data structures. For example, a flag may be set when a file is empty; a local data structure may serve as a buffer that contains the last 100 records acquired from a central database.
3. For every variable (within the program) that represents an array or file, list all other variables that have a logical connection to it.

These steps enable a software engineer to identify classes within the program that interact with the global data structures.

9.19.2 Database Structure

Regardless of its logical organization and physical structure, a database allows the definition of data objects and supports some method for establishing relationships among the objects. Therefore, reengineering one database schema into another requires an understanding of existing objects and their relationships. The following steps may be used to define the existing data model as a precursor to reengineering a new database model:

1. **Build an initial object model.** The classes defined as part of the model may be acquired by reviewing records in a flat file database or tables in a relational schema. The items contained in records or tables become attributes of a class.
2. **Determine candidate keys.** The attributes are examined to determine whether they are used to point to another record or table. Those that serve as pointers become candidate keys.
3. **Refine the tentative classes.** Determine whether similar classes can be combined into a single class.
4. **Define generalizations.** Examine classes that have many similar attributes to determine whether a class hierarchy should be constructed with a generalization class at its head.
5. **Discover associations.** Use techniques that are analogous to the CRC approach to establish associations among classes.

Once information defined in the preceding steps is known, a series of transformations can be applied to map the old database structure into a new database structure.

9.20 REVERSE ENGINEERING USER INTERFACES

Sophisticated GUIs have become de rigueur for computer-based products and systems of every type. Therefore, the redevelopment of user interfaces has become one of the most common types of reengineering activity. But before a user interface can be rebuilt, reverse engineering should occur.

To fully understand an existing user interface (UI), the structure and behaviour of the interface must be specified. Merlo and his colleagues suggest three basic questions that must be answered as reverse engineering of the UI commences:

- What are the basic actions (e.g., keystrokes and mouse clicks) that the interface must process?

- What is a compact description of the behavioural response of the system to these actions?
- What is meant by a "replacement," or more precisely, what concept of equivalence of interfaces is relevant here?

Behavioural modeling notation can provide a means for developing answers to the first two questions. Much of the information necessary to create a behavioural model can be obtained by observing the external manifestation of the existing interface. But additional information necessary to create the behavioural model must extracted from the code.

It is important to note that a replacement GUI may not mirror the old interface exactly (in fact, it may be radically different). It is often worthwhile to develop new interaction metaphors. For example, an old UI requests that a user provide a scale factor (ranging from 1 to 10) to shrink or magnify a graphical image. A reengineered GUI might use a slide-bar and mouse to accomplish the same function.

9.21 CLEAN-ROOM REVERSE-ENGINEERING

Reverse-engineered software is said to be clean-room reverse-engineered if its creators avoid directly examining the software that is emulated. This can be done by the use of published specifications and test programs. Using clean-room reverse-engineering technique prevents the developers from including pieces of the software to be emulated in the emulated software. It does not prevent the developers from infringing on existing registered patents or infringing on look-and-feel copyrights.

Clean-room reverse-engineering can sure be a labour intensive methodology. Any behaviour that is either not documented or incorrectly documented can lead the developers into writing, running and analysing complex tests to determine the true behaviour of the system being emulated. Although Apple's Classic Macintosh Operating System is fairly well documented by Apple in the Inside Macintosh series of books, each error and omission has either resulted in an incompatibility in Access to Research for Development and Innovation's (ARDI) software or the expenditure of engineering time searching for better documentation or spent creating new, often esoteric, tests.

9.21.1 Dirty-Room/Clean-Room Reverse-Engineering

Directly examining the thing to be emulated is dirty-room reverse-engineering. For example, looking at the individual instructions that constitute a computer program, even if only to determine specifications that are not publicly available, is an example of dirty-room reverse engineering. Dirty-room reverse engineering done by the same engineers who createemulationsoftwarewill alwaysrun therisk of deliberate or accidental copyright violations by incorporating portions of the software to be emulated in the emulator. To carefully avoid this kind of risk, dirty-room reverse engineering has to be done in conjunction with clean-room reverse engineering by using two physically and electronically isolated teams so that one team does dirty-room engineering and the other does clean-room engineering.

In strictly clean-room reverse engineering, the moment it is determined that the specification that the clean-room engineers are working from is insufficient to produce the degree of compatibility desired, the only recourse is to search for additional documentation or to write additional tests. In dirty-room/clean-room reverse engineering, the clean-room engineers have to write a description of the portion of the specification that needs to be elaborated or clarified. The dirty-room engineers then have to use that request to create additional functional specifications. These functional specifications should not reveal, in any way, the way in which the emulated software was written as such revelations would defeat the whole purpose of having separate clean-room and dirty-room engineers. One way of preventing such contamination is to disallow direct communication between the clean-room and dirty-room engineers. Instead, all communication between the two teams has to be passed through an intermediary who enforces protocol. Specifically the role of the intermediary is to insure that only functional specifications are passed from the dirty-room to the clean-room. Any implementation detail coming from the dirty-room should be intercepted and prevented from ever being seen by the clean-room.

9.21.2 Strictly Clean-Room Reverse-Engineering

Strictly clean-room reverse-engineering is when only a clean-room team is used – without the use of any dirty-room team. To date, ARDI has strictly used clean-room reverse engineering in the construction of its software, even though doing so has been less efficient than using dirty-room/clean-room reverse engineering. The benefit of such a technique to ARDI is that ARDI has constantly avoided the overhead of having separate dirty-room engineers as intermediaries. The significant drawback has been that ARDI's lower operating system layers are not sufficiently compatible to allow Apple's upper operating system layers to work with them. Such compatibility measures have easily provided dirty-room/clean-room reverse engineering more clear goals and compatibility.

SUMMARY

Reengineering occurs at two different levels of abstraction. At the business level, reengineering focuses on the business process with the intent of making changes to improve competitiveness in some area of the business. At the software level, reengineering examines information systems and applications with the intent of restructuring or reconstructing them so that they exhibit higher quality.

Business process reengineering defines business goals, identifies and evaluates existing business processes (in the context of defined goals), specifies and designs revised processes, and prototypes, refines, and instantiates them within a business. BPR has a focus that extends beyond software. The result of BPR is often the definition of ways in which information technologies can better support the business.

Software reengineering encompasses a series of activities that include document restructuring, reverse engineering, program and data restructuring, and forward engineering. The intent of these activities is to create versions of existing programs that exhibit higher quality and better maintainability—programs that will be viable well into the twenty-first century.

Document restructuring creates a framework of documentation that is necessary for the long-term support of an application. Reverse engineering is the process of analysing a program in an effort to extract data, architectural, and procedural design information. Finally, forward engineering reconstructs a program using modern software engineering practices and information learned during reverse engineering.

The cost/benefit of reengineering can be determined quantitatively. The cost of the status quo, that is, the cost associated with on-going support and maintenance of an existing application, is compared to the projected costs of reengineering and the resultant reduction in maintenance costs. In almost every case in which a program has a long life and currently exhibits poor maintainability, reengineering represents a cost-effective business strategy.

EXERCISES

1. What is reengineering?
2. Explain the taxonomy of software engineering?
3. What are the various benefits of reengineering?
4. What are the general objectives of reengineering?
5. Explain the software reengineering cycle?
6. Explain the general model of software reengineering?
7. Give a comparison of Reverse Engineering, Forward Engineering, and Reengineering?
8. Explain the three different approaches to software re-engineering?
9. Explain the reengineering development phases?
10. Explain the concept of Business process reengineering?
11. Explain the concept of reengineering economics?
12. Explain the cost/benefit analysis model?
13. What are the various risks of reengineering?
14. What do you mean by restructuring?
15. Explain the code and data restructuring?
16. What do you mean by reverse engineering?
17. Explain the procedure of reverse engineering?
18. Explain the reverse engineering to understand data?
19. Explain the reverse engineering user interfaces?
20. Explain the concept of clean-room reverse-engineering?
21. Explain the strictly clean-room reverse-engineering?

❑

Software Reengineering Process

10

10.1 INTRODUCTION

This chapter provides a general overview of the software re-engineering process. Its main purpose being to give a brief high-level guide on how old, poorly documented, poorly structured code can be brought up to an acceptable and maintainable standard. It also touches on issues that could possibly be addressed during this process. It is very much a generic overview and as such does not make reference to any specific platform or development tools.

Generally poorly maintained and controlled code consists of a large number of program files spread over a number of locations or a single very large file with thousands of lines of code. There may appear to be a number of copies of the same file, all of which are subtly different. On viewing these files it is found that many have little or no comments and those comments that do exist are either meaningless or appear to bear no relationship to the code itself. Any associated documentation is out of date and refers to the initial version of the application that has undergone many undocumented modifications since then. What does exist, though, is an executable file that is widely used to produce data upon which many decisions are made or actions taken. A decision is then reached that some control over the application is required as it is about to be updated, ported or passed over to another person or department to maintain. This decision may well be related to the common situation where the only person in the company who knows anything about the application has handed in their notice or is approaching retirement. Also it is possible that the existing tools or platform it is being run on are about to be phased out due to obsolescence. It is important that at this stage the actual objectives of any software reengineering are identified. The cause of the decision may be obvious but there may be other underlying problems that have been around for years that now have the opportunity of being addressed. For example there may have been a problem with the existing application that users of the application have been consistently working around (e.g. It always produces a blank output page after every tenth sheet, It always takes 10 minutes to start up after I have run application A or Don't press button B after doing that it always crashes.) It may also present the opportunity of adding in those extra features which have been waiting around for ages and everyone would really like to see implemented, or even to enhance or add in any security elements.

10.2 SOFTWARE REENGINEERING PROCESS

A re-engineering process, which can be used to take control of the situation, can be divided into eleven basic steps. These are:

1. Identification of Existing Source Code/Documentation
2. Verification of Identified Code and Setting up of a Baseline
3. Familiarization with the Existing Application
4. Identification of Re-engineering Requirements
5. Writing a Re-engineering Plan
6. Production of a Test Plan, Test Data and Script
7. Producing Test Results for Original Version
8. Producing Test Results for Original Ported Version (unmodified) if applicable
9. Restructuring the Code (in identifiable phases)
10. Testing the Code (after each phase)
11. Updating/Writing Documentation

It cannot be over emphasized that time spent on the initial stages can save a lot of effort later on. Cutting back on time in these stages can lead to major costs later on if it is found that you have been re-engineering the wrong code!

These stages will now be described in turn.

10.2.1 Identification of Existing Source Code/Documentation

The first stage of the re-engineering process is the identification of the program files that are the basis for the executable being re-engineered. The developer who is to re-engineer the application needs to identify the source files and this is best achieved in close consultation with the appropriate person in the company whose application is being re-engineered. Generally there is a person within the company who knows intimately all of the files required and can bring some logic to their existence.

Also during this stage any existing documentation should be gathered and copies of any relevant third party software required by the application identified and obtained. All this information and the identified files should be placed under a new controlled structure, which will be defined in a Configuration Plan. This plan identifies all the required components, their version numbers (if applicable) and where they reside. It will include the currently used executable. During all stages of the re-engineering process the developer should keep a log of all pertinent facts and where they originated (e.g. this file was selected because X said that it included the revised value for parameter Y. X said that he used the compiler version 1.4 to create the executable.)

10.2.2 Verification of Identified Code and Setting Up of a Baseline

Hopefully all of the required files to build the application can be identified. During this next stage the application is built to recreate the existing executable. It may require some investigation of the compilation options used to exactly recreate it and it is possible that when the existing executable was built no record was kept of these. A lot of investigative work may be required at this stage and many things can affect the created executable (e.g. the versions of third party products used, the version of the compiler, compiler options etc.)

Once what is thought to be an exact copy of the existing executable is created it should be tested against his on the same platform to verify it really is the same. This can be achieved by using sample input data or test files. Any such test files or data that is retained for future reference or testing along with the output produced and which version of the application produced this output. The source code files and any associated data files required to run the application should be documented and will form the baseline for the existing version. A copy of all these files must be kept and identified in a Baseline Description along with the version of any third party products which may be required and of any supporting documentation or development tools (i.e. compiler versions).

10.2.3 Familiarization with the Existing Application

It is now important for the developer, who is to re-engineer the code, to become familiar with it. He needs to know what it is basically trying to do and how it goes about this. This can be gained by trying the application out under a variety of situations, carrying out code reviews/walkthroughs and discussions with its users. Access to someone familiar with the code is essential at this stage. During this phase the developer can start introducing comments into the existing code which will help when coming to restructure the code. Other observations can be placed in his project log, such as ideas of improving the code, descriptions of any relevant algorithms used, a flow diagram etc. It is not uncommon that during this stage bugs are found. How these are dealt with needs to be discussed with the customer. Generally, any bugs identified will be noted at this stage and given a unique identifier and returned to during the recoding of the application.

10.2.4 Identification of Re-engineering Requirements

The next stage is to identify exactly what is required from the re-engineering process. This could be one or more of the following:

- Comment the code
- Modularize the code
- Document the code
- Enhance the code
- Identification and removal of unused code
- Identification and removal of duplicated code
- Identification and removal of duplicated parameter/data definitions
- Port the code to another platform
- Enhance the User Interface/Bring it up to date
- Bring the code up to a defined language standard
- Convert the Code into an alternative development language
- Improve/Maintain the performance
- Optimize the code
- Improve internal error handling
- Include additional functionality
- Fix existing bugs
- Use alternate third party products

Each of these can be broken down into a set of software requirements defining

10.2.5 Write a Re-engineering Plan

Once the re-engineering requirements have been identified a plan needs to be written on how these are to be implemented. To maintain control over this process it should be broken down into distinct phases, examples of which are listed in the previous section. At the end of each phase the code should be baselined, that is a copy of that code at that point in time kept. This code will then be used to recreate the executable to verify that it still agrees with the original version. Carrying this out in a phased manner means that any problems introduced during the re-engineering process can be quickly identified and the cause eliminated or addressed. This plan will need to be agreed with the customer before proceeding onto the next stage.

10.2.6 Production of a Test Plan, Test Data and Script

To enable the application to be tested and verified a test plan and script need to be written. The test plan essentially explains how testing will be carried out and the test script provides a prescriptive list of actions to carry out to perform the test. The test script consists of a list of test cases which the developer (or possibly an alternative person brought in to carry out the testing) follows and ensures that the same test can be carried out consistently each time. Generally each test case will consist of a unique identifier, a brief description of the procedure required to carry out the test, the expected result of carrying out those actions and an area where the tester can identify whether the test was successful. The test script should also allow the tester to identify the version of the application being tested, the platform (and ideally the actual machine) it was tested on, the version number of the operating system and any associated third party products used, the testers name, the current date and any other pertinent information. To assist with the testing a number of input data files will probably be required and a set of output files will be created. These output files should be stored and used to confirm agreement with the original version. By this stage any required changes to the input/output file formats need to be confirmed.

10.2.7 Producing Test Results for Original Version

The test script, using the defined input data, should be run for the original version of the application. This will produce output data or data files which will be used to verify the re-engineered code. At this stage the performance of the code may be measured if this is an issue.

10.2.8 Producing Test Results for Original Ported Version (Unmodified) If Applicable

If the code is to be ported onto a different platform then it is imperative that an unmodified version is initially ported to the new platform and run using the test script. It may not be possible to port it without making some required changes. If any changes are required these should be as few as possible and documented. Examples of such changes are having to replace the use of platform specific language extensions which may have been used. The ported code should then be run through the same test script using the same test data. It must be appreciated by the customer that porting code from one platform to another will not necessarily lead to exactly the same output results being produced. Hopefully the output should agree with the original version but this certainly may not be the case. Different platforms/operating systems handle numeric data differently and different compilers work in different ways. This may lead to small rounding error differences in the output when the application is run on the two platforms. In other applications, especially modeling applications, it is possible that in certain situations very large differences may be seen. This is generally caused by the model making use of small differences between large numbers and is a limitation of the model as represented in the application. Consequently, if large differences in the output are seen, this does not necessarily mean that the code being run on either platform is wrong but may indicate that the task being tackled has not been well represented within the code or at worse the underlying model/algorithm is not suitable for computational representation. It is also possible that the differences seen could be traced to differences in compiler options on the two platforms or related to errors introduced when modifying any platform specific code during the porting exercise. When differences are seen between the original and ported versions they need to be discussed with the customer and a course of action agreed. This may simply be to note the differences and proceed with the re-engineering. If performance is an issue then this should be measured now and compared to that on the original platform. This may lead to the identification of issues connected with running on the new platform and whether the specification of the new platform needs to be improved. Once all issues have been resolved the output produced on the ported original version will form the basis against which all re-engineered code will be compared and not the original version on the original platform.

10.2.9 Restructuring the Code (In Identifiable Phases)

The original code should now be re-engineered according to the phases identified. During the restructuring, software tools may be used to help identify or investigate the code coverage, hot spots, unused variables, checking the code conforms to a coding standard etc. Manual code inspections can also be used to help identify and then remove duplicated code, optimize array storage, collate parameter definitions etc. The restructuring of the code is an ideal opportunity to improve its performance. There are many not so obvious issues that can significantly affect the performance of written code. An example is in the storing and accessing of data in arrays. Different languages store array data in a computer's memory in different ways. The way this data is accessed can have a drastic effect on the applications performance in some cases. This is something very well known to the seasoned developer but may not have been appreciated by the original code writer. Other performance improvements can be obtained if a more recent version of the programming language is being used during the re-engineering as this may offer faster ways of handling certain aspects of the original design.

10.2.10 Testing the Code (After Each Phase)

After each phase is complete the system test script should be run on the reengineered code and the output compared to that produced by the original code. Only after agreement is reached should the next phase be started. After each stage the code should be baselined and an identifiable copy kept along with the test associated results. The storing of baseline copies of the code will allow the developer to return easily to an exact copy of the code as it existed at the end of any of the defined phases. This is very useful for tracking bugs that may appear later and to identify at what point they were introduced. It also offers the customer the opportunity to formally release a copy of the code at the end of any of the defined phases. Such a release may not always be planned in advance and it is possible that there may be a sudden requirement to have an intermediate release as soon as possible (or even instantly). In these cases the developer can simply return to the last baselined version and be confident it will work and thereby keep the customer very happy with a very fast response to their request.

10.2.11 Update/Write Documentation

Finally once the re-engineering process has been completed and tested any existing system documentation should be updated or, if none exists, written. Documentation is a very important part of the re-engineering process as it, along with the comments within the code, is the primary source of information that will assist in the future support and maintenance of the application. A typical customer requirement put forward when re-engineering existing code is the desire to move away from the dependence on a single person for its support and future development. Adequate documentation and commented code should mean that any developer familiar with the appropriate programming language can quickly get up to speed with the code and provide a high level of support in a short period of time. The content of the documentation is very dependent on the type of application that has been re-engineered and of other supporting documentation that may already exist. One area, though, that should be covered is a description of any fundamental changes that were introduced during the re-engineering process. It should also refer to or include the details of the configuration plan and the defined baselines that were created during the re-engineering process.

Other areas which should be documented, if appropriate, include:

- Description on how to install/uninstall the application and how to verify which version is installed.
- A quick guide which describes how to use the application.
- An overview of the application design. (This can be more detailed if required).
- Details on how to build the application ready for release.

The final re-engineered code should be baselined along with the associated documentation and the project log. The re-engineered application is now ready for release and is in a well-defined state which will make any future support and maintenance much less arduous.

10.3 DETAILED DESCRIPTION OF REENGINEERING PROCESS

Figure 10.1 illustrates a possible re-engineering process. The input to the process is a legacy program and the output is a structured, modularised version of the same program. At the same time as program re-engineering, the data for the system may also be re-engineered.

The activities in this re-engineering process are:

- **Source code translation:** The program is converted from an old programming language to a more modern version of the same language or to a different language.
- **Reverse engineering:** The program is analysed and information extracted from it which helps to document its organisation and functionality.
- **Program structure improvement:** The control structure of the program is analysed and modified to make it easier to read and understand.
- **Program modularisation:** Related parts of the program are grouped together and, where appropriate, redundancy is removed. In some cases, this stage may involve architectural transformation.
- **Data re-engineering:** The data processed by the program is changed to reflect program changes.

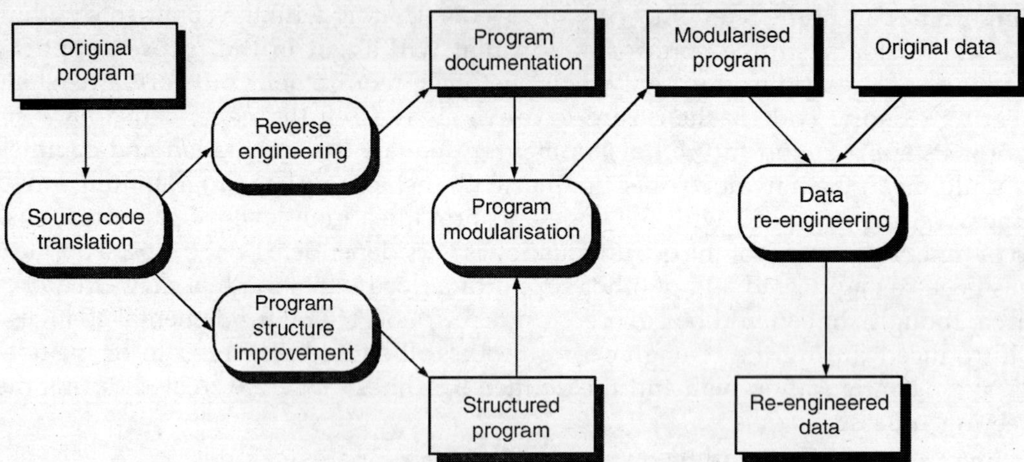

Figure 10.1: The Re-engineering Process

Program re-engineering may not necessarily require all of the steps in Figure 10.1. Source code translation may not be needed if the programming language used to develop the system is still supported by the compiler supplier. If the reengineering relies completely on automated tools then recovering documentation through reverse engineering may be unnecessary. Data re-engineering is only required if the data structures in the program change during system re-engineering. However, software re-engineering always involves some program re-structuring.

The costs of re-engineering obviously depend on the extent of the work that is carried out. There is a spectrum of possible approaches to re-engineering as shown in Figure 10.2. Costs increase from left to right so that source code translation is the cheapest option and re-engineering as part of architectural migration is the most expensive.

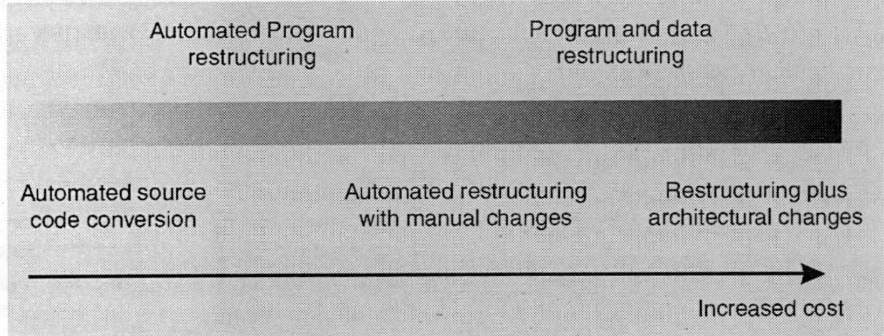

Figure 10.2: *Reengineering approaches*

Apart from the extent of the re-engineering, the principal factors that affect re-engineering costs are:

- *The quality of the software to be re-engineered.* The lower the quality of the software and its associated documentation (if any), the higher the reengineering costs.
- *The tool support available for re-engineering.* It is not normally cost-effective to re-engineer a software system unless you can use CASE tools to automate most of the program changes.
- *The extent of data conversion required.* If re-engineering requires large volumes of data to be converted, this significantly increases the process cost.
- *The availability of expert staff.* If the staff responsible for maintaining the system cannot be involved in the re-engineering process, this will increase the costs. System re-engineers will have to spend a great deal of time understanding the system.

The main disadvantage of software re-engineering is that there are practical limits to the extent that a system can be improved by re-engineering. It isn't possible, for example, to convert a system written using a functional approach to an object-oriented system. Major architectural changes or radical re-organising of the system data management cannot be carried out automatically so involve high additional costs. Although re-engineering can improve maintainability, the reengineered system will probably not be as maintainable as a new system developed using modern software engineering methods.

10.3.1 Source Code Translation

The simplest form of software re-engineering is program translation where source code in one programming language is automatically translated to source code in some other language. The structure and organisation of the program itself is unchanged. The target language may be an updated version of the original language (e.g. COBOL-74 to COBOL-85) or may be a translation to a completely different language (e.g. FORTRAN to C).

Source level translation may be necessary for the following reasons:

- *Hardware platform update:* The organisation may wish to change its standard hardware platform. Compilers for the original language may not be available on the new hardware.
- *Staff skill shortages:* There may be a lack of trained maintenance staff for the original language. This is a particular program where programs were written in a non-standard language that has now gone out of general use.

- *Organisational policy changes:* An organisation may decide to standardise on a particular language to minimise its support software costs. Maintaining many versions of old compilers can be very expensive.
- *Lack of software support:* The suppliers of the language compiler may have gone out of business or may discontinue support for their product.

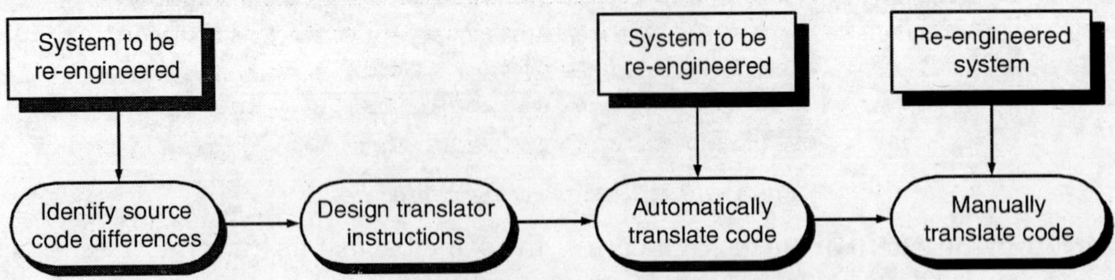

Figure 10.3: *The Program Translation Process*

Figure 10.3 illustrates the process of source code translation. There may be no need to understand the operation of the software in detail or to modify the system architecture. The analysis involved can focus on programming language considerations such as the equivalence of program control constructs.

Source code translation is only economically realistic if an automated translator is available to do the bulk of the translation. This may be a specially written program, a bought-in tool to convert from one language to another or a pattern matching system. In the latter case, a set of instructions how to make the translation from one representation to another has to be written. Parameterised patterns in the source language are defined and associated with equivalent patterns in the target language.

In many cases, completely automatic translation is impossible. Constructs in the source language may have no direct equivalent in the target language. There may be embedded conditional compilation instructions in the source code which are not supported in the target language. In these circumstances, you need to do make changes manually to tune and improve the generated system.

10.3.2 Reverse Engineering

Reverse engineering is the process of analysing software with the objective of recovering its design and specification. The program itself is unchanged by the reverse engineering process. The software source code is usually available as the input to the reverse engineering process. Sometimes, however, even this has been lost and the reverse engineering must start with the executable code.

Reverse engineering is not the same thing as re-engineering. The objective of reverse engineering is to derive the design or specification of a system from its source code. The objective of re-engineering is to produce a new, more maintainable system. Of course, as we can see from Figure 10.1, reverse engineering to develop a better understanding of a system is often part of the re-engineering process.

Reverse engineering is used during the software re-engineering process to recover the program design which engineers use to help them understand a program before re-organising its structure. However, reverse engineering need not always be followed by re-engineering:

- The design and specification of an existing system may be reverse engineered so that they can serve as an input to the requirements specification for that program's replacement.
- Alternatively, the design and specification may be reverse engineered so that they are available to help program maintenance. With this additional information, it may not be necessary to re-engineer the system source code.

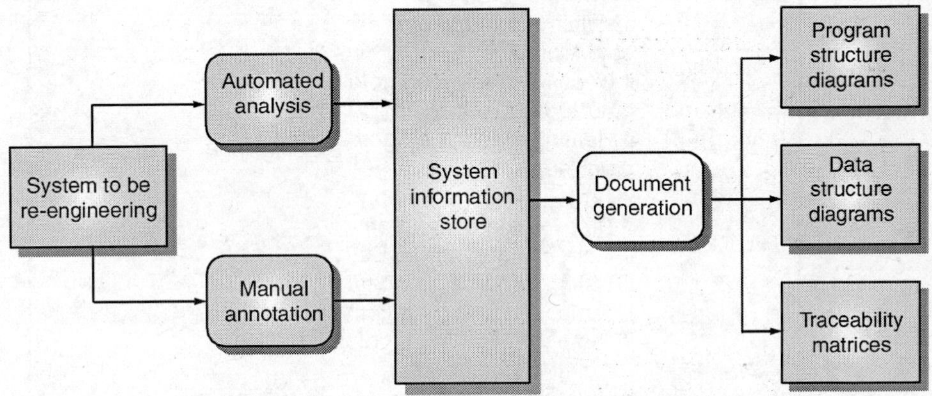

Figure 10.4: *The Reverse Engineering Process*

The reverse engineering process is illustrated in Figure 10.4. The process starts with an analysis phase. During this phase, the system is analysed using automated tools to discover its structure. In itself, this is not enough to re-create the system design. Engineers then work with the system source code and its structural model. They add information to this which they have collected by understanding the system. This information is maintained as a directed graph that is linked to the program source code.

Information store browsers are used to compare the graph structure and the code and to annotate the graph with extra information. Documents of various types such as program and data structure diagrams and traceability matrices can be generated from the directed graph. Traceability matrices show where entities in the system are defined and referenced. The process of document generation is an iterative one as the design information is used to further refine the information held in the system repository.

Tools for program understanding may be used to support the reverse engineering process. These usually present different system views and allow easy navigation through the source code. For example, they allow users to select a data definition then move through the code to where that data item is used.

After the system design documentation has been generated, further information may be added to the information store to help re-create the system specification. This usually involves further manual annotation to the system structure. The specification cannot be deduced automatically from the system model.

10.3.3 Program Structure Improvement

The need to optimise memory use and the lack of understanding of software engineering by many programmers has meant that many legacy systems are not well-structured. Their control structure is tangled with many unconditional branches and unintuitive control logic. This structure may also have been degraded by regular maintenance. Changes to the program may have made some code unreachable but this can only be discovered after extensive analysis. Maintenance programmers often dare not remove code in case it may be accessed indirectly.

```
Start:     Get (Time-on, Time-off, Time, Setting, Temp, Switch)
           if Switch = off goto off
           if switch = on goto on
           goto Cntrld
off:       if Heating-status = on goto Sw-off
           goto loop
on:        if Heating-status = off goto Sw-on
           goto loop
Cntrld:    if Time = Time-on goto on
           if Time = Time-off goto off
           if Time < Time-on goto Start
           if Time > Time-off goto Start
           if Temp > Setting then goto off
           if Temp > Setting then goto on
Sw-off :   Heating-status := off
           goto Switch
Sw-on:     Heating-status := on
Switch:    Switch-heating
loop:      goto Start
```

***Figure 10.5:** A control program with spaghetti logic*

Figure 10.5 illustrates how complex control logic can make a relatively simple program difficult to understand. The program is written in a notation similar to FORTRAN which was often used to write this type of program. However, the program has not even been made more difficult to understand by using cryptic variable names. The example in Figure 10.5 is a controller for a heating system. A panel switch may be set to On, Off or Controlled. If the system is controlled, then it is switched on and off depending on a timer setting and a thermostat. If the heating is on, Switch-heating turns it off and vice-versa.

Typically, programs develop this complex logic structure as they are modified during maintenance. New conditions and associated actions are added without changing the existing control structure. In the short-term, this is a quicker and less risky solution as it reduces the chances of introducing faults in the system. In the long-term, however, it leads to incomprehensible code. Complex code structures can also arise when programmers tried to avoid duplicating code. This was sometimes necessary when programs were constrained by limited memory.

```
loop
    -- The Get statement finds values for the given variables from the system's
    -- environment
    Get (Time-on, Time-off, Time, Setting, Temp, Switch);
    case Switch of
        when On ⇒ if Heating-status = off then
                        Switch-heating ; Heating-status : = on ;
                  end If ;
        when Off ⇒ if Heating-status = off then
                        Switch-heating ; Heating-status : = off ;
                  end If ;
        when controlled
            if Time >= Time-on and Time < = Time-off then
                if Temp > Setting and Heating-status = on then
                    Switch-heating; Heating-status = off;
                elsif Temp < Setting and Heating-status = off then
                    Switch-heating; Heating-status := on ;
            end if ;
        end if ;
    end case ;
end loop ;
```

Figure 10.6: *A structured control program*

Figure 10.6 shows the same control system which we have re-written using structured control statements. The program may be read sequentially from top to bottom so it is much easier to understand. The three switch positions, on; off and controlled are clearly identified and linked to their associated code. We have not used Java here as the original program is not object-oriented. As well as unstructured control, complex conditions can also be simplified as part of the program re-structuring process. Figure 10.7 shows how a conditional statement including 'not' logic may be made more understandable.

```
- - Complex condition
if not (A > B and (C < D or not ( E > F ) ) ) ...

- - Simplified condition
if A <= B and (C >= D or E > F) ...
```

Figure 10.7: *Condition simplification*

Bohm and Jacopini proved that any program may be rewritten in terms of simple if-then-else conditionals and while loops and that unconditional goto statements were not required. This theorem is the basis for automatic program re-structuring. Figure 10.8 shows the stages in the automatic restructuring of a program. It is first converted to a directed graph then a structured equivalent program, without goto statements, is generated.

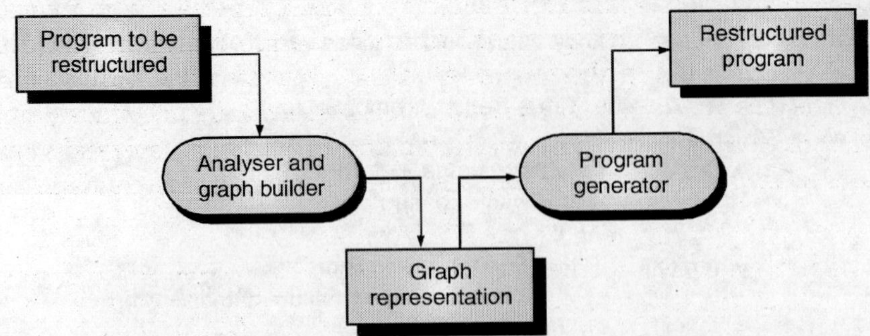

Figure 10.8: Automated Program Restructuring

The directed graph that is generated is a program flow graph which shows how control moves through the program. Simplification and transformation techniques can be applied to this graph without changing its semantics. These detect and remove unreachable parts of the code. Once simplification has been completed, a new program is generated. While loops and simple conditional statements are substituted for goto-based control. This program may be in the original language or in a different language (e.g. FORTRAN may be converted to C).

Problems with automatic program re-structuring include:

- *Loss of comments:* If the program has in-line comments, these are invariably lost as part of the re-structuring process.
- *Loss of documentation:* Similarly, the correspondence between external program documentation and the program is also lost. In many cases, however, both the comments and the documentation of a program are out-of-date so this is not an important factor.
- *Heavy computational demands:* The algorithms embedded in re-structuring tools are complex. Even with fast, modern hardware it can take a long time to complete the re-structuring process for large programs.

If the program is data-driven with components tightly coupled through shared data structures, re-structuring the code may not lead to a significant improvement in understandability. Program modularisation, as discussed in the following section, may also be necessary. If the program is written in a non-standard language dialect, standard re-structuring tools may not work properly and significant manual intervention may be required.

In some cases, it may not be cost-effective to re-structure all of the programs in a system. Some may be of better quality than others and some may not be subject to frequent change. Arthur suggests that a data should be collected to help identify those programs which could benefit most from restructuring. For example, the following metrics may be used to identify the candidates for restructuring:

- Failure rate.
- Percentage of source code changed per year.
- Component complexity.

Other factors such as the degree to which programs or components meet current standards might also be taken into account in making re-structuring decisions.

10.3.4 Program Modularisation

Program modularisation is the process of re-organising a program so that related program parts are collected together and considered as a single module. Once this has been done, it becomes easier to remove redundancies in these related components, to optimise their interactions and to simplify their interface with the rest of the program. For example, in a program that processes seismographic data, all operations associated with graphical presentation of the data may be collected together into a single module. If the system is to be distributed, the modules created can be encapsulated as objects and accessed through a common interface.

Several different types of module may be created during the program modularisation process. These include:

- *Data abstractions:* These are abstract data types that are created by associating data with processing components.
- *Hardware modules:* These are closely related to data abstractions and collect together all of the functions which are used to control a particular hardware device.
- *Functional modules:* These are modules which collect together functions which carry out similar or closely related tasks. For example, all of the functions concerned with input and input validation may be incorporated in a single module. This type of modularisation should be considered where it is impractical to recover program data abstractions.
- *Process support modules:* These are modules where all of the functions and the specific data items required to support a particular business process are grouped. For example, in a library system, a process support module may include all of the functionality required to support the issue and return of books.

Program modularisation is usually carried out manually by inspecting and editing the code. To modularise a program, you have to identify relationships between components and work out what these components do. Browsing and visualisation tools help but it is impossible to completely automate this process.

10.3.4.1 Recovering Data Abstractions

To save memory space, many legacy systems rely on the use of shared tables and common data areas. The information in these areas is globally accessible and may be used by different parts of the system in different ways. Making changes to these global data areas is expensive because of the costs of analysing change impacts across all uses of the data.

To reduce the costs of change to these shared data areas, the program modularisation process may focus on the identification of data abstractions. Data abstractions or abstract data types collect together data and associated processing and are resilient to change. Data abstractions hide the data representation and provide constructor and access functions to modify and inspect the data. So long as the interface is maintained, changes in the data type should not affect other parts of the program.

The steps involved in converting shared global data areas to objects or abstract data types are:

- Analyse common data areas to identify logical data abstractions. It will often be the case that several abstractions are combined in a single shared data area. These should be identified and logically re-structured.

- Create an abstract data type or object for each of these abstractions. If the programming language does not have data hiding facilities, simulate an abstract data type by providing functions to update and access all fields of the data.
- Use a program browsing system or cross-reference generator to find all references to the data. Replace these with calls to the appropriate functions.

This process seems to be time-consuming but relatively straightforward. In practice, however, it can be very difficult because of the ways in which shared data areas are used. In older versions of languages like FORTRAN which have limited data structuring facilities, programmers may have designed complex data management strategies which they have implemented using shared arrays. The array therefore may actually be used as a different kind of data structure. Further problems are caused by indirect addressing of shared structures and addressing by offsets from some other structure.

If the target machine for the original program had a limited memory, this causes other problems. The programmers may have used knowledge about data lifetimes and embedded this in the program. To avoid allocating extra space, they use the same data area to store different abstractions at different points in the program. These can only be discovered after a detailed static and dynamic analysis of the program.

10.3.5 Data Re-engineering

So far, most of the discussion of software evolution has focused on the problems of changing programs and software systems. However, in many cases, there are associated problems of data evolution. The storage, organisation and format of the data processed by legacy programs may have to evolve to reflect changes to the software. The process of analysing and re-organising the data structures and, sometimes, the data values in a system to make it more understandable is called *data re-engineering*.

In principle, data re-engineering should not be necessary if the functionality of a system is unchanged. In practice, however, there are a number of reasons why you may have to modify the data as well as the programs in a legacy system:

1. *Data degradation:* Over time, the quality of data tends to decline. Changes to the data introduce errors, duplicate values may have been created and changes to the external environment may not be reflected in the data. This is inevitable because data lifetimes are often very long. For example, personal banking data comes into existence when an account is opened and may have to persist for at least the lifetime of the customer. As the customer's circumstances change, these changes may not be properly included in the bank's data. Program re-engineering can bring data quality problems to light and thus highlight the need for associated data re-engineering.
2. *Inherent limits that are built into the program:* When originally designed, developers of many programs included built-in constraints on the amount of data which could be processed. However, programs are now often required to process much more data than was originally envisaged by their developers. Data re-engineering may be required to remove the limitations. For example, Rochester and Douglas describe a funds management system that was originally designed to handle up to 99 funds. The company running the system were managing more than 2000 funds and had to run 23 separate copies of the system. They therefore decided to reengineer the system and its associated data.

3. *Architectural evolution:* If a centralised system is migrated to a distributed architecture it is essential that the core of that architecture should be a data management system that can be accessed from remote clients. This may require a large data re-engineering effort to move data from separate files into the server database management system. The move to distributed program architecture may be initiated when an organisation decides to move from file-based data management to a database management system.

As with program re-engineering, there are a spectrum of approaches to data reengineering which reflect the reasons why data re-engineering may be required. These are shown in Figure 10.9.

Approach	Description
Data cleanup	The data records and values are analysed to improve their quality. Duplicated are removed, redundant information is deleted and a consistent format applied to all records. This should not normally require any associated program changes.
Data extension	In this case, the data and associated programs are re-engineered to remove limits on the data processing. This may require changes to programs to increase field lengths, modify upper limits on the tables etc. The data itself may then have to be rewritten and cleaned up to reflect the program changes.
Data migration	In this case, data is moved into the control of a modern database management system. The data may be stored in separate files or may be managed by an older type of DBMS. This situation is illustrated in Figure 10.10.

Figure 10.9: *Approaches to Data Re-engineering*

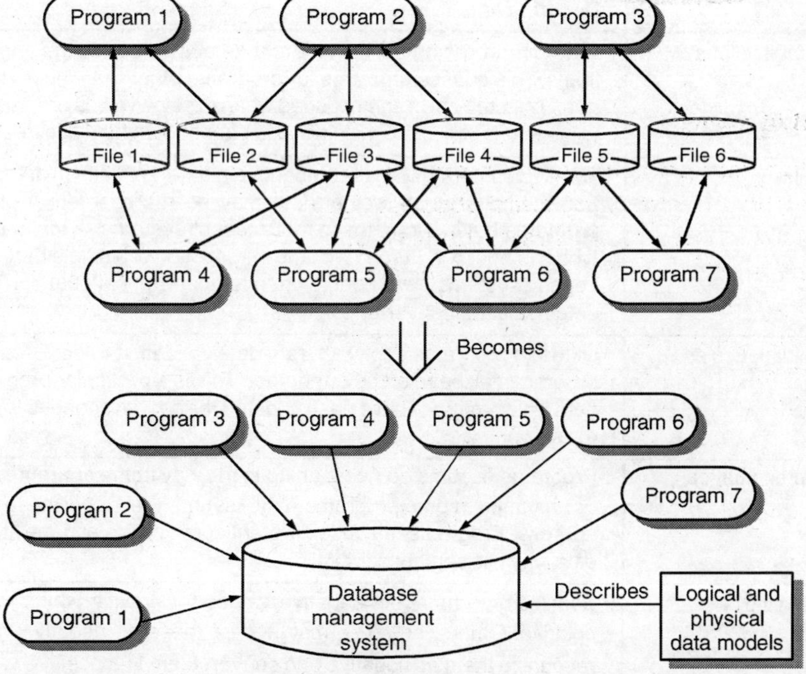

Figure 10.10: *Data Migration*

Rickets describe some of the problems with data which can arise in legacy systems made up of several cooperating programs:

1. *Data naming problems* Names may be cryptic and difficult to understand. Different names (synonyms) may be given to the same logical entity in different programs in the system. The same name may be used in different programs to mean different things.
2. *Field length problems* This is a problem when field lengths in records are explicitly assigned in the program. The same item may be assigned different lengths in different programs or the field length may be too short to represent current data. To solve this problem, other fields may be re-used in some cases so that usage of a named data field across the programs in a system is inconsistent.
3. *Record organisation problems* Records representing the same entity may be organised differently in different programs. This is a problem in languages like COBOL where the physical organisation of records are set by the programmer and reflected in files. It is not a problem in languages like C++ or Java where the physical organisation of a record is the compiler's responsibility.
4. *Hard-coded literals* Literal (absolute) values, such as tax rates, are included directly in the program rather than referenced using some symbolic name.
5. *No data dictionary* There may be no data dictionary defining the names used, their representation and their use.

As well as inconsistent data definitions, data values may also be stored in an inconsistent way. After the data definitions have been re-engineered, the data values must also be converted to conform to the new structure. Rickets *et al.* also describe some possible data value inconsistencies. These are shown in Figure 10.11.

Data Inconsistency	**Description**
Inconsistent default values	Different programs assign different default values to the same logical data items. This causes problems for programs other than those that created the data. The problem is compounded when missing values are assigned a default value that is valid. The missing data cannot then be discovered.
Inconsistent units	The same information is represented in different units in different programs. For example, in US weight data may be represented in pounds in older programs but in kilograms in more recent systems. A major problem of this type has arisen in Europe with the introduction of a single European currency. Legacy systems have been written to deal with national currency units and data has to be converted to euros.
Inconsistent validation rules	Different programs apply different data validation rules. Data written by one program may be rejected by another. This is a particular problem for archival data which may not have been updated in line with changes to data validation rules.
Inconsistent representation semantics	Programs assume some meaning in the way items are represented. For example, some programs may assume that upper-case text means an address. Programs may use different conventions and may therefore reject data which is semantically valid.
Inconsistent handling of negative values	Some programs reject negative values for entities which must always be positive. Others, however, may accept these as negative values or fail to recognize them as negative and convert them to a positive value.

Figure 10.11: *Data Value Inconsistencies*

Detailed analysis of the programs that use the data is essential before data reengineering. This analysis should be aimed at discovering the function of identifiers in the program, finding the literal values which should be replaced with named constants, discovering embedded data validation rules and data representation conversions. Tools such as cross-reference analysers and pattern matchers may be used to help with this analysis. A set of tables should be created which show where data items are referenced and the changes to be made to each of these references.

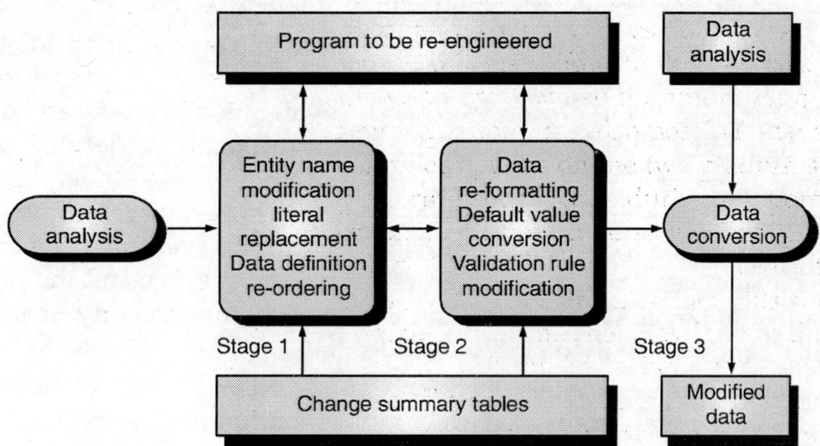

Figure 10.12: *The Data Re-engineering Process*

Figure 10.12 illustrates the process of data-re-engineering, assuming that data definitions are modified, literal values named, data formats re-organised and the data values converted. The change summary tables hold details of all the changes to be made. They are therefore used at all stages of the data re-engineering process.

In Stage 1 of this process, the data definitions in the program are modified to improve understandability. The data itself are not affected by these modifications. It is possible to automate this process to some extent using pattern matching systems such as awk to find and replace definitions or to develop XML descriptions of the data and use these to drive data conversion tools. However, some manual work is almost always necessary to complete the process. The data re-engineering process may stop at this stage if the goal is simply to improve the understandability of the data structure definitions in a program. If, however, there are data value problems as discussed above, Stage 2 of the process may then be entered.

If an organisation decides to continue to Stage 2 of the process, it is then committed to Stage 3, data conversion. This is usually a very expensive process. Programs have to be written which embed knowledge of the old and the new organisation. These process the old data and output the converted information. Again, pattern matching systems may be used to implement this conversion.

10.4 DATA MIGRATION OVERVIEW

Data migration is the process of transferring data between storage types, formats, orcomputersystems.Datamigrationisusuallyperformedprogrammaticallytoachievean *automated migration*, freeing up human resources from tedious tasks. It is required when organizations or individuals change computer systems or upgrade to new systems, or when systems merge (such as when the organizations that use them undergo a merger or takeover).

To achieve an effective data migration procedure, data on the old system is mapped to the new system providing a design for data extraction and data loading. The design relates old data formats to the new system's formats and requirements. Programmatic data migration may involve many phases but it minimally includes *data extraction*wheredataisreadfrom the old system and *data loading*wheredataiswrittentothenewsystem.

If a decision has been made to provide a set input file specification for loading data onto the target system, this allows a pre-load 'data validation' step to be put in place, interrupting the standard E(T)L process. Such a data validation process can be designed to interrogate the data to be transferred, to ensure that it meets the predefined criteria of the target environment, and the input file specification. An alternative strategy is to have on-the-fly data validation occurring at the point of loading, which can be designed to report on load rejection errors as the load progresses. However, in the event that the extracted and transformed data elements are highly 'integrated' with one another, and the presence of all extracted data in the target system is essential to system functionality, this strategy can have detrimental, and not easily quantifiable effects.

After loading into the new system, results are subjected to data verification to determine whether data was accurately translated, is complete, and supports processes in the new system. During verification, there may be a need for a parallel run of both systems to identify areas of disparity and forestall erroneous data loss.

Automated and manual data cleaning is commonly performed in migration to improve data quality, eliminate redundant or obsolete information, and match the requirements of the new system.

Data migration phases (design, extraction, cleansing, load, verification) for applications of moderate to high complexity are commonly repeated several times before the new system is deployed.

10.4.1 Benefits of Data Migration

StorVault, offers comprehensive, reliable data migration that help you cost-effectively manage the impact of switching storage platforms, and maintain business continuity in the process. We make it easy to consolidate disparate media to a common format and type.

Benefits

- Manage legacy data cost-effectively
- Easily access formerly difficult-to-reach data
- Ensure business continuity

Data Migration is the process of transferring data between storage types, formats, or computer systems. It is often required when organizations change computer systems or upgrade to new systems. Usually, specialized software tools are used to automate migrations. In the process, legacy data stored in out-of-date or obsolete formats is evaluated, indexed, and de-duplicated. Then it is migrated to newer, more cost-effective and reliable media.

If your business maintains legacy data on tapes or other outmoded media, we can move it to disk drives, making it much more accessible and reliable, better indexed, and more cost-effective to store.

We utilize a four-step process to migrate your data:

1. Working with you, we evaluate your media and determine your requirements. We can access data from any brand or type of media. We decide on the target media for delivering your data including disk or other formats.
2. We then migrate your data from its original sources and, as necessary, recover data from damaged media, restoring individual files.
3. Your data is indexed and de-duplicated, and unnecessary files are purged to reduce your storage footprint.
4. Data is delivered to you on new storage media and is ready for accessing.

10.5 DATA MIGRATION

Data migration is a key element to consider when adopting any new system, either through purchase or new development. One would think that any two systems that maintain the same sort of data must have performed similar tasks. Therefore, information from one system should map to the other with ease. However, this is rarely the case.

Although migrating data can be a fairly time-consuming process, the benefits can be worth the cost for those that "live and die" by trends in data. Additionally, old applications need not be maintained.

Some key terms in understanding data migration are:

- *Legacy data* is the recorded information that exists in your current storage system, and can include database records, spreadsheets, text files, scanned images and paper documents. All these data formats can be migrated to a new system.
- *Data migration* is the process of importing legacy data to a new system. This can involve entering the data manually, moving disk files from one folder (or computer) to another, database insert queries, developing custom software, or other methods. The specific method used for any particular system depends entirely on the systems involved and the nature and state of the data being migrated.
- *Data cleansing* is the process of preparing legacy data for migration to a new system. Because the architecture and storage method of new or updated systems are usually quite different, legacy data often does not meet the criteria set by the new system, and must be modified prior to migration. For example, the legacy system may have allowed data to be entered in a way that is incompatible with the new system. Architecture differences, design flaws in the legacy system, or other factors can also render the data unfit for migration in its present state. The data cleansing process manipulates, or cleans, the legacy data so it conforms to the new system's requirements.

10.5.1 Do We Migrate Legacy Data?

The *"Do we migrate legacy data?"* question has been asked ever since the first companies put data in one repository and decided to change systems. Here are some commonly asked questions:

- Should we bring the data over to the new system?
- If so, should we bring all or part of the data?
- If just part, which parts? - based on creation date? based on status of case open or closed? ÷ or some combination of these?
- If we choose to bring over data on or after a certain date, which should it be - last 3 months, last 6 months, last year?...should it be all the data?
- Should we filter in or out specific data?
- Are our desired criteria extractable from the existing database?
- Are the desired fields of data importable into the new system?
- Is data migration from our legacy system included in the purchase of the new system?
- If not, do we have the expertise in-house to script an automated process to migrate the data?
- If not, will we hire someone to do this?
- Will we perform this task manually?

When deciding on data migration, all factors should be examined before making the assumption that the whole dataset or none of the dataset should be moved over to the new system. The proof is in whether these data records will be used and acted upon when the new system and process is in place. Two key variables to consider in deciding on data migration include data volume and data value.

Data volume is the easiest variable in the decision process. How many data records are we talking about: 1000, 10,000, 100,000, 250,000? How many are expected to come into the new system on a weekly/monthly basis to replenish this supply? Check to see if there are any technical barriers to bringing over a certain amount of data and also if large databases will affect performance of system functions like searching. If not, then 10 records or 100,000 records should not make any difference.

If volume is low, then it may be well worth doing a migration so there is some database for users and for trend analysis. If volume is high, then it may make sense to examine the age/value of the data and start filtering on certain criteria.

Data value is a much harder variable in the decision process. Many times there are different perceptions concerning what value the existing data provide. If users are not working with older data in the current system, chances are they may not work with older data in the new system even with improved search functionality. If migrating, you may want to look at shorter-term date parameters - why bog down a system's performance with data that are never used?

Criteria, as discussed in the questions above, can be date parameters, but can also include other factors. Extracting the exact data based on some of these factors will depend on the abilities of your current system and database as well as the ability to write the detailed extraction script. Keeping it simple when possible is the best approach. However, there may be circumstances where filtering data may make sense.

Once you have determined which data you want to migrate, then determining what parts of the data record will also be important.

10.5.2 How Do We Migrate Data?

Once the decision is made to perform data migration and before migration can begin the following analyses must be performed:

- Analyze and define source structure (structure of data in the legacy system)
- Analyze and define target structure (structure of data in the new system)
- Perform field mapping (mapping between the source and target structure with data cleansing, if necessary)
- Define the migration process (automated vs. manual)

To analyze and define source and target structures, analysis must be performed on the existing system as well as the new system to understand how it works, who uses it, and what they use it for. A good starting point for gathering this information is in the existing documentation for each system. This documentation could take the form of the original specifications for the application, as well as the systems design and documentation produced once the application was completed. Often this information will be missing or incomplete with legacy applications, because there may be some time between when the application was first developed and now.

You may also find crucial information in other forms of documentation, including guides, manuals, tutorials, and training materials that end-users may have used. Most often this type of material will provide background information on the functionality exposed to end-users but may not provide details of how the underlying processes work.

For this part of the analysis, you may actually need to review and document the existing code. This may be difficult, depending on the legacy platform. For example, if data are being migrated from an AS/400 application written in RPG, assistance from an experienced RPG programmer will be required, if those skills are not available in-house. This can be an expensive part of the analysis process, because a resource to perform this analysis for you may be necessary, but it is a vital part of the process, especially if the application has been running and maintained over a long period of time. Undocumented code or fixes that are critical to the application and that have not been documented elsewhere may exist.

Another key area to examine is how the data in the system are stored (i.e., in flat files, files, or tables). What fields are included in those files/tables and what indexes are in use? Also, a detailed analysis of any server processes that are running that may be related to the data must be performed (e.g., if a nightly process runs across a file and updates it from another system).

Now that the source and target structures are defined, the mapping from the legacy to the target should fall into place fairly easily. Mapping should include documentation that specifically identifies fields from the legacy system mapped to fields in the target system and any necessary conversion or cleansing.

Once the analysis and mapping steps are completed, the process of importing the data into the new system must be defined. This process may be a combination of automation and manual processes or may be completely automated or may be completely manual. For example, a process may:

- Create data extractions from the legacy system
- Cleanse the data extractions according to mapping guidelines
- Import the data extractions into the new system using that system's import feature
- Verify and test samplings of the data in the new system by comparing data reports to the old system

Bottom Line: Data migration is a key element to consider when adopting any new system either through purchase or new development. Data migration is not a simplistic task and if not given due consideration early in the process of developing or purchasing a new system it could become a very expensive task.

10.6 DATA MIGRATION PROCESS

Following figure 10.13 shows the data migration process:

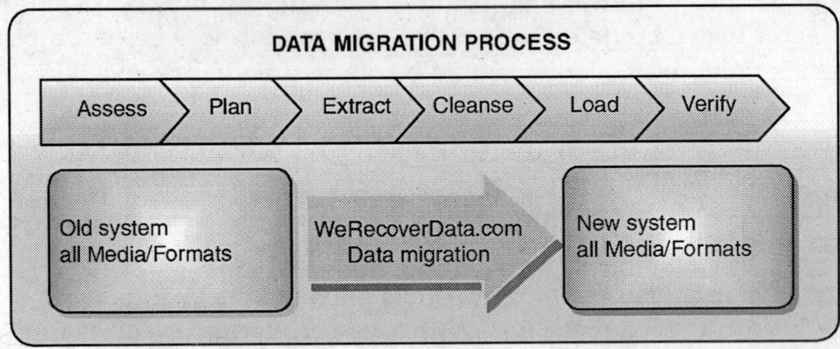

Figure 10.13: *Data Migration Process*

- **Assess.** In the initial assessment phase, we ascertain the scenario and evaluate the data migration requirements.
- **Plan.** Then, we plan a performance driven & cost effective data migration procedure in accordance to your budget guidelines.
- **Extract.** Our highly trained professionals use state-of-the-art technology in retrieving the best quality of data from the sources.
- **Cleanse.** The data is cleaned from any potential problems to ensure accurate data translation maintaining a high quality of data.
- **Load.** Then, the data is loaded in the new system / format / device.
- **Verify.** The loaded data is validated for accuracy and optimized application performance.

10.7 RISKS OF IMPLEMENTING AN EFFECTIVE DATA MIGRATION STRATEGY

Migrating data brings many risks and challenges:

- Migration might be done as part of a larger chain of dependencies (operating system upgrades, application upgrades or implementations, database structural changes, etc.) – thereby increasing complexity.
- Data requirements are not clearly defined - data rules for integrity, controls, security, availability and recoverability are often ill-defined. In the absence of such rules, data is migrated incorrectly.

- Migration acceptance criteria may not be defined.
- Data is often too distributed to be migrated easily (think end-user computing).
- Budgets may limit technology options for performing migrations.
- Expertise in data migration and management may not be present.
- Management attention might be insufficient (migrations are typically "routine" operations and not major attention-getting projects).
- There could be poor support from the storage vendor(s), making migrations all the more taxing.

10.8 THE EFFECTIVE DATA MIGRATION STRATEGY

The business driver for effective data migrations is to strike the optimal balance between data accuracy, migration speed, low or no downtime, and minimum costs. We will see how to formulate such a strategy.

To a large extent the enterprise's storage technology, storage management tools, and storage network capabilities define the range of possibilities for data migration strategies. Selection of such is out of scope of this note; however, we will introduce a methodology for data migration strategy that can work under most technology environments.

10.8.1 Analyze Phase

The first stage of data migration is data classification. It is important to know how and where data is stored, backed up, and archived. Data structures must be well understood, and there should be visibility into the data's usage, capacity, and growth patterns. Various interfaces and reports utilizing the to-be-migrated data must be considered. It is also important to understand the network connections between data points (especially required bandwidth and controls). Data classification also describes conditions for data access, retention requirements and control & security measures such as encryption. Next, migration requirements are determined. Beyond the "top three" requirements of what must be migrated, how much downtime is acceptable, and how much budget is available, there are other needs that must be considered. These can include quality requirements, new or modified service-level agreements, expectations for the new storage infrastructure, and objectives such as reduced management costs, reduced storage expenditures, greater insight into expenditure, a simplified vendor model or greater technical flexibility or stability. If the organization has standards or policies concerning data, these must be factored in. Finally, analysts must take into account historical data to be migrated (which is often forgotten until it is late in the game).

Then there are technology considerations, such as:

- How old is the operating system(s) under which data is to be migrated? Some migration tools do not support legacy operating systems.
- Which storage tiers and devices are involved?
- Can identical data structures be used for the target data (this will reduce the time and complexity of migration)?
- What staging area requirements are present, given current technologies and data migration requirements?

- Do you need or want the option to recover quickly from the source disk, or to fall back to the original storage device as a fail-over? There are both procedural and technological ways of accomplishing this.
- Is a central console needed to manage data migrations across multiple servers?
- Is there a need to control the data migration from a local server – or a remote server? If remote, which protocols must be supported?
- Is there a requirement to throttle or control data flows between servers?
- Must data integrity be checked during (not just after) migration?
- Which staff or consultants are available to assist with migration analysis, design, and deployment?

Data may be migrated in several ways:

- All at once
- In logical sections (by application, operating system, database, business function, etc.)
- Via a pilot migration or parallel run for "proof of concept" or risk mitigation.
- In phases (first critical data, then less critical or historical data).

Acceptance Test Considerations

The Analyze Phase is complete when data has been classified, data migration requirements are clear, and technology considerations have been considered. For organizations with an established data classification program (that typically includes government entities, regulated firms, and enterprises complying with quality standards) this can be done in a week or two. If a full data classification must be done as well, that can add another few weeks.

Key analysis milestones

Milestones in the Analysis Phase typically include the following:

- Legacy data and report analysis and profiles has been completed.
- There is an updated data classification document.
- The data migration strategy document has been written.
- Data exception report requirements are clear.
- Audit and reconciliation report requirements are defined.
- Data migration requirements (business and technology) are documented.

10.8.2 Design Phase

The design phase involves taking the data classification and requirements defined in the analysis phase and puts definition around how these will be realized:

- The responsibilities, roles and tasks for each individual, department, or external consultant involved in migration are determined.
- Data elements are mapped from source to target.
- A plan for freezing physical data structures during the migration is put together.
- Any tools to be used in the migration (data transformation tools, migration options, data mapping tools, CASE or other data modeling tools, simple spreadsheets, etc.) are identified or acquired.

- Any software to facilitate data extraction or checking is developed.
- Clear acceptance criteria are determined and agreed.

Where economically viable (large volumes of data to migrate, frequent mission-critical migrations, complex data structures, high data quality requirements) data transformation tools can offer the following advantages over simple spreadsheets:

- They provide flexible reporting of data elements and rules.
- They can generate migration code or scripts directly from the mapping rules.
- They can detect data integrity violations.

Acceptance Test Considerations

The Design Phase is complete when migration staffing has been confirmed, data mapping is complete, a plan for freezing data structures is in place, tools have been identified, and acceptance criteria have been agreed. The length of the design phase depends mainly on the need to acquire additional migration tools and the need to develop extraction, loading, and quality checking software. If such tools and software are in place and simply need to be customized, the design phase can take place in a few weeks; otherwise, this process can take a few months.

Key design milestones

Milestones in the Design Phase include the following:

- Roles, responsibilities, and task assignments are clear and accepted.
- Data elements are mapped from source to target.
- A plan for freezing physical data structures during the migration is put together.
- Migration tools are identified.
- Migration software is developed.
- A migration strategy is chosen.
- Acceptance criteria are agreed.
- Funding for staff, consultants, and tools has been secured.

10.8.3 Deploy Phase

The first step in the design stage is to put together a project plan and structure. As part of this process there should be close analysis of any dependencies in data migrations; where possible, such dependencies and complexities should be reduced to better manage deployment risk. During the deploy phase the following occurs:

- Physical data structures are frozen on source and target.
- Interfaces and processing on source and target are brought down where required.
- Data is staged from the source location.
- Quality reports are run and any data errors or inconsistencies identified.
- Data quality issues are fixed in the staging area.
- A preliminary reconciliation takes place in the staging area, and any reconciling items are investigated and resolved.
- Data is migrated to the target location.
- Reconciliation reports are run.

- Acceptance criteria are check; if reconciliation errors or other criteria are not met, the system is rolled back to the original data source. Otherwise, interfaces and processing from the source is discontinued and then activated on the target.
- The above may be conducted in phases, or as part of a parallel run or pilot depending upon the migration approach chosen.

Acceptance Test Considerations

Testing and implementation are inseparable in a data migration. Physical errors are typically syntactical in nature and can be easily identified and resolved through syntax corrections in the migration scripts. Logical errors are due to problems with the data mapping. Looking into these requires asking questions like:

- How many records did we expect this script to create?
- Did the correct number of records get created? If not, why?
- Has the data been loaded into the correct fields?
- Is the data load complete – or are certain fields missing?
- Has the data been formatted correctly?
- Are any post-migration clean-up tasks in order?

The goal of a successful data migration is to keep the length of the deploy phase(s) to a minimum. What is acceptable depends upon the organization – some will want this phase to last no more than a day (or less), others can tolerate a deployment that lasts a few days if availability is not a major concern.

Key deployment milestones

Milestones in the Deploy Phase include the following:

- Project plan in place and agreed.
- Project team is formed.
- A test plan is written.
- The migration takes place.
- Reconciliation / data checking reports are run.
- Acceptance criteria and performance metrics are evaluated.
- A go / no-go decision takes place.
- Data issues may be resolved post-migration.

10.9 HOW TO MIGRATE YOUR DATA IN SEVEN STEPS

Finding a data migration process that balances cost and rapid delivery

Historically, data migration projects have had a tendency to fail. According to Bloor Research, as many as 60 percent do not succeed. How can you prevent failure when migrating your data?

Follow this seven-step process:

1. **Source system exploration**

   The first phase of a data migration project is to identify and explore the source data. The most appropriate route for identification is to group data, customer names, addresses and product descriptions based on the target model.

Although the source systems may contain thousands of fields, some might be duplicates or not be applicable to the target system. In this stage, it is critical to identify which data is required and where it is, as well as what data is redundant and not required for the migration. Conversely, if the initially identified sources do not contain all of the data required for the target model, a gap is identified. In this case, you may have to consolidate data from multiple sources to create a record with the correct set of data to fulfill the requirements of the target. Using multiple data sources allows you to add another element of data validation and a level of confidence in your data.

At the end of this phase, you will have identified the source data that will populate the target model. You will also have identified any gaps in the data and, if possible, included extra sources to compensate. Optimally, you will have broken down the data into categories that enable you to work on manageable and possible parallel tasks.

2. **Data assessment**

The next logical phase is to assess the quality of this source data. If the new system fails due to data inconsistencies, incorrect or duplicate data, there is very limited value in migrating data to the target system. To assess the data, we recommend profiling the data.

Data profiling is the process of systematically scanning and analyzing the contents of all the columns in tables of interest. Profiling identifies data defects at the table and column level. Data profiling is integral to the process of evaluating the conformity of the data and ensuring compliance to the requirements of the target system.

The profiling functions include examining the actual record value and its metadata information. Too many data migration initiatives begin without first examining the quality levels of the source data. By including data profiling early in the migration process, the risks of project overruns, delays and potentially complete failures are reduced.

Through the use of data profiling, you can:

- Immediately identify whether the data will fit the business purpose.
- Accurately plan the integration strategy by identifying data anomalies up front.
- Successfully integrate the source data using an automated data quality process.

The output of this phase of the project is a thorough understanding of the data quality in the source systems, identification of data issues and a list of defined rules to be built to correct them. You will have identified and defined your data quality rules and mappings from the sources to the target model. At this point you will also have a good idea, at a high level, of the design of the integration processes.

3. **Migration design**

In the migration design phase, the main tasks will be to define the technical architecture and design of the migration processes. In addition, you will define the testing processes and how to transition them to the production system. You will also determine whether there will be a parallel run, a zero-downtime migration, or whether you will be expecting to complete the migration and simply "decommission" the old system.

In this phase, it's important to put your plans for the next four steps down on paper. Include timelines, technical details and any other concerns or approval requirements so that the entire project will be documented.

4. **Migration build**

   Be careful about using a "just enough" development approach with your data migration, simply because the migration will be executed only once and there will be limited reuse of the code. These assumptions explain why data migrations are prone to failure.

   A typical sequence to follow when developing a migration is to subset the data and test one category of data at a time (e.g., product or customer). In the case of larger projects, you can develop and test each category in parallel. Testing the migration solution is usually an iterative approach. Start by checking the components individually in small subsets to ensure the mappings, transformations and data cleansing routines are working. Then, increase the data volumes and eventually link all of the components together into a single migration job.

   Output from this phase results in a fully tested data migration process that is scalable, reliable and can deliver the migration within the allocated time.

5. **Execution**

   After comprehensive testing, the time comes to run the migration. In the majority of cases, the source systems are shut down while the migration executes. To minimize impact, this is likely to occur over a weekend or public holiday. In some cases, where the source applications are required to run 24/7, 365 days a year, a zero-downtime migration approach may be needed. This requires a tool to provide the initial load processes, with additional data synchronization technology to capture any changes that took place during the initial load; then, it requires synchronizing the source and target data after the initial load finishes.

6. **Transition**

   At some point after the data has been migrated, decide when to move to the new system, and where appropriate, retire the old system. During the execution phase, audit trails and logs will be created to ensure that all data has been correctly migrated and, when appropriate, that the correct synchronization has been achieved. Finally, after reviewing the audit trails and logs, you will be prepared to make the decision to transition users to the new system. Note that although audit trails and logs are invaluable, it also may be worth profiling the current source and target systems to ensure synchronization is correct.

   In the case of a zero-downtime migration, this becomes more complex because updates on the systems may be occurring while a synchronization check is occurring. As a result, there may always be some delay in the synchronization. In this case, tools can verify synchronization by taking into account the lag between source system changes and data replication into the target system.

7. **Production**

   As part of the design process, a system retirement policy will be created to address the old system. There will also be ongoing data quality enhancements. Remember that because not all source systems will be retired, data quality issues may be identified and will need rectifying in several of the source systems. You will also need to manage ongoing improvements and monitor the data quality of the new system.

   Before you know it, there will be the inevitable next migration project. At this point, it is well worth identifying existing components that can be reused, as well as possible improvements that can be applied to the next migration solution.

10.10 MIGRATION STRATEGIES TO CONSIDER

The next step is to consider the strategies available for achieving migration. We will take a look at complete migration, iterative migration, limited migration, vertical migration, and horizontal migration. Organizations determine which of these strategies to use based on factors such as system qualities, manageability, training, and cost.

10.10.1 Complete Migration

In complete migration, all of the components in the application are migrated as a whole. This strategy does not allow for intermediate validation of the migration process or the business rules. The only way to know if the application is suitable for the business requirements is to evaluate it once the migration is completed. Complete migration requires significant effort and is potentially expensive and risky. This strategy does enable immediate enhancement with new and added functionality. For example, VB 6.0 application functionality is improved when migrated to the .NET environment. Directly integrated into their new .NET environment, these applications gain new versatility, and if deployed on new hardware or new Windows operating systems, will not require further migration or recompilation. Complete migration is an expensive strategy, but is also the most desirable strategy to adopt since it provides application adaptability to future needs.

10.10.2 Iterative Migration

An iterative migration strategy allows for a more controlled migration process since the application is migrated component-by-component, with each newly migrated component rolled out as a phase. This strategy is only feasible if the existing application is composed of distinct components. Interoperability techniques are key, as the migrated and un-migrated components must function together. Iterative migrations provide an acceptable alternative to a complete migration, and are often the option for a large-scale legacy application migration. With this strategy, there is greater control over the cost and progress of the entire migration project. Each phased rollout, or iteration, minimizes risk since the application is returned to a stable production- quality state. Iterative migration also allows the flexibility to migrate only certain portions of the application that have immediate relevance to the business. Improved performance and scalability are immediately realized in the migrated components.

10.10.3 Limited Migration

Limited migration is different from the iterative migration process in that only a component of the application is migrated. The migrated portion is then modified to interoperate with the un-migrated part of the application. Interoperability is the key issue in this type of migration. A business may not need to migrate the entire application, so this type of migration allows an organization to port only the components of the application that is actually required.

10.10.4 Vertical Migration

Vertical migration differs from the other migrations in that the process is performed tier-by-tier. Vertical migration involves isolating and replacing a portion of an application through all n-tiers. The developer determines which component of an application has the least interaction with the other components and performs the migration. The migration is then completed on all tiers for a particular module prior to proceeding to the next module.

This strategy is advantageous when portions of an application are well isolated from other portions of the same application. In these instances, the isolated components share little state information with the rest of the application and can undergo easy migration with minimal impact on the rest of the system. Vertical migration is also an effective option when ActiveX Data Objects (ADO) recordsets are used between tiers. Many applications pass disconnected ADO record sets from the data and business tiers to the presentation tier. They then iterate through the recordsets and generate HTML tables. This type of application is well suited to a vertical migration because migrating vertically minimizes the work involved in achieving interoperability with ADO.

10.10.5 Horizontal Migration

Horizontal migration involves replacing an entire tier of an application without immediately migrating the other tiers. For example, a developer may choose to initially replace the ASP code within a Web-based presentation tier or replace the COM code within the middle tier as the initial migration step. For a business migrating to the .NET environment, the migration is performed a single tier at a time, taking advantage of the features of the .NET framework specific to a particular tier. In this instance, no application code is modified and no operations are affected on another application tier. Horizontal migration is beneficial for infrastructures containing large numbers of servers, large amounts of shared code, heavy ASP application or session state use, and complex middle tiers.

10.11 DATA MIGRATION CHALLENGES

Data Migration is the process of transferring data from one system to another while changing the storage, database or application. In reference to the ETL (Extract-Transform-Load) process, data migration always requires at least Extract and Load steps.

Typically data migration occurs during an upgrade of existing hardware or transfer to a completely new system. Examples include: migration to or from hardware platform; upgrading a database or migrating to new software; or company-mergers when the parallel systems in the two companies need to be merged into one.

There are three main options to accomplish data migration:

1. Merge the systems from the two companies into a brand new one
2. Migrate one of the systems to the other one.
3. Leave the systems as they are but create a common view on top of them - a data warehouse.

Let us describe the data migration challenges in little more detail. Data migration can be a simple process, however there are challenges one may face in implementation.

10.11.1 Storage Migration

Storage migration can be handled in a manner transparent to the application so long as the application uses only general interfaces to access the data. In most systems this is not an issue. However, careful attention is necessary for old applications running on proprietary systems. In many cases, the source code of the application is not available and the application vendor may not be in market anymore. In such cases storage migration is rather tricky and should be properly tested before releasing the solution into production.

10.11.2 Database Migration

Database migration is rather straight forward, assuming the database is used just as storage. It "only" requires moving the data from one database to another. However, even this may be a difficult task. The main issues one may encounter include:

- Unmatched data types (number, date, sub-records)
- Different character sets (encoding)

Different data types can be handled easily by approximating the closest type from the target database to maintain data integrity. If a source database supports complex data formats (e.g. sub-record), but the target database does not, amending the applications using the database is necessary. Similarly, if the source database supports different encoding in each column for a particular table but the target database does not, the applications using the database need to be thoroughly reviewed.

When a database is used not just as data storage, but also to represent business logic in the form of stored procedures and triggers, close attention must be paid when performing a feasibility study of the migration to target database. Again, if the target database does not support some of the features, changes may need to be implemented by applications or by middleware software.

ETL tools are very well suited for the task of migrating data from one database to another i. Using the ETL tools is highly advisable particularly when moving the data between the data stores which do not have any direct connection or interface implemented.

10.11.3 Application Migration

If we take a step back to previous two cases, you may notice that the process is rather straight forward. This however, is extremely uncommon in the case of application migration. The reason is that the applications, even when designed by the same vendor, store data in significantly different formats and structures which make simple data transfer impossible. The full ETL process is a must as the Transformation step is not always straight forward. Of course, application migration can and usually does include storage and database migration as well. The advantage of an ETL tool in this instance is its ready-to-use connectivity to disparate data sources/targets.

Difficulty may occur when migrating data from mainframe systems or applications using proprietary data storage. Mainframe systems use record based formats to store data. Record based formats are easy to handle; however, there are often optimizations included in the mainframe data storage format which complicate data migration. Typical optimizations include binary coded decimal number storage, non-standard storing of positive/negative number values, or storing the mutually exclusive sub-records within a record. Let us consider a library data warehouse as an example. There are two types of publications - books and articles. The publication can be either a book or an article but not both. There are different kinds of information stored for books and articles. The information stored for a book and an article are mutually exclusive. Hence, when storing a book, the data used has a different sub-record format for a book and an article while occupying the same space. Still the data is stored using rather standard encoding. On the Contrary, proprietary data storage makes the Extract step even more complicated. In both cases, the most efficient way to extract data from the source system is performing the extraction in the source system itself; then converting the data into a printable format which can be parsed later using standard tools.

10.11.4 Character Encoding

Most of the systems developed on PC-based platform use ASCII encoding or national extension based on ASCII. The latest one is UTF-8 which keeps ASCII mapping for alpha and numerical characters but enables storage of characters for most of the national alphabets including Chinese, Japanese and Russian. Mainframe systems are mostly based on EBCDIC encoding which is incompatible with ASCII and conversion is required to display the data. ETL tools should support the conversions between character sets, including EBCDIC.

10.12 HYBRID RE-ENGINEERING

The SATC has coined the phrase "Hybrid Re-engineering" to mean a reengineering process that uses not just a single, but a combination of abstraction levels and alteration methods to transition an existing system to a target system. Projects doing hybrid re-engineering choose a combination of abstraction levels based on the condition of the legacy system, the needs of the project and its budget and schedule.

In Hybrid Re-engineering, legacy systems are re-engineered using the approach shown in Figure 10.14, an adaptation of the General Model for Software Re-engineering given in chapter 9. In Figure 10.14, three development tracks are utilized. The first track is a translation from existing code to a new language, operating system or hardware platform with no abstraction. The second track uses the existing code to identify requirements that can be satisfied by the application of COTS packages. The third track is the more standard re-engineering process, the development of new code for project requirements that cannot be satisfied by either of the other tracks, and to "glue" together the translated and COTS components.

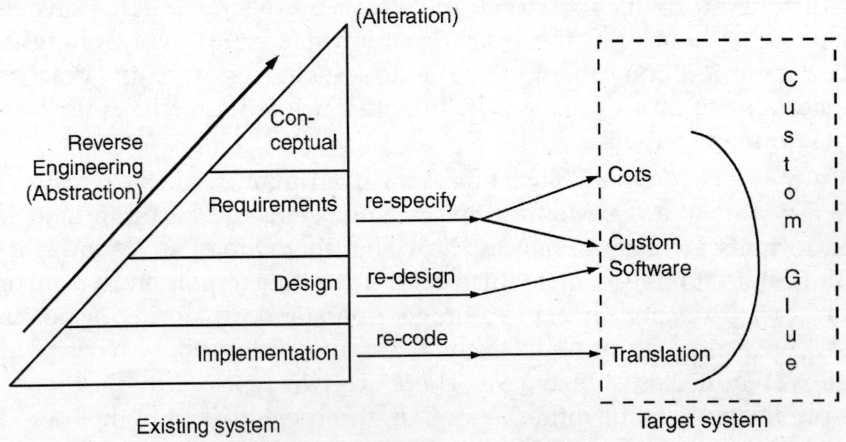

Figure 10.14: Hybrid Re-engineering Tracks

Re-engineering as a development methodology has inherent risks, such as schedule, functionality, cost, and quality. Hybrid re-engineering was developed to decrease some of these risks since COTS packages are expected to have high reliability and require minimal development time. Another method of decreasing time and cost through Hybrid re-engineering while maintaining functionality is through a straight translation of part of the current code to the new language or operating system.

Hybrid re-engineering is innovative, combining three distinct re-engineering efforts; hence the risks generally associated with re-engineering can increase by combining the risks inherent to each track. Since hybrid re-engineering is combining products from different development tracks (COTS, custom software and translated software), one new risk is the interface and interoperability of the products. For example, data transfer between products can cause compatibility and timing problems; COTS packages may not work exactly as anticipated.

In general metrics can be used by management to improve software development efforts and minimize the risks. Metrics can indicate how well a project is meeting its goals. In hybrid reengineering, metrics can support the justification for decisions on track selection for different software functions and components.

10.13 HYBRID RE-ENGINEERING TRACKS

The following sections describe each of the three hybrid re-engineering tracks. After each track is described, the risks associated with the track are identified and appropriate metrics defined.

10.13.1 Translation Track Hybrid Re-engineering

Figure 10.16 is a diagram of a "typical" software system that has been in use for some period of time. In this re-engineering example, we assume the project is moving from FORTRAN to C++ (but not necessarily to an object-oriented design).

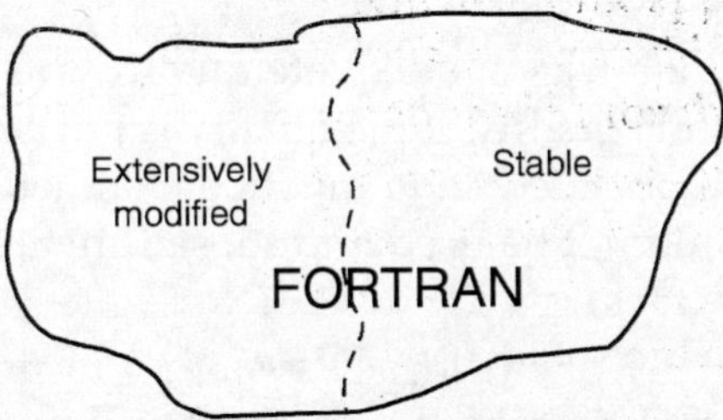

Figure 10.15: *Current Software System*

In looking at the current software system, the manager sees two classifications of code, stable code that has had minimal modifications and whose requirements have remained unchanged, and some code that has under-gone multiple changes and has become unstable, unreliable, and costly to maintain. Re-engineering the stable code may not require total reverse engineering; it might be feasible to simply re-code this portion into the new language or new environment. This process constitutes the translation track of hybrid re-engineering.

In this track, shown in Figure 4, the code in the existing system that is relatively stable, having had minimal changes to the original design and architecture must be identified. This can be accomplished by an analysis of the code and of change reports. Prior to re-engineering, in identifying candidates for translation, metrics such as the logical and calling complexities provide valuable information on structure and coupling and suggest candidates for translation. In identifying components that have been extensively maintained, change or problem reports supply the data. Tracking the criticality of functions will assist in making tradeoff decisions.

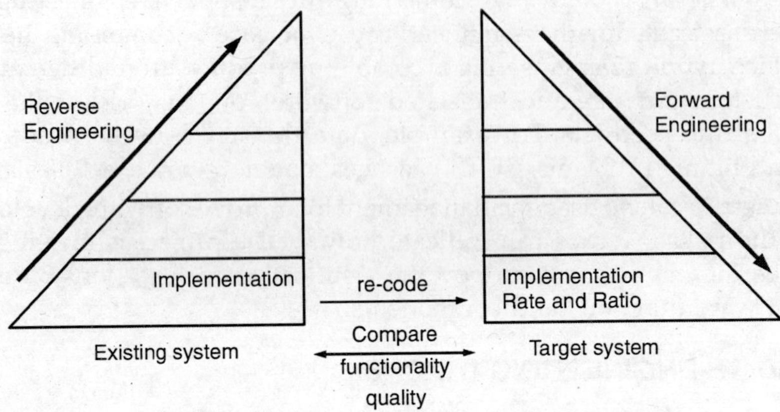

***Figure 10.16:** Translation Track Hybrid Re-engineering*

In the Translation track, the primary risk is the quality of the resulting code. When transitioning from one language to another, the code can have the syntax of the new language but none of the structures or new features. Many source code translators are available to support the transport of code from one language or operating system to another. Source code translators may not solve this problem, since line-by-line translators don't take advantage of target language semantics, constructs, etc., often resulting in code know as "C-TRAN" - C syntax on FORTRAN structures.

While the initial legacy code was of adequate quality, this does not guarantee that the resulting code will have the same quality. If the quality is not adequate, code may have to be improved. If 20 - 30% of the translated code must be changed to improve its quality or to meet standards, the code should not be used and those functions or components should be re-engineered using another track.

Quantifying the functionally of the legacy system will provide a basis for estimating how complete the new system is during development and provide estimations as to when the target system will be complete. One method being tested by the SATC and other companies to track progress in re-engineering uses function points as a measure of functionality. In this application, using the basic function point counting method described by Albrecht, an approximate estimate can be gleaned as to the type and count of tasks. This can be used as a starting point in comparing progress in transferring functionality between the original system and the target system. Tools are available to count function points from COBOL code and the SATC is working to develop a tool for FORTRAN and C. In evaluating the progress of the translation, one measure might be the rate at which functionality, approximated through function points, is moving from the existing system to the target system. The ratio of code translated can also serve as a measure of progress.

Once the re-engineering is complete, it is important to verify that the functionality is retained in the new system, as well as the quality of the code has improved, hence implying improved maintainability. There is no simple method to ensure functionality has transitioned between systems. The most commonly used method involves running test cases on the original system and then repeating the tests on the completed target system. It is also important to make sure that documentation is up to date. Documentation that originally applied presumably still does; this translated code represents the most stable part of the system. An added advantage of the translation track is that maintenance personnel will still understand the program flow and existing documentation since it remains basically unchanged. This will aid them in becoming effective in the new language and system.

10.13.2 COTS Track Hybrid Re-engineering

In the COTS track of Hybrid re-engineering, shown in Figure 10.17, requirements and functions must be identified that can feasibly be implemented using COTS.

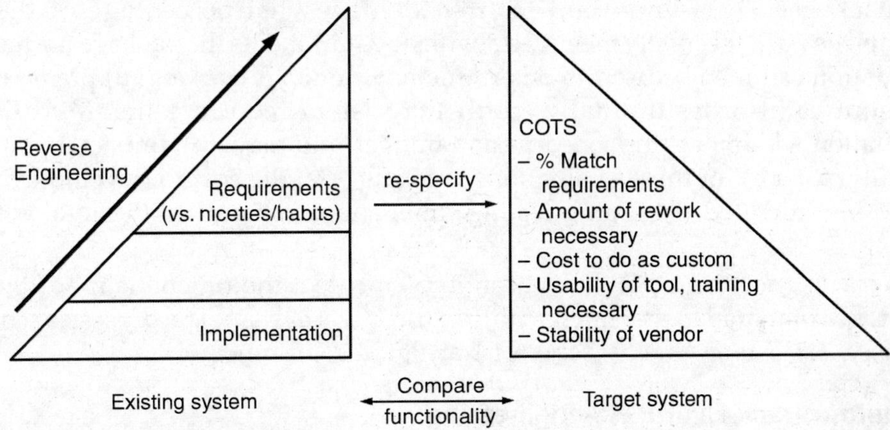

Figure 10.17: *COTS Track Hybrid Re-engineering*

After applying the techniques of Reverse Re-engineering to identify the requirements, it is important to separate those requirements that must be contained in the target system from those requirements that users want in the new system because they have become habits or are comfortable with those features. This separation of requirements into "necessary" and "nice" is critical to COTS selection.

The advantage to using COTS is the decreased development time and increased reliability. Testing is still needed during integration, but less than for code developed from scratch. The disadvantage can be the number of requirements satisfied by the package. For example, if in the existing system a specific field has 10 characters and the COTS package only allows 8, is this acceptable? Was the 10 character field arbitrary or does it represents a "hidden" business requirement that should not be altered? In addition, users are often resistant to change, even ones that have little impact, such as different icons or keystrokes to call a function. This must be taken into account for the package to have comparable usability and functionality.

Although the use of COTS software decreases the development time and increases the reliability, COTS also introduce additional risks. A major risk is that the package will not perform as anticipated or advertised, that it is unreliable, immature or incomplete. The package may also undergo frequent manufacturer version enhancements requiring constant upgrading. In the worse case, changes may alter or remove functions needed for the system. The COTS may require modifications or supplementation to match the requirements, causing increases in schedule and decreasing reliability. In addition, the use of COTS may limit further enhancements to the system, since changes in the COTS provided functions may not be possible due to legal issues.

The stability of the vendor should also be part of the evaluation process since it may be necessary for them to make later required changes. An additional cost may be incurred due to the unfamiliarity with the COTS. Simple changes to usability, such as new icons, will require additional training time.

Some metrics are applicable to assist in decreasing the risks associated with the selection of COTS packages,. It is important to first identify what percentage of the desired requirements the package totally meets, and which requirements the package partially meets. This information can then be used to determine how much rework or supplementation the package requires in order to totally fulfill the system requirements. Modification or supplementation will impact the schedule and budget, and may well impact maintainability and reliability. After all of these evaluations are complete, the cost to develop from scratch should also be estimated, including testing time, and compared to the total costs of the COTS.

In this track, once the COTS have been implemented, the functionality of the existing system must be compared to the functionality of the target system. The process of comparison must be based on testing, as was done for translated code functions.

10.13.3 Custom Track Hybrid Re-engineering

The Custom track of Hybrid Re-engineering, shown in Figure 10.18, is similar to traditional reengineering since new code is derived from the existing legacy system.

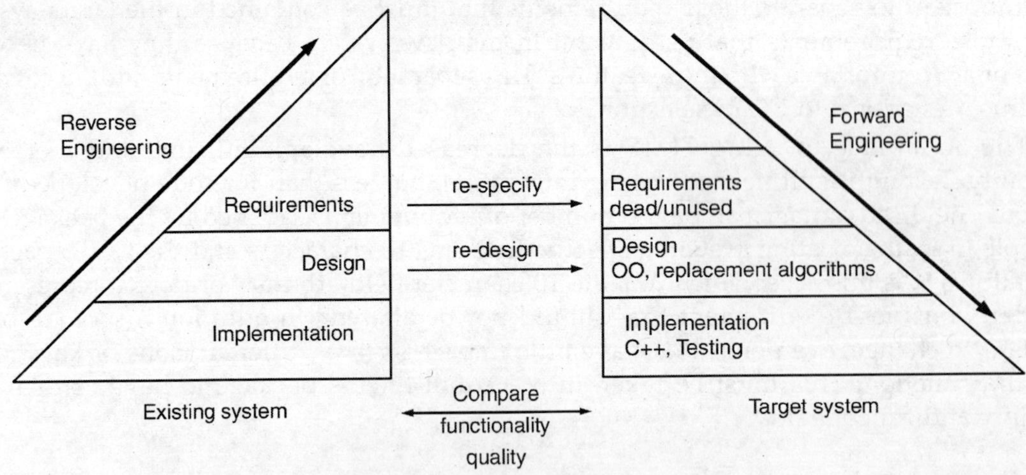

Figure 10.18: *Custom Track Hybrid Re-engineering*

In this track, reverse engineering is first performed. Those functions that are not satisfied by COTS packages or through translated code must be identified, and their requirements and design extracted. Forward engineering is then performed. This begins with requirements analysis, with the objective of identifying requirements that are not needed. The process is then similar to any development process, beginning with developing a new design, with object-oriented structure if desired, then implementing the code and doing comprehensive testing.

The advantages to the custom track are that the resulting code should meet its requirements exactly. The developed code should be of high quality and well structured, requiring little corrective maintenance. The disadvantages are similar to standard software development, in that the code might not be reliable, requiring additional testing, and that the development/testing process may exceed time and cost budgets.

Custom code has the same inherent risks that any code has, to quality, reliability, and schedule. Since most of the functions of the legacy system identified as unique to the system will be done with custom code, the risk is that one of the unique features will not be identified and hence the functionality of the new system will be incomplete. Features identified as critical to the system that are accomplished with custom code will require extensive testing.

Metrics for this track are a combination of both process and product metrics. Prior to reverse engineering, the quality of the existing system should be evaluated for later comparison to the target system (as discussed previously). Effort expended should be tracked to assist in the evaluation of the cost to re-engineer. This can also be used to approximate schedule completion using the estimate that 60% of the time is in reverse engineering. Once requirements are re-specified, their quality can be evaluated to determine testability. Also discussed previously was the use of function points as a means of calculating the rate of functionality transfer to the target system. Code analysis tools can be used to evaluate the quality of the code as it is being developed and identify the risks. In testing, discrepancy or error rates help in evaluating reliability. In this track, both the functionality and the quality are compared between the existing system and the target system.

10.14 HYBRID RE-ENGINEERING APPROACH

Hybrid re-engineering requires an approach similar to traditional re-engineering, but with additional considerations. When starting to re-engineer, initial justifications for re-engineering such as costs and quality are developed and expectations, such as return on investment, are stated. An analysis of the legacy system should be done to determine the feasibility of hybrid reengineering.

The analysis of the legacy system should provide a guideline in identifying optimal strategies (translation, COTS, etc.), and projecting the cost of the target system. Once the decision on using a hybrid re-engineering approach is made, additional analysis is needed. The first step in a hybrid re-engineering approach is to investigate the requirements and constraints of the development. These factors include setting a time table for reverse and forward engineering. Time must be built in to investigate available COTS, including hands-on testing of the COTS. While forward engineering development time should decrease with the use of COTS and the translation of code, additional time will be needed for testing the integration and interface of the products of the three tracks. Budget constraints must also be considered; how much can be spent on COTS that provide required features versus those that provide desired features. Management mandated and organization needs must also be identified. As the three tracks are developed, tradeoffs will be necessary so it is important to prioritize requirements. The next step is to do an in-depth analysis of the legacy system, focusing on functionalities and code segments suitable for each of the three tracks (Translation, Custom, COTS). In generic reengineering, an analysis of the existing system is usually done to provide an evaluation of the quality of the existing system and maintenance costs. This information is used to justify the costs and improvements at the conclusion of the re-engineering effort. While these reasons are still relevant in hybrid re-engineering, additional features of the legacy system must now be investigated. During the assessment of the legacy system, sections and functionalities must be identified. These must be further assessed to determine what documentation is available to identify the required features versus what is no longer needed or what users have become accustomed to. Code sections must be ordered by the cost of maintenance, and the quality of the current structure. Functions that are unique to this project must be identified. All of these components will be used to identify which hybrid re-engineering track will be applied to the code section.

Once the code has been divided into the development tracks, each track will proceed independently as discussed. The schedule for track completion will differ based on tasks. As the tracks conclude various tasks, the merging of the final products can begin. For example, the custom glue can be started once the COTS have been selected. Training on these packages can also begin.

Once the system is complete and all tracks merged, two tasks remain: testing and justification. First, comprehensive System and Integration testing must be performed to ensure all components work together as a cohesive unit and to ensure all functionality of the existing system was transferred to the new system. Second, justification for the re-engineering is usually required – do the benefits gained justify the cost. Some anticipated benefits, such as improved maintenance and operational costs, can only be demonstrated indirectly through the improved quality. Improved quality can initially be demonstrated by a metric analysis of the legacy system compared to the new system. As the new system is put into operation, additional metrics can be used to verify the improvements.

10.15 HYBRID RE-ENGINEERING RISKS

All software development has inherent risks to schedule and cost. Hybrid re-engineering, as a software development methodology, is also susceptible to them. Hybrid re-engineering, because of its composition of the three diverse development tracks, is subject to all of the risks that were discussed within each track description. Also, Hybrid re-engineering as a unique software reengineering methodology has additional risks to functionality and quality; the functionality of the existing system must be preserved in the new system, and the quality must improve, implying a decrease in operational and maintenance costs. With all of the risks in Hybrid re-engineering, why bother, why not just treat it as a new software development effort and omit the reengineering all together? Because of the benefits.

10.16 HYBRID RE-ENGINEERING BENEFITS

In general, re-engineering is performed as opposed to building a new system because of the invisible business application procedures and logic that are built into the software. These processes might be deeply embedded in business procedures as simple as a field length or as complicated as a mathematical algorithm; the only source of this information is in the legacy code. A second justification for re-engineering versus building is the development and maintenance costs of the legacy system; the time spent developing logic and components should not be wasted. In re-engineering, the existing system is re-implemented and instilled with good software development methodologies, properties, and new technology while maintaining existing functionality. Reliability and maintainability are also improved.

Hybrid re-engineering has the additional benefits of a reduced development schedule, hence reduced costs. The development schedule is shortened first by minimizing the amount of reverse engineering (recall, reverse engineering is 60% of the effort). The translation track uses minimal reverse engineering time since work is done in the lowest level (Figure 10.15). The use of COTS decreases the forward engineering development and test time and thus the costs. The use of properly selected COTS also increases the reliability since these packages have been extensively tested.

10.17 HYBRID RE-ENGINEERING METRICS

Metrics, when properly applied, provide managers information about their project to help mitigate risks. It is logical therefore, to discuss some of the re-engineering phases where metrics provide valuable information. Previously we have identified metrics applicable for each track in hybrid re-engineering. In this section, we will discuss metrics applicable to the entire project, not just one track. Metrics provide information on the quality, functionality, and on track selection, a prime area of risk.

At the start of the re-engineering effort, the legacy system must be quantified. There are two objectives: identify the amount of functionality and the quality of the existing system. By quantifying the functionality, scheduling estimates are more accurate; during development, completion can be estimated by the percentage of functionality transferred to the new system.

Functionality is also important at the conclusion of the project, measuring how much functionality is contained within the new system. The SATC and others are working with function points as a means of estimating functionality. Function points are comparable across languages, and time estimates based on function points are available. For COTS packages, functionality might be measured by the number of requirements satisfied.

Quality is harder to measure and few software developers agree totally on the appropriate metrics. The SATC has a group of metrics it applies to projects to evaluate the quality. These metrics evaluate the project at the module level (procedure, function, class or method). The size is measured by counting the number of executable statements. The readability is measured by the comment percentage. The complexity is measured by the cyclomatic complexity (McCabe). The coupling is measured by the calling complexity (fan in / fan out). Although there are many other metrics available, these have been successfully applied to many projects at GSFC NASA. One final measure of quality is the reliability, the number of errors found, and the projected number of errors remaining. These metrics can be used for both the translation track and the custom code track. When the components are combined, the numbers of errors found and the projected number of errors remaining can be applied to the whole system.

SUMMARY

This chapter provides a general overview of the software re-engineering process. Its main purpose being to give a brief high-level guide on how old, poorly documented, poorly structured code can be brought up to an acceptable and maintainable standard. It also touches on issues that could possibly be addressed during this process. It is very much a generic overview and as such does not make reference to any specific platform or development tools. Although re-engineering can improve maintainability, the reengineered system will probably not be as maintainable as a new system developed using modern software engineering methods. Data migration is usually performed programmatically to achieve an *automated migration,* freeing up human resources from tedious tasks. It is required when organizations or individuals change computer systems or upgrade to new systems, or when systems merge (such as when the organizations that use them undergo a merger or takeover).

EXERCISES

1. Explain the software reengineering process?
2. Explain the detailed description of reengineering process?
3. Explain the concept of source code translation?
4. What do you mean by reverse engineering?
5. Explain the improvement of program structure?
6. Explain the process of Program modularization?
7. What do you mean by data reengineering?
8. What is data migration?
9. What are the benefits of data migration?
10. How do we migrate data?
11. Explain the process of data migration?
12. Explain the risks of implementing an effective data migration strategy?
13. Explain the effective data migration strategy?
14. How to migrate your data?
15. Explain the strategies available for achieving migration?
16. Explain the various challenges of data migration?
17. What do you mean by hybrid reengineering?
18. Explain the three hybrid re-engineering tracks?
19. Explain the various approaches of hybrid re-engineering?
20. Explain the benefits of hybrid reengineering?
21. Explain the metrics of hybrid reengineering?

❑

Software Reuse 11

11.1 INTRODUCTION

Code scavenging, using source code generators, or reusing knowledge can contribute to increased productivity in software development. The reuse of life cycle objects, primarily code, is often done in an informal and haphazard way. If done systematically, software reuse has many benefits.

In the subsequent two subsections we discuss definitions and motivations for software reuse.

11.2 REUSE DEFINITIONS

Many different viewpoints exist of what software reuse is. We give a few examples from the literature.

For Freeman reuse is the use of any information which a developer may need in the software creation process. Similarly Basili and Rombach see software reuse as the use of everything associated with a software project, including knowledge. For Tracz reuse is the use of software that was designed for reuse. Braun defines reuse as the use of existing software components in a new context, either elsewhere in the same system or in another system.

An important aspect is whether software to be reused may be modified. Cooper defines software reuse as the capability of a previously developed software component to be used again or used repeatedly, in part or in its entirety, with or without modification. Lim mentions work products (i.e., products or by-products of the software development process, e.g., code, design, test plans) that are to be used in the development of other software without modification. **We adopt Krueger's general view of software reuse:**

"Software reuse is the process of creating software systems from existing software rather than building them from scratch."

Additionally, we affirm McIlroy's vision of reuse: the goal is the use of of-the-shelf components as building blocks in new systems with modifications occurring in a controlled way. It is not always possible to simply reuse components. Development of components and/or systems is still necessary. Other than compositional reuse, e.g., generative reuse is useful as well. But when we succeed in defining standards for component composition, this kind of reuse will increase software productivity considerably.

Research work in software reuse includes the development of new technology, but also the extraction of reusable parts from existing, possibly old systems. Prieto-Diaz has documented a historical overview of software reuse and described the evolution of a definition.

11.2.1 Motivation

Hardware engineers have succeeded in developing increasingly complex and powerful systems. Of course, hardware engineering cannot simply be compared with software engineering. But software engineers, too, are faced with a growing demand for complex and powerful software systems. New products have to appear more rapidly and product cycles seem to decrease to almost nothing. Advances in software engineering have contributed to increased productivity. Examples include high-level programming languages, object-oriented technology, prototyping-oriented software development, and computer-aided software engineering.

Studies on reuse have shown that 40% to 60% of code is reusable from one application to another, 60% of design and code are reusable in business applications, 75% of program functions are common to more than one program, and only 15% of the code found in most systems is unique and novel to a specific application. According to Mili et al. rates of actual and potential reuse range from 15% to 85%. Maximizing the reuse of tested (if not verified or certified) source code and minimizing the need to develop new code alone can bring improvements in cost, time and quality, and reusing source code is only the (low-level) beginning of reuse. Practicing reuse systematically requires additional effort, e.g., managerial and organizational changes. Although systematic software reuse is not the concept to solve all problems, it promises to have positive impacts on development costs, productivity, functionality, quality, reliability, portability, efficiency and maintainability of software. This is discussed in more detail in the next section.

11.3 BENEFITS OF SOFTWARE REUSE

Software reuse has a positive impact on software quality, as well as on software costs, and productivity. Reuse benefits have been treated in the literature many times, for example, in the Encyclopedia of Software Engineering, in the NATO Standards for Software Reuse, in Ph.D. dissertations, and in various overviews of software reuse, i.e., in journals, in reuse books, and in software engineering books. In the following we elaborate on quality improvements and effort reduction in more detail. Examples from industry that demonstrate such benefits are mentioned at the end of this section.

11.3.1 Quality Improvements

Software reuse results in improvements in quality, productivity, performance, reliability and interoperability.

1. **Quality:** Error fixes accumulate from reuse to reuse. This yields higher quality for a reused component than would be the case for a component that is developed and used only once. However, this requires the administration and maintenance of components and is not achieved by simply reusing.

2. **Productivity:** A productivity gain is achieved due to less code that has to be developed. This results in less testing efforts and also saves analysis and design labor, yielding overall savings in cost. When reuse is being installed, productivity may decrease shortly due to increased learning effort and the need to develop reusable components. This temporary decrease in productivity should easily be compensated by a long-term increase.
3. **Performance:** Extensive reuse can be worth the effort invested in optimizations. This may yield better performance of a reused component than might be practical for a component that is developed and used only once. However, generalizations that make components more reusable can have a negative influence on overall performance. For example, Bardo et al. have reported an estimated 15 to 25 percent penalty in load module size with minimal overhead in execution for avionics simulator software.
4. **Reliability:** Using well-tested components increases the reliability of a software system. Furthermore, the use of a component in several systems increases the chance of errors to be detected and strengthens confidence in that component.
5. **Interoperability:** Various systems can work better together if their interfaces are implemented consistently. This is the case when they use the same components for these interfaces. Even though written standards improve interoperability, different implementations might differently interpret parts of these standards.

Bauer provides an example of improved quality due to software reuse. The quality of reused components (numbers of errors per lines of code) was about 9 times better during component test and about 4.5 times better during system test. In another project there were even no errors found in reused components during the entire life cycle of the project. The components reused in these projects were macros implementing abstract data types. Unfortunately, there is no information given on the amount of reuse.

11.3.2 Effort Reduction

Software reuse provides a reduction in redundant work and thus development time, which yields to a shorter time to market. This is especially important considering the importance of good timing, i.e., early availability for software systems. Additionally, documentation and costs as well as team sizes can be reduced.

1. **Redundant work, development time:** Developing every system from scratch means redundant development of many parts like user interfaces, communication, basic algorithms, etc. This can be avoided when these parts are available as reusable components and can be shared, resulting in less development and less associated time and costs.
2. **Time to market:** The success or failure of a software product is very often determined by its time to market. Using reusable components will result in a reduction of that time. As much as a 42% reduction has been reported on a specific project.
3. **Documentation:** Even though documentation is very important for the maintenance of a system, it is often neglected. Reusing software components reduces the amount of documentation to be written but compounds the importance of what is written. Only the overall structure of the software system and the newly developed components has to be documented. The documentation of reusable components can be shared among many software systems.

4. **Maintenance costs:** Fewer defects can be expected to occur when proven components have been used, and less of the software system must be maintained. The reusable components are maintained by a separate group rather than separately in each software system.
5. **Training costs:** Over time, software engineers become familiar with the reusable components available for their development efforts. So they have a good working knowledge of many components of these systems when they are starting to design and develop new systems.
6. **Team size:** Large development teams suffer from a communication overload. Doubling the size of a development team does not result in doubled productivity. If many components can be reused, then software systems can be developed with smaller teams, leading to better communication and increased productivity.

11.3.3 Other Benefits

The support of rapid prototyping and expertise sharing are amongst additional benefits of software reuse.

1. **Rapid prototyping support:** Reusable components can provide an effective basis for quickly building a prototype of a software system. This provides the opportunity to get customer feedback early in the life cycle, thus supporting the conception of the requirements. This can also help to uncover hidden requirements.
2. **Expertise sharing:** Good designs can only be learned from good designers. It is important that software engineers study the designs of excellent peers in order to improve their design skills. Software reuse supports this very naturally. This does not mean that we should study the implementation details of all the components we reuse; the interfaces alone can reveal important information about how a component and its interoperability have been designed.

Reuse benefits are not completely independent from each other, but rather influence each other.

11.3.4 Industry Examples

Reuse benefits have been reported in various industrial settings.

- An empirical study from a NASA software production environment has shown that modules reused without modifications (revisions) had less interaction with other modules, simpler interfaces, less interaction with human users, and higher ratios of commentary compared to newly developed or modified (revised) modules. In this study 25 software projects (ranging from 3,000 to 112,000 source code lines) were considered. An average of 32% of software had been reused or modified from previous systems.
- At Motorola software reuse is considered a candidate technology for initiatives and goals to improve productivity and quality.
- At Hewlett-Packard a reuse assessment of two reuse programs has indicated higher quality (reduction in defect density ranging from 24% to 76%) and a 40% to 57% increase in productivity.

- IBM has formed the Reuse Technology Support Center, involving close to 30 of their sites worldwide. Their best programs report savings in the millions of dollars, with reuse accounting for 20% to 30% of the software.

Other industry examples are cited by Braun:

- Raytheon Missile Systems has reported an average of 60% reuse and a 50% increase in net productivity in new developments (1979).
- NEC Software Engineering Laboratory has reported a 6.7 to 1 productivity improvement and a 2.8 to 1 quality improvement (1987).
- Fujitsu has experienced an improvement from 20% of projects on schedule to 70% on schedule (1987).
- GTE has reported 14% reuse and savings of $1.5 million, with projected figures of 50% reuse and savings of $10 million (1987).
- SofTech, Inc. has reported an increase in productivity to 10 to 20 times the industry average (1987).
- Universal Defense Systems has reported 60% reuse in a system of 700,000 lines of Ada code (1991).
- Celsius Technology has experienced a 250% increase in productivity, projecting an additional increase of about 300% (1992).

Experience reports cited by Mili also document increases in productivity and quality.

11.4 OBSTACLES TO SOFTWARE REUSE

Despite the benefits of software reuse, it is not as widely practiced as one might assume. There are many factors that directly or indirectly influence the success or failure of reuse. These factors can be of conceptual, technical, managerial, organizational, psychological, economic or legal nature. In this section we list examples of such obstacles and divide them into various groups, even though sometimes an assignment to one of these groups is ambiguous. In the literature obstacles to software reuse have been described by various authors, e.g., Braun, Griss, Horner, Jones and Prieto-Diaz.

The subsequent sections describe managerial, organizational, economic and technical obstacles to software reuse.

11.4.1 Managerial and Organisational Obstacles

Reuse is not just a technical problem that has to be solved by software engineers. Management support and adequate organizational structures are equally important. Common reuse obstacles are:

1. **Lack of management support:** Since software reuse causes up-front costs, it cannot be widely achieved in an organization without support of top-level management. Managers have to be informed about initial costs and have to be convinced about expected savings.
2. **Project management:** Managing traditional projects is not an easy task. We have even less experience with projects exploiting reuse. Making the step to large-scale software reuse has an impact on the whole software life cycle.

3. **Lack of explicit procedures:** Software development is a complex process involving many activities. Successful software reuse has effects on the whole software life cycle, design methods, project planning and estimating. Models for such processes are used to determine various steps to be accomplished in a certain order. If these models do not explicitly consider software reuse, it is likely that it will not happen in practice.
4. **Inadequate organizational structures:** Organizational structures must consider different needs that arise when explicit, large-scale reuse is being adopted. For example, a separate team may be installed for gathering, maintaining and providing reusable components.
5. **Not invented here:** People may feel hindered in their creativity and independence by reusing someone else's software. They want to develop their own new software rather than maintaining software from someone else. They may also be biased against someone else's software through a lack of trust. This is called the not-invented-here syndrome.
6. **Legal issues:** The more widespread software reuse becomes, the more legal and business issues have to be addressed, e.g. liabilities and data rights. Increased use of third-party software increases the significance of these issues.
7. **Lack of management incentives:** Lack of incentives prohibits managers from letting their developers spend time in making components of a system reusable. Their success is often measured only in the time needed for completing a project. Doing any work beyond that, although beneficial for the company as a whole, diminishes their success. Even when components are reused by accessing software repositories, the gained benefits are only a fraction of what could be achieved by explicit, planned and organized reuse. It is not sufficient to simply access components in a repository. Well-designed components have to be systematically developed and used following a careful reuse-based process.

11.4.2 Economic Obstacles

Reuse can save money in the long run, but it is not for free. Costs associated with reuse are:

- costs of making something reusable,
- costs of reusing it, and
- costs of defining and implementing a reuse process (installing reuse).

Reuse requires up-front investments in infrastructure, methodology, training, tools and archives, with payoffs being realized only years later. Developing components for reuse is more expensive than developing them for single use only. Higher levels of quality, reliability, portability, maintainability, generality and more extensive documentation are necessary. Such increased costs are not justified when a component is used only once. Constructing a set of reusable components is not possible without long-term support from upper management.

11.4.3 Conceptual and Technical Obstacles

Most research is being done on technical support for software reuse. Object oriented programming is an example of technological support for reuse. However, just using object-oriented technology is by far insufficient for effective reuse.

1. **Difficulty of finding reusable software:** Software cannot be reused unless it can be found. Reuse is unlikely to happen when a repository does not have sufficient information about components or when the components are poorly classified. Suppose we know that someone has written a software component that exactly matches our needs. Finding it is impossible unless we have a well-organized repository containing that particular component with some means of accessing it.
2. **Nonreusability of found software:** Easy access to existing software does not necessarily increase software reuse. Unintentionally, software is seldom written in a way so that others can reuse it. Modifying and adapting someone else's software can become even more expensive than programming the needed functionality from scratch.
3. **Legacy components not suitable for reuse:** Reusing components is hard or impossible unless they have been designed and developed for reuse. Simply gathering existing components from various legacy software systems and trying to reuse them for new developments is not sufficient for systematic reuse. Re-engineering can help in extracting reusable components from legacy systems. However, the efforts needed for the extraction and transformation to useful components might be considerable.
4. **Object-oriented technology:** It is widely believed that object-oriented technology has a positive influence on software reuse. Unfortunately and wrongly, many also believe that reuse depends on this technology or that adopting object-oriented technology suffices for software reuse.
5. **Modification:** Components will not always be exactly the way we want them. If modifications are necessary, we should be able to determine their effects on the component and its previous verification results.
6. **Integration:** Sometimes components are available with the functionality that is needed for a new software system. Still if it is not possible to integrate components into the system, they are of no use. Unfortunately most components are ill-equipped to cope with integration requirements. Software components must be constructed in a way that subsequent reuse can be efficient and straightforward.
7. **Garbage reuse:** Certifying reusable components to certain quality levels helps in minimizing possible defects. Poor quality control is one of the major barriers to reuse. A reusable component has to perform its claimed functions. We need some means of judging whether the required functions match the functions that are provided by a component.

More basic technical difficulties with software reuse have been addressed by Taivalsaari and include:

- agreeing on what a reusable component constitutes,
- understanding what a component does and how to use it,
- understanding how to interface reusable components to the rest of a design,
- designing reusable components so that they are easy to adapt and modify (in a controlled way), and
- organizing a repository so that programmers can find and use what they need.

Risks of software reuse include the unavailability of technology and resources, lack of management support, sluggishness of people to change and the instability of domains.

Additionally, risks can evolve from legal aspects, e.g., liability issues or repository agreements. Software risk analysis, legal advice and incremental introduction of reuse programs help in avoiding or reducing these risks.

11.5 TECHNICAL ASPECTS OF SOFTWARE REUSE

Software reuse has many technical and non-technical aspects, for example, ad-hoc reuse, institutionalized reuse, black-box reuse, white-box reuse, source code reuse, design reuse. In this chapter we describe various technical aspects of software reuse.

Table 11.1: Facets of software reuse

Facet	Examples
Substance	ideas, concepts, artifacts, components, procedure, skills
Scope	vertical, domain-specific, horizontal, general-purpose, internal, external small-scale, large-scale
Mode	planned, systematic, institutionalized, ad-hoc, opportunistic, individual
Technique	compositional, generative
Intention	black-box, white-box, glass-box, as-is, by adaptation, modified
Product	specification, design, source code, architectures, documentation, text

11.5.1 Reuse Facets

Prieto-Diaz identified six perspectives from which to view software reuse. The resulting facets are:

- Substance defines the essence of reused items.
- Scope defines the form and extent of reuse.
- Mode defines how reuse is conducted.
- Technique defines the approach that is used to implement reuse.
- Intention defines how elements will be used.
- Product defines what is reused.

Table 11.1 shows these facets with examples. Reuse substances, reuse scopes, reuse techniques, reuse intentions, and reuse products are described in subsequent sections.

11.5.2 Reuse Substances

The essence of reused items is manifold. For example, we mentioned earlier that ideas and concepts are often taken (and reused) from books about algorithms. Ideas and concepts can also be 'retrieved' from experienced software engineers who had been asked for advice. Information about procedures and skills can be represented in expert systems, but is also often reused on an ad-hoc and individual basis.

Concentrating on the reuse of components does not mean excluding the reuse of ideas and concepts. The reuse of a component automatically means the reuse of ideas and concepts that are built into the component. The advantage is that reusers do not have to worry about them. They do not have to understand the concepts involved in the development of the components, yet they implicitly reuse them through the component. For example, reusing the idea for hash tables requires a thorough understanding of the concepts required in order to implement them. If a component already provides the functionality of hash tables and exports a clean interface, we can simply reuse the underlying ideas and concepts.

Freeman argues that with source code alone we miss the opportunity of explicitly reusing analysis and design information. We have to consider higher levels of components that cover more than pure source code. Naturally, not everything can be packed into components. Thus reusing components does not cover all aspects of software reuse. For example, it is difficult to reuse procedures and skills by means of components because they cover some kind of meta-information. However, the reuse of components provides prerequisites for planned and systematic reuse.

11.5.3 Reuse Scopes

The amount of possible software reuse depends on the degree of commonalty among applications that share software. A domain is an area of activity or knowledge containing applications that share a set of common capabilities and data. If the majority of applications are in a specific domain, a higher degree of reuse is probable than among applications across a broad range of different applications. Domain-specific reuse and general-purpose reuse are often called vertical and horizontal reuse, respectively.

Another possible differentiation of scope is distinguishing between internal and external reuse. Internal reuse means the multiple use of a component within a software system for which it was originally written. External reuse is the use of a component originally written for another software system. Small-scale reuse is reusing small code components like subroutines, functions, modules, and classes. Compared to the efforts needed to build large software systems, the net win is marginal. Unfortunately, small-scale software reuse is an everyday occurrence, whereas large-scale software reuse too often remains an elusive and unrealized goal. Large-scale reuse requires the consideration of many non-technical issues, as described in next sections.

11.6 REUSETECHNIQUES

Various techniques or approaches can be used in order to achieve software reuse. Compositional reuse supports bottom-up development of systems from a repository of available lower-level components; classification and retrieval is important in this context. Generative reuse is often domain-specific, adopting standard system structures (reference architectures or generic architectures) and standard interfaces for components. A combined approach is also possible.

11.6.1 Abstraction

Abstraction is essential in any software reuse technique. As Wegner states, abstraction and reusability are two sides of the same coin. Krueger states that\without abstraction developers would be forced to sift through a collection of reusable artifacts trying to figure out what each artifact did, when it could be reused, and how to reuse it."

Raising abstraction levels is a major challenge in software engineering. The relation between abstraction and reuse gives a first hint about the difficulties we face in software reuse.

Every software abstraction has two levels: specification (what is done by the abstraction) and realization (how is it done). The realization of one level of abstraction is the specification of the next lower level of abstraction. Every abstraction contains a hidden part (not visible in the specification), a fixed part, and a variable part. The variable part maps into the collection of possible realizations. The creator of an abstraction can decide in which part to put certain information, e.g., the size of a stack could be variable, fixed or hidden. The specification must contain all the information needed by the reuse of its realization.

Finding concise abstractions for components is a difficult task. The best known successes are in application domains with application-specific, one word abstractions, e.g.: sine, matrix (in numerical analysis), stack, list (in abstract data types).

11.6.2 Compositional Reuse

Compositional reuse is based on the idea of reusable components that (ideally) remain unmodified in their reuse. Higher-level or more complex components are built by combining lower-level or simpler components. Only if needed components are not available and cannot be created by modification of existing components are they built from scratch or constructed from lower-level components. The components suitable for reuse are collected in repositories.

Compositional reuse is based on component repositories (e.g., function libraries) or on principles of organization and composition, like pipe architectures or the object-oriented construction of software systems.

Component repositories: Successful reuse requires having a wide variety of high-quality components, proper classification and retrieval mechanisms, sufficient and proper documentation of components, a flexible means for combining components, and a means of adapting components to specific needs. In an ideal scenario reused components are largely atomic and remain unmodified. However, often this ideal cannot be achieved and the components have to modified and changed in order to fit the reusers' special needs. During composition components are regarded as passive elements that are combined by predefined principles which are crucial for systems being built from existing components.

Today, the nature of a reusable component technology strongly depends on the programming languages used. Components can be reusable functions, e.g., statistics libraries, numerical libraries, or packages, modules, subsystems and classes. The latter can include data-centered artifacts like abstract datatypes. Challenges in the context of repositories are techniques to locate components efficiently, e.g., classification schemes, retrieval techniques, and to integrate them in software systems. This leads to the next aspect of compositional reuse, component composition.

Component composition: Software components exist in many different forms. They cannot be arbitrarily assembled and expected to communicate and cooperate. In order to enable the combination of components they must rely on the same kind of composition technique.

Module interconnection languages and the UNIX pipe mechanism are examples of possible composition of reusable components. The UNIX pipe mechanism is one of the well-known examples of a simple, yet powerful composition and integration technique where complex programs can be built out of simpler ones. The alliance of components is accomplished by connecting the output of one component to the input of another.

Incompatibilities of components are among the main hindrances of successful component reuse. **Code and design scavenging:** Scavenging fragments from existing software systems and using them as part of new software development is an ad-hoc and unsystematic, although effective approach to reusing software system designs and source code. In this scenario reused components are fragments taken from various locations of other systems rather than self-contained, tested and documented components from a repository. Nevertheless, it is a kind of composition, and experienced programmers can gain high productivity increases. We distinguish between code and design scavenging:

- Code scavenging

Blocks of source code are copied from an existing system.

- Design scavenging

Large blocks of code are copied. Many of the internal details are deleted. The global template of the design is retained.

There is no abstraction involved in scavenging. The developer is forced to become closely involved with implementation details of the reused fragments.

11.6.3 Generative Reuse

Generative reuse is based on the reuse of a generation process rather than the reuse of components. Large frame structures are used as invariants, i.e., reused without change. Variant functionality must be added to customize the invariant parts. The components that are reused are not concrete and self-contained as in the compositional approach. The parts to be reused are incorporated into a program that generates reusable patterns.

Typical examples of this kind of reuse are generators for lexical analyzers, parsers, and compilers (e.g., lex and yacc on the UNIX platform), conventional application generators (e.g., fourth-generation languages), expert system generators, and structure-oriented editor generators.

Generators that synthesize software from reuse libraries to construct systems for a target domain compose prefabricated, interchangeable components and thus contain compositional aspects also. Subsequently, we distinguish between application generators, language-based generators, and transformation systems. Programming languages can be seen as low level specification languages. This is briefly sketched at the end of this section.

Application generators: Application generators reuse complete software system designs. They are appropriate in application domains where:

- many similar software systems are written,
- one software system is modified or rewritten many times during its lifetime, and/or
- many prototypes of a system are necessary to converge on a usable product.

Application generators allow inexperienced people to generate customized applications. In application generators, reusable patterns exist in the generator itself in the form of source code. Application generators currently provide only small coverage for software development. But the focus on narrow domains is also an advantage. Highly productive creation of quality commercial software with application generators has been reported.

Language-based generators: Language-based generators provide a specification language that represents the problem domain and simultaneously hides implementation details from the reuser. Specification languages allow developers to create software systems using constructs that are considered high-level relative to programming languages. They are also known as executable specification languages.

Specification languages help in reusing implementation patterns of programming languages, similar to programming languages that help in reusing assembler patterns. These languages typically have mathematical abstractions that are not widely used in the conventional software life cycle. Specification languages are used to describe abstract specifications, from which executable programs are automatically generated. Language-based generators differ from application generators mainly in that they use general-purpose, application-independent abstractions rather than application-specific ones. The primary concern is development and modification efficiency rather than high execution speed. This may eliminate them as development vehicles for several of today's production systems, but they can be used as a basis for rapid prototyping and validation of software systems.

The Setl optimizer is an example of this kind of generation. It is based on representing computations as operations on mathematical sets.

Transformation systems: With transformation systems, software is developed in two phases: describing the semantic behavior of a software system and applying transformations to the high-level specifications. For example, abstract programs are transformed into their concrete counterparts in an approach described by Cheatham.

Martin distinguishes the subcategories skeleton approach, kitchen sink approach, parameterized approach, and stepwise refinement approach:

- **Skeleton approach:** In the skeleton approach, the reuser starts with a generic application skeleton and fills in details and missing parts. The generic part may cover many aspects of an application, e.g., user interface details or event handling.
- **Kitchen sink approach:** The kitchen sink approach works the other way around. The reuser starts with a detailed and extensive framework and prunes parts away that are not needed for the current application.
- **Parameterized approach:** The parameterized approach provides certain parameters to modify the resulting software.
- **Stepwise refinement approach:** In the stepwise refinement approach, reusers refine the software's behavior in incremental steps.

The Draco system generates applications from domain-oriented specifications. It can be regarded as application generator and as transformation system that use patterns within transformation rules.

Programming languages: Programming languages such as C, C++ and Ada are usually not treated as examples of software reuse. But their goals and achievements have strong parallels to the current-day aspirations of software reuse researchers.

In the same way as we regard language-based generators, application generators, and transformation systems in the context of software reuse, with programming languages we do not reuse software itself, but rather we reuse language patterns. The artifacts to be reused are assembly language patterns. Of course, these languages provide only a relatively low level of abstraction. However, they provide a factor of 5 speedup in writing source code.

As with generators, programmers use variant and invariant parts of the abstraction and do not have to worry about all the assembly language details that are actually reused. The compiler provides the transformation from the specification (programming language) to the implementation (assembly or machine language).

11.6.4 Generation Versus Composition

Generation-based systems have the advantage that the reused patterns can be designed and implemented carefully by experienced programmers. But they are applicable only to a certain domain and are typically restricted to the reuse of source code. Also, they cannot be applied easily in all situations. Often they are too general or to specific for applications under consideration. Components are applicable to a wider variety of applications. Additionally, they are more modular and self-contained and thus maintainable. Their disadvantage is that they are seldom perfect or general enough. This might lead to many modifications, which reduces productivity gains and can lead to immense numbers of components in repositories.

Table 11.2 summarizes the comparison of compositional and generative reuse. Compositional reuse provides the more general approach. The generative approach is useful in specific domains and can be built on top of components.

Table 11.2: Comparison of Compositional and Generative Reuse

Reuse Technique	**Composition**	**Generation**
Reuse Component	building blocks	Patterns
Nature of components	atomic and immutable, passive	diffuse and malleable, active
Emphasis	component repositories, composition principles (code/design scavenging)	application generators language based generators, transformation systems
Examples	function/class libraries unix filters	parser generators 4th generation languages

11.7 REUSE INTENTIONS

Depending on whether the internals of a software component are visible to reusers we speak of black-box or white-box reuse. If a component is a black box we cannot modify its internals: we use it as is. White-box components are usually modified, even though this is not necessarily the case. They offer both as-is reuse and reuse by adaptation. The term glass-box reuse means white-box visibility but black-box reuse.

11.7.1 Black-Box Reuse

Reusing a component as a black box means using it without seeing, knowing or modifying any of its internals. The component provides an interface that contains all the information necessary for its utilization. The implementation is hidden and cannot be modified by the reuser. Thus reusers get the information about what a component is doing, but they do not have to worry about how this is achieved. The implementation can be changed without any effects on reusers.

Usually a black box is reused as-is. Object-oriented techniques allow modifications of black boxes by making modifications and extensions to a component without knowing its internals. This is one of the major contributions of object-oriented programming to software reuse. However, components have to be designed so that such modifications become viable.

11.7.2 White-Box Reuse

White-box reuse is the typical case in the unplanned ad-hoc reuse that is still widespread today. It means reuse of components of which internals are changed for the purpose of reuse. White boxes are typically not reused as is, but by adaptation. They create more opportunities for reusers due to the ease of making arbitrary changes. On the negative side of white-box reuse, it requires additional testing and costlier maintenance. Unlike black boxes, a new component derived by modifications to an existing component must be regarded as a new component and thoroughly tested. Additionally, the new component requires separate maintenance. If many copies of a component exist with slight modifications, it becomes burdensome to fix errors that affect all of them. If the changes made to a component are only minor, e.g., a few variable renamings or changes in procedure calls, the term grey-box reuse is also used.

11.7.3 Glass-Box Reuse

The term glass-box reuse is used when components are used as-is like black boxes, but their internals can be seen from outside. This gives the reuser information about how the component works without the ability to change it. But this information may be crucial for understanding how certain tasks are carried out. It may also give the reuser some confidence from being able to see inside the component and capture how it works. Additionally, getting internal information provides some kind of knowledge transfer and, for example, can help in building new components. Glass-box reuse has its negative sides. It may lead to dependencies on certain implementation details which become fatal when the internals of the component are changed. Unfortunately, giving reusers detailed information about a component's internals often serves as compensation of nonexistent or insufficient documentation.

11.7.4 Generative Reuse

Generative reuse is itself a reuse technique, but it can be seen as kind of black box reuse. Instead of picking one of several existing black boxes, a component's specification is created and its implementation automatically generated by a program generator. The program generator is a black box; its internals are of no interest to the reuser. Also, the generated implementation will not be modified. If changes are necessary, they will be made in the specification and the implementation is recreated. (In practice, however, modifications to the generated implementation are sometimes made due to shortcomings in the generator.)

11.7.5 Black-Box Versus White-Box Reuse

Black box reuse is more difficult to achieve than white-box reuse but promises higher quality and reliability of the resulting software system. The potential of customizing black-box components can increase their reuse potential but has to be carefully considered and designed. Black-box components have the advantage of possible verification and certification. Even though we are far from having a market of verified and certified components, such attributes will become essential in the future.

11.8 Reuse Products

There are many work products that can be reused, e.g., source code, documentation, designs, specifications, objects, text and architectures. Source code is the most common reuse product. However, higher increases in productivity will result from reusing higher levels of abstraction. This can mean that source code is generated automatically from higher levels of abstractions.

The abstraction level of the source code also plays a major role in the benefit of the reuse process. For example, object-oriented programming techniques allow the construction of application frameworks that facilitate not only source code reuse but also design reuse. Design patterns have recently emerged and help to reuse the knowledge of experienced designers of object oriented software systems. In the context of source code reuse, documentation reuse also becomes important. This affects not only system documentation for the source code but also specifications as well as user documentation and project documentation.

Different categorizations for reuse products have been proposed, most of them relying on one or more of the following factors:

- the stage of development at which the knowledge is produced and/or used, e.g., design vs. implementation,
- the level of abstraction, e.g., source code vs. tools, and
- the nature of knowledge, e.g., artifacts vs. skills.

Without systematic planning, reuse seldom goes beyond the implementation stage and the source code level. Types of reusable artifacts can comprise data reuse (e.g., standardization of data formats), architecture reuse (e.g., standardization of design and programming conventions), design reuse (e.g., for common applications like GUI), and program reuse (e.g., executable code).

In this section we give examples of what can be reused for software development. The most prominent examples of today's reuse include algorithms, function libraries, class libraries, application frameworks and design patterns. Other examples include project plans, cost estimates, requirements, designs, architectures, user documents and test cases.

11.8.1 Algorithms

Algorithms have a long tradition of successful reuse. Numerous books contain a variety of useful algorithms. A prominent example is Knuth's "The Art of Computer Programming". Many of these books contain algorithms and data structures in certain programming languages. They allow the reuse of these algorithms with only minor modifications. Often they are depicted in some sort of pseudocode and have to be translated to a specific programming language. As-is reuse is rarely possible. Often adaptations and modifications have to be made, especially concerning the data structure to be processed by a certain algorithm. For example, an algorithm in a book may depict sorting algorithms by sorting integer values. If customer records have to be sorted, then slight modifications of the algorithms will be necessary.

Advances in programming languages have made the need to adapt and modify less painful. Generic implementations and templates make algorithms work with different data structures without explicit modification. Concepts of object-oriented programming allow the most elegant kind of algorithm reuse. By inheritance, implemented algorithms can be made to work with objects not foreseen at the time these algorithms were implemented. This evolution in programming languages has brought a rise in the abstraction level from the reuse of concepts and ideas to the reuse of source code without the need for modifications (but still reusing the concepts and ideas).

11.8.2 Function Librarires

Functions are the most common form of reusable components. For many programming languages, standard libraries have been defined, for example, for input/output or mathematical functions. A few decades ago languages had much functionality defined in the language itself, e.g., PL/I. Later on, the trend was towards lean languages with standard libraries for various functionalities, e.g., Modula-2. There are many example of function libraries, from collections of standard routines (e.g., the C standard libraries) to domain-specific libraries (e.g., for statistics or numerical purposes).

11.8.3 Class Libraries

Class libraries are the object-oriented version of function libraries. Classes provide better abstraction mechanisms, better modifiability and adaptability than functions do. Reusability has greatly benefited from concepts like inheritance, polymorphism and dynamic binding. In many class libraries there are classes devoted to generic data structures like lists, trees and queues.

The major problem with class libraries is that they consist of families of related components. Thus members of different families have incompatible interfaces. Often several families implement the same basic abstraction but have different interfaces. This makes libraries hard to use and makes interchanging components difficult. Also, most class libraries are not scalable.

11.8.4 Software Architectures and Designs

A software architecture is the global structure of a software system with its major subsystems, including the specifications of these subsystems and their interrelationships. It includes the collection of components and their interactions. A description of a software system's architecture usually contains the collection of its components at the highest level of abstraction. For example, if the system consists of independent processes, then the description of the architecture contains these processes with a description of their functionality and the interactions among them. If a software system runs as a single process, then its subsystems are considered as being the architecture. These can be modules and classes or subsystems containing several such modules and/or classes. The next lower level is generally considered as being part of the software design.

A series of common patterns for the global structure of software systems has been successful and reused repeatedly. Such patterns include communicating processes, hierarchical layers, pipes and filters, clients and servers, and interpreters. The reuse of software architectures is possible through generic architectures for certain application domains. A high-level generic design for a family of applications can be defined to meet requirements within the domain.

Software design incorporates the activities of creating the software architecture of a system plus decomposing software components. This is repeated until the level of detail allows the coding of the specified components. The steps involved include the design of the architecture of the whole system or subsystems, component interfaces, component implementations, data structures and algorithms. Software design is a matter of practice and experience. It is learned not from reading a book but from studying existing, well-designed systems. Reuse of software design is mainly reuse of knowledge. However, with application frameworks it is possible to reuse not only source code but also the design (see below). Thus components are capable of supporting the reuse of software design.

Software architectures and software designs complement each other in that behind most design methods are preferred architectural styles. Design methods can also evolve from a specific architectural style.

11.8.5 Framework Classes

For large-scale reuse, isolated classes are small-scale primitives that are too fine-grained. To boost productivity, systems have to be built out of large scale composites. Thus we have to focus on sets of classes that collaborate to carry out a common set of responsibilities, rather than on individual classes. Frameworks are flexible collections of abstract and concrete classes designed to be extended and refined for reuse. Components of class libraries can serve as discrete, stand-alone, context-independent parts of a solution to a large range of different applications, e.g., collection classes. Components of frameworks are not intended to work alone; their correct operation requires the presence of and collaboration with other members of the framework components. Reusers of framework classes \inherit" the overall design of an application made by experienced software engineers and can concentrate on the application's functionality. They do not have to worry about user interfaces, window systems, event handling, refreshing, etc.

The major advantage of framework classes over library classes is that frameworks are concerned with conventions of communication between the components. Today the combination of components from different class libraries is the exception rather than the rule. This is because there is some implicit understanding of how components work together. High cohesion and low coupling increase the reusability of components. But unless the component does have extensive functionality, it is required to cooperate and communicate with many others. In a framework this interaction is built in and eases interaction of its components.

11.8.6 Design Patterns

Software design patterns capture the intent behind the design of a software system. They standardize piecework to larger units. For example, many times there exists a special arrangement of classes and/or objects in order to avoid reuse errors.

A subsystem is a set of classes with high cohesion among themselves and low coupling to classes outside the subsystem. Design patterns can correspond to subsystems, but often they have a finer level of granularity. Design patterns have been identified to avoid dependence on classes when creating objects, on particular operations, on specific representation or implementation, on particular algorithms, and on inheritance as the extension mechanism. Design patterns have been described by various authors, e.g., Coad, Gamma and Pree. Research work on design patterns is still going on, and it is not yet clear which patterns will become widely accepted. Gamma et al. have presented an extensive collection of design patterns. These patterns promise to be one further step in increasing the abstraction level in software development. They can help both in improving the development process and in recapturing design decisions behind the structure of certain parts in a system.

We see design patterns as a means of transferring design knowledge. Thus design patterns provide an efficient means of studying and later reusing the designs of experienced software engineers. Patterns can help to improve productivity by shortening the learning curve for novice and intermediate programmers and by yielding simpler, more resilient systems. In contrast to methodologies that tell us how to do something, design patterns show us how to do it. They are standard techniques for software development similar to algorithms, which operate on a lower level.

11.8.7 Applications

Entire applications can be thought of as components that provide well-defined services. They can reference or embed other applications and invoke services by sending messages. Besides production gains, reusing applications offers the flexibility to customize environments and let users stick to their preferred tools, e.g., the Emacs text editor. Applications are reused as black boxes.

They have to provide an interface to allow other applications to interact with them, e.g., to send commands. Increasing capabilities of applications to interoperate are providing alternatives to large monolithic applications. Composing applications from fine-grained applications rather than building one big closed system provides many possibilities for reuse.

11.8.8 Documentation

Documentation is an important part of a software system. We distinguish between product documentation and process documentation. Product documentation describes how to use a system (e.g., user interface description, functional description, reference manual) and how it is implemented (e.g., system architecture, design, component implementations). Process documentation describes the process of creation (e.g., plans, estimates, schedules). Documentation is hard to reuse in a systematic way. The usual case is copying a document and editing it. The reuse of components should involve the reuse of their documentation as well. If components are integrated into a software system, so should be their documentation. Chapter 20 describes how this can be accomplished.

11.9 NONTECHNICAL ASPECTS OF SOFTWARE REUSE

Many nontechnical aspects have to be considered in order to improve systematic software reuse and to make it the normal way of software creation. Technical aspects are important prerequisites for successful reuse. However, they do not suffice to make software reuse happen. Systematic reuse requires long-term, top-down management support because:

- years of investment may be required before it pays off,
- legal issues may have to be considered, and
- changes in organizational funding and management structures may be necessary.

In this section we outline various nontechnical aspects that influence the software reuse process, including legal, economic, organizational and measurement issues.

11.10 LEGAL ISSUES

Many legal issues in the context of software reuse are still diffuse. For example, what exactly are the rights and responsibilities of providers and consumers of reusable components? What happens if a reused component fails in a critical application? Such issues are not so important for reuse within companies or organizations, but may be a hindrance for reuse across such boundaries. Software is legally protected as intellectual property. Laws for this protection may differ among various countries. The following types of protection are usually provided for software: trade secret protection, copyright protection and patent protection. They are all legal concepts and apply to different aspects of software.

11.10.1 Trade Secret Protection

Trade secret protection is for the \know-how" that is embodied in software. Know-how in this context is substantial and secret information that is proprietary and leads to a commercial advantage. This becomes a problem when software is transferred to others, as is the case with intercorporation reuse. In this case the reuser is obliged to sign a nondisclosure agreement before the components to be reused are delivered. If, despite signing a nondisclosure agreement, the reuser does not keep the information confidential, damages may be claimed. However, others cannot be prevented from using the knowledge unless a patent protection is in effect.

11.10.2 Patent Protection

Patents are granted for technical inventions that are new and involve inventive steps. The decision whether something is patentable is often difficult and requires legal advice. For example, patents are granted for processes or methods which describe how products work. A computer is a product and an algorithm is such a process.

11.10.3 Copyright Protection

Copyright protection is the most common form of protection for software. It covers the software itself but not any underlying ideas and principles, which may be protected by patents. Copyright owners hold the right to reproduce their software, to reuse, maintain and adapt it, to reverse engineer it, to make backup copies, and to authorize third parties to perform such activities.

Buyers of copyright protected software are allowed to make backup copies and to study the software, especially to get information about interoperability, unless this is provided by other means.

11.10.4 Responsibilities and Liabilities

In the context of software reuse, questions about responsibilities and liabilities have to be addressed. Especially for reuse across company boundaries, questions about a guarantee that the software works become important. Who will fix it in case it does not work? Who is liable in case the reused component malfunctions? So far, software is usually reused at one's own risk. This is especially true if the reused software is in the public domain. It is the responsibility of the reuser to check whether reused components fulfill quality standards and meet specifications. Careful testing of software before it is reused may also be important in this context. If software to be reused is purchased, such issues should be addressed in the purchase agreement.

Cooper states that the risks of liability deserve serious management attention but do not appear to offer a significant impediment to software reuse. A main distinction has to be made whether reused software has been modified in a new system. In case of modifications by the reuser, the reuser bears the primary liability. This is similar to the situation when vendor-supplied hardware components are integrated into one's system.

11.11 ECONOMIC ISSUES

Costs associated with software reuse must be justified by the expected benefits; i.e., there must be sufficient return on investment. The following questions have to be answered:

- How can the expected benefits be measured and priced?
- How are the various abstract levels of software reuse measured?
- What is the potential extent of reuse for a particular software component?
- What is the projected shelf-life for that component?
- How frequently will the requirements of that component change?

The reuse process is an economic model of supply and demand. The model includes producers, consumers and a distribution mechanism. How much producers are able to transfer depends on how well their products match what the consumers need. The following factors affect this:

- the quality and reusability of the producer's software
- the skill and knowledge of the consumer about reuse and the reusable software
- the degree of congruence between the producer's and consumer's project requirements

Costs incurred by a project creating reusable components must be recovered from the reusers of those components.

11.11.1 Initial Investments

Initial investments are needed in order to install a reuse program. These investments include costs that do not directly support the completion of a company's primary development goals. Instead, money is invested to make components of this development effort more reusable. The completion of maintenance investments is the starting point of reuse investments.

Separating these costs may be difficult. Making software maintainable is often an integral part of the development process, whereas making its components reusable is not. However, maintenance will also benefit from money being spent for software reuse. The reuse benefit can be calculated by comparing costs for activities done with reuse and those done without reuse, e.g., comparing the costs for developing a software system from scratch to the costs of developing this software system utilizing reusable components from a repository. Reuse investments are cost effective when they are smaller than the sum of all reuse benefits. The benefits can only be estimated at the time the investments have to be made. If early estimations indicate that benefits will be small, then only limited investments should be made.

11.11.2 Reuse Effectiveness

Making reuse cost-effective can be accomplished by increasing the level of reuse, by reducing the average cost of reuse, and by reducing investments to achieve reuse benefits. Early in the development phase the merit of investing in certain components must be identified and their reuse potential must be determined. Buying components from the commercial software market may be taken into consideration. Even if the initial cost is higher, it might turn out that in the long run a commercial product might prove more effective if it is well documented, generalized and of high quality. Reuse effectiveness can be improved by reducing reuse costs and reuse investments (without reducing reuse). Reuse costs can be reduced by making components easy to find, adapt and integrate into new systems. Investments can be reduced by accurately predicting future needs.

11.12 ORGANIZATIONAL ISSUES

Organizational factors can greatly affect the implementation of reuse programs. Findings indicate that organizational changes will be required before the full potential of software reuse can be realized. Project managers want their projects to succeed, probably even at the expense of other groups in the same company. In fact, this enhances their career opportunities because it makes them more successful than their direct competitors. In such a corporate culture, development groups are not encouraged to build generalized software components that may be reused not only in their own future projects but also in projects of other groups. Building generalized components for the sake of reusability decreases productivity of their current project and increases productivity in projects where these components can be reused, i.e., possibly in other groups.

In this section we describe different reuse modes, organizational models, producer and consumer models, and reuse maturity models.

11.12.1 Reuse Modes

Different modes of performing software reuse comprise planned, systematic and institutionalized reuse versus ad-hoc, opportunistic and individual reuse. The most common form of reuse is informal and ad-hoc, where no methods for reuse are defined. It is the responsibility of the individual software developer to possibly identify and locate reusable components. The productivity increase is only marginal.

Systematic reuse requires up-front efforts to define guidelines and procedures, and to measure reuse performance. It means a change of software development methods. Establishing a reuse program is a long-term process and is not easy. Systematic software reuse requires appropriate organizational structures. The Reuse Adoption Process of the Software Productivity Consortium focuses on the transfer of reuse technologies like processes, methods, and tools into an organization. Navarro has described the Flexible Software Factory (FSF) Adoption Strategy, which is used to initiate and guide the transformation of a software engineering organization to a state where software reuse is instrumental to the production process. The goal is to have an organization that aligns work, objectives, intentions and any resources to support software reuse. This strategy consists of various phases and activities. The purpose is to understand the software engineering organization, determine needed changes, and finally to effectively incorporate reuse into the production process.

11.12.2 Organizational Models

Large-scale reuse in an organization cannot be adopted without organizational changes. Technology is an important prerequisite for reuse, but people make it work. Reuse in an organization can only be achieved when people cooperate. Producing valuable and reusable software components is not enough. We must ensure their transfer to the consumers.

Various models for organizations that support software reuse exist. These models influence development practices and are an indicator of reuse maturity in a software company. In practice, a company might reflect some combination of these models.

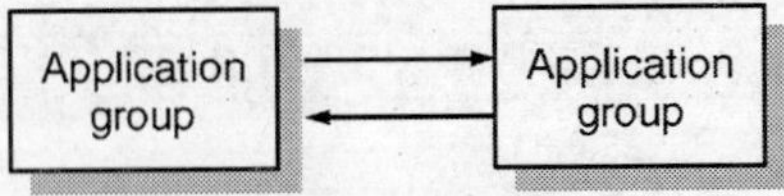

Figure 11.1: *Ad-hoc reuse*

We distinguish four different models which are described subsequently:

1. Ad-hoc reuse among application groups
2. Repository-based reuse among application groups
3. Centralized reuse with a component group
4. Domain-based reuse

1. **Ad-hoc reuse among application groups:** Frequently companies use organizations based on projects. If there is no explicit commitment to reuse then reuse can happen in an informal and haphazard way at best. Most of the reuse, if any, will occur within projects (see Figure 11.1).

   The reuse of components from different projects may occur but is the exception. Goldberg and Rubin call this "reuse in the hallway" and describe the situation with the following short story:

   An engineer is pacing around his office late at night-mumbling to himself-until a colleague bumps into him:

   "What are you doing?" she asks.

   "Thinking," he says.

   "What about?" she asks.

He explains his problem. She smiles. She has solved a similar problem.
"Come along," she urges. "I will show you my solution."
And together they go to her office to find the solution.

2. **Repository-based reuse among application groups:** The situation slightly improves when a component repository is used and can be accessed by various application groups (see Figure 11.2). However, no explicit mechanism exists for putting components into the repository and no one is responsible for the quality of the components in this repository. This can lead to many problems and hamper software reuse. The repository-based reuse approach is based on quantity because any components can be put into the repository and there is no control over their quality and usefulness. If no effort had been made to make the components reusable, then reusers must be cautious. And as there is no control over the input and no maintenance of the components, reusers have to be cautious even when the components had been prepared with high quality and reusability in mind.

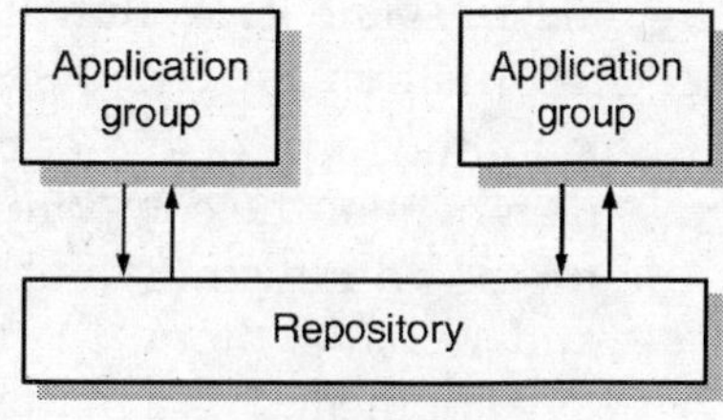

Figure 11.2: *Repository-based reuse*

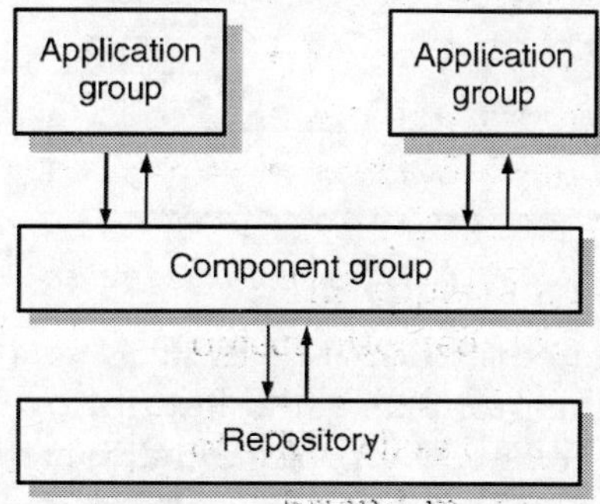

Figure 11.3: *Centralized reuse*

Goldberg and Rubin distinguish between the ad-hoc model and the supply and demand model. In the former there is no control over what goes into and out of the repository. In the latter, components are encouraged to enter the repository and compete for attention. Components that are not reused by others are removed from the repository.
The reuse of a central repository may yield to a large number of available components. Unfortunately, reusers cannot trust these components since no quality control is in effect.

3. **Centralized reuse with a component group:** In this scenario a component group is explicitly responsible for the repository (see Figure 11.3). The group determines which components are to be stored in the repository, ensures the quality of these components and the availability of necessary documentation, and helps in retrieving suitable components in a particular reuse scenario. This amounts to centralized production and management of reusable software components. Application groups are separated from the component group, which acts as a kind of subcontractor to each application group. An objective of the component group is to minimize redundancy. In the expert services model members of the component group (called reuse team by Goldberg and Rubin)

work on specific projects also. Especially during start-up of a new project, the knowledge of members of his group about the availability of reusable components is invaluable. The component group can also gain knowledge about components in the project that are possible candidates for inclusion in the repository. They also gain first-hand information about problems and possible improvements of existing components.

Another form of the component group is the product center model. In this model members of the component group are not loaned to projects; the group is responsible for the administration of the central repository, but does not give support in retrieving and reusing them. In this case reuse is viewed as a standard part of software development. It is a matter of course that application groups use the existing repository and do not need any explicit help in doing so.

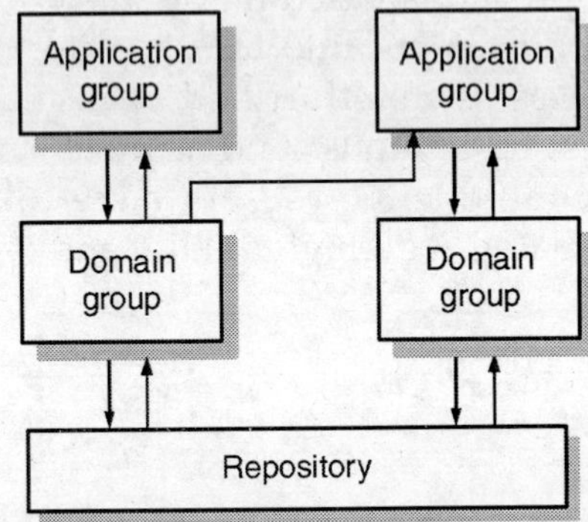

Figure 11.4: Domain-based reuse

Having a central component group raises the question of who pays for it. The organization can regard the group as some kind of overhead or investment and pay for it; or the costs can be covered by projects that benefit from that group by reusing components.

4. **Domain-based reuse:** The specialization of component groups amounts to domain-based reuse, as depicted in Figure 11.4. Each domain group is responsible for components in its domain, e.g., network components, user interface components, database components. Application groups may build their applications by integrating components from different domains. This organization yields to the acquisition of specific skills and knowledge of specific software domains. One possible drawback may be an overhead in communication between project and domain groups.

Resume: As software companies increase their commitment to reuse, they will pass from ad-hoc reuse with application groups only through domain-based reuse with domain groups and application groups. Adopting domain-based reuse requires sufficient company size to maintain specialized groups. Component groups are responsible for developing reusable components. Domain groups are also responsible for the development of reusable components; in addition, they have to gain knowledge about their specific domain. Application groups are obligated to develop applications by using components created by these specialized groups. These subareas, component engineering (design for reuse), application engineering (design with reuse) and domain engineering (design for reuse in a certain domain).

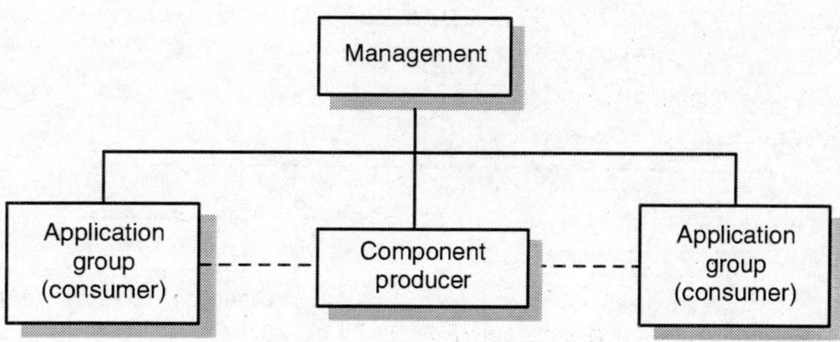

Figure 11.5: Lone producer

11.12.3 Producers and Consumers

Having one or several groups for component administration creates a distinction between producers and consumers of components. Producers (component groups) design and develop reusable components. Consumers (application groups) design and develop products with reusable components. The relationship between consumers and producers is essential. Producer groups can be located at different organizational levels. Four models of these producer/ consumer relationships have been identified at Hewlett-Packard and are depicted by Fafchamps:

1. **Lone producer**

   A single individual handles the reuse needs of several application groups (see Figure 11.5). The lone producer's primary role is to design, develop and/or maintain reusable components. Maintenance is typically done by newly hired programmers, whereas design and development activities are performed mostly by experienced programmers. Lone producers face the problems of informal change requests, work overload, isolation and communication overload.

2. **Nested producer**

   Each application group has an individual who provides reuse services and expertise. Nested producers are members of the application group and contribute to the development of this product (see Figure 11.6). However, their reuse position may be at risk when managers of the application group face critical phases in product development and divert reuse efforts toward product needs.

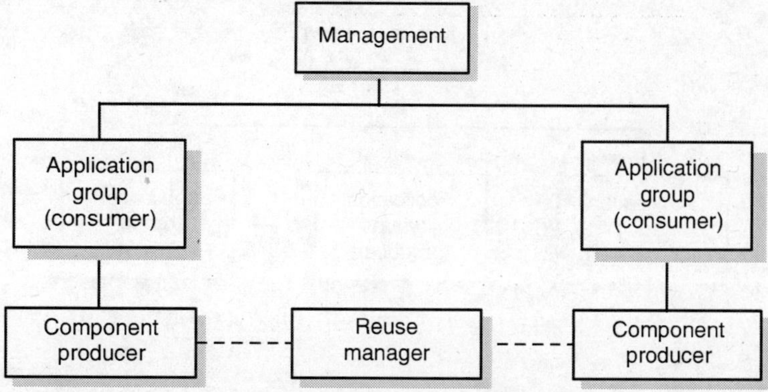

Figure 11.6: Nested producer

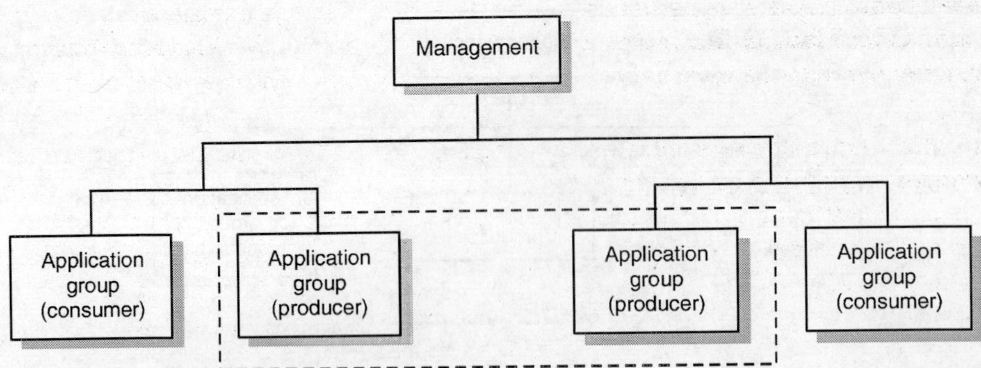

Figure 11.7: Pool producer

3. **Pool producer**
   Two or more groups collaborate to produce and share components (see Figure 11.7). Pool producers belong to a stable and identifiable organizational group. The communication overhead may be high in this model, because the groups may be at geographically different locations. Communication increases with the number of groups and product lines.
4. **Team producer**
   Groups of producers interact with groups of consumers. Consumer groups develop products; they are inwardly oriented. A producer group interacts with the consumer groups; they are outwardly oriented. Producer groups have a dedicated manager; their own budget and a typical group structure (see Figure 11.8).

These consumer/producer models have various advantages and disadvantages. For example, Fafchamps reports that the nested producer model did not work well at Hewlett-Packard. This is most likely due to "double management" in this model. The most important thing for all these models is that the right people are selected for the producer groups (i.e., highly skilled and experienced in software techniques, in the application domains, and also in communication and interpersonal relationships), that change requests are managed properly, that ownership and responsibilities are clarified, and that conflict-resolution strategies are established.

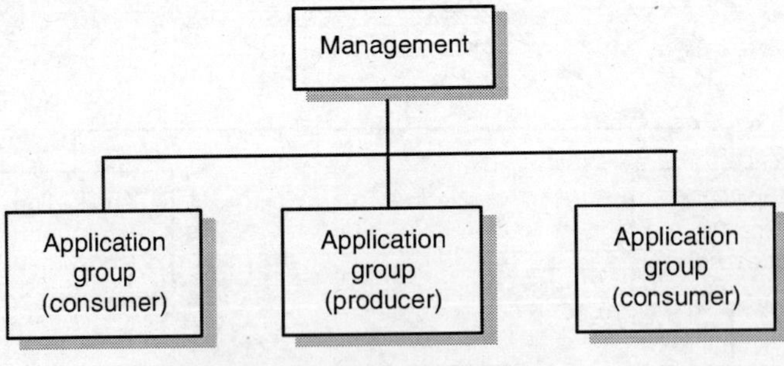

Figure 11.8: Team producer

Prieto-Diaz has also identified specific roles that are crucial in a reuse infrastructure: librarians, asset managers and reuse managers:

Librarian

The librarian is responsible for the promotion of reuse by making components easily available to potential reusers.

Asset manager

The asset manager controls compliance with quality standards of reusable components.

Reuse manager

The reuse manager coordinates the overall reuse effort and supports the collection of relevant data needed as feedback for domain analysis. Librarians and asset managers are members of the component group and/or the domain group. Reuse managers are responsible for one or more such groups.

These roles complement the tasks of the domain analyst, domain expert and domain engineer, who are members of a domain group.

11.12.4 Reuse Maturity

Reuse maturity is a measure of the effectiveness of an organization's reuse activities. The evaluation of reuse maturity can be an incentive to take steps for increasing it. The presence or absence of adequate organizational structures is a good indicator for reuse maturity in organizations. Assigning an organization to one of the models described in the previous sections gives a first clue about the maturity reached.

A five-level maturity model has been proposed by Koltun and Hudson. In this model the five levels are distinguished by motivation, planning for reuse, breadth of reuse involvement, responsibility for making reuse happen, process by which reuse is leveraged, reuse inventory, classification activity, technology support, metrics, and legal/accounting considerations.

The five levels are initial/chaotic, monitored, coordinated, planned and ingrained. Table 11.3 gives an overview of the characteristics of the various levels of this maturity model.

Similar models have been developed by other authors and/or organizations, for example, a five-stage maturity model by the Software Productivity Consortium. The proposed stages are ad-hoc reuse, repeatable reuse, portable reuse, architectural reuse, and systematic reuse. An overview of various models is given by Griss.

Table 11.3: Characteristics of reuse maturity levels

Level	Characteristics
1. Initial/Chaotic	Short-term thinking reuse costs are feared resistance to reuse reuse is individualized, uncoordinated, unmonitored

2. Monitored	Managerial awareness little active promotion of reuse reuse costs are known individual achievements
3. Coordinated	Organizational responsibility domain analyses for product line reuse tactics payoff of reuse is known component standardization,
4. Planned	Life cycle view of reuse reports of reuse costs and savings reuse is supported and encouraged reuse across all functional areas
5. Ingrained	Corporation wide view reuse is regular business domain analyses across all products lines corporation wide definitions, guidelines, standards

11.13 MEASUREMENT ISSUES

It is often said that we cannot manage what we cannot measure. Software reuse is no exception to the rule. Reuse spans multiple projects and has an influence even on organizational structures of companies. To manage such enterprise-wide activities requires some kind of monitoring. Software metrics can be used to estimate costs, cost savings, and the value of software practices. In the following subsections we describe various measures that are useful in the context of software reuse.

11.13.1 Reuse Level

The amount of software reuse (the reuse level) in a certain software system can be determined by the ratio of reused components (or their lines of code) to the total components of the system (or total amount of code lines). This measure does not consider more subtle aspects like adaptation costs, but it is objective.

$$\text{Reuse level} = \frac{\text{number of reused components}}{\text{total number of components}}$$

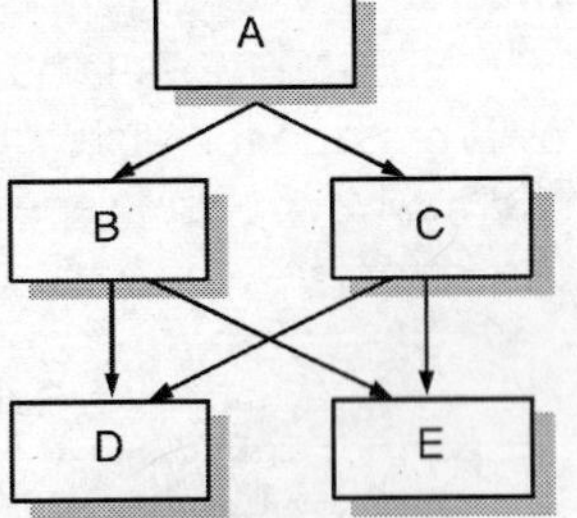

Figure 11.9: Sample system with five components

A proposal that reuse be measured as the number of lines of code incorporated in a system without modification, divided by the total number of lines of code in the system has also been made by the Software Productivity Metrics Working Group of the IEEE. We can further distinguish between external and internal reuse and determine these levels. The internal and external reuse levels consider components that have been developed for the system or outside the system, respectively.

Example: A small system consists of five components, say A, B, C, D and E (see Figure 11.9). Component A calls components B and C; both B and C call D and E. If D and E are reused and the other three components have been developed from scratch, we get a reuse level of 2/5 or 0.4.

Object-oriented systems: Object-oriented software development allows the simple modification and extension of components through inheritance. In this case a new component reuses a fraction of the component it inherits from. Different ways of calculating reuse levels are possible. We can simply regard the components as either new or reused or do a more subtle distinction by considering how often a component is reused through inheritance, or even how often and how many of its functions are called.

11.13.2 Line and Word Runs

A reuse measurement based on lines and words for a low-level determination of white-box reuse has been proposed by Childs and Sametinger. The number of lines that are identical in file a and file b as opposed to the total number of lines (of file a) gives an indication of how much of file a has been reused in file b.

$$\text{Line reuse percentage} = \frac{\text{number of identical lines}}{\text{total number of lines}} \times 100$$

This formula can be used in both directions, i.e., to determine how much of file a is being reused in file b and to determine how much of file b originates from file a (by using the total number of lines of file b).

Comparing lines and words gives a good indication about white-box reuse. Let Rl and Rw denote the reuse percentage of lines and words, respectively. As it turns out, usually Rl and Rw do not differ much, with Rw slightly higher than Rl. If both Rl and Rw are high, then obviously reuse had been achieved. If Rl is low, but Rw is high, then reuse had been achieved, but the reused text had been modified on a more local basis, which leads to many different lines (and a lower Rl), but still leaves many equal words (leading to a higher Rw). Finally, if both Rl and Rw are low, then apparently there is only little reuse.

If several consecutive lines are identical in two files, it is likely that they were reused. If there is a solitary identical line, it might have been reused, but it also might have nothing to do with reuse at all. For example, consider lines in C and cplusplus source code containing closing braces ('}'). In some cases such lines may be regarded as being reused in a certain context, i.e., when the surrounding lines are reused as well. We obtain a modified reuse percentage by only considering lines (or words) when they are part of a run of certain length.

11.13.3 Return on Investment

Henderson-Sellers suggest metrics based on reuse savings and generalization costs. The return-on-investment metric is defined as follows:

$$\text{Return on investment} = \frac{\text{reuse savings}}{\text{generalization costs}}$$

It is important that long-term generalization costs not exceed long-term reuse savings; otherwise reuse is not recommended. Reuse savings can be determined by estimating the costs for developing all components anew and subtracting the costs necessary for partly new development plus costs for finding reusable components and for their modification (if needed). Generalization costs are difficult to assess, but will somehow depend on the size of components.

Regarding a single project only would suggest that components from a repository are reused without providing components for the repository, thus minimizing generalization costs. Therefore, return on investment has to be assessed over a number of projects.

It is also important to consider the whole spectrum of life cycle costs, e.g., costs for testing, verification and maintenance. On the one hand, these costs will hopefully be reduced by reusing a component. On the other hand, despite cost reductions during development, the integration of a component may have an impact on the overall system design and a negative impact on software maintenance.

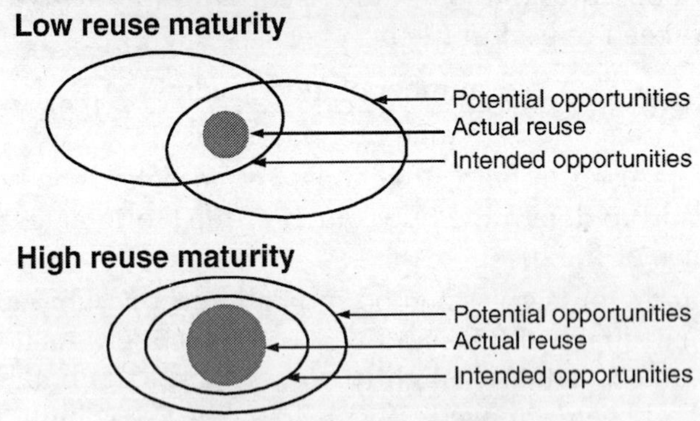

Figure 11.10: Reuse maturity

11.13.4 Reuse Maturity

Section 11.3.1 described reuse maturity levels. It is difficult to quantify these levels. Organizations often measure their reuse efforts by the ratio of reused source code lines to the total number of source code lines. This is not sufficient for the measurement of reuse maturity because it does not reflect how many reuse opportunities had been missed.

Reuse maturity can be seen as the range of expected results in reuse efficiency, reuse proficiency and reuse effectiveness that can be achieved in an organization by following a reuse process. But even though we give formulas below, it is difficult to determine the results unless high reuse maturity has been achieved by an organization. Otherwise the input parameters are not readily available and have to be based on estimated numbers.

Figure 11.10 shows two examples of low and high reuse maturity. In the upper example potential and intended opportunities do not match each other well. Thus actual reuse is limited from the start. In the lower example these opportunities match better, facilitating higher actual reuse. It is crucial for organizations to recognize existing reuse opportunities and to exploit them systematically. Failing to recognize them leads to fruitless efforts.

Reuse efficiency. Reuse efficiency measures how much of the intended reuse opportunities have actually been exploited by an organization. It is determined by the ratio of the percentage of exploited reuse opportunities to the percentage of intended reuse opportunities. If the intended reuse is 50% (i.e., the organization aims at exploiting 50% of the reuse opportunities) and the actual reuse is 25%, then the reuse efficiency is 25/50 or 0.5.

$$\text{reuse efficiency} = \frac{\text{exploited reuse opportunities}}{\text{intended reuse opportunities}}$$

Reuse proficiency. Reuse proficiency is the ratio of actual reuse to potential reuse, i.e., the ratio of the percentage of exploited reuse opportunities to the percentage of potential reuse opportunities. If the potential reuse is 75% and actual reuse is 25%, reuse proficiency is 25 75 or 0.33.

$$\text{reuse proficiency} = \frac{\text{exploited reuse opportunities}}{\text{potential reuse opportunities}}$$

Reuse effectiveness. Reuse effectiveness is the ratio of reuse benefits to reuse costs. It can be measured by the ratio of the difference between what the development of a new component would have cost to what it costs to reuse the component times the number of its reuse to the investments costs to acquire or develop the reusable component. Consider the following example: the development of a new component costs USD 10,000; the development to make it reusable costs USD 13,000; to reuse the component costs USD 1,000. If the component is used twice, then the reuse effectiveness is $2 \times \frac{10{,}000 - 1{,}000}{13{,}000}$ or 1.38.

$$\text{reuse effectiveness} = \text{no. of reuses} \frac{\text{cost of development} - \text{cost of reuse}}{\text{cost of acquisition or development}}$$

11.13.5 Industrial Example

Significant and largely positive effects of software reuse on software development have been found in two reuse programs at Hewlett-Packard [Lim94]. Metrics were collected in these programs and demonstrated that reuse can provide a substantial return on investment. Findings indicated that software reuse positively influenced quality, productivity and development time. Returns on investment (savings/costs) were 216 and 410 percent with gross savings of 5.6 and 4.1 million US dollars, respectively. The relative cost of creating reusable code components was about twice as high as creating these components without supporting their reuse. The relative cost to reuse these components, i.e., integrate them into new systems, was only about a quarter to a fifth of the costs to develop them anew. The FAGQM (Framework Assisted Goal Question Metric) model is presented and illustrated by Vaishnavi and Bandi. It suggests metrics for the perspective of development for reuse and development with reuse. A framework for setting up a software measurement program is described by Goldberg and Rubin.

11.14 INSTALLING A REUSE PROGRAM

The benefits of reuse are quite apparent. So the question is not whether to install a reuse program but rather how to install it. Some of the benefits of reuse can certainly be realized by casual approaches. However, adopting large-scale, institutionalized reuse requires many steps and is not trivial at all. Reuse programs should start small and gain experience through pilot projects in order to be successful and effective. A common misconception is that object-oriented programming will bring software reuse for free. In this chapter we describe how to install a reuse program. Steps that have to be undertaken to install a reuse program are depicted in Section 11.14.1. A reuse program should be installed in progressive steps, where each step sets the basis for the following steps. This enables starting a reuse program and learning from it.

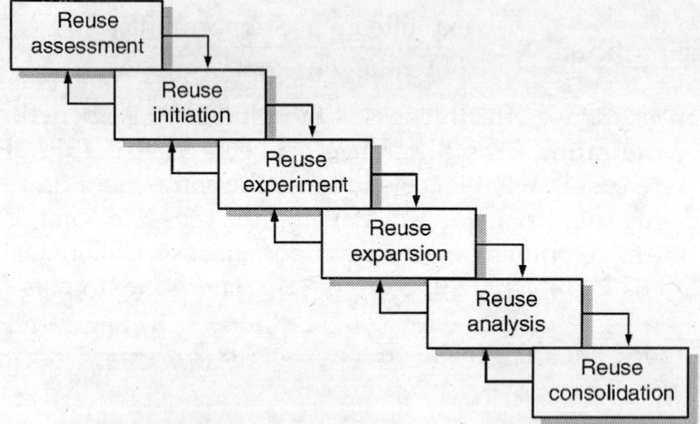

Figure 11.11: Steps to install a reuse program

Advantages for this incremental approach are:

- immediate return on investment,
- confidence within the organization,
- ease of management,
- possibility to tune and refine the reuse program, and
- possibility to monitor and evaluate reuse.

Additionally, the process should be systematic and formal, i.e., consistent, repeatable and decomposable into well-defined steps. These steps may be carried out repeatedly, increasing the scope of reuse in case its adoption has been successful so far. The steps for adding the practice of reuse to an organization are described in the subsequent sections. An overview of these steps is depicted in Figure 11.11.

Reuse programs can be tuned to benefits that fit the business objectives of an organization. The objectives should be clearly defined, e.g., productivity/quality improvements, time to market.

11.14.1 Reuse Assessment

Despite of the apparent benefits of reuse, its potential in a certain organization have to be understood and should be assessed before a reuse program is installed. The potential payoff/cost to the organization has to be analyzed. The following questions should be addressed during this phase:

- Is software reuse feasible in our organization?

Is software production large enough to justify a reuse program? Will management support a reuse program? Are there enough (human and financial) resources for a reuse program? Can we afford a reuse program? How many similar systems will be produced? Are reusable assets already available? What do we want to reuse?

- Is our domain suitable for reuse?

How broad/complex is the domain? Is the domain mature and well understood? Is it stable or rapidly changing?

- How is the cost/benefit relation?

What is the desired level of reuse? How much will the reuse program cost? Is it economically justified?

- How will we implement reuse?

What are the steps to implement the reuse program?

In case an organization is developing software in more than one domain, it is recommended to identify those which are well understood, have applications with similar requirements, and are important for the organization. Initial reuse installment can be restricted to only one or several of these domains.

11.14.2 Reuse Initiation

Existing software has to be analyzed in order to find, evaluate and select potentially reusable software components. The components may need to be generalized and/or complemented with specific reuse documentation. Then they need to be stored in a repository to serve as the base of reusable components in the organization. The effort needed for performing these tasks will vary depending on the scope of the reuse program to be installed. This may range from a part-time individual at almost no cost to the installment of a separate organizational unit. Especially in the latter case, support from top management is essential because initial costs face a slow return on investment.

Not every component that is reusable will be considered in this initiation step. Thus categories of reusable components should be identified and prioritized. It is important to acquire components that are important for the business. Assigning components to different levels of generality can be useful in this context. Examples of such levels are: components of interest to any business, components of interest to any company within the industry, and components specific to the company.

11.14.3 Reuse Experiment

Risks and costs are reduced by starting with a reuse experiment. This will facilitate learning about technical and organizational issues that impede the reuse program. The experiment can be done with an ongoing project as well as with a new one that is to be approached with reuse.

It is important that success criteria be defined and measurements be taken for the experiment. The project should not be too long, so that results are not delayed too long.

Depending on the results, the reuse program should be extended (positive results) or reworked (unsatisfactory results).

11.14.4 Reuse Expansion

If the reuse experiment has been successful, a commitment to change has to be institutionalized. Other applications have to be integrated into the reuse efforts and the repository of reusable components has to be extended and consolidated. Incentives to support the program should be provided until reuse becomes part of the culture.

Other domains can be considered for reuse either by doing an experiment in that domain also, or, in case reuse benefits are convincing enough, by developing the needed resources right away.

11.14.5 Domain Analysis

Domain analysis is necessary in order to institute systematic reuse. It comprises activities to identify needs that are common to multiple projects in a certain domain.

11.14.6 Reuse Consolidation

Institutionalized reuse requires adjustments of organizational structures and additional activities like domain analysis and administrating the component repository. Software development processes have to be adapted. Reuse training for engineers as well as tool support for reuse has to be established. Steps for installing reuse may be rerun even if reuse has been installed successfully already. For example, the abstraction level of reused components should be as high as possible. In a first step the reuse of function libraries may be considered. In a next installation cycle, object-oriented technology may be considered as well. Depending on the maturity of component technology, further component types should be included in the reuse program.

SUMMARY

Software reuse is the process of creating software systems from existing software rather than building them from scratch. In this chapter we have provided several other definitions of software reuse, various benefits, and obstacles to reuse. The most common benefits of software reuse are quality improvement and effort reduction. Obstacles to reuse are of managerial, organizational, economic and technical nature. The essence of reuse comprises ideas, artifacts, and skills. By reusing components, which are artifacts, we cannot reuse any skills. But we are able to reuse ideas and concepts, which, to some degree, can be incorporated into components. The form and extent of reuse, defined by reuse scope, is strongly dependent on nontechnical measures that are taken. The same holds for reuse modes, e.g., individual and systematic reuse. Reuse techniques include generative and compositional reuse. Reuse intentions define how components are to be reused, i.e., as black boxes, grey boxes, glass boxes or white boxes. The reuse products we mentioned contained various products of the software life cycle like algorithms and class libraries. The only way to overcome these obstacles is to systematically install a reuse program.

EXERCISES

1. What do you mean by reuse?
2. Explain the various benefits of software reuse?
3. Explain the various obstacles to software reuse?
4. Explain the technical aspects of software reuse?
5. What are the various techniques of software reuse?
6. Distinguish between Compositional and Generative Reuse?
7. Explain the prominent examples of today's reuse?
8. Explain the non-technical aspects of software reuse?
9. Explain the issues of software reuse economics?
10. Explain the various organizational issues of software reuse?
11. Explain the organizational models of software reuse?
12. Explain the various measurement issues of software reuse?
13. Explain the procedure to install a reuse program?

❑

UNIT 5
OBJECT ORIENTED MEASUREMENTS

Object Oriented Metrics

12

12.1 INTRODUCTION

Object-Oriented Analysis and Design of software provide many benefits such as reusability, decomposition of problem into easily understood object and the aiding of future modifications. But the OOAD software development life cycle is not easier than the typical procedural approach. Therefore, it is necessary to provide dependable guidelines that one may follow to help ensure good OO programming practices and write reliable code. Object-Oriented programming metrics is an aspect to be considered. Metrics to be a set of standards against which one can measure the effectiveness of Object-Oriented Analysis techniques in the design of a system.

Five characteristics of Object Oriented Metrics are as following:

- Localization *operations used in many classes*
- Encapsulation *metrics for classes, not modules*
- Information Hiding *should be measured & improved*
- Inheritance *adds complexity, should be measured*
- Object Abstraction *metrics represent level of abstraction*

We can signify nine classes of Object Oriented Metrics. In each of then an aspect of the software would be measured:

- Size
  - Population (# of classes, operations)
  - Volume (dynamic object count)
  - Length (e.g., depth of inheritance)
  - Functionality (# of user functions)
- Complexity
  - How classes are interrelated
- Coupling
  - # of collaborations between classes, number of method calls, etc.
- Sufficiency
  - Does a class reflect the necessary properties of the problem domain?
- Completeness
  - Does a class reflect all the properties of the problem domain? (for reuse)

- Cohesion
  - Do the attributes and operations in a class achieve a single, well-defined purpose in the problem domain?
- Primitiveness (Simplicity)
  - Degree to which class operations can't be composed from other operations
- Similarity
  - Comparison of structure, function, behavior of two or more classes
- Volatility
  - The likelihood that a change will occur in the design or implementation of a class

It is clear that software measurement is necessary for the software development process to be successful. The main goals of the software measurement are:

- Evaluate the software systems.
- Improve quality of software systems.
- Identify and correct problems early.
- Defend and justify decisions.

One side of the concept of software engineering is the idea that the software should be under control. As De Marco said "You cannot control what you cannot measure". Fenton and Pfleeger added "You cannot predict what you cannot measure".

Most of the measure strategies have as the main goal to evaluate the different characteristics of software quality, such as reliability, ease of use, maintainability, robustness, etc.

12.2 METRICS

Metric is a quantitative measure of the degree to which a given attribute is possessed by a system or its component or by a process. Software metrics are measures that are used to quantify different attributes of a software product, software development resource and software development process.

*Software metrics:*deals with the estimation and measurement of different attributes of the software product and the software development process.

12.2.1 Measurement History

The earliest software measure is the Measure LOC (Lines of Code). The basis of the Measure LOC is that program length can be used as a predictor of program characteristics such as reliability and ease of maintenance.

Then in the 70's, they tried to set the relation between the programs size and the needed effort to write and maintain them (COCOMO).

In the 80's they studied more about complexity metrics, module and structured design, cost estimation and time used to develop the software projects. By this time the norm ISO 9000 appeared.

In the 90's they tried to center in the classification, study and validity of the software metrics. COCOMO model was reviewed (COCOMO II) to show the big changes in the development techniques during the last ten years.

12.3 METRICS PROPERTIES

Following are the properties of metrics:

Factors in software quality

Quality factors are usually attributes in a high level of abstraction, as reliability, ease of use, ease of maintenance. The McCall quality software model defines three aspects or important characteristics of a product: operational characteristics, of modification and transaction, and each of them are broken down in quality factors of high level. These are broken down in quality criterion. And these are associated to an attributes set named quality metrics.

- **Operational characteristics**
  - *Reliability:*
    - o Correctness: a program is correct when it make his work without errors.
    - o Strength: ability of a program to answer to non-predicted situations.
  - *Efficiency:* to offer the maximum of performance qualities with the minimum resources.
  - *Ease of use:* needed effort to learn to control a program
  - *Integrity:* control the access to software or data by non-authorized people.
- **Modification characteristics**
  - *Ease of maintenance:* the needed effort to modify a program.
  - *Expandable:* possibility of add new functionality of an easy way.
  - *Ease of testing:* the needed effort to test a program in a way that this testing assures that the program works well.
- **Transition characteristics**
  - *Portability:* possibility of execution in different platforms without changes.
  - *Re-usability:* property of software components. These components can be used in other tasks from which they were built.
  - *Interoperability:* the systems should be able to inter-operate with other software components.

There are two kinds of attributes:

- **Internal attributes:** those which can be measured with the own product independently of his behaviour.
- **External attributes:** those which can only be measured when it relates with the environment.

The measurement of internal and external attributes is considered as the basis to improve the quality of software products.

12.3.1 Measurement and Metrices Properties

Measurement is "the process by which numbers or symbols are assigned to attributes of entities in the real world in such a way as to describe them according to clearly defined rules". An entity may be a person, a developed program or the development process. An attribute of entity may be the weight of a person or the length of the development process. The goal of the metrics use is evaluate systems to get high quality, strength and ease of maintenance.

Since object oriented system is becoming more pervasive, it is necessary that software engineers have quantitative measurements for accessing the quality of designs at both the architectural and components level. These measures allow to designer to access the software early in the process, making changes that will reduce complexity and improve the continuing capability of the product. The measurement process is to drive the software measures and metrics that are appropriate for the representation of software that is being measured. Suitable metrics are analysed based on pre-established guidelines and past data.

Metrics can be applicable to one or more steps in the life cycle of software development: requirement specification, analysis, design, implementation, etc.

There are two kinds of metrics:

- **Direct metrics:** those which only need an attribute to measure it.
- **Indirect metrics:** those which need more than one attribute to measure it. It needs a combination of some metrics.

12.4 METRICS VALIDATION

A measure is valid if it accurately characterizes the real world behaviour it claims to measure.

As Kitchenham says, in order for a measure to be valid, both of the following conditions must hold:

- The measure must not violate any necessary properties of its elements.
- Each model used in the measurement process must be valid.

And to decide whether a measurement is valid we need to confirm:

- **Attribute validity:** whether the attribute in which we are interested is actually exhibited by the entity we are measuring. Attribute validity must be considered both for directly measurable attributes and for indirectly measurable attributes that are derived from other attributes.
- **Unit validity:** whether the measurement unit being used is an appropriate means of measuring the attribute.
- **Instrument validity:** whether any model underlying a measuring instrument is valid and the measuring instrument is properly calibrated.
- **Protocol validity:** whether an acceptable measurement protocol is adopted.

12.5 METRICS HIERARCHY

We categorized metrics into two groups: project based metrics and design based metrics. Project based metrics contain process, product and resources; these are discussed in next sub section. Design based metrics contain traditional metrics and object oriented metrics. In traditional metrics, we will discuss complexity metrics, SLOC (Source lines of code), and CP (Comment percentage) metric. Object oriented metrics are discussed in next sections. The following figure 12.1 shows metrics hierarchy according to our categorization.

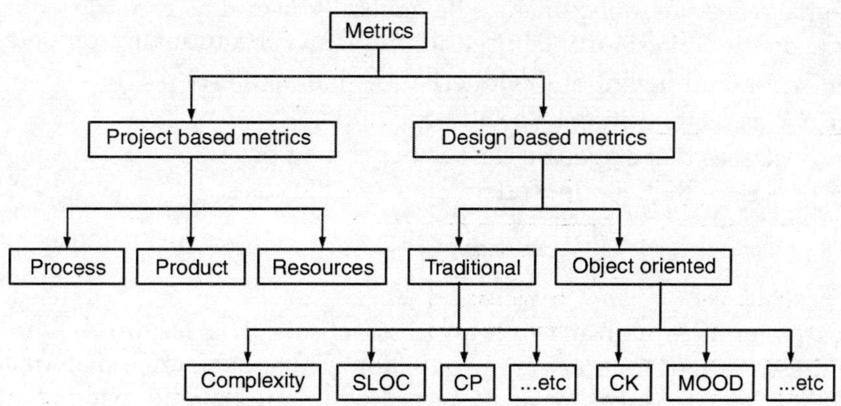

***Figure 12.1:** Metrics Hierarchy*

Norman E. Fenton proposes three kinds of entities and attributes to measure in software design. The entities are process, product, resources and attributes are internal and external attributes.

12.5.1 Process

Processes are set of software related activates which are used to measure the status and progress of the system design and to predict future effects. A process is usually related with some timescale. The timing can be explicit, as when an activity must be finished by a specific date, or implicit, as when one activity must be finished before another can begin. The following examples of a process related metrics that it is proposed to collect when working with object oriented software engineering (OOSE).

- Total development time,
- Development time in each process and subprocess,
- Time spent to modify models from previous processes,
- Time spent in all kinds of subprocess, such as use case specification, object specification, use case design, block design, block testing and use case testing for each particular object,
- Number of different kind of fault found during reviews,
- Number of change proposals on previous models,
- Cost for quality assurance,
- Cost for introducing new development process and tools.

12.5.2 Products

Product metrics are used to control the quality of the software product. These metrics are applied to incomplete software products in order to measure their complexity and to predict properties of the final product. Products are any artefacts, deliverables or documents that result from a process activity. Products are not restricted to the items that management is committed to deliver to the customer. Any artefact or document produced during the software life cycle can be measured. Various kinds of product related metrics are proposed.

None of these have been demonstrated to be generally useful as overall quality predictor. However, some quality criteria can be used to predict a certain quality property as follow:

- Number, width and height of the inheritances hierarchies,
- Number of classes inheriting a specific operation,
- Number of classes that a specific class is dependent on,
- Number of classes that are dependent on a specific class,
- Number of direct users of a class or operation.

12.5.3 Resources

Resources are entities required by a process activity. The resources that we want to measure include any input for software production. Thus, personnel, materials, tools, and methods are candidates for measurement. According to internal and external attribute each class of entity can be distinguish.

12.5.3.1 Internal Attributes

Internal attributes of a product, process or resource are those that can be measured purely in terms of the product, process, or resource itself. In other words, an internal attribute an be measured by examining the product, process or resource on its own.

12.5.3.2 External Attributes

External attributes of a product, process or resource are those that can be measured only with respect to how the produce process or resource, relates to its environment. Here, the behavior of the process, product or resource is important, rather than the entity itself. Table 1 represents a classification of software metrics. Essentially any software metrics is an attempt to measure or predict some internal or external attribute of some product, process, or resource. The table provides a feel for the board scope of software metrics, and clarifies the distinguished between the attributes.

Table 12.1: Components of software measurements

Entities	**Attributes**	
	Internal	**External**
Products		
Specification	Size, reuse, modularity, redundancy, functionality, syntactic correctness.	Comprehensibility, maintainability,
Design	Size, reuse, modularity, coupling, cohesiveness, inheritance, functionality.	Quality, complexity, maintainability.
Code	Size, reuse, modularity, coupling, functionality, algorithmic complexity, control-flow structuredness.	Reliability, usability, maintainability, reusability.
Test data	Size, coverage level.	Quality, reusability.

Process		
Constructing Specification	Time, effort, number of requirements changes.	Quality, cost, stability.
Detailed design	Time effort, number of specification faults found.	Cost, cost-effectiveness.
Testing	Time, effort, number of coding faults found.	Cost, cost-effectiveness, stability, ...
Resources		
Personnel	Age, price.	Productivity, experience, intelligence.
Terms	Size, communication level, structuredness.	Productivity, quality.
Organization	Size, ISO Certification, CMM level.	Maturity, profitability.
Software	Price, size.	Usability, reliability.
Hardware	Price, speed, memory size.	Reliability.
Offices	Size, temperature, light.	Comfort, quality.

12.6 MEASURING QUALITY

Measurement enables to improve the software process, assist in the planning, tracking the control of a design. A good software engineer uses measurements to asses the quality of the analysis and design model, the source code, the test cases, etc. What does quality mean?

"Quality refers to the inherent or distinctive characteristics or property of object, process or other thing. Such characteristics or properties may set things apart from other things, or may denote some degree of achievement or excellence".

Many quality measures can be collected from literature, the main goal of metrics is to measure errors and defects. The following quality factor should have every metrics:

- Efficiency – Are the constructs efficiently designed? The amount of computing resource and code required by a program to perform its function.
- Complexity – Could the constructs be used more effectively to decrease the architectural complexity?
- Understandability – Does the design increase the psychological complexity?
- Reusability – Does the design quality support possible reuse?
- Extent to which a program or part of a program can be reused in other application, related to the packaging and scope of the functions that the program performs.
- Testability/Maintainability – Does the structure support ease of testing and changes?

Effort required locating and fixing an error in a program, as well as effort required to test a program to ensure that it performs its intended function. How do we know that our metrics measure the desired design qualities? We should establish the objectives of measurements before data collection begins and then we should define each and every metrics in a way that measure the quality of a design.

12.7 OBJECT ORIENTED METRICS TAXONOMY

Software Engineering introduces the measures in each step in a life cycle of a software project, independently of the used model: waterfall, spiral, etc. Then, the metrics can be viewed from a three-dimensional approach, with the next dimensions:

- Software attribute to measure (complexity, re-usability, ...)
- Step in the life cycle in which is done the measure (design, analysis, ...)
- Granularity level in which the measure is taken (system level, program level, class level, ...)

Metrics cannot be applied to any software attribute that want to be measured indiscriminately. The typical case of a mistaken measure is to measure the lines of code (LOC) as a complexity program measure, when this is valid as a measure of the size program, not as complexity program measure. In another way, all the metrics don't have to be taken in the implementation stage, although part of them are taken from this step. It should be desirable to get them in the earlier design step.

Chidamber and Kemerer proposed six metrics for object oriented design:

- Metric 1: Weighted Methods Per Class (WMC)
- Metric 2: Depth of Inheritance Tree (DIT)
- Metric 3: Number Of Children (NOC)
- Metric 4: Coupling Between Objects (CBO)
- Metric 5: Response For a Class (RFC)
- Metric 6: Lack of Cohesion in Methods (LCOM)

The appearance of the Unified Modelling Language (UML) as a standard of modelling object oriented information systems have provided a great contribution toward building quality object oriented systems. In propose a set of metrics in order to assess the complexity of UML class diagrams from the relations in UML, such as association, aggregation, etc.

Briand made a study about the coupling in object oriented systems:

- There are different types of coupling among classes, methods, attributes.
- Classes and methods can be coupled more or less strongly, depending on:
  - The type of connections between them
  - The frequency of connections between them
- A distinction can be made between import and export coupling.
- Both direct and indirect coupling may be relevant.
- The server class can be stable or unstable.
- The effect of inheritance on coupling has to be considered.

The study of Abreu and Melo is based in a suit of metrics called MOOD, with the next motivations:

- coverage of the basic structural mechanisms of the object oriented paradigm as encapsulation, inheritance, polymorphism and message-passing.
- formal definition to avoid subjectivity of measurement and thus allow replicability
- size independence to allow inter-project comparison, thus fostering cumulative knowledge

- language independence to broad the applicability of this metric set by allowing comparison of heterogeneous system implementations.

In the next sections taxonomy of metrics will be presented, grouped with the main characteristic of the object oriented approach that is wanted to measure, showing in each of them the granularity level and the step in the life cycle in which it is measured.

12.7.1 Coupling

It is viewed as a measure of the complexity increment, reducing the encapsulation and his possible reutilization; limiting the ease of understanding and system maintenance.

12.7.1.1 Coupling Between Objects (CBO)

CBO of a class is the number of classes to which a particular class is coupled, without have inheritance relations with it. A class is coupled with another class if either one accesses a method or attribute of the other.

- *Valuation*: if an object is more independent, more easily is to reuse it in another application. When the coupling is reduced, the complexity is reduced, the modularity is improved and the encapsulation is promoted. A coupling method is useful to know the complexity of the necessary testing of the different parts of the design.
- *Granularity level:* class, program, system.
- *Life cycle:* design.

12.7.1.2 Coupling Factor (COF)

COF is the proportion between the real number of coupling and the maximum possible number of coupling in the system. It shows the communication between classes.

- *Valuation:* COF may be an indirect measure of the attributes in which is related: complexity, lack of encapsulation, lack of re-usability, ease of understanding and bit ease of maintenance. With the coupling increment between classes, density of faults is increased and ease of maintenance is reduced.
- *Granularity level:* class, program, system.
- *Life cycle:* design.
- *Related with:* complexity, encapsulation, re-usability.

12.7.2 Cohesion

Cohesion, originating from the structured design, refers to the relatedness of the elements in a module. A highly cohesive module is one whose elements have a close relationship among them in order to provide the sole functionality of the module. On the contrary, a low cohesive module has some elements that have little relation with others, which indicates that the module seems to provide several unrelated functionalities. It is widely accepted that the higher the cohesion of a module is, the easier the module is to develop, maintain, and reuse, and the less fault prone it is.

12.7.2.1 Lack of Cohesion in Methods (LCOM)

LCOM is the number of local method groups which don't access to common attributes.

- *Valuation:* it shows the quality of the abstraction done in the class. It uses the concept: rate of similarity methods. If there is not common attributes, the similarity rate is zero. A low cohesion increases the complexity and the ease to make faults during the development process. These classes probably can be divided in two or more subclasses increasing the cohesion of the final classes. It is desirable a high cohesion in the methods inside a class, because it cannot be divided promoting encapsulation.
- *Granularity level:* class.
- *Life cycle:* design, implementation.

12.7.3 Complexity Methods

Following are the various complexity methods:

12.7.3.1 Response for a Class (RFC)

RFC is a set of methods that can potentially be executed in response to a message received by an object of that class. The cardinality of this set is a measure of the attributes of objects in the class. Since it specifically includes methods called from outside the class, it is also a measure of the potential communication between the class and other classes.

- *Valuation:* is a measure of the class complexity with the number of methods and the communications with another, because it includes methods called from outside the class. When the RFC is larger, more complexity has the system, because it is possible to invoke more methods as answers to a message, with larger understanding, which involve more time and effort of testing and debugging.
- *Granularity level:* class, program, system.
- *Life cycle:* design.
- *Related with:* coupling.

12.7.3.2 Weighted Methods Per Class (WMC)

Consider a class C1, with methods M1, ..., Mn and c1, ..., cn the complexity of the methods. WMC is defined as the sum of the complexity of each method in a class. If all methods are considered the same complexity, then c1 = 1 and WMC = n (number of methods).

- *Valuation:* describe the algorithm complexity of a class in terms of the complexity of all his methods. It is linked with the quality of the complexity method definition (ci). The authors simplify it, assigning 1 to each method, then it is a counter of methods number in a class.
- *Granularity level:* class, program, system.
- *Life cycle:* design

12.7.3.3 Average (V(G))

Average is the ciclomatic complexity average of the methods in the class. The ciclomatic complexity v(G) of a method is the number of independent ways in the method. In structured methods, v(G)= number of decision nodes plus one.

- *Valuation:* is a measure of structural complexity. The measure in more complex methods is the maximum ciclomatic complexity (Maximum v(G)). It is useful to know the diifficult of testing and maintenance of a program.
- *Granularity level:* class, program, system.
- *Life cycle:* implementation.

12.7.4 Encapsulation

Information hiding is a way of designing routines such that only a subset of the module's properties, its public interface, is known to users of the module. Information hiding gives rise to encapsulation in object-oriented languages. Encapsulation means that all that is seen of an object is its interface, namely the operations we can perform on the object. Information hiding is a theoretical technique that indisputably proven its value in practice. Large programs that use information hiding have been found to be easier to modify — by a factor of 4 — than programs that don't.

12.7.4.1 Method Hiding Factor (MHF)

MHF is the proportion between the invisibility degree of methods in all classes and the total number of defined methods in the system. Method invisibility degree is the percentage over the total number of classes from where a method is not visible. It is to say, MHF is the proportion between the protected and private methods and the total number of methods.

- *Valuation:* MHF is proposed as a measured encapsulation, relative amount of hiding information. When MHF is increased, density of faults and the needed effort to correct them should decrease. Inheritance methods are not considered.
- *Granularity level:* class.
- *Life cycle:* implementation.

12.7.4.2 Attribute Hiding Factor (AHF)

AHF is the proportion between the invisibility degree of attributes in all classes and the total number of defined attributes in the system. The invisibility degree of an attribute is the percentage over the total number of classes from where an attribute is not visible. It is to say, AHF is the proportion between the protected and private attributes and the total number of attributes.

- *Valuation:* Ideally this metric value should always be 100%, trying to hide all the attributes. Public attributes should not be used, because it violates the encapsulation principles. To improve the performance, sometimes it is avoided the use of methods that access or modify attributes directly.
- *Granularity level:* class.
- *Life cycle:* implementation.

12.7.5 Inheritance

The inheritance use has to be shown as a compromise between the ease of re-usability that it provides and the ease of understanding and maintenance. High inheritance levels show complex objects, which can be difficult to testing and reusing. Low inheritance levels could show that the code is written in a functional way, without use the inheritance property provided by the object oriented programming.

12.7.5.1 Method Inheritance Factor (MIF)

MIF is the proportion between the sum of all inherited methods in all classes and the total number of methods (locally defined plus inherited methods) in all classes.

- *Valuation:* is an indicator of the re-usability level. It is proposed as a help to evaluate the amount of resources needed to testing.
- *Granularity level:* class, program, system.
- *Life cycle:* design, implementation.
- *Related with:* re-usability.

12.7.5.2 Attribute Inheritance Factor (AIF)

AIF is the proportion between the number of inheritance attributes and the total number of attributes.

- *Valuation:* is an indicator of the re-usability level.
- *Granularity level:* class, program, system.
- *Life cycle:* design, implementation.
- *Related with:* re-usability.

12.7.5.3 Specialisation Index Per Class (SIX)

SIX shows how the subclasses redefine the behaviour of the super-classes.

- *Valuation:* when frameworks are used, some methods has to be redefined: these methods has not to be taken in account when this metric is calculated. SIX is proposed as a inheritance quality measure. SIX can shows when there are too much redefined methods, in a way that some abstractions have to change their behaviour. In general, a sub-class should extend the behaviour of the superclass with new methods instead of modify the existing methods, redefining them.
- *Granularity level:* class.
- *Life cycle:* design, implementation.

12.7.5.4 Depth of Inheritance (DIT)

DIT measure the maximum level in inheritance hierarchy. It is the count of the levels in the inheritance hierarchy. In level zero there is the root class.

- *Valuation:* DIT is proposed as a complexity class measure, design complexity and potential re-usability, because when a class is more depth in the hierarchy, higher is the probability of inherit more methods. Systems built from frameworks often show high inheritance levels, because the classes are built from an existing hierarchy. In languages as Java or Smalltalk, classes always inherit from Object class, which plus one to DIT.
- *Granularity level:* class.
- *Life cycle:* design.

12.7.6 Polymorphism: Polymorphism Factor (POF)

POF is the proportion between the real number of possible polymorph situation for a class Ci and the maximum number of possible polymorph situations in Ci. It is to say, it is the number of inherited redefined methods divided by the maximum number of possible polymorph situations.

- *Valuation:* POF is a polymorphism measure and it is an indirect measure of dynamic association in a system. Polymorphism is due to inheritance. In some cases, overloading methods reduces the complexity, and then, it is increased the ease of maintenance and understanding of the system.
- *Granularity level:* class.
- *Life cycle:* design, implementation.
- *Related with:* inheritance.

12.7.7 Re-Usability: Number of Children (NOC)

NOC is the number of subordinate subclasses in a class hierarchy, it is to say, the amount of subclasses that belong to a class.

- *Valuation:* it is an indicator of re-usability level, the possibility of create mistaken abstractions, and it is and indicator of required testing. A high number of children require more testing in the method of this class, and a high difficulty to modify a class, because it influences in all the children of this class. Classes in a high level of the hierarchy should have more subclasses than the classes in a lower level in the hierarchy. NOC may be an indicator of the mistaken use of inheritance. It is a potential indicator of the influence than a class can have over the system design. If the system depends a lot of re-usability by inheritance, maybe would be better to divide the functionality in some classes.
- *Granularity level:* class.
- *Life cycle:* design.

12.7.8 SIZE: Lines of Code Per Method (LOC)

LOC is the number of active lines of code (executable lines) in a method.

- *Valuation:* the method size is used to evaluate the understanding ease, re-usability capacity and maintenance ease of code. It depends on the programming language and the methods complexity. In object oriented systems the lines of code number should be low. It is not a recommended metric to use in object oriented systems, but it is easy to get and use.
- *Granularity level:* method, class, program, system.
- *Life cycle:* implementation.

12.7.8.1 Number of Messages Send (NOM)

- NOM measure the number of sent messages in a method, classified by the message type. Types:
  - Unary: messages without arguments.
  - Binary: messages with one argument which belongs to a special type.
  - Password: messages with one or more arguments.

- *Valuation:* NOM quantifies the method size of a slant way. A high value can show functional style and/or poor responsibility assignment.
- *Granularity level:* method.
- *Life cycle:* implementation.

The figure 12.2 below summarizes the metrics discussed above. It illustrates, in general, whether a high or low value is desired from a metric for better code quality. However, one still must exercise judgment when determining the best approach for the task at hand.

Metric	Desirable value
Coupling Factor	Lower
Lack of Cohesion of Methods	Lower
Cyclomatic Complexity	Lower
Attribute Hiding Factor	Higher
Method Hiding Factor	Higher
Depth of Inheritance Tree	Low (tradeoff)
Number of Children	Low (tradeoff)
Weighted Methods Per Class	Low (tradeoff)
Number of Classes	Higher
Lines of Code	Lower

Figure 12.2: Summary of Metrics

12.8 TESTING COVERAGE METRICS

It is oriented to white-box testing. There are some types:

- **Sentences set coverage:** is the ratio of executed sentences set by testing set to total number of program sentences. A sentences set is a piece of code which is executed sequentially, without branches.
- **Branches coverage:** is the ratio of the number of branches in the testing set to total number of program branches.
- **Ways coverage:** any set of sentences defined by the control flow is a possible way.
- **Data flow coverage:** is the ratio of pairs variables definition-use and data structures in the testing set to total number of pairs definition-use of the program.

Testing has to be designed with the goal of find the maximum number of faults with the minimum amount of effort and time. But in object oriented, traditional coverage is not enough, because when a method is inherited by a class is necessary an additional test.

Polymorphism and encapsulation are main characteristics of object oriented design, and coverage metrics have to consider these characteristics in the software testing. An extension to traditional structural coverage in the form of object oriented context coverage is shown here, being divided in three types:

12.8.1 Inheritance Context Coverage (ICC)

ICC considers the methods execution in the base class context and in all derived classes context.

- *Valuation:* it helps to measure if the polymorphed calls in the system have been tested correctly. Harrold proposes the execution of hierarchical integration testing (HIT), that as the first step executes all methods in the context of a particular class. This proposal has effect in all classes, of such way that redefinitions of a method in a derived class (overload method) are tested with the same detail level that the original base class
- *Granularity level:* method, class.
- *Life cycle:* implementation.

12.8.2 State-Based Context Coverage (SCC)

SCC considers the method execution in the class context which are described as state machines, which behaviour depends on particular state in each moment.

- *Valuation:* it helps to measure if have been done coverage testing for each possible state in a class. A difficulty in implementation used to be the non-availability of actual class state, and usually the code should be changed in order to the class returns the possible states.
- *Granularity level:* class.
- *Life cycle:* implementation.

12.8.3 Multi-Threaded Context Coverage (UCC)

UCC considers the method execution in the multi-threaded context, maintaining coverage information for each thread.

- *Valuation:* if allows to apply the context coverage approach in other cases in which traditional coverage is not appropriate.
- *Granularity level:* class.
- *Life cycle:* implementation.

12.9 GOAL QUESTION METRIC

Basili developed GQM (Goal Question Metric) approach. This approach was originally defined for evaluating defects for a set of projects in the NASA Goddard Space Flight Center environment. It provides a framework involving three steps:

1. List major goals of the development or maintenance project.
2. Derive from each goal the questions that must be answered to determine if the goals are being met.
3. Decide what must be measured in order to be able to answer the questions adequately.

He has also provided a series of templates which are useful for designers. The goals of GQM can be expressed by means of a template which covers purpose, perspective and environment; a set of guidelines also proposed for driving question and metrics. The following discussion is a summary of basili's.

12.9.1 Purpose

The purpose template is to articulate what is being analyzed, for example it is used to characterize, evaluate, predict, motivate from the process, product, model, and metric. This template also expresses what purpose it will be used. For example, a designer might want to evaluate the maintenance process in order to improve.

12.9.2 Perspective

The perspective template focuses on the factors which are important within the process or product that is being evaluated, for example cost, effectiveness, correctness, defects, changes, product measures, maintainability, testability, usability. Customers and developers are the main two perspective of software development process. A developer might examine the cost from the viewpoint of the manager.

12.9.3 Environment

The environment template consists of the process factors, people factors, problem factors, methods, tools constraints as for example the type of the computer system that is being used, the skills of the stuff involves, the amount of trained resource available. For example, the maintenance staffs are poorly motivated programmers who have limited access to tools.

When the purpose, perspective and environment of a goal have been specified, the process of questioning and metric development can begin. As for example, an application of the template for the goal definition is as follow.

Purpose:

Analyze: design documents

For the purpose of: evaluation

Perspective:

From the view point of: developer

With respect to: correctness

Environment:

In the following context: academy, master thesis

***Figure** 12.3: Goal Template*

The result of the application of the GQM approach application is the specification of a measurement system targeting a particular set of issues and a set of rules for the interpretation of the measurement data. The GQM approach has three levels as follows:

1. **GOAL** (Conceptual level): A goal is defined for an object, for a variety of reasons, with respect to various models of quality, from various points of view, relative to a particular environment. Objects of measurement are products, processes and resources.
2. **QUESTION** (Operational level): A set of questions is used to characterize the way the assessment/achievement of a specific goal is going to be performed based on some characterizing model.
3. **METRIC** (Quantitative level): A set of data is associated with every question in order to answer it in a quantitative way. The data can be objectives and subjective.
   - This data is said to be objective if they depend only on the object that is being measured and not on the viewpoint from which they are taken. For example, number of versions of a document, staff hours spent on a task, size of a program.
   - The data is said to be subjective if they depend on both the object that is being measured and the viewpoint from which they are taken. For example, readability of a text, level of user satisfaction.

The GQM approach define some goals, refine those goals into a set of questions, and the questions are further refined into metrics. Consider the following figure 12.4, for a particular question; G1 and G2 are two goals, Q2 in common for both of these goals. Metric M2 is required by all three questions. The main idea of GQM is that each metric identified is placed within a context, so metric M1 is collected in order to answer question Q1 to help achieve the goal G1.

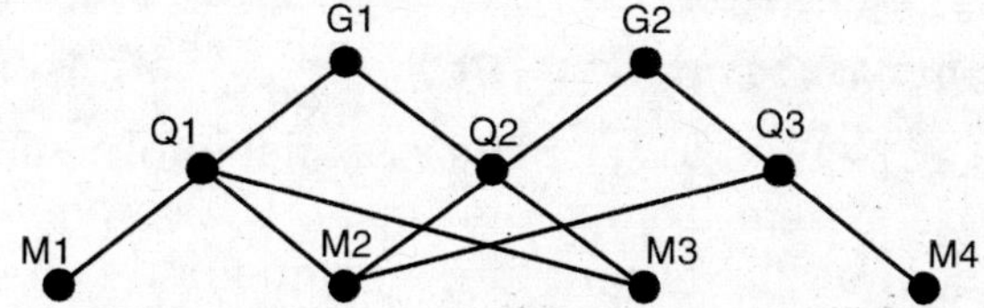

Figure 12.4: *Goal-Question-Metrics hierarchy*

Consider a goal is to evaluate the effectiveness of using a coding standard. To decide if the standard is effective, we have to check some questions. A question might be 'who is using the standard' because it is important to know what proportion of coders is using the standard. The metric might be the proportion of coders using the standard, and so on. A number of measurements may be needed to answer a single question; on the other hand, a single measurement may be applied to more than one question. The following figure 12.5 shows how different metrics might be generated from a single goal.

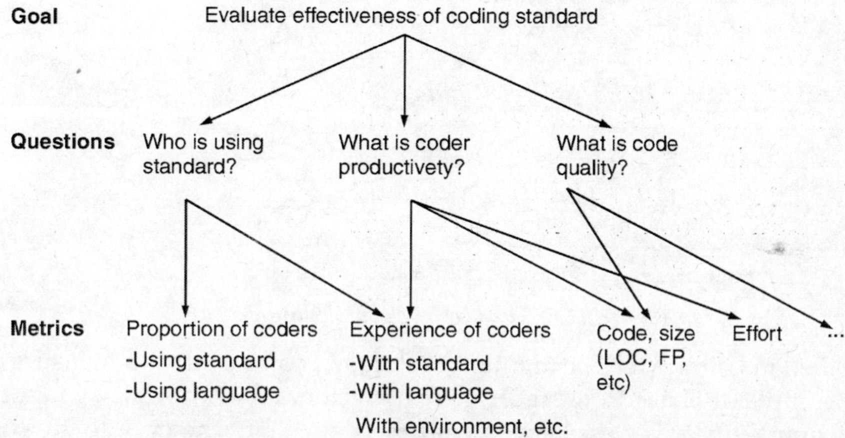

Figure 12.5: *Example of deriving metrics from goal and questions.*

12.10 METRICS FOR OO DESIGN MODEL

A significant number of object oriented metrics have been developed in literature. For example, metrics proposed by Abreu, C.K metrics, Li and Henry metrics, MOOD metrics, Lorenz and Kidd metrics etc. C.K metrics are the most popular (used) among them. Another comprehensive set of metrics is MOOD metrics. This subsection will focus on traditional metrics and above mention metrics (mainly C.K and MOOD metrics).

12.10.1 Traditional Metrics

In an object-oriented system, traditional metrics are generally applied to the methods that comprise the operations of a class. Methods reflect how a problem is broken into segments. Traditional metrics have been applied for the measurement of software complexity of structured systems since 1976. The following discussion shows three popular traditional metrics.

12.10.1.1 McCabe Cyclomatic Complexity (CC)

Complexity metrics can be used to calculate essential information about constancy and maintainability of software system from source code. It also provides advice during the software project to help control the design. In the testing and maintain phase, complexity metrics provide detail information about software module to identify the areas of possible instability.

Cyclomatic complexity (McCabe) can be used to evaluate the complexity of a method. This metric measures the complexity of a control flow graph of a method or procedure. The idea is to draw the sequence a program may take as a graph with all possible paths. The complexity is calculated as "connections – nodes + 2" and will give a number denoting how complex the method is. See the following figure 12.6. Since complexity will increase the possibility of errors, a too high McCabe number should be avoided.

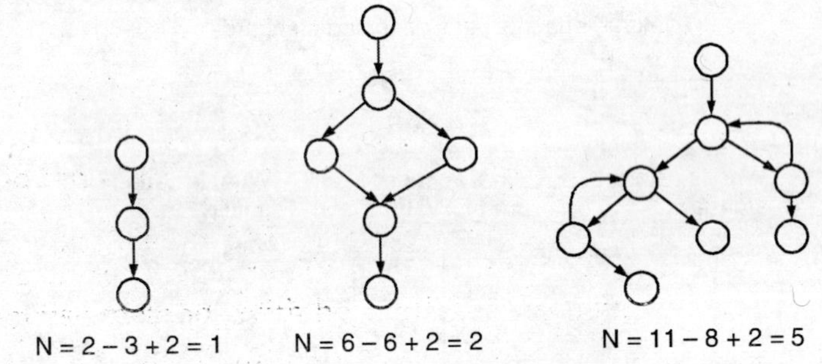

Figure 12.6: The McCabe complexity metrics

As described in Laing, McCabe mention cyclomatic complexity is a measure of a module control flow complexity based on graph theory. Cyclomatic complexity cannot be used to measure the complexity of a class because of inheritance, but the cyclomatic complexity of individual methods can be combined with other measures to evaluate the complexity of the class. A high cyclomatic complexity indicates that the code may be of low quality and difficult to test and maintain.

12.10.1.2 Source Lines of Code (SLOC)

SLOC is used to estimate the total effort that will be needed to develop a program, as well as to calculate approximate productivity. The SLOC metric measures the number of physical lines of active code, that is, no blank or commented lines code. Logical SLOC measures the number of statements, but their specific definitions are fixed to specific language for example, in C programming language logical SLOC measure the terminating semicolon.

Since functionality is not as much interconnected with SLOC, expert developers may be capable to develop the same functionality with less code. So one program with less SLOC may show more functionalities than another similar program. Programs with larger SLOC values usually take more time to develop. Therefore, SLOC can be very effective in estimating effort. Thresholds for evaluating the SLOC measures vary depending on the coding language used and the complexity of the method.

12.10.1.3 Comment Percentage (CP)

The CP metric is defined as the number of commented lines of code divided by the number of non-blank lines of code. The comment percentage is calculated by the total number of comments divided by the total lines of code less the number of blank lines. The SATC has found a comment percentage of about 30% is most effective.

12.10.2 Chidamber and Kemerer Metrics Model

Chidamber and Kemerer define the so called CK metric suite. This metric suite offers informative insight into whether developers are following object oriented principles in their design. They claim that using several of their metrics collectively helps managers and designers to make better design decision. CK metrics have generated a significant amount of interest and are currently the most well-known suite of measurements for OO software. Chidamber and Kemerer proposed six metrics; the following discussion shows their metrics.

12.10.2.1 Weighted Method Per Class (WMC)

WMC measures the complexity of a class. Complexity of a class can for example be calculated by the cyclomatic complexities of its methods. High value of WMC indicates the class is more complex than that of low values. So class with less WMC is better. As WMC is complexity measurement metric, we can get an idea of required effort to maintain a particular class.

12.10.2.2 Depth of Inheritance Tree (DIT)

DIT metric is the length of the maximum path from the node to the root of the tree. So this metric calculates how far down a class is declared in the inheritance hierarchy. The following figure 12.7 shows the value of DIT for a simple class hierarchy. This metric also measures how many ancestor classes can potentially affect this class. DIT represents the complexity of the behaviour of a class, the complexity of design of a class and potential reuse.

If DIT increases, it means that more methods are to be expected to be inherited, which makes it more difficult to calculate a class's behavior. Thus it can be hard to understand a system with many inheritance layers. On the other hand, a large DIT value indicates that many methods might be reused.

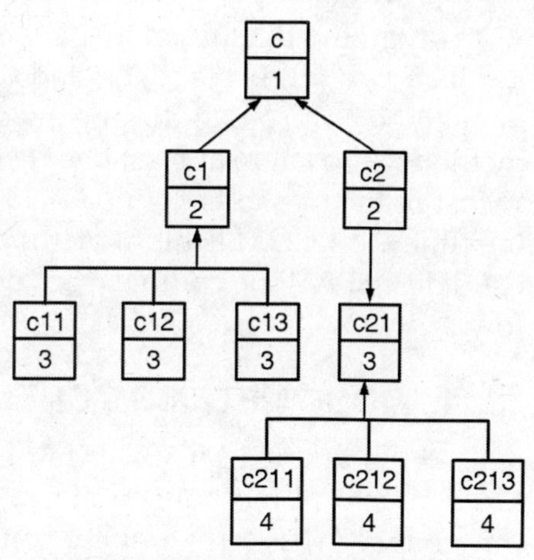

Figure 12.7: The value of DIT for the class hierarchy

12.10.2.3 Number of Children (NOC)

This metric measures how many sub-classes are going to inherit the methods of the parent class. As shown in above figure12.7, class C1 has three children, subclasses C11, C12, and C13. The size of NOC approximately indicates the level of reuse in an application. If NOC grows it means reuse increases. On the other hand, as NOC increases, the amount of testing will also increase because more children in a class indicate more responsibility. So, NOC represents the effort required to test the class and reuse.

12.10.2.4 Coupling Between Objects (CBO)

The idea of this metrics is that an object is coupled to another object if two object act upon each other. A class is coupled with another if the methods of one class use the methods or attributes of the other class. An increase of CBO indicates the reusability of a class will decrease. Thus, the CBO values for each class should be kept as low as possible. CBO metric measure the required effort to test the class.

12.10.2.5 Response for a Class (RFC)

RFC is the number of methods that can be invoked in response to a message in a class. Pressman States, since RFC increases, the effort required for testing also increases because the test sequence grows. If RFC increases, the overall design complexity of the class increases and becomes hard to understand. On the other hand lower values indicate greater polymorphism. The value of RFC can be from 0 to 50 for a class, some cases the higher value can be 100- it depends on project to project.

12.10.2.6 Lack of Cohesion in Methods (LCOM)

This metric uses the notion of degree of similarity of methods. LCOM measures the amount of cohesiveness present, how well a system has been designed and how complex a class is. LCOM is a count of the number of method pairs whose similarity is zero, minus the count of method pairs whose similarity is not zero.

Raymond discussed for example, a class C with 3 methods M_1, M_2, and M_3. Let I_1 = {a, b, c, d, e}, I_2= {a, b, e}, and I_3= {x, y, z}, where I_1 is the set of instance variables used by method M_1. So two disjoint set can be found: $I_1 \cap I_2$ (= {a, b, e}) and I3. Here, one pair of methods who share at least one instance variable (I_1 and I_2). So LCOM = 2 – 1 =1. Riel states "Most of the methods defined on a class should be using most of the data members most of the time". If LCOM is high, methods may be coupled to one another via attributes and then class design will be complex. So, designers should keep cohesion high, that is, keep LCOM low.

12.11 MOOD METRICS MODEL

Abreu defined MOOD (Metrics for Object Oriented Design) metrics. MOOD refers to a basic structural mechanism of the object-oriented paradigm as encapsulation (MHF, AHF), inheritance (MIF, AIF), polymorphism (POF), and message passing (COF). Each metrics is expressed as a measure where the numerator represents the actual use of one of those feature for a given design. In MOOD metrics model, two main features are used in every metrics; they are methods and attributes. Methods are used to perform operations of several kinds such as obtaining or modifying the status of objects.

Attributes are used to represent the status of each object in the system. Each feature (methods and attributes) is either visible or hidden from a given class. We will discuss MOOD metrics in the context of encapsulation, inheritance, polymorphism, and coupling. These are discussed below.

12.11.1 Encapsulation

The Method Hiding Factor (MHF) and Attribute Hiding Factor (AHF) were proposed together as measure of encapsulation. MHF and AHF represent the average amount of hiding between all classes in the system.

12.11.1.1 Method Hiding Factor (MHF)

The MHF metric states the sum of the invisibilities of all methods in all classes. The invisibility of a method is the percentage of the total class from which the method is hidden. Abreu States, the MHF denominator is the total number of methods defined in the system under consideration. The MHF metric is defined as follows:

$$\text{MHF} = \sum_{i=1}^{TC} M_h(C_i) / \sum_{i=1}^{TC} M_d(C_i)$$

Here, $M_d(C_i) = M_v(C_i) + M_h(C_i)$

$M_d(C_i)$ = the number of methods defined in class Ci

$M_v(C_i)$ = the number of methods that visible in the class Ci

$M_h(C_i)$ = the number of methods hidden in Ci

Where the summation occurs over i=1 to TC. TC is defined as total number of classes.

If the value of MHF is high (100%), it means all methods are private which indicates very little functionality. Thus it is not possible to reuse methods with high MHF. MHF with low (0%) value indicate all methods are public that means most of the methods are unprotected.

12.11.1.2 Attribute Hiding Factor (AHF)

The AHF metric shows the sum of the invisibilities of all attributes in all classes. The invisibility of an attribute is the percentage of the total classes from which this attribute is hidden. MHF and AHF represent the average amount of hiding among all classes in the system. The AHF metric is defined as follows.

$$\text{AHF} = \sum_{i=1}^{TC} A_h(C_i) / \sum_{i=1}^{TC} A_d(C_i)$$

Here, $A_d(C_i) = A_v(C_i) + A_h(C_i)$

$A_d(C_i)$ = the number of attributes defined in class Ci

$A_v(C_i)$ = the number of attributes that visible in the class Ci

$A_h(C_i)$ = the number of attributes hidden in Ci

Where the summation occurs over i=1 to TC. TC is defined as total number of classes.

If the value of AHF is high (100%), it means all attributes are private. AHF with low (0%) value indicates all attributes are public.

12.11.2 Inheritance

Inherited features in a class are those which are inherited and not overridden in that class. Method Inheritance Factor (MIF) and Attribute Inheritance Factor (AIF) are proposed to measure inheritance.

12.11.2.1 Method Inheritance Factor (MIF)

The MIF metric states the sum of inherited methods in all classes of the system under consideration. The degree to which the class architecture of an object oriented system makes use of inheritance for both methods and attributes. MIF is defined as the ratio of the sum of the inherited methods in all classes of the system as follow.

$$\text{MIF} = \sum_{i=1}^{TC} M_i(C_i) / \sum_{i=1}^{TC} M_a(C_i)$$

Here, $M_a(C_i) = M_d(C_i) + M_i(C_i)$

$M_a(C_i)$ = the number of Methods defined in class Ci

$M_d(C_i)$ = the number of Methods declared in the class Ci

$M_i(C_i)$ = the number of Methods inherited in Ci

Where the summation occurs over i=1 to TC. TC is defined as total number of classes.

If the value of MIF is low (0%), it means that there is no methods exists in the class as well as the class lacking an inheritance statement.

12.11.2.2 Attribute Inheritance Factor (AIF)

AIF is defined as the ratio of the sum of inherited attributes in all classes of the system. AIF denominator is the total number of available attributes for all classes. It is defined in an analogous manner and provides an indication of the impact of inheritance in the object oriented software. AIF is defined as follows

$$\text{AIF} = \sum_{i=1}^{TC} A_i(C_i) / \sum_{i=1}^{TC} A_a(C_i)$$

Here, $A_a(C_i) = A_d(C_i) + A_i(C_i)$

$A_a(C_i)$ = the number of available attributes defined in class Ci

$A_d(C_i)$ = the number of attributes that declared in the class Ci

$A_i(C_i)$ = the number of inherited inherited in Ci

Where the summation occurs over i=1 to TC. TC is defined as total number of classes.

If the value of AIF is low (0%), it means that there is no attribute exists in the class as well as the class lacking an inheritance statement.

12.11.3 Polymorphism

Polymorphism is an important characteristic in object oriented paradigm. Polymorphism measure the degree of overriding in the class inheritance tree.

12.11.3.1 Polymorphism Factor (POF)

The POF represents the actual number of possible different polymorphic situation. It also represents the maximum number of possible distinct polymorphic situation for class Ci. The POF is defined as follows.

$$\text{POF} = \sum_{i=1}^{TC} M_0(C_i) / \sum_{i=1}^{TC} [M_n(C_i) * DC(C_i)]$$

Here, $M_0(C_i) = M_n(C_i) + M_0(C_i)$
$M_n(C_i)$ = the number of new methods defined in class Ci
$M_0(C_i)$ = the number of overriding methods in the class Ci
$DC(C_i)$ = the descendants count in Ci

The numerator represents the actual number of possible different polymorphic situation and the denominator represents the maximum number of possible distinct polymorphic situation for class Ci. The value of POF can be varies between 0% and 100%. If a project have 0% POF, it indicates the project uses no polymorphism and 100% POF indicates that all methods are overridden in all derived classes.

12.11.4 Coupling

Coupling shows the relationship between modules. A class is coupled to another class if it calls methods of another class.

12.11.4.1 Coupling Factor (COF)

The COF is defined as the ratio of the maximum possible number of couplings in the system to the actual number of coupling is not imputable to inheritance. The COF is defined as follows.

$$\text{COF} = \sum_{i=1}^{TC} \left[\sum_{i=1}^{TC} \text{is\_client}(C_i, C_j) \right] / (TC^2 - TC^2)$$

Here is_client (Ci,Cj) = 1 if and only if, a relationship exists between the client class, Cc and the server class Cs and Cc not equal to Cs.

And is_client (Ci,Cj) = 0, otherwise Where the summation occurs over i=1 to TC. TC is defined as total number of classes.

Pressman argues that, although many factors affect software complexity, understandability, and maintainability. It is reasonable to conclude that as "the COF value" increases, the complexity of object oriented design will also increase, and as a result the understandability, maintainability, and the potential for reuse may suffer. The value of COF can be varies between 0% and 100%. 0% COF indicates no classes are coupled and 100% COF indicates all classes are coupled with all other classes. High values of COF should be avoided.

The idea in COF metric is as same idea used in CBO metrics because they both use coupling factor. The main difference between COF and CBO is, in COF metric all variable accesses are counted whereas CBO metric does not count variables.

12.12 LORENZ AND KIDD´S METRICS

Lorenz and Kidd proposed a group of metrics called "design metrics", which deal with the static characteristics of software design.

Table 12.2: Design Metrics Suite by Lorenz and Kidd

Method size	Number of messages sent Number of statements Lines of code Average method size
Method internals	Method complexity Strings of message sent
Class size	Number of public instance methods Number of instance methods Average number of instance methods Number of instance variables Average number of instance variables Number of static methods Number of static variables
Class inheritance	Class hierarchy nesting level Number of abstract classes Use of multiple inheritance
Method inheritance	Number of methods overriden by a subclass Number of methods inherited by a subclass Number of methods added by a subclass Specialization index
Class internals	Class cohesion Global usage Average number of parameters per method Use of friend functions Percentage of function-oriented code Average number of comment lines per method Average number of commented method Number of problem reports per class
Class externals	Class coupling Number of times a class is reused Number of classes/methods thrown away

12.12.1 Method Size

A method's size can be measured in many ways. Lorenz and Kidd show four different ways of quantifying an individual method in a class. These include traditional LOC, but also message passing is considered.

1. **Number of message-sends (NMS)**: The metric is designed to measure the size of a method. According to its authors, NMS measures the size of the method in a rather unbiased way as it is unaffected by developer style. Its authors state that the messages should be segregated by type of message. They define three types of messages, viz., unary (without parameters), binary (with one parameter), and keyword (with more than one parameter). Its authors do not explain how the message type is to be integrated into the metric. Only one number is generated and only one threshold is given by its authors. Therefore, assume that all message types are to be treated the same. NMS is a positive integer and ranges from 0 to *N* where *N* is a count of the outgoing messages without regard to type.
   NMS is presented as a rather unbiased measure of method size. Three types of messages are listed but not differentiated by the authors. If the measurer can accept that the method size is not influenced by the type of message, NMS may be used as a ratio scale.
2. **Number of statements (NOS):** The number of statement metric measure the size of a method code in a less biased manner.
3. **Lines of code (LOC):** The lines of code metric measure the number of lines of active code that are in a method.
4. **Average method size:** The average method size metric is one indication of the quality of the design from an object perspective.

12.12.2 Method Internals

Method internals describe the internal characteristics of methods in a class. Traditional complexity metrics are first discussed and then a new approach is taken.

1. **Method complexity (MC):** This metric is used for computing the complexity. It involves length of method, number of arguments, coupling to other methods, etc.
2. **Strings of message-sends (SMS)**: SMS is presented by its authors as a measure of complexity even though they state that they are unsure of the usefulness of this metric. SMS is a count of the number of messages strung together each feeding the next with an intermediate result. This form of coding makes intelligent error recovery more difficult. SMS ranges from 1 to N, where N is a positive integer. The complexity that SMS proposes to measure is that caused by the links among message calls inherent in strings of message calls. Instead of counting the message calls, this measure would better gauge complexity if the links were counted. Call this new measure string of message links (SML). SML possesses a natural zero which is missing from the original measure. This new metric would fit the ratio scale but SMS does not.

12.12.3 Class Size

The size of a class can be measured in many ways. Lorenz and Kidd list different approaches: methods vs. variables, public vs. private, static vs. instance.

1. **Number of Public Instance Methods in a Class:** Number of Public Instance Methods in a Class (PIM) is defined as the total number of public instance methods in a class. Public methods are those that are available as services to other classes. The number of public instance methods in a class is a good measure of the amount of responsibility in the class. It helps in estimating the amount of work needed to develop a class.
2. **Number of Instance Methods in a Class:** The Number of Instance Methods in a Class (NIM) counts all the public, protected, and private methods defined for class´ instances. The number of methods in a class relates to the amount of collaboration being used. Larger classes may be trying to do too much of the work themselves instead of putting the responsibilities where they belong. They are more complex and harder to maintain. Smaller classes tend to be more reusable, since they provide one set of cohesive services instead of a mixed set of capabilities. It suggests examining patterns of instance variable usage to see if there are useful ways to split the class.
3. **Number of Instance Variables in a Class:** The Number of Instance Variables in a Class (NIV) is defined as the total number of instance variables in a class. Instance variables include private and protected variables available to the instances. The fact that a class has more instance variables indicates that the class has more relationships to other objects in the system. It suggests that classes are more reusable when they have fewer instance variables.
4. **Number of Class Methods in a Class:** The Number of Class Methods in a Class (NCM) is defined as the total number of class methods in a class. A class method is a method that is global to its instances. This number should generally be relatively small compared to the number of instance methods. The number of class methods can indicate the amount of commonality being handled for all instances.
5. **Number of Class Variables in a Class:** The Number of Class Variables in a Class (NCV) is defined as the total number of class variables in a class. Class variables are often used to provide customizable constant values that are used to affect the behaviour of all the instances. The average number of class variables should be low. In general there should be fewer class variables than instance variables.
6. **Average number of instance methods per class (AIM)**: The parent (NIM) can be assigned to a ratio scale and the average (AIM) may also be assigned to a ratio scale.
7. **Average number of instance variables per class (AIV)**: The parent metric (NIV) can be assigned to a ratio scale and the average (AIV) may also be assigned to a ratio scale.

12.12.4 Class Inheritance

Inheritance is one of the core concepts of OO paradigm, so many metrics can be evolved around it. These metrics deal, like DIT and NOC by CK, with classes inheriting other classes.

1. **Class hierarchy nesting level (HNL)**: HNL has been proposed as an indicator of complexity. HNL is a surrogate for the number of ancestor classes that could affect a class.

   It suggests:

   (1) the deeper a class resides in the hierarchy the more methods it is likely to inherit and

(2) the more methods inherited by a class, the more difficult it is to predict its behavior. It seems reasonable that complexity increases (decreases) as classes are added to (deleted from) an existing hierarchy chart. However, let the new class be added as a subclass of B or C and the program's maximum HNL does not increase. The measurer must decide if the complexity of the program increased. HNL has other problems which would keep it from becoming other than a nominal scale. HNL within a given project tend to cluster around one level and thus fail to discriminate one class from another.

2. **Number of abstract classes:** An abstract class exists to facilitate reuse of methods and state data among its subclasses. The number of abstract classes is an indication of the successful usage of inheritance and the effort that has been spent looking for general concepts in the problem domain.
3. **Use of multiple inheritance (MUI)**: MUI is presented as a measure of complexity. Their assertion that multiple inheritance should be avoided could lead us to treat MUI as a dichotomous indicator which gets set on whenever multiple inheritance is present within a project. Of course it would also be possible to count the classes which have more than one superclass. Since a dichotomous indicator is looked at elsewhere and all dichotomous indicators function identically, the later definition for MUI will be assumed. MUI ranges from 0 to N where N is a positive integer. It admits that there have been times when allowing multiple inheritance would have allowed them to construct a "(seemingly) more elegant design."

12.12.5 Method Inheritance

CK metrics didn't take into account how methods are involved in inheritance. These metrics count the number of overriden, inherited and added methods.

1. **Number of Methods Overridden:** The Number of Methods Overridden metric (NMO) is defined as the total number of methods overridden by a subclass. A subclass is allowed to define a method of the same name as a method in one of its superclasses. This is called overriding the method. This metric looks at the quality of the classes' use of inheritance. It examines superclass-subclass inheritance relationships. A large number of overridden methods indicate a design problem.
2. **Number of Methods Inherited:** The Number of Methods Inherited metric (NMI) is defined as the total number of method inherited by a subclass. This metric looks at the quality of the classes' use of inheritance. It examines superclass-subclass inheritance relationships. The number of methods inherited from superclasses indicates the strength of subclassing by specialization.
3. **Number of Methods Added:** The Number of Methods Added (NMA) is defined as the total number of methods defined in a subclass. This metric looks at the quality of the classes´use of inheritance. It examines superclass-subclass inheritance relationships. Subclasses should define new methods, extending the behaviour of the superclasses. A class with no methods is certainly questionable. The number of new methods should usually decrease as you move down through the layers of the hierarchy.
4. **Specialisation Index:** The Specialisation Index (SIX) for each class is defined thus:

(Number of overridden Methods × Hierarchy Nesting level) / Total number of Methods

This metric looks at the quality of the classes´use of inheritance. The specialisation index measures to what extent subclasses redefine the behaviour of their superclasses. This weighted calculation has done a good job on identifying classes worth looking at for their placement in the inheritance hierarchy and for design problems.

12.12.6 Class Intervals

This set of metrics looks at the design of the classes' internals - how they use their instance variables, what external referenced they make, and so on.

1. **Class cohesion:** The degree to which the methods within a class are related to one another. Here, cohesion is limited to cohesion within a class.
2. **Global usage:** GUS is proposed as a measure of unnecessary coupling. This metric is a count of the total number of global variables in a system. This count includes system variables which are global to the entire system, class variables which are global to the instances of a class, and pool directories which are global to any classes which include them. GUS ranges from 0 to N, where N is a positive integer. Adding a system global variable which potentially affects every class in the system adds as much to GUS as adding a class global variable which effects only the class within which it is declared. Since the system global variable is not counted once for each method which references it (or at least once for each class within the system) it is not weighted, in proportion to its potential impact, relative to a class global variable. Unless one can accept that each system global variable contributes equally with each class global variable to unnecessary coupling, GUS cannot be accepted as an ordinal scale.
3. **Average number of parameters per method (PPM)**: PPM is defined as the total number of method parameters divided by the number of methods. More parameters place a higher burden on the user of the code. PPM is a positive real number and ranges from 0 to N.

   The Average Parameters per Method (APPM) is defined thus:

   Total of Methods Parameters/ Total Number of Methods

   This metric looks at the design of the class´internals. It suggests that parameters require more effort from clients, and high and low numbers of parameters imply a style of design. They also suggest an upper threshold of 0.7 parameters per method.
4. **Use of friend functions:** Some programming languages, such as C++ allow you to write code that breaks the concepts of encapsulation of objects. Friend functions allow encapsulation to be violated. Hey are needed in few cases, such as support for commutative expressions.
5. **Percentage of function-oriented code (FOC)**: FOC is presented by the authors as a measure of possible design problems. This metric is defined as the percentage of code written outside of objects, e.g., the C++ *main ()* routine and other non-member functions. The measurement of the code is left to us; the authors do not elaborate on a measurement procedure. The most obvious measure of code is LOC. Although the name of the metric implies multiplication by 100, there is no apparent benefit in the conversion from proportion to percentage. Therefore, FOC as described in this section is a positive real number and ranges from zero to one.

LOC has been shown to be assignable to a ratio scale. Hence, LOC non object-oriented code can also be assignable to the ratio scale and the proportion FOC can also be assigned to a ratio scale. Functional (non object-oriented) code is required in some languages, e.g., the C++ *main ()* routine. However, functional code should be kept to a minimum. Therefore, FOC should be as small as possible.

6. **Average number of comment lines per method (CLM)**: CLM is presented by its authors as one measure of documentation. CLM is defined as the number of explanatory comments divided by the number of methods. The number of explanatory comments is defined as the total number of comment lines minus comments due to coding convention or automatic insertion. CLM is a positive real number and ranges from 0 to N.

   Explanatory comments are those lines placed in the code not as functional code but to explain the functionality of the method or function. Identifying comments, such as comments which merely report the date or the programmer's name or initials, should not be counted as explanatory comments. When CLM is used as a measure of the documentation of a method, CLM can be used on a ratio scale.
7. **Average number of commented methods (PCM)**: PCM is presented by its authors as one measure of documentation. PCM is more accurately the proportion of methods in the class being measured which contain at least one explanatory comment line. PCM is the number of methods within a class which contain at least one explanatory comment line divided by the total number of methods in the class. This gives the developer an indicator of the completeness of a class' documentation where documentation is defined as the percentage of methods containing explanatory comment lines. PCM is a positive real number and ranges from 0 to 1. PCM may not be assigned to the ordinal scale.
8. **Number of problem reports per class:** Certainly, classes with larger numbers of problem reports against them are candidates for rewrite, due to:
   - Additional unplanned requirements
   - Poor design

12.12.7 Class Externals

This set of metrics describes how classes relate to other classes, subsystems and so on.

1. **Class coupling (CCP):** CCP is the summation of the number of methods within the measured class which access other classes and the number of methods within the measured class which are accessed by other classes. The number of methods within the measured class which both access a method in another class and are accessed by the method in the other class are counted only once. Its authors call this last type of method cooperated methods but they give no example. If co-operated methods are included in the first two counts, the number of methods within the measured class which are cooperated with other classes has to be subtracted from the sum of the first two counts. If a class is entirely self-contained, the CCP for that class is zero. The method coupling metric ranges from 0 to N, where N is a positive integer. It is possible (or even probable) that the inter-object complexity of a class may well be related to the number of inter-object links identified with the class. However, based on the measurement theory

validation of CCP, because CCP cannot account for the methods in one class called by the other class when two classes are merged, CCP is a valid measurement only on the ordinal scale.

2. **Number of times a class is reused:** The amount of software reuse (the reuse level) in a certain software system can be determined by the ratio of reused components (or their lines of code) to the total components of the system (or total amount of code lines). This measure does not consider more subtle aspects like adaptation costs, but it is objective. There are number of ways to count reuse:
   - **White box reuse:** It means reuse of components of which internals are changed for the purpose of reuse. White boxes are typically not reused as is, but by adaptation. They create more opportunities for reusers due to the ease of making arbitrary changes. On the negative side of white-box reuse, it requires additional testing and costlier maintenance.
   - **Black box reuse:** Reusing a component as a black box means using it without seeing, knowing or modifying any of its internals. The component provides an interface that contains all the information necessary for its utilization. The implementation is hidden and cannot be modified by the reuser. Thus reusers get the information about what a component is doing, but they do not have to worry about how this is achieved. The implementation can be changed without any effects on reusers.
3. **Number of classes/methods thrown away (NCT)**: NCT is presented by the authors as a measure of the maturity of the system design. NCT is a count of classes or methods which have been rewritten for a given project. NCT functionality in the form of processing speed, resilience and over-all quality can be realized by throwing away classes and methods which were not designed correctly the first (or subsequent) time. NCT ranges from 0 to *N*, where *N* is a positive integer. Although one might be tempted to argue that small NCT indicates a good initial design, Lorenz and Kidd argue that developers do not get designs correct the first time and part of the design is learning about the domain and building it better the next time. Likewise, one might be tempted to argue that a large NCT indicates poor design or lousy programmers, but Lorenz and Kidd argue that true iterations on designs are essential to the development of elegant solutions.
   - **Goal.** Lorenz and Kidd s metrics were defined to measure the static characteristics of software design, such as the usage of inheritance, the amount of responsibilities in a class, etc.
   - **Theoretical validation.** To our knowledge no work related to the theoretical validation of these metrics has been published.
   - **Empirical validation.** After applying these metrics to 5 real projects (written in Smalltalk and C++), Lorenz and Kidd have provided some recommendations, such as:
     - An inheritance hierarchy that is too shallow or too deep has quality repercussions.
     - No instance methods or too many instance methods can indicate non-optimal allocation of responsibility (related to the NIM metric).

  - Large numbers of instance variables can indicate too much coupling with other classes and reduce reuse (related to the NIV metric).
  - The average number of class variables should be low. In general there should be fewer class variables than instance variables.
  - Too many class methods indicate inappropriate use of classes to do work instead of instances (related to the NCM metric).
  - Overriding methods, especially deeper in the hierarchy, can indicate poor subclassing (related to the NMO metric).
  - Specialization index has done a good job on identifying classes worth looking at, for their placement in the inheritance hierarchy and for design problems.
  - They also suggest an upper threshold of 0.7 parameters per method (related to the APPM metric).
- **Tool.** A tool called OOMetric was developed to collect these metrics, applied to code written in Smalltalk and C++.

12.13 OBJECT ORIENTED APPROACH

One of the problems of any software project is to be able to manage the concepts, flow of control, and data. The solution to this problem may be the object oriented approach, which groups both data and procedures into and entity called and object. These objects allow a programmer, designer, and analyst to examine larger cognitive blocks of a project, and thus clarify the programming process.

12.13.1 Elements of the Object Oriented Approach

The main elements in the object oriented approach are:

- **Identity**. Data is organized in entities called objects.
- **Objects**. Each object has his own identity which distinguish from another one even if both have the same values in their attributes.
- **Classification**. Objects with the same attributes and behaviour are grouped in classes.
- **Class**. A class is an abstraction which describes the important properties of a set of objects for an application.
- **Polymorphism**. The ability of two or more objects to interpret a message differently at execution, depending upon the superclass of the calling object.
- **Inheritance**. A relationship among classes, wherein one class shares the structure or methods defined in one other class or in more than one other class.
- **Abstraction**. The essential characteristics of an object that distinguish it from all other kinds of object.
- **Encapsulation**. The process of bundling together the elements of an abstraction that constitutes its structure and behaviour.
- **Information hiding**. The process of hiding the structure of an object and the implementation details of its methods. An object has a public interface and a private representation; these two elements are kept distinct.
- **Specialization**. Get subclasses from a superclass.

12.14 OBJECT ORIENTED DESIGN

Object oriented design is concerned with developing an object-oriented module of a software system to apply the identified requirements. Designer will use OOD because it is a faster development process, module based architecture, contains high reusable features, increases design quality and so on.

"Object-oriented design is a method of design encompassing the process of objects oriented decomposing and a notation for depicting both logical and physical as well as static and dynamic models of the system under design".

Objects are the basic units of object oriented design. Identity, states and behaviors are the main characteristics of any object. A class is a collection of objects which have common behaviors.

"A class represents a template for several objects and describe how these objects are structured internally. Objects of the same class have the same definition both for their operation and for their information structure".

There are several essential themes in object oriented design. These themes are mostly support object oriented design in the context of measuring. These are discussing in next sub section.

12.14.1 Internal Quality of OOD

Following are the internal qualities of OOD:

12.14.1.1 Cohesion

Cohesion refers to the internal consistency within the parts of the design. Cohesion is centred on data that is encapsulated within an object and on how methods interact with data to provide well-bounded behaviour. A class is cohesive when its parts are highly correlated. It should be difficult to split a cohesive class. Cohesion can be used to identify the poorly designed classes.

"Cohesion measures the degree of connectivity among the elements of a single class or object".

12.14.1.2 Coupling

Coupling indicates the relationship or interdependency between modules. For example, object X is coupled to object Y if and only if X sends a message to Y that means the number of collaboration between classes or the number of messages passed between objects. Coupling is a measure of interconnecting among modules in a software structure.

12.14.1.3 Inheritance

Inheritance is a mechanism whereby one object acquires characteristics from one, or more other objects. Inheritance occurs in all levels of a class hierarchy.

"Inheritance is the sharing of attributes and operations among classes based on a hierarchical relationship".

In general, conventional software does not support this characteristic because it is a pivotal characteristic in many object oriented systems as well as many object oriented metrics focus on it.

12.14.1.4 Encapsulation

Encapsulation is a mechanism to realize data abstraction and information hiding. Encapsulation hides internal specification of an object and show only external interface.

"The process of compartmentalizing the elements of an abstraction that constitute its structure and behaviour; encapsulation serves to separate the contractual interface of an abstraction and its implementation".

Encapsulation influences metrics by changing the focus of measurement from a single module to a package of data.

12.14.1.5 Information Hiding

Booch States that, information hiding is the process of hiding all the secrets of an object that do not contribute to its essential characteristics. An object has a public interface and a private representation; these two elements are kept distinct. Information hiding acts a direct role in such metrics as object coupling and the degree of information hiding.

"All information about a module should be private to the module unless it is specifically declared public".

12.14.1.6 Localization

In object oriented design approach localization is based on objects. In a design, if there is some changes in the localization approach, the total plan will be violated, because one function may involve several objects, and one object may provide many functions. *"Localization is the process of gathering and placing things in close physical proximity to each other".*

Metrics should apply to the class as a complete entity. Even the relationship between functions and classes is not necessarily one-to-one. For that reason, metrics that reflect the manner in which classes collaborate must be capable of accommodating one-to-many and many-to-one relationships.

12.15 PRINCIPLES OF OOD

This section shows some OO design principles, which are used for support in OO design. Object oriented principles advise the designers what to support and what to avoid. We categorized all design principles into three groups in the context of design metrics. These are general principles, cohesion principles, and coupling principles. These principles are collected by Martin. The following discussion is a summary of his principles according to our categories.

12.15.1 General Principles

The Open/Closed Principle (OCP): Open close principle states a module should be open for extension but closed for modification i.e. Classes should be written so that they can be extended without requiring the classes to be modified.

The Liskov Substitution Principle (LSP): Liskov Substitution Principle mention subclasses should be substitutable for their base classes i.e. a user of a base class instance should still function if given an instance of a derived class instead.

The Dependency Inversion Principle (DIP): Dependency Inversion Principle state high level classes should not depend on low level classes i.e. abstractions should not depend upon the details. If the high level abstractions depend on the low level implementation, the dependency is inverted from what it should be.

The Interface Segregation Principle (ISP): Interface Segregation Principle state Clients should not be forced to depend upon interfaces that they do not use. Many client-specific interfaces are better than one general purpose interface.

12.15.2 Cohesion Principles

Reuse/Release Equivalency Principle (REP): The granule of reuse is the granule of release. Only components that are released through a tracking system can be efficiently reused. A reusable software element cannot really be reused in practice unless it is managed by a release system of some kind of release numbers. All related classes must be released together.

Common Reuse Principle (CRP): All classes in a package should be reused together. If reuse one of the classes in the package, reuse them all. Classes are usually reused in groups based on collaborations between library classes.

Common Closure Principle (CCP): The classes in a package should be closed against the same kinds of changes. A change that affects a package affects all the classes in that package. The main Goal of this principle is to limit the dispersion of changes among released packages i.e. changes must affect the smallest number of released packages.

Classes within a package must be cohesive. Given a particular kind of change, either all classes or no class in a component needs to be modified.

12.15.3 Coupling Principles

Acyclic Dependencies Principle (ADP): The dependency structure for a released component must be a Directed Acyclic Graph (DAG) and there can be no cycles.

Stable Dependencies Principle (SDP): The dependencies between components in a design should be in the direction of stability. A component should only depend upon components that are more stable than it is.

Stable Abstractions Principle (SAP): The abstraction of a package should be proportional to its stability. Packages that are maximally stable should be maximally abstract. Instable packages should be concrete.

12.16 SYMPTOMS OF BAD DESIGN

Designers can perform a good OO design by following the OOD principles discussed above. If designers know the reasons for and symptoms of bad design then it is helpful for them to avoid the bad design. There are some reasons for bad design, as for example: changing technology, domain complexity, lack of design skills and design practices and so on.

Technology is "constantly changing". So for a good design, it is usual to adapt with new technologies. Now it is the era of OOD, because various properties of OOD (Inheritance, modularity etc) support the modification without changing the previous or existing modules. But one should always be careful about some properties of OOD, which can make the design more complex, for example "inheritance" property. Designers cannot be able to use OOD in such a way that it will help him in case of later with the change of technologies but will not make the program more complex. Too much method makes a system complex. Martin proposes four primary symptoms tell whether designs are rotting. They are not orthogonal, but are related to each other in ways that will become obvious. They are: rigidity, fragility, immobility, and viscosity. The following is a summary of his work:

1. **Rigidity:** The concept of rigidity is if the design change in simple way the entire design will be change, i.e. a design is rigid if a single change causes a cascade of subsequent change in dependent modules. More module changes in a design indicates more rigid the system.
2. **Fragility:** The idea of fragility is that changes cause new bugs i.e. the tendency of a program to break in many places when a single change made. Martin states the new problem are in areas that have no conceptual relationship with the area that was changed, fixing those problems leads to even more problem and the development team begins to resemble a dog chasing its tail.
3. **Immobility:** Immobility means unsuccessful to reuse software from different or same design. Sometimes it happens that one designer will find out that he needs a module which is already written by another designer. It means similar module in a design makes immobile.
4. **Viscosity:** Martin states viscosity comes in two forms: viscosity of the design and viscosity of the environment. Designers always look for more options to make changes their design if they need to change something. In any cases designers maintain their design. According to Martin, viscosity of design indicates, "when the design preserving methods are harder to employ than the hacks, and then the viscosity of the design is high". It is easy to do the wrong thing, but hard to do the right thing. Viscosity of environment indicates slow and inefficient environment in a design.

Object oriented design is fundamentally different from software developed using conventional methods (procedural methods). The purposes of design principles are to mark poor use of inheritance and poor dependencies of design structure, along with among other kinds of design errors. The knowledge of Bad Design Symptom assists to the designer to perform better. The metrics for object oriented system focus on measurements that are applied to the class and the design characteristics, for example encapsulation, information hiding, inheritances, localization, etc. So Object oriented metrics are usually used to assess the quality of software designs. Next section we will discuss metrics and their quality.

12.17 OBJECT ORIENTED ISSUES AND MEASURES

This section summarizes the state of the practice for measurement of object-oriented software development projects.

Practical Software Measurement (PSM) describes a generic process for selecting and tailoring measures based on project management issues. This section highlights some of the new issues that the introduction of object-oriented technology introduces. The general process for measuring OO software development is the same as that for measuring any other type of software. However, the specific size and quality measures, algorithms, and normative values of parameters must be adjusted to reflect the nature of the software and the development method applied. The estimation and tracking approach described here is based on the generic process presented in PSM.

Estimation typically produces projections of the software size, effort, and schedule required to complete the project. Sometimes, projections of software quality are also produced. These estimates form the basis for initial project plans and subsequent replans. The initial round of estimation often occurs during the proposal phase, before the detailed information needed to accurately size the project has been developed. The nature of software engineering, whether or not OO methods are used, makes early estimates imprecise and requires that estimation be repeated throughout the project life cycle.

Poor estimates and misconceptions about the estimating process often contribute to the failure of software projects. PSM identifies several common contributors to poor estimates. Many of these have been exacerbated by the transition to OO methods. This section attempts to address as many of them as possible. The following list describes the common estimation problems and the effect of the transition to OO development on them:

- **Lack of historical data on which to base estimates.** Since OO methods are relatively new, few organizations have a significant amount of data from these projects.
- **Lack of estimating experience. Only time can solve this.** As managers get more experience in estimating OO projects they will get better at it. Nevertheless, defining a repeatable estimation process makes learning from that experience more likely.
- **Lack of a systematic estimation process, sound techniques, or models suited to object-oriented development.** While the available OO estimation techniques may not be widely known, several useful techniques have been developed.
- **Failure to include essential project activities and products within the scope of the estimates.** Every estimation model makes assumptions about the scope covered by the estimates. The OO development model differs in significant ways from structured development models.
- **Unrealistic expectations or assumptions.** Misunderstanding the capabilities of OO methods leads to infeasible plans. Aggressive claims have been made for the levels of productivity, quality, and reuse obtained from OO methods. They are not always realized.
- **Failure to recognize and address the uncertainty inherent in software estimates.** The increased uncertainty due to the factors discussed above makes understanding the confidence associated with an estimate more important for OO development.

Generally, the same factors that are estimated need to be tracked in order to manage a project effectively. Detailed plans are based on the overall estimates. Changes or mistakes in the assumptions driving the plans must be recognized as early as possible so that corrective action can be taken. Tracking the status of the project relative to the plans provides the insight necessary to effective management.

While many projects do not address quality in any terms other than tracking problem reports, there is increasing recognition that, like effort and schedule, software quality must be managed rigorously to ensure project success. Although there are numerous dimensions of software quality (e.g., portability and maintainability), this chapter focuses on the dimension of functional correctness, whose absence can be measured by the presence of defects.

Many studies indicate that most defects in software applications are found in only a few of a system's components. The early identification of these components allows an organization to take mitigating actions, such as focus defect detection activities on high risk components, for example by optimally allocating testing resources, or redesigning components that are likely to cause field failures.

For object-oriented systems, one approach to identify classes with defects early in development is to construct prediction models using object-oriented *design* measures (i.e., the object-oriented measures serve as leading indicators of a class' *defect-proneness*). Such models are developed using historical data, and can then be applied for identifying classes with defects in future applications or future releases. The use of design measures allows the organization to take mitigating actions early and consequently avoid costly rework (as opposed to, for example, code measures where the mitigating actions would be taken later in the project). Also, the total number of defects expected in each phase can be estimated so that rework effect can be allocated appropriately during planning.

Many of the information needs of managers of object-oriented software projects are the same as those experienced by the managers of other software-intensive development projects. PSM defines seven common issue areas (or types of information needs). However, the transition to object-oriented development may introduce additional issues and measures for consideration during the measurement planning activity.

Examples of issues driving the need to modify the typical measurement system to address object-oriented development include:

- New processes and work products mean new entities with different measurement opportunities
- Expectations for established measures may be invalid
- Motivation for adopting object-oriented methods (e.g., reuse) may require focused feedback

The following table (Figure 12.8) shows how the issues specific to object-oriented development are linked to recommended measures via the PSM mechanisms of common issue areas and measurement categories.

Object Oriented Issue	Common Issue Area	Measurement Category	Measures	Associated Base Measure
How to access the size of OO software	Product growth and stability	Physical size and stability	Source lines of code	• Class SLOC including external libraries • Class SLOC excluding external libraries
			Number of classes in the system	• Number of language classes • Number of library classes • Number of project classes
			Design size	• Number of events • Number of states • Number of use cases

How to access the quality of OO software	Product quality	Supportability Maintainability	Source lines of code per class	• Total source lines of code • Total number of classes
			Number of attributes per class	• Total number of attributes • Total number of classes
			Number of methods per class	• Total number of methods • Total number of classes • Total cyclomatic complexity
			Inheritance	• Depth of inheritance tree • Number of children
			Coupling	Import coupling to ancestors • Class-Attribute • Class-Method • Method-Method
				Import coupling to other classes • Class-Attribute • Class-Method • Method-Method
				Export coupling to other classes • Class-Attribute • Class-Method • Method-Method
				Export coupling to descendents • Class-Attribute • Class-Method • Method-Method
How to access reuse in OO software	Process performance	Process efficiency	Cost of reuse	• Cost of producing reusable assets • Cost of consuming reusable assets
			Reuse potential	• Depth of inheritance tree • Number of children
			Amount of black-box reuse	• Number of class reused verbatim • SLOC reused vibratim
			Amount of white-box reuse	• Percentage of a class that is modified for reuse • Size of a class

Figure 12.8: *Mapping of Issues to Object Oriented Measures*

12.18 ESTIMATION PROCESS FOR OBJECT-ORIENTED SOFTWARE

This section describes a general process for estimating OO software, based on the estimation process defined in *Practical Software Measurement*. This process involves four basic activities as shown in Figure 12.9. First, select an estimation approach. Next, map and calibrate the project's activity structure and relevant historical data to the selected approach. Scope and data might be considerations in selecting the model as well. Then, compute estimates using the selected approach. Finally, evaluate the estimates and compare them with project constraints. If the estimate does not satisfy the project constraints, make appropriate adjustments and repeat the computation. Any adjustment that is not supported by some reasonable action should be documented as a risk.

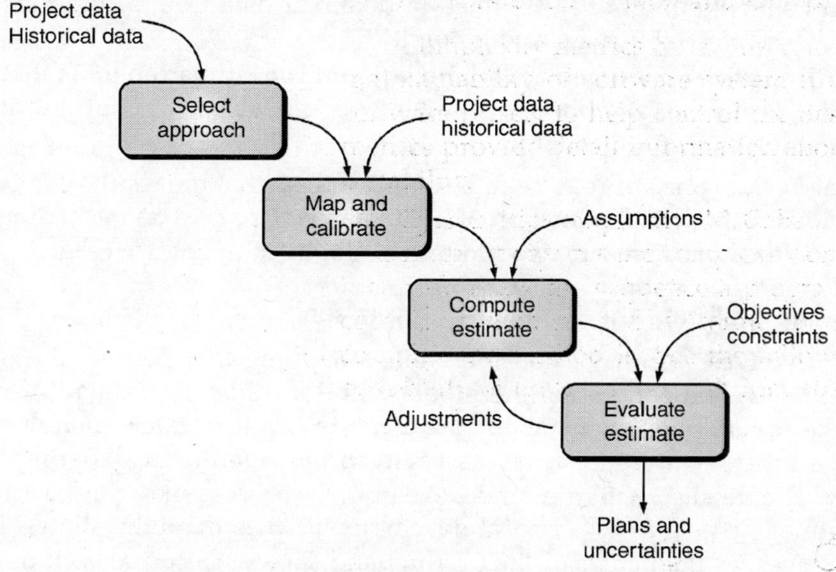

Figure 12.9: *Generic Estimation Process (from PSM)*

Reestimates should be performed periodically throughout the project life cycle. Typically reestimates are performed at major milestones and when requirements significantly change. As the project progresses and more information become available about actual project performance, the accuracy of estimates should increase.

12.18.1 Select an Estimating Approach

The first activity in the estimation process involves selecting an appropriate estimation approach (or approaches). Remember that no matter how elaborate and sophisticated the model, the results will be no better than the data and assumptions provided as input to it.

Some specific factors to consider in selecting an estimation approach include

- **Range of activities covered by the model or approach.** Does it match the activities to be estimated for the project under study? Documentation, requirements analysis, and final qualification testing are some of the activities that models often fail to include.
- **Scope of support.** Does the approach address estimating size, effort, schedule, quality, and reuse? Does it provide guidance for periodic re-estimation of these dimensions.
- **Empirical validation of the model.** Is the model a theoretical exercise, or has it been proven in software engineering situations? Consider the depth of data, number of users/evaluators, and robustness of the evaluation methods.

- **Availability of appropriate local historical data to calibrate the model or approach.** Is data available from past projects for the specific parameters used in the model?
- **Ability to capture the necessary data from the current project.** Does the OO development method used produce the artifacts, such as "key classes," that get counted to drive the model?
- **Ability to approximate input parameters.** Is there a reasonable method for approximating the values of parameters for which no historical data is available? A sample of software might be examined in detail, or data from a commercial database could be used to establish a starting point.
- **Availability, prices, documentation, and support for estimation tools that implement the model, if any.** We describe some of the tools available to support estimation of OO projects at the end of the chapter.

Ideally, more than one approach will be employed, so that the results can be compared. Few models address both the estimation of quality as well as cost and schedule, so in most cases it will be necessary to select two models to obtain complete coverage.

12.18.2 Map and Calibrate the Estimating Approach

Tailoring involves two major considerations: mapping the scope of the model to the scope of the project, and calibrating the model with local historical data. Most estimation methods make some assumptions about the activities and products included within the scope of the estimate. Differences may be resolved by inflating or deflating the estimate appropriately. The detailed activities and development process may not be known during the initial estimate (e.g., during proposal development). The mapping should be reviewed during later stages, as the nature of the product and process becomes well understood.

The models described in the next sections probably were developed in environments significantly different from the one in which a current project will be developed. Calibration adapts the model to a new environment. Those models supported by tools may have an automatic calibration feature. Other models will require computations by the analyst. Historical data that is as similar as possible to the proposed project should be used. The simplest method of calibration is to determine the average error of the model for past projects, using that to adjust estimates for new projects. Better results are obtained by processing current project data through the algorithm originally used to develop the model. Once the project is underway, data from early activities can be used to calibrate the estimation approach. For example, the actual productivity experienced on the first build can be inserted into the estimating relationship for planning subsequent builds.

12.19 COMPUTE THE ESTIMATE

Three dimensions of a software project must be estimated to provide an adequate basis for project planning. These are size, effort, and schedule. Optionally, quality (e.g., number of defects) may be estimated. During project planning, the effort estimate is converted into dollars and combined with other costs to establish the project budget. At each stage of estimation, the degree of uncertainty should be captured. This may be accomplished by defining best case, worst case, and nominal scenarios, or by computing the standard deviation for any statistical results obtained.

12.19.1 Size Estimating (New and Reused)

Typically, estimation begins by projecting the amount of software to be produced. Software size may be estimated in terms of functional size (the amount of capability to be delivered), physical size (the amount of software product to be delivered), or both. Getting a good size estimate is essential to getting good estimates of effort, schedule, and quality. The first step in size estimation is to select a size measure. Historically, the two most widely used size measures are source lines of code and function points. However, the most common measure of size for OO software is the number of classes. An initial estimate can be made based on the number of "key" or "top-level" classes, but as the design progresses the actual number of planned classes should be substituted. The total number of classes seems to range from two to four times the number of key classes. Systems with more complex interfaces tend toward the larger number, as reported by Nesi and Lorenz and Kidd. The size of a class in terms of source lines of code or other attributes may be used to weight the class in computing overall software size or complexity.

Reducing cost by increasing reuse provides one of the strongest motivations for adopting OO techniques. The amount of reused software expected is estimated separately during the sizing step. Counting the depth of inheritance and the number of children gives an indication of the degree of reuse achieved, but unless the origin of the top-level classes is recorded, internal reuse cannot be distinguished from external reuse. While most of the effort associated with reusing software comes from integrating that software with the developed code, rather than from designing or coding, that cost can be significant. Modifying the reusable software will increase the effort required significantly.

Top-level (or key) classes that are reused from previous applications should generate considerable savings. Instantiation of those classes should not be substantially different from instantiating new top-level classes. Generally, separate size estimates also should be made for each language type. The actual amount of software produced in each language and from each source should be tracked separately so that deviations from the estimates can be recognized early. As Lorenz and Kidd observe, the characteristics of Smalltalk and C++ programs differ significantly in terms of the size of classes and the effort required to implement them.

12.19.2 Effort Estimation

Effort estimation is the best understood part of the estimation process, as it is the focus of most traditional estimation models. This step converts the software size estimate into an estimate of effort by applying an appropriate estimating relationship. For example, dividing the size estimate (e.g., number of classes) by productivity (e.g., classes/hour) yields effort (e.g., total hours). More complex classes may require more effort. Nesi and Querci reported that the number of attributes and the number of interfaces were the best predictors of the effort required to implement a class.

Some estimation models use a non-linear relationship between size and effort, assuming that as software size increases the effort required per class increases. If multiple types of software (e.g., reuse and new development) are included in the estimate, then the effort for each type must be estimated separately and the results added together. Alternatively, the sizes can be converted to a common unit by a weighting algorithm, and then used as the basis for effort estimation.

Most popular estimation models also provide for other adjustments to productivity. These adjustments, or performance factors, generally fall into two categories: process and product factors. Process factors capture characteristics of the project software development process (e.g., tools and skill levels). Product factors capture the nature of the prospective software in operation (e.g., required reliability and application complexity). The values of these parameters are selected as part of the estimation process to raise or lower the productivity to more accurately reflect expected project conditions. While estimation models may provide from 15 to 100 adjustment factors, most organizations will find that their performance is only affected by a few of them. The survey of estimation models for OO development shows that the two most commonly used adjustment factors were team experience (or expertise) and application type (complexity or difficulty). If complexity was considered as an adjustment during the software-sizing step, it should not be factored in again in this step.

Comparison of results from Nesi and Lorenz and Kidd also suggest that the effort to implement a class in Smalltalk is greater than the effort to implement a class in C++. Nesi notes that productivity declines as teams get larger than four persons.

Documentation still needs to be considered in planning OO projects. Nesi and Querci report that 36% of effort was spent on documentation for one industrial project.

12.19.3 Schedule Estimation

Most commonly, schedules are determined by working backward from a delivery date set by the customer or by marketing. However, estimation models may help to negotiate more realistic dates than those typically set. The estimation models already in widespread use (e.g., COCOMO) provide an estimate of project duration as a function of the estimated effort required for the project. (Again, such models should be calibrated with local data.)

Depending on the sizing method, either use cases or classes may be prioritized and allocated to the system increments, each of which is associated with part of the project schedule. Jacobson recommends that each increment (or cycle or spiral) manage the detailed analysis, design, implementation, and testing of 5 to 20 use cases, with each increment lasting 3 to 6 months.

12.19.4 Quality Estimation

Object-oriented software projects usually are concerned with two dimensions of software quality, functional correctness and maintainability. Estimating them requires measures of outcomes (e.g., defects and change effort) as well as predictors (e.g., size and complexity).

The task of estimating functional correctness may be approached from two complementary perspectives. The total number of defects expected to be encountered in each phase may be predicted (defect profile) and/or the classes most likely to contain defects may be identified (defect-prone classes). Understanding the number of defects to be handled in each phase helps to allocate rework effort appropriately across the life-cycle. Determining the defect prone classes helps to focus testing or inspection effort within a phase on the part of the software where it will provide the greatest yield.

Both of these approaches require historical data to give good results. Best results usually come from using data from a previous release of the same product within the same organization and process, or a similar product also within the same organization and process. The historical number of defects can also be normalized by a size measure to obtain a defect density that can be used to obtain estimates for different sizes of products.

Maintainability is typically measured as change effort. Change effort can mean either: (a) the average effort to make a change to a class, or (b) the total effort spent on changing a class. The latter accounts for the number of changes that a class undergoes (i.e., across many changes), whereas the former is specific to a single change. Changes can be classified into change types for estimation purposes. For example, one can estimate maintenance effort for corrective changes only or for functionality enhancement changes only (where "corrective" and "functionality enhancements" are two different types of changes). In addition, for corrective changes, changes to fix different types of defects can be distinguished, for example, fixes of "data" type and "memory" type defects.

Depending on the objectives of estimation, one may be interested in estimating functional correctness or maintainability for each class in a system individually, or for the whole system in aggregate. For example, one can estimate the number of post-release defects for each individual class in an application. Alternatively, one can sum up all of these individual estimates to come up with the estimated number of defects for the whole system.

Another strategy is to classify the classes into "high" and "low" risk. A "high" risk class is one where the intention is to take action once it is identified. For example, a "high" risk class may have more than five pre-release defects or takes more than 40 person-hours on average to make a single change to. In such a case, one can estimate the proportion (or number) of classes in a system that are "high" risk. This can serve as another quality measure for individual classes (i.e., is it "high" risk) or for the whole system.

The earlier the quality estimates can be made the better. Therefore, it is most desirable to use object-oriented measures that can be collected at the design or even analysis stages.

However, it should also be noted that analysis and design models may either:

- Evolve over time as the project progresses. Therefore, estimates made using design measures one year ago may not be accurate anymore because the design itself has changed.
- Remain static and fail to reflect the actual evolution of the system. Therefore, reliance on design measures to estimate and re-estimate may be inappropriate.

When making quality estimates, it is important to be cognizant of which of the above two situations you are in, because this will impact how much you can trust the estimates.

Generally, the scope of the quality estimate should make clear what parts of the system are under consideration. If an external library is used, for example, it must be clear whether the library is within the scope of the estimate or not. Especially for design measures, it is not difficult to collect many useful coupling and inheritance measures from class signatures only. Therefore, it is possible to collect data on external libraries, but in some cases you may want to treat these differently.

12.19.5 Review Estimates

The estimates resulting from the preceding steps should be reviewed by the project manager, customer (or marketing), and staff responsible for implementing the software. If the team developing the estimate does not have a substantial background in OO development (a common situation during proposal development), then the reviewers should include someone with that background.

PSM suggests the following three major areas of concern:

- **Quality of the estimate.** Are the resulting estimates complete, consistent, and reliable? Is the degree of uncertainty in the estimates understood?
- **Satisfaction of constraints.** Are the estimates within project constraints in terms of overall budget and schedule?
- **Documentation of the estimate.** Are the bases for the estimates, assumptions, and the results fully recorded?

The quality of the estimate depends on the appropriateness of the model selected, the amount and relevance of historical data, and the expertise of the estimator. However, even a quality estimate may yield results outside these constraints of the project budget and schedule. In this situation, trade-offs are preferable to arbitrary adjustments. For example, reducing schedule and functionality may be an effective strategy for reducing cost to stay within the project budget. Whenever an adjustment is made, ensure that a strategy for achieving that delta is in place, and that any resulting dependencies are tracked as risks.

Good documentation of the estimates helps improve the estimation process and facilitates periodic reestimation. This is especially important in a situation such as OO development, where the data and experience needed for estimating are limited. For small projects, current performance may be extrapolated to reestimate the project. For example, if 25% of the work has been done to date using X amount of effort, the estimate to complete the project would be 3X. However, diseconomies of scale apply to large projects. As the size increases, productivity declines. Consequently, if the project has experienced size growth, the productivity observed to date may be overly optimistic. The total project should be reestimated with the new size and other updated assumptions, then that effort expended to date is subtracted from that result to get an estimate to completion.

12.20 PERFORMANCE ANALYSIS MODEL

Measures should be selected to address project issues. Issues include objectives, risks, uncertainties, and problems that may affect the success of the project. The PSM structured analysis model in Figure 12.10 shows the relationship between common types of project issues. The model provides a useful performance analysis "roadmap" showing how problems in one area may affect another.

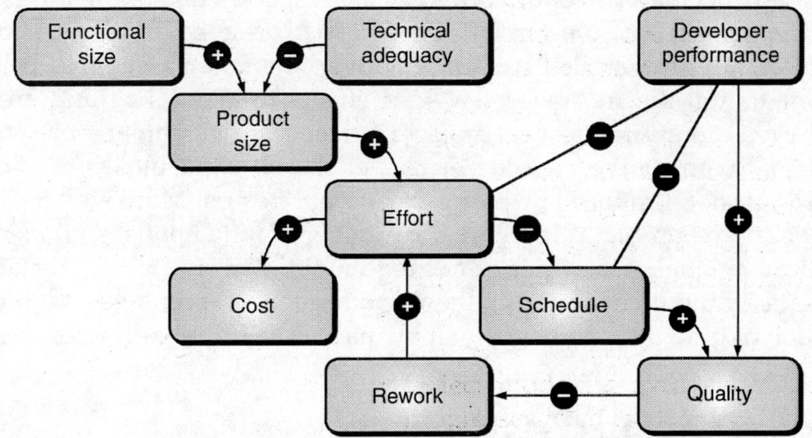

Figure 12.10: PSM Performance Analysis Model

The plus and minus symbols along the arrows indicate the nature of the relationship between two components. A plus sign signifies that the two quantities move in the same direction. As the quantity of the first element of the pair increases (or decreases), the second element also increases (or decreases) correspondingly. For example, as functional size increases, product size is also likely to increase, as more structural components are usually needed to implement increased functionality or requirements. The minus sign signifies that the two quantities move in opposite directions. For example, as product quality increases, rework should decrease.

This performance analysis model suggests the need for several different types of **measurement indicators.** Projects need current measurement indicators in order to monitor the performance of identified high-priority issues. These indicators also are useful in monitoring downstream events for potential problems.

- **Leading indicators.** Projects should consider monitoring elements that are upstream of the project's primary issues of concern, because they represent leading indicators for that issue. For example, if the primary concern is staying within a fixed cost ceiling, effort should be measured, along with software size, developer performance, and technical adequacy.
- **Early warning.** Analysing performance for an issue's leading indicators should provide an early warning to identify problems related to that issue.
- **Tradeoffs.** The tradeoffs between issues must be considered when evaluating alternatives. Attempting to optimize a project in one area may result in a negative impact elsewhere. For instance, attempting to make up a schedule slippage by increasing the number of personnel on the project also increases overall cost.

The analysis roadmap helps to sort out different potential causes of trouble by using a set of distinct measures. Interpretation problems often result from combining multiple factors into a single measure. Goldberg and Rubin describe a case study of a C++ project that tracked progress in terms of the percentage of classes produced out of the refined estimate of total classes. The domain model identified 75 classes; the design model grew to 425 classes. The project decided to report progress against 500 classes for the target system. Monthly status reports showed the percentage of classes designed, implemented, unit tested, and integrated. Before the detailed design was over, the 500 classes had been exceeded. During implementation the number grew, and efforts to generalize and create reusable objects created even more. An alarmed project manager and customer froze the number of classes in an effort to control the project. The classes soon became bloated and complex. The progress-tracking strategy ended up driving the system design. Moreover, it did not clearly indicate the cause of the problem. Tracking the number of (and changes to) use cases would have given a clearer signal of whether or not requirements were stable. Tracking the actual number of classes (without constraining them), rather than percentages, would have given a better indication of growth, whether driven by inaccurate initial estimates or requirements changes.

12.21 PERFORMANCE ANALYSIS PROCESS

PSM defines a systematic process for collecting, analysing, and using software measurement data for project management purposes. This section summarizes the part of the PSM process that concerns tracking project performance. Figure 12.11 illustrates the steps of this subprocess. The analysis subprocess is executed periodically, typically monthly. Planned and actual values of the selected measures are inputs to the process. Problems requiring management attention are outputs from it.

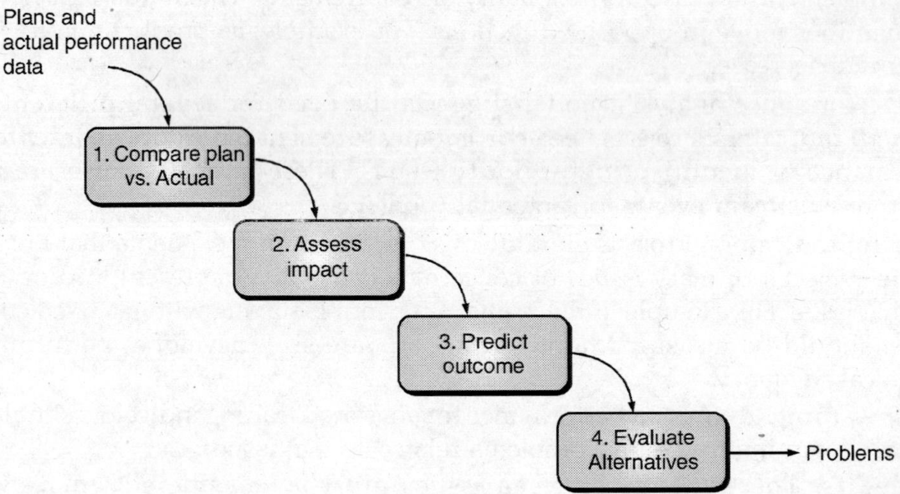

Figure 12.11: Performance Analysis Subprocess

Several of these performance analysis tasks involve collecting additional non-measurement information. Decisions cannot be based solely on quantitative data. Project context information may be collected from staff feedback, technical and management reviews, document reviews, and risk analyses. Gathering and integrating appropriate non-quantitative information is essential to the successful application of measurement techniques.

Step 1: Compare Plan Versus Actual

The first task in evaluating performance status is to examine the basic indicators that correspond to each issue.

Problems are recognized by quantifying the difference between plans and actuals, or between plans and other baselines. If the difference between these values exceeds the pre-defined threshold acceptable to management, then the situation should be investigated further. Consider not only the absolute magnitude of the difference, but also the trend. If a variance has been growing steadily larger over time, it should be investigated even if it has not yet exceeded a pre-defined threshold.

Unfortunately, by the time that a size, effort, schedule, or quality problem becomes visible, the problem has likely become one of major proportion. Thus, in evaluating performance, the relationships among multiple indicators also must be considered. Some of the things to look for in performance analysis are

- **Leading indicators.** Often problems will become visible in upstream issues before they translate into a measurable problem in the issue of immediate concern. For example, requirements changes usually precede size and effort increases. Even if resources are not currently a problem on a project, a large number of requirements changes indicates that resources will become a problem if action is not taken. Use the structured analysis model to identify likely sources of prospective problems.
- **Critical path items.** Even if high-level indicators suggest the project is moving ahead smoothly, delays and quality problems in a critical path item that are not recognized and countered early can have a ripple effect late in the project. A good example might be the failure to resolve interface issues on time. Even though overall design might be progressing, implementation and testing of large parts of the system may be delayed as a consequence of delays in this critical design item.
- **Inconsistent trends.** Sometimes two related indicators will suggest that different situations exist. Neither variance taken alone may be large enough to suggest a problem, but taken together they indicate that some element of the process is not working as planned.
- **Outliers.** Individual points that are not part of a trend, but show unusual behaviour also should be investigated. These could include a large change in productivity, defect rate, or complexity.

One of the common motivations for adopting OO methods is to facilitate reuse. Failure to achieve planned levels of reuse frequently is a leading indicator of cost, schedule, and quality problems. Carefully tracking the level of reuse achieved enables departures from the plan to be recognized and addressed as early as possible.

Step 2: Assess Impact

The first step in assessing the impact of a performance problem is to determine which parts of the project are affected. This may require collecting additional data specific to the problem. Usually, separating the data by subsystem will highlight the focus of the problem. Next, the magnitude of the problem must be assessed. Sometimes a substantial difference between planned and actual values may be caused by outliers, which are values that do not appear to be consistent with the other data collected. For example, the scope of an important "engine" class may be significantly larger than others, resulting in the expenditure of additional time and effort. Productivity and progress should not be estimated for the whole project based on that example, unless it is typical of that system. Nevertheless, implementation of that specific class may require additional attention in order to prevent it from delaying the project as a whole.

Step 3: Predict Outcome

Understanding the significance of a problem requires projecting its impact into the future. Eventual project outcomes can be predicted by projecting current trends or by reestimating effort, size, and schedule with new information about project performance. Observed trends in measures such as work unit progress, size growth, and requirements changes can be projected into the future as straight lines. Unless some specific counteraction is taken, the variance is due to an outlier, or some other transient factor exists. The current performance of the project should be assumed to be typical of future performance.

Step 4: Evaluate Alternatives

When the predicted outcome does not satisfy project objectives, investigate alternative courses of action. For example, if the projected cost based on the work done to date exceeds the project budget, consider reducing the functional requirements of the project. Productivity might be enhanced by increasing the level of automation, if the project has a tool gap and it can be filled in time to affect the outcome. Keep in mind that just changing the assumptions behind the project plan does not make the plan any more likely to be realized. For example, assuming increased productivity in the plans without taking any real action to improve performance will not change the outcome of the project.

12.22 OBJECT-ORIENTED MEASUREMENT TOOLS

Measurement and analysis of objected-oriented software can be facilitated by tools that help to collect data as well as tools that help to perform estimates with the resulting data. This section provides some suggestions in each area.

Many factors that come into play when selecting a tool. The following issues should be considered when selecting a data collection tool issues:

- **Does the tool collect useful measures?** Some tool vendors advertise that their tools collect a large number of measures. This is irrelevant. Many measures are simply measuring size. So you can have hundreds of size measures. A subset of useful measures is all you need. In fact, in practice you will only need about a dozen measures to start off with (import coupling, export coupling, size, and inheritance measures), which could be reduced to 3 or 4 when validating the measures in your organization.
- **How easy is it to integrate the tool into your development environment?** Many measurement tools parse source code. Some of these tools have poor parsers that work only for certain flavours of a language (e.g., with extensions that work on a certain platform or from a specific manufacturer). If that is the case, then they are not very useful. It is therefore important to get an evaluation version of the tool and make sure that it works with *your* code. It is not unheard of that someone spends months with an automated tool trying to get it to work in a particular project.

- **Can it handle large code?** Yes, it is true. Some analysers cannot deal with larger amounts of code. Because many measures require cross-referencing classes in the whole system, some tools simply cannot scale up to systems with thousands of classes.
- **Can it export data?** Although some tools have the facility to plot graphs of your object-oriented measurement data, and do basic queries on the data, you really need to have a professional analysis and plotting package. You will likely want to look at subsets of classes, group them by some criterion, such as subsystem, produce categorized plots, and so on. This is much easier to do with analysis software (good analysis software will support database queries as well). So it is important to check that the measurement tool can export the data in a format that you can actually use in an analysis package with minimal manual conversion. Also, the analysis and plotting capabilities of the measurement tools are not really that critical if you can export your data to a professional analysis package.
- **Can you develop your own measures?** At some point, after reaching a certain level of sophistication, you may want to develop some measures that make more sense in your particular organization. Some tools collect cross-referencing information in a database and allow the user to define their queries on this database to calculate their own measures. If a tool allows you to do that, then this is a big plus. However, this is really a feature for power users. For most projects, a basic set of coupling measures will work reasonably well (i.e., the pay-off will be evident from using these measures).

The vendor market is constantly changing. Therefore, to deal with these changes we refer you to a web-based search engine where vendors are indexed, and where it is possible to find out what the current products, vendors, and prices are.

Estimating and planning software projects can be complex, labour-intensive tasks. Effective tool support facilitates that effort. This section describes some of the tools that are available to support the estimation approaches. The description places each tool in a methodological context, covering the major criteria identified earlier in this section. Figure 12.12 summarizes the tools, providing a side-by-side comparison. Details are provided in the following subsections. Contact the vendor for the latest pricing information.

Tool Name	Estimation Model	Uses	Size Measure	Effort Measure	Schedule Prediction	Tracking	Other Measures
SOMATIK	Ian Graham's SOMA	SOMA Task Object Model and Business Object Model	Task points number of classes	Not computed	Not compared	Available by exporting snapshot files into a spreadsheet	Complexity, coupling, inheritance based on C&K metrics
ANGEL	Analogy	Template files	Based on similarity to historical data	Based on similarity to historical data	Based on Similarity to historical data	Available by storing snapshots is a data model	Error analysis, attribute optimization

Price S	Empirical knowledge base	Microsoft Project98 files	Lines of code, function points, predictive object points	Predicted from a database of empirical data	Predicted from a Systems empirical data	Contact Price Systems	Contact Price Systems
ma	System Meter Method	PRE and DOME specification on files of analysis and design models	System meters, LOC, function points	Predicted from a database of empirical data (the predictor model)	Predicted from a database of empirical data (a sample is provided)	Based on comparing result model to predictor model	C&K metrics and simple descriptive statistics
Optimize	Object Metrix approach	User input or casetool output	Scope elements	Person-days	Predicted from team size, skill level, schedule, and budget	Estimates are repeated and refined through the life cycle	Contact The Object Factory
Knowledge Plan	Analogy, Component Metric	Task hierarchies	Screens or reports, design components, LOC, function points	Predicted from the selected knowledge base	Predicted from the selected knowledge base	From predicted to actual measures	Contact Software Productivity Research

Figure 12.12: *Tools Supporting Estimation of Object-Oriented Projects*

The metrics proposed by different authors are well-known: Chidamber and Kemerer, Brito and Abreu, Lorenz and Kidd, etc. In this chapter has been reviewed the most representative metrics of these authors and others, from the perspective of the object oriented approach, more than the analysis of the metrics set of a single author.

Special interest is placed in coverage metrics. Special characteristics in object oriented as polymorphism and encapsulation suggest new focus in the test cases design to get the 100% of method coverage.

SUMMARY

Object-Oriented programming metrics is an aspect to be considered. Metrics to be a set of standards against which one can measure the effectiveness of Object-Oriented Analysis techniques in the design of a system. *Software metrics*deals with the estimation and measurement of different attributes of the software product and the software development process. There are different types of metrics like C.K., MOOD etc. Lorenz and Kidd proposed a group of metrics called "design metrics", which deal with the static characteristics of software design. There are several essential themes in object oriented design. These themes are mostly support object oriented design in the context of measuring. This describes a general process for estimating OO software, based on the estimation process defined in

Practical Software Measurement. Measurement and analysis of objected-oriented software can be facilitated by tools that help to collect data as well as tools that help to perform estimates with the resulting data.

EXERCISES

1. Explain the Five characteristics of Object Oriented Metrics?
2. What do you mean by metrics?
3. Explain the various properties of metrics?
4. Explain the properties of measurement and metrics?
5. Explain the validation of metrics?
6. Explain the metrics hierarchy in detail?
7. What do you mean by measuring quality?
8. Explain the categories of metrics?
9. Explain the taxonomy of object oriented metrics?
10. Explain the concept of coupling and cohesion?
11. Explain the various complexity methods?
12. Explain the testing coverage metrics?
13. Explain the GQM (Goal Question Metric) approach?
14. Explain the metrics for OO design model?
15. Explain the MOOD metrics model?
16. Explain the various design metrics Suite by Lorenz and Kidd?
17. What do you mean by object oriented approach?
18. Explain the concept of Object oriented design?
19. What are the internal qualities of OOD?
20. Explain the various OO design principles?
21. Explain the symptoms of bad design?
22. Explain the object oriented issues and measures?
23. Explain the estimation process for object-oriented software?
24. Explain the performance analysis model?
25. Explain the process of performance analysis?
26. Explain the measurement tools of object-oriented?

❑

UNIT 6
OBJECT-ORIENTED ANALYSIS AND DESIGN

Object Oriented Analysis and Design

13

13.1 INTRODUCTION

Systems are created to solve problems. One can think of the systems approach as an organized way of dealing with a problem. In this dynamic world, the subject System Analysis and Design (SAD) mainly deals with the software development activities.

The main purpose of this section is to introduce the readers to the concept of systems. This section starts with a description of the characteristics of systems and types of systems. A detailed description of the phases in the development of a system with the emphasis on the analysis phase is also provided. The section also describes the role of the system analysis in the development of a system.

After a discussion on systems, two major methodologies of system analysis and design are presented namely, Structured System Analysis and Design (SSAD) and Object Oriented Analysis and Design (OOAD). OOAD is the focus of discussion in this chapter. Hence this chapter forms a basis of understanding as to what we are up to.

13.2 SYSTEM

A collection of components that work together to realize some objectives forms a system. Basically there are three major components in every system, namely input, processing and output.

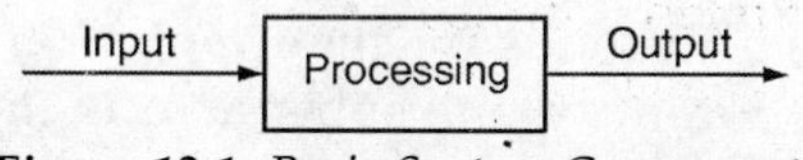

Figure 13.1: *Basic System Components*

In a system the different components are connected with each other and they are interdependent. For example, human body represents a complete natural system. We are also bound by many national systems such as political system, economic system, educational system and so forth. The objective of the system demands that some output is produced as a result of processing the suitable inputs. A well-designed system also includes an additional element referred to as 'control' that provides a feedback to achieve desired objectives of the system.

Virtually everything that we come into contact with during our day-to-day life is either a system, or a component of a system, or both. On careful observation of such systems, we find that they share common philosophies and theories.

A system can be defined as a regularly interacting or independent group of items forming a unified whole. A system is an organised set of doctrines, ideas, or principles that explains the arrangement of a systematic whole.

There should be some characteristics present in all systems, some of which are as follows:

- **Central Objective:** The last characteristic of a system is its central objective. Objectives may be real or stated. Although a stated objective may be the real objective, it is not uncommon for an organization to state one objective and operates to achieve another. The important point is that users must know the central objective of a computer application early in the analysis for a successful design and conversion. Political as well as organizational considerations often cloud the real objective. This means that the analyst must work around such obstacles to identify the real objective of the proposed change.
- **Organization:** Organization implies structure and order. It is the arrangement of components that helps to achieve objectives. In the design of a business system, for example, the hierarchical relationships starting with the president on top and leading downward to the blue – collar workers represents the organization structure. Such an arrangement portrays a system – subsystem relationship, defines the authority structure, specifies the formal flow of communication and formalizes the chain of command. Like – wise, a computer system is designed around an input device, a central processing unit, an output device and one or more storage units. When linked together they work as a whole system for producing information.
- **Interaction:** Interaction refers to the manner in which each component functions with other components of the system. In an organization, for example, purchasing must interact with production, advertising with sales and payroll with personnel. In a computer system, the central processing unit must interact with the input device to solve a problem. In turn, the main memory holds programs and data that the arithmetic unit uses for computation. The interrelationship between these components enables the computer to perform.
- **Interdependence:** Interdependence means that parts of the organization or computer system depend on one another. They are coordinated and linked together according to a plan. One subsystem depends on the input of another subsystem for proper functioning: that is, the output of one subsystem is the required input for another subsystem. This interdependence is crucial in systems work.
- **Integration:** Integration refers to the holism of systems. Synthesis follows analysis to achieve the central objective of the organization. Integration is concerned with how a system is tied together. It is more than sharing a physical part or location. It means that parts of the system work together within the system even though each part performs a unique function. Successful integration will typically produce a synergistic effect and greater total impact than if each component works separately.

13.2.1 Elements of a System

In most cases, systems analysts operate in a dynamic environment where change is a way of life. The environment may be a business firm, a business application, or a computer system. To reconstruct a system, the following key elements must be considered:

- **Outputs and Inputs:** A major objective of a system is to produce an output that has value to its user. Whatever the nature of the output (goods, services, or information), it must be in line with the expectations of the intended user. Inputs are the elements (material, human resources, and information) that enter the system for processing. Output is the outcome of processing. A system feeds on input to produce output in much the same way that a business brings in human, financial, and material resources to produce goods and services. It is important to point out here that determining the output is a first step in specifying the nature, amount, and regularity of the input needed to operate a system. For example, in systems analysis, the first concern is to determine the user's requirements of a proposed computer system – that is, specification of the output that the computer is expected to provide for meeting user requirements.
- **Processor(s):** The processor is the element of a system that involves the actual transformation of input into output. It is the operational component of a system. Processors may modify the input totally or partially, depending on the specifications of the output. This means that as the output specifications change so does the processing. In some cases, input is also modified to enable the processor to handle the transformation.
- **Control:** The control element guides the system. It is the decision – making subsystem that controls the pattern of activities governing input, processing, and output. In an organizational context, management as a decision – making body controls the inflow, handling and outflow of activities that affect the welfare of the business. In a computer system, the operating system and accompanying software influence the behaviour of the system. Output specifications determine what and how much input is needed to keep the system in balance.

  In systems analysis, knowing the attitudes of the individual who controls the area for which a computer is being considered can make a difference between the success and failure of the installation. Management support is required for securing control and supporting the objective of the proposed change.
- **Feedback:** Control in a dynamic system is achieved by feedback. Feedback measures output against a standard in some form of cybernetic procedure that includes communication and control. Output information is fed back to the input and / or to management (Controller) for deliberation. After the output is compared against performance standards, changes can result in the input or processing and consequently, the output.

  Feedback may be positive or negative, routing or informational. Positive feedback reinforces the performance of the system. It is routine in nature. Negative feedback generally provides the controller with information for action. In systems analysis, feedback is important in different ways. During analysis, the user may be told that the problems in a given application verify the initial concerns and justify the need for change. Another form of feedback comes after the system is implemented. The user informs the analyst about the performance of the new installation. This feedback often results in enhancements to meet the user's requirements.
- **Environment:** The environment is the "suprasystem" within which an organization operates. It is the source of external elements that impinge on the system. In fact, it

often determines how a system must function. For example, the organization's environment, consisting of vendors, competitors, and others, may provide constraints and, consequently, influence the actual performance of the business.

- **Boundaries and interface:** A system should be defined by its boundaries – the limits that identify its components, processes and interrelationship when it interfaces with another system. For example, a teller system in a commercial bank is restricted to the deposits, withdrawals and related activities of customers checking and savings accounts. It may exclude mortgage foreclosures, trust activities, and the like.

  Each system has boundaries that determine its sphere of influence and control. For example, in an integrated banking – wide computer system design, a customer who has a mortgage and a checking account with the same bank may write a check through the "teller system" to pay the premium that is later processed by the "mortgage loan system." Recently, system design has been successful in allowing the automatic transfer of funds form a bank account to pay bills and other obligations to creditors, regardless of distance or location. This means that in systems analysis, knowledge of the boundaries of a given system is crucial in determining the nature of its interface with other systems for successful design.

13.2.2 Types of Systems

Systems are broadly characterized as follows:

- **Natural Systems:** These systems already exist in nature. Natural systems can be physical systems like geological and molecular systems or living systems like plant and animal systems. These natural systems interact with man-made and automated systems. These systems can also be a component of automated systems.
- **Man-Made Systems:** These systems are designed by human-beings. Some examples of such systems are social, communication, transportation, financial, and manufacturing systems.
- **Automated Systems:** Man-made systems controlled by computers are called automated systems. These systems are comprised of computer hardware, software, people, data and procedures. Automated systems are categorised as follows:
  - *Batch Systems:* Batch systems retrieve information on a sequential basis.
  - *On-line Systems:* On-line systems interact with the surrounding environment by accepting input and supplying output to it.
  - *Real-Time Systems:* These systems control the environment by receiving data, processing it and returning the results in a time efficient manner.
  - *Decision-Support Systems:* These systems help managers and other professional 'knowledge workers' in an organization to make intelligent and informed decisions about the various aspects of operation.
  - *Knowledge-Based Systems:* These systems try to imitate the intelligent tasks performed by human beings.

13.3 SYSTEM ANALYSIS

The various phases involved in system development are survey, analysis, design, implementation, testing, installation and maintenance. The people connected with the activity of the system development are users, managers, and technical experts. Analysis activity transforms the policies of the user and the characteristics of the system into a structured specification. System analysis helps us gain a better knowledge of the components in the system and their functionalities. Indeed, this method of splitting up the system into components and studying their behaviour has existed since nineteenth century, to improve the performance of man-made systems like labour organizations. The science of system analysis has also developed along with IT applications.

The process of system analysis deals with the following activities:

- Identification of the functionalities of the existing system.
- Understanding the operation of the existing system.
- Understanding the user's needs.
- Identification of the functionalities of the new system.
- Deciding the operations of the new system.

Analysis plays a very important part in the life cycle of the system as this activity relates to all other activities and subjects participating in the system. Around 50% of faults originate due to deficiencies in system analysis. Thus, a thorough analysis of the system can speed up other phases of software development like system design, implementation and testing. Programmers can also ensure that the developed system has met the user requirements using complete analysis documentation.

Systems analysis is a process of collecting factual data, understand the processes involved, identifying problems and recommending feasible suggestions for improving the system functioning. This involves studying the business processes, gathering operational data, understand the information flow, finding out bottlenecks and evolving solutions for overcoming the weaknesses of the system so as to achieve the organizational goals. System Analysis also includes subdividing of complex process involving the entire system, identification of data store and manual processes.

The major objectives of systems analysis are to find answers for each business process: What is being done, How is it being done, Who is doing it, When is he doing it, Why is it being done and How can it be improved? It is more of a thinking process and involves the creative skills of the System Analyst. It attempts to give birth to a new efficient system that satisfies the current needs of the user and has scope for future growth within the organizational constraints. The result of this process is a logical system design. Systems analysis is an iterative process that continues until a preferred and acceptable solution emerges.

The person who does system analysis is called a system analyst. A system analyst is a key member of any systems development project. The various roles performed by a systems analyst are:

- A system analyst performs the tasks of an archaeologist as he maintains a clear and concise documentation of business policies.
- A system analyst identifies the true causes of the user's problems and identifies solutions to overcome these problems.
- A system analyst acts as a mediator who tries to compromise on the conflicting views of the users, managers, programmers, and auditors.

- Usually, a system analyst also performs the role of a project leader who manages the activities of the project.

To perform these roles, the system analyst should be able to:

- Model the system diagrammatically.
- Interview the users and mediate disagreements.
- Understand the users' business needs.
- Analyse the system from different perspectives.
- Understand both the abstract and physical view of the system.

Analysis of systems was initially performed in an unorganized manner. Due to thus the software developed was unsuccessful. Hence following a structured methodology for system analysis is highly essential to develop efficient and successful applications.

13.4 SYSTEM DESIGN

Based on the user requirements and the detailed analysis of the existing system, the new system must be designed. This is the phase of system designing. It is the most crucial phase in the developments of a system. The logical system design arrived at as a result of systems analysis is converted into physical system design. Normally, the design proceeds in two stages:

- **Preliminary or General Design:** In the preliminary or general design, the features of the new system are specified. The costs of implementing these features and the benefits to be derived are estimated. If the project is still considered to be feasible, we move to the detailed design stage.
- **Structured or Detailed Design:** In the detailed design stage, computer oriented work begins in earnest. At this stage, the design of the system becomes more structured. Structure design is a blue print of a computer system solution to a given problem having the same components and inter-relationships among the same components as the original problem. Input, output, databases, forms, codification schemes and processing specifications are drawn up in detail. In the design stage, the programming language and the hardware and software platform in which the new system will run are also decided.

There are several tools and techniques used for describing the system design of the system. These tools and techniques are:

- Flowchart
- Data flow diagram (DFD)
- Data dictionary
- Structured English
- Decision table
- Decision tree

Some of the above tools for designing will be discussed in detailed in the next sections. The system design involves:

(i) Defining precisely the required system output
(ii) Determining the data requirement for producing the output

(iii) Determining the medium and format of files and databases
(iv) Devising processing methods and use of software to produce output
(v) Determine the methods of data capture and data input
(vi) Designing Input forms
(vii) Designing Codification Schemes
(viii) Detailed manual procedures
(ix) Documenting the Design

Before discussing the techniques of system analysis and design, here we present a brief overview of the need for various systematic analysis and design techniques.

13.5 SYSTEMS ANALYST

The systems analyst systematically assesses how users interact with technology and businesses function by examining the inputting and processing of data and the outputting of information with the intent of improving organizational processes.

Many improvements involve better support of users' work tasks and business functions through the use of computerized systems. This definition emphasizes a systematic, methodical approach to analyzing—and potentially improving—what is occurring in the specific context experienced by users and created by a business.

Our definition of a systems analyst is necessarily broad. The analyst must be able to work with people of all descriptions and be experienced in working with computers. The analyst plays many roles, sometimes balancing several at the same time. The three primary roles of the systems analyst are consultant, supporting expert, and agent of change.

13.5.1 Systems Analyst As Consultant

The systems analyst frequently acts as a systems consultant to humans and their businesses and, thus, may be hired specifically to address information systems issues within a business. Such hiring can be an advantage because outside consultants can bring with them a fresh perspective that other people in an organization do not possess. It also means that outside analysts are at a disadvantage because the true organizational culture can never be known to an outsider. As an outside consultant, you will rely heavily on the systematic methods discussed throughout this text to analyze and design appropriate information systems for users working in a particular business. In addition, you will rely on information systems users to help you understand the organizational culture from others' viewpoints.

13.5.2 Systems Analyst As Supporting Expert

Another role that you may be required to play is that of supporting expert within a business for which you are regularly employed in some systems capacity. In this role the analyst draws on professional expertise concerning computer hardware and software and their uses in the business. This work is often not a full-blown systems project, but rather it entails a small modification or decision affecting a single department.

As the support expert, you are not managing the project; you are merely serving as a resource for those who are. If you are a systems analyst employed by a manufacturing or service organization, many of your daily activities may be encompassed by this role.

13.5.3 Systems Analyst As Agent of Change

The most comprehensive and responsible role that the system analyst takes on is that of an agent of change, whether internal or external to the business. As an analyst, you are an agent of change whenever you perform any of the activities in the systems development life cycle (discussed in the next section) and are present and interacting with users and the business for an extended period (from two weeks to more than a year). An agent of change can be defined as a person who serves as a catalyst for change, develops a plan for change, and works with others in facilitating that change.

Your presence in the business changes it. As a systems analyst, you must recognize this fact and use it as a starting point for your analysis. Hence, you must interact with users and management (if they are not one and the same) from the very beginning of your project. Without their help you cannot understand what they need to support their work in the organization, and real change cannot take place.

If change (that is, improvements to the business that can be realized through information systems) seems warranted after analysis, the next step is to develop a plan for change along with the people who must enact the change. Once a consensus is reached on the change that is to be made, you must constantly interact with those who are changing.

As a systems analyst acting as an agent of change, you advocate a particular avenue of change involving the use of information systems. You also teach users the process of change, because changes in the information system do not occur independently but cause changes in the rest of the organization as well.

13.5.4 Qualities of the Systems Analyst

From the foregoing descriptions of the roles the systems analyst plays, it is easy to see that the successful systems analyst must possess a wide range of qualities. Many different kinds of people are systems analysts, so any description is destined to fall short in some way. There are some qualities, however, that most systems analysts seem to display.

Above all, the analyst is a *problem solver*. He or she is a person who views the analysis of problems as a challenge and who enjoys devising workable solutions. When necessary, the analyst must be able to systematically tackle the situation at hand through *skillful* application of tools, techniques, and experience. The analyst must also be a *communicator* capable of relating meaningfully to other people over extended periods of time. Systems analysts need to be able to *understand* humans' needs in interacting with technology, and they need enough computer experience to program, to understand the capabilities of computers, to glean information requirements from users, and to communicate what is needed to programmers. They also need to possess strong personal and *professional ethics* to help them shape their client relationships.

The systems analyst must be a self-disciplined, self-motivated individual who is able to manage and coordinate other people, as well as innumerable project resources. Systems analysis is a demanding career, but, in compensation, an ever-changing and always challenging one.

13.6 COMPLEXITY OF SYSTEMS

We have already studied about systems. A social system like an institution has a highly complicated structure. Here, groups of people join together to accomplish tasks that cannot be done by individuals. The interactions among these people are very important for the successful functioning of the system.

The main purpose of this section is to introduce readers to the complexity of real world systems. This section clearly explains the complexity of software systems and the attributes of such a system. Methods of overcoming the complexity in such systems to facilitate their successful implementation are also provided.

13.6.1 Complexity of Software Systems

Natural systems like the circulatory system, galaxies and molecules as well as man-made systems like bridges have highly complex organization and functionality. The study of fields as diverse as astronomy and nuclear physics provide us with many other examples of incredibly complex systems.

It is very difficult to analyse and study such systems. Computer systems are devices possessing moderate complexity. A computer system is composed up of major elements like CPU, monitor, keyboard, etc. each of which is made up of minor parts. Enterprise software systems are also highly complex. The more complex the system is, the more susceptible it is to failures. Mastering the complexity of software is highly essential to prevent delivery of software that is late, over budget, and deficient in its stated requirements. This is known as software crisis.

Enterprise software exhibits a very rich set of behaviours and interacts with real world situations. Management of resources and integrity of software is of utmost importance. The main characteristic of industrial strength software is that it is extremely difficult for the developer to comprehend all the information about the entities into the design. This complexity is an essential property of all large software systems. This inherent complexity of the software systems derives from four elements. They are:

- **The Complexity of the Problem Domain:** The real world problems that are solved by software include complex elements which may have contradicting functional and non-functional requirements. This complexity usually springs from the 'communication gap' that exists between the users of a system and its developers. Further, systems also continuously evolve over time based on changing user requirements.
- **The Difficulty of Managing the Development Process:** As a team of developers are involved in software development, maintaining unity and integrity of design becomes a challenge. This problem becomes even more aggravated while considering the communication and coordination among members who are geographically dispersed.
- **The Flexibility Possible through Software:** Unlike other fields of engineering, software development does not have a well-established standard. It is still labour intensive with less reuse. This makes the system more rigid and difficult to maintain.
- **The Problems of Characterizing the Behaviour of Discrete Systems:** Analog systems such as the trajectory of a bullet are continuous systems. In a continuous system, small changes in inputs will always cause correspondingly small changes in outputs. As

software is executed on digital computers, the system is said to have discrete states. These systems have a very large number of possible states. As we cannot model the behaviour of the discrete systems complexity, the degree of correctness achieved on implementing these systems is not satisfactory.

13.6.2 Attributes of a Complex System

The attributes common to all complex systems are:

- **Hierarchic Structure:** Complexity takes the form of a hierarchy. A complex system is composed of interrelated subsystems that are in turn composed of subsystems. Finally, these subsystems are composed of elementary components. The architecture of a complex system is a function of its components as well as the hierarchical relationships among these components.
- **Relative Primitives:** The choice of what components in a system are primitive is highly dependent on the view of a particular user of the system. For example, a building may be viewed by different people in different ways. A plumber may view it as a collection of electrical components like wires, bulbs, fans, etc.
- **Separation of Concerns:** A complex system is implemented by decomposing it into subsystems and components. For a system to be efficient, intra-component linkages should be stronger than inter-component linkages. It enables the separation of high-frequency dynamics of the components (internal structure of the components) from low-frequency dynamics (interaction among components).
- **Common Patterns:** Hierarchical elements are usually composed of only a few different kinds of subsystems in various combinations and arrangements. For example, almost all plants have the same systems and subsystems. So complex systems have common patterns that promote reuse of small components.
- **Stable Intermediate Forms:** Usually complex systems are built using existing systems and components. As systems evolve, complex objects in the systems evolve into primitive objects on which more complex systems are built.

According to general principles, a complex system is made up of two hierarchies that architect the system. They are the class-structured hierarchy and the object-structured hierarchy. A class-structured hierarchy is concerned with extracting the common characteristics of classes. For example, a four wheeler is a vehicle. So it has all the characteristics of a vehicle with four wheels. It is also called as 'is-a' hierarchy. As object structured hierarchy is concerned with grouping of objects (parts) to form a whole. For example, a car is composed up of parts like engine, wheels, door, etc. It is also called as a 'part-of' hierarchy.

A complex software system that is designed to exhibit well-engineered class and object structures and embody the five attributes of complex systems is said to be successful. Even though the theoretical rules for design of successful software systems are well known, the human capacity to deal with disorganised complexity puts a restriction of the design of successful complex systems.

13.6.3 Dealing with Complexity

To deal with complexity, the divide and conquer method of decomposing a larger system into smaller parts which can be understood and refined independently is used. Decomposition can be characterized into two types. They are:

- **Algorithmic Decomposition:** Top-down structured design uses algorithmic decomposition. Here, each module in the system denotes a major step in some overall process. Here, the problem is decomposed, based on the functionality it performs.
- **Object-Oriented Decomposition:** Rather than decomposing the problem based on the functionality, decomposition can be based on the entities on the system. Here, the world is viewed as a set of autonomous agents that collaborate to perform a higher-level behaviour. These agents are objects that compose the system. As this method of decomposition is based on objects, it is called object-oriented decomposition.

We discuss both these approaches of dealing with complexity in detail in the next sections.

13.7 SYSTEM DEVELOPMENT APPROACHES

The development of software involves a variety of tasks, such as defining the problem, having a certain scope and vision, gathering detailed requirements, making the design, implementing the system with the help of programming technology, testing the developed system, delivering the product, and even maintaining it. Basically, there are two approaches of developing software.

- The first approach called traditional approach (**Structured System Analysis and Design**) is algorithmic approach in which we decompose the larger algorithm into smaller ones. The main building block of software is procedure or function. This approach is very simple. But as requirements change, the systems built with an algorithmic focus turn out to be very hard to maintain.
- The second approach which is now-a-days mostly followed is object-oriented approach (**Object Oriented Analysis and Design**). In this approach the main building block of software system is the class or object. A collection of objects having some common attributes and behavior is termed as a class. This approach is little bit complex, but changes in requirements can be easily accommodated.

Object-oriented approach methods differs from traditional approach in that the traditional techniques view software as a collection of programs (or functions) and isolated data. A software system is a set of mechanism for performing certain action on certain data, i.e. "Algorithm + Data structure = Program".

This means that there are two different, yet complementary ways to view software construction:

(1) We can focus primarily on the functions, or

(2) We can focus primarily on the data.

The heart of distinction between traditional system development methodologies and newer object-oriented methodologies lies in their primary focus, where the traditional approach focuses on the functions of the system, and object-oriented systems development centres on the object, which combines data and functionality. As we will see, this seemingly simple shift in focus radically changes the process of software development.

Let us look at both these approaches of systems development and discuss why we should study them.

13.8 STRUCTURED SYSTEM ANALYSIS AND DESIGN (SSAD)

We have studied the need for system analysis. Analysing systems in an ad hoc fashion increases the error rate in the systems developed. Hence, an organised way of analysing systems has to be followed. This gave rise to the SSAD methodology. The drive behind structured system analysis is that the principles of structured analysis can also be applied to analysis and designing stage.

SSAD advocates a top-down approach in system development. **Some of the characteristics of this methodology are as follows:**

- This method promotes the partitioning of an application into chapters and analysing each part separately.
- This method facilitates the easy updating of an existing system.
- This method promotes the usage of tools, techniques and models to record and analyse the current system.
- This method of analysis and design clearly differentiates between the physical model and logical models of a system. A physical model is used in surveying the current system and designing the new system while a logical model is used in analysing system's requirements.
- The role of the users is clearly differentiates between the physical model and logical models of a system. A physical model is used in surveying the current system and designing the new system while a logical model is used in analysing system's requirements.
- The role of the users is clearly understood in different stages of the system development. Hence, parallel execution of different stages is possible in SSAD methodology.
- Feedback obtained from one stage can be used to improve upon the output of the previous stage. This improves the traceability of the system.

The objectives of SSAD methodology are:

- To develop systems of good quality.
- To foster effective staff management.
- To enable successful execution and maintenance of projects.
- To promote the development of systems using tools.
- To improve communication between participants in a project.

Widely used SDLC models in SSAD are the waterfall and the spiral models. In the waterfall model, the different phases in software development life cycle like survey, requirements, analysis, design, implementation, design, testing, installation and maintenance are performed one after the other by a separate group of experts. The spiral model is the basis for iterative development systems. In this approach, the system development process is divided into different steps and smoothened after repetitive steps. So, the system becomes more perfect after these repetitive steps. **The major steps in SSAD methodology are listed below:**

- **Feasibility Study:** This step determines the cost effectiveness of the proposed system.
- **Requirements Analysis:** This step identifies the system requirements using which the proposed system can be modelled.
- **Requirements Specification:** It identifies the functional and non-functional requirements of the system.
- **Logical System Specification:** It is used to create the logical design of the system.
- **Physical Design:** It includes database and program design. Physical design is done using the logical system specification and technical system specification.

In the process of system analysis, analysts often construct models to give an overview on aspects of the whole system. **Models facilitate the following:**

- They allow the user to abstract the important features of the system, ignoring the unwanted details.
- They permit the easy incorporation of changes in the system.
- They enable the analyst to have a complete understanding of the user's requirements.

SSAD analyses the system using three different modeling techniques. They are:

- **Logical Data Modeling:** This model identifies and documents the data requirements of the system being designed. Data is separated into entities. As this model identifies the relationships between these entities, it gives the structural specification of the system.
- **Data Flow Modeling:** This model is concerned with the movement of the data around the information system by examining processes, data stores, external entities, and data flows. This model gives the functional specification of the system.
- **Entity Behaviour Modeling:** This model identifies and documents events with respect to the entities in the system and the order in which these events take place. This model gives the process specification of the system.

These models are explained in the following subsections.

13.8.1 Data Flow Modeling

This model gives the functional specification of the system. It is represented using Functional Diagram (FD) and Data Flow Diagram (DFD).

13.8.1.1 Functional Diagram (FD)

A functional diagram is used to describe the functionalities of a system. A functional diagram describes what a system should do to meet the users' requirements. It analyses the system by dividing its functionality into a number of smaller functions. For example, consider an online shopping system. The main functionalities of the system are management of customers, management of goods and money transactions. Customer management activity includes adding a new customer and checking for customers as shown in Figure 1.1.

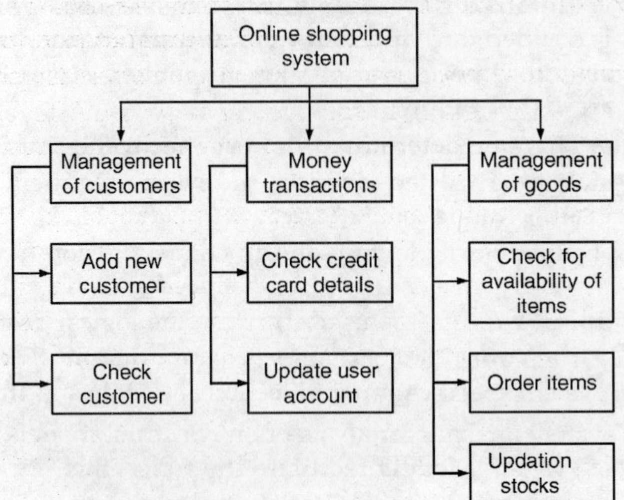

Figure 13.2: Functional Diagram of an Online Shopping System

13.8.1.2 Data Flow Diagram (DFD)

After identification of the functionalities of the system, its implementation details should be described. The modeling tool that is frequently used for this purpose is DFD. A DFD describes the information flow in the system. It describes how a given input is transformed into the output and the functions used to perform this transaction. A DFD is used for the following:

- A DFD determines the user's requirements. Hence, it can be used as a tool for analysis.
- A DFD is used in design as it aids in planning and illustrating the solutions for analysis and users.
- A DFD is simple. SO it aids the analysts to communicate their ideas to the users.
- A DFD acts as an aid in documenting both the user's requirements and the system design.

Different analysis and design methodologies follow different notations for representation of elements in the DFD. The main components of a DFD are:

- **The Process:** The process shows the part of the system that transforms a given input into the desired output. It is represented graphically as a circle or a rounded rectangle as depicted in Figure 13.3(c). The process name should describe the functionality of the process.
- **The Data Flow:** The data flow is used to describe the movement of information from one part of the system to another. It is represented graphically by a named arrow into or out of a process as depicted in Figure 13.3(e).
- **The Data Store:** The data store is used to model a collection of data packets at rest. It is represented graphically by a rectangle with one shorter edge omitted. Another line is also given to identify the data store. The flow represents data in motion, whereas the stores represent data at rest as depicted in Figure 13.3(d).

- **External Entities:** External entities can be a person, a group of persons or an organization who can act on the system. It identifies the system's relationship to the outside world. An external factor is represented by a rectangle as depicted in Figure 13.3(b).
- **Internal Entities:** Internal entities are the system functions or processes. It is represented by a rectangle, one shorter edge of which can be omitted while the other is drawn by a single line as depicted in Figure 13.3(a).

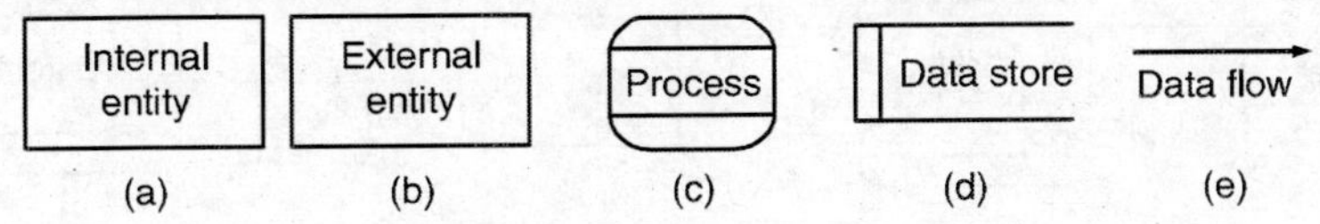

Figure 13.3: *Elements of DFD*

A DFD does not describe the data involved in the information flow. So a data dictionary is used. A data dictionary provides an organised and well-defined listing of all the data elements pertinent to the system. It provides a complete and consistent listing of all the data flows and composite data elements in the system. Building a data dictionary is one of the most time consuming activities of system analysis.

Thus the data flow diagrams illustrate how data is processed by a system in terms of inputs and outputs. Data flow diagrams are drawn in several nested layers. The functionalities of a system can be represented by different levels of DFDs. A context diagram is a top-level (Level 0) DFD. It only contains one process node (process 0) that generalizes the function of an entire system or relationship to external entities as shown in Figure 13.4(a). Now process 0 can be broken down into two processes: process 1 and process 2 as depicted in Figure 13.4(b) to form level 1 DFD. This process of decomposition can be continued until a desired level of system detail is obtained by the designer.

For example, consider the process of online shopping. The context diagram for this example consists of an external entity (customer) and a single process (online shopping process) as shown in Figure 13.4(a). In level 1, the shopping process is expanded into three processes, verification of credit card details, shipment of items and updating customer/merchant accounts. Once the customer places his order, his credit card details are verified. Then the order is shipped to the customer and his account is updated as shown in Figure 13.4(b).

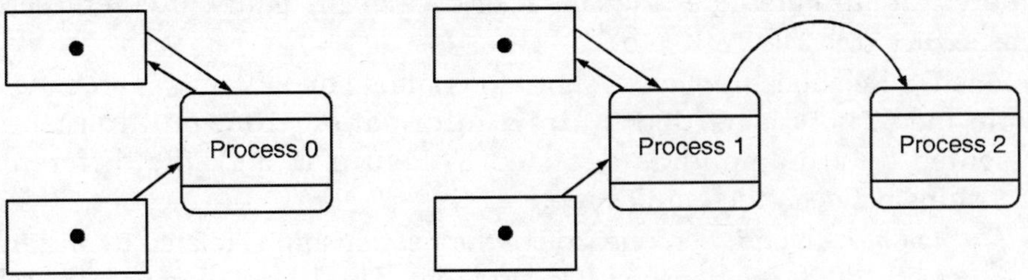

Figure 13.4: *(a) Context Diagram; (b) Level 0 DFD*

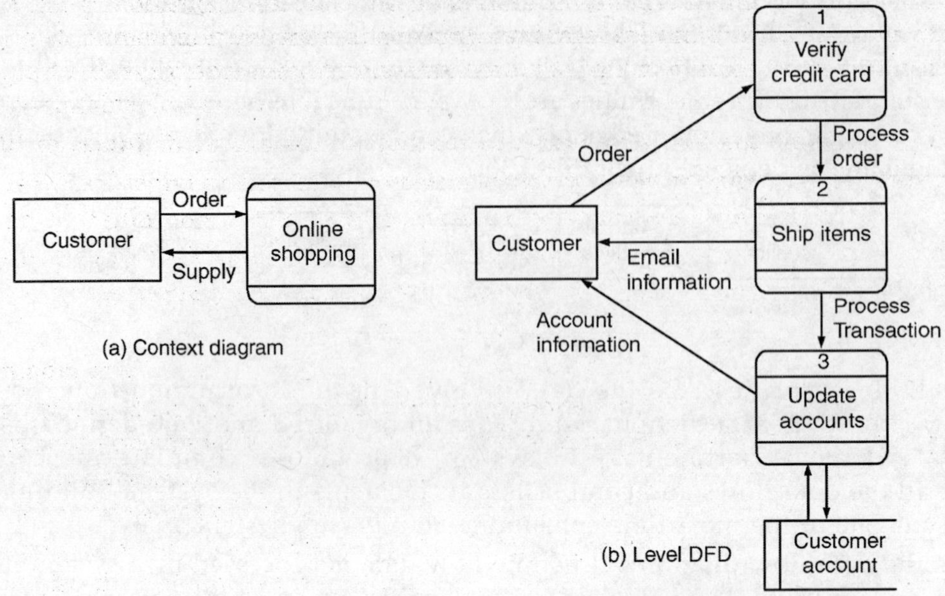

Figure 13.5: *Data Flow Diagrams for Online Shopping*

Thus at the end of function analysis phase, we have two diagrams: the function hierarchy diagram and the data flow diagram. These diagrams form the basis for finding out entities in the system and their relationships between them. This is represented by the Entity-Relationship Diagram.

13.8.2 Logical Data Modeling

Logical data modeling is performed using Entity-Relationship Diagram (ERD). ERD is a network model that describes the stored data of a system at a high level of abstraction. It highlights the relationship between data stores on DFD. The main components of an ERD include the following:

- **Entity:** An entity is a subject, a duty, or an event that has a significant meaning to the future system and is displayed by a rectangle as depicted in Figure 13.6(a).
- **Attribute:** An attribute gives the characteristics of the entity. It is represented by an oval as depicted in Figure 13.6(b).
- **Relationship:** Relationship shows connections among the system's entities. Relationships provide the structure needed to draw information from multiple entities. It is represented by a diamond as depicted in Figure 13.6(c). the different types of relationships between the entities are:
  - *One-to-One:* An entity on one side of the relationship is related to one entity on the other side of the relationship. It is represented by 1:1 notation near the relationship.
  - *One-to-Many:* An entity on one side of the relationship is related to many entities on the other side of the relationship. It is represented as 1:n.
  - *Many-to-Many:* This relationship holds between many entities on either side of the relationship. It is represented as n:n.

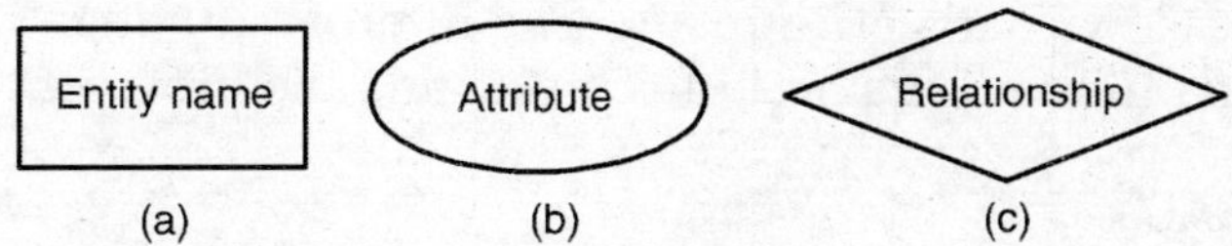

Figure 13.6: Elements of ER Diagrams

For example, consider the following statement:

Painters are treated in a single **ward** by the **doctors** assigned to them. Usually each patient will be assigned a single doctor, but in rare cases they will have two. **Health care assistants** also attend the patients; a number of these assistants are associated with each ward.

The following steps are followed in the construction of ER diagrams:

1. **Definition of Entities:** Entities are nouns used in the description of the system. It is represented in **bold** in the system description given above.
2. **Definition of Relationships:** Relationships are verbs used in the description of the system. Relationships are underlined in the system description given above.
3. **Identifying Attributes:** This is done by querying the system. It describes the variables that characterize the entities.
4. **Cardinality:** Adding cardinality to the relations. For example, patient-ward relationship is a one-to-one relationship.

The ERD of this example is depicted in Figure 13.7.

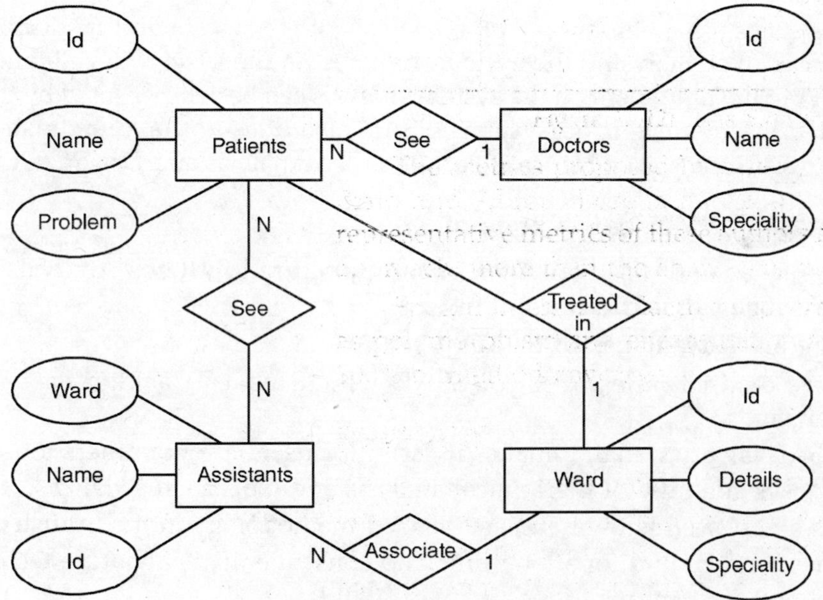

Figure 13.7: An Example ERD

13.8.3 Entity Behaviour Modeling

This model is represented using the process specification diagrams. These diagrams show the behaviour of the entity. Decision tables, flow charts, and structured English are used for this purpose. Flow charts are already used in programming. Structured English is an algorithmic notation (formal) method of representing the process.

13.8.4 Benefits of SSAD

The following are the benefits of SSAD methodology:

1. SSAD allows a person to plan, manage and control a project well. Hence, it enables the timely delivery of the product.
2. The user's needs are fully analysed. Hence thus model improves the usability of the system.
3. The progress of the project is carefully documented. So SSAD ensures that all the business objectives are fully met.
4. SSAD promotes the use of modeling tools. Hence the systems can be develops quickly and effectively.
5. Conformance to the specified quality has to be assured. Hence SSAD reduces the error rate in the systems developed.
6. SSAD enables the developers to meet the business requirements and also ensures better quality and on-time delivery of products. Hence the overall productivity of the product is ensured.
7. SSAD separates logical and physical design of the systems. Hence the same design can be reused for implementing the system over some other hardware.

As SSAD puts special emphasis on the analysis of the system and its documentation, it has the danger of over-analysing the system. As a result, the system development time and cost increases. But the time spent on the system analysis can be compensated by the amount of reuse promoted by the developed systems. SSAD also does not favour drastic changes in specifications given by the user. Hence Object-Oriented Analysis and Design (OOAD) is used.

13.8.5 Advantages and Disadvantages of SSAD

The advantages and disadvantages of the Structured Systems Analysis and Design methodology can be summarized as follows:

Following are Advantages of SSAD:

1. There are distinct milestones for SSAD which makes tracking easier for project management.
2. Since SSAD is very visual, it makes it easier for users/programmers to understand.
3. SSAD makes good use of it graphical analysis and tools such as DFD's.
4. SSAD is a very well-known and established methodology in the industry.
5. SSAD has been around for a long time and consequently is a mature technique.
6. SSAD allows for a means of requirements validation.
7. Finally SSAD is relatively simple and easy to understand.

Following are the Disadvantages of SSAD:

1. Since SSAD is process-oriented, it ignores the non-functional requirements.
2. There is less direct management involvement in SSAD.

3. Since SSAD is non-iterative like the waterfall model, so that requirements changes would mean restarting the entire process.
4. In SSAD there is some but not enough user/analyst interaction.
5. Except for the logical design and the DFD's, SSAD provides no other tools for communication with users, and therefore it is more difficult for users to measure progress.
6. In SSAD it is more difficult to decide when to stop functional decomposition and to start building the system.
7. SSAD does not always address the user's requirements.
8. Finally, SSAD is not a good fit for object-oriented programming languages, as it was originally designed for structured programming languages and not object-oriented ones.

13.9 OBJECT-ORIENTED ANALYSIS AND DESIGN

In earlier sections, we have discussed about system analysis and structured methodology of system analysis and design. The amount of reuse in this methodology is only at a higher level of abstraction. Further, SSAD views the system as a collection of functionality. But real-world systems are usually viewed in terms of entities encapsulated with their properties and behaviour. Hence object-oriented analysis came into existence. Thus section describes about the process, the need for object-oriented analysis and design, its advantages and disadvantages.

13.9.1 Object-Oriented Analysis

The method of analysis is done by identifying the classes in the system and their responsibilities. It answers the 'what' aspects of the system.

The activities that should be performed as a part of OOA are:

- Determining the functionality of the system. This is called requirements analysis.
- Creating a list of classes that are part of the system. It also enlists the classes that are not part of the system.
- Distributing the functionality of the system among the list of classes. A piece of functionality assigned to a specific class is called a responsibility.

The characteristics of a good OOA are as follows:

- Classes should be relatively small and generalised. This increases reuse by permitting the classes to be used again in a future project.
- Responsibility and control should be distributed.
- OOA describes the world. It is not a computer science jargon.
- Every object in the system should have some responsibility.
- Updation and maintenance of the system is minimized. Using OOA, the existing parts of the design would change minimally, even if the requirements are changed or enhanced.
- This approach avoids redundancy of information.

13.9.2 Object-Oriented Design

OOD specifies the design of the system. It deals with 'how' the functionality is performed by the system. The primary goal of the OOD phase is to convert the analysis specifications of the system obtained in OOA into a design that can be easily implemented.

The characteristics of OOD are as follows:

- To decompose the analysed system, thus making it easier for implementing the system.
- To depict the logical and physical as well as static and dynamic structures of the system.
- To identify the flow of information through the system. OOD decides on the information each class should know. It also decides the information that other classes need to know.

To design the static structure of the system, attributes and services have to be assigned to classes. Further, links have to be assigned to pass messages between these classes.

Design takes care of the activities explained below:

- **Assigning Attributes and Services:** *Attributes* represent the state of the object. It tells us what the object 'knows'. An attribute should not contain the name of another object in the system. If an attribute has sufficient details to form its own class, it should be identified as a separate class. This helps to improve the modifiability of the system. For example, consider a pen object. The attributes of a pen include make, model, owner, etc. A *service* represents the functionality the object should perform. It is implemented as a method. An object typically does those things that are done to the real-world object it represents. For example, the services offered by a pen object are writing, filling ink, etc.
- **Assigning Links:** A *link* represents a connection between two classes. It shows how the classes share information between them. For example, consider pen and ink objects. Filling ink into the pen is the link between them.

13.9.3 Object-Oriented Programming (OOP)

OOP is an organization of programs into a co-operative collection of objects with a class hierarchy. OOP is mainly based on objects and not on algorithm or procedures.

Some of the characteristics of object-oriented programs are given below:

- Object-oriented programs encourage encapsulation. Encapsulation also brings about data hiding. Here, the details of an objects implementation are hidden from other objects.
- They are easier to debug and maintain.
- Object-oriented programs encourage modularity. This means that pieces of the program do not depend on other pieces of the program.
- Classes formed can be reused in future projects. This makes it easier to build new projects.
- It works very well for implementation of large and complex systems.

13.10 OBJECT MODELING

Usually analysis is performed to obtain the static, dynamic and functional views of a system. The static model used in OOAD methodology is called the object model. Object-oriented models are useful for understanding problems, communicating with application experts, modeling enterprise, preparing documentation, and designing programs and databases. Object-oriented modeling and design provides better understanding of requirements, cleaner design and more maintainable systems.

The following steps are carried out to establish an object model:

- Identification of classes and objects from the given requirement specification.
- Identification of operations that can be performed by the object.
- Establishment of the visibility of the operations and attributes in the object.
- Establishment of the interface that exposes the services offered by an object.
- Implementation of the objects.

Some characteristics of an object model are:

- Object modeling is about finding objects, their attributes and their operations, and tying them together as a model. It is based on entities with hidden state and operations on that state. Objects communicate using messages.
- In an object model, all data is stored as attributes of some object.
- An object model comprehensively and competently defines the system's functionality by specifying not only the data but also the operations on the data.
- The attributes of an object are manipulated only by making use of its operations. The only way of accessing the values of an object's attribute is through its operation. This brings about data hiding.
- An object can manipulate another object only through an operation offered by that object or using an object's interfaces.
- The process of object-oriented analysis and design is one of elaborating object model, increasing its detail and scope until enough information is obtained to construct the state model of the system. The object model is the principal output of an analysis and design process.
- The distinction between analysis and design is much greyer in object-oriented development. Objects identified during analysis are fully decomposed and expanded in the design phase.
- The object model is the central pillar of an analysis or design. It defines the computable entities in the system.
- The dynamic and functional models can also operate on the objects, attributes and operations being defined in the object model.
- OOAD views the software as a set of interacting objects, SSAD methodology views the software as a set of functions.
- An object-oriented model uses information hiding to minimize dependence on global state information.
- It uses various object-oriented abstractions like classification, inheritance, aggregation, and polymorphism.
- Abstraction in object model aid to cope up with the complexity inherent in many kinds of system.
- There is a clear separation between the internal and external behaviour of the system in an object model

Advantages of object modeling are:

- Shared data areas are eliminated in an object model. Objects communicate by exchanging messages. This reduces the overall system coupling.
- Objects are independent entities. Object models clearly separate external and internal behaviour of the system using interfaces. Hence, changes in implementation of a class do not impact on the design of the entire system. This enhances the reuse of the system.
- Objects can execute either sequentially or in parallel.
- For many systems, there is a clear mapping between real world entities and objects within the system. This improves the understandability of the design.
- Objects formed are relatively stable over time. This in turn aids in reuse of results of analysis.
- Object modeling avoids shifting the underlying representation of the system as it progresses from analysis to design to implementation. Object-oriented concepts can be used to provide a smooth transition between the different stages of system development, like analysis, design and implementation stages.
- It creates building blocks from object and groupings of objects. SSAD methodology uses chunks of data and/or functions as the basic building blocks. Hence it provides a higher level of abstraction.

13.11 OBJECT-ORIENTED CONCEPTS

The main objective of analysis is to capture a complete, unambiguous and consistent picture of the requirements of the system. It is an iterative and creative process that demands a complete understanding of the problem. When object orientation is applied in the initial stages of software life cycle, like analysis and design, it fosters the development of high quality and reusable systems.

Object-oriented analysis is a method of analysis that examines requirements from the perspective of classes and objects found in the vocabulary of the problem domain. Here we organize the system as a collection of discrete objects that incorporate both data and functionality.

Object-oriented analysis and design fosters the following concepts:

- **Information Hiding:** Information hiding is the key to object-oriented thinking. It stressed on hiding the unnecessary information from the user. It simplifies the design of the system and reduces ripple effect. Objects are like black boxes that hide the implementation details of their functionality from the users. For example, consider a bank account object. Bank customers are aware of the functionalities that it offers like opening an account, depositing/withdrawing money, inquiring for current balance, etc. But they do not know how these functionalities are to be carried out.
- **Abstraction:** Abstraction is the process of supressing the inessential details of the system while focusing on the essential details of the system. Higher levels of abstraction focus on the important characteristic of an entity, while lower levels of abstraction focus on its construction. For example, consider an automobile. At its higher level of abstraction, it is viewed as a mode of transportation. At its lower level, it is viewed in terms of its components like engine, transmission system, electrical system, etc. and their connections. Abstraction can be categorized as follows:

  - *Functional Abstraction:* It provides information on what functionality is being offered by the system, while suppressing the details of its implementation. For example, consider a sorting functionality. Functional abstraction provided by the developer hides what type of sorting algorithm is used from the customer.
  - *Data Abstraction:* It is built on top of functional abstraction. The attributes of an object are accessible only through the functionalities offered by the object. Thus the information (data) is an abstraction. It is only accessible through a well-defined interface comprised of operations.
  - *Process Abstraction:* It deals with how an object handles itself in parallel processing environment with more than one thread of control.
- **Encapsulation:** Localization is the process of gathering and placing things in close physical proximity to each other. Encapsulation is the process of logically and/or physically packaging items so that they may be treated as a section. While functional decomposition localizes information around functions and data-driven decomposition localizes information around data, object-oriented approaches localize information around objects. Classes provide a powerful encapsulation of data and functionality.
- **Concurrency:** It enables parallel execution of processes. Object-oriented approach can simplify the development of concurrent systems to great extent.

Object oriented approaches emphasize on the following:

- Using an object as the essential section.
- Using three complementary views of a system: static model, dynamic model and process or functional models.
- Using models at every life cycle stage.

Static data models aim at identifying the conceptual entities (objects) and the static relationships between them. In these models, the focus is on abstracting the entities conceptually into objects, and their attributes. The associations that exist among the entities are formalised as relationships that are based on policies, rules, and physical laws that prevail the real world. The dynamic model describes the behaviour of every object in the system over time. For this reason, concepts describing the dynamic aspects of systems, such as states, events, activities, and actions, are introduced. The functional/process model gives the details of how actions change the numerical attributes or drive output values from imported values.

These and several other object-oriented concepts are discussed in detail in the next chapter.

13.12 OOAD METHODS

The term Object Oriented Analysis and Design (OOAD) was coined in order to differentiate it from the classical analysis and design techniques, such as SSAD. OOAD has attracted a lot of interest in the last few years, and it has become the de facto standard for majority of newly undertaken software projects.

The structure and organization of OOAD is actually not significantly different from SSAD. Both the techniques involve a similar series of steps called phases, namely, Analysis, Design, Coding, Testing and Implementation. However, where OOAD differs from SSAD is in terms of what is done in these phases. The approach and mindset that the analyst is expected to have in OOAD is quite different from the one she is expected to exhibit in case on SSAD.

OOAD has evolved over several years. There have been many methodologies that have been proposed. OOAD as it stands today is actually a mixture of these methodologies. We shall discuss some of the main OOAD methodologies in brief. This will provide us a good background in terms of understanding how and why OOAD is the way it is today. Of the people who have done solid groundwork in the area of OOAD are Grady Booch, Evor Jaobson, and James Rambaugh. Their methodologies are still studied separately to gain an insight into their work. However, more often, a combination of these methods is now studied and applied, as it combines the best features of all of them.

Our focus would be to present a brief yet crisp overview of these methodologies, and in the later sections, show how these converge to a single method called as Rational Unified Process (RUP).

Many methodologies are available to choose from for system development. Each methodology is based on modeling the business problem and implementing the application in an object-oriented fashion; the differences lie primarily in the documentation of information and modeling notations and language. An application can be implemented in many ways to meet the same requirements and provide the same functionality. The largest noticeable differences will be in the trade-offs and detailed design decisions made. Two people using the same methodology may produce application designs that look radically different. This does not necessarily mean that one is right and one is wrong, just as they are different.

In the following section, we look at the methodologies and their modeling notations developed by ***Rumbaugh***, ***Booch*** and ***Jacobson***, which are origins of the ***Unified Modeling Language*** (UML). Their methodologies are still studied separately to gain an insight into their work. However, more often a combination of these methods is now studied and applied, as it combines the best features of all of them. Combining, we call it as ***Rational Unified Process*** (RUP).

Each model has its strengths. The Rumbaugh method is well-suited for describing the object model or the static structure of the system. The Jacobson method is good for producing user-driven analysis models. The Booch method produces detailed object-oriented design models.

13.12.1 Rumbaugh's Object Modeling Technique

The Object Modeling Technique (OMT) presented by Jim Rumbaugh and his co-workers describes a method for the analysis, design, and implementation of a system using an object-oriented technique. OMT is a fast, intuitive approach for identifying and modeling all the objects making up a system. Details such as class attributes, method, inheritance, and association also can be expressed easily. The dynamic behaviour of objects within a system can be described using the OMT dynamic model. This model lets you specify detailed state transitions and their descriptions within a system. Finally, a process description and consumer-producer relationships can be expressed using OMT's functional model.

OMT consists of four phases, which can be performed iteratively:

1. **Analysis:** The results are objects and dynamic and functional models.
2. **System Design:** The results are a structure of the basic architecture of the system along with high-level strategy decisions.
3. **Object Design:** This phase produces a design document, consisting of detailed objects static, dynamic and functional models.
4. **Implementation:** This activity produces reusable, extendible, and robust code.

OMT separates modeling into three different parts:

1. An *object model*, presented by the object model and the data dictionary.
2. A *dynamic model*, presented by the state diagrams and event flow diagrams.
3. A *functional model*, presented by data flow and constraints.

13.12.1.1 The Object Model

The object model describes the structure of objects in a system: their identity, relationships to other objects, attributes, and operations. The object model is represented graphically with an object diagram as shown in Figure 13.8. The object diagram contains classes interconnected by association lines. Each class represents a set of individual objects. The association lines establish relationships among the classes. Each association line represents a set of links from the objects of one class to the objects of another class.

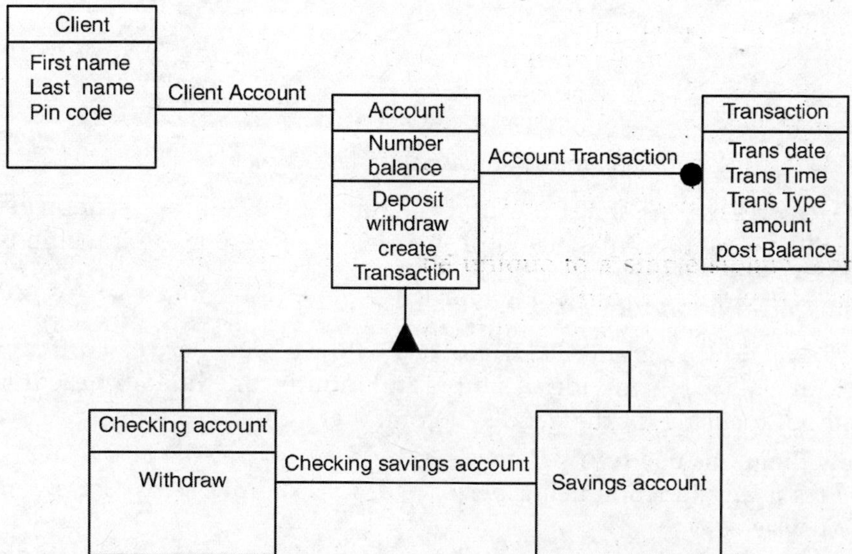

Figure 13.8: *The OMT Model of a Bank System*

In Figure 13.8 is depicted an OMT model of a bank system. The boxes represent classes and the filled triangle represents specialization. Association between Account and Transaction is One-to-Many; since one account can have many transactions. The filled rectangle represents many (Zero or More). The relationship between Client and Account classes is One-to-One, as a client can have only one account and an account can belong to only one person.

13.12.1.2 The OMT Dynamic Model

OMT provides a detailed and comprehensive dynamic model, in addition to letting you depict states, transitions, events, and actions. The OMT state transition diagram is a network of states and events, as depicted in Figure 13.9. Each state receives one or more events, at which time it makes the transition to the next state. The next state depends in the current state as well as the events.

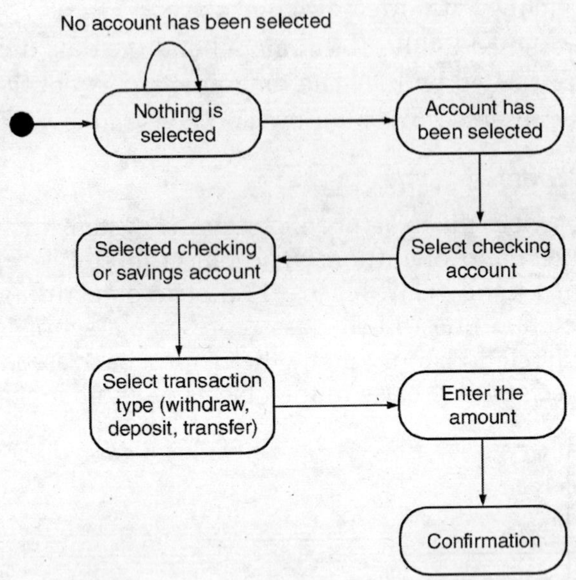

Figure 13.9: State Transition Diagram

Figure 13.9 represents the state transition diagram for the Bank application user interface. Here the round boxes represent states and the arrows represent the transitions.

13.12.1.3 The OMT Functional Model

The OMT data flow diagram (DFD) shows the flow of data between different processes in a business. An OMT DFD provides a simple and intuitive method for describing business processes without focusing on the details of computer systems.

Data flow diagrams use four primary symbols:

1. The *process* is any function being performed; for example, verify Password or PIN in the ATM systems.
2. The *data flow* shows the direction of data elements movement; for example PIN code.
3. The *data store* is a location where data are stored; for example, account is a data store in the ATM example.
4. An *external entity* is a source or destination of a data element; for example, the ATM card reader.

Overall, the Rumbaugh OMT methodology provides one of the strongest tools sets for the analysis and design of object-oriented systems, and thus forms the basis of discussion in this book. The next sections describe the three OMT models in detail.

For a better comparison, let us have a look at other object oriented design techniques also.

13.13 THE BOOCH METHOD

The Booch method is a well-known OO method, which helps us in designing a system using objects. It covers the analysis and design aspects of an OO system.

Booch has defined many symbols to document possibly every design decision. The main aspect of the Booch method is that the method is descriptive. In other words, Booch explains what we can do in terms of system definition, but he does not provide if any guidelines regarding what we should do as to come up with a better analysis and design model of the system.

The Booch method begins with class and object diagrams in the analysis phase. That is, we first try and find out all the possible classes and objects in a given system. We draw diagrams to document them. Later on, we refine these diagrams through various steps, by means of an evolutionary approach. Only when the code is about to be written, we add design symbols. In other words, the design symbols depict the very final implementation decisions. Thus, in the Booch method, it is possible to sully document the OO code.

Booch defines different models to describe an OO system. These models are:

- **Physical Model:** The physical model describes the various processes and modules that the system will have at a later stage.
- **Logical Model:** The logical model describes the classes and objects in the system. In other words, it describes the problem domain. It discusses the classes and objects in a system.
- **Static Model:** The static model describes how the classes and objects in a system are related to each other.
- **Dynamic Model:** This model shows how the classes, objects, and other aspects of a system work together to produce the desired results. It talks of the various scenarios that a system would depict, and how these would be depicted.

As mentioned earlier, Booch makes extensive use of diagrams. The designer of a system can use a variety of symbols and diagrams to depict the underlying design.

The examples of such diagrams are:

- The Class Diagram
- The Object Diagram
- The Module Diagram
- The State Diagram
- The Interaction Diagram
- The Process Diagram

The designer supports these with specifications that describe the symbols in the diagrams. However, we should realize that there may not be an exact one-to-one relationship between a model and a particular view of that model. Some diagrams and/or textual descriptions can contain information from several models. On the other hand, some models can incorporate details that are captured across several diagrams. Each model component and their relationships can appear in zero, one or several model diagrams.

Booch uses a cloud symbol to depict a class. An example of this is shown in Figure 13.10.

The interaction between classes is shown with the help of a connector line that joins the two classes. This connection is based on calling a particular method of the classes. For example, let us assume that we have two classes named A and B. Let us suppose furthermore that class A wants to get in touch with class B, by calling the method M of class B. Then we show an arrow from A and B, indicating the direction of processing.

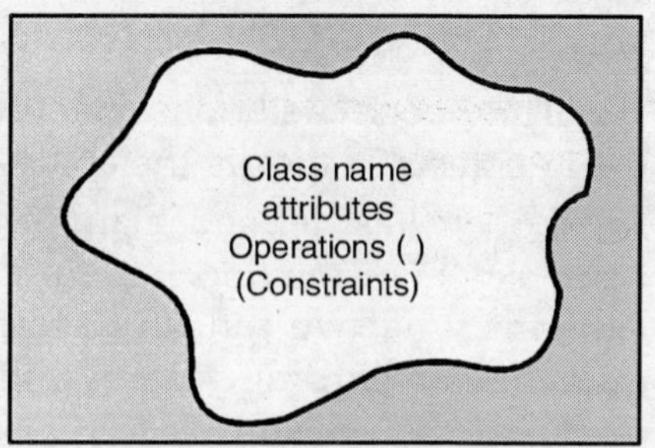

Figure 13.10: *Class Symbol*

Let us now describe the essence of the Booch method. The Booch methodology focuses on some key areas of object technology, as follows.

1. **Abstraction**

   Abstraction denotes the essential characteristics of an object that distinguish it from all other kinds of objects. Furthermore, it provides crispy defined conceptual boundaries, relative to the perspective of the viewer. Booch recommends that the designer identify these boundaries as soon as possible, and that the programming languages that transform this design into actual code should also respect these boundaries, and implement them. For this purpose, it is important to identify four important artifacts of a system:

   (a) Instance methods: These method are accessible to any object (i.e. any instance) of a class.

   (b) Instance attributes: These attributes are accessible to any object (i.e. any instance) of a class.

   (c) Class attributes: These attributes are accessible to all the objects (i.e. all the instances) of a class, but all the instances share the same value of a given attribute.

   (d) Class methods: These methods are accessible to all the objects (i.e. all the instances) of a class, but they all can be used independently of any object.

2. **Modularity**

   Modularity is the property of a system that has been decomposed into a set of cohesive and loosely coupled modules. In other words, the programming implementation of an object-oriented design should provide for the classification of related classes and objects into packages or files. This helps in terms of a better organization and logical referencing of classes.

3. **Encapsulation**

   Encapsulation is the process of hiding all the details of an object that do not contribute to its essential characteristics. That is, the designer should not classify the attributes and methods of a class into various categories:

   (a) Private: Those attributes and methods that should belong only to the class and no other class should even know about their existence.

   (b) Protected: Those attributes and method that also belong to a class and should only be known to that class, but with one exception. When the class is inherited by another class, the child class can also access these attributes and methods.

   (c) Public: Those attributes and methods that are declared in a class, but are globally accessible to all other classes in the system.

4. **Hierarchy**
   Hierarchy builds an order or a rank of the various abstractions. This is mainly implemented in the form of inheritance relationships, which can grow down to multiple levels.
5. **Typing**
   Typing is the enforcement of an object in such a way that objects of different type may not be swapped. At the most, they might be swapped in very restricted manners.
6. **Concurrency**
   Concurrency distinguishes one object that is active from an inactive object.
7. **Persistence**
   Persistence is the characteristic of an object through which it always exists. That is, even when the creator of an object no longer exists, the object continues to exist.

13.13.1 The Booch Methodology

The Booch methodology is a widely used object-oriented method that helps you design your system using the object paradigm. It covers the analysis and design phases of an object-oriented system. Booch sometimes is criticized for his large set of symbols.

- Class Diagrams
- Object Diagrams
- State Transition Diagrams
- Module Diagrams
- Process Diagrams
- Interaction Diagrams

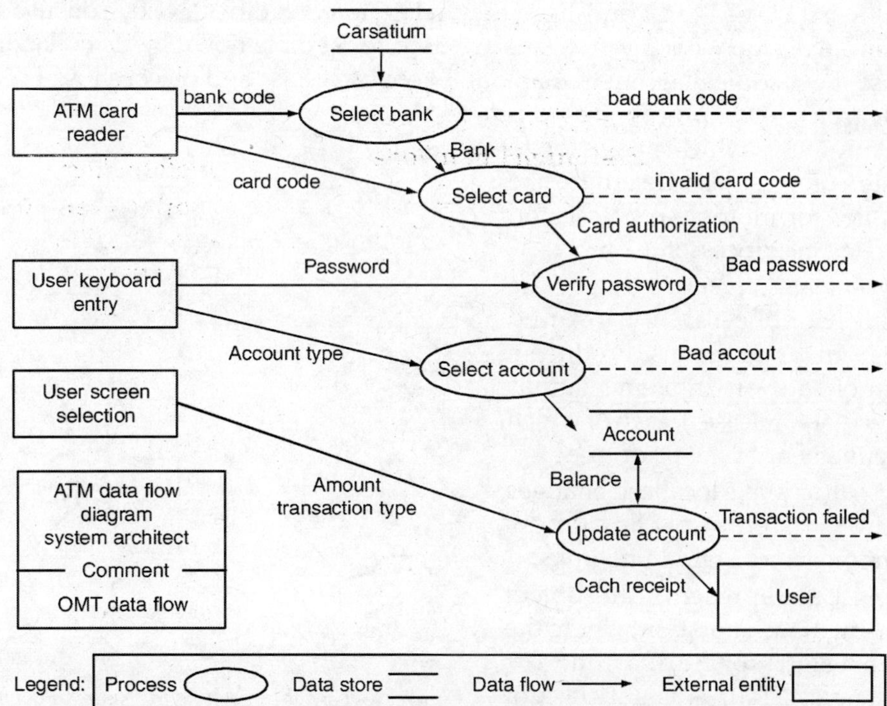

Figure 13.11: *OMT DFD of the ATM system*

The data flow lines include arrows to show the direction of data element movement. The circles represent processes. The boxes represent external entities. A data store reveals the storage of data.

The Booch methodology prescribes a macro development process and a micro development process.

13.13.1.1 The Macro Development Process

The macro process serves as a controlling framework for the micro process and can take weeks or even months. The primary concern of the macro process is the technical management of the system. Such management is interested less in the actual object-oriented design than in how well the project corresponds to the requirements set for it and whether it is produced on time. In the macro process, the traditional phases of analysis and design to a large extent are preserved.

The macro development process consists of the following steps:

1. *Conceptualization:* During conceptualization, you establish the core requirements of the system. You establish a set of goals and develop a prototype to prove the concept.
2. *Analysis and development of the model:* In this step, you use the class diagram to describe the roles and responsibilities objects are to carry out in performing the desired behaviour of the system. Then, you use the object diagram to describe the desired behaviour of the system in terms of scenarios or, alternatively, use the interaction diagram to describe behaviour of the system in terms of scenarios.
3. *Design or create the system architecture:* In the design phase, you use the class diagram to decide what classes exist and how they relate to each other. Next, you use the object diagram to decide what mechanisms are used to regulate how objects collaborate. Then you use the module diagram to map out where each class and object should be declared. Finally, you use the process diagram to determine to which processor to allocate a process. Also, determine the schedules for multiple processes on each relevant processor.
4. *Evolution or implementation:* The system is successively refined through many iterations. Produce a stream of software implementations (or executable releases), each of which is a refinement of the prior one.
5. *Maintenance:* Make localised changes to the system to add new requirements and eliminate bugs.

Figure 13.12 represents the object modeling using Booch notation, where the arrows represent specialization; for example, the class Taurus is subclass of class Ford.

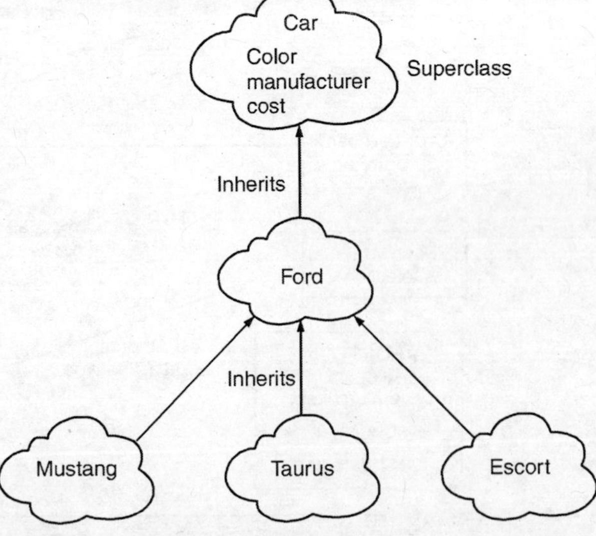

Figure 13.12: *Object Modeling using Booch Notation*

13.13.1.2 The Micro Development Process

The macro development process has its own micro development processes. The micro process is a description of the day-to-day activities by a single or small group of software developers, which could look blurry to an outside viewer, since the analysis and design phases are not clearly defined.

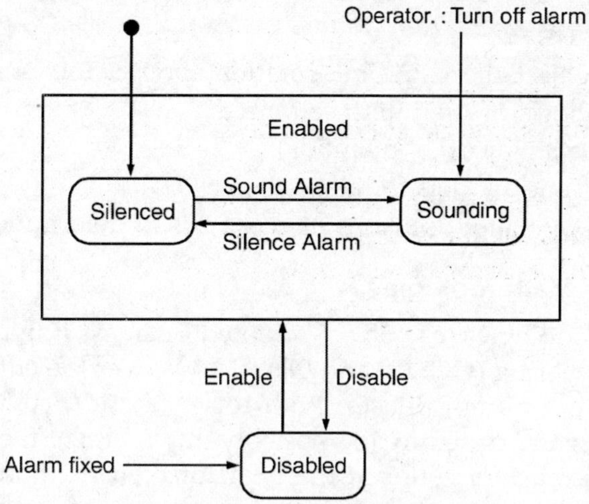

Figure 13.13: *An alarm class state diagram with Booch notation*

Such diagrams can capture the state of a class based on a stimulus. For example, in Figure 13.13, a stimulus causes the class to perform some processing, followed by a transition to another state. In this case, the alarm silenced state can be changed to alarm sounding state and vice-versa.

The micro development process consists of the following steps:

1. Identify classes and objects.
2. Identify class and object semantics.
3. Identify class and object relationships.
4. Identify class and object interfaces and implementation.

13.14 JACOBSON METHOD

The Jacobson method concentrates primarily on the concept of use cases. A use case is an operation, or a transaction performed in a system. For example, *Prepare pay-slips* can be considered a use case in payroll application. The Jacobson method begins by identifying the users (called as the actors) of the system. It then goes on to find out their responsibilities. The next step in this method is to build a model of the user's requirements.

For this purpose, the following steps are performed:

- Define the actors and their responsibilities.
- Identify use cases for each actor.
- Prepare initial view of system objects and relationships.
- Review model using use cases as scenarios to determine validity.

Thus, we begin by identifying the users of the system, here called as actors. These actors can be human or non-human. For example, a person preparing pay-slips is a human actor. On the other hand, a scanner digitizing a document is an example of a non-human actor. Having identified the actors, we then identify what tasks each of these actors would perform (i.e. the use cases). Then we create a relationship between these actors and the use cases. Finally, we create scenarios to validate these relationships.

Thus, we can summarize:

- Identify interface objects by using information about actors and their interactions.
- Create structural views of the interface objects.
- Represent object behaviour (i.e. methods)
- Isolate subsystems and models for all of them.
- Review the model by using use cases as scenarios to determine validity.

13.14.1 The Jacobson Methodologies

The Jacobson methodologies (e.g. object-oriented Business Engineering (OOBE), object-oriented Software-Engineering (OOSE), and Objectory) cover the entire life cycle and stress traceability between the different phases, both forward and backward. This traceability enables reuse of analysis and design work, possibly much bigger factors in the reduction of development time than reuse of code. At the heart of their methodologies is the use-case concept, which evolved with Objectory (Object factory for Software Development).

13.14.1.1 Use Cases

Use cases are scenarios for understanding system requirements. A use case is an interaction between users and a system. The use-case model captures the goal of the use and the responsibility of the system and its users as depicted in the Figure 13.14.

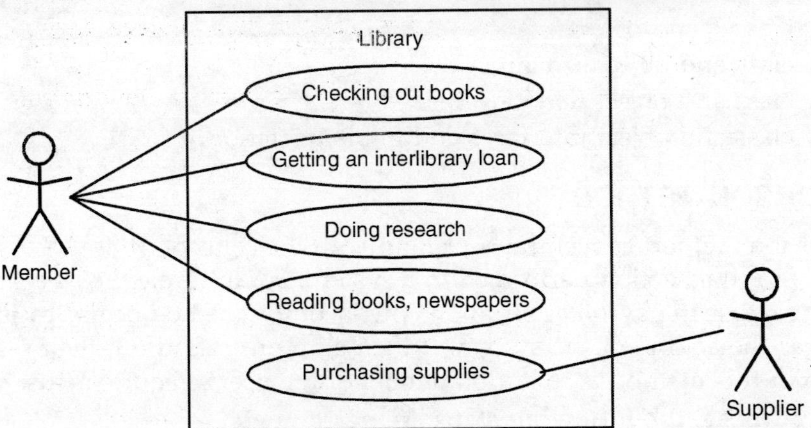

Figure 13.14: *Some uses of a library.*

As it can be seen in Figure 13.14, these are external views of the library system from an actor such as a member. The simpler the use case, the more effective it will be. It is unwise to capture all of the details right at the start, as it should be done later.

In the requirements analysis, the use cases are described as one of the following:

- Nonformal text with no clear flow of events.
- Text, easy to read but with a clear flow of events to follow (this is a recommended style).
- Formal style using pseudo code.

The use case description must contain:

- How and when the use case begins and ends.
- The interaction between the use case and its actors, including when the interaction occurs and what is exchanged.
- How and when the use case will need data stored in the system or will store data in the system.
- Exceptions to the flow of events.
- How and when concepts of the problem domain are handled.

Every single use case should describe one main flow of events. An exceptional or additional flow of events could be added. The exceptional use case extends another use case to include the additional one. The use-case model employs extends and uses relationships. The 'extends' relationship is used when you have one use case that is similar to another use case but does a bit more. In essence, it extends the functionality of the original use case (like a subclass). The 'uses' relationship reuses common behaviour in different use cases.

Use cases could be viewed as concrete or abstract. An abstract use case is not complete and has no actors that initiate it but is used by another use case. This inheritance could be used in several levels. Abstract use cases also are the ones that have uses or extends relationships.

13.14.1.2 Object-Oriented Software Engineering: Objectory

Object-oriented software engineering (OOSE), also called Objectory, is a method of object-oriented development with the specific aim to fit the development of large, real-time systems. The development process, called *use-case driven development*, stresses that use cases are involved in several phases of the development as depicted in Figure 13.15, including analysis, design, validation, and testing. The use-case scenario begins with a user of the system initiating a sequence of interrelated events.

The system development method based on OOSE< Objectory, is a disciplined process for the industrialized development of software, based on a use-case driven design. It is an approach to object-oriented analysis and design that centers on understanding the ways in which a system actually is used. By organizing the analysis and design models around the sequences of user interaction and actual usage scenarios, the method produces systems that are both more usable and more robust, adapting more easily to changing usage. Jacobson's Objectory has been developed and applied to numerous application areas and embodied in the CASE tool systems.

Objectory is built around several different models:

- *Use case model:* The use case model defines the outside (actors) and inside (use case) os the system's behaviour.

- *Domain object model:* The objects of the 'real' world are mapped into the domain object model.
- *Analysis object model:* The analysis object model presents how the source code (implementation) should be carried out and written.
- *Implementation model:* The implementation model represents the implementation of the system.
- *Test model:* The test model constitutes the test plans, specifications, and reports.

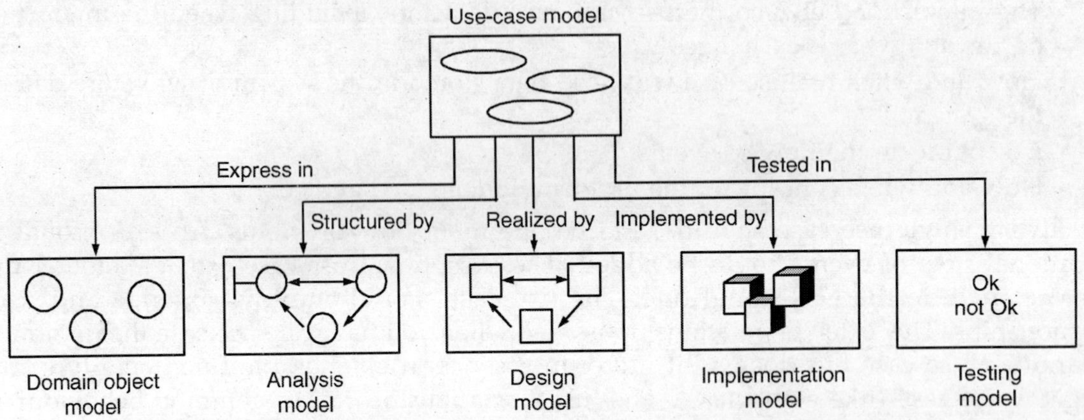

Figure 13.15: *The use-case model is considered in every model and phase*

The maintenance of each model is specified in its associated process. A process is created when the first development project starts and is terminated when the developed system is taken out of service.

13.14.1.3 Object-Oriented Business Engineering

Object-oriented business engineering (OOBE) is object modeling at the enterprise level. Use cases again are the central vehicle for modeling, providing traceability throughout the software engineering process.

- *Analysis phase:* The analysis phase defines the system to be built in terms of the problem domain object model, the requirements model, and the analysis model. The analysis process should not take into account the actual implementation environment. This reduces complexity and promotes maintainability over the life of the system, since the description of the system will be independent of hardware and software requirements. Jacobson does not dwell on the development of the problem domain object model, but refers the developer to Coad and Yourdon's or Booch's discussion of the topic, who suggest that the customer draw a picture of his view of the system to promote discussions. In their view, a full development of the domain model will not localize changes and therefore will not result in the most 'robust and extensible structure'. This model should be developed just enough to form a base of understanding for the requirements model. The analysis process is iterative but the requirements and analysis models should be stable before moving on the subsequent models. Jacobson suggests that prototyping with a tool might be useful during this phase to help specify user interfaces.

- *Design and implementation phases:* The implementation environment must be identified for the design model. This includes factors such as Database Management System (DBMS), distribution of process, constraints due to the programming language, available component libraries, and incorporation of graphical tools. It may be possible to identify the implementation environment concurrently with analysis. The analysis objects are translated into design objects that fit the current implementation environment.
- *Testing phase:* Finally, Jacobson describes several testing levels and techniques. The levels include unit testing, integration testing, and system testing.

13.15 THE COAD-YOURDON METHOD

Coad-Yourdon methodology has its primary strength in system analysis. Their methodology is based on a technique called "SOSAS", which stands for the five steps that help make up the analysis part of their methodology. The first step in system analysis is called "Subjects", which are basically data flow diagrams for objects. The second step is called "Objects", where they identify the object classes and the class hierarchies. The third step is called "Structures", where they decompose structures into two types, classification structures and composition structures. Classification structures handle the inheritance connection between related classes, while composition structures handle all of the other connections among classes. The next step in analysis is called "Attributes", and the final step is called "Services", where all of the behaviours or methods for each class are identified. Following analysis, Coad and Yourdon define four parts that make up the design part of their methodology.

The steps of system design are:

- *The problem domain component* - This will define the classes that should be in the problem domain.
- *The human interaction component* - These steps defines the interface classes between objects.
- *The task management component* - This is where system-wide management classes are identified.
- *The data management component* - This design step identifies the classes needed for database access methods.

13.16 THE SHLAER-MELLOR METHOD

Shlaer-Mellor methodology has its primary strength in system design and is considered somewhat weak on analysis. The Shlaer-Mellor methodology includes three models; the information model, the state model, and the process model. The information model contains objects, variables, and all the relationships between the objects, and is basically a data model for the system. The state model records the different states of objects and changes that can occur between the objects. The process model is really not much more than a traditional data flow diagram.

13.17 RATIONAL UNIFIED PROCESS METHOD

The Rational Unified Process (RUP) model is essentially a combination of the above three methods (and also of a few more methods less well known). The RUP method talks about four distinct steps of a software project, as follows:

- **Inception:** This step deals with the initial high-level planning of the project. We determine the scope of the project here. We also discuss some of the business decisions and their impacts. Other factors such as costing, estimation, and projected revenue also come into picture.
- **Elaboration:** This step deals with the requirements gathering, analysis, and design phases of a project. We also develop an outline for the construction phase of the project here. The risks pertaining to the project are also identified and a risk mitigation plan prepared. The risks can be of various natures, such as technological, business-related, skills-related, requirements-related, and technology models, and the risk mitigation plan.
- **Construction:** In this phase, the use cases are transformed into actual code. It is quite possible that the analysis and design steps refined here, as more clarity is needed in order to perform the actual construction activities. Software testing also plays a crucial role. The product should be tested as much and as early as possible.
- **Transition:** This is the phase just as before the main release of the software product. Here things like scalability, optimization, performance etc. are primarily addressed. The steps necessary to transform the product from a piece of software to something that can actually use and feel are carried out in this phase.

13.18 ADVANTAGES AND DISADVANTAGES OF OOAD

The advantages and disadvantages of the Object-Oriented Analysis and Design methodology can be summarized as follows:

Following are the advantages of OOAD:

1. OOAD significantly simplifies the development of the system compared to SSAD.
2. In comparison to SSAD, the development time, the level of organization, the robustness, and the code reuse are all greatly enhanced by the OOAD methodology.
3. In OOAD there is no separation between the analysis and design phases, which improves communication between the users from beginning to end of project development.
4. In OOAD analysts and programmers are not bound by the constraints of system implementation, so that they can formulate designs that conform to different execution environments.
5. Since objects relate to entities (things) with which we commonly interact there is usually a clear mapping between the real-world entities and the corresponding objects in the system. This significantly improves understanding of the design.
6. In OOAD the software is resilient to change, resulting in a higher level of confidence in the correctness of the software which helps to reduce the risks in developing complex systems.
7. In OOAD, when developing objects with complex interactions, the analyst thinks on a different level of detail than is possible with structured code. In this case the analyst thinks about which attributes the object needs to know and how it will act on those attributes.
8. Since objects are independent encapsulations of data and methods, they are reusable and can be used in other projects in addition to the one for which they were originally created. This will reduce design, programming and validation costs.

9. OOAD improves the quality of the system due to program reuse. Vivek Shah says in his paper that "If 90% of a new application consists of proven, existing components, then only the remaining 10% of the code has to be tested from scratch. That observation implies an order-of-magnitude reduction in defects".
10. OOAD enables the standardization of objects which increases design understanding and decreases the risk associated with project development.
11. Object decomposition enables the analyst to break down the problem into independent and manageable parts. Many times the work shifts from developing new code to bringing together existing objects in creative ways to solve the problem. Thus OOAD methodology cuts down development time and costs which will stimulate and induce market and competitive advantage. This results in a very flexible, easily changed and more maintainable system.
12. The systems designed using OOAD are closer to the real world as the real world functioning of the system is directly mapped into the system designed using OOAD. Because of this, it becomes easier to produce and understand designs.
13. The objects in the system are immune to requirement changes because of data hiding and encapsulation features of object-orientation. Here, encapsulation we mean a technique that allows the programmer to hide the internal functioning of the objects from the users of the objects. Encapsulation separates the internal functioning of the object from the external functioning thus providing the user flexibility to change the external behavior of the object making the programmer code safe against the changes made by the user.
14. OOAD designs encourage more reusability. The classes once defined can easily be used by other applications. This is achieved by defining classes and putting them into a library of classes where all the classes are maintained for future use. Whenever a new class is needed the programmer first looks into the library of classes and if it is available, it can be used as it is or with some modification. This reduces the development cost & time and increases quality.
15. Another way of reusability is provided by the inheritance feature of the object-orientation. The concept of inheritance allows the programmer to use the existing classes in new applications i.e. by making small additions to the existing classes can quickly create new classes. This provides all the benefits of reusability discussed in the previous point.
16. As the programmer has to spend less time and effort so he can utilize saved time (due to the reusability feature of the OOAD) in concentrating on other aspects of the system.
17. OOAD approach is more natural as it deals with the real world objects. So, it provides nice structures for thinking and abstracting and leads to modular design.

Following are the disadvantages of OOAD:

As new software development technologies are adopted, an enthusiasm develops as is often the case, and many expectations are brought to the surface. Like an empty glass, developers and managers may fill it up not knowing whether the technology will, in fact, deliver what it is supposed to. Lack of understanding and unrealistic expectations seems to be common denominators. So there is a delay of their proper use. These problems can be minimized, even avoided, by having a clear understanding of the problems and pitfalls that programmers face when adopting these technologies. Most problems have two things in common: confusion about what OOAD is and what it entails.

1. In OOAD the initial designs for the system may be too simplified to be adequate.
2. In OOAD there tends to be much more focus on code than in SSAD.
3. In OOAD there is not as much emphasis on team work as in SSAD.
4. In OOAD it is not an easy task to determine all the necessary classes and objects needed for the system.
5. Many times object-oriented programming is used in conjunction with analyzing the various functions of the system; however, these function based methods are inappropriate in OOAD.
6. Another major disadvantage of OOAD is the overemphasis of this object methodology in general where, in fact, another approach might be much better to use for the design and development of a system, depending on the particular circumstances.
7. OOAD necessitates a new kind of project management which involves a different type of analysis from the traditional functional decomposition approach and structured programming methods. Consequently, for project development teams that have a long history of using the SSAD methodology, the transition to the OOAD methodology is extremely difficult and time consuming.
8. Another shortcoming of the OOAD methodology is the concept of reuse. Reuse is considered one of the major benefits of this methodology and a reason for converting to OOAD. However, without an explicit reuse procedure in place many of the systems developed with this methodology do not lead to successful reuse on a large scale.
9. Project managers and programmers may confuse style with substance. Some developers and managers today believe that OOAD simply means defining classes, objects, and methods. It is like what happened when structured programming development became popular. Developers and managers at first thought that structured development simply meant that one had to remove GOTO statements and increase the use of subroutines. While these steps helped, they were just surface features of a deeper group of more significant principles.
10. Managers and developers may not recognize all the implications of OOAD. They often assume that using OOAD will eliminate development bottlenecks. This is due to expectations that OOAD will reduce the complexity of programs and will provide architectural modularity. This different approach to architecture may work better with different management and scheduling techniques.
11. Managers may be tempted to ignore or abandon traditional software design and engineering processes. OOAD is often adopted because of the promise of increased productivity coupled with a shortened development schedule. However, a sufficientamountof developmenttime isoftennotallowed thatwill makesure the design processes are followed correctly. This may actually result in bigger problems.Theseincludemisseddeadlines,scheduleslippage,andprojectfailures.
12. Finally, one of the disadvantages of object oriented analysis and design is that developers maygetsome educationabout OOAD, but not enough. A false sense of

programmingconfidencemaystemfromjustreadingarticles,orevenabook,ortaking a class in it. Programmers will need time to immerse themselves in the nuances of OOAD.

13.19 ADVANTAGES AND PITFALLS OF OOAD

Some of the advantages of the object-oriented analysis and design methodology are listed below:

- It fosters the use of 'modern' software engineering methodologies.
- It promotes and facilitates software re-usability. Industrial Revolution started off with the need for interchangeable parts as it increases re-usability. These interchangeable parts are nothing but objects.
- It facilitates interoperability. Interoperability in a software system is brought about by polymorphism. Polymorphism is a measure of the degree of difference between the items in a specified collection of items at a given level of abstraction. For example, the word 'drive' could mean 'driving a car', 'driving a cycle', or 'driving a bus'. Object-oriented approaches often stress on polymorphism, which in turn facilitates interoperability.
- It produces solutions that resemble the real-world problems. People view the real world in terms of objects and its functionalities.
- It facilitates modification, extension, and maintenance of software. As an object encapsulates related functionalities, it aids in modular development of the system. Hence it fosters easy modification and extension of the existing systems, using hierarchical relationships.
- It reduces problems faced while integrating systems. This is mainly because objects offer clear interfaces, using which they can be integrated into the system.
- It improves traceability of the system. Traceability is the degree of ease with which a concept can be followed from one point in a process to either a succeeding or preceding point in the same process. For example, a user's requirements can be traced in the other phases of software engineering.
- It results in a smooth transition between analysis, design and implementation phases of software engineering.
- It reduces the overall time taken to develop the system by promoting reuse.
- It improves the quality of the system developed. If a new system is developed using objects from an existing system, the number of errors can be minimized and hence better quality systems can be developed.
- Object orientation focuses on data relationships represented using ER diagrams. An OO model provides the insight of an ER diagram and contains additional information related to the methods to be performed on the data.

Potential of OOAD are listed below:

- **Conceptual Pitfalls:** These pitfalls mainly result due to the misunderstanding of the objects oriented approaches. Some developers think that object-oriented development is just defining objects, classes and methods, while others have a view that these approaches always reduce the developmental complexity of the systems. Project managers also do not provide sufficient time to ensure that sufficient procedures are followed to ensure increased productivity of the systems. Often developers do not have a thorough knowledge of object-oriented development approaches. To ensure success in OOAD, more time has to be spent in the initial stages (analysis and design) of development. This time spent can be gained during implementation. A complete cooperation between management and developers, education and experience, are the keys to the success of any OOAD project.

- **Political Pitfalls:** Organizational politics also plays a major role in deciding the success of OOAD. An organization may resist object-oriented approaches due to many reasons. It is the duty of the developer to educate the management and the users on the need for OO approaches to software development.
- **Analysis and Design Pitfalls:** These pitfalls result due to the complex nature of the systems and lack of complete knowledge of object technology. Many organizations follow conventional approaches to analysis and design and then attempt to implement it using object-oriented techniques. Some developers may try to implement classes and their hierarchies based on their functionalities while using OOAD approaches. Both these approaches result in poor solutions. While using OOAD, an iterative bottom-up approach is to be followed. This involves breaking the system into subsystems, their representation and interactions.
- **Environment, Language and Tool Pitfalls:** The boundaries between the three are not always clear. Some of the factors that should be taken into account while selecting environment, language and tools include technology, compatibility, economic issues and integration with the existing systems.
- **Implementation Pitfalls:** In rapid application development, a prototype of the system is developed. Such a prototype possesses only the essential features. Hence more time is needed to incorporate new features or change the existing features. For object-oriented development to be successful, it is important that analysis and design should be sufficiently completed. It is also important to define design, implementation, documentation and coding standards for each subsystem and class before coding and implementation take place.
- **Class and Object Pitfalls:** These pitfalls mainly result due to the lack of knowledge on the subject. Some of the common reasons for these pitfalls are due to the lack of complete understanding of the following concepts:
  - is-a, has-a and using relationships
  - interface and implementation inheritance
  - use of multiple inheritance
  - encapsulation

  To overcome this, developers should use class hierarchies to identify classes and determine the relationships with existing classes.
- **Re-use Pitfalls:** One of the primary goals of OOAD is reuse of code. Re-use of code, rather than design, usually leads to unnecessary delays and slipped schedules. Hence the reusability of objects must be documented in the design of a system itself.

- **Lack of Functional Models:** A weakness of the OO method is that it only builds functional models within the objects. It does not provide a complete functional model. Use cases address this problem to some extent.
- **Performance Pitfalls:** Communication between objects cannot be easily described using OO models. While this leads to a flexible design, performance modeling cannot be handled readily.
- **Pitfalls in Object Identification:** The OOAD does not provide methods to identify the objects automatically to suite optimal system design.
- **Complexity:** The overhead of OOAD is the complexity of the learning curve.

13.20 A COMPARISON OF SSAD AND OOAD

Structure methodology is not 'the wrong way' to analyse and design a system. Similarly, object-oriented methodology is not necessarily 'the right way'. The previous sections described two major methodologies in system analysis and design: SSAD and OOAD. This section compares the feature of both these approaches.

A clear comparison of the features of structured and object-oriented approaches in analysis and design of systems are listed below:

1. SSAD is top-down in nature, while OOAD is bottom-up in nature.
2. The basic building blocks of SSAD are functions in contrast to data in OOAD.
3. SSAD uses functional decomposition, whereas OOAD identifies objects with similar functionalities and groups them together.
4. The basic level of abstraction in OOAD is an object, whereas in SSAD it is a module.
5. The module summary in SSAD is purely textual and descriptive in nature. OOAD uses class diagrams in the analysis phase itself to show the classes in the system and their relationships.
6. In SSAD, the requirements specification has to be confirmed in all the phases of software development. In OOAD, use cases act as a link to check-up original system requirements. All models formed are verified using use case diagrams.
7. In SSAD, product cost and time increases exponentially with the complexity of the system. So OOAD approaches are preferred for larger and more complex systems.
8. SSAD has a narrow orientation. It depends on the application and the data structure used. Hence re-use and maintenance in this approach is less when compared to OOAD methodology.
9. Natural systems follow a top-down approach. So OOAD is preferred to SSAD as it follows a bottom-up approach.
10. As objects are the level of abstraction in OOAD, it facilitates easy extension and maintenance compared to SSAD approach.
11. As OOAD has a higher level of reuse, it reduces the time to market. Further, the system developed has a higher level of productivity when compared to SSAD methodology.
12. OOAD spends more time in design when compared to implementation. In SSAD, less time is spent on design stage.

13. As good design documentation is available in OOAD, errors can be identified and corrected in early stages.
14. The following is a comparison of modeling diagrams offered by these approaches:
    (a) Use cases in OOAD model requirement are equivalent to requirements document in SSAD.
    (b) Class diagrams in OOAD perform better when compared to module summary in SSAD.
    (c) There are no scenarios in SSAD.
    (d) The ER diagrams in structured models play a similar role to the static models in object-oriented modeling.
    (e) Data flow diagrams perform similar roles as functional models in the object-oriented modeling.
    (f) SSAD lacks models corresponding to the dynamic models in OOAD. Hence it lacks the capability to capture the dynamic aspects of systems.

As object-oriented analysis and design is becoming such a popular and widely used technology all over, we dedicate the next chapter to the detailed discussion of object oriented concepts and design techniques.

SUMMARY

Systems are created to solve problems. One can think of the systems approach as an organized way of dealing with a problem. In this dynamic world, the subject System Analysis and Design (SAD) mainly deals with the software development activities.

The main purpose of this section is to introduce the readers to the concept of systems. This section starts with a description of the characteristics of systems and types of systems. A detailed description of the phases in the development of a system with the emphasis on the analysis phase is also provided. The section also describes the role of the system analysis in the development of a system. We have already studied about systems. A social system like an institution has a highly complicated structure.

After a discussion on systems, two major methodologies of system analysis and design are presented namely, Structured System Analysis and Design (SSAD) and Object Oriented Analysis and Design (OOAD). OOAD is the focus of discussion. Hence this chapter forms a basis of understanding as to what we are up to.

EXERCISES

1. What do you mean by system?
2. What are the elements of a system?
3. What are the types of systems?
4. Explain the concept of system analysis?
5. Explain the concept of system design?
6. Explain systems analyst in detail?
7. What do you mean by complexity of systems?

8. What are the attributes of a complex system?
9. How can you deal with complexity?
10. What are the different approaches of system development?
11. Explain the structured system analysis and design (SSAD)?
12. Explain the data flow modeling in detail?
13. What are the various benefits of SSAD?
14. What are the advantages and disadvantages of SSAD?
15. Explain the concept of object-oriented analysis and design?
16. What is object oriented programming?
17. What do you mean by object modeling?
18. Explain the concept of object oriented?
19. Explain the various methods of OOAD?
20. Explain the Rumbaugh's object modeling technique?
21. Explain the concept of Booch methodology?
22. Explain the Jacobson method in detail?
23. Explain the Coad-Yourdon methodology?
24. Explain the model of Rational Unified Process (RUP)?
25. What are the advantages and disadvantages of OOAD?
26. What are the advantages of advantages and pitfalls of OOAD?
27. Distinguish between SSAD AND OOAD techniques?

❑

Elements of an Object Oriented Model

14.1 INTRODUCTION

The object-oriented approach was invented (or, rather, it evolved) because of the difficulties people were having trying to get good quality systems produced on time and within budget, especially for large systems with many people involved.

Here are some of the justifications typically given for object orientation:

- *Objects are easier for people to understand:* This is because the objects are derived from the business that we're trying to automate, rather than being influenced too early by computer-based procedures or data storage requirements. For example, in a bank system, we program in terms of bank accounts, bank tellers and customers, instead of diving straight into account records, deposit and withdrawal procedures, and loan qualification algorithms.
- *Specialists can communicate better:* Over time, the software industry has constructed career ladders that newcomers are expected to climb gradually as their knowledge and experience increases. Typically, the first rung is **programmer**: fixing faults (bugs) in the code written by others. The second rung is **senior programmer**: writing the code itself. The third is **designer**: deciding what code needs to be written. Finally comes the role of **analyst**: talking to customers to discover what they need and then writing down a specification of what the finished system must be able to do.

  Such a career ladder may not be a bad idea in itself. The problem comes when you realize that each specialist is expected to learn a whole new set of concepts and techniques, depicting their conclusions using notations that are tailored to their specialty. This means that there's a big gap in understanding between the different roles, made worse by the fact that the documents are being passed down the career ladder rather than up, so we tend to have to read documents without understanding the techniques used to produce them. This can lead to 'throw it over the wall' syndrome: the analyst produces a large amount of documentation, throws it over the wall to the designer and walks away. The designer, after weeks of effort, produces even more documentation, using completely different techniques, and throws it over the wall to the programmers. The programmers then start all over again.

  With the object-oriented approach, everyone is dealing with the same concepts and notations. Moreover, there are generally fewer concepts and fewer notations to deal with in the first place.

- *Data and processes are not artificially separated:* In traditional methods, the data that needs to be stored is separated early on from the algorithms that operate on that data and they are then developed independently. This can result in the data being in inconvenient formats or inconvenient locations, with respect to the processes that need access. With object-oriented development, data and processes are kept together in small, easy-to-manage packages; data is never separated from the algorithms. We also end up with less complex code that is less sensitive to changes in customer requirements.
- *Code can be reused more easily:* With the traditional approach, we start with the problem that needs to be solved and allow that problem to drive the entire development. We end up with a monolithic solution to today's problem. But tomorrow always brings a different problem to solve; no matter how close the new problem is to the last one we dealt with, we're unlikely to be able to break open our monolithic system and make it fit – we hamper ourselves by allowing a single problem to influence every part of the system.

  With object-oriented development, we're constantly looking for objects that would be useful in similar systems. Even when a new system has minor differences, we're much more likely to be able to change our existing code to fit, because objects are like the pieces in a jigsaw puzzle: if one piece is changed, it might affect a few pieces next to it, but the rest of the puzzle will remain intact.

  When we build an object-oriented system, we try to find existing objects (written by us, by our colleagues or by third parties), before we consider writing any code ourselves. As one sage put it, 'object-oriented programming is about *not* writing code'.
- *Object orientation is mature and well proven:* This is not a new fad. The programming concepts emerged in the late 1960s while the methodologies have been around for at least a decade. Applying objects in such areas as software, databases and networks is now well understood.

  The object model forms a conceptual framework that brings about object orientation. It helps the analyst to concentrate on the similarities and ignore the differences between entities. Abstraction is the basic principle behind object models. The elements in the object oriented model are categorised into major and minor elements. The major elements are mandatory and emphasize on the necessary conditions, while the minor elements emphasize on the sufficient conditions. The minor elements can be absent in an object model. But, if these elements are present in the model then it is useful. This chapter explores the major as well as minor elements of an object-oriented model.

14.2 OBJECT TECHNOLOGY BASICS

Many people have an apprehension about object technology for a strange reason. This technology comes with such a big list of terminology, buzzwords, jargon and vocabulary that it is actually quite normal to get frightened. Therefore, our objective would be to simplify and clearly demystify all these terms in a very simple manner.

The fundamental principle in object technology is an **object**. At the simplest level, everything that we see, feel, touch, or smell is an object. For instance, the book you are holding and reading now is an object, each page in the book is also an object, and you and me are also objects. Actually, this is a fairly informal definition of the term object. So let us be somewhat more technical, and understand what an object means, soon.

The origins of object technology can be found in the 1960s with reference to a programming language called as Simula. The name Simula was an abbreviation of the term Simulation language. This language first introduced the principles of object technology. Simula's purpose was quite clear. This language was designed to build accurate models of complex and huge physical systems (e.g. big buildings, aircrafts, machines, etc.). These systems could consist of hundreds of components. In Simula, models were created as objects. For instance, a floor in a building could be an object, which could be accessed by another object called as elevator, and so on. An object is a self-sufficient entity. It hosts operations as well as data. We will quickly notice that this is remarkably different from what we have been observing so far. In the procedural world, the emphasis is on operations. Data comes at the very end. Operations and data are separate aspects of a program. In the context of object technology, we are considering operations and data as two portions of a single an object. Data is no longer considered separately, it is tightly coupled with the operations on an object. This concept is illustrated in Figure 14.1.

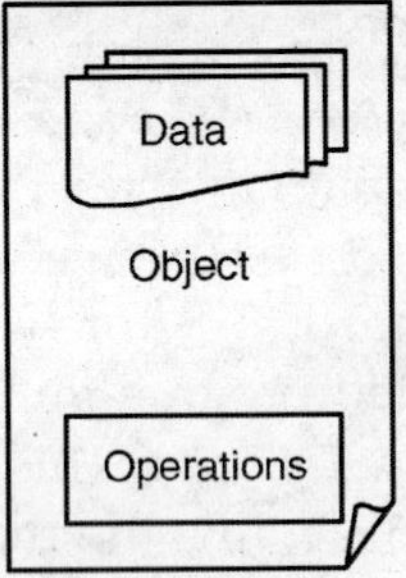

***Figure 14.1:** Object = Data + Operations*

We should state one more observation. Here, we have not talked about the term program. Instead we are discussing about objects. We need to note that this is also a big change from our discussion so far. But it also means that we need to know how objects relate to a program. In object technology, a program is simply a collection of well-designed objects. We do not think of a program as a group of data items and operations. Rather, we think of it as a group of objects, as shown in Figure 14.2.

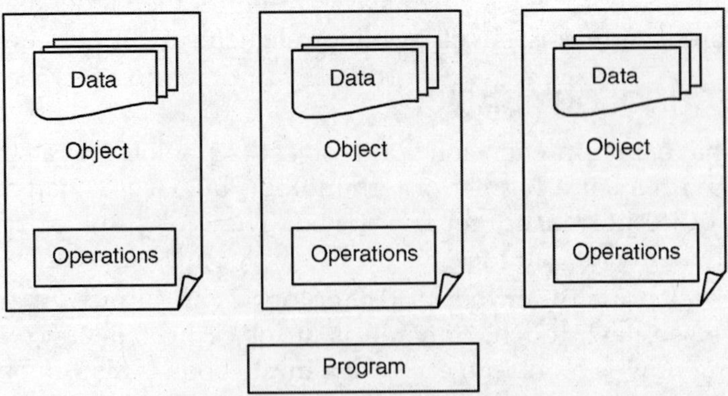

***Figure 14.2:** Program in Object Technology*

As an illustration, in a payroll application, the objects could be employee, department, manager, salary, etc. All these objects would interact with each other on a needs basis, to create one or more application programs. In an electrical application, the various objects could be wire, voltage, appliance, etc.

Let us examine a few more important terms now.

- In object oriented technology, operations are called as **methods**. Note that these are also called as functions or procedures in the traditional systems.
- Data items or variables are called as **attributes**.

As an example, if we consider a horse as an object, the horse's eyes, ears, nose, etc. are all its attributes. Some of these are shown in Figure 14.3. Also eating, running, standing still etc. are horse object's methods.

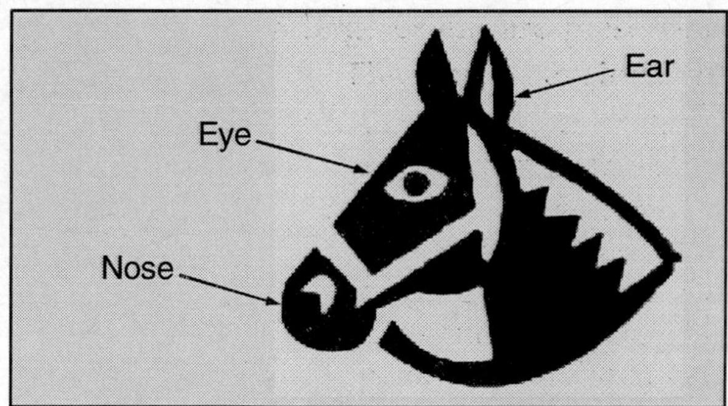

Figure 14.3: *Horse Object and Its Attributes*

This nature of objects makes them self-sufficient. For instance, as soon as we imagine a horse, we can describe everything about it. These are the attributes and methods of that objects. There is nothing extra, which is missing here. This principle of object technology is quite interesting and useful. As far as a designer is concerned, this means that an object no longer depends on other objects for its own features and characteristics. When this leads to the development stage, a programmer can look at an object as a black box. It is a self-contained unit, which can be protected from the outside world. This also means that one object cannot, intentionally or otherwise, affect the internals of another object. As we shall study later, this has far reaching consequences in the area if software development.

One interesting question emerges at this juncture. We know that objects are self-sufficient. But then how do we interact with it? For instance, we know that a horse can run. But how can we instruct a horse to run? If we are not able to do so, the horse object would be quite useless to the rest of the world. This means that we have to be able to instruct the horse to perform the desired action, such as asking it to run. Of course, object technology takes care of this aspect by providing **messages**. We can pass a message to an object, requesting it to perform a specific task. For example, we can send a message to the horse object, asking it to run.

We can imagine that in the real computing world, objects need to interact with each other in a number of ways, and for a variety of reasons. In order to make this possible, one object can send a message to another object. This message requests the called object to execute one of its methods. For example, we can send a message to another object called as dog, which results into it invoking its run method.

Note that we could have sent the same message to the horse object as well. That would cause the horse to run, instead of the dog running. In effect, different objects can have the same method and can receive the same message from the external world. Their responses would also be quite similar to each other. What would differ, though, is the precise execution of these methods.

However, this discussion raises another question. How do we know in the first place that a horse or a dog can run? In real life, we would actually know this, but consider another object called *employee*. Let us imagine that we are interested in finding out the salary of the employee. What message do we need to send to the employee object, so that it can provide us with this information? We cannot take for granted or hope that the employee name contains a method for this purpose. As a result, every object must inform the external world which methods it provides. In the absence of this, it is not possible for other objects in the system to send any messages. The idea to achieve this objective is actually quite straightforward. Every object must publish a list of methods that it supports. This enables other objects to consult this list, and send it appropriate messages. This concept is shown in Figure 14.4.

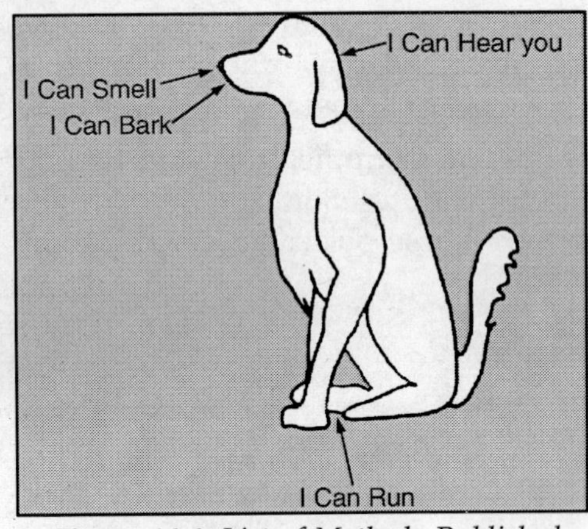

Figure 14.4: *List of Methods Published by the Dog Object*

If we consider two objects X and Y, we can imagine that object X can send a message to object Y. This can be for requesting it to execute one of its methods. Similarly, object Y can invoke any method of object X by sending it a message, as shown in Figure 14.5.

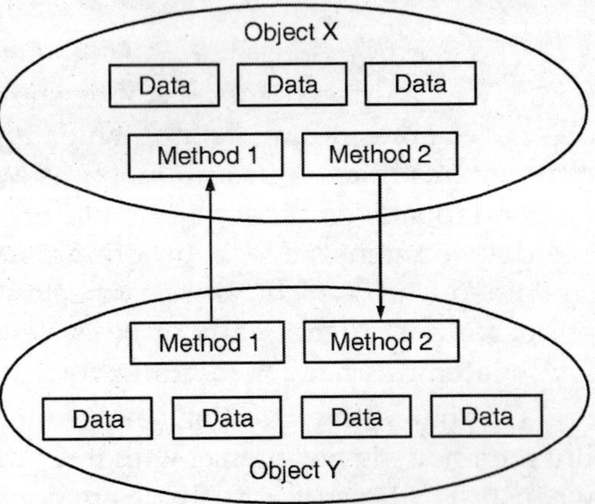

Figure 14.5: *Objects Send Messages to Each Other to Call Each Other's Messages*

The diagram also illustrates a very critical concept. Objects can call he methods of other objects by sending messages to each other. However, an object does not have any direct access to the data portion of another object. An object protects or hides its data from the outside world. On the other hand, it publishes data to the entire world. In the real world, there are minor variations of this concept. For the time being, it is safe to imagine that an object protects its data, and does not allow another object to access it. However, it exposes its methods to everyone else so that they can call any of those methods.

We have been discussing the significant effects of global data in the procedural technology. Providing for common data access to more than one program almost always leads to some sort of problems. Object technology makes the boundaries between different objects quite crisp and explicit in relation to the data items. Since objects are supposed to be self-sufficient entities, it is very important that their internal details are protected from other objects. Otherwise, this self-sufficient nature of objects may be in danger. It is, therefore, quite essential to protect the internal details of objects from other objects.

14.3 FUNDAMENTAL CHARACTERISTICS OF AN OBJECT-ORIENTED METHODOLOGY

Systems analysis and design is a complex process. Accommodating this complex process requires systems analysts to exploit commonly understood characteristics or principles for managing complexity. As cited earlier, today's information systems are complex and involve tens of thousands, hundreds of thousands, or millions of lines of programming code. For example, some knowledgeable software developers have estimated that Microsoft's popular Windows Operating System has more than 35 million lines of programming source code. In fact the systems being developed today are far more sophisticated than those of just five years ago. A personal computer word processor was "feature poor" back then compared to the ones currently available for purchase. Shrink-wrap software has moved into the competitive arena of hundreds of thousands or even millions of units in commercial sales. As a result, each new version or release of the software must exceed the features and benefits of the older version. Not only that, new releases often must exceed the capability of their strongest software competitor's currently selling software version.

Some common characteristics for managing complexity during systems analysis and design are available for systems analysts to use to one degree or another regardless of the SDLC used to develop the information system. At least eight characteristics or principles for managing complexity are also considered foundational and are generally accepted characteristics of object-oriented analysis, design, and programming. Each of these common characteristics is presented here for your consideration. You may already be familiar with many of them because they often have a much broader applicability to your own personal life, not just to software development. They are:

1. Common methods of organization
2. Abstraction
3. Encapsulation or information hiding
4. Inheritance
5. Polymorphism
6. Message communication
7. Associations
8. Reuse

Not all object-oriented books discuss all eight of these characteristics. However, because we believe they are important, we have included them here. These eight concepts are not necessarily new to object-oriented systems development as other older methodologies incorporate one or more of them in some way. However, together all eight form the fundamental building blocks for object-oriented technologies. Each is discussed next.

1. ***Common methods of organization*** assist with organizing an information system's model as well as the software that is ultimately written. The common methods of organization that are applicable here are:

(i) **Objects and attributes** or **characteristics**. For example, you could be the object and your name, address, height, weight, color of eyes, date of birth, and so on are some of your attributes or characteristics.

(ii) **Wholes and parts**. For example, your television set is the "whole" and the individual parts that make up the television set are the "parts." A personal computer system—the whole—usually consists of a box with all kinds of hardware in it, a printer, a monitor, a keyboard, and a mouse—the parts.

(iii) **Groups and members**. Conceptually this is similar to wholes and parts, but its examples are often different and do not seem to fit neatly into a "wholes and parts" classification. For example, a computer club would be a group and the individual members of the computer club would be the members. Your Systems Analysis and Design course would be the group and the students in the course would be the members.

People in general are quite familiar and comfortable with the above common methods of organization; therefore they will be able to related to our Systems Analysis and Design models that take advantage of these concepts.

2. ***Abstraction*** is the principle of ignoring those aspects of a problem domain that are not relevant to the current purpose in order to concentrate more fully on those that are. Abstraction is a concept that you use every day. It has to do with the amount of detail you care to get involved in. In systems analysis and design, this is called **levels of abstraction**. Let's say that your friend decides to bake a cake. He offers you the choices of both helping him bake the cake and then helping him eat it or just helping him eat it. If you choose the first option, you are demonstrating a detailed level of abstraction because you have chosen to get involved with the details of making a cake. If you choose the second option, you are demonstrating a generalized level of abstraction because you chose not to deal with the details of baking the cake, only eating it. Telling your father that you love him is abstract, or generalized, while telling him one or more of the reasons why you love him is specific and thus a more detailed level of abstraction.

   In systems analysis and design, abstraction is used to identify essential information system requirements while simultaneously postponing or eliminating non-essential aspects. An abstraction intentionally ignores some qualities, attributes, or functions of an information system in order to focus attention on others. An abstraction is also a summary, covering the highlights and leaving out the details. It also omits the pieces of the system that are not necessary for understanding the system at a given level of detail. Maps typically represent a good example of abstraction. You can get maps of the United States, individual states, counties, cities, zip codes, and so on. Each map cited here in succession is less abstract and hence more detailed than the prior one. In addition, a city map intentionally leaves off the details of the surrounding county, state, and country that it is a part of in order to allow you to focus on the details of the city. Another example of abstraction would be to view an aerial picture of your entire university campus. Such a picture would not have detailed information regarding a specific office on a specific floor within a specific building on the campus. Abstraction has been a common characteristic in all of the prevailing information systems analysis and design methodologies. Therefore, experienced systems analysts can continue to utilize this system-building characteristic as they transition to an object-oriented methodology.

3. ***Encapsulation*** or ***information hiding*** is the notion that a software component (module, subroutine, operation, method, and so on) should isolate or hide a single design decision. This notion is based on the work of David Pamas dating back to the early 1970s. An example of programming encapsulation may illustrate this notion best. The creation and subsequent use of a single software component to look up student account numbers in a student database isolates this lookup feature from the rest of the software that makes up the information system. Each time the information system needs to look up a student account number, this routine is used, since the logic to look up student account numbers has been encapsulated within this one routine. If a new lookup routine is created, tested, and used each time there is a new requirement to look up a student account in the database, two potentially negative things happen. First, prior work—software construction and testing as a minimum—is replicated. Second, additional maintenance activity will be required for the information system should it ever be necessary to alter the student lookup routine(s).

   In systems analysis and design, systems analysts decompose the problem domain into small, encapsulated units. These analysis and design decisions eventually become software modules. Encapsulation helps to localize their volatility when changes and maintenance are required after they have become software modules.

   A further elaboration of encapsulation or information hiding is any mechanism that allows certain portions of the information system to be "hidden." This can be useful in at least two different situations:

   (a) When it is important that people only use or have access to a certain subset of the complete information system. For example, while an information system is being developed, development team members may be assigned to work on a certain part of the system and not allowed access to other parts of the system being worked on by other team members. Once the information system is operational, certain users may only be allowed to use a few of the features of the information system while other users may have access to many more features.

   (b) To purposely prevent other components of the information system from being aware of or unable to take advantage of certain other components in the system. This situation addresses another aspect of encapsulation—assignment of responsibilities. Just as in real life you have certain responsibilities, a specific component of an information system has its responsibility, say dispensing cash in an ATM, while other components of the same system have their responsibilities, which exclude the dispensing of cash since that function is done by another component.

   Another way to think about encapsulation is from a programming perspective, which has long since advocated the creation and use of small blocks of function-specific code (e.g., procedure, subroutine, paragraph, and so on) that can be assembled into a working computer program in a modular fashion, much like the plug-compatible stereo components in homes today. Each of these blocks has encapsulated within it one or a few design functions. For example, each of the following functions could be represented by a small block of computer programming code and then bundled together to perform a higher-level function, such as registering for courses for this coming school year — "get student identification (Id) number," "validate student Id number," "check student Id number for outstanding fines," "get course Id to add to student's schedule," "determine if a seat is available for this course Id," "determine student Id number's eligibility to take this course Id," and so on.

Finally, encapsulation has been a common characteristic in all of the prevailing information systems methodologies. Therefore, experienced systems analysts can continue to utilize this system-building characteristic as they transition to an object-oriented methodology. There is one subtle difference. With the older, more mature methodologies, encapsulation was usually limited to encapsulation of functions separately from encapsulation of data. With the object-oriented methodology, encapsulation incorporates both functions and data together into objects. This notion will be discussed in more detail later in the book.

4. ***Inheritance*** is a mechanism for expressing similarity. Just as you inherited certain physical features from your mother and certain ones from your father, so also can information system components inherit certain things from related components. For example, Figure 14.6 shows that a hierarchical or parent-child relationship exists between a group called Person and groups of Faculty, Administrator, and Student. We purposely are using the singular for each of these words in keeping with the notation that is used throughout the book, but keep in mind that Administrator means one or more administrators, as does student and faculty.

A sibling relationship exists between Faculty, Administrator, and Student. There are certain characteristics that can be associated with Person and thus inherited by all the children in the hierarchy—Faculty, Administrator, and Student—such as name, address, phone number, and date of birth to name a few. Other characteristics may be unique to a single sibling. For example, office hours may only be applicable to Faculty, job title may only be applicable to Administrator, and grade point average may only be applicable to Student. These characteristics would be associated with the specific child node in the hierarchy. Similarly, there are certain things that a Person can do that would be common to Faculty, Administrator, and Student, such as eating at the cafeteria and walking on campus. Likewise, there are certain things that are unique to each of the children nodes. For example, a Faculty person may assign grades and add students to the class, whereas an Administrator person may manage people and key in administrative data to the computer, while a Student person could register for courses and take an exam. These actions would be associated with the specific child node that each belongs to.

As is usually the case in real life, inheritance in systems development is a one-way street—**down** the hierarchy—from the "parent" node to each of the "children" (siblings) nodes. However, as you view Figure 14.6 you observe three arrows—each pointing upwards toward the "parent." The explanation for this is that each of Faculty, Administrator and Student "extends from" or "is an extension of" or "is a specialization of" or "inherits from" the Person—hence the upward-pointing arrows.

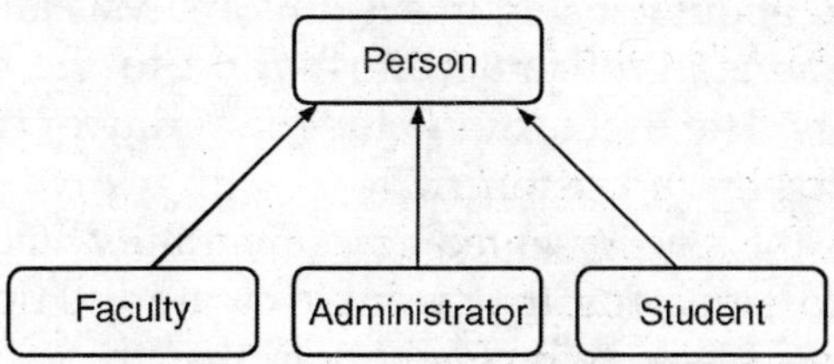

Figure 14.6: *Inheritance Hierarchy*

5. ***Polymorphism*** in the general sense is the ability to take on different forms. For example H_2O can take on three forms—water, steam, or ice. In a sense, you could say that you are polymorphic with respect to your behavior when approaching a traffic signal in your car. You respond differently depending on the status of the signal light. In software, for example, the *print* operation associated with textual characters and numbers can print textual characters and numbers "because it knows how to do this". The print operation associated with graphic symbols and images can print graphic symbols and images "because it knows how to do this". Each of the *print* operations just described will print something on a printer in the abstract sense; however, at the detail level each of these *print* operations does its job a little differently because what is being printed is of a different type—textual characters and numbers, graphic symbols, and images. Because of the differences at the detail level, the print operation is considered polymorphic. Polymorphism in computer programming isn't new, but its use during object-oriented analysis and design by systems analysts probably is.
6. ***Message communication*** is the way objects in an object-oriented methodology communicate with each other. It is similar to a subroutine call with parameters or a paragraph or procedure call in some other conventional programming languages such as Fortran, COBOL, C, or Pascal. This concept is widely understood by practicing systems analysts so it, too, can be directly transferred into an object-oriented methodology by them.
7. ***Associations*** are useful to assist with relating things in an information system to each other. Things that happen at the same time could be associated as well as things that happen under similar conditions. For example, VISA, MasterCard, Discover, and other credit card companies send out periodic statements showing us our balance owing. These companies often take this opportunity to insert a number of advertisements along with the statement, since the postage is often the same with or without the advertisements. Also, Figure 14.6's hierarchy is an example of association.
8. ***Reuse.*** Everywhere you look in your world you see reuse in one form or another. The same power cord can often be used for your computer, your monitor, or your printer. Apartment windows often come in standard sizes, and dozens of a certain size window are used in a large apartment complex. The can of orange juice you bought last time probably looks just like the one you bought today. How many shirts or blouses do you have that reuse the same type of button? How often do you reuse a textbook that was used by some other student before you? Have you ever reused a videocassette to record over some other event that you recorded at a previous time?

Reuse is a much talked about concept in systems analysis and design, but one which is still struggling to make a significant contribution to the development process due primarily to two factors. The first factor is the retraining of the mind-set of the analysts and programmers who are accustomed to creating their own systems models and code. This translates to the "not invented here" mentality held by some systems analysts and programmers. In other words, they want to create and debug their own "whatever" rather than use someone else's "whatever" that does the same thing. Management can address and overcome this problem given proper amounts of time, retraining, and other motivators for the systems analysts and programmers who are resistant to reuse.

The second factor relates to the administrative factors that must be established for setting up a library of reusable models and code. This is no easy task for a variety of reasons including strategy to accomplish, personal, organizational, cultural, and legal aspects.

As used in our everyday world, reuse can take one of three forms: ***(1) sharing, (2) copying*** or ***cloning,*** or ***(3) adjusting***. Each is discussed here.

An example of **sharing** is when you use a textbook and then sell it back to the bookstore, which in turn resells it to another student. Or everyone living in or visiting your apartment or home shares (reuses) the telephone you have. In software development, a subroutine, module, paragraph, procedure, service, or file definition are all potentially reusable. A small procedure could be created that only looks up student identification numbers in a student database and then responds with valid or invalid. Such a procedure could be used over and over again, intact, within an information system.

An example of **copying** or **cloning** is what is done every day in the manufacturing industry. An automobile model is prototyped and then moved into production to produce thousands of that model. In software development, we could have a paragraph of a COBOL program that we copy and put into another COBOL program, giving two paragraphs that are identical.

An example of **adjusting** is a variation on the copying or cloning. Using the automobile example, as a certain model moves down the manufacturing assembly line, standard features for this automobile are assembled (copying) as well as different combinations of options are assembled such as air conditioner, CD player, spoiler, tinted glass, and so on (adjusting). It is granted that these options are standard reusable components just assembled in different combinations in the particular automobile. However, the final product, the automobile, is a variation on the standard make and model.

A variation of the adjusting type of reuse is the situation in which the standard item is actually changed and then used in some other application. For example, a computer modem cable can have two of its wires physically swapped within the cable housing, and then this cable becomes a different kind of modem cable called a null modem cable—an adjustment to the standard cable.

An example of adjusting in systems analysis and design is when a programmer locates a subroutine, module, or paragraph, and so on from a library of reusable components. The subroutine becomes the programmer's beginning point for creating a new subroutine, somewhat similar to the original library version. Then the programmer begins making adjustments to the subroutine, such as removing some of the code in the subroutine, changing other parts of the code, and adding new code to this new subroutine to meet a specific purpose. The end result is a new subroutine.

The eight characteristics described above play pivotal parts in the object-oriented systems analysis and design methodology. This is indeed good news because most people—software developers and users of computers—are already familiar with most of them.

14.4 OBJECT-ORIENTED APPROACH

Object-oriented development offers a different model from the traditional software development approach, which is based on functions and procedures. In simplified terms, object-oriented systems development is a way to develop software by building self-contained modules or objects that can be easily replaced, modified, and reused. Furthermore, it encourages a view of the world as a system of cooperative and collaborating objects. In an object-oriented environment, software is a collection of discrete objects that encapsulate their data as well as the functionality to model the real-world 'objects'. An object orientation yields benefits to the practice of software construction.

Object-orientation is so called because this method sees things that are part of the real world as objects. A phone is an object in the same way as a bicycle, a human being, or an insurance policy, all are objects. In everyday life, we simplify objects in our thinking as we work with models. Software development does essentially the same: objects occurring in reality are reduced to a few features that are relevant in the current situation. Instead of real objects, we work with symbols. Properties and composition of objects correspond only roughly to reality; the model selects only those aspects that are useful for carrying out a specific task. In Figure 14.7, we use model to describe a reality that a teacher owns a bicycle and he reads a book.

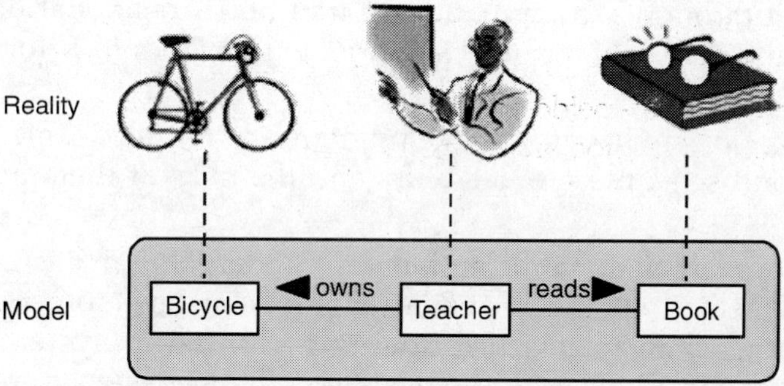

Figure 14.7: *Complex Realities are made more manageable by Abstract Models*

All object-orientation experts agree that a good methodology is essential for software development, especially when working in teams. Thus, quite a few methodologies have been invented over the last decade. Broadly speaking, all object-oriented methodologies are alike – they have similar phases and similar artifacts – but there are many small differences. Object-oriented methodologies tend not to be too prescriptive: the developers are given some choice about whether they use a particular type of diagram, for example. Therefore, the development team must select a methodology and agree which artifacts are to be produced, before they do any detailed planning or scheduling.

In general, each methodology addresses:

- The philosophy behind each of the phases.
- The workflows and the individual activities within each phase.
- The artifacts that should be produced (diagrams, textual descriptions and code).
- Dependencies between the artifacts.
- Notations for the different kinds of artifacts.
- The need to model static structure and dynamic behavior.

Static modeling involves deciding what the logical or physical parts of the system should be and how they should be connected together. Dynamic modeling is about deciding how the static parts should collaborate. Roughly speaking, static modeling describes how we construct and initialize the system, while dynamic modeling describes how the system should behave when it is running. Typically, we produce at least one static model and one dynamic model during each phase of the development.

Some methodologies, especially the more comprehensive ones, have alternative development paths, geared to different types and sizes of development. The object-oriented approach uses a set of diagramming techniques known as the Unified Modeling Language or UML. It focuses on the three architectural views of a system: functional, static, and dynamic. The functional view describes the external behavior of the system from the perspective of the user. Use cases and use-case diagrams are used to depict the functional view. The static view is described in terms of attributes, methods, classes, relationships, and messages. Class responsibility-collaboration (CRC) cards, class diagrams, and object diagrams are used to portray the static view. The dynamic view is represented by sequence diagrams, collaboration diagrams, and state charts. All diagrams are refined iteratively until the requirements of the information system are fully understood. Finally, the information system is developed through a combination of traditional relational database and object-oriented programming rather than true object-oriented methodology for both programming and database.

The benefits of Object-Oriented Development are reduced time to market, greater product flexibility, and schedule predictability and the risks of them are performance and start-up costs.

Software development is dynamic and always undergoing major change. Today a vast number of tools and methodologies are available for system development. *System development* refers to all activities that go into producing information system solution. System development activities consist of system analysis, modelling, design, implementation, testing and maintenance. A software development methodology is series of processes that, if followed, can lead to the development of an application. The original goal based on the system requirements. Further we study about the unified approach, which is the methodology used for learning about object oriented system development. Object-Oriented (OO) systems development is a way to develop software by building self-contained modules that can be more easily:

- Replaced,
- Modified, and
- Reused.

14.4.1 Abstraction

Abstraction is the presentation of simple concept (or object) to the external world. Abstraction concept is to describe a set of similar concrete entities. It focuses on the essential, inherent aspects of an entity and ignoring its accidental properties. The abstraction concept is usually used during analysis: deciding only with application-domain concepts, not making design and implementation decisions.

Two popular abstractions: *procedure abstraction* and *data abstraction*. Procedure abstraction is to decompose problem to many simple sub-works. Data abstraction is to collect essential elements composing to a compound data. These two abstractions have the same objective: reusable and replaceable. Figure 14.8 shows an example of data abstraction to abstract doors as a data structure with essential properties.

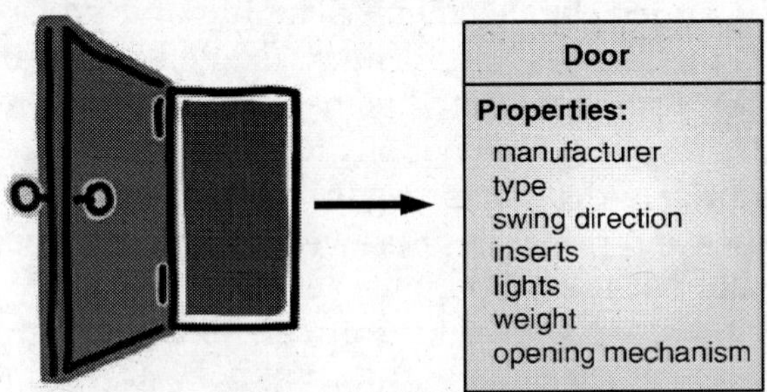

Figure 14.8: *Example of Data Abstraction*

14.4.2 Encapsulation

Encapsulation means as much as shielding. Each object-oriented object has a shield around it. Objects can't 'see' each other. They can exchange things though, as if they are interconnected through a hatch. Figure 14.9 shows the concept of the encapsulation. It separates the external aspects of an object from the internal implementation details of the object, which are hidden from other objects. The object encapsulates both data and the logical procedures required to manipulate the data.

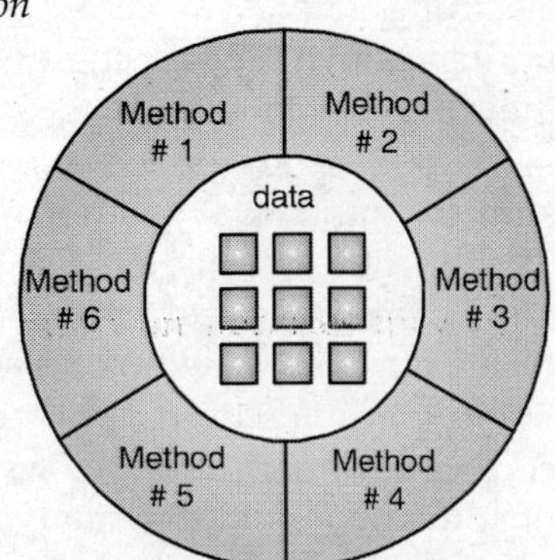

Figure 14.9: *Example of Encapsulation Concept*

14.5 OBJECT-ORIENTED DEVELOPMENT

The traditional view of a computer program is that of a process that has been encoded in a form that can be executed on a computer. This view originated from the fact that the first computers were developed mainly to automate a well-defined process (i.e. an algorithm) for numerical computation, and dates back to the first stored-program computers. Accordingly, the software creation process was seen as a translation from a description in some 'natural' language to a sequence of operations that could be executed on a computer. As many would argue, this paradigm is still the best way to introduce the notion of programming to a beginner, but as systems become more complex; its effectiveness in developing solutions became suspect. This change of perspective on part of the software developers happened over a period of time and was fuelled by several factors including the high cost of development and the constant efforts to find users for software in new domains. One could safely argue that the software applications developed in later years had two differentiating characteristics:

- Behaviour that was hard to characterise as a process.
- Requirements of reliability, performance, and cost that the original developers did not face.

The 'process-centered' approach to software development used what is called 'top-down functional decomposition'. The first step in such a design was to recognize what the process had to deliver (in terms of input and output of the program), which was followed by decomposition of the process into functional modules. Structures to store data were defined and the computation was carried out by invoking the modules, which performed some computation on the stored data elements. The life of a process-centered design was short because changes to the process specification (something relatively uncommon with numerical algorithms when compared with business applications) required a change in the entire program. This in turn resulted in an inability to reuse existing code without considerable overhead. As a result, software designers began to scrutinize their own approaches and also study design processes and principles that were being employed by engineers in other disciplines. Cross-pollination of ideas from other engineering disciplines started soon after, and the disciplines of 'software design' and 'software engineering' came into existence.

In this connection, it is interesting to note the process used for designing simple electromechanical systems. For several decades now, it has been fairly easy for people with limited knowledge of engineering principle to design and put together simple systems in their backyards and garages. So much so, it has become a hobby that even a ten-year old could pursue. The reasons for this success are easy to see: easily understandable designs, similar (standards) solutions for a host of problems, an easily accessible and well-defined 'library' of 'building-blocks', inter-changeability of components across systems, and so on. Some of the pioneers in the field of software design began to neither ask whether they could nor also design software using such 'off-the-shelf' components. The object-oriented paradigm, one could argue, has really evolved in response to this outlook. There are, of course, several differences with the hardware design process (inevitable, because the nature of software is fundamentally different from hardware), but parallels can be drawn between many of the defining characteristics of hardware design and what today's advocates of good software design recommend. This methodology provides us with a step-by-step process for software design, a language to specify the output from each step of the process so that we can transition smoothly from one stage to the next, the ability to reuse earlier designs, standards solutions that adhere to well-reasoned design principles and, even the ability to incrementally fix a poor design without breaking the system.

The overall philosophy here is to define a software system as a collection of objects of various types that interact with each other through well-defined interfaces. Unlike a hardware component, a software object can be designed to handle multiple functions and can therefore participate in several processes. A software component is also capable of storing data, which adds another dimension of complexity to the process. The manner in which all of this has departed from the traditional process-oriented view is that instead of implementing an entire process end-to-end and defining the needed data structures along the way, we first analyse the entire set if processes and from this identify the necessary software components. Each component represents a data abstraction and is designed to store information along with procedures to manipulate the same. The execution of the original processes is then broken down into several steps, each of which can be logically assigned to one of the software components. The components can also communicate with each other as needed to complete the process.

14.5.1 Object

An **object** is a thing, an entity, a noun, something you can pick up or kick, anything you can imagine that has its own identity. Some objects are living, some aren't. Examples from the real world include a car, a person, a house, a table, a dog, a pot plant, a check book or a raincoat.

All objects have **attributes**: for example, a car has a manufacturer, a model number, a colour and a price; a dog has a breed, an age, a colour and a favourite toy. Objects also have **behaviour**: a car can move from one place to another and a dog can bark.

In object-oriented software, real world objects migrate into the code. In programming terms, our objects become stand-alone modules with their own knowledge and behaviour (or, if you prefer, their own data and processes). It's common to think of a software object as a robot, an animal, or a little person: each object has certain knowledge, in the form of attributes, and it knows how to perform certain **operations** for the benefit of the rest of the program. For example, a person object might know its title, first name, last name, date of birth and address; it would be able to change its name, move to a new address, tells us how old it is, and so on.

By concentrating on the characteristics of a person when we write the code for the Person object, we can put the rest of the system out of our mind – this makes our programming simpler than it would otherwise be (it also helps that we have a real-world concept to get us started). If we decide later that our Person needs to know its height, we can add that extra knowledge (and associated behaviour) directly to the Person code. Only the code in the rest of the system that needs to use the height attribute has to be modified; all other code would remain unchanged. Simplicity and localization of change are important characteristics of object-oriented software.

It's easy enough to think of a living thing as some kind of robot. It is a little strange, though, when we try to think of a lifeless object as having behaviour. We wouldn't normally consider a video capable of changing its price or giving itself a new advert. However, when it comes to object-oriented software, that's exactly what we need to do. The key is that if the video didn't do those jobs, some other part of the system would have to. This would lead to video characteristics leaking into other parts of the code, so we'd start to lose the simplicity and locality that we crave (we would be going back to 'the old way of doing things'). Don't be put off by the **anthropomorphism** (the assignment of human characteristics to inanimate objects or animals) that's common in object-oriented development, imagining software objects as little people.

Figure 14.10: Objects in the Real World

Figure 14.10 shows some real-world objects that would make good software objects. It turns out that almost anything would make a good object in some context or another. A bad object is one that merges several concepts, for example, a bank account object that has been polluted with the knowledge and behaviour that belongs to a bank clerk. Always keep in mind that separate concepts in the real world suggest separate concepts in the program.

Before we go any further, it's important to note that we're not trying to **simulate** the real world that would be far too difficult. We're simply trying to make sure that our software is influenced by real-world concepts, so that it is easier to produce and easier to change. The needs of the system and the needs of computers are important influences too. Some developers are uncomfortable with the close proximity of the real world and software; however, an object-oriented system developed for a hospital that *didn't* include some kind of Patient object would be of little use.

You shouldn't think that it's possible to code the ideal Person object or any other kind of perfect object. There are simply too many characteristics and capabilities that can be applied to real-world objects – if we tried to capture them all, we'd never get as far as coding the second object in our system.

Most aspects of a real-world object are not needed for a typical program, especially since software systems tend to address a single problem area. For example, a bank system will be interested in the age and salary of a customer, but not their shoe size or favourite colour. It's quite reasonable to code an object that is useful for *many* systems, especially for well understood areas of programming: for example, all systems with a user interface are likely to be able to make use of the same 'scrollable list' object. The trick is to start by considering the business you're dealing with, to ask yourself 'If I worked in this business area, what would a "person" mean to me: a customer, an employee, a patient, or what?' All good software developers start by modeling the business.

A **model** is a representation of a problem domain or a proposed solution that allows us to talk, or reason, about the real thing. This allows us to increase our understanding and avoid potential pitfalls. Think of an architect's model of a new concert hall: it allows the architects to say 'This is what the finished concert hall will look like' and it helps them to come up with new ideas, such as 'I think we're going to need a steeper roof'. A model allows us to learn a lot without actually building anything. Much of software development involves creating and refining models, rather than cutting lines of code.

14.5.1.1 Depicting Objects

Once we've decided to work with objects, we need some way of showing them on a diagram so that we can describe them and think about them. Figure 14.11 shows how we can draw an object. The notation used here is a UML **object diagram**.

anObject
attribute 1 attribute 2
Operation 1() Operation 2() Operation 3()

Figure 14.11: *An Object*

The three parts of the box show the object's *name* (which is underlined), its *attributes* (its knowledge) and its *operations* (its behaviour). (Showing operations on an object diagram is not actually legal UML, but it suits our purposes for now.) The parentheses next to the operation names indicate any parameters that are required: even though none of the operations shown here have parameters, it's a good idea to keep the parentheses so that operation names stand out from attribute names (this becomes even more important when we omit one or more parts of the box).

The attributes are hidden inside the object; the only way to access them is via the operations. This is reasonable from analogy with the real world: most of us are much more interested in the fact that a television has a 'change channel' operation than we are in the fancy electronics inside the box that actually perform the change.

Let's examine a coffee machine object. First, we should decide what operations a coffee machine needs:

- display drinks
- select drink
- accept money
- dispense drink

Next, we should think about what the coffee machine needs to know in order to perform these operations:

- available drinks
- drink prices
- drink recipes

Having designed our coffee machine object, we can record our findings on an object diagram, like the one shown in Figure 14.12.

aCoffeMachine
drinkPrices availableDrinks drinkRecipes
displayDrinks() selectDrink() dispenseDrink() acceptMoney()

Figure 14.12: *A Coffee Machine Object*

14.5.1.2 Interaction Between Object

An object can be considered a "thing" that can perform a set of activities. The set of activities that the object performs defines the object's behaviour. For example, a "Student Status" object can tell you its grade point average, year in school, or can add a list of courses taken. A "Student" object can tell you its name or its address.

Objects are the basic run-time entities in an object-oriented system. Programming problem is analyzed in terms of objects and nature of communication between them. When a program is executed, objects interact with each other by sending messages. Different objects can also interact with each other without knowing the details of their data or code.

The object's interface consists of a set of commands, each command performing a specific action. An object asks another object to perform an action by sending it a *message*. The requesting (sending) object is referred to as *sender* and the receiving object is referred to as *receiver*.

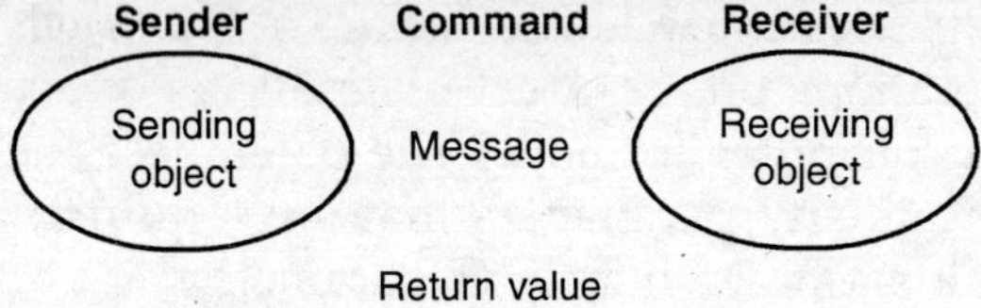

Figure 14.13: *Sending and receiving object*

Control is given to the receiving object until it completes the command; control then returns to the sending object.

For example, a **School** object asks the **Student** object for its *name* by sending it a *message* asking for its name. The receiving **Student** object returns the *name* back to the sending object.

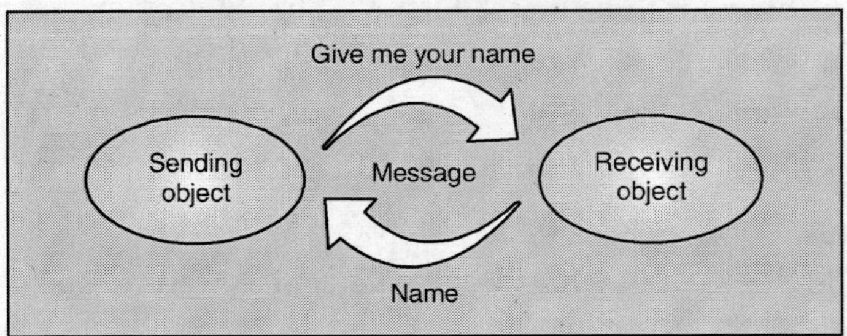

Figure 14.14: *Sender sending message to receiver*

A message can also contain information the sending objects needs to pass to the receiving object, called the *argument* in the message. A receiving object always returns a *value* back to the sending object. This returned value may or may not be useful to the sending object.

For example, the **School** object now wants to change the student's name. It does this by sending the **Student** object a message to set its name to a new name. The new address is passed as an argument in the message. In this case, the **School** object does not care about the return value from the message.

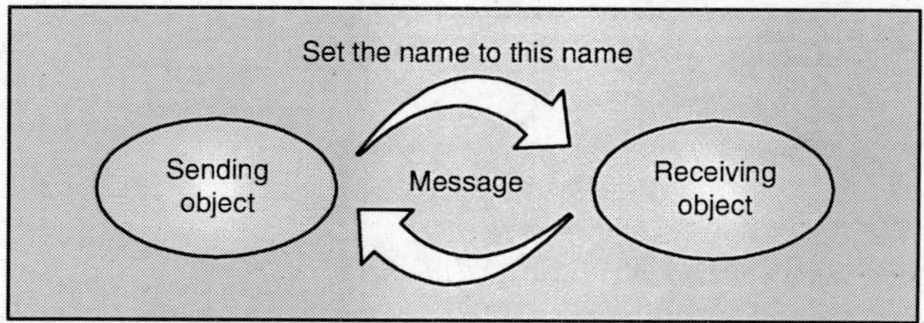

Figure 14.15: *Interaction between objects*

14.5.1.3 Sequential Operation

It is very common that a message will cause other messages to be sent, either to itself or to other objects, in order to complete its task. This is called ***sequential operation***. Control will not return to the original sending object until all other messages have been completed. For example, in the following diagram, Object A sends a message to Object B. For Object B to process that message it sends a message to Object C. Likewise, Object C sends a message to Object D. Object D returns to Object C who then returns to Object B who returns to Object A. Control does not return to Object A until all the other messages have completed.

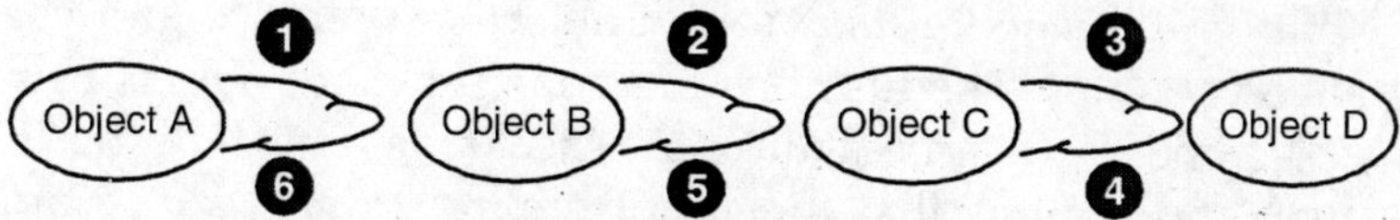

Figure 14.16: *Sequential operation of objects*

14.5.1.4 Method

How do receiving objects interpret messages from the senders? How are the messages processed?

Each message has code that associated with it. When an object receives a message, code is executed. In other words, these messages determine an object's behaviour and the code determines how the object carries out each message. The code that is associated with each message is called a *method*. The message name is also called the *method name* due to its close association with the method.

When an object receives a message, it determines what method is being requested and passes control to the *method*. An object has as many methods as it takes to perform its designed actions.

Refer to the following diagram, **name**, **name:**, and **name:address** are method names for the **Student** object. When the **Student** object receives the **name** message, the **name** message passes control to the *name* method defined in **Student**.

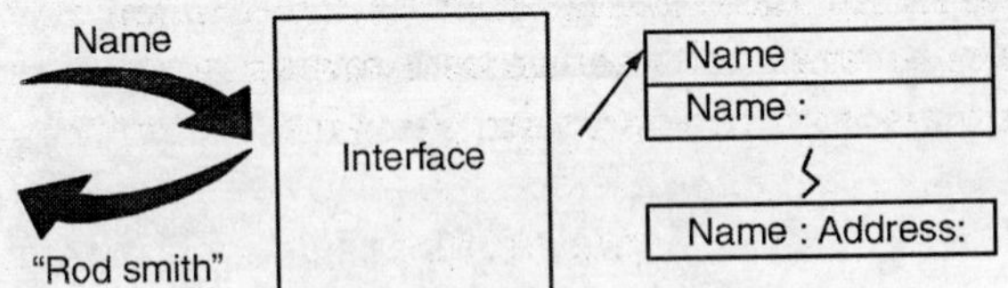

Figure 14.17: Interfacing between objects

Methods that operate on specific objects are instance methods and messages that invoke instance methods are called instance message. Methods that operate on specific classes are class methods. This will be discussed in more details in later chapter.

Methods are similar to subroutines, procedures, or functions found in procedural languages (C, Pascal). For example, a method name equates to a subroutine name, and the code for the method equates to the code found in a subroutine. Sending a message to an object is similar to calling a subroutine.

14.5.1.5 Object's Data

Each object need to keep the information on how to perform its defined behaviour. Some objects also contain variables that support their behaviour. These variables are called *instance variables*. Only the *instance method* for an object can refer to and change the values stored in the instance variables. The instance methods for other objects cannot refer to this object's data. An object may only access another object's data by sending it messages. This is called *encapsulation* and assures that there is a secure process for getting to an object's data.

Refer to the following diagram, the instance variables *variableOne* through *variableX* can only be accessed by the sender via instance methods *methodOne* through *methodN*. The sender can not refer to the variables directly by itself. Unlike procedural programming where common data areas are often used for sharing information, object-oriented programming discourages direct access to common data (other than the use of *global variables*) by other programs. Only the object that "owns" the data can change its content. Other objects can view or change this data by sending message to the "owner."

The instance variable names can be identical to the method names that associate with them. For example, the **Student** object has methods of **name**, **address**, and **major** as well as instance variables of *name, address*, and *major*. Smalltalk distinguishes variable identifier and a method identifier by the identifier's position in the expression.

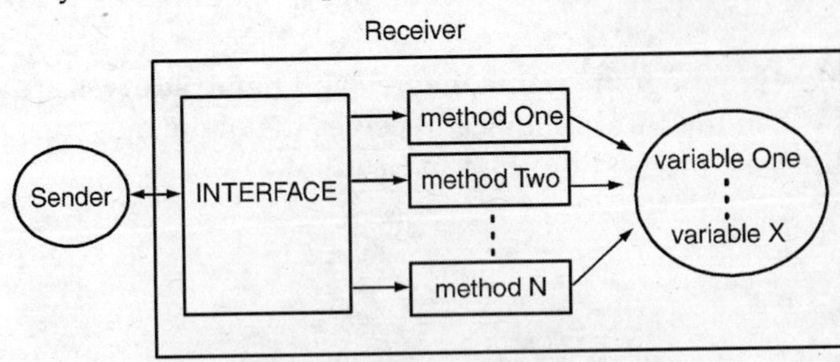

Figure 14.18: Representing different methods

The **figure 14.19** below illustrates diagrammatically what a programming shell in an object oriented programming environment "looks" like:

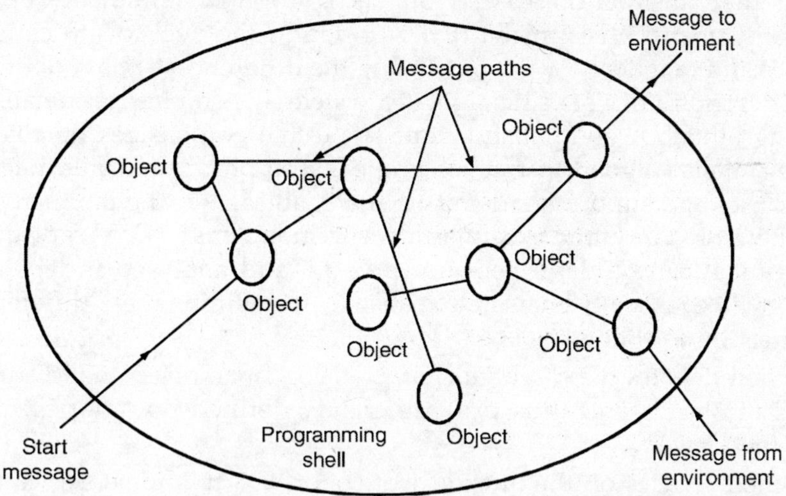

Figure 14.19: *Diagram of objects created in an object oriented programming shell*

Each object would have the following (diagrammatic) form:

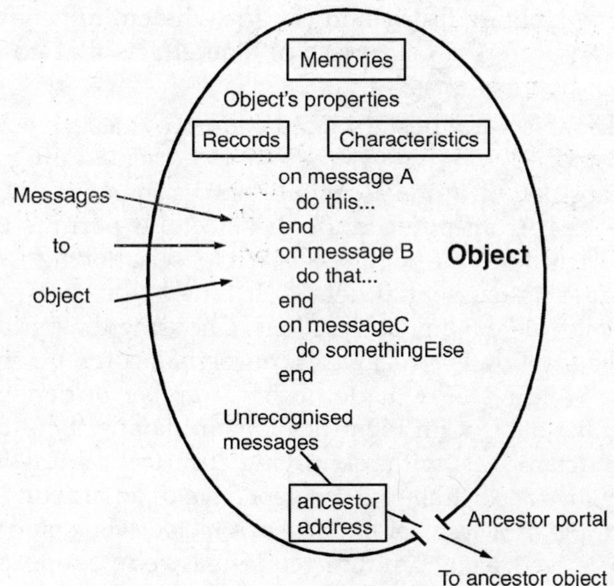

Figure 14.20: *Diagram of an abstract object*

Once you have understood that OOPS isn't about programming per se, you can then concentrate your thinking upon your ideas and your imagination. You will then discover the real power of OOPS.

14.5.2 Abstraction

Abstraction is one of the fundamental ways that we as humans cope with complexity. Hoare suggests that 'abstraction arises from recognition of similarities between certain objects, situations, or processes in the real world, and the decision to concentrate upon these similarities and to ignore for the time being the differences'. Shaw defines abstraction as 'a simplified description, or specification, of a system that emphasises details or properties while supressing others. A good abstraction is one that emphasizes details or properties while supressing others'. A good abstraction is one that emphasizes details that are significant to the reader or user and suppresses details that are, at least for the moment, immaterial or diversionary. Berzins, Gray and Naumann recommend that 'a concept qualifies as an abstraction only if it can be described, understood, and analysed independently of the mechanism that will eventually be used to realise it'. Combining these different viewpoints, we define abstraction as follows:

An abstraction denotes the essential characteristics of an object that distinguish it from all other kinds of objects and thus provide crisply defined boundaries, relative to the perspective of the viewer.

An abstraction focuses on the outside view of an object, and so serves to separate an object's essential behaviour from its implementation. Abelson and Sussman call this behaviour/ implementation division an abstraction barrier achieved by applying the principle of least commitment, through which the interface of an object provides its essential behaviour, and nothing more. We like to use an additional principle that we call the principle of least astonishment, through which an abstraction captures the entire behaviour of some object, no more and no less, and offers no surprises or side effects that go beyond the scope of abstraction.

In object-oriented analysis and design, abstraction provides a mechanism for managing and communicating complexity of the system. In object-oriented programming, abstraction aids in reuse and encapsulation. An abstraction denotes the essential characteristics of an object that distinguishes it from other kinds of objects. It permits us to concentrate on similarities between objects. For a particular view, it exposes only the essential characteristics of an object while hiding its inessential details. It thus helps us to model the real world object. A single entity may have many abstractions. Choosing the attributes and behaviours to be included in the abstraction is critical. It is the job of a software engineer. For example, consider the plan of a building. It is made up of a number of details. The point of view (abstraction) of a plumber deals with identification and laying the pipelines, taps, etc. The abstraction of the electrician deals with identifying electrical cabling, fan and light fittings etc. Thus abstraction varies according to the perspective of a particular viewer of the object. Consider another example of a web server. The abstracted web server requires details like accepting requests for a web page, sending requested web page to client and permitting multiple connections. The less essential details of a web server are port details and maintenance of concurrent connections. Similarly, consider a pen. The user of a pen is concerned with how it writes. The manufacturer of the pen is concerned with its cost, components that a pen is made up of and so on. Thus the pen is abstracted on different ways by different people.

The principle of least astonishment states that an abstraction captures the entire behaviour of certain objects, no more or no less. It offers no side effects that go beyond the scope abstraction. Abstraction ensures major and minor elements of the object model like Classification, Class hierarchy, Encapsulation, Polymorphism, Aggregation, Association and Collaboration.

In the early design stage, models provide an abstraction of the system. Code is an abstraction in the implementation stage. Software is abstracted into attributes and behaviour as depicted in Figure 14.21. While attributes of an abstraction are mapped to a set of data called fields, behaviour of an abstraction is mapped to a set of methods.

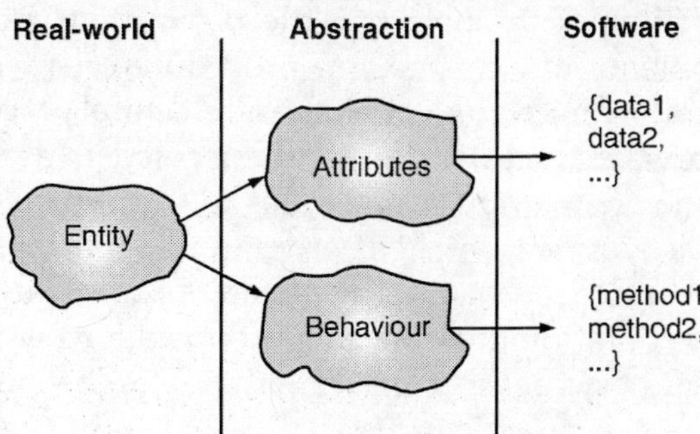

Figure 14.21: Abstraction

The properties of a good abstraction are:

- Abstractions should be well named. The meanings, intuitions, impressions, and expectations implied by a name accurately reflect the use of the abstracted entity.
- Abstractions should be coherent. It has related set of attributes and behaviour that make sense from the viewpoint of the user. For example, the details of the building from the plumber's viewpoint should be separated from the details of the building from the electrician's viewpoint.
- Abstraction should be accurate. The abstraction contains only those attributes or behaviour that is part of the entity being modeled. For example the web server should not maintain a utility to rename files (namely, file system utility).
- An abstraction should have only the minimal details of the entity. The abstraction should not contain unnecessary attributes or behaviour. For example, a pen does not need a description of its owner.
- An abstraction should be complete. It should encompass all the attributes and behaviour necessary for the object to perform an action. For example, a verification of the availability of details necessary to send the requested information through HTTP should be confirmed for a web server.

Abstraction can be categorised as:

(a) Entity Abstraction: An object that represents a useful model of a problem domain or solution domain entity is known to be entity abstraction.

(b) Action Abstraction: An object that provides a generalized set of operations, all of which perform the same kind of function is known to be action abstraction. An abstraction that collects objects based on the output produced is an apt example of action abstraction.

(c) Coincidental Abstraction: An object that packages a set of operations that have no relation to each other is known to be coincidental.

(d) Virtual Machine Abstraction: An object that groups operations that are all used by some superior level of control, or operations that all use some junior level set of operations is known to be virtual machine.

All abstractions have static as well as dynamic properties. For example, a file object takes up a certain amount of space on a particular memory device; it has a name, and it has contents. These are all static properties. The value of each of these properties is dynamic, relative to the lifetime of the object: A file object may grow or shrink in size, its name may change, its contents may change. In a procedure-oriented style of programming, the activity that changes the dynamic value of objects is the central part of all programs; things happen when subprograms are called and statements are executed. In a rule-oriented style of programming, things happen when new events cause rules to fire, which in turn may trigger other rules, and so on. In an object-oriented style of programming, things happen whenever we operate on an object (i.e. when we send a message to an object). Thus, invoking an operation on an object elicits some reaction from the object. What operations we can meaningfully perform on an object and how that object reacts constitute the entire behaviour of the object.

14.5.2.1 How Types of Abstractions Differs

There are two broad types of abstraction; **functional abstraction** and **data abstraction**. The main difference between functional abstraction and data abstraction is that functional abstraction refers to a function that can be used without taking into account how the function is implemented. Data abstraction refers to the data that can be used without taking into account how the data are stored. There is also a difference in the way the access takes place in functional abstraction and data abstraction. In functional abstraction, access to the function is provided through a specific interface defined to invoke the function. In contrast, in data abstraction, access to the data is provided through a specific set of operations defined to examine and manipulate the data. For instance, when a programmer is using C++ standard data types, this means that users are using the concept of data abstraction. When using data types, the users are not concerned with how the data is stored but they are concerned with what operations are provided and what properties are supported.

14.5.2.2 Reasons for the Ned Abstraction

Following are the reason for the need of abstraction:

1. **Flexibility in approach:** By hiding data or abstracting details that are not needed for presentation, the programmer achieves greater flexibility in approach.
2. **Enhanced Security:** Abstraction gives access to data or details that are needed by users and hide the implementation details, giving enhanced security to application.
3. **Easier Replacement:** With the concept of abstraction in object-oriented programming language, it is possible to replace code without recompilation. This makes the process easier and saves time for users.
4. **Modular Approach:** In object-oriented programming language C++, the abstraction concept helps users to divide the project application into modules and test each of them separately. Then all modules are integrated and ultimately tested together. This approach makes the application development easier.

14.5.2.3 Data Abstraction

Data Abstraction increases the power of programming language by creating user defined data types. Data Abstraction also represents the needed information in the program without presenting the details.

The public interface, formed by the collections of messages understood by an object, completely defines how to use this object. Programs that want to manipulate an object only have to be concerned about which messages this object understands, and do not have to worry about how these tasks are achieved or the internal structure of the object. The hiding of internal details makes an object abstract, and the technique is normally known as data abstraction.

With abstraction you create a well-defined entity which can be properly handled. These entities define the data structure of a set of items. An entity with the properties just described is called an ***abstract data type*** **(ADT)**. However, data abstraction and data hiding are almost same.

For example: Car is a physical object which abstracts the details of engine, braking system, suspension, fuel injection etc. **Figure 14.22** represents abstract car without showing its parts explanations.

Figure 14.22: *Abstract car*

Figure 14.23 is representing car with its explanations:

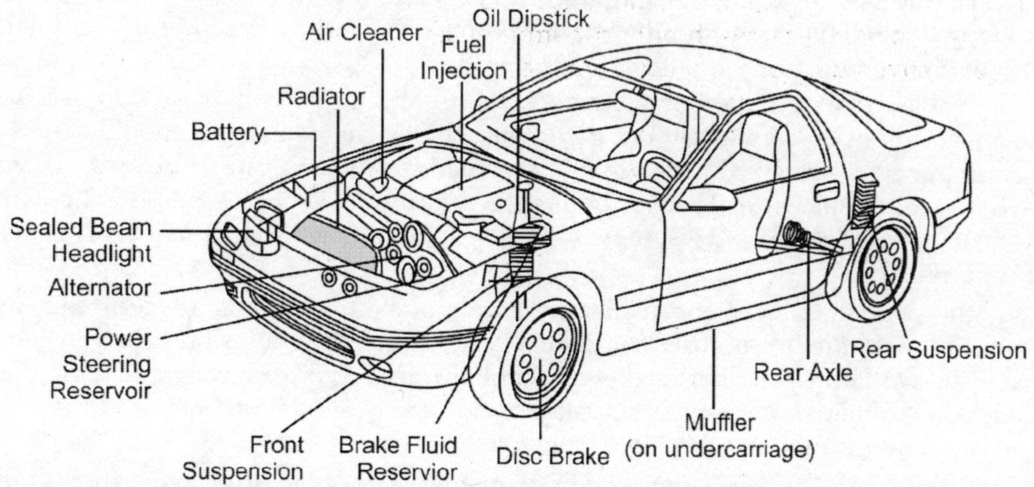

Figure 14.23: *Car representing its background details or explanations*

Abstraction refers to the act of representing essential without including the background details or explanations. Classes use the concept of abstraction and are defined as a list of abstract attribute such as size, weight and cost, and functions to operate on these attributes. Data abstraction ensures security of data from being unexpected viewing or changing or manipulating. Both the term data abstraction and data hiding are closely related and are often understood as one which is very much correct.

Abstract Data Type or Data Abstraction is a wide asked and thought question even in procedural or structured languages as data security or data hiding is essential for corporate users and to ensure the irrational manipulation or processing of data by other calls because of dynamic binding and multiple calls or value passing i.e. messages.

14.5.3 Encapsulation

Encapsulation refers to an object hiding its attributes behind its operations (it seals the attributes in a capsule, with operations on the edge). Hidden attributes are said to be **private**. Some programming languages (for example, Smalltalk) automatically make attributes private and some languages (for example, Java) leave it to the programmer.

Encapsulation is one of the ways that a programming language protects programmers from themselves: if programmers could bypass the operations, they would become dependent on the attributes that were being used to represent the object's knowledge. It would then be much harder to change the internal representation of the object in the future, because we'd have to find all the pieces of code that access the attributes directly and change those too. Without encapsulation we would lose simplicity and locality.

As an example of why encapsulation is a good idea, consider an object representing a circle. A circle would be likely to have operations allowing us to discover its radius, diameter, area and perimeter. What attributes would we need to store in order to support this behaviour? Well, we could store the radius and calculate the other attributes on demand. Or, we could store the diameter and calculate the other attributes from that. In fact, we could store any one of the four attributes and calculate the other three on demand. (Our choice may depend on personal preference or it may depend on predicting how the circle will normally be used.)

Let's say we choose to store the diameter. Any programmer who was allowed to access the diameter might do so, rather than going via the 'get diameter' operation. If, for a later version of our software, we decided that we wanted to store the radius instead, we would have to find all the pieces of code in the system that used direct access to the diameter, so that we could correct them (and we might introduce faults along the way). With encapsulation, there's no problem.

Another way to think of encapsulation is to imagine that objects are courteous to one another. If you wanted to borrow some money from a colleague to buy food in the staff canteen, you wouldn't grab their wallet and look through it to see if they had enough cash. Instead, you would ask them whether they could lend you some money and they would look in their own wallet.

Abstraction and encapsulation are complementary concepts: Abstraction focuses on the observable behaviour of an object, whereas encapsulation focuses on the implementation that gives rise to this behaviour. Encapsulation is most often achieved through information hiding (not just data hiding), which is the process of hiding all the secrets of an object that do not contribute to its essential characteristics; typically, the structure of an object is hidden, as well as the implementation of its methods. 'No part of a complex system should depend on the internal details of any other part'. Whereas abstraction 'helps people to think about what they are doing', encapsulation 'allows program changes to be reliably made with limited effort'.

Encapsulation provides explicit barriers among different abstractions and thus leads to a clear separation of concerns. For example, consider the structure of a plant. To understand how photosynthesis works at a high level of abstraction, we can ignore details such as the responsibilities of plant roots or the chemistry of cell walls. Similarly, in designing a database application, it is standard practice to write programs so that they don't care about the physical representation of data but depend only on a schema that denotes the data's logical view. In both of these cases, objects at one level of abstraction are shielded from implementation details at lower levels of abstraction.

'For abstraction to work, implementations must be encapsulated'. In practice, this means that each class must have two parts: an interface and an implementation. The interface of a class captures only its outside view, encompassing our abstraction of the behaviour common to all instances of the class. The implementation of a class comprises the representation of the abstraction as well as the mechanisms that achieve the desired behaviour. The interface of a class is the one place where we assert all of the assumptions that a client may make about any instances of the class; the implementation encapsulates details about which no client may make assumptions.

To summarize, we define encapsulation as follows:

Encapsulation is the process of compartmentalizing the elements of an abstraction that constitute its structure and behaviour; encapsulation serves to separate the contractual interface of an abstraction and its implementation.

These encapsulated elements are also called the 'secrets' of an abstraction.

14.5.3.1 Features and Advantages of the Concept of Encapsulation

Encapsulation in OOP-terminology means that an object has something like a shell around it protecting the attributes or status variables from being accessed from outside of the object.

Following are the various features of encapsulation:

1. **Makes Maintenance of Application Easier:** Complex and critical applications are difficult to maintain. The cost associated with maintaining the application is higher than that of developing the application properly. To resolve this maintenance difficulty, the object-oriented <u>programming</u> language C++ created the concept of encapsulation which bundles data and related functions together as a unit called class. Thus, making maintenance much easier on the class level.
2. **Improves the Understandability of the Application**
3. **Enhanced Security:** There are numerous reasons for the enhancement of security using the concept of Encapsulation in C++. The access specifier acts as the key strength behind

the concept of security and provides access to members of class as needed by users. This prevents unauthorized access. If an application needs to be extended or customized in later stages of development, the task of adding new functions becomes easier without breaking existing code or applications, there by giving an additional security to existing application.

In order to benefit from the powerful feature of encapsulation in object-oriented programming language C++, the programmer must use encapsulation properly. To maximize the benefits of encapsulation, the user must minimize the implementation details in external interfaces as needed.

14.5.3.2 Encapsulation: Information Hiding

Encapsulation is a method for protecting data from unwanted access or alteration by packaging it in an object where it is only accessible through the object's interface.

Encapsulation is often referred to as ***information hiding***. But both are different. Infact information hiding is actually the result of Encapsulation. Encapsulation makes it possible to separate an object's implementation from its original behaviour - to restrict access of its internal data. This restriction facilitates certain details of an object's behaviour to be hidden. This allows protecting an object's internal state from corruption by its user.

It is the mechanism by which Abstraction is implemented. In other words you can say that it is the result of the Encapsulation. For example, the Laptop is an object that encapsulates many technologies/hardware that might not be understood clearly by most people who use it.

14.5.3.3 Encapsulation: Data Hiding

Data encapsulation, sometimes referred to as ***data hiding***, is the mechanism whereby the implementation details of a class are kept hidden from the user. The user can only perform a restricted set of operations on the hidden members of the class by executing special functions commonly called *methods*. The actions performed by the methods are determined by the designer of the class, who must be careful not to make the methods either overly flexible or too restrictive. This idea of hiding the details away from the user and providing a restricted, clearly defined interface is the underlying theme behind the concept of an *abstract data type*.

The advantage of using data hiding comes when the *implementation* of the class changes but the *interface* remains the same. For example, to create a stack class which can contain integers, the designer may choose to implement it with an array, which is hidden from the user of the class. The designer then writes the push() and pop() methods which puts integers into the array and removes them from the array respectively. These methods are made accessible to the user. Should an attempt be made by the user to access the array directly, a compile time error will result. Now, should the designer decide to change the stack's implementation to a linked list, the array can simply be replaced with a linked list and the push() and pop() methods rewritten so that they manipulate the linked list instead of the array. The code which the user has written to manipulate the stack is still valid because it was not given direct access to the array to begin with.

The concept of data hiding is supported in C++ through the use of the public, protected and private keywords which are placed in the declaration of the class. Anything in the class placed after the public keyword is accessible to all the users of the class; elements placed after the protected keyword are accessible only to the methods of the class or classes derived from that class; elements placed after the private keyword are accessible only to the methods of the class.

As a convention, calling a method of an object instantiated from a class is commonly referred to as sending a *message* to that object.

14.5.3.4 Coupling

The degree to which a module (class) depends on other classes. In a good design, you should try to minimize coupling. Classes should be self-contained units that have a low dependence on other classes, meaning understanding and using one class should not require an understanding of another. With low coupling a change in a module will not require changes in other modules.

Related to the concept of coupling is information hiding. Information hiding is the hiding of the implementation in a class or module that is most likely to change; this protects other parts of the program from change if the implementation is changed. Protecting an implementation involves providing a stable interface which other classes can use to access services provided by the class. Often encapsulation and information hiding are used interchangeably.

Example: Car and Driver

14.5.3.5 Cohesion

Cohesion is the measure within a module (class) of how well the members work together to provide a specific piece of functionality. Cohesion is measured by how strongly related and focused the responsibilities of a single class are. In good design, the cohesion should be maximized. Cohesion is decreased if the methods of a class have little in common, or methods carry out many activities.

If cohesion is low, modules may be difficult to understand, maintenance is difficult, because change may affect many modules, and modules cannot be reused, because it is unlikely that another application will have a use for the random grouping of functionality.

Example: Oven that has built-in radio and alarm clock.

14.5.4 Modularity

Modularity is the act of partitioning a program into individual components can reduce its complexity to some degree. Although partitioning a program is helpful for this reason, a more powerful justification for partitioning a program is that it creates a number of well defined, documented boundaries within the program. These boundaries, or interfaces, are invaluable in the comprehension of the program. In some languages, such as Smalltalk, there is no concept of a module, and so the class forms the only physical unit of decomposition. In many others, including Object Pascal, C++, CLOS, and Ada, the module is a separate language construct, and therefore warrants a separate set of design decisions. In these languages, classes and objects form the logical structure of a system; we place these abstractions in *modules* to produce the system's physical architecture. Especially for larger applications, in which we may have many hundreds of classes, the use of modules is essential to help manage complexity.

Modularization consists of dividing a program into modules which can be compiled separately, but which have connections with other modules. The connections between modules are said to be the assumptions which the modules make about each other. Most languages that support the module as a separate concept also distinguish between the interface of a module and its implementation. Thus, it is fair to say that modularity and encapsulation go hand in hand.

Deciding upon the right set of modules for a given problem is almost as hard a problem as deciding upon the right set of abstractions. Zelkowitz is absolutely right when he states that "because the solution may not be known *hen the design stage starts, decomposition into smaller modules may be quite difficult. For older applications (such as compiler writing), this process may become standard, but for new ones (such as defence systems or spacecraft control), it may be quite difficult".

Modules serve as the physical containers in which we declare the classes and objects of our logical design. This is no different than the situation faced by the electrical engineer designing a board-level computer. NAND, NOR, and NOT gates might be used to construct the necessary logic, but these gates must be physically- packaged in standard integrated circuits, such as a 7400, 7402, or 7404. Lacking any such standard software parts, the software engineer has considerably more degrees of freedom - as if the electrical engineer had a silicon foundry at his or her disposal.

For tiny problems, the developer might decide to declare every class and object in the same package. For anything but the most trivial software, a better solution is to group logically-related classes and objects in the same module, and expose only those elements that other modules absolutely must see. This kind of modularization is a good thing, but it can be taken to extremes. For example, consider an application that runs on a distributed set of processors and uses a message passing mechanism to coordinate the activities of different programs. In a large system, it is common to have several hundred or even a few thousand kinds of messages. A naive strategy might be to define each message class in its own module. As it turns out, this is a singularly poor design decision. Not only does it create a documentation nightmare, but it makes it terribly difficult for any users to find the classes they need. Furthermore, when decisions change, hundreds of modules must be modified or recompiled. This example shows how information hiding can backfire.

Arbitrary modularization is sometimes worse than no modularization at all. In traditional structured design, modularization is primarily concerned with the meaningful grouping of subprograms, using the criteria of coupling and cohesion. In object-oriented design, the problem is subtly different: the task is to decide where to physically package the classes and objects from the design's logical structure, which are distinctly different from subprograms.

14.6 ASSOCIATION AND AGGREGATION

No object is an island. All objects are connected to other objects, directly or indirectly, strongly or loosely. By connecting objects, we make them more powerful. Connections allow us to navigate around to find extra information and behaviour. For example, if we were processing a Customer object representing Freda Bloggs and we wanted to send Freda a letter, we would need to know that Freda lives at 42 Acer Road. We would expect the address information to be stored in some kind of Address object, so we would look for a connection from the Customer to the Address, to find out where to send the letter.

When we're modeling with objects, we can connect them in two principal ways: association or aggregation. It's sometimes hard to spot the difference between the two, but here are some ideas.

- Association is a weak form of connection: the objects may be part of a group, or family, of objects but they're not completely dependent on each other. For example, consider a car, a driver, a passenger and another passenger. When the driver and the two passengers are in the car, they're associated: they all go in the same direction; they occupy the same volume in space, and so on. But the association is loose: the driver can drop off one of the passengers to go their separate way, so that the passenger is no longer associated with the other objects. Figure 14.24 shows how we can draw an association on an object diagram – the attributes and operations have been omitted here in order to emphasize the structure.

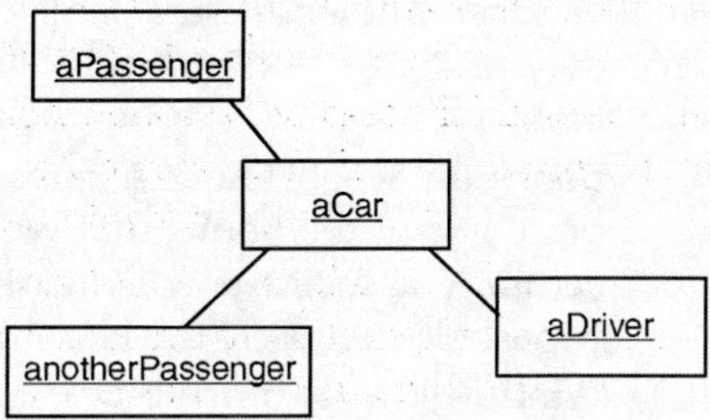

Figure 14.24: *Association*

- Aggregation means putting objects together to make a bigger object. Manufactured items usually form aggregations: for example, a microwave is made up of a cabinet, a door, an indicator panel, buttons, a motor, a glass plate, a magnetron, and so on. Aggregations usually form a **part–whole** hierarchy. Aggregation implies close dependency, at least of the whole to the part; for example, a magnetron is still a magnetron if you take it out of its microwave, but the microwave would be useless without the magnetron, because it wouldn't be able to cook anything.

Figure 14.25 shows how we can draw a house as an aggregation: in order to emphasize the difference between this kind of connection and an association, we place a white diamond on the 'whole' end.

As suggested, the distinction between association and aggregation can be subtle.

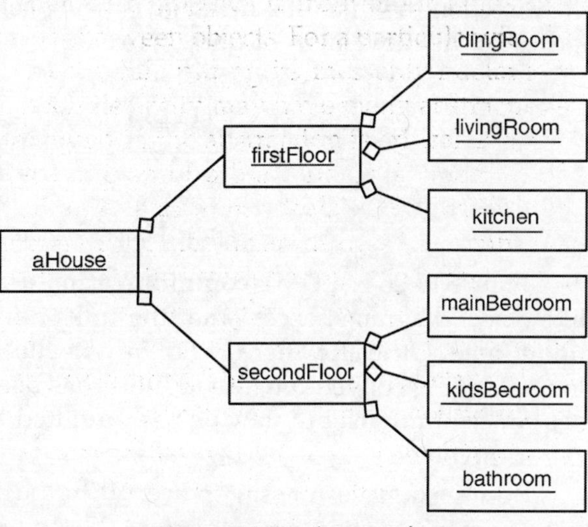

Figure 14.25: *Aggregation*

The 'What happens if you remove one of the objects?' test can be helpful, but it doesn't always solve the problem: hard thinking and experience are often needed.

We often need to choose between aggregation and association, because the choice can affect the way we design our software. Here are some examples:

- Friends: We would expect friends to be an association: there is no sense in which we could put the friends together to make a larger friend; friends come and go over time.
- Components in a television set: This is one of the easier ones to reason about because it's the classic part–whole hierarchy: you put the buttons and the knobs together to make the control panel; you put the glass screen, the electron gun and the magnetic coils together to make the tube; once the small parts have been assembled, then assembled into bigger components, you put everything into the cabinet and screw the back on. The end users see a single television object: if one of the components fails, they probably don't think they have a television set anymore, just a useless heap of junk.
- Books on a bookshelf: A bookshelf doesn't need books to be a bookshelf, it's just a place to put the books that we own. Conversely, when a book is on a bookshelf, it is certainly associated with it (if you move the bookshelf, the book moves too; if the bookshelf collapses, the book falls). This is a classic association.
- Windows in an office block: The windows are part of the office block. Although we could remove a broken window, leaving the office one window short, we would expect a replacement to be provided soon afterwards. This is probably aggregation.

14.7 COLLABORATION AMONG OBJECTS

Every object is connected to at least one other object: an isolated object wouldn't be much use to anyone. Once objects are connected, they can **collaborate**, to perform more complex tasks than they could on their own. Objects collaborate by sending **messages** to each other, as shown in Figure 14.26. The message is shown next to a solid arrow indicating the direction in which the message is being sent; the reply is shown next to a 'tadpole' that indicates the movement of data.

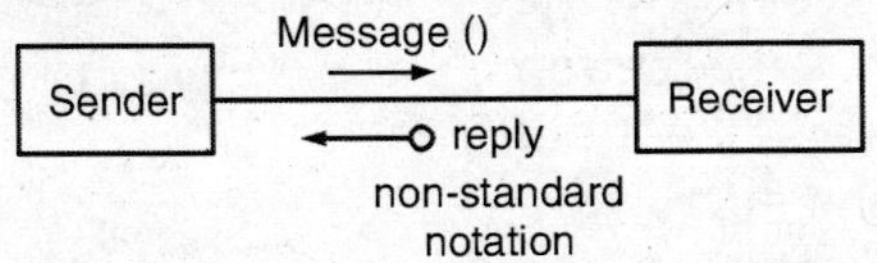

Figure 14.26: *Collaboration using messages*

Figure 14.26 is a UML **communication diagram**. Communication diagrams look rather like object diagrams, except that the links have no direction and the object names are not underlined. Officially, there is no way to show replies on a communication diagram, so a long-standing convention, the tadpole, has been used instead. Ideally, we would also show **sequence numbers**, but they've been omitted here, because the UML numbering scheme is rather involved.

Some example messages are: 'What's the time?', 'Start the engine' and 'What is your name?', as shown in Figure 14.27. As you can see, the receiving object may or may not need to provide a reply: we would expect replies to 'What's the time?' and 'What is your name?', but not to 'Start the engine'.

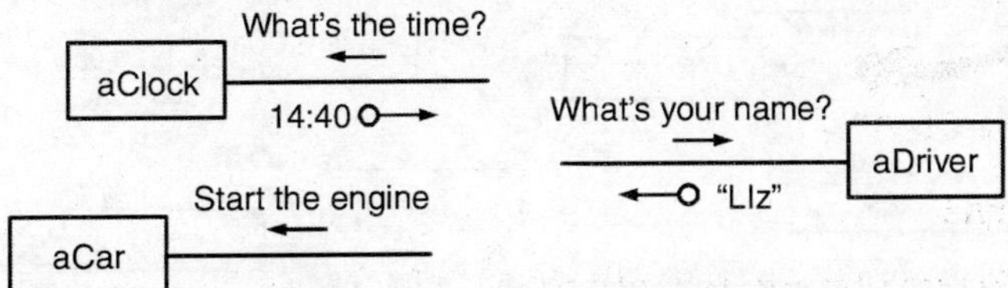

***Figure 14.27:** Some example messages*

Objects are courteous, i.e. when an object receives a message; it carries out the request without question. This way, the sending object doesn't need to cope with the possibility of a message being refused. In practice, some requests can't be carried out, despite the best intentions of the receiver.

Sometimes, we can't allow things to fail: we would be rather disappointed if a fly-by-wire plane crashed because of a software fault. Ensuring success under such circumstances is a specialist area, **software reliability**. Just to give you an idea, here's one strategy for reliability: install three computers on the plane and get them to vote on what to do next; if one computer says 'fly to the left' but the other two say 'fly to the right', the plane flies to the right. Now that you've seen why messages can fail, you should put the problem out of your mind for the time being and assume that messages always succeed.

14.8 CLASSES

A class encapsulates characteristics common to a group of objects. There are a number of ways you could think of a class – some of them are illustrated in Figure 14.28.

***Figure 14.28:** Different ways of thinking about a class*

Putting this picture into words:

- A factory manufactures objects according to some blueprint.
- A set specifies what features its member objects will have.
- A template allows us to produce any number of objects of a given shape.
- A dictionary definition describes an object as precisely as possible.

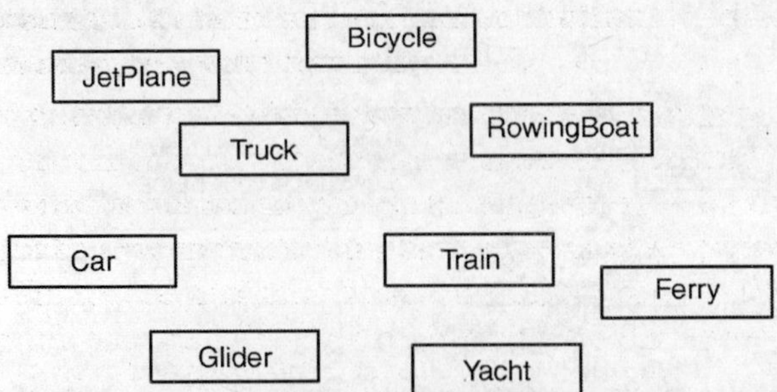

Figure 14.29: Some example classes

Figure 14.29 shows some example classes. In UML, classes are drawn as boxes on a **class diagram**. So that we can easily tell the difference between classes and objects, class names (on class diagrams) are not underlined, while object names (on object diagrams) are. Classes and objects are rarely mixed on the same diagram: it turns out that we can do most of our modeling in terms of classes, reserving object diagrams for illustration and verification purposes. Object-oriented programmers are often heard to say 'Every object is an instance of a class', hence the use of the term **instance** as a synonym for object.

By convention, class names start with a capital letter. On a class diagram, they're shown in bold, although, admittedly, that may be tricky when drawing by hand. In an object-oriented context, class names tend to be short and in the singular.

Classification – grouping things into classes – is something that humans are rather good at. We start doing it from the age of 12–18 months – 'toy', 'food', 'girl', 'boy', 'doggy' – so it's nice to see it in programming, which is not otherwise known for its accessibility or its closeness to nature. Object-oriented software development is meant to be natural: close to the real world and close to the way that we reason about it. Since, in the real world, classes are the next major step after objects, that should be justification enough for introducing them into our programs. Another justification for having classes, from a software point of view, is that they allow us to share the definition of elements between related objects, so that we don't have to repeat ourselves.

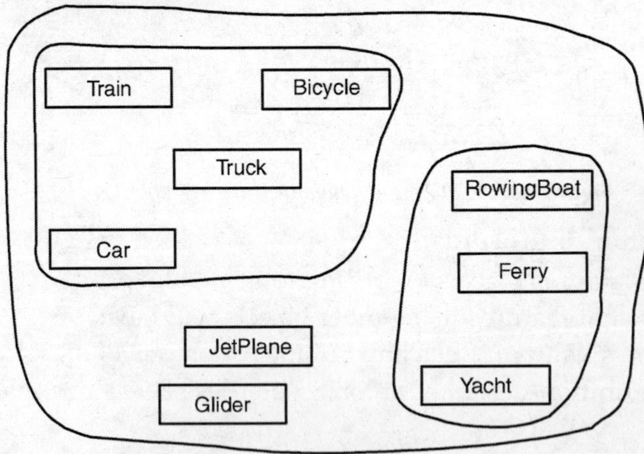

Figure 14.30: Groups of classes

Looking at Figure 14.29 again, can you spot any similarity between the classes? You would probably conclude that they're all kinds of vehicle: some work on water, some on land and so on. By drawing lines to show how the classes are related, we come up with the picture shown in Figure 14.30.

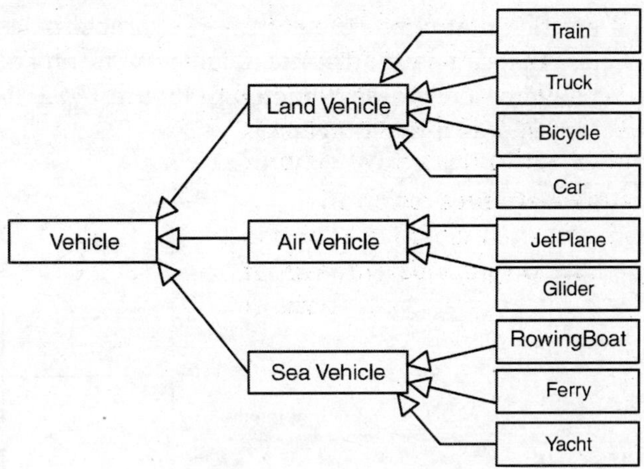

Figure 14.31: *A class hierarchy*

This picture shows a hierarchy of classes, a point that should be obvious when the relationships are redrawn using the proper UML notation, as in Figure 14.31. Here, a white arrow-head is used to point from each detailed concept to the less detailed one on its left. Just like the aggregation hierarchy we saw earlier, with its common name 'part–whole hierarchy', there are a few common names for this kind of hierarchy too:

- Inheritance: Trains **inherit** the characteristics of land vehicles.
- Generalization/specialization: A train is more **specialized** than a land vehicle; a land vehicle is more **generalized** than a train.
- Parent/child: LandVehicle is the **parent** of Train; Train is a **child** of LandVehicle.
- Superclass/subclass: LandVehicle is the **superclass** of Train; Train is a **subclass** of LandVehicle.
- Base/derived: LandVehicle is the **base** from which Train is **derived**.

Given below are some examples of class data type:

	class car **Properties:** company, model and colour **Behaviour:** speed and average
	class laptop **Properties:** company, hard disk, RAM size and price **Behaviour:** processing and resolution
	class CD **Properties:** company, size and capacity **Behaviour:** storing and retrieving

14.9 MAJOR ELEMENTS OF OBJECT MODEL

In this section, we describe some of the elements which are necessary to establish the characteristics of the object model. They are classification, encapsulation, modularity, and hierarchy. The details of these elements are given below:

Classification: The entities that share the common characteristics are grouped into a class. Consider a person class that can have attributes such as name and address. The instances of this class (objects) can be Hem, Joe, etc. as depicted in Figure 14.32. It can also be said that Joe, Hem, and Akil are classified as a person class.

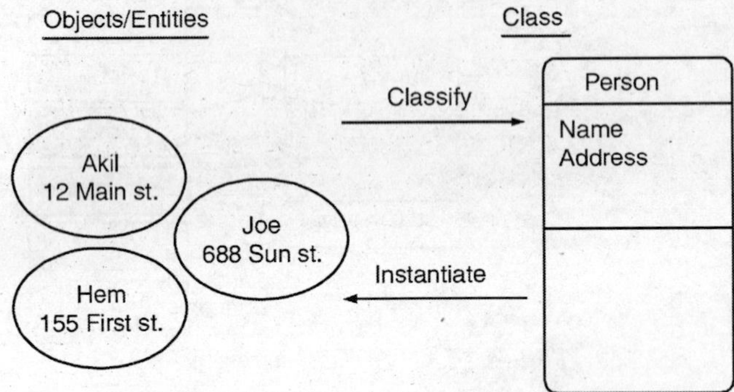

Figure 14.32: Classification and Instantiation

(i) Encapsulation: Encapsulation is the mechanism that binds together code and the data it manipulates and keeps both safe from outside interference and misuse. For example, in the person class of Figure 14.32, setName() operation can only set/modify the name of the person while getName() operation is used to obtain the name of the person. Encapsulation thus aids in data hiding by providing access to an object's data only through the operations it offers. This is called an interface. These external interfaces provide a set of methods that accepts and responds to a particular kind of message. It thus separate interface (external) details from the implementation (internal) details of an object. For example, a remote acts as an interface to the TV operations. To operate a washing machine, it is not necessary to study the internal working of the system. An understanding of the set of interfaces like buttons or switches provided by the washing machine is sufficient to operate the system. From the implementation point of view encapsulation specifies the scope of the data. A private data is accessed only by its class members, while a public data can be globally accessed by any class. Protected data is accessed only by the members of the class and its child classes.

(ii) Modularity: Modularity deals with partitioning a program into individual components to reduce the complexity of the system developed. Modularity is the property by which a system can be decomposed into a set of cohesive and loosely coupled modules. These modules can be implemented, compiled and tested separately. Then they can be linked together to form a complete executable program. Encapsulation and modularity provide a bar around the abstraction.

(iii) Hierarchy: Hierarchy is the ranking or ordering of abstraction. In complex systems, there are two most important hierarchies. They are the class structure and the object structure hierarchies. Class hierarchy is a mechanism that is used to express the similarity between classes. It portrays the generalization/specialization relationship, making common attributes and services explicit within a class hierarchy. Generalization tells us what the similarities between classes are. Specialization tells us what the differences between classes are. A generalized class is a superclass, while a specialized class is a subclass. For example Person is a generalized class and Employee and Student are specialized classes of the Person.

The object hierarchy is represented using aggregation. Aggregation is used to treat a collection of objects as a single object. It groups logically related structures. For example, a car consists of tyres and an engine as depicted in Figure 14.33(b). Decomposition is opposite of aggregation.

An association can be viewed as a weak form of aggregation as data-oriented relationship between two entities. For example, Figure 14.33(c) shows the association between a car and its owner.

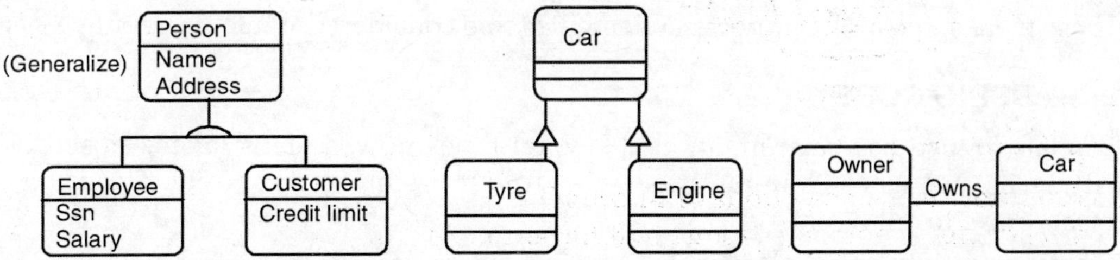

Figure 14.33: *(a) Class Hierarchy (b) Object Hierarchy (c) Association*

14.10 MINOR ELEMENTS OF OBJECT MODEL

The various minor elements of the object model are explained as follows:

(i) Persistence: Every object in a system takes up some amount of space and exists for an amount of time. Persistence is the property by which an object transcends time and/or space. Here the object maintains its state even after its creator ceases to exist. The object's location also moves from the address space in which it was created to another address space. The different types of persistence usually offered by programming languages are:

- Maintenance of transient results in expression evaluation.
- Maintenance of local variables in procedure activations.
- Maintenance of global variables and heap items.

In the domain of database technology, persistence is offered by the data that:

- exists between executions of a program.
- exists between different versions of the program.
- outlives the life of a program.

(ii) Typing: Typing of a class prevents objects of different types from being interchanged. Binding is the association of the variables or classes to their types. The programming languages can be categorised as strongly typed or weakly types languages. In strongly typed languages, the violation of type conformance can be detected at compile time. This type of binding variables to their types is called static binding or early binding. In weakly typed language, the violation of type of conformance cannot be detected until runtime. Here variables are bound to their type only at execution time. This is called as dynamic or late binding. Static binding is fast but rigid, whereas dynamic binding is slow but flexible. Dynamic binding also promotes expandability of the system.

Connected with typing is polymorphism. Polymorphism is the quality that allows one name to be used for more than one different purpose. Polymorphism can be statically or dynamically implemented. For example, different shapes like circle, triangle, etc. have the same draw functionality. But this draw functionality is implemented in different ways for each object.

(iii) Concurrency: This property distinguishes an active object from an inactive one. Concurrency is the property by which a program has several threads of control. These portions can be executed in parallel. To maintain consistency between these parallel threads of execution, locking mechanism is used.

These were some of the important elements to be considered while designing a system.

14.11 REUSING CODE

The term **reuse** has been mentioned several times now, so let's take a closer look at what it means and what its implications are. To put it simply, reuse refers to using code more than once, resulting in:

- Faster and simpler development.
- Easier maintenance (less code to harbour faults).
- More robust code (every time it is reused, it is retested and, over time, more and more faults are squeezed out).

There are historical and technical reasons why reuse has taken a long time to emerge. From a historical point of view, the software industry was initially preoccupied with the problem of how to program computers at all (starting with machine code), then with how to program them more efficiently and then with how to develop large systems in a reliable, systematic way.

The potential of reusing code in different contexts became apparent as more and more systems were constructed – millions upon millions of lines of code being written every year over many decades. Surely there couldn't be that many distinct systems that needed writing, could there? Since most software was written in software departments behind the closed doors of individual companies, using a variety of different programming languages, it's easy to see why reuse was rare. Even when packaged software started making it out through company doors, the source code, and even the binaries, was kept a closely guarded secret. Even so, protecting a company's commercial advantage and intellectual property doesn't justify failing to reuse code within the company itself.

From a technical point of view, reuse was difficult because of an attitude in development teams and central to the development methodology that 'We only need to solve today's problem'. This was exacerbated by the lack of facilities provided in programming languages and methodologies to promote reuse: there was a tendency to scatter the data and operations in small pieces throughout the system, making it difficult to collect related pieces into a larger chunk that would be worth reusing.

Because object orientation is driven by the modeling of general concepts from an entire domain, it's much more likely that reuse opportunities will emerge. For example, developing a payroll system would normally involve the development of an Employee class. Since the development should be driven by 'What does the employee concept mean to this company?' rather than 'What employee information does the payroll system need?', the end result is likely to be applicable to other systems developed by the same company. In addition, the modularity of objects reduces the tendency to spread attributes and operations around the system, making it easier to extract and refine the Employee code.

Gradually, the situation has improved, to the extent that, often, we will only need to write the parts of the system that are unique to our problem – the rest of the system can be implemented using prewritten code. This is especially true for common, well understood, application areas such as: user interfaces; database access; distributed programming; input/output; network access; e-commerce; access to legacy (pre-existing) systems; security (authentication, authorization, privacy, integrity checking, origin checking); text processing; mathematics; games; service look-up; sound synthesis and playback; 2D graphics; 3D graphics; e-mail; image processing; multimedia encoding and decoding; messaging; transaction processing; telephony; speech synthesis and recognition; and integration with digital TV broadcasts.

Reuse opportunities can be summarized into the categories listed below:

- *Reusing functions within a system:* The simplest form of reuse (used in traditional systems development) involves writing utility functions that are called from various places. For example, you may discover that various parts of your system need to search through a list of customer names, so you write a general search function that can be called from each context. Writing reusable functions is different from writing functions that break a complex process into simpler steps.
- *Reusing methods within an object:* Methods encapsulated within an object can be invoked from other methods. For example, a nonpublic drawFilledRectangle method inside a GUIComponent class can be used by any GUIComponent method that needs to fill an area of the screen with the current background colour. You should aim to reuse methods within an object whenever possible. Non-public methods within an object are often used to break up a complicated process, in traditional fashion.
- *Reusing classes within a system:* Many of the classes that we define can be used in different parts of our system. For example, if you define a Customer class for use in a marketing system, you expect the same Customer object to appear in many different pieces of system code. This kind of reuse is fundamental to the object-oriented approach.
- *Reusing functions across systems:* General functions can be reused (in traditional systems development as well as in object-oriented development) in other systems that you and your colleagues produce. For example, you might write a function that extracts the year that an employee joined the company from the employee's payroll number. For such a function to be reused by your colleagues, you would have to make them aware of it, preferably by putting it in a **reuse repository**: a database of useful functions that developers are expected to peruse when they're writing new code.

- *Reusing classes across systems:* We can publish and reuse a whole class (with all its attributes and operations) rather than just a single function. An example would be an Employee object that encapsulates the employee attributes used throughout the company, along with a useful set of operations. Object-orientation enthusiasts were the ones who popularized the idea of a **reuse repository** containing classes rather than functions. In order to get developers to put in the extra effort required to make their classes reusable enough for a repository, it's a good idea to offer some kind of reward (a mug with a humorous logo on it is a common choice). Access to class repositories may be offered to third parties, perhaps for a fee. Reusing classes across your own systems is not difficult, once you have a little practice.
- *Reusing classes across all systems:* A software component is analogous to a hardware component. Software components are designed to be reusable in any context; are strongly encapsulated (clients can't see the inner workings); come with a standard style of interface; and are available from third parties, usually in return for payment. Every object-oriented programming language has its own form of software component, for example, Java has JavaBeans. There is no real equivalent of software components in the traditional arena, because a handful of related functions would not be of much use to third parties. Examples of software components include a spreadsheet that can be dropped into any office productivity suite and an income tax object that can be dropped into any home tax package. A software component is really just an object that obeys sensible rules about its style of interface (as in using naming conventions to identify getters and setters).
- *Function libraries:* Related, high quality functions can be grouped into a **library**, so that they're available all at once. An example would be the studio function library, originating on Unix systems, that provides input/output facilities for C programmers. Function libraries are used in both traditional systems development and object-oriented development. Well-designed libraries sometimes become standardized by bodies such as ISO or ANSI. Function libraries may be internal to a company, free, or sold for profit.
- *Class libraries:* An improvement on function libraries, class libraries offer whole classes rather than mere functions. Writing a class library requires lots of experience. A good example is the **Java 2 Enterprise Edition (J2EE)** library, which provides code for all of the well-understood reuse areas listed above. Just like function libraries, class libraries may be internal to a company, free, or sold for profit.
- *Design patterns:* A design pattern is a description of how to create part of an object-oriented system elegantly and effectively. Since their introduction, patterns have also been applied to other areas such as system architectures. Each pattern has a short description, a detailed description, advice on where to use it, and code samples. For example, the description of the Adapter pattern is 'An adapter translates the interface of one object into another interface that clients expect'. Designing patterns requires a lot of experience, but less than producing a class library.
- *Frameworks:* A framework, as its name suggests, is a pre-existing structure to which you attach your own code. In the object-oriented case, a framework consists of a number of prewritten classes, along with a document describing the construction rules that must

be followed by the developer. A large example is the **Enterprise Java Beans (EJB)** framework: this consists of the J2EE library plus a document, hundreds of pages long, that specifies how programmers should write reusable enterprise components and how third parties should implement Java application servers. Most frameworks are designed by gurus (a guru is an expert's expert).

So, how should you design for reuse? We'll leave aside the issues of designing patterns and frameworks, since such techniques are beyond the scope of this book, and concentrate instead on writing reusable classes. Even a single reusable class will often have one or two closely collaborating classes – thus, we might produce a small family of reusable classes rather than just one. **Here are some tips:**

- *Always follow style guidelines:* Style guidelines are recommendations for how you should write your classes. If you write your classes in an exotic or personal style, potential reusers of your software will quickly move on to look at other code, rather than learn your personal idiosyncrasies. Style guidelines may originate from your company, or they be more widely accepted. For example, since Sun has control over the Java standard, whatever Sun says is good style is normally accepted by the Java community. As well as having a plethora of object-orientation gurus and experts of its own, Sun pays close attention to the opinions of external experts and gurus.
- *Be thorough with your documentation:* Few programmers will be able to understand how your classes should be reused just by reading the source code. At the very least, your class should have an explanatory name, a short comment (one or two sentences) summing up the class, a longer comment (maybe several paragraphs) describing how the class should be used and a short comment alongside each public message describing how the method should be used. Your comments should always describe the contract between the object and its clients, setting out the obligations on both sides. Documentation that is separate from the classes, such as design or tutorial information, should also be provided.
- *Be prepared to write more code than you need:* Often, when you're implementing a class for a particular system, you will find yourself thinking along the lines of 'I bet a foo method would come in handy here'. For example, even if you currently only need a getRadius message for your Circle class, it would be a good idea to add a getDiameter message too, making the class more useful in other systems.
- *Use patterns and frameworks:* Patterns and frameworks reduce your workload, but they're also understood by other developer, which means that the other developers will have less to learn before reusing your code.
- *Design client–supplier objects:* If you have two-way, or even cyclical, collaborations between your objects, you may end up with what is referred to in the trade as **code spaghetti**. Things will be a lot simpler if you design your objects as a client–supplier hierarchy. For example, a reusable Employee does not make any assumptions about its context; instead, it provides public messages that are generally useful. Taking this idea further, the Employee would be in control of its EmploymentHistory, but the EmploymentHistory would not know about the Employee. Imagine that your objects are servants that do what they're told, without caring about who asked them to do it. To compensate for their servile lives, the objects have servants of their own to control.

- *Make each object single-purpose:* This is referred to as **high cohesion**. Avoid coding objects that serve multiple purposes, such as maintaining an employee's personal information as well as their employment history.
- *Separate the interface from the business behaviour:* A reusable object should be usable in any context. For example, the object might need to be used, directly or indirectly, in many different kinds of interface (workstation, mobile phone, or Web server). If you pollute the object with the details of a particular interface, you will run into problems. Therefore, write business objects that contain only business behaviour. You can also provide interface objects to view your business objects, but that's optional. Such interface objects will become reusable in their own right.
- *Design for questions and commands:* Objects are simpler if their messages are either questions – 'What's the time?' – or commands – 'Set the time to . . . ' Although messages that are questions and commands at the same time are occasionally useful, you should consider their use to be an advanced technique. Combined messages, such as 'Set the time to . . . and tell me what the time was before I set it', can be confusing.

14.12 BENEFITS OF OBJECT ORIENTATION

Object-oriented methods enable us to create sets of objects which work together synergistically to produce software that better model their problem domains than similar systems produced by traditional techniques. The systems are easier to adapt to changing requirements, easier to maintain, more robust, and promote greater design and code reuse. Object-oriented development allows us to create modules of functionality. Once the objects are defined, it can be taken for granted that they will perform their desired functions and they can be sealed off like black boxes. The attention of a programmer thus shifts to what they do rather than how they do it.

We present some reasons why object orientation works:

- **Higher level of abstraction:** The op-down approach supports abstraction at the function level. The object-oriented approach supports abstraction at the object level. Since objects encapsulate both data (attributes) and functions (methods), they work at a higher level of abstraction. The development can proceed at the object level and ignore the rest of the system for as long as necessary. This makes designing, coding, testing, and maintaining the system much simpler.
- **Seamless transition among different phases of software development:** The traditional approach to software development requires different styles and methodologies for each step of the process. Moving from one phase to another requires a complex transition of perspective between models that almost can be in different worlds. This transition not only can slow the development process but also increases the size of the project and the chances of errors introduced in moving from one language to another. The object-oriented approach, on the other hand, essentially uses the same language to talk about analysis, design, programming and database design. This seamless approach reduces the level of complexity and redundancy and makes for clearer, more robust system development.
- **Encouragement of good programming techniques:** A class in an object-oriented system carefully delineates between its interface (specifications of what the class can do) and the implementation of that interface (how the class does what it does). The routines

and attributes within a class are held together tightly. In a properly designed system, the classes will be grouped into subsystems but remain independent; therefore, changing one class has no impact on other classes, and so, the impact is minimized. However, the object-oriented approach is not a panacea, as nothing is magical here that will promote perfect design or perfect code. But, by raising the level of abstraction from the function level to the object-oriented method tends to promote clearer designs, which are easier to implement, ad provides for better overall communication. Using object-oriented language is not strictly necessary to achieve the benefits of an object-orientation. However, an object-oriented language such as C++, Smalltalk, or Java adds support for object oriented design and makes it easier to produce more modular and reusable code via the concept of class and inheritance.

- **Promotion of reusability:** Objects are reusable because they are modeled directly out of a real-world problem domain. Each object stands by itself or within a small circle of peers (other objects). Within this framework, the class does not concern itself with the rest of the system or how it is going to be used within a particular system. This means that classes are designed generically, with reuse as a constant background goal. Furthermore, the object orientation adds inheritance, which is a powerful technique that allows classes to be built from each other, and therefore, only differences and enhancements between the classes need to be designed and coded. All the previous functionality remains and can be reused without change.

14.13 APPLICATIONS OF THE OBJECT MODEL

The object model has proven applicable to a wide variety of problem domains. Figure 14.34 lists many of the domains for which systems exist that may properly be called object-oriented. Object-oriented analysis and design may be the only method we have today that can be employed to attack the complexity inherent in very large systems. In all fairness, however, the use of object-oriented development may be ill-advised for some domains, not for any technical reasons, but for nontechnical ones, such as the absence of a suitably trained staff or a good development environment.

Air traffic control	Investment strategiei
Animation	Mathematical analysis
Avionics	Medical electronics
Banking and insurance software	Music composition
Business data processing	Office automation
Chemical process control	Operating systems
Command and control systems	Petroleum engineering
Computer aided design	Reusable software components
Computer aided education	Robotics
Computer integrated manufacturing	Software development environments
Databases	Space station software
Document preparation	Spacecraft and aircraft simulation
Expert systems	Telecommunications
Film and estage storyboarding	Telemetry systems
Hipermedia	User interface design
Image recognition	VLSI design

Figure 14.34: *Applications of the Object Model*

SUMMARY

Many people have an apprehension about object technology for a strange reason. This technology comes with such a big list of terminology, buzzwords, jargon and vocabulary that it is actually quite normal to get frightened. Therefore, our objective would be to simplify and clearly demystify all these terms in a very simple manner.

Some common characteristics for managing complexity during systems analysis and design are available for systems analysts to use to one degree or another regardless of the SDLC used to develop the information system. The object model forms a conceptual framework that brings about object orientation. It helps the analyst to concentrate on the similarities and ignore the differences between entities. Abstraction is the basic principle behind object models. The elements in the object oriented model are categorised into major and minor elements. The major elements are mandatory and emphasize on the necessary conditions, while the minor elements emphasize on the sufficient conditions. The minor elements can be absent in an object model. But, if these elements are present in the model then it is useful.

EXERCISES

1. What are the basics of object technology?
2. What are the characteristics of an object-oriented methodology?
3. What do you mean by object oriented approach?
4. Explain the concept of object oriented development?
5. What are objects? Also explain depicting objects?
6. Explain the concept of abstraction in detail?
7. Why we need abstraction?
8. What do you mean b data abstraction?
9. Explain the concept of encapsulation?
10. What do you mean by information hiding?
11. What do you mean by data hiding?
12. What do you mean by modularity?
13. Explain the concept of association and aggregation?
14. Explain the collaboration among objects?
15. Explain the classes in detail?
16. Explain the major elements of object model?
17. Explain the minor elements of object model?
18. Explain the concept of reusing code?
19. What are the benefits of object orientation?
20. What are the various applications of the object model?

❑

UNIT 7
SOFTWARE AGENTS

Software Agents 15

15.1 INTRODUCTION

An agent is simply another kind of software abstraction, an abstraction in the same way that methods, functions, and objects are software abstractions. An object is a high-level abstraction that describes methods and attributes of a software component. An agent, however, is an extremely high-level software abstraction which provides a convenient and powerful way to describe a complex software entity. Rather than being defined in terms of methods and attributes, an agent is defined in terms of its behaviour. This is important because programming an agent-based system is primarily a matter of specifying agent behaviour instead of identifying classes, methods and attributes. It is much easier and more natural to specify behaviour than to write code.

There is a minimum set of common features that typify a software agent. A software agent is autonomous; the agent is capable of operating as a standalone process and performing actions without user intervention. A software agent is communicative; it communicates with the user, other software agents, or other software processes. A software agent is perceptive; it is able to perceive and respond to changes in its environment.

Software agents, like people, can possess different levels of competence at performing a particular task. For example, one email software agent might be quite dumb and capable of only forwarding email to a few specified locations. A second, smarter email agent might have the ability to automatically detect and delete spam. While software agents must be autonomous, communicative, and perceptive, they can have different levels of competence (intelligence) as determined by their programs - i.e., their behavioural specifications.

Software agent technology is a rapidly developing area of research. In this chapter, we provide the developers with an overview of the evolving area of software agents. The over-use of the word 'agent' has tended to mask the fact that, in reality, there is truly heterogeneous body of research being carried out under this banner. This chapter provides an overview of the rationales, hypothesis, goals and state-of-the-art demonstrators of the various agent types which are currently under investigation by researchers.

15.2 AGENT

We are all in one sense familiar with the concept on agent. Consider for instance the role undertaken by a travel or estate agent. Both these organisations have a representative role, i.e. they both ***act on behalf of others***, in the case of the estate agents this is the actual owners of the property, for travel agents the hotels and flight companies. We claim acting on behalf of another entity is the first fundamental property of agency. The agents discussed above also exhibit a second fundamental agent characteristic, namely, they both enjoy at least a variable degree of autonomy. For example, estate agents can generally make viewing appointments for unoccupied properties without reference to the owners. A third important aspect of an agent's behaviour is the degree of ***proactivity*** and ***reactivity*** present in their behaviour. For instance, an estate agent who simply places a 'For Sale' sign outside a property for sale and waits for purchasers to come into his shop is behaving in a much more reactive fashion, than an agent who proactively advertises the property in the local press. It should be noted however that reactivity and proactivity are not flip sides of the same coin. The same agent can display high amounts of both proactivity and reactivity at different times. Finally, agents also exhibit some level of a number of attributes, the key ones of which are ***learning***, ***cooperation*** and ***mobility***.

The above discussion is equally true of *computational agents* in general. The term 'agent' in this context has its background in the early work on AI when researchers concentrated on trying to create artificial entities which mimicked human abilities. In its strictest sense, the term can be applied to a wide range of entities including the software systems which have become synonymous with the term as well as autonomous robots and biological organisms. In essence, therefore, we believe that the concept of agenthood can be summed up by the following definition.

"An agent is a computational entity which:

- ***acts on behalf of other entities in an autonomous fashion***
- ***performs its actions with some level of proactivity and/or reactiveness***
- ***exhibits some level of the key attributes of learning, co-operation and mobility."***

15.2.1 Definitions and Concepts

Outside the realm of computers, the term *agent* is well defined. It is derived from the concept of *agency*, which is to employ someone (such as a theatrical, literary, or boxing agent) to act on your behalf. An agent represents a person or organization and interacts with others to accomplish a predefined task.

Definitions proposed by different authors:

S. Russell and P. Norvig: An agent is anything that can be viewed as perceiving its environment through sensors and acting upon that environment through effectors.

P. Maes: Autonomous agents are computational systems that inhabit some complex, dynamic environment, sense and act autonomously in this environment, and by doing so realize a set of goals or tasks that they are designed for.

H.S. Nwana: When we really have to, we define an agent as referring to a component of software and/or hardware which is capable of acting exactingly in order to accomplish tasks on behalf of its user.

S. Franklin and A. Graesser: An autonomous agent is a system situated within and part of an environment that senses that environment and acts on it, over time, in pursuit of its own agenda and so as to effect what it senses in the future.

Y. Shoham: An agent is an entity whose state is viewed as consisting of mental components such as beliefs, capabilities, choices, and commitments.

N.R. Jennings and M. Wooldridge: An agent is a computer system that is situated in some environment, and that is capable of autonomous action in this environment in order to meet its design objectives.

FIPA1 (standard)[Poslad, Buckle]: An agent is an encapsulated software entity with its own state, behavior, thread of control, and an ability to interact and communicate with other entities – including people, other agents, and legacy systems.

In the computer realm, things are not so simple. There are almost as many definitions for the term **software (intelligent) agent** as there are people employing it.

The following are some examples:

"An agent is anything that can be viewed as perceiving its environment through sensors and acting on that environment through effectors"

"Autonomous agents are computational systems that inhabit some complex dynamic environment, sense and act autonomously in this environment, and by doing so realize a set of goals or tasks for which they are designed".

"An intelligent agent is software that assists people and acts on their behalf. Intelligent agents work by allowing people to delegate work that they could have done to the agent software. Agents can, just as assistants can, automate repetitive tasks, remember things you forgot, intelligently summarize complex data, learn from you, and even make recommendations to you".

"[An agent is] a piece of software that performs a given task using information gleaned from its environment to act in a suitable manner so as to complete the task successfully. The software should be able to adapt itself based on changes occurring in its environment, so that a change in circumstances will still yield the intended result".

Software agents can be distinguished from regular computer software programs along several dimensions, as shown in table.

Software agents versus traditional software programs

Characteristics	Regular Software	Software Agents
Nature	Static	Dynamic
Focus	Perform tasks; a solution engineered by a developer who has analyzed a problem.	Work toward a goal; about what to accomplish rather than how to go about it.
Manipulation	Direct: User initiates every action.	Indirect: Autonomous
Interactivity	Noninteractive	Dialogues are fully interactive. Actions may be initiated by either the user or the agent system. Interacts with user and with other agents.
Flexibility	Never changes, unless changed by a human or an error in the program.	Adapts, learns.

Temporal continuity	Runs one time, then stops to be run again when called.	Persistent: Continues to run over time.
Response	Predictable: Does what you tell it to, even if you didn't mean what you said.	Interprets what you mean, not what you say. In the best of circumstances, actions are based on rules, but they may change over time or in reaction to different circumstances.
Autonomy, independence	Follows instructions.	May initiate actions, as well as respond to instructions.
Mobility	Stays in one place.	May be mobile, travelling to other servers.
Concurrency	Generates process in one dedicated server with limited processing power.	Dispatches messages simultaneously to accomplish various parts of a task in parallel.
Local interaction	Network Table (NTBL): Accesses data across network client-server architecture.	Can travel and interact with local entities, as database, file servers, and stationary agent, through message passing.

In addition to the differing definitions, individual researchers have also invented a variety of synonyms for the term *agent* in order to promote their particular brand of software agency. Included among the alternatives are *intelligent agent, software robot, knowbot* (knowledge-based robot), *softbot* (intelligent software robot), *taskbot* (task-based robot), *autonomous agent, personal assistant*, and *digital proxy*. The different terms can be confusing, but they do serve a purpose.Not only do they capture our attention—the term *knowbot* is certainly more engaging than *agent*—but they also denote the character of the various agents, the roles they play (e.g., performing tasks), and the features they possesses (e.g., intelligence).

15.2.2 Levels of Intelligence

How agents are defined depends greatly on the agent's level of intelligence. The levels of agent intelligence are as follows:

Level 0 (the lowest): These agents retrieve documents for a user under straight orders. Popular Web browsers fall into this category. The user must specify the URLs where the documents are. These agents help people navigate the Web.

Level 1: These agents provide a user-initiated searching facility for finding relevant Web pages. Internet search agents such as Google, AltaVista, and Lycos are examples. Information about pages, titles, and word frequency is stored and indexed. When the user provides keywords, the search engine matches them against the indexed information. These agents are referred to as *search engines.*

Level 2: These agents maintain users' profiles. They then monitor the Internet and notify the users whenever relevant information is found. An example of such an agent is WebWatcher (search for WebWatcher at cs.cmu.edu). Agents at this level are frequently referred to as *semi-intelligent* or *software* agents.

Level 3: Agents at this level have a learning and deductive component to help users who cannot formalize a query or specify a target for a search. DiffAgent (CMU) and Letizia

(MIT) are examples of such agents. Agents at this level are referred to as *learning* or *truly intelligent* agents.

Similar to the concept of intelligence levels is the idea of "agent generation."

15.2.3 Major Characteristics of Different Kinds of Agents

An agent system is essentially a component system exhibiting several of the characteristics. There are six orthogonal characteristics work together to make agent-oriented systems more flexible and robust to change. These characteristics are supported by mechanisms and interfaces in the underlying infrastructure and by models and policies configured in each agent or group of agents.

1. *Adaptability:* the degree to which an agent's behavior may be changed after it has been deployed.
2. *Autonomy:* the degree to which an agent is responsible for its own thread of control and can pursue its own goal largely independent of messages sent from other agents.
3. *Collaboration:* the degree to which agents communicate and work cooperatively with other agents to form multi-agent systems working together on some task.
4. *Knowledgeable:* the degree to which an agent is capable of reasoning about its goals and knowledge.
5. *Mobility:* the ability for an agent to move from one executing context to another, either by moving the agent's code and starting the agent afresh, or by serializing code and state, allowing the agent to continue execution in a new context, retaining its state to continue its work.
6. *Persistence:* the degree to which the infrastructure enables agents to retain knowledge and state over extended periods of time, including robustness in the face of possible run-time failures.

15.3 SOFTWARE AGENT

Software agents (often simply termed agents) are software systems that loosely conform to the above definition and can basically be described as inhabiting computers and networks, assisting users with computer-based tasks. Why is it that in the closing years of the 20th century the need for software agents is becoming so urgent? In today's modern world, computers are now as ubiquitous as cars or televisions, but exploiting their capabilities is a problem we still need to tackle. As this technology proliferates, the gap between millions of untrained users and an equal number of sophisticated microprocessors will become even more apparent. Computers currently respond only to what interface designers call direct manipulation. Nothing happens unless a person gives commands from a keyboard, mouse or touch screen. The computer is merely a passive entity waiting to execute specific, highly detailed instructions; it provides little help for complex tasks or for carrying out actions that may consume a large proportion of the user's time (e.g., searching for information). Researchers and software companies have set high hopes on these so-called *software agents*, which "know" users' interests and can act autonomously on their behalf. Instead of exercising complete control, people will be engaged in a cooperative process in which both human and computer agents initiate communications, monitor events and perform tasks to meet users' goals.

In essence, we need software agents because:

- more and more everyday tasks are computer-based
- the world is in a midst of an information revolution, resulting in vast amounts of dynamic and unstructured information
- increasingly more users are untrained
- and therefore users require agents to assist them in order to understand the technically complex world we are in the process of creating.

Software agents (often simply termed agents) are software systems that loosely conform to the above definition and can basically be described as inhabiting computers and networks, assisting users with computer-based tasks. Why is it that in the closing years of the 20th century the need for software agents is becoming so urgent? In today's modern world, computers are now as ubiquitous as cars or televisions, but exploiting their capabilities is a problem we still need to tackle. As this technology proliferates, the gap between millions of untrained users and an equal number of sophisticated microprocessors will become even more apparent. Computers currently respond only to what interface designers call direct manipulation. Nothing happens unless a person gives commands from a keyboard, mouse or touch screen. The computer is merely a passive entity waiting to execute specific, highly detailed instructions; it provides little help for complex tasks or for carrying out actions that may consume a large proportion of the user's time (e.g., searching for information).

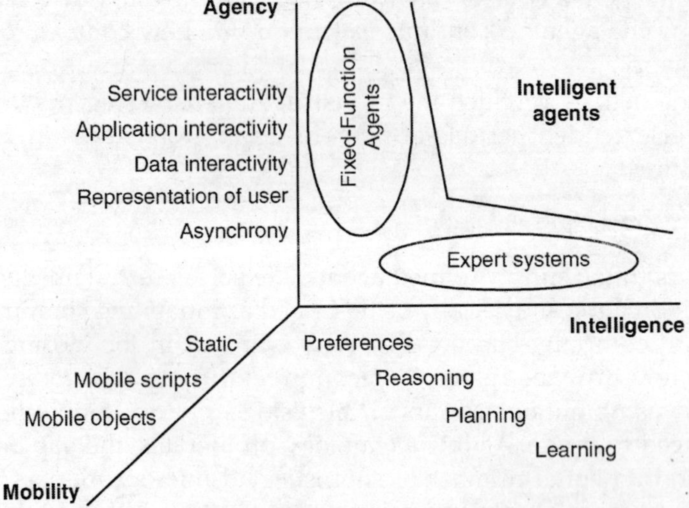

Figure 15.1: Scope of intelligent agents

Researchers and software companies have set high hopes on these so-called *software agents*, which "know" users' interests and can act autonomously on their behalf. Instead of exercising complete control, people will be engaged in a cooperative process in which both human and computer agents initiate communications, monitor events and perform tasks to meet users' goals.

In essence, we need software agents because:

- more and more everyday tasks are computer-based

- the world is in a midst of an information revolution, resulting in vast amounts of dynamic and unstructured information
- increasingly more users are untrained
- and therefore users require agents to assist them in order to understand the technically complex world we are in the process of creating.

The number and type of application domains in which agent technologies are being applied to or investigated include workflow management, network management, air-traffic control, business process re-engineering, data mining, information retrieval/management, electronic commerce, education, personal digital assistants (PDAs), scheduling/diary management, etc. Indeed as Guilfoyle (1995) notes,

"In 10 years' time most new IT development will be affected, and many consumer products will contain embedded agent-based systems".

A software agent can be described as an independently executing program which is able to handle autonomously (i.e. without direct input at run time from a human) the selection of actions when expected or limited unexpected events occur. Software agents can be of differing abilities, but typically possess appropriate 'expertise' to deal with their own world. Table 15.1 summarizes some of the attribute of agency that researchers have highlighted.

Table 15.1: Properties that Software Agents can Exhibit

Property	Description
Social ability	A software agent is able to use communication as a basis to signal interest or information to either homogeneous or heterogeneous agents that constitute a part of its environment. The agents may work toward a single goal global goal or separate individual goals.
Autonomy	Agents should operate without the intervention of external elements (other agents or humans). They have some kind of control over their actions and internal states.
Reactivity	Agents perceive their environment and respond in a timely fashion to changes that may occur.
Adaptability	Agents are characterized by their flexibility, adaptation and facility to set up their own goals based on their implicit purpose (interests). One of the major characteristics is their ability to acquire and process information about the situation, both spatially and temporally.
Agent Granularity Degrees	Agents may have degrees of complexity; Most simple agents are characterized by the lack of intelligence regarding their behaviour. These agents are called reactive. More complex agents are called cognitive or intelligent agents. They are characterised by their ability to know their environment, to act on themselves and on the environment; their observed behaviour is a consequence of their perception, knowledge, and interactions.

Learning	Either the agency itself may perform some learning ability (as a society) or each individual agent may be embedded with a learning algorithm (e.g. a Neural Network or other re-enforcement algorithm). Learning often allows the agent to alter its future action sequences and behaviour such that future mistakes can be alleviated. Learning is often a factor that provides an agent's ability to demonstrate adaptive behaviour.
Pro-activity	Agents should exhibit goal directed behaviour such that their performed actions cause beneficial changes to the environment. This capability often requires the agent to anticipate future situations (e.g. using predictions) rather than just simple responding to changes within their environment.

Summarizing some characteristics, it is told that an agent is:

- *Autonomous* - proactive, goal-directed, long-lived;
- *Adaptive* - adapt to their environment and users and learn from their users, other agents and their own experience;
- *Cooperative* - cooperates with human agents and other software agents, utilize various agent communication languages, advertise their capabilities and understand the capabilities of other agents.

Thus, we define an agent as referring to a component of software and/or hardware that is capable of acting exactingly in order to accomplish tasks on behalf of its user. Given a choice, we would rather say that it is an umbrella term that covers a range of other more specific agent types, and then go on to a list and define these other agent types.

15.4 NWANA'S PROPERTIES OF AN AGENT

Nwana considers that a truly intelligent agent (the ideal agent) should equally be characterised by three primary attributes i.e. autonomy, cooperation and learning while any system that does not exhibit these three properties (more or less emphasized) should not be considered an agent at all. Figure 15.2 summarizes all the properties associated with the notion of agency and provides an explanation for each.

Property	Other name(s)	Explanation	Comments
Autonomy		An agent can operate on its own without the intervention of humans or other systems.	Generally accepted
Reactivity	Situationness or Sensing and acting	An agent perceive is environment: it receives input from the environment and is able to change the environment by performing some actions.	
Pro-activeness	Goal-directed behaviour	An agent has the ability to take the initiative in order to accomplish its design objectives.	Considered by Nwana a key element of autonomy.

Cooperation	Communication or Social Ability	An agent is capable of interacting with other agents and/or humans in order to accomplish its design objectives.	Viewed by most researchers as a crucial attribute of an intelligent agent.
Flexibility		Defined by Wool/dridge and Jennings using three other properties i.e. reactivity, pro-activeness and cooperation.	Flexibility is not a new property but instead incorporates three properties already defined.
Learning	Adaptability	An agent can learn and improve with experience.	Considered by Nwana a key attribute of an intelligent agent.
Mobility		An agent has ability to move from one machine to another in a network.	
Temporal continuity		An agent persists over long periods of time.	
Personality	Character	An agent demonstrates a "believable" personality and emotional state.	

Figure 15.2: Properties of an agent

Wooldridge (as well as other researchers) indicates that the various properties of an agent (described above) are of differing importance for different domains. Therefore, learning can be considered very important for some applications while others may consider it really detrimental. Table 15.2 presents the definition of an agent based on a list of the properties the agent should have proposed by different authors.

Table 15.2: Various definitions of an agent using a list of properties

Author	Properties used in the definition of an agent
H.S. Nwana	Autonomy (which includes pro-activeness) Cooperation Learning
S. Franklin A. Graesser	Autonomy Reactivity Pro-activeness Temporal Continuity
N.R. Jennings M. Wooldridge	Autonomy Reactivity Pro-activeness } Flexibility Social Ability

15.5 MAIN ATTRIBUTES OF AGENTS

Software agents are an innovative technology designed to support the development of complex, distributed, and heterogeneous information systems. There is however no complete standard/consensus definition of an agent. As a result, agents tend to be characterised in terms of a number of their behavioural attributes.

Commonly cited main attributes of agents include the following:

- *Autonomy:* the ability to act autonomously to some degree on behalf of users for example by monitoring events and changes within their environment.
- *Pro-activity:* the ability to pursue their own individual set goals, including by making decisions.
- *Re-activity*: the ability to react to and evaluate external events and consequently adapt their behaviour and make appropriate decisions to carry out the tasks to help them achieve their goals.
- *Communication and Co-operation:* the ability to behave *socially*, to interact and communicate with other agents (in multiple agent systems (MAS)) i.e. exchange information, receive instructions and give responses and co-operate when it helps them fulfil their own goals.
- *Negotiation:* the ability to conduct organized conversations to achieve a degree of co-operation with other agents
- *Learning:* the ability to improve performance over time when interacting with the environment in which they are embedded.

15.6 CHARACTERISTICS OF SOFTWARE AGENTS: THE ESSENTIALS

Although there is no commonly accepted definition for the term *software agent*, people think of several possible traits when they discuss software agents. Four of these traits—autonomy, temporal continuity, reactivity, and goal driven—are essential to distinguish agents from other types of software objects, programs, or systems. Software agents possessing only some of these traits are often labeled *simple* or *weak*. Virtually all commercially available software agents are of this sort. Beside these essential traits, a software agent may also possess additional traits such as adaptability, mobility, sociability, and personality. Typically, these latter traits are found in more advanced research prototypes. In this section, we will consider the essential traits first.

15.6.1 The Essential Traits of Software Agents

The following are the major traits of software agents.

1. **Autonomy**

   Autonomous software agents can perform certain tasks automatically according to the rules and inference mechanisms given by the designer. As Maes points out, regular computer programs respond only to direct manipulation. In contrast, a software agent senses its environment and acts autonomously upon it. A software agent can initiate communication, monitor events, and perform tasks without the direct intervention of humans or others.

Autonomy implies that an agent takes initiative and exercises control over its own actions and thus displays the following characteristics:

- **Goal orientation.** Accepts high-level requests indicating what a human wants and is responsible for deciding how and where to satisfy the requests. These are referred to as *homeostatic goal(s).*
- **Collaboration.** Does not blindly obey commands but can modify requests, ask clarification questions, or even refuse to satisfy certain requests.
- **Flexibility.** Actions are not scripted; the agent is able to dynamically choose which actions to invoke, and in what sequence, in response to the state of its external environment.
- **Self-starting.** Unlike standard programs directly invoked by a user, an agent can sense changes in its environment and decide when to act. Autonomous agents can be resident or mobile.

2. **Temporal Continuity**

   A software agent is a program to which a user assigns a goal or task. The idea is that once a task or goal has been delegated, it is up to the agent to work tirelessly in pursuit of that goal. Unlike regular computer programs that terminate when processing is complete, an agent continues to run—either actively in the foreground or sleeping in the background—monitoring system events that trigger its actions. You can think of this attribute as "set and forget."

3. **Reactivity**

   A software agent responds in a timely fashion to changes in its environment. This characteristic is crucial for delegation and automation. The general principle on which software agents operate is "When X happens, do Y," where X is some system or network event that the agent continually monitors.

4. **Goal Driven**

   A software agent does more than simply respond to changes in its environment. An agent can accept high-level requests specifying the goals of a human user (or another agent) and decide how and where to satisfy the requests. In some cases, an agent can modify the goals or establish goals of its own.

15.6.2 Other Common Traits

Some software agents also possess other common traits.

1. **Communication (Interactivity)**

   Many agents are designed to interact with other agents, humans, or software programs. This is a critical ability in view of the narrow repertoire of any given agent. Instead of making a single agent conduct several tasks, additional agents can be created to handle undelegated tasks. Thus, communication is necessary in these instances. Agents communicate by following certain communication languages and standards, such as Agent Communication Language (ACL) and Knowledge Query and Manipulation Language (KQML).

2. **Intelligence and Learning**

Currently, the majority of agents are not truly intelligent because they cannot learn; only some agents can learn. This learning goes beyond mere rule-based reasoning because the agent is expected to use learning to behave autonomously. Although many in the artificial intelligence (AI) community argue that few people want agents who learn by "spying" on their users, the ability to learn often begins with the ability to observe users and to predict their behavior. One of the most common examples of learning agents is the *wizards* found in many commercial software programs (e.g., in Microsoft Office applications). These wizards offer hints to the user based on patterns the program detects in the user's activities. Some of the newer Internet search engines boast intelligent agents that can learn from previous requests the user has made.

15.7 MORE FEATURES OF AGENTS

Depending on different usages of agents, they can have a lot of different features. Such features are often used for classification as well. We have already discussed different basic architectures. Next we describe mobility, size intelligence and ability to adapt and to learn. Relations to other agents are described later in the section on Multi-Agent Systems. A collection of agent features will be given in table 15.3.

1. **Mobility** - Agents can be *static* or *mobile*. Static agents are permanently located at one place, while mobile agents can change their location. When a static agent wants some action to be executed at a remote site, it will send a message to an agent at that location with the request for the action. In a similar situation, a mobile agent would transmit itself to the remote site and invoke the action execution. There are a lot of benefits from usage of mobile agents but if we wanted to get all of these benefits without a mobile agent, we would need a large amount of work and it would be practically almost impossible. The advocated utility of mobile agents is to support optimization of sophisticated operations that may require strong interactivity between components or special computing facilities as encountered e.g. in negotiation, network management and monitoring, and load balancing for scientific computing. Mobility of software agents is closely related to the problem of code mobility in distributed programming with applications in operating systems and computer networks. Some problems related with mobile agents concern security and safety.
2. **Size and Intelligence** - Agents can be of various sizes and can possess various amounts of intelligence. Generally, intelligence of a software agent is proportional to its size, so we can distinguish: *big-sized*, *middle-sized* and *micro agents*. It is difficult to make clear boundaries among these categories.
    1. A big-sized agent occupies and controls one or more computers. It possesses enough competence to be useful even if it acts alone, without the other agents in a MAS. A big-sized agent can be as big and as intelligent as an expert system with competencies for expert problem solving, e.g. distributed medical care or plane ticket reservation.
    2. A middle-sized agent is the one that is not useful without the other agents in a MAS or without additional software. However, it is able to perform some non-trivial task(s). A user-interface agent that acts without other agents and performs

some simple actions can also be classified as a middle-sized agent. Mobile agents are usually middle-sized agents.

3. Micro agents (also called the Society of Mind agents) do not possess any intelligence. Minsky followed the idea that the intelligence emerges as a global effect of the overall activity of many simple and unintelligent agents.

3. **Adaptation** – Adaptive agents can adapt their behavior to different situations and changes in the environment. For example, a navigation system can adapt to changes in traffic (e.g. a traffic jam) and propose alternative routes. This makes adaptive agents more robust to non-predicted changes in a dynamic environment.
4. **Learning** - Agents can use learning capabilities for better performance. Learning can be done online, e.g. by data mining from data which are constantly collected through interaction with users (e.g. for profiles). Offline learning refers to training processes (e.g. for pattern recognition) prior to productive agent usage. Agents may possess many features in various combinations.

Table 15.3: Agent's Features

Adaptivity	**Agents can adapt to unpredicted changes**
Autonomy	An agent can act without direct intervention by humans or other agents and that it has control over its own actions and internal state.
Benevolence	It is the assumption that agents do not have conflicting goals and that every agent will therefore always try to do what is asked of it.
Character (personality)	An agent has a well-defined, believable "personality" and emotional state.
Competitiveness	An agent is able to coordinate with other agents except that the success of one agent may imply the failure of others.
Cooperation or collaboration	An agent is able to coordinate with other agents to achieve a common purpose; non-antagonistic agents that succeed or fail together.
Coordination	An agent is able to perform some activity in a shared environment with other agents. Activities are often coordinated via plans, workflows, or some other process management mechanism.
Credibility	An agent has a believable personality and emotional state.
Deliberation	A deliberate agent decides for its action by reasoning processes which may involve metal categories like goals, plans etc.
Embodiment	An embodied agent can interact with its environment by physical processes. This allows for emergent controls guided by sensor data without internal representations.
Emergent behaviour	More complex behaviour emerges by interaction of (simple) agents with each other (swam intelligence) or with the environment (embodied agents, situation agents).

Flexibility	The system is responsive (the agents should perceive their environment and respond in a timely fashion to changes that occur in it), pro-active and social.
Goal directed	Agent behaviour is guided by mental qualities like goals, which are results of deliberation. Then the agent tries to achieve the goal by appropriate actions.
Hybrid architecture	Combination of different architectures. Often with simple (reactive, stimulus response) control for low level behaviour and deliberative control for high level behaviour.
Inferential capability	An agent can act on abstract task specification using prior knowledge of general goals and preferred methods to achieve flexibility; goes beyond the information given, and may have explicit models of self, user, situation, and/or other agents.
Intelligence	An agent's state is formalized by knowledge and that agent interacts with other agents using symbolic language.
Interpretation ability	An agent is interpretive if it can correctly interpret its sensor readings.
"Knowledge-level" communication ability	The ability to communicate with persons and other agents with language more resembling human-like "speech acts" than typical symbol-level program-to-program protocols.
Learning	An agent is capable of learning from its own experience, its environment, and interactions with others.
Mobility	An agent is able to transport itself from one machine to another and across different system architectures and platforms.
Prediction ability	An agent is predictive if its model of how the world works is sufficiently accurate to allow it to correctly predict how it can achieve the task.
Proxy ability	An agent can act on behalf of someone or something acting in the interest of, as a representative of, or for the benefit of, some entity.
Personality (character)	An agent has a well-defined, believable "personality" and emotional state.
Proactiveness	An agent does not simply act in response to its environment; it is able to exhibit goal-directed behaviour by taking the initiative.
Rationality	It is the assumption that an agent will act in order to achieve its goals, and will not act in such a way as to prevent its goals being achieved—at least insofar as its beliefs permit.
Reactivity	An agent receives some form of (sensory) input from its environment, and it performs some action that changes its environment in some way.
Resource limitation	An agent can only act as long as it has resources at its disposal. These resources are changed by its acting and possibly also by delegating.
Reusability	Processes or subsequent instance can require keeping instance of the class 'agent' for an information handover or to check and to analyze them according to their results.

Ruggedization	An agent is able to deal with errors and incomplete data robustly.
Sensor-actor coupling	Agent act by (direct) connections between sensors and actors. This can be used for reactive controls.
Situatedness	An agent (robot) is situated in its environment. Its behavior can be guided by physical interactions (e.g. sensor-actor coupling). This can be an efficient alternative to control using internal representations.
Social ability	An agent interacts and this interaction is marked by friendliness or pleasant social relations; that is, the agent is affable, companionable or friendly.
Sound	An agent is sound if it is predictive, interpretive and rational.
Stimulus	A stimulus response agent has no internal state It means that its responses are equal for equal response inputs.
Temporal continuity	An agent is a continuously running process, not a "one-shot" computation that maps a single input to a single output, then terminates.
Transparency and accountability	An agent must be transparent when required, but must provide a log of its activities upon demand.
Trustworthiness	An agent adheres to laws of robotics and is truthful.
Unpredictability	An agent is able to act in ways that are not fully predictable, even if all the initial conditions are known. It is capable of nondeterministic behavior.
Veracity	It is the assumption that an agent will not knowingly communicate false information.

15.8 INTELLIGENT USER INTERFACES

Before considering this field in any detail it is worth setting the scene by attempting to clarify exactly what is meant by the term "Intelligent Interface Agent". The first point to note is that there is a pre-existing body of work concerning Intelligent User Interfaces (IUI). It doesn't seem unreasonable to characterise such systems as being user adaptive. By adaptive it is meant of course that such systems attempt to modify their behaviour to maximise the productivity of the current user's interaction with the system. Obviously, for any such adaptation to be viable, it must be based upon information gathered concerning the current users behaviour. Given this, three interesting questions arise.

- What aspects of the user's behaviour are useful to capture?
- What information such behaviour gives us on the actual intentions and preferences of the user?
- Finally, what use can be made of any such information captured?

Intelligent (User) Interface Agents are fairly recent developments that use an agent oriented approach to the construction of such systems. The major factors that distinguish Interface Agents from any other IUI is the fact that agents are *proactive* and enjoy a degree of *autonomy*. These properties could manifest themselves in a number of different ways, for instance, there are a number of systems which perform an information filtering role, some of which filter in an autonomous fashion, only presenting the user with information it considers to be of interest to them. Similarly, this same type of system can also be proactive in that it actively searches for information that it judges would be of interest to its users.

15.9 AN AGENCY

Software agents, like people, can be most useful when they work with other software agents in performing a task. A collection of software agents that communicate and cooperate with each other is called an **agency**. System designers using agents must consider the capabilities of each individual agent and how multiple agents can work together. The agent-based approach allows the system designer to implement the system using multiple agents, with each agent specialized for a particular task. For example, an electronic commerce application might have buyer agents, seller agents, stocking agents, database agents, email agents, etc. All of these agents need to communicate with each other and must have the capability of working together to achieve a common set of goals.

15.10 THE STRUCTURE OF AN AGENT SYSTEM

The term *Agency* refers to the conceptual and physical location in which agents reside and execute. The heart of the agency is the *agent platform*, the component model infrastructure that provides local services for agents and includes proxies to access remote services. An agent system can provide particular services using *service agents*, such as a Broker, Auctioneer or Community Maker agents; these service agents form the component infrastructure. The interaction standard of a component model defines the nature of an interface. An agent system is composed of components with simple interfaces, but complex behaviour results from the messages that the components process and communicate with each other. The agents are only able to communicate with each other because they all conform to some common, well-defined interaction standard.

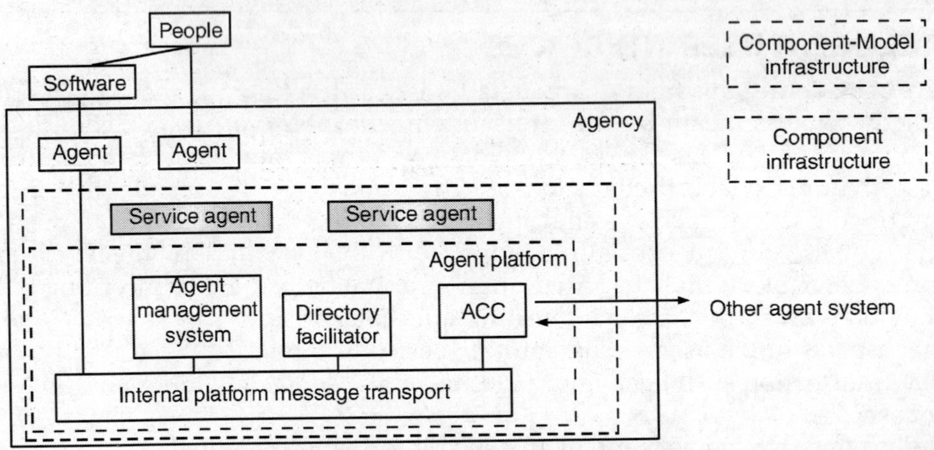

Figure 15.3: Agency Reference Model

The agency serves as a "home base" for locating and messaging mobile and detached agents, and collecting knowledge about groups of agents. Services include agent management, security, communication, persistence, naming, and agent transport in the case of mobile agents. In addition to basic agent infrastructure and agent communication, a FIPA compliant agent system, such as Zeus, provides additional services in the form of specialized agents, residing in some (possibly remote) agency. Figure 15.3 summarizes the overall agent system architecture:

1. *Agent Management System (AMS)* - controls creation, deletion, suspension, resumption, authentication, persistence and migration of agents. Provides "White Pages" to name and locate agents.
2. *Agent Communication Channel (ACC)* - routes messages between local and remote FIPA agents, realizing messages using an agent communication language.
3. *Directory Facilitator (DF)* - provides "Yellow Pages" service for FIPA agents that register agent capabilities so an appropriate task-specific agent to handle the task can be found.
4. *Internal Platform Message Transport* - provides communication infrastructure.

Many agent capabilities for naming and communication can be implemented by using HTTP and XML, such as XML structured documents for messages, and URL/URIs for naming and locating. Agents may have a globally unique name or they may have one or more local names based on the agency or agent group. To provide a systematic and consistent way for agents to exchange messages with each other, most agent systems use a special Agent Communication Language (ACL); the ACL becomes associated with the component model. The agent platform and additional service agents can monitor and control these message exchanges to insure that they conform to a desired protocol, or at least do not violate "rules of engagement".

15.11 TYPES OF SOFTWARE AGENTS

There are several dimensions to classify existing software agents. Some of the dimensions are listed below:

- ***Static and Mobile Agents***

  The agents may be classified by their *mobility*, i.e. by their ability to move around some network. This yields the classes of static or mobile agents.
- ***Deliberative and Reactive Agents***

  They may be classed as either deliberative or reactive. Deliberative agents derive from the deliberative thinking paradigm which holds that agents possess an internal symbolic reasoning model, and they engage in planning and negotiation with other agents in order to achieve their goals. Work on reactive agents originates from research carried out by Brooks and Agre and Champman. These agents do not have any internal, symbolic models of their environment, and they act using a stimulus/response type of behaviour by responding to the present state of the environment in which they are embedded.
- ***Collaborative, Interface, and Smart Agents***

  Agents may also be classified along several attributes which ideally they should exhibit. There have been identified a list of three such attributes, namely autonomy, learning, and cooperation. *Autonomy* refers to the principle that agents can operate on their own without the need for human guidance, even though this would sometimes be invaluable. A key element of autonomy is proactiveness, i.e. 'the ability to take the initiative'. *Cooperation* with the other agents is paramount, i.e. it is the reason for existence for having multiple agents. Further, the communication required to ensure cooperation generally involves high-level messages. Lastly, for agents to be truly 'intelligent', they would have to *learn* as they react and/or interact with their external environment, such that with time, their performance increases. We use these three characteristics in Figure 15.4 to derive three types of agents: *collaborative agents, interface agents* and truly and truly *smart agents*.

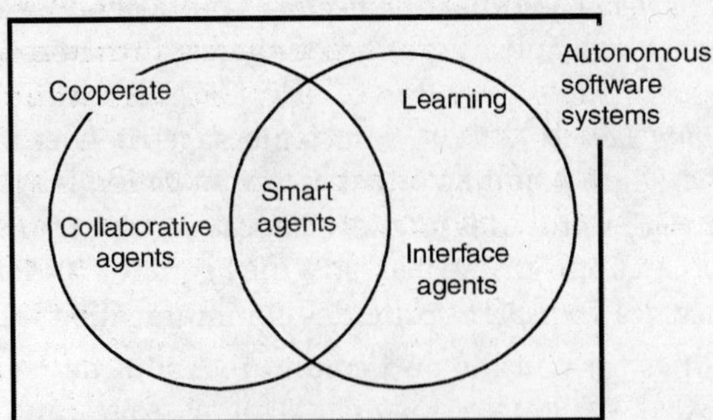

Figure 15.4: Agent Typology

We must emphasize that these distinctions are not definitive. For example, with collaborative agents, there is more emphasis on cooperation and autonomy than on learning; but we do not imply that collaborative agents never learn. We do not consider anything else lying outside the 'circles' to be agents. For example, most expert systems are largely autonomous; but typically, they do not cooperate or learn. Ideally, agents should do all three equally well, but this is the aspiration rather than the reality. Truly smart agents do not yet exist.

- ***Information or Internet Agents***

  Agents may sometimes be classified by their roles (particularly, if the roles are major ones), e.g. World Wide Web (WWW) information gathering agents. Essentially, such agents help manage the vast amount of information in wide area networks like the Internet. We refer to this class of agents as information or Internet agents. Again, information agents may be static or mobile and deliberative or reactive.

- ***Hybrid Agents***

  We also have included the category of hybrid agents that combine two or more agent philosophies in a single agent.

There are other attributes of agents that we consider secondary to those already mentioned above. For example, is an agent versatile (i.e. does it have many goals or does it engage in a variety of tasks?). Is an agent benevolent or unhelpful, antagonistic or altruistic? Does an agent lie knowingly or is it always truthful? Is it temporally continuous? Some researchers also attribute emotional attributes to agents, i.e. do they get 'fed up' when asked to do the same thing time and time again. Some agents are also imbued with mentalistic attitudes such as beliefs, desires, and intentions. Such attributes are these provide for a stronger definition of agenthood.

In essence, agents exist in a truly multi-dimensional space. However, for the sake of clarity of understanding, we have collapsed this space into a single list. Hence, we identify seven types of agents as follows:

- Collaborative agents
- Mobile agents
- Reactive agents
- Smart agents
- Interface agents
- Information/Internet agents
- Hybrid agents

There are applications that combine agents from two or more of these categories, and we refer to these as *heterogeneous agent systems.*

The next section gives an overview of all the types of agents identified above in terms of some or all of the following: their essential metaphors, hypothesis/goals, motivations, roles, prototypical examples, and potential benefits. We do not overview smart agents on the grounds that this is the aspiration of great researchers rather than the reality.

15.12 CLASSIFICATION OF SOFTWARE AGENTS

Classification refers to the study of types and entities. There are several dimensions to classify existing software agents. They can be classified according to: the tasks they perform; their control architecture; the range and effectiveness of their actions; the range of sensitivity of their senses; or how much internal state they posses. In this section we classify agents, along several ideal and primary characteristics that agents should exhibit. We identify three characteristics: *autonomy, learning,* and *cooperation.* Let us start by elaborating a bit more on these characteristics. Autonomy refers to the characteristic that an agent can operate on its own without the need for human guidance. In other words, an agent has a set of internal states and goals; it acts in such a manner to meet its goals on behalf of the user. In order to do so, an agent has to be proactive in the sense that it has the ability to take the initiative rather than acting simply in response to its environment. Cooperation with other agents is necessary to accomplish a complicated task. In order to cooperate however, an agent must posses a social ability that allows it to interact with other agents. Finally, an agent is intelligent if it is able to learn and sense as it acts and reacts to its external environment. These three characteristics of agents are used to derive some types of agents to include in our classification as shown in Figure 15.5.

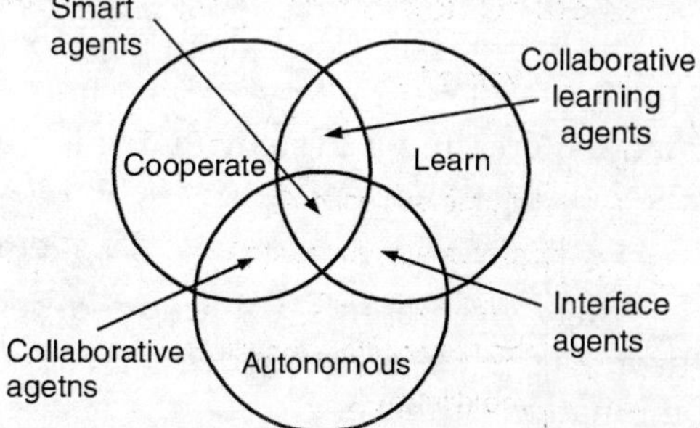

Figure 15.5: *A partial view of agent classification*

Overview all the types of agents identified in our typology of the previous section bar smart agents. Figure 15.6 summarizes these types and lists the order in which they are surveyed. In particular, we would overview them in terms of *some*or *all* of following: their essential metaphors, hypotheses/goals, motivations, roles, prototypical examples, potential benefits, key challenges, and some other general issues about the particular agent type. We do not overview the shaded type, smart agents, on the grounds that this is the *aspiration*of agent researchers rather than the *reality.*

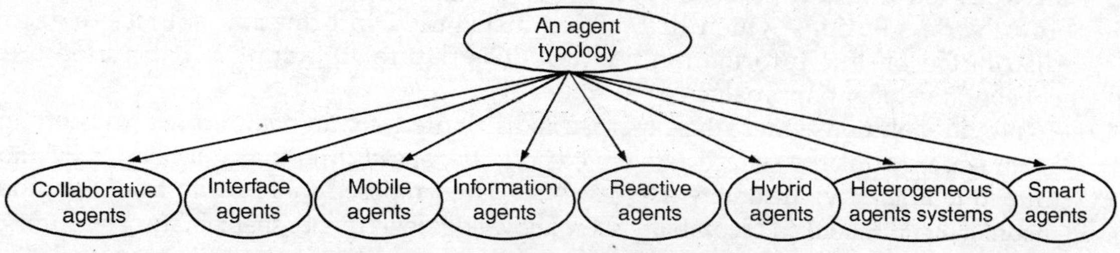

Figure 15.6: *A Classification of Software Agents*

15.13 COLLABORATIVE AGENTS

Collaborative agents emphasize autonomy and cooperation with other agents in order to perform tasks for their owners in open and time-constrained multi-agent environments. They may learn, but this aspect is not typically a major emphasis on their operation, though some perform limited parametric or rote learning. To coordinate their activities, they may have to negotiate in order to reach mutually acceptable arguments. Collaborative agents tend to be static, large, coarse-grained agents. They may be benevolent, rational, truthful, some combination of these, or none of them. As noted earlier, some researchers give stronger definitions of such agents, hence, the class of collaborative agents may itself be perceived as a broad grouping.

In brief the key general characteristics of these agents include autonomy, social ability, responsiveness and proactiveness. Hence, they are (or should/would be) able to act rationally and autonomously in open and time-constrained multi-agent environments. They tend to be static, large coarse-grained agents. They may be benevolent, rational, truthful, some combination of these or neither. Typically, most currently implemented collaborative agents do not perform any complex learning, though they may or may not perform limited parametric or rote learning.

15.13.1 Hypothesis/Goal

The hypothesis, rationale or goal for having collaborative agent systems is a specification of the goal of Distributed Artificial Intelligence (DAI). Paraphrasing these authors, it may be stated as 'creating a system that interconnects separately developed collaborative agents, thus enabling the ensemble to function beyond the capabilities of any of its members'. Formally,

$$V(\Sigma \text{agent}_i) > \max(V(\text{agent}_i))$$

where V represents 'value added-ness'. This could have an arbitrary definition involving attributes such as speed, worst-case performance, reliability, adaptability, accuracy or some combination of these.

15.13.2 Motivation

The motivation for having collaborative agent systems may include one or several of the following (they are a specialisation of the motivations for DAI):

- To solve problems that are too large for a centralised single agent to do due to resource limitations or the sheer risk of having one centralised system;
- To allow for the interconnecting and interoperation of multiple existing legacy systems, e.g. expert systems, decision support systems, etc.;
- To provide solutions to inherently distributed problems, e.g. distributed sensor networks or air-traffic control;
- To provide solutions which draw from distributed information sources, e.g. for distributed on-line information sources, it is natural to adopt a distributed and collaborative agent approach;
- To provide solutions where the expertise is distributed, e.g. in health care provisioning;
- To enhance modularity (which reduces complexity), speed (due to parallelism), reliability (due to redundancy), flexibility (i.e. new tasks are composed more easily from the more modular organisation) and reusability at the knowledge level (hence shareability of resources);
- To research into other issues, e.g. understanding interactions among human societies.

15.13.3 A Prototypical Example: CMU's Pleiades System

The Pleiades project at CMU directed by Tom Mitchell and Katia Sycara has, as one of its objectives, to investigate methods for automated negotiation among collaborative agents, in order to improve their robustness, effectiveness, scalability and maintainability. The project applies collaborative agents in the domain of Organisational Decision Making over the "InfoSphere" (which refers essentially to a collection of internet-based heterogeneous resources). This infosphere is ripe for the application of these class of agents not least because it is inherently a distributed set of on-line information sources.

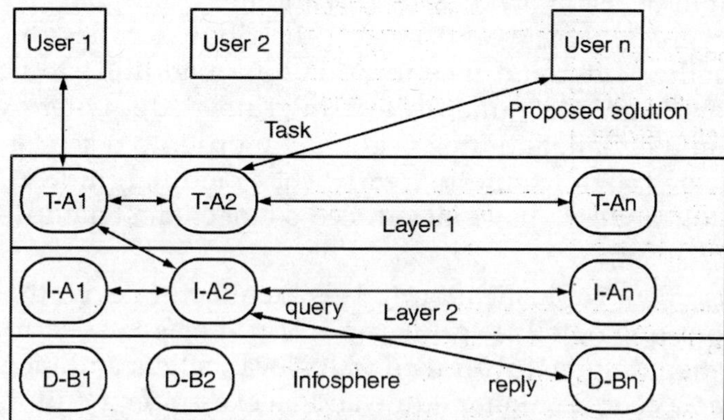

Figure 15.7: *The Pleiades Distributed System Architecture*

Pleiades is a distributed collaborative agent-based architecture which has two layers of abstraction: the first layer which contains *task-specific* collaborative agents and second layer which contains *information-specific* collaborative agents as depicted in Figure 15.7. Task-specific agents, depicted as task-assistants (T-A) in the figure, perform a particular task for its user, e.g. arranging appointments and meetings with other task-specific agents. These agents coordinate and schedule plans based on the context. They collaborate with one another (at level 1) in order to resolve conflicts or integrate information. In order to garner the information required at this level, they request information from information-specific agents, depicted as information assistants (I-A) in Figure 15.7. Information-specific agents, in turn, may collaborate with one another (i.e. within layer 2) in order to provide the information requested back to the layer 1 requesting agent. The sources of the information are the many databases (D-B) in the infosphere. Ultimately, the task agent proposes a solution (sometimes an intermediate one) to its user.

Task-specific agents have the following knowledge: a model of the task domain, knowledge of how to perform the task, knowledge of how to gather the information for the task, knowledge of other task-specific or information-specific agents it must coordinate with in order to meet the task, protocols that enable coordination with other agents and, lastly, strategies for conflict resolution and information fusion. They also possess some learning mechanisms, e.g. when an agent needs to learn the preferences of its user. On the contrary, information-specific agents know of the following: knowledge of the databases that it is associated with (in addition to details such as their size, average time it takes to answer a query and monetary costs for query processing), knowledge of how to access the databases, knowledge of how to resolve conflicts and information fusion strategies, and protocols for coordination with other relevant software agents. These agents are also 'smart' enough to cache answers to frequently asked queries, and can also induce database regularities which they use during inter-agent interactions.

The main rationale of the architecture is to provide software agents for retrieving, filtering and fusing information from distributed, multi-modal sources and that the agents should assist in decision making. Sycara and her colleagues hypothesised that in order to meet their goals, they would need a distributed collection of collaborative agents which can gather, filter and fuse information in addition to being able to learn from their interactions. Agents communicate using Knowledge Query and Manipulation Language (KQML) and e-mail, and they negotiate in order to reach agreements in cases of conflicts. The layered architecture is clearly very modular, indeed modular enough for Sycara and her colleagues to have introduced connectionist modules in the design of other systems.

Clearly, there is much sophistication to this architecture even though we have left out much more interesting details (e.g. *how* and *what* the agents learn). Individually, an agent consists of a planning module linked to its local beliefs and facts database. It also has a local scheduler, a coordination module and an execution monitor. Thus, agents can instantiate task plans, coordinate these plans with other agents and schedule/monitor the execution of its local actions.

Interestingly, the architecture has no central planner and hence agents must all engage in coordination by communicating to others their constraints, expectations and other relevant information.

The Pleiades architecture shows clearly how collaborative agents can operate in concert such that their ensemble functions beyond the capabilities of any individual agent in the set-up. Apart from the visitor hosting system, other systems have also been developed using this architecture/methodology in the domains of financial portfolio management, emergency medical care and electronic commerce. In addition to these domains, there are others ripe for exploiting collaborative agents including workflow management, network management and control, telecommunication networks and business process engineering. In all these domains, collaborative agents may provide much 'added value' to current single agent-based applications.

15.13.4 Collaborative Agents: Some Key Challenges

Despite successful demonstrators like the Pleiades system and MII, these agents have been deployed in none but a few real industrial settings though this situation is changing. There are still many teething problems; we mention several here. Note that these are not necessarily specific to collaborative agents only:

- **Engineering the construction of collaborative agent systems:** The Pleiades system is a good step in this direction but there is much more research to do. To paraphrase BT's Prof. Robin Smith, we must move away from point solutions to point problems, and design methodologies/meta-tools which allow for quicker implementation of collaborative agent-based systems;

- **Inter-agent coordination:** This is a major issue in the design of these systems. Coordination is essential to enabling groups of agents to solve problems effectively. Without a clear theory of coordination, anarchy or deadlock can set in easily in collaborative agent systems? Furthermore, should agents be totally truthful when negotiating with others or should they be allowed to 'lie' when it suits them? Coordination is also required due to the constraints of resource boundedness and time. Much experimental and/or formal work is still required to address these issues of coordination and negotiation.
- **Stability, Scalability and Performance Issues:** These issues have yet to be acknowledged, yet alone tackled in collaborative agent systems research. Empirical investigations need to be carried out to establish suitable minimum levels of performance and, clearly, these systems have to be stable. Alternatively, their stabilities would need to be proven formally. Though, these issues are *non-functional*, they are crucial nonetheless;
- **Legacy systems:** The thorny issue of what to do with legacy systems is still with us and will always be a problem. Established techniques and methodologies for integrating agents and legacy systems are still required;
- How do these systems learn? Would learning not lead to instability? What are the appropriate architectures for different types of problems? How do you ensure an agent does not spend much of its time learning, instead of participating in its set-up?
- **Evaluation of collaborative agent systems:** This problem is still outstanding. How are they verified and validated to ensure they meet their functional specifications? Are unanticipated events handled properly? How else would you trust such systems to run power stations, nuclear installations and chemical plants?

In conclusion, despite the criticisms of collaborative agents by those within and without other agent camps, there are many industrial applications which would benefit significantly from them, in just the same way as there are applications which would benefit from reactive agents. For example, at BT, we see a potential major role for them in managing telecommunications networks and in business process management.

15.14 INTERFACE AGENTS

Interface agents emphasize autonomy and learning in order to perform tasks for their owners. Maes points out that the key metaphor underlying interface agents is that of a personal assistant who is collaborating with the user in the same work environment. Note the subtle emphasis and distinction between collaborating with the user and collaborating with other agents as is the case with collaborative agents. Collaborating with a user may not require an explicit agent communication language as one required when collaborating with other agents.

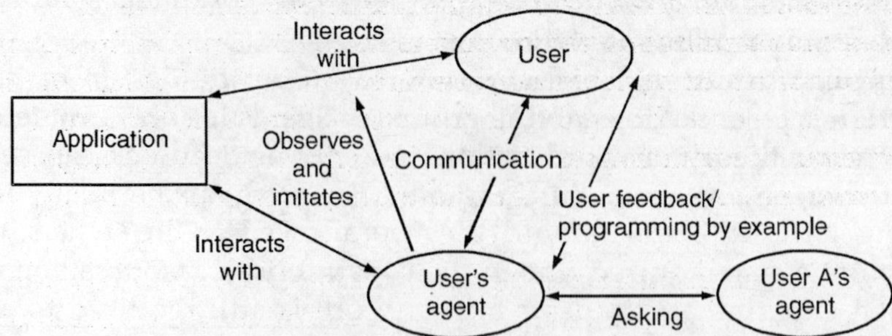

***Figure 15.8:** Working of Interface Agents*

Figure 15.8 depicts the functioning of interface agents. Essentially, interface agents support and provide proactive assistance, typically to a user learning to use a particular application such as a spreadsheet or an operating system. The user's agent observes and monitors the actions taken by the user in the interface (i.e. it watches over the shoulder of its user), learns new shortcuts, and suggests better ways of doing the task. As for learning, typically, interface agents learn to assist their users in the following four ways: (1) by observing and imitating the user, (2) through receiving positive and negative feedback from the user, (3) through receiving explicit instructions from the user, and (4) by asking other agents for advice. Generally, the learning modes are by rote-memory based learning or parametric, through other techniques such as evolutionary learning are also being introduced. Their cooperation with other agents, if any, is limited typically to asking for advice. The learning modes are typically by rote (memory-based learning) or parametric, though other techniques such as evolutionary learning are also being introduced.

In summary a learning interface agent, as opposed to any kind of agent, is one that uses machine-learning techniques to present a pseudo "intelligent" user interface for its actions.

15.14.1 Hypothesis/Goal

The objective of interface agent's research is to work towards Alan Kay's dream of having indirectly managed human-computer interfaces. The argument goes as follows. Current computer user interfaces only respond to direct manipulation, i.e. the computer is passive and always waits to execute highly specified instructions from the user. It provides little or no *proactive* help for complex tasks or for carrying out actions such as searches for information that may take an indefinite time. In the future, there will be millions of untrained users attempting to make use of computers and networks of tomorrow.

Therefore, instead of a user issuing direct commands to some interface, he could be engaged in cooperative process in which human and software agents can initiate communication, perform tasks and monitor events. This cooperation between human and agent would benefit the human in using this application.

Hence, the *goal* is to migrate from the direct manipulation metaphor to one that delegates some of the tasks to (proactive and helpful) software interface agents in order to accommodate novice users. The *hypothesis* is that these agents can be trusted to perform competently some tasks delegated to them by their users. More specifically, that "under certain conditions, an interface agent can "program itself" (i.e., it can acquire the knowledge it needs to assist its user). The agent is given a minimum of background knowledge, and it learns appropriate "behaviour" from the user and from other agents".

Maes specifies two preconditions to be fulfilled by suitable application programs for interface agents. Firstly, that there is substantial repetitive behaviour in using the application program (otherwise, the agent will not be able to learn anything) and secondly, that this repetitive behaviour is potentially different for different users (otherwise, use a knowledge-based approach).

15.14.2 Motivation

To recap, an interface agent is a quasi-smart piece of software which assists a user when interacting with one or more computer applications. Therefore, the *motivating*, underlying principle of interface agents seems to be that there is no inherent merit in drudgery. Where boring and laborious tasks (particularly, but not exclusively at the user interface) could be delegated to interface agents, they should be - in order to eliminate the tedium of humans performing several manual sub-operations say. A motivating reason for the choice of domains that Maes' group has tackled has been their dissatisfaction with the ways that tasks in these domains are handled currently. For example, she explains that valuable hours are wasted managing junk mail, scheduling and rescheduling meetings, searching for information among heaps of it, etc.

15.14.3 Benefit/Roles

The general benefits of interface agents are threefold. First, they make less work for the end user and application developer. Secondly, the agent can adapt, over time, to its user's preferences and habits. Finally, know-how among the different users in a community may be shared (e.g. when agents learn from their peers). Perhaps these will be better understood by discussing a few of the roles for which interface agents have been built.

- *Eager assistants*

  Maes describes an interface agent, Calendar Agent that assists its user in scheduling meetings. Over time, it can learn the preferences and commitments of its user, e.g. he does not like to attend meetings on Friday evenings, he prefers meetings in the morning, etc. The learning techniques employed are memory-based learning and reinforcement learning.
- *Guides*

  Liebermann describes Letizia, a keyword and heuristic-based search agent, which assists in web browsing. Since most browsers encourage depth-first browsing, Letizia conducts a breadth-first search concurrently for other useful locations that the user may be interested in. It does this by 'guessing' the user's intention from her browsing behaviour, e.g. he keeps returning to some particular page, and proceeding to search using the search engine. This enables it to recommend some particular page, and proceeding to search using the search engine. This enables it to recommend some other useful, serendipitous locations.

- *Memory aids*
  The Remembrance Agent is attached currently to an Emacs editor. As the user composes some e-mail message, say, the agent is able to carry out a keyword search and retrieve the five most relevant e-mails in her directory relating to this e-mail being composed. It is really successful when it recommends continuously and unobtrusively invaluable documents, e-mails or files which you would otherwise have forgotten when, for example, you are composing some new document. It can also be used, conceivably when browsing the web or writing a paper; in the latter case, the remembrance agent may recommend other researchers' papers which should be consulted. Hence, its role is clearly that of a *memory* aid.
- *Filter/critics*
  Maes describe a news filtering agent, called NewT, whose role is that of helping the user filter and select articles from a continuous stream of Usenet Netnews. The idea is to have the user create one or many "news agents" (e.g. one agent for sports news, one for financial news, etc.) and train them by example (i.e. by presenting to them positive and negative examples of what should/or should not be retrieved). It is message-content, keyword-based but it also exploits other information such as the author and source. NewT is even more complicated because a user's population of information filtering agents evolve with time using genetic computing techniques. Indeed, some similar new work at MIT is investigating agents that 'breed' in their environment, i.e. information agents, given feedback on the information returned, breeds progressively more of those which return 'good quality' information, and purges the rest that do not.
- *Matchmaking/referrals*
  Foner reports on his Yenta/Yenta-lite matchmaking agent prototype whose goals scenarios include being able to match buyers and sellers of some item and introducing them to one another, finding and grouping people with compatible professional or personal interests, or building coalitions of people interested in the same topics. Each user in the community has a Yenta agent. Yenta agents are able to carry out referrals which work in the same fashion as word-of-mouth recommendations used by people daily. Yenta deals currently with text such as electronic mail messages, the contents of a user's files in a directory, etc. For example, two users, A and B, are deemed to share the same interest if A has at least one granule of interest as B. A granule may represent the fact that a user reads regularly newsgroups on politics say. Matchmaking presents some challenging problems which are covered in Foner's paper.
- *Buying/selling on your behalf*
  Chavez & Maes describe some preliminary ideas on Kasbah, a classified ads service on the WWW that incorporates interface agents. Kasbah is meant to represent a 'market place' (a web site) where Kasbah agents, acting on behalf of their owners, can filter through the ads and find those that their users may be interested in, and then proceed to negotiate, buy and sell items. Kasbah-like agents may, in the future, render middlemen or brokers redundant.
- *Entertainment*
  Last, but by no means least, is the entertainment selection agent which Maes believes has the best potential of all her application domains to be the next "killer application".

For example, the Ringo/HOMR system is a personalised recommendation system for music albums and artists, which exploits interface agents. These agents work by social filtering, i.e. a user's agent finds other agents which are correlated, and recommends whatever films their users like to its own user. Hence, like Yenta agents, Ringo's working is similar to a word-of-mouth approach. Maes also describes the ALIVE system which is "a virtual environment which allows wireless full-body interaction between a human participant and a virtual world which is inhabited by autonomous agents". However, it presents a much more challenging illustration of how autonomous interface agents may be used in entertainment. Essentially, ALIVE demonstrates how agents can form a link between animated characters, based of Artificial Life models, and the entertainment industry.

We hope it is clear that the potential for these interface agents are large. All these demonstrators have been or are being evaluated with users and the results so far are, in the main, quite promising. For example, Ringo has been used by more than 2000 people.

15.14.4 Interface Agents: Some Challenges

Following on from the last section, some challenges for interface agents include:

- Demonstrating that the knowledge learned with interface agents can truly be used to reduce users' workload, and that users, indeed, want them;
- Carrying out hundreds of experiments using various machine learning techniques (including soft and evolutionary learning techniques) over several domains to determine *which* learning techniques are preferable for *what* domains and *why*;
- Analysing the effect of the various learning mechanisms on the responsiveness of agents;
- Extending interface agents to be able to negotiate with other peer agents;
- Enhance continually the *competence* of interface agents so that their users' *trust* in them builds up over time. Other issues which Maes notes include guaranteeing the users' privacy and the legal quagmire which may ensue following the fielding of such agents.
- Extending the range of applications of interface agents into other innovative areas such as entertainment.

However, having stated these, there is no denying the fact that interface agents can/will be deployed in real applications in the short term because they are simple, operate in limited domains and do not, in general, require cooperation with other agents.

15.15 MOBILE AGENTS

Agents can be classified into two major categories: resident and mobile. **Resident agents** stay in the computer or system and perform their tasks there. For instance, many of the wizards in software programs are designed to carry out very specific tasks while a person is using his or her computer. **Mobile agents**, however, move to other systems, performing tasks there. A *mobile agent* can transport itself across different system architectures and platforms. EC agents are mobile.

Mobile agents are computational software processes capable of roaming wide area networks (WANs) such as the WWW, interacting with foreign hosts, gathering information on behalf of its owner and coming 'back home' having performed the duties set by its user. These duties may range from a flight reservation to managing a telecommunications network. However, *mobility is neither a necessary nor sufficient condition for agenthood.* Mobile agents are agents because they are autonomous and they cooperate, albeit differently to collaborative agents. For example, they may cooperate or communicate by one agent making the location of some of its internal objects and methods known to other agents. By doing this, an agent exchanges data or information with other agents without necessarily giving all its information away. This is an important point, not least because the public perception of agents (thanks to the popular computing press) is almost synonymous with mobile agents. For example, Peter Wayner's agent text (and there are almost no other agent texts about currently) is titled 'Agents Unleashed: A Public Domain Look at Agent Technology', but it is all about mobile agents. Whilst the 'unleashed' in the title gives it away, it is rather subtle - so, Wayner could be accused of reinforcing this rather jaundiced view, that agents equals mobile pieces of software.

Another myth to slay is that mobile agent's equals Telescript, the current leading mobile agent operating environment invented at General Magic (Mountain View, CA). Through some very clever marketing, General Magic has managed to put mobile agents 'on the map' and link their name simultaneously and inextricably to it. But other mobile agent demonstrators or applications not based on Telescript do exist.

15.15.1 Characteristics of Mobile Agents

Mobility refers to the degree to which the agents themselves travel through the network. Some agents are very mobile; others are not. *Mobile scripts* can be composed on one machine and shipped to another for execution in a suitably secure environment; in this case, the program travels before execution, and therefore, no static data need to be attached. Finally, agents can be *mobile with state,* moving from machine to machine in the middle of execution and carrying accumulated state data with them. Such agents can be viewed as mobile objects that travel to agencies (other agents or computing systems representing other entities) where they can present their "credentials" and obtain access to services and data managed by the agencies. Agencies can also serve as brokers or matchmakers, bringing together agents with similar interests and compatible goals and providing a meeting point at which they can safely interact.

Mobile agents can move from one Web site to another and send data to and retrieve data from the user, who can focus on other tasks in the meantime. This can be very helpful to a user. For example, if a user wanted to continuously monitor an electronic auction that takes a few days, the user essentially would have to be online continuously for days. Software applications that automatically watch auctions and stocks are readily available. For example, a mobile agent that watches stocks travels from site to site, looking for information on a certain stock as instructed by the user. If the stock price hits a certain level or if there is news about the stock, the agent alerts the user. What is unique about a mobile agent is that it is a software application that moves on its own to different computers to execute its task. Resident (nonmobile) agents can be defined along two dimensions (see Exhibit C.2a), whereas mobile agents are defined in a three-dimensional space (Exhibit C.2b). For example, in Exhibit C.2, note that expert systems, which are not mobile, may fall below the threshold line and, thus, are regular (nonmobile) software agents. True intelligent agents are listed above the threshold line.

Description of mobile agents in (a) Two dimensions and (b) Three dimensions.

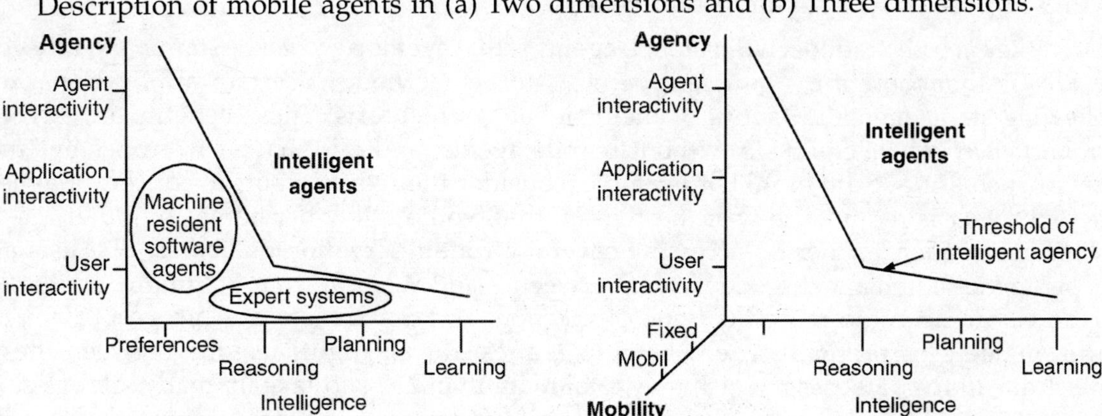

(a) 2-D space

(b) 3-D space

15.15.2 Advantages of Mobile Agents

Mobile agents seem to be useful for many different applications. One may however, claim that virtually any task that can be performed with mobile agents can be performed with other technologies (e.g. remote method invocation). Despite the fact that there are not many distributed computing problems that cannot be solved without mobile agents, nevertheless mobile agents make certain applications easier to develop and may improve reliability and efficiency. Table 15.4, which contain some of the claimed advantages of mobile agents over conventional approaches.

Table 15.4: Advantages of mobile agents over conventional approaches

Advantage	Justification
Efficiency	Mobile agents consume fewer network resources since they move the computation to the data instead of the data to the computation.
Less Bandwidth	Most communication protocols involve several interactions, which cause a lot of network traffic. Mobile agents consume bandwidth only when they move.
Robustness and Fault Tolerance	The ability of mobile agents to react dynamically to adverse situations make it easier to build fault tolerance behaviour in complex distributed systems.
Support for Heterogeneous Environment	Mobile agent systems are computer and network independent. Therefore, a Java mobile agent can target any system that has a Java Virtual Machine.
Support for Electronic Commerce	Mobile agents are being used to build electronic markets since they embody the intentions, desires, and resources of the participants in the market.
Easier Development Paradigm	The construction of distributed systems can be made easier with agents. Mobile agents are inherently distributed in nature. Therefore, they are a natural view of a distributed system.

15.15.3 Hypothesis, Motivation and Benefits

The key *hypothesis* underlying mobile agents is that agents need *not* be stationary; indeed, the idea is that there are significant benefits to be accrued, in certain applications, by eschewing static agents in favour of their mobile counterparts. These benefits are largely *non-functional*, i.e. we could do without mobile agents, and only have static ones but the costs of such a move are high. For example, consider the scenario borrowed from Wayner where the user is required to write a program that would allow her home computer make a flight reservation for her by accessing several airline reservation databases. She lists all her preferences: nonsmoking, departure between 7 and 9.30 am from Baltimore, arrival at Austin before noon, no more than one connection, and no changes at Chicago O'Hare. A static single-agent program would need to request for all flights leaving between these times from all the databases, which may total more than 200 and take up many kilobytes. It would also require a list of all the connections and proceed to narrow down the search. Each of these actions involves sifting through plenty of extraneous information which could/would clog up the network. Besides, she is probably paying for this network time.

Consider the alternative. She encapsulates, object-oriented style, her entire program within an agent which consumes probably less than 2K which roams the network of airline reservation systems, arrives safely and queries these databases locally, and returns ultimately to her home computer, with a schedule which she may confirm or refute. This alternative obviates the high communications costs of shifting, possibly, kilobytes of information to her local computer - which presumably she cannot cope with. Hence, mobile agents provide a number of *practical*, though *non-functional*, advantages which escape their static counterparts. So their motivation includes the following anticipated benefits.

Reduced communication costs: there may be a lot of raw information that need to be examined to determine their relevance. Transferring this raw information can be very time-consuming and clog of the networks. Imagine having to transfer many images just to pick out one. It is much more natural to get your agents to "go" to that location, do a local search/pruning and only transfer the chosen compressed image back across the network. It obviates the need for costly network connections between remote computers as required in remote procedure calls (RPC). It provides a much cheaper alternative as we pay increasingly for network bandwidth and time as CompuServe users already do. In the future we would almost certainly be charged by the byte for bandwidth, though others maintain that bandwidth would be free.

- Limited local resources: the processing power and storage on the local machine may be very limited (only perhaps for processing and storing the results of a search), thereby necessitating the use of mobile agents.
- Easier coordination: it may be simpler to coordinate a number of remote and independent requests and only collate all the results locally.
- Asynchronous computing: you can 'set off' your mobile agents and do something else and the results will be back in your mailbox, say, at some later time. They may operate when you are not even connected.
- It provides a natural development environment for implementing 'free market' trading services. New services can come and go dynamically and much more flexible services may co-exist with inferior ones, providing more choices for consumers.

- A flexible distributed computing architecture: mobile agents provide a unique distributed computing architecture which functions differently from the static set-ups. It provides for an innovative way of doing distributed computation.
- Lastly, mobile agents represent an opportunity for a radical and attractive rethinking of the design process in general. Following on from the latter, it turns the conventional design process 'on its head', and some truly innovative products should/would emerge out of mobile agent technology.

15.15.4 How Mobile Agents Work: A Brief Telescript View

Telescript is an interpreted object-oriented and remote programming language which allows for the development of distributed applications. The interpreter and runtime development environment for the Telescript language is called the *Telescript engine* and a given host can support simultaneously multiple Telescript engines. Figure 15.9 summarises a part view of the Telescript architecture. It shows just one of these Telescript engines integrated onto an operating system via a programming interface called the Telescript application programmer interface (API).

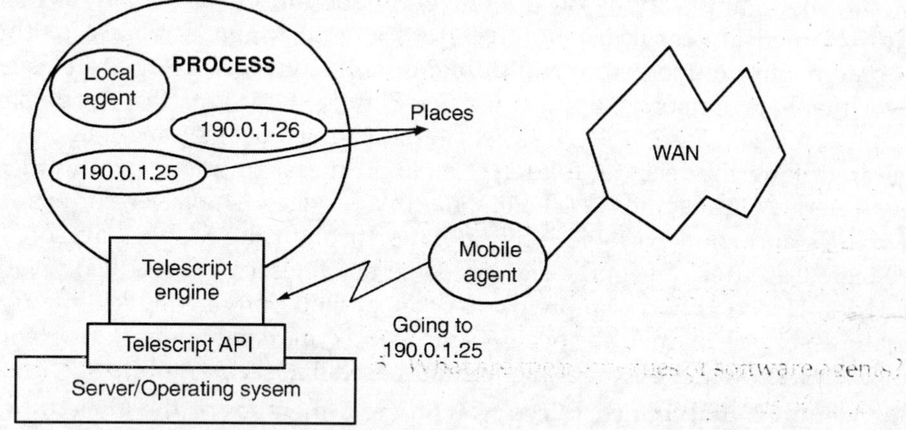

Figure 15.9: *A Part View of Telescript Architecture*

Telescript applications consist of Telescript agents operating within a 'world' or cyberspace of places, engines, clouds and regions. All of these are objects. For example, a *place* is an instance of some class within the engine whose definition inherits operations which can be called on that place. The top class in Telescript's object hierarchy is the *process*. A Telescript engine is itself a multitasking interpreter which can run multiple processes and switches pre-emptively between them. Hence, the engine can host multiple agents that share data/information between themselves. Furthermore, a place is itself a process which can contain an arbitrary number and depth of other places. Figure 15.9 also shows a local agent process. *Agent* processes, unlike *place* processes, are objects which cannot contain other processes, but they can 'go' from place to place (note that places have unique network addresses as shown in Figure 15.9). An agent requiring a service defined at some given place must go to that place and call the operations there.

So to affect remote programming, Telescript makes use of these three language concepts: *places*, *agents* and *"go"*. "Go" is the primitive which allows for inter-process communication. Two or more agent processes can meet (in one place using the *meet* command) and make use of each other's services. They do this by setting up a communication channel - this is the basis for cooperation. Indeed, by agents moving places, they can exploit the services implemented at these places.

A "go" requires a destination space and the host engine packages up the agent along with all its data, stack and instruction pointer and ships it off to its destination place which may be across a vast WAN. At its destination, the other Telescript-enabled engine unpacks it, checks its authentication, and it is then free to execute at its new place. When it finishes, it returns to its original host having performed the task required by its owner. Non-cooperation occurs when a place refuses to accept an incoming agent process. In the free market model, services would be located at places, and it is up to the agent processes to 'go' there, 'negotiate' for the services, use them, pay and return to their owners.

15.15.5 Mobile Agent Applications

Mobile agent applications do not currently abound but are likely to increase to be in the short to medium term, especially after General Magic's release of their Telescript Development Environment into the public domain with their Open Telescript Initiative. However, the first commercial application was Sony's Magic Link PDA or personal intelligent communicator (PIC). Essentially, it assists in managing a user's e-mail, fax, phone and pager as well as linking the user to Telescript-enabled messaging and communication services such as America Online and AT&T PersonaLink Services. The latter, for example, can carry text, graphics and sound. Magic Link operates through the Magic Cap software platform, and a Magic Cap user can send executable agents (Telescript processes) via e-mail through the network. Hence, if two or more users connect their Sony's Magik Link PDAs to AT&T's PersonaLink services (which supports Magic Cap's e-mail messaging), it provides a platform for an application which could exploit email-based Telescript mobile agents.

Plu mentions that France Telecom, who are a member of the General Magic Alliance and therefore had access to Telescript technology, has prototyped some services based on Telescript. In one of their demonstrators, they have used mobile Telescript agents to integrate railway ticketing and car renting services, and the prototype is able to propose an optimal solution depending on price and time. IBM plans to launch their ICS system which uses mobile agents for providing a communications super-service: capable of routeing and translating communications from one service and medium to another, e.g. mobile to desktop, PDA to fax, speech to text, etc.

As we write, many others applications are in the pipeline. Telescript technology is now also evolving into active web tool technology.

According to Yeo, mobile agents are well suited to the following applications:

E-commerce: A commercial transaction may require real-time access to remote resources, such as stock quotes and, perhaps, even agent-to-agent negotiations. For applications in auctions, for comparison shopping agents, for intelligent product brokering and tracking, for e-payment systems, and for secure agents for EC applications.

M-commerce: Intelligent agents can facilitate m-commerce, operating in a wireless environment.

Personal assistance: Mobile agents' ability to execute on remote hosts makes them suitable assistants for performing tasks in the network on behalf of their creators. Mobile agents acting remotely operate independently of their limited network connectivity; their creators can even turn off their computers. For example, to bid in an auction, a user can send a mobile agent to interact with the bidding agent to monitor the price change and to perform auto bidding according to the instructions of the creator.

Procurement and logistics: A large number of applications of both individual and multiagent systems deal with e-procurement and logistics.

Secure brokering: An interesting application of mobile agents is in collaborations in which not all the collaborators are trusted. In such a scenario, parties could let their mobile agents meet on a mutually agreed upon trusted and secure host. Collaboration could then take place at the host without risk of the host's taking the side of one of the visiting agents.

Workflow applications and groupware: The nature of workflow applications includes support for the flow of information among coworkers. Mobile agents are especially useful here because, in addition to mobility, they provide a degree of autonomy to the workflow item. Individual workflow items fully embody the information and behavior they need to move through the organization independent of any particular application.

Searching and filtering: Collecting information from a network often amounts to searching through vast amounts of data for a few relevant pieces of information. On behalf of a user, a mobile agent could visit many sites, search through the information available at each site, filter out the irrelevant information, and build an index of links to pieces of information that match a search criterion.

Monitoring and notification: Sometimes information is not spread out across space but across time (e.g., financial data). New information is constantly being produced and published on the network. Agents can be sent out to wait for certain kinds of information to become available.

Interface agents: Agents may interface with databases. Such agents facilitate access to databases and certain applications and resources. They make access to these resources easy—almost automatic.

Customer service: Many companies are using intelligent agents, including avatars, to facilitate customer service. Here is how Wydham Hotels does it.

Example: Wyndham Uses Intelligent Agents in Its Call Center

Wyndham Hotels & Resorts (wyndham.com) is a hotel chain based in Dallas. It owns, leases, manages, and franchises hotels and resorts in the United States, Canada, Mexico, the Caribbean, and Europe. More than 2 million prospective customers contacted Wyndham's call center in 2005, making it one of the hotel's most critical services.

In order to enhance customer service, Wyndham deployed intelligent agent technology from Voxify (voxify.com) to serve its customers. This automated agent uses speech technology to greet guests, help locate hotels, book reservations, and update guests' loyalty program information. The software agent is most suitable for rapidly confirming reservations, whereas the live agents are best for helping a guest with an unusual question. Callers are given the option to reach a human agent if they do not like the computer agent.

15.15.6 Use of Mobile Agents in E-Commerce

Mobile agents are useful in the context of e-commerce for a number of reasons (Yeo 2002):

- **They reduce the network load.** The distributed system model used in the business world today often generates considerable network traffic, which is due to the interaction of applications with the server. Mobile agents allow the interaction to take place locally by dispatching themselves to the destination host. This means that the computations are moved to the data rather than the data to the computer.
- **They overcome network latency.** Critical real-time systems in e-business, such as online stock trading, require immediate response to events, with no delay. Mobile agents offer a solution to this need because they can be dispatched from a central controller to act locally and directly execute the controller's command.
- **They execute asynchronously and autonomously.** Mobile devices often require an established connection with a server to perform their function. However, maintaining the connection for mobile devices could be very expensive or technically infeasible. Mobile agents can work independently of the mobile device asynchronously and autonomously so that the mobile device can reconnect to the server at a later time to transmit the data.
- **They are naturally heterogeneous.** Computer networks are heterogeneous. Different business entities have different standards on their networks. Mobile agents are generally computer- and transport-layer independent and depend only on the execution environment (e.g., Java Run Time Environment). Therefore, they can work within a wide range of computer systems and with different hardware configurations.

15.15.7 Mobile Agents: Some Challenges

We list here the major challenges associated with mobile agents. They include the following. As usual, they are not exhaustive.

- **Transportation:** how does an agent move from place to place? How does it pack up and move?
- **Authentication:** how do you ensure the agent is who it says it is, and that it is representing who it claims to be representing? How do you know it has navigated various networks without being infected by a virus?
- **Secrecy:** how do you ensure that your agents maintain your privacy? How do ensure someone else does not read your personal agent and execute it for his own gains? How do ensure your agent is not killed and its contents 'core-dumped'?
- **Security:** how do you protect against viruses? How do you prevent an incoming agent from entering an endless loop and consuming all the CPU cycles?
- **Cash:** how will the agent pay for services? How do you ensure that it does not run amok and run up an outrageous bill on your behalf?

In addition to these are the following:

- **Performance issues:** what would be the effect of having hundreds, thousands or millions of such agents on a WAN?
- **Interoperability/communication/brokering services:** how do you provide brokering/ directory type services for locating engines and/or specific services? How do you

execute an agent written in one agent language on an agent engine written in another language? How do you publish or subscribe to services, or support broadcasting necessary for some other coordination approaches?

Having listed these, it must be noted that some of them are already being addressed successfully in development environments like TDE using various techniques including the following: using ASCII-encoded, Safe-TCL scripts or MIME-compatible e-mail messages for transportation; using public-key and private-key digital signature technology for authentication, cash and secrecy; and providing limited and/or interpreted languages that will prevent illegal instructions from being executed, for security; for example, environments would typically not allow an agent to write to memory as viruses do. As a result, much software and hardware (e.g. new consumer electronics products) which exploit mobile agent-based services are currently in the pipeline.

15.16 INFORMATION/INTERNET AGENTS

Information agents have come about because of the sheer demand for tools to help us manage the explosive growth of information we are experiencing currently, and which we will continue to experience henceforth. Information agents perform the role of managing, manipulating or collating information from many distributed sources.

However, before we proceed, perhaps we should clarify that there is, yet again, a rather fine distinction, if any, between information agents and some of those which we have earlier classed as interface or collaborative agents. For example, we saw the presence of 'information-specific' collaborative agents in the Pleiades distributed architecture (as depicted in Figure 15.7). In the previous sections, we described briefly a news filtering agent, NewT, which helps filter and select articles from a continuous stream of Usenet Netnews. We also discussed briefly the Letizia search agent and the remembrance agent. We would not attempt to argue with any researcher who would rather class all these agents as information agents. Interface or collaborative agents started out quite distinct, but with the explosion of the WWW and because of their applicability to this vast WAN, there is now a significant degree of overlap. This is inevitable especially since information or internet agents are defined using different criteria. They are defined by what *they do*, in contrast to collaborative or interface agents which we defined by what *they are*. Many of the interface agents built at the MIT Media Labs, for example, are autonomous and learn, but they have been employed in WWW-based roles; hence, they are, in a sense, information agents. This is a rather subtle distinction, but it must be clarified.

15.16.1 Hypothesis, Motivation and Benefits

According to John Naisbitt and Megatrends, "We are drowning in information but starved of knowledge". Similarly, vis-à-vis the WWW, it is also the case that we are drowning in data but starved of information. The underlying *hypothesis* of information agents is that, somehow, they can ameliorate, but certainly not eliminate, this specific problem of information overload and the general issue of information management in this information era. We agree with Tom Henry, vice president of SandPoint, who is quoted in Indermaur as saying that the biggest challenge is to create a simple user interface so that information search and retrieval using information agents will become as natural for people as picking up a phone or reading a newspaper. Though Henry is quoted in Indermaur's article in the context of 'assistant' agents, we believe this is the ultimate *goal* for information agents. Your information agents would, perhaps, put together your own personal newspaper, just as you want it. The information agents would have to be endowed with the capabilities of knowing *where* to look, *how* to find the information and how to collate it.

The case for having information agents should be clearer from the following. Davies & Weeks report that in 1982, the volume of scientific, corporate and technical information was doubling every 5 years. Three years later, i.e. 1988, it was doubling every 2.2 years, and by 1992 every 1.6 years. This trend suggests that it should now be doubling every year. What is more, much of this information is now accessible electronically on the WWW, whose phenomenal growth over the last 5 years has astonished most. Nicholas Negroponte, head of MIT's Media Labs, claimed in a recent talk at BT Labs that the web was doubling every fifty days. This latter figure is arguable (we believe it is overly optimistic) but the explosive growth of information and the WWW is unquestionable.

The *motivation* for developing information/internet agents is at least twofold. Firstly, there is simply a yearning need/demand for tools to manage such information explosion. Everyone on the WWW would benefit from them in just the same way as they are benefiting from search facilitators such as Spiders, Lycos or Webcrawlers. As Bob Johnson, an analyst at Dataquest

Inc., notes: "in the future, it [agents] is going to be the only way to search the Internet, because no matter how much better the Internet may be organised, it can't keep pace with the growth in information".

Secondly, there are vast financial benefits to be gained. Recall that Netscape Corporation grew from relative obscurity to a billion dollar company almost overnight - and a Netscape or Mosaic client offers generally browsing capabilities, albeit with a few add-ons. Whoever builds the next killer application - the first usable Netscape equivalent of a proactive, dynamic, adaptive and cooperative agent-based WWW information manager - is certain to reap enormous financial rewards. Furthermore, $21 billion was spent by Internet users on purchasing air tickets including hotel bookings, car rentals, etc. in 1995 alone. This compares significantly with the US/European market totals of $170 billion.

15.16.2 How Information Agents Work

As noted earlier, information agents have varying characteristics: they may be static or mobile; they are non-cooperative or social; and they may or may not learn. Hence, there is no standard mode to their operation.

Internet agents could be mobile, i.e. they may be able to traverse the WWW, gather information and report what they retrieve to a home location. However, this is not the norm as yet. Figure 15.10 depicts how the typical static ones work. It shows how an information agent, typically within some browser like Netscape, uses a host of internet management tools such as Spiders and search engines in order to gather the information. The information agent may be associated with some particular indexer(s), e.g. a Spider. A Spider is an indexer able to search the WWW, depth-first, and store the topology of the WWW in a database management system (DBMS) and the full index of URLs in the WAIS. Other search/indexing engines or spiders such as Lycos or WebCrawler can be used similarly to build up the index. Indeed, there are currently more than twenty spiders on the WWW.

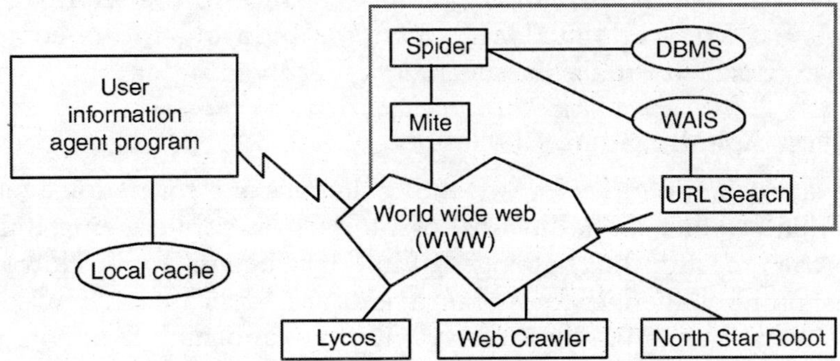

Figure 15.10: *Working of Information Agents*

The user information agent, who has been requested to collate information on some subject, issues various search requests to one or several URL search engines to meet the request. Some of this search may even be done locally if it has a local cache. The information is collated and sent back to the user.

15.16.3 A Prototypical Example: The Internet Softbot

Etzioni & Weld describes a state-of-the-art agent called the internet softbot (software robot). It is a fully implemented agent which allows a user to make a high-level request, and the softbot is able to use search and inference knowledge to determine *how* to satisfy the request in the internet. In doing so, it is able to tolerate ambiguity, omissions and the inevitable errors in the user's request. In their paper, Etzioni & Weld use a strong analogy to a real robot in order to describe their softbot-based interface to the internet. For example, they describe the softbot's *effectors* to include ftp, telnet, mail and numerous file manipulation commands including mv or compress. The *sensors* provide the softbot with information about the external world and they include internet facilities such as archie, gopher and netfind and other UNIX commands such as mv or compress; netfind, for example, is used to determine some user's e-mail address.

The contribution of softbot, in its designers' view, is threefold. Firstly, it provides an integrated and expressive interface to the internet. Secondly, it chooses dynamically which facilities to invoke *when* and in *what* sequence. Thirdly, if a UUCP gateway goes down during a search, it is able to backtrack from one facility to another, at run-time in order to try an alternative to meet its goal. This is quite important, not least because the softbot is very goal driven. *Prima facie*, the softbot presents a menu-based interface through which users can compose queries (users are also allowed to use the first-order logic based notation which supports negation, conjunction, quantification and disjunction, but studies have shown that they are uncomfortable with it). However, at its core, the softbot is a goal-driven planner. It translates the filled-in menu form into a softbot goal which it tries to satisfy.

Softbots may be implemented for a host of other problems including filtering e-mails, scheduling meetings and performing system maintenance tasks. We classed the softbot as an information agent rather than as an interface agent because learning is not *the* crucial feature of it, though it does some limited memory-based learning. For example, returning to an example given earlier, the softbot is able to record for future reference that it is now familiar with all the Mitchells at CMU - hence, obviating the need to carry out a disambiguation process next time a similar query is received.

15.16.4 Information Agents: Some Challenges

This section is much briefer. As regards the challenges of information agents, we believe that they are essentially either similar to those of interface or mobile agents. If the information agents are static, then most of the challenges of interface agents apply. However, if they are mobile, then most of the challenges for mobile agents are applicable. Likewise, the criticisms of information agents are similar to those of interface and mobile agents depending on whether they are static or mobile respectively.

15.17 REACTIVE SOFTWARE AGENTS

Reactive agents represent a special category of agents which do *not* possess internal, symbolic models of their environments; instead they act/respond in a stimulus-response manner to the present state of the environment in which they are embedded. Reactive agents work dates back to research such as Brooks and Agre & Chapman, but many theories, architectures and languages for these sorts of agents have been developed since. However, a most important point of note with reactive agents are not these (i.e. languages, theories or architectures), but the fact that the agents are relatively simple and they interact with other agents in basic ways. Nevertheless, complex patterns of behaviour *emerge* from these interactions when the ensemble of agents is viewed globally.

Maes highlights the three key ideas which underpin reactive agents. Firstly, 'emergent functionality' which we have already mentioned, i.e. the dynamics of the interaction leads to the emergent complexity. Hence, there is no *a priori* specification (or plan) of the behaviour of the set-up of reactive agents. Secondly, is that of 'task decomposition': a reactive agent is viewed as a collection of modules which operate autonomously and are responsible for specific tasks (e.g. sensing, motor control, computations, etc.). Communication between the modules is minimised and of quite a low-level nature. No global model exists within any of the agents and, hence, the global behaviour has to emerge. Thirdly, reactive agents *tend* to operate on representations which are close to raw sensor data, in contrast to the high-level symbolic representations that abound in the other types of agents discussed so far.

15.17.1 Hypothesis, Motivation and Benefits

The essential *hypothesis* of reactive agent-based systems is a specification of the *physical grounding hypothesis*, not to be confused with the *physical symbol system hypothesis*. Traditional AI has staked most of its bets on the latter which holds that the necessary and sufficient condition for a physical system to demonstrate intelligent action is that it be a physical symbol system. On the contrary, the physical grounding hypothesis challenges this long-held view arguing it is flawed fundamentally, and that it imposes severe limitations on symbolic AI-based systems. This new hypothesis states that in order to build a system that is intelligent, it is necessary to have representations grounded in the physical world. This hypothesis is quite radical and it turns, literally, the physical symbol system hypothesis 'on its head'. Brooks argues that this hypothesis obviates the need for symbolic representations or models because the world becomes its own best model. Furthermore, this model is always kept up-to-date since the system is connected to the world via sensors and/or actuators. Hence, the reactive agent's *hypothesis* may be stated as follows: smart agent systems can be developed from simple agents which do not have internal symbolic models, and who's 'smartness' derives from the emergent behaviour of the interactions of the various modules.

It is important to note that all current reactive software agents do not necessarily possess actuators and sensors which connect them to the physical world, though Brooks would insist on them. Indeed, in a paper titled 'Intelligence without Robots', Etzioni has argued that software environments "circumvent many thorny but peripheral research issues that are inescapable in physical environments".

However, the essence of the physical grounding hypothesis still holds with such reactive agents: no explicit symbolic representations, no explicit (abstract) symbolic reasoning and an emergent functionality. Reactive agents are simple and easy to understand, and their 'cognitive economy' is very low; this is because they have to 'remember' little. They are situated, i.e. they do not plan ahead or revise any world models, and their actions depend on what happens at the present moment.

The key *benefits* which motivates reactive agents work, in addition to the hypothesis mentioned earlier, is the hope that they would be more robust and fault tolerant than other agent-based systems, e.g. an agent may be lost but without any catastrophic effects. Other benefits include flexibility and adaptability in contrast to the inflexibility, slow response times and brittleness of classical AI systems. Another benefit, it is hoped, is that this type of work would address the *frame problem* which has so far proved intractable with traditional AI techniques such as non-monotonic reasoning.

15.17.2 Reactive Agent Applications

It must be stated that there are a relatively few number of reactive software agent-based applications. Partly, due to this reason, there is no standard mode to their operation; rather, they tend to depend on the reactive agent architecture chosen. We describe briefly two of these architectures below.

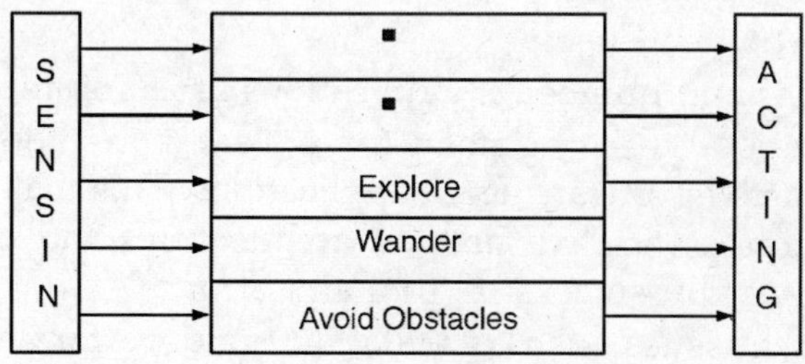

Figure 15.11: *Brook's Subsumption Architecture*

Perhaps the most celebrated of them all, is Brook's *subsumption architecture.* Though Brook's architecture has been used to implement physical robots (i.e. tightly connecting perception to action), it could also be exploited in purely reactive software agents. The architecture consists of a set of modules, each of which is described in a subsumption language based on augmented finite state machines (AFSM). An AFSM is triggered into action if its input signal exceeds some threshold, though this is also dependent on the values of suppression and inhibition signals into the AFSM. Note that AFSMs represent the only processing units in the architecture, i.e. there are no symbols as those in classical AI work. The modules are grouped and placed in layers (which work asynchronously) such that modules in a higher level can inhibit those in lower layers as shown in Figure 15.11. Each layer has a hard-wired purpose or *behaviour*, e.g. to avoid obstacles or to enable/control wandering. This architecture has been used to construct, at least, ten mobile robots at MIT. Steels uses similar agents to Brooks' in order to investigate cooperation between distributed simulated robots using self-organisation.

Arguably, the most basic reactive architecture is that based on situated-action rules which, in turn, derives from some work carried out in by Suchman. Situated action agents act essentially in ways which is 'appropriate' to its situation, where 'situation' refers to a potentially complex combination of internal and external events and states. Situated-action 'agents' have been used in PENGI, a video game designed as part of Agre's doctoral thesis, and SONJA. Researchers at Philips research laboratories in Redhill, UK, have implemented a situation-action based language called the RTA programming language. Indeed, they have used this language to implement characters in computer games which they have since integrated into CD-i titles. Kaebling & Rosenschein have proposed another language based on a modal logical formalism, which in turn is based on a paradigm called *situated automata*. Agents written in this language are compiled into digital circuits which implement the reactive agent system.

In summary, few applications based on reactive software agents exist currently but this situation will change before the millennium. A favourite application area for them seems to be the games or entertainment industry, which of course is a multi-billion pound industry. For example, the Philips researchers are already working on digital video and 3-D graphics-based, reactive agent animations.

15.17.3 Reactive Agents: Some Challenges

This list of criticisms above is not exhaustive but it provides some of the challenges for reactive agent researchers to address. In summary, we see the main challenges to include the following:

- Expanding the range and number of applications based on reactive agents;
- *Methodology:* there is a yearning need for a clearer methodology to facilitate the development of reactive software agent applications. This may or may not require the development of more associated theories, architectures and languages. Much of the current approaches, sadly, smacks of 'trial and error';
- *Non-functional issues:* issues such as scalability and performance would need to be addressed, though these are unlikely to be important until clearer methodologies have been developed and evaluated.

Despite these challenges, we would expect more applications to be 'hand-crafted' in the medium term.

15.18 HYBRID AGENTS

Hybrid Agents refer to those agents whose constitution is a combination of two or more agent philosophies within a singular agent. These philosophies may be mobile, interface, information, collaborative, ... etc. The goal of having hybrid agents is the notion that the benefits accrued from having the combination of philosophies within a single agent is greater than the gains obtained from the same agent based on a singular philosophy.

15.18.1 Hypothesis, Motivation and Benefits

So far, we have reviewed five types of agents: collaborative, interface, mobile, internet and reactive agents. The debates as to which of them is 'better' are rather academic, and frankly, sterile - and rather too early to get into. Since each type has (or promises) its own strengths and deficiencies, the trick (as always) is to maximise the strengths and minimise the deficiencies of the most relevant technique for your particular purpose. Frequently, one way of doing this is to adopt a *hybrid* approach, like Maes, which brought together some of the strengths of both the deliberative and reactive paradigms. Hence, hybrid agents refer to those whose constitution is a combination of two or more agent *philosophies* within a singular agent. These philosophies include a mobile philosophy, an interface agent philosophy, collaborative agent philosophy, etc.

The key *hypothesis* for having hybrid agents or architectures is the belief that, for some application, the benefits accrued from having the combination of philosophies within a singular agent is greater than the gains obtained from the same agent based entirely on a singular philosophy. Otherwise having a hybrid agent or architecture is meaningless. Clearly, the *motivation* is the expectation that this hypothesis would be proved right; the ideal *benefits* would be the set union of the benefits of the individual philosophies in the hybrid. Consider the obvious case of constructing an agent based on both the collaborative (i.e. deliberative) and reactive philosophies. In such a case the reactive component, which would take precedence over the deliberative one, brings about the following benefits: robustness, faster response times and adaptability. The frame problem is also better ameliorated by the reactive component. The deliberative part of the agent would handle the longer term goal-oriented issues. Typically, such hybrid architectures end up having a layered architecture as is evidenced by Muller *et al.*'s InteRRaP, Ferguson's Touring Machines, and Hayes-Roth's architectures. We describe them briefly below.

15.18.2 Hybrid Agent Architectures

As is the case with reactive agents, there are just but a few hybrids agent architectures. A prototypical example of a hybrid example is Muller *et al.*'s layered InteRRaP architecture shown in Figure 15.12 developed at the German Research Centre for AI. It is an architecture that implements a layered approach to agent design.

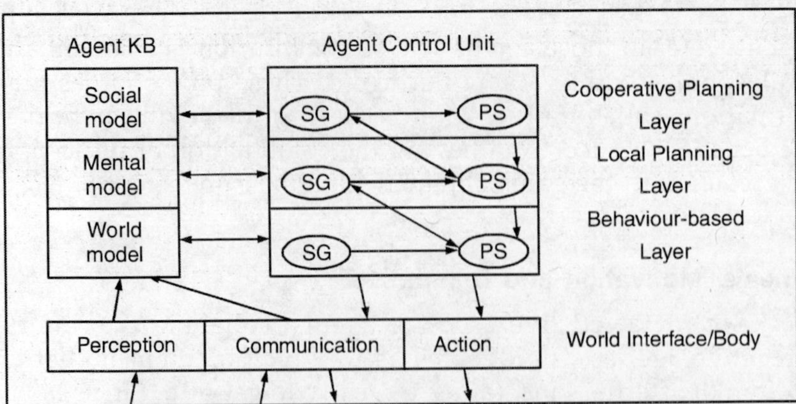

Figure 15.12: *The InteRRaP Hybrid Architecture*

This architecture can be used to construct an agent such as an autonomous robot. As shown, it consists of an agent knowledge base and its associated control unit sitting 'on top' of the perception-action component which also handles the low-level communications. There are three control layers in this architecture: the behaviour-based layer (BBL), the local planning layer (LPL) and the cooperative planning layer (CPL). Clearly, the architecture marries the deliberative and the reactive philosophies. The reactive part of the framework which allows for efficiency, reactivity and robustness are implemented by the BBL which contains a set of patterns of behaviour (PoBs), in effect, situation-action rules. These describe the agent's reactive skills which implements fast situation recognition in order to react to time-critical situations. The intermediate LPL implements local goal-directed behaviour while the topmost CPL enables the agent to plan/cooperate with other agents in order to achieve multi-agent plans, as well as resolve conflicts. LPL and CPL allow for more deliberation. These layers all work with different models in the agent's knowledge base: BBL, LPL and CPL operate with the world, mental and social models respectively. Each InteRRaP layer also consists of two processes, SG and PS, which interact with each other as well as with neighbouring layers.

These layers work asynchronously. The InteRRaP architecture has been evaluated by constructing a FORKS application which simulates forklift robots working in an automated loading dock environment.

Ferguson's *Touring Machines* architecture is another good example of a hybrid "architecture for dynamic, rational and mobile agents", though the word 'mobile' does not refer to mobile agents as in Telescript agents, but to mobile agents as in autonomous robots. This architecture, which is similar to Brook's subsumption architecture, consists of three control layers: the reactive layer, the planning layer and the modelling layer which all work concurrently. A key distinction between Touring Machines and Brook's subsumption architecture on the one hand, and InteRRaP on the other is that the former are *horizontal* architectures while the latter is a *vertical* architecture. This means that all the layers in Touring Machines and the subsumption architecture have access to the perception/sensing data and all the layers can contribute to the actions, while only the bottom layer in InteRRaP receives and acts on the perceptual data (see Figure 15.12). Therefore to achieve coordination in Touring Machines, Ferguson has control rules capable of suppressing the input to a certain layer, much similar to the suppression/inhibition mechanisms in the subsumption architecture.

Hayes-Roth's integrated architecture for intelligent agents consists of two layers: the physical layer which performs perception-action coordination, i.e. it senses, interprets, filters and reacts to the dynamic environment in which the agent is embedded; the cognitive layer receives perceptual input from the physical controller to construct an evolving model, and to perform interpretation, reasoning and planning. Her goal is to provide an architecture for constructing adaptive intelligent agents which can operate in specialised, but challenging, "niches"; indeed, she argues cogently that AI agents must, of necessity, be niche-bound because they are knowledge-bound. The fundamental theoretical concept which underlies her architecture captures succinctly the hybridism that belies it: to construct an agent which "dynamically constructs explicit control plans to guide its choices among situated-triggered behaviours". Hence, the physical layer implements reactive situated behaviour while the cognitive layer performs some longer term, deliberative planning and scheduling, drawing from the evolving model. Though the Hayes-Roth paper was largely a design proposal (aiming to provide sophisticated adaptive, intelligent, versatile and coherent agents), Hayes-Roth reports that the architecture has not only been implemented, but has also been used to implement several experimental agents. For example, she reports on an agent, Guardian, which has been constructed for one niche - Intensive Care Unit (ICU) monitoring. Guardian is currently able to monitor on the order of twenty continuously sensed patient data variables amongst several other occasionally sensed ones. A new demonstrator, Guardian, under development will monitor on the order of a hundred variables. She also reports that she has begun applying the architecture to other niches including Aibots - adaptive intelligent robots. Hayes-Roth *et al.* report on an evolving testbed application - an animated improvisational theatre company for children. The idea is to have animated characters (hybrid agents) which can display spontaneous, situated, opportunistic and goal-directed behaviour. The agents collaborate via *directed improvisation* and the goal is to have the animated characters produce "a joint performance that follows the script and directions in an engaging manner".

There are a few other hybrid architectures which we do not review here, an obvious one being the *procedural reasoning system* (PRS) in which the OASIS prototype was implemented. Another hybrid system is CIRCA.

15.19 HETEROGENEOUS AGENT SYSTEMS

Heterogeneous agent systems, unlike hybrid systems described in the preceding section refers to an integrated set-up of at least two or more agents which belong to two or more different agent classes. A heterogeneous agent system may also contain one or more hybrid agents. As for the other classes, we next discuss their motivation, benefit, how they work, an example and some challenges.

15.19.1 Hypothesis, Motivation and Benefits

Genesereth & Ketchpel articulate clearly the *motivation* for heterogeneous agent systems. The essential argument is that the world abounds with a rich diversity of software products providing a wide range of services for a similarly wide range of domains. Though these programs work in isolation, there is an increasing demand to have them *interoperate* - hopefully, in such a manner such that they provide 'added-value' as an ensemble than they do individually. The *hypothesis* is that this is plausible. Indeed, a new domain called *agent-based software engineering* has been invented in order to facilitate the interoperation of miscellaneous software agents. A key requirement for interoperation amongst heterogeneous agents is having an agent communication language (ACL) via which the different software 'agents' can communicate with each other. The potential *benefits* for having heterogeneous agent technology are several:

- Standalone applications can be made to provide 'value-added' services by enhancing them in order to participate and interoperate in cooperative heterogeneous set-ups;
- The legacy software problem may be ameliorated because it could obviate the need for costly software rewrites as they be given 'new leases of life' by getting them to interoperate with other systems. At the very least, heterogeneous agent technology may cushion or lessen the blow or effect of routine software maintenance, upgrade or rewrites;
- Agent-based software engineering provides a radical new approach to software design, implementation and maintenance in general, and software interoperability in particular. Its ramifications (e.g. moving from passive modules in traditional software engineering to proactive agent-controlled ones) would only be clear as this methodology and its tools become clearer.

Genesereth & Ketchpel note that agent-based software engineering is often compared to object-oriented programming in that an agent, like an object, provides a message-based interface to its internal data structures and algorithms. However, they note that there is a key distinction: in object-oriented programming, the meaning of a message may differ from object to object (this is the principle of polymorphism); in agent-based software engineering, agents use a common language with an agent-independent semantics. They highlight three important questions raised by the new agent-oriented software engineering paradigm. They include:

- What is an appropriate agent communication language?
- How are agents capable of communicating in this language constructed?
- What communication architectures are conducive to cooperation?

In their paper, they begin addressing such issues via ACL - an agent communication language they have been developing as part of a DARPA initiative. ACL, *inter alia*, consists of the Knowledge Interchange Format (KIF), the Knowledge Query and Manipulation Language (KQML) and Ontolingua.

15.19.2 How Heterogeneous Agent Systems Work

To commence, we provide the rather *specific* definition of the word 'agent' proffered in agent-based software engineering. It defines a software agent as such "if an only if it communicates correctly in an agent communication language".

If new agents are constructed such that they abide by this dictum, then putting them together in a heterogeneous set-up is possible, though not trivial. However, with legacy software, they need to be converted into software agents first. The latter authors note that there are three ways of doing this conversion. Firstly, the legacy software may totally be rewritten to meet the criteria for agenthood - a most costly approach. Secondly, a *transducer* approach may be used. The transducer is a *separate* piece of software which receives messages from other agents and translates them into the legacy software's native communication protocol, and passes the messages into the program. Likewise, it also translates the program's responses into ACL which is sent on to other agents. This is the favoured approach in many situations where the code may be too delicate to tamper with or is unavailable. Lastly, another approach is the *wrapper* technique. In this approach, some code is "injected" into the program in order to allow it communicate in ACL. The wrapper can access directly and modify the program's data structures. This is clearly a more interventionist approach which requires the code to be available, but offers greater efficiency than the transduction approach.

Once the agents are available, there are two possible architectures to choose from: one in which all the agents handle their own coordination or another in which groups of agents can rely on special system programs to achieve coordination. The disadvantage of the former is that the communication overhead does not ensure scalability which is a necessary requirement for the future of agents. As a consequence, the latter federated approach as shown in Figure 15.13 is preferred typically.

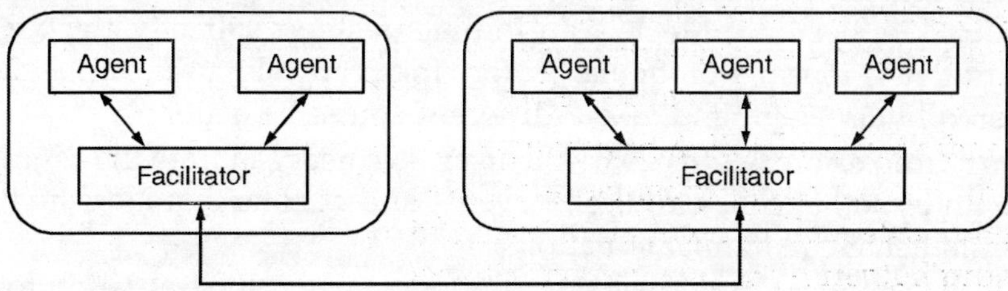

Figure 15.13: *A Federated System*

In the above federated set-up, there are five agents distributed in two machines, one with two agents and the other with three. The agents do not communicate directly with one another but do so through intermediaries called facilitators which are similar to Wiederhold's *mediators*. Essentially, the agents surrender some of their autonomy to the facilitators who are able to locate other agents on the network capable of providing various services. They also establish the connection across the environments and ensure correct 'conversation' amongst agents. ARCHON used such architecture.

15.20 LEARNING AGENTS

Software agents are called *intelligent agents* or **learning agents** if they have the capacity to adapt or modify their behavior—that is, to learn. Simple software agents, such as e-mail agents, lack this capacity. If a simple software agent has any intelligence at all, it is found in the subroutines or methods that the agent uses to do pattern matching. However, these subroutines or methods are built into the program and cannot be modified by the agent. Currently, few, if any, commercially available agents have the ability to learn. However, some research prototypes have this capability.

15.20.1 The Characteristics of Learning Agents

A number of prototypes have been developed at the MIT Media Lab. Researchers, inspired by the metaphor of a "personal assistant," have used machine learning techniques to create a series of "user interface" agents. According to Maes, Initially, a personal assistant is not very familiar with the habits and preferences of his or her employer and may not even be very helpful. The assistant needs some time to become familiar with the particular work methods of the employer and organization at hand. However, with every experience the assistant learns, either by watching how the employer performs tasks, by receiving instructions from the employer, or by learning from other more experienced assistants within the organization. Gradually, more tasks that were initially performed directly by the employer can be taken care of by the assistant.

As Maes suggests, an interface agent can modify its behavior in four ways:

1. **"Look over the shoulder" of the user.** An agent can continually monitor the user's interactions with the computer. By keeping track of the user's actions over an extended period of time, the agent can discern regularities or recurrent patterns and offer to automate these patterns.
2. **Direct and indirect user feedback.** The user can provide the agent with negative feedback either in a direct or an indirect fashion. Directly, the user can tell the agent not to repeat a particular action. Indirectly, the user can neglect the advice offered by an agent and take a different course of action.
3. **Learn from examples given by the user.** The user can train the agent by providing it with hypothetical examples of events and actions that indicate how the agent should behave in similar situations.
4. **Ask the agents of other users.** If an agent encounters a situation for which it has no recommended plan of action, it can ask other agents what actions they would recommend for that situation. Examples of commercial personal assistants are Cybelle (agentland.com), Imp (inchain.com.au), and Noa (madoogali.com). Guan and Zhu developed an agent system in which agents can enhance their knowledge base by exchanging knowledge with other agents. It has been suggested that this capability can be used for product brokering. (See earlier discussion on recommendation systems.)

15.20.2 LEARNING AGENTS: AN EXAMPLE

The major difference between the operation of an intelligent learning agent and the workings of a simple software agent is in how the if/then rules are created. With a learning agent, the onus of creating and managing rules rests on the shoulders of the agent, not the end user. To understand this difference, let us examine the operation of an intelligent e-mail agent.

An E-mail Agent That Learns from Experience

Maxim is a classic intelligent e-mail agent that operated on top of the Eudora e-mail system. This agent relies on a form of learning known as *case-based reasoning*. Maxim continually monitors what the user does and stores this information as examples. The situations are described in terms of fields and keywords in the message (i.e., the "From," "To," and "Cc" lists; the keywords in the "Subject" field; and so on), and the actions are those performed by the user with respect to the message (e.g., the order in which the user reads it, whether the user deleted or stored it, and so on). When a new situation occurs, the agent analyzes its features based on its stored cases and suggests an action to the user (such as read, delete, forward, or archive). The agent measures the *confidence,* or fit, of a suggested action to a situation. Two levels of confidence are used to determine what the agent actually does with its suggestion. If the confidence is above the "do-it" threshold, the agent automatically executes the suggestion. If the confidence is above the "tell-me" threshold, the agent will offer a suggestion and wait for input from the user.

15.20.3 Value of Learning Agents

Learning agents also address the problem of end-user competence. With simple software agents, the end user is required to recognize when an agent should be used, create the agent, specify the rules to be used by the agent, and modify or edit the rules to account for changing interests and work patterns. Learning agents remove all of these impediments (although they are not a total panacea). Learning agents such as Maxim operate on the assumptions that the application involves a substantial amount of repetition and that the repetition does not vary considerably from one end user to another. Without these assumptions, there is no way to build the requisite levels of confidence, nor is there any need to learn the underlying rules if a general set of rules cannot be applied to all users. Additionally, critics argue that most people do not want intelligent agents "looking over their shoulders". They contend that simple software agents that require end users to fill out forms are easy to use and provide enough utility for the average end user.

Our discussion so far has pertained to individual software agents. But as we illustrate next, agents can also work in pairs or in groups.

15.21 MULTIAGENTS AND COMMUNITIES OF AGENTS

Agents can communicate, cooperate, and negotiate *with other agents.* The basic idea is that it is easy to build an agent that has a small amount of specialized knowledge and then group several agents to create a system where each agent is assigned to a simple subtask. However, in executing complex tasks that require much knowledge, it frequently is necessary to employ several software agents in one application. These agents need to *share* their knowledge, or the results of applying this knowledge together may fail. Multiagent systems tend to work without intervention from humans and are "self-organizing" systems.

An example of a multiagent system is routing among telecommunications networks. Information can pass through a network controlled by one company into a network controlled by another company. Computers that control a telecommunications network might find it beneficial to enter into agreements with other computers that control other networks about routing packets more efficiently from source to destination.

Another example is wireless devices, which are continuously increasing their functionality.

Wireless devices offer more than Internet access and e-commerce support; they also enable device-to-device communication. You can take a photograph with your digital camera in one location and transmit pictures wirelessly, in seconds, to your office. Intelligent agents embedded in such devices facilitate this interaction.

Each of these situations is an instance in which computers control certain resources and might be able to help themselves by strategically sharing this resource with other computers. With wireless devices, the resource might be a person's time, whereas with a telecommunications network, the resource might be communication lines, switching nodes, or short- and long-term storage. In each situation, the computers that control these resources can do their own job better by reaching agreements with other computers.

15.21.1 Multi-Agent Systems

With **multiagent systems (MASs)**, no single designer stands behind all of the agents. Each agent in the system may be working toward different goals, even contradictory ones. Agents either compete or cooperate. For example, a customer may want to place a long-distance call. Once this information is known, agents representing the carriers submit bids simultaneously. The bids are collected, and the best bid wins. In a complex system, the customer's agent may take the process one step further by showing all bidders the offers, allowing them to rebid or negotiate. A complex task is broken into subtasks, each of which is assigned to an agent that works on its task independently of others and is supported by a knowledge base. Acquiring and interpreting information is done by knowledge-processing agents that use deductive and inductive methods, as well as computations. The data are refined, interpreted, and sent to the coordinator, who transfers whatever is relevant to a specific user's inquiry or need to the user interface. If no existing knowledge is available to answer an inquiry, knowledge creating and collecting agents of various types are triggered. Of the many topics related to MASs, we present the following ones: negotiation in e-commerce, coordination, collaboration, communities of agents, and agent networking. Up until now, we have concerned ourselves mainly with solitary agents. However there is a growing need for situated agents that can interact with other actors, both human and artificial. Multi-Agent Systems (MAS) are systems wherein multiple (software) agents can potentially interact. The corresponding subfield of artificial intelligence that deals with the principles and design of multi-agent systems is called distributed artificial intelligence. Multi-agent systems provide several advantages over 'single-agent systems'.

Below we shall discuss some of these advantages.

- ***Efficiency***
  Having a system with multiple agents allows for parallel and asynchronous computation. In a multi-agent system tasks can be broken down into several independent tasks and computed simultaneously by different agents.
- ***Robustness***
  Multi-agent systems can have built-in redundancy. If the responsibility for certain tasks is shared among different agents, the system can tolerate failures from individual agents. By contrast when a single-agent system or program fails, the entire system fails. Although a multi-agent system need not be implemented on multiple processors, to provide full robustness against failure, its agents should be distributed across several machines.
- ***Scalability***
  Multi-agent systems are more flexible and scalable than single-entity (monolithic) systems. As a result of the modular approach of multi-agent systems, new agents can easily be introduced in the system giving it added capabilities.

- ***Simpler Programming***
  The modularity of multi-agent systems makes programming easier and allows for better control of the programming tasks. Rather than handling the whole task with a centralised agent, programmers can identify subtasks and assign control of those subtasks to different agents.
- ***Emergent Behaviour***
  By letting multiple (reactive) agents interact within an agent system, 'smartness' can arise out of the emergent behaviour of the interactions of the various modules. This 'bottom-up' approach to artificial intelligence is steadily gaining prominence and is considered to be valuable alternative to the 'top-down' approach of fully programming an artificial system using symbolic reasoning and symbolic representation.

Multiagent Negotiation in E-Commerce

A considerable amount of research and development is being done on multiagent negotiation in e-commerce. Consider a situation in which agents cooperate to arrange for a person's summer vacation in Hawaii: The person's agent notifies sellers' agents about the potential traveler's needs for a hotel, plane tickets, and a rental car, and the sellers' agents submit bids. The person's agent collects the bids and tries to get lower rebids. The sellers' agents can use rules for the negotiations. The process of negotiation and its relationship to bidding processes are being studied by researchers. Two issues that are being examined include the following: Can automated agents learn strategies that enable them to effectively participate in typical, semi structured, and multi-issue business negotiations? What is required and how does it work? For an example of automated online bargaining. Related to negotiation is intermediation, which is an advanced EC feature. Bohte and La Poutre describe a multiagent system that incorporates intermediation. For an example of automated negotiation.

15.21.1.1 Architecture and Standardisation

In order for agents and agent systems to interact they must be interoperable. While many different multi-agent systems are currently being developed independently, the use of common agent standards will improve interoperability and stimulate overall system integration.

There are two main standardisation efforts with regard to software agents and multi-agent systems, namely FIPA and KQML. The latter is part of the larger DARPA-sponsored Knowledge Sharing Effort focused on developing techniques and tools to promote the sharing of knowledge in intelligent systems. KQML, short for Knowledge Query and Manipulation Language, was designed to enable sharing and reuse of knowledge bases and knowledge-based systems but was rapidly adopted by agent researchers. The Foundation of Intelligent Physical Agents (FIPA) was formed in 1996 to produce software standards for heterogeneous and interacting agents and agent-based systems. FIPA currently has the broadest user base, so we shall use the FIPA standard set to discuss multi-agent system architecture further.

The FIPA standardisation effort is based around FIPA Abstract Architecture that acts as an overall description of the FIPA standard set. The primary focus of the Abstract Architecture is to create a (semantically) meaningful message exchange between agents that may be using different meaningful message exchange between agents that may be using different messaging transports, different communication languages, or different content languages. The Abstract Architecture focuses on the core interoperability of agents by providing designers with abstract agent-architecture components on which to base their concrete multi-agent-system implementations.

The management of agents is the main topic of the FIPA Agent Management Specification. The Agent Management Specification defines (1) the type of environment that an agent inhabits, (2) the services that are expected to be available to it, and (3) the management actions that can be carried out by them or for them. One of the elements often used in concrete implementations of the Abstract Architecture is the agent platform as described in the Agent Management Specification. Agent platforms are commonly used to provide the following services:

- creating and running an agent;
- searching for an agent;
- migrating agents to other platforms;
- enabling communication with other agents hosted by an agent platform.

In order for agents to interact on a given agent platform they must be able to communicate with each other. Effective interaction is the exchange (communication) of information and knowledge that can be mutually understood. To this end agents must share a common language and have a common understanding of terms used in a given context. A third requirement is the ability to exchange both the message and the meaning between each other.

There are a number of FIPA standards that deal with agent communication. A common language is provided in the form of FIPA ACL. Common understanding (i.e. semantics) is provided in the form if a library of communicative acts or performatives that define formal and informal meanings for a set of different communicative acts specified by FIPA. The ability to exchange messages is standardised by the FIPS Agent Message Transport Service.

Apart from these core specifications, there are numerous other FIPA specifications (ninety six in total, some of which are obsolete) that govern multi-agent-system design.

15.21.1.2 Multi-Agent Coordination

Coordination is a key factor in the success of MASs. The purpose of the coordination mechanism is to manage problem solving so that cooperating agents work together as a coherent team. Coordination is achieved by exchanging data, providing partial solution plans, and enforcing constraints among agents. Coordination can be done by analyzing related activities; for example, coordination is part of order processing, synchronization, structured group mediation, and information sharing.

While some agents are used individually, several agents can collaborate to perform more complex tasks. For example, to purchase books, a group of agents will exchange messages in a conversation to find the best deal, bid in an auction, arrange financing, select a shipper, and track the order. Multi-agent systems (groups of agents collaborating to achieve some purpose) are critical for large-scale Ecommerce, especially B2B interactions such as service provisioning, supply chain, negotiation, and fulfilment. The grouping can be static or dynamic. The conversation can include interactions between people and agents, or between agents. We need to coordinate the interactions between the agents to achieve a higher-level task, such as requesting, offering and accepting a contract for some services. We call this "choreography" or "conversation management." An agent group will have a series of stylized message exchanges to accomplish this task, perhaps by advertising and using a brokered service (Figure 15.14), bidding during an auction, responding to a call for proposals, or negotiating a price.

There are several possible levels of choreography of the expected message sequences, depending on the need for a relatively "loose" or more "tight" control of allowed interactions. These include:

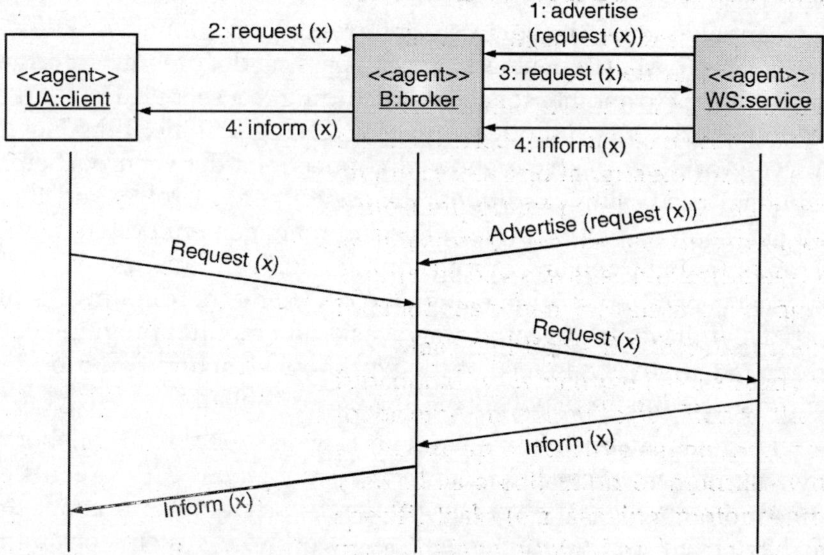

Figure 15.14: *Message Sequencing*

1. *Built-in message type assumptions* - The message type itself directly suggests a standard expected message sequence. The agent system can monitor compliance. For example, an agent might issue a "request" to one or more agents. Other agents would respond, either to "inform" of their ability to provide this service, or to indicate that they "did not understand" the message. The system can also monitor timeouts, using the "reply-by".
2. *Rules* - A set of rules can be defined for any agent, or community of agents. For example, one could customize an agent's time to wait for a response, the number of other agents it can talk to at one time, and what sort of responses to make to a specific message from various types of agent. Not all request/response patterns are constrained by the rules. A standard rule language can be used, such as the forward chaining rule system provided by Zeus.
3. *Conversation protocols* - Often a group of agents must "lock-step" through a standard protocol of messages; if A says "x" then B says "y"; for example, bidding during an

auction, or responding to a call for proposals. These protocols can be expressed as finite state machines, UML state charts or petrinets. Each participant can have the same or a compatible model, stepped through explicitly to determine the action and response any incoming message. Figure 15.14 shows UML diagrams of the "broker" message type, used by a weather service agent, WS. First, WS advertises to broker B that it can respond to certain requests by sending the message "advertise(request(x))" to B. User agent, UA, issues a "broker(request(x))"; it will obtain the answer from WS, via a "request(x)" which then responds with "inform(answer)". B relays this to UA with its own "inform(answer)".

4. *Workflow* - When the conversation coordination for interactions of multiple agents and humans needs to be more complex and precise, a workflow system can be used. A workflow system allows the explicit definition (e.g. as a graphical model) and control of a group of participants that execute a (business) process. Many E-commerce applications involve some form of inter- or intra- organizational workflow. A workflow system automates (part of) a business process, passing documents, information or tasks from one participant to another for action, according to a set of rules. Workflow systems such as ActionWorks Metro, Endeavours, HP ChangeEngine, IBM FlowMark, Little-JIL, or Verve Workflow describe allowed connections between participants, desired and exceptional processing conditions, the assignment of roles, and the request and allocation of resources. For example, a telecom management system alerting a human operator, or assigning a repair or provisioning engineer. This use of workflow can be seen as a "next generation scripting language". A single coordinating agent ("workflow manager") with full workflow, could assign tasks and monitor progress for each member of the group; alternatively a piece of the workflow structure could be assigned to an agent with the role it is to play (say as "buyer" or "seller").

Workflow and agents can be combined in several ways. Agents can collaborate to perform a workflow, *e.g., telecom provisioning (BT), or service provisioning (HP).* Agents can represent the participants and resources, the society of agents collaborate to enact the workflow. Agent systems have been used to implement new workflow systems or augment existing workflow systems. Agents can be used to make workflow more intelligent, e.g., by adding negotiation, reasoning at decision points. Other examples include the Little-JIL process programming language demonstrates how a workflow language can be used to coordinate agents. Worklets is an agent-like light-weight process workflow system implemented in Java and the JPython.

15.21.1.3 Multi-Agent Coolaboration

Lotus Notes/Domino is a comprehensive collaborative software product. It includes Notes Agents, which operate in the background to automatically perform routine tasks for the Notes user, such as filing documents, sending e-mail, looking for particular topics, or archiving older documents. These agents can be created by designers as part of an application for automating routine tasks, such as progress tracking or serving as reminders of overdue items, or for performing more powerful functions, such as manipulating field values and bringing data in from other applications. Agents can be *private*, created by the user and used only by the user, or they can be *shared*, created by a designer and used by anyone who has access to the application or database. Because an agent typically represents an individual user's interests, collaboration is a natural area for agent-to-agent interaction and communication. IBM, for example, is exploring multiagent interaction through several research efforts.

Another example of collaborating agents is provided by Bose, who proposed a framework for automating the execution of collaborative organizational processes performed by multiple organization members. The agents emulate the work and behavior of human agents. Each agent is capable of acting autonomously, cooperatively, and collectively to achieve the collective goal. The system increases organizational productivity by carrying out several tedious watchdog activities, thereby freeing humans to work on challenging and creative tasks. Bose describes an example of a travel authorization process that can be divided into subtasks delegated to agents.

Another example involves scheduling a meeting. Several agents can cooperate in proposing meeting times and places until a mutually acceptable schedule is found. Note that a simpler case is that of a single agent that checks the calendars of the participants to determine when all of them are free and then books a free meeting room and notifies the participants.

In an EC environment, the third-party logistics (3PL) takes charge of the logistics design, delivery, storage, and transportation in a supply chain with its professional and complete value-added services. Ying and Dayong suggest that only when the 3PL reengineers its logistics business process to accommodate the customer will it maximize the value of the customer. Five intelligent agents—order management agent, logistics process reengineering agent, resource scheduling agent, dynamic union management agent, and simulating and evaluating agent—are designed to form an EC-based 3PL system, which with the collaboration of the five agents constructs a virtual private logistics teamwork suitable for a certain customer's needs and realizes the win-win between the customer and the logistics service vendor. A multiagent system for assigning air cargo to airline flights in creative ways. Yet another example was proposed by Wang et al. for a "society" of agents to monitor financial transactions for irregularities. The concept of agent societies (see the following discussion) also is discussed by Huhns. Finally, Wu and Sun describe collaboration in multiagent bidding for EC. A successful commercial system was developed by IBM for improved planning and scheduling of operations for certain papermaking plants. For a multiagent system for auction-based services; for a multiagent system for product customization. Below figure 15.15 shows an example of a multiagent system called Genie, in which four agents (calendar, identification, database, and Web) interact and collaborate. The identification agent identifies a user, the calendar agent schedules events, the database agent provides relevant data, and the Web agent provides the interaction support.

15.21.2 Communities of Agents

Elofson introduced the concept of communities of agents behaving in believable ways in the entertainment industry. *Communities of agents* are groups of agents that collaborate to complete a complex task. They may work as one entity, or they may represent several entities (e.g., buyers, sellers, and support services). Agents, by definition, represent someone or something. There is great potential for more sophisticated agents of this form to be used in movies and games, possibly even generating a new genre of interactive movies. This concept was expanded to a *society of agents* by Huhns. A *society of agents* is a broader grouping than a community of agents; a society may include several (or many) communities of agents.

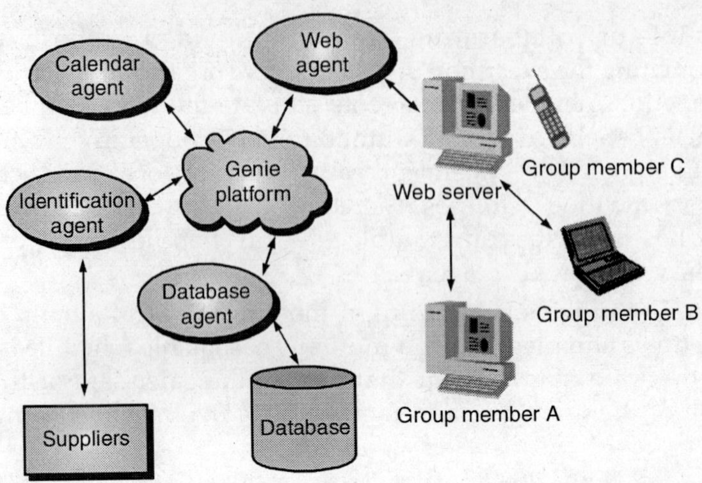

Figure 15.15: A sample multiagent system

15.21.2.1 Agent Networking

A system for implementing "ecology of distributed agents" was created at the MIT Media Lab. The system supports applications of distributed agents in various environments, including wireless ones.

15.22 STANDARDS FOR SOFTWARE AGENTS

Standards for software agents are needed for improving communication, collaboration, and use. Some important representative standards are described in this section.

15.22.1 Communication Languages

The development of an effective, rich *agent communication language (ACL)* is one of the keys to the success of intelligent agents. KQML is the first ACL that has seen substantial use. It is the de facto standard for agent communication languages. However, there are still no fixed specifications, no interoperable implementations, and no agreed-upon semantics. The Foundation for Intelligent Physical Agents (FIPA, fipa.org) is currently addressing all of these problems with its FIPA ACL, which is a well-specified standard based on formal semantics. A newer language is Formal Language for Business Communication (FLBC).

In addition to standardizing the agent communication language, FIPA also seeks to standardize other aspects of agent technology. These include architectural guidelines and specifications for constricting agents and agent platforms, defining open-standard interfaces for accessing agent management services, the human–agent interaction part of an agent system, security management and facilities for securing interagent communication, software agent mobility, and technologies enabling agents to manage explicit, declaratively represented ontologies. Standardization efforts also are underway within the Object Management Group (omg.org) and the Mobile Agent System Interoperability Facility (MASIF).

15.22.2 Open Profiling Standard

The **Open Profiling Standard (OPS)** provides Internet site developers with a uniform architecture for using personal profile information to offer individuals tailored content, goods, and services that match their personal preferences while protecting their privacy.

The idea works like this: Individuals have a Personal Profile that contains their personal information. A user may be asked to answer a series of questions, or the user's movements on the Net can be followed in order to construct the profile. The user's computer stores this profile (the user can also specify that the profile be stored securely in a corporate-wide or global directory). The first time that an individual visits a Web site that supports OPS, the Web site will request information from the Personal Profile. The individual has the choice of releasing all, some, or none of the requested information to the Web site. In addition, if the Web site collects additional information about the individual's preferences, it can (with the individual's permission) store that information in the Personal Profile for future use. On subsequent visits, the individual can authorize the Web site to retrieve the same personal information without having to ask permission.

15.22.3 AgentX

The Internet Engineering Task Force's AgentX (objs.com/survey/ietf.htm) is a standardized framework for extensible Simple Network Management Protocol (SNMP) agents, the network management protocol for TCP/IP. It defines processing entities called *master agents* and *subagents;* a protocol, AgentX, which is used to communicate between them; and the procedure by which the extensible agent processes SNMP protocol messages. In SNMP, agents can monitor the activity in the various devices on the network and report to the network console workstation.

15.23 THE FUTURE OF AGENTS

As told by Norman, "**Smart agents** are here to stay. Once unleashed, technologies do not disappear." We agree fully with these sentiments, which is why we believe agent technology is not a passing fad. We have now overviewed a broad range of work which goes under the banner of 'agents'. We have outlined their various promises as well as their challenges. However, apart from such technical issues, there is also a range of societal (i.e. social) and ethical problems which are looming. Donald Norman writes:

"Probably all the major software manufacturers are exploring the use of intelligent agents. Myths, promises, and reality are all colliding. But the main difficulties we foresee are social, not technical. How will intelligent agents interact with people and perhaps more importantly, how might people think about agents?"

We disagree with Norman as regards the major technical hurdles ahead; as shown in the previous section, there are some extremely demanding technical issues to be resolved in most of the agent classes reviewed. However, we agree that he poses an extremely pertinent question. There are issues which society would have to grapple with through various legislations and they would be very thorny.

They include the following:

- *Privacy:* how do you ensure your agents maintain your much needed privacy when acting on your behalf?
- *Responsibility which goes with relinquished authority:* when you relinquish some of your responsibility to software agent(s) (as you would do implicitly), be aware of the authority that is being transferred to it/them. How would you like to come back home after a long hard day at work being the proud owner of a used car negotiated and bought for, courtesy of one of your (Kasbah) software agents? How do you ensure the agent does not run amok and run up a huge credit card bill on your behalf?
- *Legal issues:* following on from the latter, imagine your agent (which you probably bought off-the-shelf and customised) offers some bad advice to other peer agents resulting in liabilities to other people, who is responsible? The company who wrote the agent? You who customised it? Both? We envisage a new raft of legislation would need to be developed in the future to cover software agents.
- *Ethical issues:* these would also need to be considered. Already, David Eichmann is already concerned enough about the ethics of software agents that he has proposed an agent etiquette for information service and user agents as they gather information on the WWW. They include the following:
  - Agents must identify themselves;
  - They must moderate the pace and frequency of their requests to some server;
  - They must limit their searches to appropriate servers;
  - They must share information with others;
  - They must respect the authority placed on them by server operators;
  - An agent's services much be accurate and up-to-date.

Etzioni & Weld have proposed others including:

- *Safety:* the agent should not destructively alter the world;
- *Tidiness:* the agent should leave the world as it found it;
- *Thrift:* the agent should limit its consumption of scarce resources;
- *Vigilance:* the agent should not allow client actions with unanticipated results.

However, such issues are not that critical immediately, but would be in the medium to long terms. In the short term, we expect some basic agent-based software to be rolled out e.g. some basic interface agents such as mail filtering or calendar scheduling agents. More basic mobile agent services would also be provided in the short term. We can also predict comfortably that many vendors would claim that their products are agent-based even though they most certainly are not. For example, we are already hearing of 'compression agents' and 'system agents' when 'disk compressers' and 'operating systems' would do respectively, and have done in the past. As Guilfoyle warns: "there is a danger, however, that customers may be disappointed by the gap between colourful press reports about smart agents handling half the work, and the reality of 'if-then' rules for message routing".

In the medium term (3 to 5 years), some more decent agent applications would be rolled out for most of the classes of agents overviewed in this paper. Perhaps, there would be collaborative agents and/or integrated heterogeneous agent applications doing limited, but *real* workflow or air traffic management or controlling real telecommunication networks say, etc., rather than just simulations. Useful, but limited, interface agents should be available which perform roles including the following: eager assistants, WWW guides, memory aids, entertainment and WWW filters/critics. Indeed, the HOMR/Ringo system is already being marketed as Firefly by Agents Inc. - a Boston-based agents company. Open Sesame– another interface agent which employs a neural network learning technique is already on the market from Charles River Analytics. More mobile and information agent applications and languages would soon be rolled out by vendors. We expect reactive and/or hybrid agent technology to start delivering some real everyday industrial applications during this period. Furthermore, during this medium term, we expect the WWW to be commercialised, to some degree, enabling agents of different classes to play a role in paying for services and performing some restricted buying and selling on our behalf, as Kasbah agents propose to do. We would also start seeing a proliferation of specialist agent's conferences: agents in the aviation industry, agents in law, etc. We also envisage that the new domain of agent-based software engineering will grow from strength to strength. In the long term (> 7 years), we would expect to see agents which *approximate* true 'smartness' in that they can collaborate and learn, in addition to being autonomous in their settings. They would possess rich negotiation skills and some may demonstrate what may be referred to, arguably, as 'emotions'. We caution against the usage of such words as the latter, not least because the agent literature abounds with such vocabulary which have subtle and complex meanings in the human context. However, it is also at this stage society would need to begin to confront some of the legal and ethical issues which are bound to follow the large scale fielding of agent technology. In the long term too, agents would also provide another design approach to constructing complex pieces of software.

Indermaur writes: "they can't fly yet, but intelligent agents and smart software are beginning to walk". Our view is different: using Indermaur's metaphor, we argue that limited software agents are just about to 'crawl' out of research laboratories; apart from a few interface and information agents, there is still a very long way, yet, to them 'walking', yet alone to their adolescence.

In summary, we believe, like Greif, that agents can have an enormous effect, but that this will appear in everyday products as an *evolutionary* process, rather than a *revolutionary* one predicted by much press coverage. Greif notes correctly that agents would initially leverage simpler technologies available in most applications (e.g. word processors, spreadsheets or knowledge-based systems). Then agents would gradually be evolved into more complicated applications. We hope the over optimistic claims about agent technology are moderated. It is a sad fact that the only jarring voices in this hymn of confident approbation about agent technology come from those doing the *real* research, and who know what some of the real technical, social and ethical challenges are.

SUMMARY

An agent is simply another kind of software abstraction, an abstraction in the same way that methods, functions, and objects are software abstractions. A software agent is autonomous; the agent is capable of operating as a standalone process and performing actions without user intervention. A software agent is communicative; it communicates with the user, other software agents, or other software processes. A software agent is perceptive; it is able to perceive and respond to changes in its environment.

Software agents, like people, can possess different levels of competence at performing a particular task. For example, one email software agent might be quite dumb and capable of only forwarding email to a few specified locations. A second, smarter email agent might have the ability to automatically detect and delete spam. While software agents must be autonomous, communicative, and perceptive, they can have different levels of competence (intelligence) as determined by their programs - i.e., their behavioural specifications.

Software agent technology is a rapidly developing area of research. In this chapter, we provide the developers with an overview of the evolving area of software agents. The over-use of the word 'agent' has tended to mask the fact that, in reality, there is truly heterogeneous body of research being carried out under this banner. This chapter provides an overview of the rationales, hypothesis, goals and state-of-the-art demonstrators of the various agent types which are currently under investigation by researchers.

Then agents would gradually be evolved into more complicated applications. We hope the over optimistic claims about agent technology are moderated. It is a sad fact that the only jarring voices in this hymn of confident approbation about agent technology come from those doing the *real* research, and who know what some of the real technical, social and ethical challenges are.

EXERCISES

1. What is agent?
2. What are software agents?
3. Explain the level of agent intelligence?
4. What are the major characteristics of different kinds of agents?
5. What are the properties of software agents?
6. What are the different properties of different kinds of agents?
7. Explain the various features of agents?
8. Explain the main attributes of agents?
9. What are the essential traits of software agents?
10. Explain the concept of Intelligent User Interfaces?
11. What is agency? Explain the structure of an agency?
12. Explain the types of software agents?
13. Explain the classification of software agents?
14. What are Collaborative agents?
15. What are key challenges of collaborative agents?
16. What are the benefits of interface agents?
17. What are the challenges of interface agents?
18. What are mobile agents? Explain the various characteristics of mobile agents?
19. What are advantages of mobile agents?

20. How mobile agents work?
21. What are the various applications of mobile agents?
22. Explain the use of mobile agents in E- Commerce?
23. What are the various challenges of mobile agents?
24. What are information agents?
25. How information agents work?
26. What are reactive software agents?
27. What are the applications of reactive agents?
28. What are the challenges of reactive agents?
29. What are hybrid agents?
30. Explain the hybrids agent architectures?
31. What are the Heterogeneous agent systems?
32. How heterogeneous agent systems work?
33. What are learning agents?
34. Explain the characteristics of learning agents?
35. Explain the concept of multiagents and communities of agents?
36. Explain the architecture, collaboration and coordination of multiagent systems?
37. Explain the future of agents?

❑

Applications of Software Agents

16

16.1 INTRODUCTION

Intelligent agents are a new paradigm for developing software applications. More than this, agent-based computing has been hailed as 'the next significant break-through in software development', and 'the new revolution in software'. Currently, agents are the focus of intense interest on the part of many sub-fields of computer science and artificial intelligence. Agents are being used in an increasingly wide variety of applications, ranging from comparatively small systems such as email filters to large, open, complex, mission critical systems such as air traffic control. At first sight, it may appear that such extremely different types of system can have little in common. And yet this is not the case: in both, the key abstraction used is that of an agent. Our aim in this article is to help the reader to understand why agent technology is seen as a fundamentally important new tool for building such a wide array of systems.

More precisely, our aims are five-fold:

- to introduce the reader to the concept of an agent and agent-based systems,
- to help the reader to recognize the domain characteristics that indicate the appropriateness of an agent-based solution,
- to introduce the main application areas in which agent technology has been successfully deployed to date,
- to identify the main obstacles that lie in the way of the agent system developer, and finally
- to provide a guide to the remainder of this book.

Before we can discuss the development of agent-based systems in detail, we have to describe what we mean by such terms as 'agent' and 'agent-based system'. Unfortunately, we immediately run into difficulties, as some key concepts in agent- based computing lack universally accepted definitions. In particular, there is no real agreement even on the core question of exactly what an agent is. However, we believe that most researchers would find themselves in broad agreement with the following definitions.

First, an agent is a computer system situated in some environment, and that is capable of autonomous action in this environment in order to meet its design objectives. Autonomy is a difficult concept to pin down precisely, but we mean it simply in the sense that the system should be able to act without the direct intervention of humans (or other agents), and should have control over its own actions and internal state. It may be helpful to draw an analogy between the notion of autonomy with respect to agents and encapsulation with respect to object-oriented systems. An object encapsulates some state, and has some control over this state in that it can only be accessed or modified via the methods that the object provides. Agents encapsulate state in just the same way. However, we also think of agents as encapsulating behavior, in addition to state. An object does not encapsulate behavior: it has no control over the execution of methods – if an object x invokes a method m on an object y, then y has no control over whether m is executed or not – it just is. In this sense, object y is not autonomous, as it has no control over its own actions. In contrast, we think of an agent as having exactly this kind of control over what actions it performs. Because of this distinction, we do not think of agents as invoking methods (actions) on agents – rather, we tend to think of them requesting actions to be performed. The decision about whether to act upon the request lies with the recipient.

Of course, autonomous computer systems are not a new development. There are many examples of such systems in existence.

Examples include:

- any process control system, which must monitor a real-world environment and perform actions to modify it as conditions change (typically in real time) – such systems range from the very simple (for example, thermostats) to the extremely complex (for example, nuclear reactor control systems),
- software daemons, which monitor a software environment and perform actions to modify the environment as conditions change – a simple example is the UNIX xbiff program, which monitors a user's incoming email and obtains their attention by displaying an icon when new, incoming email is detected.

It may seem strange that we choose to call such systems agents. But these are not intelligent agents. An intelligent agent is a computer system that is capable of flexible autonomous action in order to meet its design objectives.

By flexible, we mean that the system must be:

- *responsive:* agents should perceive their environment (which may be the physical world, a user, a collection of agents, the Internet, etc.) and respond in a timely fashion to changes that occur in it,
- *proactive:* agents should not simply act in response to their environment, they should be able to exhibit opportunistic, goal-directed behavior and take the initiative where appropriate, and
- *social:* agents should be able to interact, when they deem appropriate, with other artificial agents and humans in order to complete their own problem solving and to help others with their activities.

Hereafter, when we use the term 'agent', it should be understood that we are using it as an abbreviation for 'intelligent agent'. Other researchers emphasizc different aspects of agency (including, for example, mobility or adaptability). Naturally, some agents may have additional characteristics, and for certain types of applications, some attributes will be more important than others. However, we believe that it is the presence of all four attributes in a single software entity that provides the power of the agent paradigm and which distinguishes agent systems from related software paradigms – such as object-oriented systems, distributed systems, and expert systems.

By an agent-based system, we mean one in which the key abstraction used is that of an agent. In principle, an agent-based system might be conceptualized in terms of agents, but implemented without any software structures corresponding to agents at all. We can again draw a parallel with object-oriented software, where it is entirely possible to design a system in terms of objects, but to implement it without the use of an object-oriented software environment. But this would at best be unusual, and at worst, counterproductive. A similar situation exists with agent technology; we therefore expect an agent-based system to be both designed and implemented in terms of agents. A number of software tools exist that allow a user to implement software systems as agents, and as societies of cooperating agents. Note that an agent-based system may contain any non-zero number of agents. The multi-agent case – where a system is designed and implemented as several interacting agents, is both more general and significantly more complex than the single-agent case. However, there are a number of situations where the single-agent case is appropriate. A good example, as we shall see later in this chapter, is the class of systems known as expert assistants, wherein an agent acts as an expert assistant to a user attempting to use a computer to carry out some task.

16.2 AGENT APPLICATION DOMAIN CHARACTERISTICS

Now that we have a better understanding of what the terms 'agent' and 'agent-based system' mean, the obvious question to ask is: what do agents have to offer? For any new technology to be considered as useful in the computer marketplace, it must offer one of two things:

- the ability to solve problems that have hitherto been beyond the scope of automation – either because no existing technology could be used to solve the problem, or because it was considered too expensive (difficult, time-consuming, risky) to develop solutions using existing technology; or
- the ability to solve problems that can already be solved in a significantly better (cheaper, more natural, easier, more efficient, or faster) way.

16.2.1 SOLVING NEW TYPES OF PROBLEM

Certain types of software system are inherently more difficult to correctly design and implement than others. The simplest general classes of software systems are functional. Such systems work by taking some input, computing a function of it, and giving this result as output. Compilers are obvious examples of functional systems. In contrast, reactive systems, which maintain an ongoing interaction with some environment, are inherently much more difficult to design and correctly implement. Process control systems, computer operating systems, and computer network management systems are all well-known examples of reactive systems. In all of these examples, a computer system is required that can operate independently, typically over long periods of time. It has long been recognized that reactive systems are among the most complex types of system to design and implement, and a good deal of effort has been devoted to developing software tools, programming languages, and methodologies for managing this complexity – with some limited success. However, for certain types of reactive system, even specialized software engineering techniques and tools fail – new techniques are required.

We can broadly subdivide these systems into three classes:

- open systems,
- complex systems, and
- ubiquitous computing systems.

16.2.1.1 Open Systems

An open system is one in which the structure of the system itself is capable of dynamically changing. The characteristics of such a system are that its components are not known in advance, can change over time, and may be highly heterogeneous (in that they are implemented by different people, at different times, using different software tools and techniques). Computing applications are increasingly demanded by users to operate in such domains. Perhaps the best-known example of a highly open software environment is the Internet – a loosely coupled computer network of ever expanding size and complexity. The design and construction of software tools to exploit the enormous potential of the Internet and its related technology is one of

the most important challenges facing computer scientists in the 1990s, and for this reason, it is worth using it as a case study. The Internet can be viewed as a large, distributed information resource, with nodes on the network designed and implemented by different organizations and individuals with widely varying agendas. Any computer system that must operate on the Internet must be capable of dealing with these different organizations and agendas, without constant guidance from users (but within well-defined bounds). Such functionality is almost certain to require techniques based on negotiation or cooperation, which lie very firmly in the domain of multi-agent systems.

16.2.1.2 Complex Systems

The most powerful tools for handling complexity in software development are modularity and abstraction. Agents represent a powerful tool for making systems modular. If a problem domain is particularly complex, large, or unpredictable, then it may be that the only way it can reasonably be addressed is to develop a number of (nearly) modular components that are specialized (in terms of their representation and problem solving paradigm) at solving a particular aspect of it. In such cases, when interdependent problems arise, the agents in the systems must cooperate with one another to ensure that interdependencies are properly managed. In such domains, an agent-based approach means that the overall problem can be partitioned into a number of smaller and simpler components, which are easier to develop and maintain, and which are specialized at solving the constituent sub-problems. This decomposition allows each agent to employ the most appropriate paradigm for solving its particular problem, rather than being forced to adopt a common uniform approach that represents a compromise for the entire system, but which is not optimal for any of its subparts. The notion of an autonomous agent also provides a useful abstraction in just the same way that procedures, abstract data types, and, most recently, objects provide abstractions. They allow a software developer to conceptualize a complex software system as a society of cooperating autonomous problem solvers. For many applications, this high-level view is simply more appropriate than the alternatives.

16.2.1.3 Ubiquity

Despite the many innovations in human-computer interface design over the past two decades, and the wide availability of powerful window-based user interfaces, computer-naïve users still find most software difficult to use. One reason for this is that the user of a software product typically has to describe each and every step that needs to be performed to solve a problem, down to the smallest level of detail. If the power of current software applications is ever to be fully utilized by such users, then a fundamental rethink is needed about the nature of the interaction between computer and user. It must become an equal partnership – the machine should not just act as a dumb receptor of task descriptions, but should cooperate with the user to achieve their goal. As Negroponte wrote, 'the future of computing will be 100% driven by delegating to, rather than manipulating computers'. To deliver such functionality, software applications must be:

- *autonomous:* given a vague and imprecise specification, it must determine how the problem is best solved and then solve it, without constant guidance from the user,
- *proactive:* it should not wait to be told what to do next, rather it should make suggestions to the user,
- *responsive:* it should take account of changing user needs and changes in the task environment, and
- *adaptive:* it should come to know user's preferences and tailor interactions to reflect these.

In other words, it needs to behave as an intelligent agent. These considerations give rise to the idea of an agent acting as an 'expert assistant' with respect to some application, knowledgeable about both the application itself and the user, and capable of acting with the user in order to achieve the user's goals.

16.2.2 Improving the Efficiency of Software Development

Agent technology gives us the tools with which to build applications that we were previously unable to build. But it can also provide a better means of conceptualizing and/or implementing a given application. Here, three important domain characteristics are often cited as a rationale for adopting agent technology:

- data, control, expertise, or resources are inherently distributed,
- the system is naturally regarded as a society of autonomous cooperating components, or
- the system contains legacy components, which must be made to interact with other, possibly new software components.

16.2.2.1 Distribution of Data Control, Expertise, or Resources

When the domain involves a number of distinct problem solving entities (or data sources) that are physically or logically distributed (in terms of their data, control, expertise, or resources), and which need to interact with one another in order to solve problems, then agents can often provide an effective solution. For example, in a distributed health care setting, general practitioners, hospital specialists, nurses, and home care organizations have to work together to provide the appropriate care to a sick patient.

In this domain, there is:

- distribution of data: the general practitioner has data about the patient, which is very different from that of the hospital nurse – even though it concerns the same person,
- distribution of control: each individual is responsible for performing a different set of tasks,
- distribution of expertise: the specialist's knowledge is very different from that of either the general practitioner or the nurse, and
- distribution of resources: a specialist is responsible for the beds required by their patients, a general practitioner for paying hospital bills, etc.

In cases like this, agents provide a natural way of modeling the problem: real-world entities and their interactions can be directly mapped into autonomous problem solving agents with their own resources and expertise, and which are able to interact with others in order to get tasks done. Also, in the case of distributed data sources, and seismic monitoring, the use of agents means that significant amounts of processing can be carried out at the data source, with only high-level information exchanged. This alleviates the need to send large amounts of raw data to a distant central processor, thus making more efficient use of communications bandwidth.

16.2.2.2 Natural Metaphor

The notion of an autonomous agent is often the most appropriate metaphor for presenting a given software functionality. For example:

- a program that filters email can be presented to its user via the metaphor of a personal digital assistant and
- meeting scheduling software can naturally be presented as an empowered, autonomous, social agent that can interact with other similar agents on the user's behalf.

In such applications, the fact that these functions are implemented through a series of local agents also means that they can be personalized to reflect the preferences of their user. Finally, in computer games and virtual reality systems, characters can naturally be represented as agents.

16.2.2.3 Legacy Systems

Large organizations have many software applications (especially information systems) that perform critical organizational functions. To keep pace with changing business needs, these systems must be periodically updated. However, modifying such legacy systems is in general very difficult: the system's structure and internal operation will become corrupted with the passage of time, designs and documentation are lost, and individuals with an understanding of the software move on. Completely rewriting such software tends to be prohibitively expensive, and is often simply impossible. Therefore, in the long term, the only way to keep such legacy systems useful is to incorporate them into a wider cooperating community, in which they can be exploited by other pieces of software. This can be done, for example, by building an 'agent wrapper' around the software to enable it to interoperate with other systems. The process of transforming a software application such as a database into an agent is sometimes referred to as agentification.

16.2.3 The Limitations of Agent Solutions

Although agent technology has an important role to play in the development of leading-edge computing applications, it should not be oversold. Most applications that currently use agents could be built using non-agent techniques. Thus the mere fact that a particular problem domain has distributed data sources or involves legacy systems does not necessarily imply that an agent-based solution is the most appropriate one – or even that it is feasible. As with all system designs, the ultimate choice is dictated by many factors. This section has identified the types of situation in which an agent-based solution should be considered, as opposed to those in which it should be deployed. Moreover, it should be noted that the very nature of the agent paradigm leads to a number of problems, common to all agent-based applications:

- **No overall system controller.** An agent-based solution may not be appropriate for domains in which global constraints have to be maintained, in domains where a real-time response must be guaranteed, or in domains in which deadlocks or livelocks must be avoided.
- **No global perspective.** An agent's actions are, by definition, determined by that agent's local state. However, since in almost any realistic agent system, complete global knowledge is not a possibility, this may mean that agents make globally sub-optimal decisions. The issue of reconciling decision making based on local knowledge with the desire to achieve globally optimal performance is a basic issue in multi-agent systems research (Bond and Gasser, 1988).
- **Trust and delegation.** For individuals to be comfortable with the idea of delegating tasks to agents, they must first trust them. Both individuals and organizations will thus need to become more accustomed and confident with the notion of autonomous software components, if they are to become widely used. Users have to gain confidence in the agents that work on their behalf, and this process can take time. During this period, the agent must strike a balance between continually seeking guidance (and needlessly distracting the user) and never seeking guidance (and exceeding its authority). Put crudely, an agent must know its limitations.

16.3 AGENT APPLICATION DOMAINS

Agents are the next major computing paradigm and will be pervasive in every market by the year 2000. There are several orthogonal dimensions along which agent applications could be classified. They can be classified by the type of the agent, by the technology used to implement the agent, or by the application domain itself. We choose to use the domain type, since this view fits best with the objectives and structure of the rest of this chapter. Our aim in producing this classification scheme is simply to give a feel for the breadth and variety of agent applications.

16.3.1 Industrial Applications

Industrial applications of agent technology were among the first to be developed: as early as 1987, Parunak reports experience with applying the contract net task allocation protocol in a manufacturing environment. Today, agents are being applied in a wide range of industrial applications.

16.3.1.1 Process Control

Process control is a natural application for intelligent agents and multi-agent systems, since process controllers are themselves autonomous reactive systems. It is not surprising, therefore, that a number of agent-based process control applications should have been developed. The best known of these is ARCHON, a software platform for building multi-agent systems, and an associated methodology for building applications with this platform. ARCHON has been applied in several process control applications, including electricity transportation management (the application is in use in northern Spain), and particle accelerator control. ARCHON also has the distinction of being one of the earliest field-tested multi-agent systems in the world. Agents in ARCHON are fairly heavyweight computational systems, with four main components: a high-level communication module (HLCM), which manages inter-agent communication; a planning and coordination module (PCM), which is essentially responsible for deciding what the agent will do; an agent information management module (AIM), which is responsible for maintaining the agent's model of the world, and finally, an underlying intelligent system (IS), which represents the agent's domain expertise. The HLCM, PCM, and AIM together constitute a kind of 'agent wrapper', which can be used to encapsulate an existing intelligent system (or indeed any pre-existing software application) and turn it into an agent.

16.3.1.2 Manufacturing

We have the YAMS (Yet Another Manufacturing System), which applies the well-known Contract Net protocol (Smith, 1980) to manufacturing control. The basic problem can be described as follows. A manufacturing enterprise is modeled as a hierarchy of workcells. There will, for example, be workcells for milling, lathing, grinding, painting, and so on. These workcells will be further grouped into flexible manufacturing systems (FMS), each of which will provide a functionality such as assembly, paint spraying, buffering of products, and so on. A collection of such FMSs is grouped into a factory. A single company or organization may have many different factories, though these factories may duplicate functionality and capabilities. The goal of YAMS is to efficiently manage the production process at these plants. This process is defined by some constantly changing parameters, such as the products to be manufactured, available resources, time constraints, and so on. In order to achieve this enormously complex task, YAMS adopts a multi-agent approach, where each factory and factory component is represented as an agent. Each agent has a collection of plans, representing its capabilities. The contract net protocol allows tasks (i.e., production orders) to be delegated to individual factories, and from individual factories down to FMSs, and then to individual workcells. The contract net is based on the idea of negotiation, and hence YAMS views the problem of deciding how best to process a company's product manufacturing requirements as a negotiation problem. A some-what similar approach was developed in, where the problem of determining an optimal production sequence for a factory was analyzed using the tools of game and negotiation theory.

16.3.1.3 Air Traffic Control

We have a sophisticated agent-realized air traffic control system known as OASIS. In this system, which is undergoing field trials at Sydney airport in Australia, agents are used to represent both aircraft and the various air traffic control systems in operation. The agent metaphor thus provides a useful and natural way of modeling real-world autonomous components. As an aircraft enters Sydney airspace, an agent is allocated for it, and the agent is instantiated with the information and goals corresponding to the real-world aircraft. For example, an aircraft might have a goal to land on a certain runway at a certain time. Air traffic control agents are responsible for managing the system. OASIS is implemented using the AAII's own dMARS system. This system allows an agent to be implemented using the belief-desire-intention model of agency – one of the most popular approaches to reasoning about agents in theoretical multi-agent systems.

16.3.2 Commercial Applications

Following are the various commercial applications:

16.3.2.1 Information Management

As the richness and diversity of information available to us in our everyday lives has grown, so the need to manage this information has grown. The lack of effective information management tools has given rise to what is colloquially known as the information overload problem. Put simply, the sheer volume of information available to us via the Internet and World Wide Web (WWW) represents a very real problem. The potential of this resource is immediately apparent to anyone with more than the most superficial experience of using the WWW. But the reality is often disappointing. There are many reasons for this. Both human factors (such as users getting bored or distracted) and organizational factors (such as poorly organized pages with no semantic markup) conspire against users attempting to use the resource in a systematic way.

We can characterize the information overload problem in two ways:

- **Information filtering.** Every day, we are presented with enormous amounts of information (via email and newsnet news, for example), only a tiny proportion of which is relevant or important. We need to be able to sort the wheat from the chaff, and focus on information we need.
- **Information gathering.** The volume of information available prevents us from actually finding information to answer specific queries. We need to be able to obtain information that meets our requirements, even if this information can only be collected from a number of different sites.

One important contributing factor to information overload is almost certainly that an end user is required to constantly direct the management process. But there is in principle no reason why such searches should not be carried out by agents, acting autonomously to search the Web on behalf of some user. The idea is so compelling that many projects is directed at doing exactly this. **Three such projects are described below:**

- **Maxims:** Maes describes an electronic mail filtering agent called Maxims. The program 'learns to prioritize, delete, forward, sort, and archive mail messages on behalf of a user'. It works by 'looking over the shoulder' of a user as he or she works with their email reading program, and uses every action the user performs as a lesson. Maxims constantly makes internal predictions about what a user will do with a message. If these predictions turn out to be inaccurate, then Maxims keeps them to itself. But when it finds it is having a useful degree of success in its predictions, it starts to make suggestions to the user about what to do.
- **Newt:** Maes also describes an example of an Internet news filtering program called Newt. This program, implemented in C++ on a UNIX plat-form, takes as input a stream of usenet news articles and as output gives a subset of these articles that it is recommended the user reads. The Newt agent is 'programmed' by means of training examples: the user gives Newt examples of articles that would and would not be read, and this feedback is used to modify an internal 'model' (we use the term very loosely) of the user's interests. The user can, if desired, explicitly program Newt by giving it precise rules (e.g., "give me all articles containing the word 'agent'"). Newt retrieves words of interest from an article by performing a full-text analysis using the vector space model for documents.
- **The Zuno Digital Library:** A digital library is an organized, managed collection of data, together with services to assist the user in making use of this data. The Zuno Digital Library (ZDL) system is a multi-agent system that enables a user to obtain a single, coherent view of incoherent, disorganized data sources such as the World Wide Web, a user's own data, collections of articles on publishing house sites, and so on. Agents in ZDL play one of three roles:
  - consumer – representing end users of the system, who can be thought of as consuming information;
  - producer – representing 'content providers', who own the information that customers consume; and
  - facilitator – mapping between consumers and producers.

Consumer agents in the system are responsible for representing the user's interests. They maintain models of users, and use these models to assist them, by proactively providing information they require, and shielding them from information that is not of interest. ZDL thus acts both as an information filter and an information gatherer.

16.3.2.2 Electronic Commerce

Currently, commerce is almost entirely driven by human interactions; humans decide when to buy goods, how much they are willing to pay, and so on. But in principle, there is no reason why some commerce cannot be automated. By this, we mean that some commercial decision making can be placed in the hands of agents. Lest the reader suppose that this is fanciful, and that no sensible commercial organization would make their decision making (and hence money spending) the responsibility of a computer program, it should be remembered that this is precisely what happens today in the electronic trading of stocks and shares. Widespread electronic commerce is, however, likely to lie some distance in the future. In the near term, electronic trading applications are likely to be much more mundane and small scale. As an example, Chavez and Maes describe a simple 'electronic marketplace' called Kasbah. This system realizes the market-place by creating 'buying' and 'selling' agents for each good to be purchased or sold respectively. Commercial transactions take place by the interactions of these agents.

16.3.2.3 Business Process Management

Company managers make informed decisions based on a combination of judgement and information from many departments. Ideally, all relevant information should be brought together before judgement is exercised. However obtaining pertinent, consistent and up-to-date information across a large company is a complex and time consuming process. For this reason, organizations have sought to develop a number of IT systems to assist with various aspects of the management of their business processes. Project ADEPT tackles this problem by viewing a business process as a community of negotiating, service-providing agents. Each agent represents a distinct role or department in the enterprise and is capable of providing one or more services. For example, a design department may provide the service of designing a telecom network, a legal department may offer the service of checking that the design is legal, and the marketing department may provide the service of costing the design. Agents who require a service from another agent enter into a negotiation for that service to obtain a mutually acceptable price, time, and degree of quality. Successful negotiations result in binding agreements between agents. This agent-based approach offers a number of advantages over more typical workflow solutions to this problem. The proactive nature of the agents means services can be scheduled in a just-in-time fashion (rather than pre-specified from the beginning), and the responsive nature of the agents means that service exceptions can be detected and handled in a flexible manner. The current version of the system has been tested on a British Telecom (BT) business process involving some 200 activities and nine departments and there are plans to move toward full scale field trials.

16.3.3 Medical Applications

Medical informatics is a major growth area in computer science: new applications are being found for computers every day in the health industry. It is not surprising, therefore, that agents should be applied in this domain. Two of the earliest applications are in the areas of health care and patient monitoring.

16.3.3.1 Patient Monitoring

The Guardian system is intended to help manage patient care in the Surgical Intensive Care Unit (SICU). The system was motivated by two concerns: first, that the patient care model in a SICU is essentially that of a team, where a collection of experts with distinct areas of expertise cooperate to organize patient health care; and second, that one of the most important factors in good SICU patient health care is the adequate sharing of information between members of the critical care team. In particular, specialists tend to have very little opportunity to monitor the minute-by-minute status of a patient; this task tends to fall to nurses, who, in contrast, often do not have the expertise to interpret the information they obtain in the way that an appropriate expert would. The Guardian system distributes the SICU patient monitoring function among a number of agents, of three different types:

- perception/action agents – responsible for the interface between Guardian and the world, mapping raw sensor input into a usable symbolic form, and translating action requests from Guardian into raw effector control commands,
- reasoning agents – responsible for organizing the system's decision making process, and
- control agents – of which there will only ever be one, with overall, top-level control of the system.

These agents are organized into hierarchies, and the system as a whole is closely based on the blackboard model of control, wherein different agents ('knowledge sources') cooperate via sharing knowledge in a common data structure known as a blackboard.

16.3.3.2 Health Care

We have a prototypical agent-based distributed medical care system. This system is designed to integrate the patient management process, which typically involves many individuals. For example, a general practitioner may suspect that a patient has breast cancer, but this suspicion cannot be confirmed or rejected without the assistance of a hospital specialist. If the specialist confirms the hypothesis, then a care programme must be devised for treating the patient, involving the resources of other individuals. The prototype system allows a natural representation of this process, with agents mapped onto the individuals and, potentially, organizations involved in the patient care process. Agents in the prototype contain a knowledge-based (intelligent) system, containing the domain expertise of the agent, a human-computer interface, allowing the user to add, remove, or view system goals, and a communications manager, which realizes the message-passing functionality of agents. The intelligent system component is based on the KADS model of expertise, and the whole agent architecture is implemented in PROLOG. Message passing is realized via extensions to standard email.

16.3.4 Entertainment

The leisure industry is often not taken seriously by the computer science community. Leisure applications are frequently seen as somehow peripheral to the 'serious' applications of computers. And yet leisure applications such as computer games can be extremely lucrative – consider the number of copies of id Software's 'Quake' sold since its release in 1996. Agents have an obvious role in computer games, interactive theater, and related virtual reality applications: such systems tend to be full of semi-autonomous animated characters, which can naturally be implemented as agents.

16.3.4.1 Games

We have several applications of agent technology to computer games. For example, they have developed a version of the popular Tetris computer game, where a user must try to make a wall out of irregularly shaped falling blocks. The agent in the game takes the part of the user, who must control where the blocks fall. Trying to program this agent using traditional symbolic AI techniques would require going through a knowledge elicitation stage, representing knowledge about the game and the role of the user in terms of symbolic data structures such as rules, and so on. This approach would be entirely un-realistic for a game like Tetris, which has hard real-time constraints. Wavish and colleagues thus use an alternative reactive agent model called RTA (Real Time Able). In this approach, agents are programmed in terms of behaviors. These behaviors are simple structures, which loosely resemble rules but do not require complex symbolic reasoning.

16.3.4.2 Interactive Theater and Cinema

By interactive theater and cinema, we mean a system that allows a user to play out a role analogous to the roles played by real, human actors in plays or films, interacting with artificial, computer characters that have the behavioral characteristics of real people. Agents that play the part of humans in theater-style applications are often known as believable agents, a term coined by Joe Bates. His vision is of [Agents that] provide the illusion of life, thus permitting ... [an] audience's suspension of disbelief. A number of projects have been set up to investigate the development of such agents. For example, describe a directed improvisation system, in which human players act out roles in a dynamic narrative, creating a new, user directed 'work'.

16.3.5 Comments

At a certain level of abstraction, many of the above applications share common features. Individual agents are designed and built to enact particular roles. These agents are autonomous, goal directed entities, which are responsive to their environment. They must typically interact with other agents in order to carry out their role. Such interactions are a natural consequence of the inevitable inter-dependencies which exist between the agents, their environment, and their design objectives. As the agents are autonomous, the interactions are usually fairly sophisticated – involving cooperation, coordination and negotiation.

Following on from this view, two important observations can be made about developing agent-based applications:

- The detailed problem solving actions of the agent can only be determined at run time. Individual behavior is regulated by a complex interplay between the agent's internal state and its external influences (its environment and the other agents). Thus the precise 'trajectory' that an agent will follow can only be discovered by running the agent in its environment.
- Because the behavior of individual agents is not uniquely determined at design time, the behavior of the system as a whole can also only emerge at run time. These points have some obvious (and perhaps alarming) implications for the use of an agent-based approach in safety-critical application domains such as air traffic control, where it is essential that the system satisfies its specification.

The above applications also illustrate that there are several different dimensions along which we can analyze agent-based systems:

- **Sophistication of the Agents.** Agents can be seen as performing three broad types of behavior. At the simplest level, there is the 'gopher' agent, which carries out comparatively simple tasks, based on well-defined, pre-specified rules and assumptions. The next level of sophistication involves 'service performing' agents, which carry out a high-level, but still well-defined task at the request of a user (e.g., arrange a meeting or find an appropriate flight). Finally, there are the predictive/proactive agents, capable of flexible autonomous behavior in the way we discussed above. Simple examples are agents that volunteer information or services to a user, without being asked, whenever it is deemed to be appropriate.

- **Role of the Agents.** Agents play many types of role. For example, in several of the industrial and commercial applications discussed above, the role of the agent system is to provide decision support functionality. The agents act autonomously and proactively to gather information and to make recommendations, but a human operator makes the ultimate decisions. In contrast, in the entertainment domain (for example), the agent completely automates a problem solving role – it is thus delegated a particular activity and is entirely responsible for carrying it out.
- **Granularity of View.** In some of the applications discussed above, the significant unit of analysis and design is the individual agent, whereas in other applications it is the society of agents that is key. The decision about whether to adopt a single-agent or multi-agent approach is generally determined by the domain, and is similar in nature to decisions about whether monolithic, centralized solutions or distributed, decentralized solutions are appropriate. Single-agent systems are in a sense much simpler than multi-agent systems, since they do not require the designer to deal with issues such as cooperation, negotiation, and so on.

16.4 THE AGENT DEVELOPMENT BOTTLENECK

At the time of writing, expertise in designing and building agent applications is scarce. There is little in the way of production-quality software support for building agent applications, and still less general understanding of the issues that need to be addressed when building such systems. Worse, most of today's agent systems are built from scratch, using bespoke tools and techniques, which cannot easily be applied to other types of system. This is particularly worrying because a lot of infrastructure is required before the main components of an agent system can be built. At the moment, most developers rebuild this infrastructure from scratch in every new case; this process is clearly not sustainable. However, there is an increasing awareness that this situation must change if agents are to make it into the mainstream of software development. Support is required throughout the agent system development process. In what follows, we use a traditional software engineering model as a basis for structuring our discussion of this issue. We begin our discussion with requirements specification, since the stage that precedes it – requirements analysis – does not differ in any significant way from that for other types of software system. The requirements analysis stage typically concludes with a user requirements document – a statement of the properties that the analyst or developer believes the user (client) wants of the new system. This document is usually written in non-technical language, so that it can be understood by both client and developer.

16.4.1 Requirements Specification

Once an understanding is reached of the client's needs with respect to the newly commissioned system, a precise statement is required of what the developers intend to build. This document tends to be written as formally as possible – it aims to be a precise statement of the properties of the system that the developers will build. A number of approaches have been developed to agent system requirements specification, and in particular to formal (mathematical) approaches. The details of these formalisms tend to be rather complex, but broadly speaking, they characterize agents as rational decision makers. By this, we mean systems whose internal state can be expressed in terms of 'mentalistic' constructs such as belief, desire, and intention. An agent's decision making can then be characterized in terms of these constructs. It may be difficult to see how one might specify a computer system in this way, but the idea is really quite straightforward. One builds a specification out of a set of 'rules' (strictly speaking, logical formulas), somewhat like this:

if agent 1 believes that agent 2 believes runway 1 is clear
then agent 1 should believe that agent 2 has erroneous information,
and agent 1 should intend that agent 2 is informed of its error.

One might wonder why terms such as 'believe' and 'intend' are used. Beliefs are generally used to refer to the information that agents have about their environment. This information can be incorrect – in just the same way that information we have about the environment (our beliefs) could be wrong. The term intention is used to refer to a goal that the agent will pursue until it either succeeds or fails completely – it admits the possibility of failure, a realistic possibility in many complex systems, one which traditional formalisms tend to ignore.

16.4.2 System Design

The design of robust, efficient systems is one of the most important issues addressed by software engineers, and a great deal of effort has been devoted to making system design a methodical, rigorous process. At the time of writing, comparatively few workers in the agent research community have considered how design methodologies might be applied to agent systems. This situation must clearly change if agent systems are to become widely used, and in particular, the following key questions need to be addressed:

- Adopting an agent-based approach. In much of the work that goes under the agent banner, the rationale behind the choice of an agent-based approach (over other, arguably simpler alternatives) is unclear. The analysis of appropriate domain properties represents a step toward this end.
- Macro-system Structure. Once given an abstract, high-level system specification, we need to transform this specification into agents, and relate these agents to one another in a system structure. This process is known as refinement. In just the same way those object-oriented design methodologies exist, which give guidelines relating to the identification of objects and object inter-dependencies, so we might expect soon to see agent-oriented design methodologies, which offer clear guidelines about how to decompose a problem into agents and what effects a given decomposition is likely to have on the system performance. The design problem is exacerbated by the fact that legacy systems often need to be incorporated in agent systems. Thus design needs to be done both from a top-down perspective (how should the problem be decomposed ideally?) and from a bottom-up perspective (what software groupings already exist and cannot be changed?). Both perspectives must be accommodated.

16.4.3 System Implementation

An agent system design will both describe the various different roles that exist within the system and characterize the relationships that exist between these roles. However, the design will not generally prescribe an implementation of these agents. So, having identified the various agent roles in a system, the next step is to determine how each of these roles can be best realized. An agent architecture needs to be devised or adopted for each role, which will deliver the required functional and non-functional characteristics of the role.

Many agent architectures have been developed by the intelligent agent's community, with many different properties. At one extreme, there are 'strong AI' systems, which allow users to build agents as knowledge-based systems, or even as logic theorem provers. In order to build agents using such systems, one goes through the standard knowledge-based system process of knowledge elicitation and representation, coding an agent's behavior in terms of rules, frames, or semantic nets. At the other extreme, there are many agent frameworks that simply offer enhanced versions of (for example) the Java programming language – they include no AI techniques at all. Neither of these extremes is strictly right or wrong: they both have merits and drawbacks. In general, of course, the simplest solution that will effectively solve a problem is often the best. There is little point in using complex reasoning systems where simple Java-like agents will do. Obviously, more detailed guidelines to assist with this decision making process are desirable.

16.4.4 System Testing, Debugging and Verification

As long ago as 1987, Les Gasser wrote:

Concurrency, problem-domain uncertainty, and non-determinism in execution together conspire to make it very difficult to comprehend the activity in a distributed intelligent system [...] we urgently need graphic displays of system activity linked to intelligent model-based tools which help a developer reason about expected and observed behavior.

Gasser's comments remain as true of agent system development in the late 1990s as they did of the mid-1980s. Sadly, testing and debugging are still much neglected areas of the agent development process. Developers need assistance with visualizing what is happening, and need debugging facilities to step through the execution and amend behavior where appropriate. Visualization is particularly important – determining what is happening in asynchronous, concurrent systems is an exceedingly difficult task. This is true both within an agent and even more so between agents. Traditional debugging features which allow execution to be stopped, internal states to be examined, states to be changed, message arrivals to be simulated, and so on are also essential. In most systems these features and tools are developed from scratch – clearly an undesirable state of affairs.

SUMMARY

Intelligent agents are a new paradigm for developing software applications. More than this, agent-based computing has been hailed as 'the next significant break-through in software development', and 'the new revolution in software'. Currently, agents are the focus of intense interest on the part of many sub-fields of computer science and artificial intelligence. Agents are being used in an increasingly wide variety of applications, ranging from comparatively small systems such as email filters to large, open, complex, mission critical systems such as air traffic control. At first sight, it may appear that such extremely different types of system can have little in common. And yet this is not the case: in both, the key abstraction used is that of an agent. By an agent-based system, we mean one in which the key abstraction used is that of an agent. In principle, an agent-based system might be conceptualized in terms of agents, but implemented without any software structures corresponding to agents at all. We can again draw a parallel with object-oriented software, where it is entirely possible to design a system in terms of objects, but to implement it without the use of an object-oriented software environment. But this would at best be unusual, and at worst, counterproductive. A similar situation exists with agent technology; we therefore expect an agent-based system to be both designed and implemented in terms of agents. A number of software tools exist that allow a user to implement software systems as agents, and as societies of cooperating agents. Note that an agent-based system may contain any non-zero number of agents. The multi-agent case – where a system is designed and implemented as several interacting agents, is both more general and significantly more complex than the single-agent case. However, there are a number of situations where the single-agent case is appropriate. Our aim in this article is to help the reader to understand why agent technology is seen as a fundamentally important new tool for building such a wide array of systems.

EXERCISES

1. What are the agent application domain characteristics?
2. Explain the open and complex systems?
3. How to improve the efficiency of software development?
4. Explain the various agent application domains?
5. Explain the commercial applications of agents?
6. Explain the various medical applications of agents?
7. Explain the applications of agents for entertainment?
8. Explain the designing and building agent applications?

❑❑❑